SPEAKING IN TONGUES

A Guide to

Research on Glossolalia

SPEAKING IN TONGUES

A Guide to

Research on Glossolalia

edited by

WATSON E. MILLS

Grand Rapids, Michigan
WILLIAM B. EERDMANS PUBLISHING COMPANY

Library of Congress Cataloging-in-Publication Data

Main entry under title:

Speaking in tongues.

Bibliography: p. 493
Includes index.
1. Glossolalia — Addresses, essays, lectures.
I. Mills, Watson E.
BL54.S64   1986   248.2′9   85-27568

ISBN 0-8028-0183-8

DEDICATION

For

Mary Mason, Martha, Brother

PREFACE

A considerable disruption occurred in mainline Christendom in the sixties and seventies. It was caused, in part, by a dispute rooted in the experiential dimension of the faith. At the center of the controversy was a practice known as glossolalia. Participants defended the practice as necessary and essential to the Christian faith. They pointed to certain biblical passages in support of their position. Opponents, with equal vigor, rejected the phenomenon as esoteric and meaningless.

In the first half of the twentieth century, American Protestantism had evolved along institutional lines so that a majority of the denominations placed little, if any, emphasis upon the role of the spirit in the Christian life. Those few groups that did emphasize the spirit, were generally viewed with suspicion, if not disdain, by the majority. Usually, groups that emphasized this area of the faith were lumped together and characterized by mainline Christians through the use of such denegrating terms as ''holy rollers.'' Today, these same groups are often referred to as ''charismatic.''

Despite the reactionary views that each held for the other's understanding of the faith, there was a certain predictability in that the lines of separation between the groups were clearly defined. The spirit's role among charismatic Christian groups was overt and central; among non-charismatics it was covert and peripheral.

In the years after 1961, however, the economy of clarity was lost as the charismatic dimension of the faith began to make significant in-roads into mainline Christianity. Older stereotypes began to crumble in the sixties and the seventies. Parish churches were divided, ministers expelled, families torn apart. The response of the institutional church, through its commissions and special review boards, was predictable: this discussion about the reality of the spirit as evidenced through the presence of glossolalia is a devilish perversion of the genuine faith, and should not be tolerated. And so it was that the expression of the reality became the substance of the discussion and any emphasis upon a theology of spirituality was minimized, if present at all.

Few other aspects of the Christian faith have been examined in such microscopic detail as has the tongues phenomenon. In the course of a quarter century of research, certain evaluatory models emerged as methods for examining the phenomenon, enabling it to be studied from different perspectives. This volume attempts to bring together typical examples of these methodological approaches so that the reader can appreciate the strengths and weaknesses of each perspective.

The attempt here is not to advocate a personal or theological position regarding glossolalia. Rather, it is to explore the available methods for evaluating a phenomenon that is practiced by a sizeable minority within Christendom. Perhaps by understanding glossolalia in-the-round a clearer understanding of its nature and essence will emerge for those who participate as well as for those who do not.

I wish to acknowledge the contribution of Ms. Irene Pace who typed all of the drafts of this manuscript and who worked faithfully proofreading the text and verifying the bibliographic data. Without her assistance this project could not have been completed; I cannot praise her work too highly. Also, Bill Stembridge read the galleys and offered many helpful suggestions. His careful eye and gentle spirit have contributed much to this volume.

Finally, I am grateful to be a part of Mercer University where the disciple of research and writing is acknowledged and appreciated by a faculty and administration committed to excellence in scholarship.

Watson E. Mills
Macon, GA
July 1985

CONTENTS

1

WATSON E. MILLS

Glossolalia:
An Introduction

The pages of the history of both Judaism and Christianity are dotted with the presence of persons who have experienced God in special and unusual ways. Today these persons are sometimes lumped together and referred to as "charismatics" (from the Greek word "charisma," "gift" as in "gift of grace"). The Old Testament, for example, contains references to a number of persons who received a gift or grace in some special or uncommon sense.[1] For instance, King Saul was "turned into another man" by the "Spirit of God" (1 Sam. 10:6). God enlisted the aid of priests from the tribe of Levi, through the presence of his Spirit, to make military and political judgments (2 Chron. 20:14-17). The book of Isaiah (Isa. 11:1-2, 42:1) speaks of the ardent expec-

---

[1]Often interpreters of the Old Testament employ the term "ecstatic" to refer to this dimension of the prophetic utterance. In fact, the history of prophetic interpretation betrays a wide range of application of the ecstatic to prophetic studies. See Theodore H. Robinson, "The Ecstatic Element in Old Testament Prophecy," *The Expositor*, 8th series, 21 (1921): 217-38.

tation of a Messianic king whose coming would establish eternal peace because the spirit of the Lord would be upon him.

The earliest Christians regarded the reception of the "Holy" Spirit as a direct sign of God's presence in their midst. In both the writings of John and Paul, the Holy Spirit is described as that driving force holding together and giving purpose to the Christian community during the interim between Jesus' resurrection and his imminent return at the end of time.

The presence of this force within the early community metamorphosized frightened disciples into effective missionaries. The text of the New Testament seeks to document the presence of the Spirit by likening it to "noise, wind, and tongues of fire" (Acts 2:1-4). The second chapter of Acts, sometimes referred to as the Pentecost narrative, describes the excitement that gripped the early disciples as they began to proclaim the gospel of Jesus Christ in many languages to people from various parts of the Roman Empire (Acts 2:9-11). This is the charismatic phenomenon that is sometimes known as "zenolalia" (zenos, "foreign" and lalein, "to babble" or to "speak"). The day on which this zenolalia occurred is the day of Pentecost (from the Greek Pentecostals, "fiftieth"). The Day of Pentecost has become a part of the calendar of the Christian church, usually celebrated as the "birthday" of the Christian church though the origin of the feast is couched in agricultural history by ancient Israel.

The narrative also indicates that some Christians on Pentecost spoke not only foreign languages of which they had had no previous training, but also certain of them spoke a "strange" tongue which no one understood—a charismatic phenomenon referred to as "glossolalia" (glossa, "tongue," and lalein). Apparently, judging from the text of Acts 2, persons who practice glossolalia are frequently ecstatic and experience feeling of great joy.

Elsewhere in the New Testament, the phenomenon of glossolalia surfaced at Corinth.[2] In the course of his correspondence there, the Apostle Paul presented to the congregation a sober assessment of the meaning of charisma. Generally, Paul took the broad approach to the subject indicating that charisma referred to a variety of specific aspects of the Christian faith, i.e., various functions within the church (Rom. 5:15; 1 Cor. 1:11,

---

[2]Zenolalia refers to an utterance in a foreign tongue with reference to the Greeks—a language that he does not know, but is readily understood by a native. Glossolalia refers to a purely ecstatic utterance that represents no human language. The Corinthian utterances were glossolalic; those referred to in Acts contained elements of both the glossolalic and zenolalic types.

12:28). Paul consistently discussed the charismata in the Christian church in the larger context of "service" and "working."

So while Paul acknowledged the experiencing of special powers through the Holy Spirit, such as speaking in tongues, he went on to indicate that these are valid only to the extent that they work for the "common good" of the entire community (1 Cor. 14:39-40). He warned the Corinthian Christians not to become self-indulgent and overly fascinated with the ecstatic powers which may be admired by pagan detractors. Rather, Paul insisted that all spiritual gifts are but an individual indication of the presence of the greatest gift of all—Jesus Christ.

The charismatic phenomena of zenolalia and glossolalia, in the history of the Christian church, have been singled out by some groups as essential marks of the faith. Generally, these groups have been referred to in the twentieth century as "Pentecostal" and consistently argue that those who compose the "true" church receive the gift of tongues accompanied by other manifestations of the Spirit, such as the power of healing, as an *indication* of the difference between worldly and otherworldly existence. Some researchers see a continuity between the earliest days of Pentecost and present-day charismatic religion by tracing the evidence of "enthusiasm" throughout the history of the Christian faith. For an example, one key to understanding Montanism is to focus upon the certainty with which they predicted the imminent culmination of the world. Similar movements have come and gone in subsequent centuries, but few have been any more radical than the Montanists.[3]

Some see the Quakers and Shakers as a link between the ancient and modern charismatics.[4] In 1774 for an example, the Shakers moved from

---

[3]Glossolalia also occurred among the Albigenses in the twelfth century in France; among the Mendicant friars in the thirteenth century; among the Jansenites and the "little prophets" of the Cévennes of the seventeenth century; and among the Irvingites of the nineteenth century. There were several isolated instances reported in the United States in the 1900s. W. Jethro Walthall, a Baptist minister, for instance, spoke in tongues in 1879. He was later ejected from his denomination and founded the Holiness Baptist Association. See J. D. Williams, "The Modern Pentecostal Movement in America: A Brief Sketch of Its History and Thought," *Lexington Theological Quarterly*, 9:2 (1974): 50-59.

[4]For a typical Pentecostal account, see Klaude Kendrick, *The Promise Fulfilled: A History of the Modern Pentecostal Movement* (Gospel Publishing House, 1961), chaps. 2-3. A good scholarly treatment is Ronald A. Knox, *Enthusiasm: A Chapter in the History of Religion with Special Reference to the Seventeenth and Eighteenth Centuries* (Oxford University Press, 1961), chap. 8. Knox also traces the link between Methodism and other revival movements.

Manchester, England, to the vicinity of Albany, New York, to found a commune under the leadership of their prophetess Ann Lee Stanley. They regarded glossolalia as a sign of the true faith and as an indication that Christ's second coming was imminent. They also demonstrated their enthusiasm through the form of religious dancing.

While, within classic Pentecostalism, there is some divergence in certain areas of theology, there is surprising agreement on most of the fundamental doctrines. This agreement includes the place and significance of glossolalia. There is, among classic Pentecostals, virtual unanimity that the modern-day experience of glossolalia extends the practice as first given by God in apostolic times.[5]

Classic Pentecostalism regards glossolalia as but *one* of the nine[6] supernatural gifts of the spirit alluded to in the New Testament.[7] As a spiritual gift, glossolalia is a normal and quantifiable feature of the New Testament. The gift functions as a *sign* (outward evidence) of the baptism of the Spirit. It is this doctrine that has occupied such a place of cardinal importance in Pentecostal theology. While some classic Pentecostal theologians deny *the connection*, most follow Horton: "it is inconceivable that a supernatural experience like the baptism [of the Holy Spirit] should exist without a distinctive supernatural evidence. Tongues is that necessary evidence."[8]

THE RISE OF CLASSIC PENTECOSTALISM

During a New Year's Eve vigil on December 31, 1900, at Bethel College in Topeka, Kansas, 40 students assembled in a prayer meeting under

---

[5]Pentecostal writers have offered various explanations as to why the manifestation of glossolalia is so infrequent between the first and twentieth centuries. Donald Gee insists that the contemporary interest in glossolalia grows out of the twentieth century penchant for experience over belief. See Donald Gee, *Concerning Spiritual Gifts* (Gospel Publishing House, n.d.), p. 62.

[6]Harold Horton, *The Gifts of the Spirit* (Assembly of God Publishing House, 1954), page 33, suggests a threefold classification of spiritual gifts: (1) gifts of revelation (wisdom, knowledge, discerning of spirits); (2) gifts of power (faith, working of miracles, healing); (3) inspiration (prophecy, glossolalia, interpretation of glossolalia).

[7]Some Pentecostal apologists label glossolalia as the "least" of the nine gifts. See Harold Horton, *What is the Good of Speaking in Tongues?* (Assembly of God Publishing House, 1960), p. 4.

[8]Ibid., p. 8.

the leadership of a former Methodist minister, Charles F. Parham.[9] Parham had left the Methodist church in 1895 searching for the ultimate charismatic experience. He wished to prepare himself to meet the challenges that would come with the new century. He had founded Bethel College and vowed to build a curriculum around its only textbook—the Bible. The focus of study was on the "baptism by the Holy Spirit." During that New Year's Eve night, Parham laid hands on one of the students, Agnes Ozman. She not only spoke in tongues, but she reportedly talked fluently in several foreign languages. For those present, there seemed to be a halo around her head and face. Many others in the prayer meeting began speaking in tongues and making sounds that were not discernible as normal language to the others present.[10]

Bethel College was closed in 1901 and Parham moved on to hold revival meetings throughout Kansas and Missouri. In 1905 he founded a Bible training school in Houston, Texas. It had an enrollment of 25 students. These students were destined to become missionaries of the new Pentecostal revival. Among his Houston students was William J. Seymour, a black man from Louisiana, who was eager to be trained in Bible study. He earnestly sought the experience of glossolalia and other charismatic manifestations of the Spirit's presence.

In 1906, Seymour went to Los Angeles and subsequently received the gift of tongues on the night of April 6. Crowds began to gather wherever Seymour preached. He finally moved into an abandoned Methodist church at 312 Azusa Street. Then he attracted large crowds that were racially mixed. In time, the term "holy rollers" was applied to those who met at the Azusa Street mission. After being featured in a story in the *Los Angeles Times* the mission became a tourist attraction.

Thousands of people flocked to the Azusa mission from all over the United States. Even Seymour's teacher, Charles Parham, visited during the

---

[9]Some authorities dispute the claim that the origin of the Pentecostal movement is traceable simply to these antecedents of the Azusa Street mission; rather, some researchers point to the influence of evangelists like Charles Finney and D. L. Moody, or to the stirrings of evangelicals in America and in Europe during the 1900's. See, for instance, V. R. Wilson, "The Pentecostal Minister: Role Conflicts and Status Contradictions," *American Journal of Sociology*, 64 (1958-59): 494-504.

[10]Newspapers such as *The Kansas City Times* reported that twenty-one languages had been spoken during that service and in subsequent revival meetings.

year 1906 and tried to curb what he regarded as the "frenzied state" of the meetings. But Seymour's disciples refused to let him stay. Despite these warnings from his teacher, Seymour's ministry continued to flourish and it spread its influence to the south and to the east as far as New York, and even abroad. Oslo, Norway, became the focus of the first Pentecostal center in Europe after a Norwegian Methodist pastor, T. B. Barratt, on tour to the United States, had received the gift of tongues in November 1906 during a revival meeting in New York City.

The 1906 Los Angeles revival on Azusa Street represents the birth of the modern Pentecostal movement. Its basic theological stance is clearly stated in the first issue of Seymour's periodical, *The Apostolic Faith*, which was published in 1906 and sent free of charge to thousands of people, especially in the south.

From its very beginnings, Seymour's Azusa mission was opposed by those who refused to regard the charismatic phenomenon of speaking in tongues as the *essential* mark of the Christian faith. One of the attempts to de-radicalize Seymour's insistence upon the essential nature of glossolalia came about when one of Seymour's disciples, W. H. Durham, along with Eudorus N. Bell, attempted to coordinate various radical views on such issues as the relationship between sin and sanctification. In April 1914 a meeting was held in Hot Springs, Arkansas, to coordinate the now flowering Pentecostal movement. Several hundred delegates from all over the United States quickly adopted a statement of policy which gave local groups complete autonomy and assigned coordinating leaders to an executive agency. This new organization called itself the Assemblies of God with headquarters in Findlay, Ohio. A statement of faith was issued which affirmed speaking in tongues and the teaching that "entire sanctification" is "progressive" rather than "instantaneous." This view had the effect of cooling down Pentecostalism's most radical assertion that baptism by the Holy spirit is the "finished work of Christ." It also served to leave the door open for union between Methodist moderates, Baptist radicals, and others.

Other controversies plagued the emerging Pentecostal groups. One such controversy was rooted in the notion that the doctrine of the Trinity had been an invention of the Bishop of Rome and that baptism should be in the name of Jesus *only*. This controversy is sometimes referred to as "Pentecostal Unitarianism" or the "Jesus Only" Theology. By 1945, these

Pentecostals were known as the United Pentecostal Church.[11]

Since the 1940s, however, there has been a growing ecumenical spirit among Pentecostal groups.[12] The World Pentecostal Fellowship was established in 1949 in Paris (in opposition to the National Council of Churches). Much of this ecumenical spirit was the result of the work of Davis J. DuPlessis. A longtime secretary of the World Pentecostal Conference, DuPlessis later served as an active participant in the Second Vatican Council.[13] His call for unity among various Pentecostal bodies proved to be a turning point. As a consequence "World" Pentecostalism became a term with meaning and specificity. By 1955 Nils Bloch-Hoell reported thirty-six Pentecostal bodies of a combined membership with approximately one million, five hundred thousand. He noted further that there were another twenty-three organizations not reporting membership statistics.[14] By the 1960s, the stage had been set for the emergence of Walter Hollenweger's epoch-making work *Enthusiastisches Christentum: Die Pfingstbeweung in Geschichte und Gegenwart.*[15]

---

[11]The Assemblies of God reaffirmed the traditional (Chalcedonian) doctrine of the Trinity in their 1916 Statement of Fundamental Truths, thus aligning themselves with ecumenical orthodoxy and rejecting Pentecostal Unitarianism in general.

[12]The most definitive classification of Pentecostal groups is that offered by Charles Edwin Jones, *A Guide to the Study of the Pentecostal Movement* 2 vols. (American Theological Library Association/Scarecrow Press, 1983). Jones' classification of the various groups along doctrinal lines is the enlargement and refinement of a system first introduced in 1954 by Everett L. Moore, "Handbook of Pentecostal Denominations," (unpublished master's thesis, Pasadena College, 1954). Moore identified three categories of Pentecostals: (1) those who hold a Keswick view of sanctification; (2) those who hold a Holiness view of "entire" sanctification; (3) those who hold a "Jesus only" view of the god-head.

[13]His autobiographical account of his work in this area is entitled *The Spirit Bade Me Go: The Astounding Move of God in the Denominational Churches*, published by the author, 1960. This popular treatment has undergone many subsequent revisions.

[14]Nils Bloch-Hoell, *The Pentecostal Movement: Its Origin, Development, and Distinctive Character* (Allen and Unwin, 1964).

[15]Walter Hollenweger's multivolume dissertation written at the University of Zurich and entitled "Handbuch der Pfingstbewegung," in all of its enormity, is a gold mine of historical and statistical information on World Pentecostalism. Happily for the layman, Hollenweger summarized that work into a German publication (1966) entitled *Enthusiastisches Christentum: Die Pfingstbewegung in Geschichte und Gegenwart*, published by Rolf Brockhaus. In 1972 this epoch-making work appeared from Augsburg Publishing House under the English title *The Pentecostals: The Charismatic Movement in the Churches*. The work contains a thirty-five-page annotated bibliography.

Today, no one doubts the size and importance of World Pentecostalism. This "new force" within Christendom, born of this century out of the dispossessed of American society, may well be one of the major contributions of America to twentieth-century Christianity.

With all the difficulties of the easy generalization, and in spite of some perplexing differences in which the emphasis upon glossolalia is explained, it is reasonable to conclude that speaking in tongues has occupied a place of central importance among all Pentecostals. Glossolalia, at the least, is regarded as a normal phenomenon, and by many, a necessary component to the reception of the Holy Spirit.

THE RISE OF NEO-PENTECOSTALISM

The "new" charismatics, as they are sometimes called, began to appear in the 50s as the older, classical Pentecostals began to share their charismatic experiences with non-Pentecostal Christians.

By the early 50s, there was a growing disenchantment in the ranks of old-line Pentecostalism. Generally, there was dissatisfaction with what was perceived as limited vision and autocratic leadership. As the body of the disenchanted grew and gained financial backing, permanent support was forthcoming to inaugurate new programs and enlist new support. The rapid growth of the Full Gospel Business Men's Fellowship International clearly indicated the potential for charismatic religion *outside* the traditional Pentecostal circles. Founded by Demos Shakarian, a successful California dairyman reared in a Pentecostal home, the FGBMFI grew naturally out of the postwar mass revivals that unified Pentecostals all over the world.[16]

In 1951 Shakarian helped to organize the Oral Roberts Los Angeles campaign. Out of this meeting came the FGBMFI. Initially, the call went out for Pentecostals who wanted the "full experience" of the Christian life but who were being held back under the burdensome restrictions of old-line Pentecostalism. Quickly, this new alliance of charismatic businessmen spread across the U.S. and around the world. From its beginning the organization reached a new type of audience in settings far removed from the camp meetings of the old-line Pentecostal denominations. Meetings of local chapters, often staged in plush hotels, displayed the traditional charismatic vigor but in radically new surroundings. A broader and much more

---

[16]"The Story of Demos Shakarian and the Full Gospel Business Men's Fellowship," *The Voice of Deliverance* (August 1953): 9.

sophisticated audience became aware of the charismatic dimension of the faith. A figure of no less prominence than Walter Hollenweger concluded that the FGBMFI can claim credit for having gained a hearing for the healing evangelists in the non-Pentecostal churches.[17] The FGBMFI was responsible for introducing charismatic religion to hundreds of thousands of middle-class Americans.

Some of the strategies in the practice of charismatic religion had to be revised, others discarded. A new breed of people were the targets for its ministry.[18]

Oral Roberts, a keen observer of the changing mix in the makeup of the charismatics, moved slowly but resolutely in the 60s to insure that no innovation escaped his close scrutiny. In 1967, for instance, he abandoned his televised healing crusades after thirteen successful years. In 1968 he joined the prestigious Boston Avenue Methodist Church in Tulsa—a decision which shocked Pentecostal observers. The dedication of Oral Roberts University in 1967 marked the unique blending of charismatic religion and higher education—in an accredited university!

Perhaps more than any other figure,[19] Oral Roberts, with a newly designed TV series airing in prime time slots in all major U.S. markets, and a going university, has put the face of respectability upon the practice of charismatic religion.[20]

---

[17]Hollenweger, *op. cit.*, p. 6.

[18]Oral Roberts established the first important magazine published by an independent charismatic ministry. His magazine went through a series of name changes: *Healing Waters* (November 1947-August 1953), *America's Healing Magazine* (September 1953-December 1955), *Healing* (January 1956-July 1956), and *Abundant Life* (July 1956-). Roberts' magazine had a number of able editors, but the evangelist himself exercised close control over its contents.

[19]Many Pentecostal scholars cite the work of David J. DuPlessis as central in introducing Pentecostalism into the mainline denominations. As a longtime executive secretary for the World Pentecostal Conference, DuPlessis was in a unique position to contact leaders in the World Council of Churches. His autobiographical *The Spirit Bade Me Go: The Astounding Move of God in the Denominational Churches* (Logos International, 1972) is still available and documents this fascinating story.

[20]In more recent years, the liberal religious press has come to show a much greater respect for the charismatic movement. A few examples might include: Allen Walker, "Where Pentecostalism is Mushrooming," *Christian Century*, 85 (January 17, 1968): 81-82; "The Gift of Tongues," *Christianity Today* (April 11, 1969): 27-28; Jeffery L. Klaiber, "Pentecostal Breakthrough," *America*, 122 (January 31, 1970): 99-102.

On another front, earlier on in the 60s, neo-Pentecostalism was recognized as a respectable component of ecumenical Christianity. In April 1960, then rector of St. Mark's Episcopal Church in Van Nuys, California, Reverend Dennis Bennett, confessed to his congregation his own personal involvement for some months with charismatic religion in general, and speaking in tongues in particular.[21] Bennett had been reared a Congregationalist but had been converted to the Episcopal church in 1951 upon completion of his theological studies at Chicago Divinity School. He vowed not to leave the Episcopal ministry even though he was asked to leave St. Mark's. By July of 1960, he was called to be the rector of St. Luke's Episcopal Church in Seattle, a church of about 200 apathetic members. Within the course of one year 80 of those members had received the baptism of the Holy Spirit. By 1968 there were more than 2,000 members at St. Luke's and Dennis Bennett was now cropping up in every major denomination.[22] As early at 1963 the spread of charismatic religion into the mainline churches received national attention in an article in the *Christian Century*.[23]

The "new penetration" of charismatic religion into mainline churches was marked by the involvement of lay leaders. One early example is Jean Stone, who was a member of Dennis Bennett's congregation at Van Nuys. She was an affluent housewife who organized The Blessed Trinity Society in 1961 after being baptized by the Spirit at a prayer meeting in 1960 at St. Mark's. The Society was aimed at emphasizing the work of the third member of the trinity. The Society published a magazine called *Trinity*. Gradually, the seminars sponsored by The Blessed Trinity Society came to be known as "charismatic clinics" because invariably they featured charismatic testimonies and speaking in tongues. In 1966 Stone divorced and remarried on her way to Hong Kong to serve as a "faith missionary" in the charismatic movement there. The Blessed Trinity Society was absorbed into

---

[21]See Dennis J. Bennett, *Nine O'Clock in the Morning* (Logos International, 1970). See also Dennis and Rita Bennett, *The Holy Spirit and You* (Logos International, 1971).

[22]Michael Harper has written the best account tracing the development of the charismatic revival among the mainline denominations: *As At the Beginning: The Twentieth Century Pentecostal Revival* (Hodder and Stoughton, 1965).

[23]Frank Farrell, "Outburst of Tongues: The New Penetration," *Christianity Today*, 7 (September 13, 1963): 3-7.

Melodyland, an organization then headed by David Wilkerson. *Trinity* became the *Logos Journal* and the *New Covenant* which remain the leading periodicals of the charismatic movement today.[24]

The Catholic charismatic movement[25] is usually traced to the involvement of lay faculty members at Duquesne University in Pittsburgh in February of 1967. The so-called "Duquesne Weekend" saw about 30 people receive the gift of the Holy Spirit. From Duquesne, Catholic interest in charismatic religion quickly spread to Notre Dame and to Michigan State University. The resulting campus charismatic groups began to meet with local chapters of the FGBMFI, and by the summer of 1967 more than 3,000 Catholic charismatics attended "Notre Dame Weekend." To the chagrin of church leaders, most were priests, nuns, or teaching monks.[26]

In general the place and importance of glossolalia is just as central in neo-Pentecostalism as in classic Pentecostalism; however, this generality is often accompanied by the caveat that some of the emotional excesses of the latter are not present in the former. Again, this assertion is *generally* true, but no would claim that neo-Pentecostalism has no room for the emotional dimension. Perhaps a more precise claim would focus on a *lesser emphasis* upon the emotional in neo-Pentecostalism than in classic-Pentecostalism.[27]

---

[24]Some of the additional, more prominent, charismatic periodicals include: *Charisma Digest*, Full Gospel Business Men's Fellowship International; *Cross and Switchblade*, Teen Challenge Publications; *Heartbeat*, Charismatic Educational Centers, Inc.; *New Nation News*, Texas Soul Clinic; *New Wine*, Holy Spirit Teaching Missions; *Voice*, Full Gospel Business Men's Fellowship International.

[25]The Catholic phenomenon is regarded here as a part of the wider neo-Pentecostal movement despite the disclaimers of some Catholic writers who reject this terminology in favor of the term "renewal."

[26]For an excellent definitive bibliography on Catholic Pentecostalism see Edward D. O'Connor, editor, *Perspectives on Charismatic Renewal* (University of Notre Dame Press, 1975), pp. 156-84. Earlier, shorter bibliographies include: John Gordon Melton, *Catholic Pentecostal Movement: A Bibliography* (Institute for the Study of American Religion, 1976); Edward D. O'Connor, *The Pentecostal Movement in the Catholic Church* (Ave Maria Press, 1971), pp. 295-301; Peter Hocken, "Pentecostals on Paper," *The Clergy Review*, 59:11 (November 1974): 750-67; 60:3 (March 1975: 161-83; 60:6 (June 1975): 344-67.

[27]Like their classic-Pentecostal counterparts, Neo-Pentecostals also may experience singing in tongues, individually or collectively. See Dennis J. Bennett, *Nine O'Clock in the Morning* (Logos International, 1970), p. 181.

GLOSSOLALIA IN RECENT RESEARCH

The earliest examinations of glossolalia were centered almost exclusively in *polemics*.[28] It was not until the debate about the *usefulnesses* of tongues subsided that researchers were motivated to put the phenomenon under the microscope and examine it as they would any other phenomenon in religious experience. The subject then became of interest to theologians, lexicographers, history of religionists, psychologists, sociologists, linguists, and behaviorists alike. Certain models and approaches have emerged in the course of these rigorous examinations. Representative examples from five of these models will be featured in this volume: (1) the exegetical model; (2) the historical model; (3) the theological model; (4) the psychological model; (5) the sociocultural model.[29] Part I begins with a careful analysis of the terminology involved in the study of glossolalia. It also contains articles that examine the occurrences of glossolalia in non-biblical writings as well as in the New Testament itself. Part II deals with the history of the phenomenon in the history of Christianity as well as in more recent manifestations such as the holiness movement, neo-Pentecostalism, black Pentecostalism, and Catholic Pentecostalism. Part III features four essays that attempt to focus the theological issues that are implicitly rooted in the discussions about glossolalia. There has been much interest in the psychological dimension of speaking in tongues. This research area is the focus of Part IV. Finally, in Part V, sociocultural research is examined.

Admittedly, the discussions about the significance of tongue speaking have ranged from hostile, to heated, to genuine give and take. These essays were chosen, not because of any theological position, but because it seemed that they have contributed significantly to the kind of discussions that inevitably lead to better focus and understanding. The approach here is that no subject, however personal or emotional, is too sacred or too profane to stand the test of rigorous critical examination. It is in that spirit that this volume of readings is offered.

---

[28]There are certain important exceptions noted in chapter 2.

[29]For a fuller discussion of these and other approaches to the study of glossolalia, see chapter 2. The bibliography will provide reference data for most works in the field.

2

WATSON E. MILLS

Glossolalia:
A Survey of the Literature

Prior to 1950 there were only a handful of studies available on the subject of glossolalia, and some of the more significant of these were not accessible to English readers.[1] Generally, the literature that is available reflects a general lack of clarity on several fronts, especially regarding the defining characteristics of glossolalia. The turbulent period of the 1960's saw deep divisions in the institutional church brought on by the rapid growth of the charismatic phenomena. As a consequence much of the writing is deeply biased with respect to the usefulness of the tongues phenomenon. Invariably, the descriptive material alternates between attempting to jus-

---

[1]Two standard works, for instance, published in the early part of the twentieth century remain untranslated today: *Das Zungenreden geschichtlich und psychologisch untersucht* by Eddison Mosiman and *De la Glossolalie chez les premiers chrétiens et des phénomènes similaires* by Émile Lombard.

tify the experience as essential or dismissing it altogether as meaningless if not psychotic.[2]

This bibliographic essay attempts to identify some of the more significant work done in the area of glossolalia studies. The traditional approaches that relate to historical, biblical, theological, psychological studies will be examined as well as the more recent approaches that are based on the clinical description of the phenomenological dimension of tongue-speaking.

PRIMARY MATERIALS

The references to glossolalia in Acts and 1 Corinthians exhaust the direct instances of the phenomenon in the canonical record. Virtually all scholars, including Pentecostals, agree that the reference to tongues in Mark 16:17 is spurious.[3] Krister Stendahl[4] presents a sensitive and fair treatment of the textual materials. This noted Roman Catholic scholar is noncharismatic, and yet realizes the importance of the questions posed by Charismatics. Stendahl begins by restating the Pauline recipe for dealing with the reality of glossolalia, and only *then* turns to Acts 2. He gives more emphasis to Paul's discussion than the Pentecostal narrative because he regards the latter to be a Lukan objectification of a symbolic event. Frank Stagg[5] focuses upon the importance of source criticism for understanding the Acts material. Taken in its present form, the Pentecost account in Acts 2 is clear enough. Almost all interpreters recognize that Luke represents the tongues on the day of Pentecost as understandable language of some kind. The disagreement arises over the historicity of the narrative. The significance of source studies is carefully documented here, and some recent solutions offered by scholarship are discussed.

---

[2]For example see Alexander Mackie, *The Gift of Tongues* (Doran, 1921).

[3]See, for example, Bastiaan Van Elderen, "Glossolalia in the New Testament," *Bulletin of the Evangelical Theological Society*, 7 (1964): 53-58.

[4]"The New Testament Evidence," in *The Charismatic Movement*, ed. Michael Hamilton (Eerdmans, 1975), 49-60.

[5]"Glossolalia in the New Testament," in *Glossolalia: Tongues Speaking in Biblical, Historical, and Psychological Perspective*, ed. Frank Stagg, E. Glenn Hinson, and Wayne E. Oates (Abingdon Press, 1967), 20-44.

Another important study is the one by D. Moody Smith.[6] He draws the necessary distinction between New Testament exegesis and Christian experience, pointing out how some tongues-speakers confuse the two at best and at worst allow the latter to dominate the former to a degree that exceeds the normative role for experience in Christian history.

The apostolic period is dealt with in an essay by Ira J. Martin.[7] The Old Testament background is important, too, for an understanding of glossolalia, and certain of its texts may be approached from the vantage point of prophetic ecstaticism.[8] Although the term *ecstasy* is sometimes regarded only as a descriptive term rather than a scientific or psychological expression, it does define clearly a general emotional state closely approximating that in which glossolalic utterances arise. Ecstasy may be likened to enthusiasm based on the way in which the adherent's mind is absorbed into that of the deity. Such a condition is apparent in certain passages relating to the Old Testament prophets. The individual who enters into an ecstatic state may be oblivious to the external world. He may lose his self-consciousness and his rational thought processes may be severely impaired.[9]

Ira J. Martin has assembled some of the ancient texts that may be glossolalic in nature.[10] Martin's work contains a series of interesting and informative appendices: (1) "Non-Christian instances of ecstatic speaking"; (2) "Historical interpretations" (a catalogue of various "interpretations" of glossolalia offered by twentieth-century scholars); (3) "Psychological Explanations" (a similar catalogue of the various psychological interpretations offered to date by researchers).

---

[6]"Glossolalia and Other Spiritual Gifts in a New Testament Perspective," *Interpretation*, 28 (1974): 307-20.

[7]"Glossolalia in the Apostolic Church," *Journal of Biblical Literature*, 63 (1944): 123-30.

[8]Cf. Alfred Guillaume, *Prophecy and Divination among the Hebrews and Other Semites* (Hodder and Stoughton, 1938).

[9]For a full discussion of the relevance of this aspect for an understanding of glossolalia, see John T. Bunn, "Glossolalia in Historical Perspective," in *Speaking in Tongues: Let's Talk about It*, ed. Watson E. Mills (Word, 1973), 36-47.

[10]*Glossolalia in the Apostolic Church: A Study of Tongue Speech* (Berea College Press, 1960). See also Nils Ivar Johan Engelsen, "Glossolalia and Other Forms of Inspired Speech According to 1 Corinthians 12-14," (Ph.D. dissertation, Yale University, 1970).

The references in the church are fathers identified and discussed thoroughly in Kenneth Bruce Welliver[11] and Carl Clemens.[12] Clemens reviews the second- and third-century references to speaking in tongues found in Origen and Irenaeus and concludes that these fathers interpret tongues as speaking in a "foreign language." He doubts, however, that these references are to an absolutely "new" language, noting that Acts 10:46 and 19:6 read "tongues" without the adjective "other." He theorizes that the term "other" may have been added to the Pentecost narrative by a later redactor in an attempt to imitate the Midrash, according to which seven voices changed into seventy tongues at Sinai. Hence before the addition, Acts 2 read "tongues" just as Acts 10:46 and 19:6.

GENERAL INTRODUCTION

One of the standard general treatments in English is George B. Cutten's *Speaking with Tongues: Historically and Psychologically Considered*.[13] Although the book is somewhat dated, it remains central for the student of glossolalia. Cutten, then president of Colgate University, typifies the prevailing attitude concerning glossolalia: he felt the experience belonged mainly to those of lower socioeconomic status. He was certain the phenomenon of tongues would never be taken seriously by the mainline denominations.

Father Morton Kelsey asserts that glossolalia is a genuine spiritual experience, and he treats the subject with a degree of Christian maturity seldom found in this kind of literature.[14] He traces the history of the phenomenon from its beginnings to its resurgence in the twentieth century. It was Kelsey's volume that paved the way for discussions among tongue-speaking and non-tongue-speaking Christians. Slowly, the dialog was moving from confrontation to understanding.

---

[11]"Pentecost and the Early Church" (Ph.D. dissertation, Yale University, 1961).

[12]"The 'Speaking With Tongues' of the Early Christians," *Expository Times*, 10 (1898): 344-52.

[13](Yale University Press, 1927).

[14]*Tongues Speaking: An Experiment in Spiritual Experience* (Doubleday, 1964).

Canon Michael Hamilton offers an interdisciplinary analysis of the strengths and weaknesses of the phenomenon.[15] It is a highly readable work consisting of four major sections with ten essays. The contributors come from both charismatic and noncharismatic traditions. In addition to bibliographies at the end of each chapter, there is a general bibliography at the conclusion of the volume together with a short phonograph record that contains a sample of tongue speech. Also of significance are six essays edited by J. Elmo Agrimson.[16] This anthology deals with the range of spiritual gifts and the ways these relate to the body of Christ. These general studies should be supplemented with the two notable foreign works by Mosiman and Lombard cited above. Both of these works remain untranslated but represent significant research on the subject.

Less technical introductions include those by Laurence Christenson[17], Watson E. Mills[18] and Alexander Mackie.[19] Christenson, an American Lutheran pastor, relates his own experience and is typical of many who were once outside of Pentecostalism but are now proponents of the movement. In my work I sought out areas of agreement between defenders and critics of tongues. Essentially I argued that each "side" needed to listen to the concerns and fears of the other. Mackie's volume is a vehement denial of the legitimacy of glossolalia. He relegates the entire experience to the realm of the demonic, and functionally describes it as a psychosis. The work is indicative of a type of the polemic that was popular during the era of confrontation and hostility.

Among notable Pentecostal assessments of the phenomenon are works edited by Wade Horton[20] and Vinson Synan.[21] These volumes offer per-

---

[15]*The Charismatic Movement* (Eerdmans, 1975). There have been a number of these volumes that attempt to set glossolalia "in-the-round." See *Aspects of the Pentecostal-Holiness Movement,*Vinson Synan, ed., (Logos International, 1975);*Speaking in Tongues: Let's Talk about It*, Watson E. Mills, ed., (Word Books, 1973).

[16]*Gifts of the Spirit and the Body of Christ: Perspectives on the Charismatic Movement*, ed. J. Elmo Agrimson (Augsburg, 1974).

[17]*Speaking in Tongues and the Significance for the Church* (Bethany, 1968).

[18]*Understanding Speaking in Tongues* (Eerdmans, 1972).

[19]*The Gift of Tongues* (Doran, 1921).

[20]*The Glossolalia Phenomenon* (Pathway, 1966).

[21]*Aspects of Pentecostal-Charismatic Origins* (Logos International, 1975).

spective and general orientation from the vantage point of classic Pentecostalism. The writers continue the discussion into its present place in neo-Pentecostalism. A study critical of some of the suppositions taken for granted in these studies is a work three seminary professors—Frank Stagg, E. Glenn Hinson, and Wayne E. Oates.[22] These three essays are sensitive and evenly balanced. Together they present a concise overview of tongues in biblical, historical and theological perspective. A book that presents articles by participants and nonparticipants alike is *Speaking in Tongues: Let's Talk about It*.[23] That such a volume is possible signals a change in attitude from the previous decade when hostility and division characterized what little communication there was between debaters.

TONGUES IN CHRISTENDOM

One approach to the study of tongue speech has been to place it within the context of Pentecostalism. The so-called "classic Pentecostals" are those Christians who are presently active in several Pentecostal groups: Assemblies of God, United Pentecostal Church, Pentecostal Church of America, The Church of God, Pentecostal Holiness, etc. Most of these groups emerged in the early twentieth century when there was a schism within the Holiness movement over the question of what constituted "proof" for baptism by the Holy Spirit. A standard treatment of the classic Pentecostal position is John T. Nichol, *Pentecostalism*.[24] The English translation of Walter Hollenweger, *Enthusiastisches Christentum: die Pfingstbewegung in Geschichte und Gegenwart* was published in 1972 as *The Pentecostals: The Charismatic Movement in the Churches* (Augsburg, 1972). The translation of this massive work signaled that Pentecostal studies were indeed becoming international in scope. Hollenweger's monumental ten volume "handbook" of the Pentecostal movement won him the doctorate from the University of Zurich in 1966. *The Pentecostals* contains much sociological material that makes lively reading even though it is interlaced with technical bibliographic information. Hollenweger's treatment of the rise of Pentecostalism in mainline Protestant churches is

---

[22]*Glossolalia: Tongues Speaking in Biblical, Historical, and Psychological Perspective* (Abingdon, 1967).

[23](Word Books, 1973).

[24](Harper & Row, 1966).

well written and deserving of a wide audience. Also pertinent is a work by Vinson Synan.[25]

The term *neo-Pentecostal* is usually used to refer to members of the historic Protestant denominations that are not noted for "charismatic interest." Only in the last two decades has tongues speaking become a factor in these groups, and the adherents are sometimes referred to as "new Pentecostals." A book that traces what Frank Farrell has called the "new penetration" is *As at the Beginning: The Twentieth Century Pentecostal Revival* by Michael Harper.[26] Another useful contribution is Russell Spittler, editor, *Perspectives on the New Pentecostalism.*[27] Catholics have been an integral part of the charismatic movement since 1967. This aspect is noted by Edward D. O'Donnell[28] and James F. Breckenridge.[29] A small paperback volume by Monsignor Vincent M. Walsh[30] provides a good overview of the charismatic movement among Catholics. Cardinal Joseph Suenens[31] focuses upon the broader area of a theology of the spirit and only then speaks to the issue of the experiential dimension of the faith.

As glossolalia began to grow within the major denominations, some official pronouncement on the subject seemed necessary. The episcopal diocese of California issued the late Bishop Pike's "preliminary report" in 1963. His "pastoral letter" grew out of the findings of the twenty-page report submitted by a panel of nine persons.[32] Other official reports include

---

[25]*The Holiness Movement in the United States* (Eerdmans, 1971).

[26](Hodder and Stoughton, 1965).

[27](Baker Book House, 1976).

[28]*The Pentecostal Movement* (Ave Maria, 1971).

[29]*The Theological Self-Understanding of the Catholic Charismatic Movement* (University Press of America, 1980). See also Kevin and Dorothy Ranaghan, *As the Spirit Leads Us* (Paulist, 1973) and Leon Joseph Suenens, *A New Pentecost* (Seabury, 1975).

[30]*A Key to Charismatic Renewal in the Catholic Church* (Abbey Press, 1971).

[31]*A New Pentecost* (Seabury Press, 1973). See also Kevin and Dorothy Ranagan, *Catholic Pentecostals* (Paulist Press, 1971); Donald Gelpi, *Pentecostalism: A Theological Viewpoint* (Paulist Press, 1971). A dated but definitive bibliography on Catholic Pentecostalism is that by J. Gordon Melton, *Catholic Pentecostal Movement: A Bibliography* (Garrett Bibliographical Lectures, No. 7, 1971).

[32]See James A. Pike, "Pastoral Letter Regarding 'Speaking in Tongues,' " *Pastoral Psychology*, 15 (1964): 55-61. See also A. W. Sadler, "Glossolalia and Possession: An Appeal to the Episcopal Study Commission," *Journal for the Scientific Study of Religion*, 4 (1964): 84-90.

those printed by study commissions of the Lutheran ("Report on Glossolalia," a report of the Commission on Evangelism of the American Lutheran Church [Minneapolis, 1962]) and Presbyterian ("Report of the
Special Study Committee on the Work of the Holy Spirit," a report of the
United Presbyterian Church of the U. S. A. [Philadelphia, 1970]) churches.

The definitive compendium of these documents is a three-volume wor-
kedited by Kilian McDonnell.[33] Volumes one and two contain eighty documents dated between 1960-1979 that are continental, national, and
regional in nature, while the eleven documents in volume three are international in scope.

A major recent report is that edited by Arnold Bittlinger, *The Church
Is Charismatic*.[34] This volume consists of documents, on-scene reports,
personal reflections, and discussions that trace the involvement of the World
Council of Churches in the Charismatic movement.

PSYCHOLOGICAL STUDIES

For orientation and reference, consult an article by E. Mansell Pattison.[35] Pattison reports on a variety of studies done on the subject as well
as contributing his own research. He concludes his essay with a commentary on the theological implications of glossolalia.

Carl Jung first referred to glossolalia in a psychological sense in his *On
Psychology and Pathology of So-Called Occult Phenomena*.[36] He explained the phenomenon as a kind of somnambulism, or multiple personality in which some center other than the ego possesses the motor centers
of the personality. Glossolalia is not necessarily pathological according to
Jung.

Alexander Mackie concluded that the behavior of the glossolalists included symptoms such as an unstable nervous system, disturbed sex life,
perversions, exhibitionism, etc. He described glossolalia as speech that
manifested imitation or simulation, a torrent of unintelligible words re-

---

[33]*Presence, Power, Praise: Documents on the Charismatic Renewal* (Liturgical Press,
1980).

[34](World Council of Churches, 1981).

[35]"Behavioral Science Research on the Nature of Glossolalia" in *Journal of the American Scientific Affiliation*, 20 (1968): 73-86.

[36](1902; reprinted by Pantheon Books, 1963).

sulting from an inner unrestrainable compulsion. He concluded that glossolalia was a symptom of emotionalism or dissociative process, and that it is definitely pathological in nature.[37]

George Cutten[38] suggests that glossolalists experience a state of personal disintegration in which the verbo-motive centers may become obedient to subconscious impulses. He linked glossolalia to hysteria, catalepsy, ecstasy, and schizophrenia. He even suggested that when the speaker used a language unknown to him, the speaker had in reality been previously exposed to it: the "foreign" language existed in his subconscious and was brought out by abnormal conditions without volition on the speaker's part.

Lincoln Vivier completed a comprehensive study that compared glossolalists with nonglossolalists.[39] His project called for the use of two control groups: twenty pro-tongue speakers and twenty members of a Christian church who did not approve of the practice of glossolalia. In addition, there was an experimental group of twenty-four glossolalists. His methods included administering the Willoughby Test, the Rosenweig Picture Frustration Test, and the Thematic Apperception Test. His findings indicated that glossolalists often came from homes in which there was a high degree of psychopathology present, resulting from alcoholism, nervous breakdowns, and so on. He further discovered that as a group, charismatics were anxious, experienced difficulty in nervous control, were often superstitious, and employed the mechanism of repression in frustrating situations. Vivier's summary characterization of glossolalists is as follows: (1) a preference for feeling rather than thought; (2) an interest in the unusual and extraordinary; (3) fewer formalized thought processes; (4) a freedom from traditional or orthodox behavior patterns.

Morton Kelsey[40] observed that glossolalia is different in kind and quality from either an ecstatic hysterical experience or a release of strong religious emotions. Kelsey attempted to define glossolalia in terms of Jung's theory of the collective unconscious. He doubts there is a causal relationship between glossolalia and schizophrenia because his research indicates

---

[37]*The Gift of Tongues* (Doran, 1921).

[38]*Speaking in Tongues: Historically and Psychologically Considered* (Yale, 1927).

[39]"Glossolalia" (unpublished doctor's dissertation, University of Vitwatersrand, 1960).

[40]*Tongue Speaking: An Experiment in Spiritual Experience* (Doubleday, 1964).

that glossolalists suffer no damage to their ego. Moreover, they remain clearly able to differentiate between reality and unreality during and after the experience. He rejects the notion that glossolalia is in fact a form of hysteria because he sees the results of the spiritual experience manifesting itself in an increased ability to cope with reality.

James N. Lapsley and John H. Simpson[41] referred to glossolalia as psychomotor behavior with similarities to trance states, somnambulism mediumship, and automatism. Most of those involved in the neo-Pentecostal movement have a deep need for personal security and emotional expression. The movement has attracted a sizable number of clergy from various denominations who have been frustrated and concerned about the nature and purpose of their work within the confines of the traditional church. Lapsley and Simpson suggest that glossolalia serves as an emotional outlet for people who often exhibit more anxiety and personality instability than non-tongue speakers.

Using Rorschach techniques, W. W. Wood compared members of a Pentecostal group with members of a non-Pentecostal group in the same cultural setting.[42] He sought to test the assumption that Pentecostalism provides a place for "intense, immediate and positive emotion" in religion. He discovered that Pentecostals lack an adequately structured value-attitude system. They often mobilize their inner resources to meet this strongly felt threat of instability. They reorganize their basic perceptual patterns to meet these concerns. They have an uncommon degree of uncertainty concerning interpersonal relationships coupled with a strong drive to feel a close fellowship with others. Wood concluded that there may be psychologically based reasons for the participation of individuals in a movement such as Pentecostalism, and that there must be differences in basic perceptual habits and consequently in personality types.

Stanley Plog[43] focused upon the economic level of two neo-Pentecostal groups by examining 272 subjects in Southern California. His 1965 sur-

---

[41]"Speaking in Tongues: Token of Group Acceptance and Divine Approval," *Pastoral Psychology*, 15 (May 1964): 48-55.

[42]*Culture and Personality Aspects of the Pentecostal Holiness Religion* (Morton, 1965).

[43]"Preliminary Analysis of Group Questionnaires on Glossolalia," (unpublished data, University of California, 1966).

vey indicated a median income of over $621 per month with a range of $100-$1600 per month. For both groups the occupational categories were as follows: "professional and technical" (34%); "housewives" (24%); "clerical-secretarial" (17%). The average ages of the two groups was 44 and 42; there were 59% women and 41% men in one group and 51% women and 49% men in the other group. Glossolalia was high in both groups (75% and 80%) as well as church attendance (95% and 100%). Plog noted evidence of improved interpersonal relationships in the lives of group members within the Pentecostal movement.

Wayne E. Oates[44] has examined the sociopsychological dimensions of glossolalia and concluded that "intellectualization, institutionalization and sophistication result in the repression of deep religious feelings, aspirations and ideas." When these emotions finally break through, the first attempts at communicating them may sound like "babble." Oates correlates glossolalia with the language of children—the infantile babble that is meaningless to an adult. These "babblings" disappear as the child matures, but may reappear as glossolalia if the individual tries to verbalize long-repressed religious convictions for the first time. Oates sees the resurgence of glossolalia in the present day, in different social strata, as the breaking through of deeply felt, long pent-up religious feelings. Glossolalists, according to Oates, tend to have weak egos, confused identities, high anxiety levels, and generally, unstable personalities. Neo-Pentecostals are often members of the affluent middle class who suffer from emotional deprivation, and for them speaking in tongues provides a form of release.

Theodore Spoerri[45] reserves the term *glossolalia* for instances of ritualized tongue speaking. Using case histories, he demonstrated how disintegration of the speech profile may arise in cases of exorcism, acute catatonic schizophrenia, and chronic schizophrenia. He analyzed examples of tongue-speaking, and found a striking resemblance to the schizophrenic dialogue in terms of sound formation, vocal color, rhythm, and speech melody.

---

[44]"Socio-Psychological Study of Glossolalia" in *Glossolalia: Tongue Speaking in Biblical, Historical, and Psychological Perspective*, ed. Frank Stagg, E. Glenn Hinson, and Wayne E. Oates (Abingdon, 1967).

[45]"Ekstatische Rede und Glossolalie," in *Beiträge zur Ekstase* (Karger, 1967).

By the late sixties the older psychological stereotype began to disappear as evident in two studies published near the end of that decade. E. Mansell Pattison[46] studied forty-three people (from a number of churches) who had been "healed by faith." Of these, thirty-nine were glossolalists. He used the Spitzer mental-status schedule, the MMPI (Minnesota Multiphasic Personality Inventory), and the Cornell Medical Index as testing devices. He found that these subjects showed a strong need for social acceptance and social affiliation. This need led to the extensive use of denial and repression as major coping mechanisms. The subjects from the lower and lower-middle classes (both rural and urban) demonstrated the overt psychopathology of a schizophrenic, hysterical, or hypochondriacal nature. The subjects from the middle and upper classes demonstrated no gross psychopathology. They were well-integrated, highly functional individuals who were clinically "normal."

Luther P. Gerlach and Virginia H. Hine[47] conducted a study to determine the factors that are crucial to the growth of the tongues movement. They interviewed 239 Pentecostals asking them to rank in importance the factors that influenced them to seek the experience of tongues. The study revealed that the most significant factor was contact with an individual who had already had the experience.

Another study done in 1969 by Felicitas D. Goodman[48] explained that "Glossolalia is a vocalization uttered while the speaker is in a state of dissociation." This researcher concluded that glossolalia is the result of the believer's being in a trance.[49]

---

[46]"Behavorial Research on the Nature of Glossolalia," *Journal of the American Scientific Affiliation*, 20 (September 1968): 73-86.

[47]"Five Factors Crucial to the Growth and Spread of a Modern Religious Movement," *Journal for the Scientific Study of Religion*, 7 (1968): 23-40.

[48]"Phonetic Analysis of Glossolalia in Four Cultural Settings," *Journal for the Scientific Study of Religion*, 8 (1969): 227-39.

[49]The same argument, presented in a more extended form, is available in Goodman, "Speaking in Tongues in Four Cultural Settings," *Confinia Psychiatrica*, 12 (1969): 113-29. William J. Samarin offers a critique of Goodman's arguments in his "Sociolinguistic Versus Neuropsychological Explanations for Glossolalia: Comment on Goodman's Paper," *Journal for the Scientific Study of Religion*, 11 (1972): 293-96. For Goodman's response, see "Altered Mental State Versus 'Style of Discourse': Reply to Samarin," *Journal for the Scientific Study of Religion*, 11 (1972): 297-99.

Three major studies were published in 1972, each representing a different and yet persistent style for interpreting the data available. John Kildahl[50] focused on the personal experiences of individuals and suggested that tongue speaking should be understood as a variety of aberrant behavior, like neuroses and other psychogenic disorders. Kildahl used psychiatric interviews and batteries of psychological tests to document his conclusion that glossolalists were more submissive, suggestible and dependent on leaders than were non-glossolalists. Glossolalists were found to initiate their speech in the presence of or by thinking and feeling emotionally "close" to some authority figure, either real or imagined. Based upon interviews, the Rorschach test, thematic appreciation test, and the MMPI, Kildahl concluded that glossolalia is an example of "regression in the service of the ego."

Felicitas Goodman[51] understands tongue speaking to be extraordinary behavior, usually associated with altered states of consciousness that may be culturally patterned and beneficial to society. From an analysis of twenty-nine case histories, Goodman pointed out that none of her informants appeared to be psychotic; however, they did have two qualities in common—fundamentalist convictions about the role and nature of the Holy Spirit and a "before and after" phase in their lives. The point of demarcation between these two phases was marked by a clear and decisive "change." Glossolalia became the means of demonstrating the effect of and the degree of intensity of this change. Goodman's study showed that glossolalists varied widely in their personality structure and in the reasons they give for joining a charismatic congregation. Goodman remarked that glossolalia should be understood as a vocalization pattern, a speech automatism, and a dissociation that reflects neurophysiologic processes present in this mental state.

The third volume produced in 1972 was William Samarin's *Tongues of Men and Angels: The Religious Language of Pentecostalism.*[52] Samarin's understanding of tongues emphasizes neither the aberrant aspects of this behavior nor its extraordinary features. Instead, Samarin sees tongue

---

[50]*The Psychology of Speaking in Tongues* (Harper and Row, 1972).

[51]*Speaking in Tongues: A Cross-Cultural Study of Glossolalia* (University of Chicago Press, 1972).

[52](Macmillan and Company, 1972).

speaking as anomalous behavior because it is different from usual speech patterns by virtue of being nonlinguistic in nature. His final judgment is that glossolalic utterances are neither abnormal, pathological, nor always an expression of an altered state of consciousness. While Samarin suggests that in some sense glossolalia is "learned behavior," he is quick to point out that it is not learned in the sense that a foreign language is learned. Rather, the tongue speaking "is the product of considerable instruction, whether or not glossolalia comes suddenly or gradually."[53]

While the earlier studies enabled critics to dismiss glossolalia as a pathological experience,[54] or some kind of general psychic catharsis akin to ecstaticism,[55] presently there is a reluctance to regard the glossolalist as more "abnormal" than the non-tongue-speaking Christian.

Julius Laffal[56] studied taped interviews of an experienced glossolalist minister to determine if communication occurs during glossolalic discourse. When these tape recordings were replayed, the listeners tended to make consistent judgments about their contents even though the meaning differed from what was in the speaker's mind. The audience tended to attribute personal and affective content to the glossolalic speech more than other kinds of informational content. Laffal concludes that although glossolalia had a noncommunicative role, it was expressive of social sharing.

Thomas I. DeVol[57] did a study on Pentecostal prayer and meditation. He judged that the altered state of consciousness achieved differs from that induced by drugs or other means since it can be induced at will. This altered state of consciousness may appear in a subject regardless of psychological sophistication or formal knowledge or training. DeVol does believe

---

[53]Also see William J. Samarin, "Glossolalia as Regressive Speech," *Language and Speech*, 16 (1973): 77-89. For a comprehensive review of Samarin's book, see Theodore Mueller, "A Linguistic Analysis of Glossolalia: A Review Article," *Concordia Theological Quarterly*, 45 (1981): 185-91.

[54]See Alexander Mackie, *The Gift of Tongues* (Doran, 1921).

[55]See Ira Martin, "Glossolalia in the Apostolic Church," *Journal of Biblical Literature*,53 (1944): 123-30.

[56]"Communication of Meaning in Glossolalia," *Journal of Social Psychology*, 92 (April 1974): 277-91.

[57]"Ecstatic Pentecostal Prayer and Meditation," *Journal of Religion and Health*, 13:4 (1974): 285-88.

that the experience has socially redeeming value because it is associated with the great ethical tradition of Christianity. He lists a number of effects on behavior such as: (1) increase in the effective use of time; (2) decreased preoccupation with bodily appetites; (3) greater sensitivity and tolerance in dealing with other people; (4) less defensiveness and greater openness; (5) an increased interest in things "religious"; (6) an increased desire to share the experience with other people.

SOCIO-CULTURAL STUDIES

Enthusiastic, ecstatic possession and other similar phenomena have long intrigued anthropologists. There have been a number of cross-cultural studies of the ethnographic data. The social function of tongue speech seems to vary with the particular social movement of which it is an expression.

R. A. Knox[58] studied the occurrences of glossolalia in the eighteenth and nineteenth centuries among the traditional Christian groups. He noted that the experiential component of religious experience had been largely displaced by "intellectual" religious practices. Knox discovered that among these traditional groups, tongue speech functioned to reestablish an experiential base for the practice of the Christian faith. Glossolalia served as "proof" of the presence of God in the believer's life. P. Worsley[59] documents how glossolalia verifies the leader's claim to authority. This particular social function of glossolalia may explain its presence among shamans and priests throughout the history of religion.[60]

Ericka Bourguignon[61] reports on studies done on religion in native societies. She notes a variety of forms of glossolalia among the primitives. In some cases, the practice was part of a pattern that included trances and the like. In other instances, tongue speech occurred as isolated behavior.

By far, the major practice of glossolalia, and all enthusiastic behavior in the Christian religion, has been by Pentecostal and Holiness groups.

---

[58]*Enthusiasm: A Chapter in the History of Religion* (Oxford, 1950).

[59]*The Trumpet Shall Sound: A Study of the "Cargo Cults" in Melanesia* (Macgibbon and Kee, 1957).

[60]See especially W. Mischel and F. Mischel, "Psychological Aspects of Spirit Possession," *American Anthropologist*, 60 (1958): 249-60.

[61]"World Distribution Patterns of Possession States," in *Trance and Possession States*, (Bucke Memorial Society, 1968) 3-34.

These groups are often characterized by their marginal socioeconomic position in society. As shown in a number of studies, the ecstatic behavior is both an outlet for repressed conflicts and a means of giving credence to the notion that one is the sole possessor of truth.[62]

BIBLICAL STUDIES

The vast amount of scholarly research that has been done in Acts studies has only rarely touched on glossolalia. The problem of the sources used in the composition of Acts, along with the role the redactor may have played, has received little attention. One notable exception is an essay by Frank Stagg[63] in which he examines the primary biblical references to glossolalia with particular attention to Acts as these bear upon the significance of tongues. Stagg recognizes that virtually all interpreters understand that Luke represents the tongues on the day of Pentecost to have been understandable languages. The disagreement among scholars arises over the question of the trustworthiness of the narrative itself. A. Q. Morton and G. H. C. MacGregor[64] claim that there was a proto-Acts and that it began with 1:12-14; 3:1-10; and 4:1-5:12a. According to their thesis, Acts did not originally contain 1:1-11; 1:15-2:47; 3:11-26; or 5:12b-42. These passages are assigned to a later, inferior source. On this reconstruction of the text, Acts 4:31 is seen as the earliest statement of what had occurred in Jerusalem. This text is universally regarded by scholars as primary. It connects normal speech—not *unintelligible* speech—with the earliest tradition about the gift of the Holy Spirit. Lindsey Dewar[65] proposes that only the apostles spoke in other tongues and that Acts 2:9-11 is an editorial addendum, and thus should not be used as the basis for suggesting that other languages were present. Dewar believes that the speaking in tongues was due to a "sudden breaking down of a repression in the unconscious minds of the apostles." This "repression" was due in part to the shock they sustained in witnessing the crucifixion of Christ.

---

[62]See V. Lanternari, *The Religion of the Oppressed* (Knopf, 1963) and B. Johnson, "Do Holiness Sects Socialize in Dominant Values?" *Social Forces*, 39 (1961): 309-16.

[63]"Glossolalia in the New Testament," in *Glossolalia: Tongue Speaking in Biblical, Historical, and Psychological Perspective* (Abingdon, 1969) 20-44.

[64]*The Structure of Luke and Acts* (Harper and Row, 1965).

[65]"The Problem of Pentecost," *Theology*, 9 (1924): 249-59.

Some interpreters have suggested that the miracle referred to by Luke in the Pentecost narrative does not reside in the *speaking* but in the *hearing*. Hubert E. Edwards[66] suggests that the *Pax Romana* brought many Diaspora Jews back to their country to live. The "miracle" was in their hearing dialects from homes left some time ago. "Other tongues," then, refers not to other languages, but to various dialects.

J. G. Davies, in "Pentecost and Glossolalia,"[67] suggests that no matter what sections of the Acts material may be excised by the source critics, the key to understanding the Pentecost narrative is in noting its relationship with the LXX passage upon which it rests, namely Genesis 11:1-9. The Tower of Babel episode functions etiologically in the Genesis narrative to account for the presence of the many language groups on the earth. Davies believes that the *opposite* is intended by Luke in Acts 2: at Babel the languages were confused to indicate God's displeasure; at Pentecost the languages were unified again through a miracle attributed to God—and likely intended to be understood as a token of divine approval.

One notable study of tongues in 1 Corinthians is Nils Ivar Johan Engelsen's doctoral dissertation.[68] Engelsen sees Paul offering the first evidence of a separation of intelligible and unintelligible speech by his distinction between prophecy and speaking in tongues. Consequently, Paul refers to prophecy as intelligible and tongues as unintelligible. Thus Paul is further defining the older use of the term in which it signified speech caused by God's spirit, regardless of its intelligibility. Engelsen understands the background for the usage of the term to be the poetic, semi-metaphorical usage found among the Old Testament sources.

R. H. Gundry[69] argues that tongues should be regarded as human speech in the New Testament. He believes that the use of the term "glossa" (γλῶσσα) in the New Testament is used for understandable language far more frequently than it is used for obscure speech. In fact, he cites only two cases in the Septuagint where it is used in the latter sense: Isaiah 29:24

---

[66]"The Tongues at Pentecost: A Suggestion," *Theology*, 16 (1928): 248-52.

[67]*Journal of Theological Studies*, 3 (October 1952): 228-31.

[68]"Glossolalia and Other Forms of Inspired Speech According to 1 Corinthians 12-14" (Yale, 1970).

[69]"Ecstatic Utterance," *Journal of Theological Studies*, 17 (1966): 299-307.

and 32:4. Even in these cases, however, the term still refers to language. Further, he notes that Paul's use of λαλειν does not militate against the notion that tongues refers to human language. Even though λαλειν can mean incoherent speech, it does not necessarily refer to incoherent, ecstatic speech (see 1 Corinthians 14:29).

One of the classic examples of biblical exegesis from the Pentecostal view point is Frederick Dale Bruner, *A Theology of the Holy Spirit, the Pentecostal Experience and the New Testament*.[70] Older, but still significant is Robert C. Dalton, *Tongues Like As Of Fire: A Critical Study of the Modern Tongues Movement in Light of Apostolic and Patristic Times*.[71] These volumes lay the exegetical basis for the Pentecostal belief in the centrality of speaking in tongues.

THEOLOGICAL STUDIES

Anthony Hoekema[72] offers a thoroughgoing diatribe, based upon his understanding of Scripture, against the major components of Pentecostal theology. His primary criticism is a fundamental one aimed at the basic presupposition of Pentecostal theology: Hoekema assails the teaching of a second blessing and offers the scriptural evidence that when a person is *first* baptized, the Holy Spirit *already* dwells within.

A conciliatory article by Wayne E. Ward[73] seeks common ground for Pentecostals and non-Pentecostals alike. He finds the basis for this commonality within the local spiritual community, where all gifts are finally measured by their capacity for building up the body of the church.

BIBLIOGRAPHIES

Extensive holdings in the area of charismatic religion in general, and glossolalia studies in particular, may be found at the following depositories:

Oral Roberts University, Tulsa, Oklahoma

---

[70](Eerdmans, 1970).

[71](Gospel Publishing House, 1945).

[72]*Holy Spirit Baptism* (Harper and Row, 1972).

[73]"The Significance of Tongues for the Church," in *Speaking in Tongues: Let's Talk about It*, Watson E. Mills, editor (Word Books, 1973), 143-51.

Church of God, Headquarters, Cleveland, Tennessee

The following bibliographical guides may be useful: Ira J. Martin, *The Gift of Tongues: A Bibliography*;[74] David W. Faupel, *The American Pentecostal Movement*;[75] Watson E. Mills, *Speaking in Tongues: A Classified Bibliography*;[76] Charles Edwin Jones, *A Guide to the Study of the Holiness Movement*.[77]

Shorter bibliographic essays include: Watson E. Mills, "Literature on Glossolalia"[78] and James T. Richardson, "Psychological Interpretations of Glossolalia: A Reexamination of Research."[79]

---

[74](Pathway Press, 1970).

[75](Society for Pentecostal Studies, 1972).

[76](Society for Pentecostal Studies, 1974).

[77](Scarecrow Press, 1974).

[78]*Journal of the American Scientific Affiliation*, 26:4 (1974): 169-73.

[79]*Journal for the Scientific Study of Religion*, 12 (1973): 199-207.

Part I
Exegetical Studies

3

ROY A. HARRISVILLE

Speaking in Tongues:
A Lexicographical Study

[Reprinted from *Catholic Biblical Quarterly*, 38:1 (January 1976): 35-48. Reprinted with permission from the Catholic Biblical Association and the author.]

The purpose of this essay is to note the frequency of usage of technical terms employed in the NT to describe the phenomenon of speaking in tongues, and from a comparison of this usage with that in the Septuagint, non-ecclesiastical Greek and para-biblical literature, to arrive at a conclusion regarding the point at which such terms may have penetrated the NT.

NT USAGE

In the NT, there are thirty-five references to what is commonly called "speaking in tongues." Twenty-eight of these are found in Paul's first letter to the Corinthians, of which twenty-three appear in the fourteenth chapter of that epistle alone,[1] and seven in the Gospel of Mark and the Book of Acts.[2]

The technical terminology used can be readily identified: In nineteen of the references cited above, speaking in tongues is referred to by use of the noun γλῶσσα (with or without the preposition ἐν) together with the verb λαλεῖν. The preponderance of these references is in 1 Corinthians.[3] The passages in Mark and Acts contain the same combination. Five times, and only in 1 Cor 14, the noun γλῶσσα appears in the singular unmodified.[4] At the same time, the noun appears in the plural without modifiers seven times in 1 Cor 12 and 14,[5] and twice in Acts.[6] The noun appears in the plural with modifiers twice in 1 Corinthians,[7] twice in Acts,[8] and in the lone passage in Mark.

There are six instances in the NT in which speaking in tongues is referred to by use of the noun γλῶσσα unmodified, but in conjunction with another noun or verb—an occurrence peculiar to 1 Corinthians.[9]

Eleven expressions in the NT are related to the use of γλῶσσα (ἐν γλώσσῃ, γλώσσαις) λαλεῖν, with or without modifiers, nine appearing in 1 Cor 14,[10] and two in Acts.[11]

---

[1]Three times in 1 Cor 14:2; 14:4; twice in 14:5; 14:6, 13, 14; twice in 14:15; 14:16, 17, 18, 19; twice in 14:21; 14:22, 23, 26, 27, 28, and 39.

[2]I.e., in the spurious ending of Mark's Gospel, 16:17, and in Acts 2:4, 6, 8, 11; 10:46 and 19:6.

[3] 1 Cor 12:31; 13:1; 14:2, 4; twice in 14:5; 14:6, 13, 18, 19, 21, 23, 27, and 39.

[4] 1 Cor 14:2, 4, 13, 19, 27.

[5] 1 Cor 12:30; twice in 14:5; 14:6, 18, 23, and 39.

[6]Acts 10:46 and 19:6.

[7] 1 Cor 13:1 and 14:21.

[8]Acts 2:4 and 11.

[9] 1 Cor 12:10 and 28: γένη γλωσσῶν; in 13:8 and 14:22 the noun appears as subject; 14:14: προσεύχωμαι γλώσσῃ and in 14:26: γλῶσσαν ἔχει.

[10] 14:2: λαλεῖ ἀλλὰ θεῷ; 14:2: πνεύματι . . . λαλεῖ μυστήρια ; 14:15: προσεύξομαι τῷ πνεύματι; 14:15: ψαλῶ τῷ πνεύματι; 14:16: εὐλογῇς ἐν πνεύματι; 14:16: ἐπὶ τῇ σῇ εὐχαριστίᾳ 14:17: εὐχαριστεῖς; 14:21: ἐν χείλεσιν ἑτέρων λαλήσω; and 14:28: ἑαυτῷ . . . λαλείτω καὶ τῷ θεῷ.

[11] 2:6, 8: τῇ ἰδίᾳ διαλέκτῳ, and in the former passage with the verb λαλεῖν;.

We may summarize findings to this point as follows: (1) References to the phenomenon or practice of speaking in tongues predominate in Paul, the ratio consisting of approximately four to one over against Acts and Mark. (2) Paul's use of the noun γλῶσσα in the plural and joined to the verb λαλεῖν far outweighs any other. (3) Wherever Paul, Mark and Acts employ the noun in the singular, they nowhere modify it. (4) Γλῶσσα in the plural together with the verb λαλεῖν predominates in Paul, and his use of the plural term unmodified is reflected in Acts. (5) The use of γλῶσσα without the verb λαλεῖν, in the singular and without modifiers, is found only in Paul. (6) The same is true of Paul's use of γλῶσσα in the plural without modifiers. (7) Use of γλῶσσα without the verb λαλεῖν, in the singular and modified, or with the feminine article,[12] occurs neither in Paul nor elsewhere in the NT. The same is true of its use without λαλεῖν in the plural and modified. As to related expressions, the Pauline letters have the lion's share.

From these more or less superficial observations, it would be but a short step to acknowledge Paul's usage as determinative for that of Acts and Mark. Indeed, a few have suggested that Paul introduced, if he did not invent, the technical term γλῶσσα (ἐν γλώσσῃ or γλώσσαις) λαλεῖν. This is the position of Paul Feine, who suggested that despite the emergence of the term within the context of Judaism, and despite Paul's dependence upon the usage of the Corinthian community and thus upon profane Greek habit, he was responsible for the appropriation and application of the term.[13] H. A. W. Meyer as well denied the originality of the use of γλῶσσα (ἐν γλώσσῃ or γλώσσαις) λαλεῖν with a modifier, and while allowing that the phenomenon could be variously described, opted for the simpler as the more original, the implication being that Paul was responsible for its introduction.[14] Since H. J. Holtzmann regarded 1 Corinthians 12-14 as the *locus classicus* of the phenomenon in primitive Christianity, the same in-

---

[12] A feature noted years ago by Heinrici, *Der erste Brief an die Korinther* (*Meyer*; 8te Auflage, 1896) 416, and Johannes Weiss, *Der erste Korintherbrief* (*Meyer*, 1910) 336.

[13] Paul Feine, "Zungenreden," *Realencyklopädie der klassichen Altertumswissenschaft* (3te Auflage, 1908), XXI, 758f.

[14] H. A. W. Meyer, *Critical and Exegetical Hand-book to the Epistles To The Corinthians*, trans. by D. Bannerman (Funk and Wagnalls, 1890) 324, n. 2.

ference may be drawn.[15] The same may be inferred from the statements of H. H. Wendt,[16] C. F. W. v. Weizäcker[17] and, in addition, from those who draw no distinction between the usage in Acts and Corinthians,[18] or who suggest that Paul, at least, recognized a longer and a shorter terminology.[19]

The difficulty facing the investigator is that inasmuch as the preponderance of use lies with Paul, the temptation is to credit him with originating the technical term or terms for its description, whether or not he is regarded as dependent on his Jewish or pagan environment.[20] This position, of course, has not gone unchallenged. Ferdinand Christian Baur regarded the phrase ἕτερος or καιναὶ γλῶσσαι (appearing in Acts and Mark) as the more original, and the Pauline expression, γλώσσαις λαλεῖν, as the abbreviated formula.[21] Blass-Debrunner also regard the Pau-

---

[15]Heinrich Julius Holtzmann, "Die Synoptiker—Die Apostelgeschichte," *Herders Theologischer Kommentar zum Neuen Testament* (J. C. B. Mohr, 1889) 330.

[16]Hans Hinrich Wendt, *Kritisch Exegetisches Handbuch über die Apostelgeschichte* (*Meyer*, 6te Auflage, 1888) 63, 65f., 68.

[17]C. F. W. v. Weizsäcker, *Das Apostolische Zeitalter der Christlichen Kirche* (J. C. B. Mohr, 1892) 567f.

[18]E.g., Sebastian Castellio in Matthew Pole, *Synopsis Criticorum Aliorumque Sacra Scripturae Interpretum et Commentatorum* (Vol. V, Sumtibus Johannis Ribbii, Johannis v. de Water, & Francisci Halma, 1686) 502; David Greene, "The Gift of Tongues," *Bibliotheca Sacra* 22 (186? 109; W. Keilbach, "Zungenreden," *Die Religion in Geschichte und Gegenwart* (3te Auflage, 1962) VI, 1941.

[19]Cf. the arguments of Meyer *vs.* Wieseler, *Epistles To The Corinthians*, 324.

[20]As does, e.g., Johannes Weiss, who writes that the original term, γλῶσσαι or γένη γλωσσῶν was not invented by Paul, but rather appropriated by him from Corinthian usage, a term, moreover, directly intelligible to the Greeks, the singular used to describe an individual utterance or a genus, and the plural various types of tongue-speaking, cf. *Korintherbrief*, 335. This view is analogous to that of Weizsäcker, who defines γένη γλωσσῶν as designating a particular gift and γλώσσαις λαλεῖν its actual use or exercise, cf. *Apostolische Zeitalter*, 567f. In a recent doctoral dissertation, Nils I. J. Engelsen, like Weiss, applies the phrase γλῶσσα λαλεῖν to the charisma in general, but the plural γλώσσαις λαλεῖν to "a series of inspired, unintelligible words *Glossolalia and Other Forms of Inspired Speech According to 1 Corinthians 12-14* (University Microfilms, 1970) 187. Otto Betz writes that the singular expression is most used by Paul in reference to the individual, whereas the plural forms the basis for the narrative in Acts 2, "Zungenreden und süsser Wein," *Bibel und Qumran, Beiträge zur Erforschung der Beziehungen zwischen Bibelund Qumranwissenschaft* (Evangelische Haupt Bibelgeselischaft, 1968) 26.

[21]F. C. Baur, *Vorlesungen über Neutestamentliche Theologie* (Friedrich Andreas Perthes, 1892) 131f.

line usage of γλώσσαις λαλεῖν as an ellipse in contrast to the more original phrase ἑτέραις γλώσσαις λαλεῖν as it appears in the narrative of its first occurrence in Acts 2:4.[22] Otto Betz, referring to the first Christians as orienting their speaking in tongues to the OT passage in Isaiah 28:11, states that the expression γλώσσαις λαλεῖν is an abbreviated rendering of ἑτέραις γλώσσαις λαλεῖν.[23] Engelsen concludes, after the manner of Baur and Blass-Debrunner, that the use of the phrase ἕτεραι or ἡμέτεραι in Acts and Mark is pre-Pauline, and that hence the Pauline use may be an ellipse, the origin of the term lying in the unrecoverable past.[24]

LXX USAGE

In the Septuagint, the term γλῶσσα appears together with the verb λαλεῖν seven times, four times in the singular unmodified,[25] and three times in the singular with modifiers.[26]

As is the case with the NT, use of the term γλῶσσα in the Septuagint is frequent in contexts which do not suggest the phenomenon under discussion. There are, however, at least twenty instances which are suggestive of the usage in 1 Corinthians, Acts and Mark, and in which one of the two chief terms in the phrase occurs. In fourteen of these, γλῶσσα appears in the singular without modifiers. The first in this category which comes to mind is Ezek 36:3 in which γλῶσσα appears with a noun derived from λαλεῖν, i.e., λάλημα, a translation of the Hebrew śāpāh in construct with lāšôn, the literal meaning of which could be: "speech of tongue," "lip of tongue," "speech of language," or "lip of language."[27] The phrase φθέγξαιτο ἡ γλῶσσά μου in Ps 118(119):172 and the τὴν γλῶσσαν ἡμῶν

---

[22]Blass-Debrunner, *Grammatik des neutestamentlichen Griechisch* (10te. Auflage; Vandenhoeck und Ruprecht, 1959) para. 480, 3.

[23]Betz, *Bibel und Qumran* 26 and 35.

[24]Engelsen, *Glossolalia* 92f., 98, 100, 161, 176 and 191. Cf. the chart indicating the frequency of the usage of γλῶσσα with and without λαλεῖν, n. 44.

[25]Job 33:2; Ps 36(37):30; 38(39):4(3) and Jer 9:4(5).

[26]Ps 108(109):2; Isa 19:18 and 28:11.

[27]Koehler-Baumgartner render the phrase "gossip of tongues," cf. *Lexicon in Veteris Testamenti Libros* (Lieferung XV; E. J. Brill, 1953) 928.

μεγαλυνοῦμεν of Ps 11(12):4 are reminiscent of Acts 2:4 and 10:46, and three further passages in the Septuagint appear to be variations on the theme of Isa 28:11 quoted in 1 Cor 14:21.[28] An additional five passages employ the noun γλῶσσα together with the verbs ἀγαλλιάω and μελετάω.[29] Finally, in Sir 17:6 and 51:22 appear references to the tongue as gift, and in Jer 23:31 γλῶσσα is used in conjunction with the noun προφητεία.

In the six instances remaining, γλῶσσα appears in the singular with modifiers.[30] In passages where γλῶσσα appears in the plural with other verbs, and without modifiers, there is little which is suggestive of NT usage.[31] In the Septuagint, γλῶσσα appears in the plural, and modified in only four instances.[32]

We summarize our conclusions regarding the use of γλῶσσα in the Septuagint, and in passages where the noun is joined to λαλεῖν. (1) Γλῶσσα λαλεῖν most often occurs in the singular and without modifiers. Admittedly, the number of such instances is miniscule—four to be exact— but they do constitute that point at which Septuagint use most approximates that of the NT. (2) In contrast to the NT, γλῶσσα joined to λαλεῖν in the Septuagint may appear in the singular with modifiers. Again, the number of such occurrences is not great—there are only three—but the contrast is present nonetheless. (3) In further contrast to NT use, γλῶσσα never appears with λαλεῖν in the plural, with or without modifiers. On the other hand, fourteen such instances were noted in 1 Corinthians, Mark and Acts.

In those passages suggestive of NT usage, some similarity with NT expressions can be noted. Γλῶσσα, when joined with other verbs, may appear in the singular without modifiers, or in the plural with or without modifiers. In six passages, however, and in contrast to NT usage, γλῶσσα joined to other verbs appears in the singular with modifiers. Because of the

---

[28]Ps 80(81):6(5): γλῶσσαν, ἥν οὐκ ἔγνω, ἥκουσεν; Zeph. 3:9: τότε μεταστπέψω ἐπι λαοὺς γλῶσσαν , and Jer 5:15: οὐκ ἀκούσῃ τῆς φωνῆς τῆς γλώσσης.

[29]Ps 15(16):9; 34(35):28; 50(51):16(14); 125(126):2 and Isa 59:3.

[30]Ps 113(114):1, Aquila's version ἑτερόγλωσσος ; Isa 33:19, Aquila's version ἑτερόγλωσσος, 45:23; Sir, Prologue 17 and 5:13, and 4 Mac. 10:21.

[31]With the possible exception of Isa 29:24.

[32]Ps 30(31):19(18); Prov 12:18; Wis 10:21 and Dan 3:29(96).

subjectivity involved in the selection of the twenty passages suggestive of NT use, however, we cannot conclude without further ado that the Septuagint usage has in any way influenced that of the NT. The similarities between the Septuagint and NT references are, in the last analysis, few and far between. Indeed, the Septuagint translator appears to have known nothing of a technical term for speaking in tongues.[33]

NON-ECCLESIASTICAL GREEK SOURCES

In profane Greek, γλῶσσα together with the verb λαλεῖν appears only once, viz., in two reconstructed lines of a hymn to Imanthes-Asclepius, contained in the library of the Oxyrhynchus Papyri.[34] In three other instances, γλῶσσα appears in the singular and modified, in a Giessen papyrus from the first century B.C.; in a sixth century find, and in Strabo.[35] In all three instances, however, the noun appears without the verb λαλεῖν.

There are at least two occurrences of γλῶσσα in the plural, modified and connected with a verb other than λαλεῖν. The first is in Polybius, and the second in the Roman strategist Onosander.[36] Three expressions in clas-

---

[33]Cf. the chart, n. 44.

[34]*The Oxyrhynchus Papyri*, Part XI, ed. by B. Grenfell and A. Hunt (The Offices of the Egypt Exploration Fund, 1915) 229, lines 199-200: Γλληυ(τ)ς δὲ π(α)σα γλῶσσα την σην λαλ(ή)(. . .)σε(τ) ιστοριαυ κ(αί) πας Ελ(λ)ην ἀνϱ τόν τ(ο)ῦ φθα σεβήσεται Γμου(θ)ηι.

[35]Γλῶσσα ξενικῆ in *Griechische Papyri im Museum des oberhessischen Geschichtsvereins zu Giessen* (O. Eger, E. Kornemann, und P. M. Meyer, 1910ff.), and in a Byzantine papyrus (Mon 13, 71) ed. by Hersinberg and Wenger, noted in Friedrich Presigke, *Wörterbuch der griechischen Papyrusurkunden*; Band Eins (Selbstverlag der Erben, 1925) 299. Ἑτερόγλωσσα in Strabo, cited in Franz Passow, *Handwörterbuch der Griechischen Sprache*, neu bearbeitet und zeitgemäss umgestaltet von Rost und Palm; Ersten Bandes Erste Abtheilung. 5te. Auflage (Fr. Chr. Wilh. Vogel, 1841) 1198. Schleusner's reference to Aristotle's *Poetics* as containing a reference to γλῶσσα in the singular and modified by ἑτερα is an error; cf. Joh. Fried. Schleusner, *Novum Lexicon Graeco-Latinum in Novum Testamentum*; Volumen Primum (Glasguae: Impensis Ricardi Priestley, 1824) 410.

[36]Polybius, *The Histories, Loeb Classical Library* trans. by W. R. Paton (Harvard University Press, 1960) Book 23, 13.2: καὶ πλείστους ἀνδράσιν ἀλλοφύλοις καὶ ἑτερογλώττοις χρησάμενος. The sentence in Onosander reads: πρὸς τὰς συμμαχίας τῶν ἐθνῶν, quoted in J. J. Wetstein, *Novum Testamentum Graecum* (Tomus II; Ex Officina Dommeriana, 1752) 163.

sical Greek which are reminiscent of Paul's usage in 1 Corinthians, and which employ one of the two chief terms in the phrase under discussion, occur in Galen, Pyrrho and Lucian.[37] In non-ecclesiastical Greek, use of γλῶσσα with other verbs, and in instances not suggestive of NT use, is, of course, legion, and the reader is referred to such lexica and etymological word-books as Frisk, Hesychius, Passow, Schleusner et al.[38]

We now summarize our observations of the use of γλῶσσα in non-ecclesiastical Greek. (1) The appearance of γλῶσσα together with λαλεῖν in the singular, modified, and in the one, lone instance of its occurrence, is in contrast to NT but not to Septuagint usage.[39] (2) The two occurrences of γλῶσσα in the singular, modified, but without λαλεῖν, are in further contrast to NT but not to Septuagint usage.[40] (3) In contrast to NT but not to Septuagint usage, γλῶσσα may appear without λαλεῖν in the plural and modified.[41] (4) Γλῶσσα never appears without λαλεῖν in the plural and unmodified—in contrast both to Pauline[42] and Septuagint usage.[43]

Because of the paucity of non-ecclesiastical Greek references to γλῶσσα (ἐν γλώσσῃ or γλώσσαις) λαλεῖν, the similarity they enjoy with Septuagint use is minimized. It is nonetheless interesting, perhaps even significant to note that when they agree, viz., in the use of γλῶσσα with or without λαλεῖν in the singular or plural with modifiers, they reflect a usage in direct contrast to that of the NT which, with five exceptions, concentrates on the use of γλῶσσα, with or without λαλεῖν, in the singular and

---

[37]Galen: τρόπος τῶν γλωσσῶν, cited in Feine, "Zungenreden" 758; Pyrrho: καὶ ἑαυτῶλαλῶν, and Lucian: ὁ λαλῶν ἑαυτῷ, cited in Wetstein, *Novum Testamentum* 163.

[38]Cf. Hjalmar Frisk, *Griechisches Etymologisches Wörterbuch* (Carl Winter, 1960) Band I, 315f.; Hesychii Alexandrini *Lexicon* (Recensuit et Emendavit Kurt Latte, Hauniae; Einar Munksgaard Editore, 1953) I, 382; Passow, *Handwörterbuch* I, 562, and Schleuner, *Novum Lexicon Graeco-Latinum* 410, 741.

[39]Cf. pp. 36 and 39.

[40]Cf. pp. 36 and 39.

[41]Cf. pp. 36 and 39.

[42]Cf. p. 36.

[43]Cf. p. 39.

plural unmodified.[44] The conclusion to be drawn here is that profane or non-ecclesiastical Greek knew of no technical term for speaking in tongues.

Unless we assign to the NT authors total responsibility for coining the nomenclature under discussion, we shall have to continue our search for that point at which the technical terms for speaking in tongues penetrated the NT.

Engelsen's study of glossolalia concludes that the term γλῶσσα λαλεῖν does not occur in literature outside the NT. The reason for this non-occurrence, Engelsen continues, is that "inarticulate or unintelligible speech is looked upon only as a feature of ecstatic speech."[45] Our study has uncovered only one exception to Engelsen's thesis, i.e., the two reconstructed lines in the Oxyrhynchus fragment cited on p. 39. Yet, while it may indeed be true that texts outside the NT do not differentiate glossolalia from the ecstatic in general, the search for the possible origins of what in Paul and the remainder of the NT appears to have become a technical term[46] ought not to be prejudiced by an opinion of the phenomenon the term describes.

---

[44]The following chart will make the situation clear:

γλῶσσα with λαλεῖν	NT	LXX	Non-ecclesiastical Greek
In the singular without modifiers:	5	4	0
In the singular with modifiers:	0	3	1
In the plural without modifiers:	9	0	0
In the plural with modifiers:	5	0	0
γλῶσσα without λαλεῖν			
In the singular without modifiers:	2	14*	0
In the singular with modifiers:	0	6*	2
In the plural without modifiers:	4	1*	0
In the plural with modifiers:	0	4	3

*suggested

[45]Cf. Engelsen, *Glossolalia* 20.

[46]Cf. Engelsen's statement to the effect that the exegesis and classification of passages in which γλῶσσα/γλώσσαις λαλεῖν appear indicate that Paul used these phrases as technical terms. This is especially clear, Engelsen adds, when γλῶσσα/γλώσσαις is used independently, not as a dative with *verba dicendi*, cf. *Glossolalia* 183.

THE LITERATURE OF QUMRAN

If we give attention to passages reminiscent of NT usage which appear in the non-Greek, para-biblical literature of Qumran, we may be nearer our goal. Such passages come first to mind for two reasons: First, because of the sect's preoccupation with Isa 28:11-13a (a preoccupation also reflected in the Septuagint)[47] and its interpretation, and second, because of the reappearance of the verses within the context of Paul's discussion of tongue-speaking. in 1 Cor 14:21. The Massoretic text translates:

> Yet he will speak with stammering lips (*b**e**la 'ăgê śāpāh*) and a strange tongue (*ûblāšôn 'aheret*) to this people, to whom he said, 'This is rest; give rest to the weary; and this is repose,' but they would not hear (*w**e**lō' 'ābû' šemôa'*). Thus Yahweh's word will be to them *ṣaw lāṣāw ṣaw lāṣāw qaw lāqāw qaw lāqāw*.

The Thanksgiving hymns dealing with the Isaiah verse translate:

> They exchanged them for lips of uncircumcision, and for the foreign tongue (*lāšôn 'aheret*) of a people without understanding, that they might come to ruin in their straying.[48]

> They come to inquire of Thee from the mouth of lying prophets deceived by error who speak (with strange) lips (*[B**e**]l[ô 'a]g śāpāh*) to Thy people, and an alien tongue (*w**e**lašôn 'aheret*) that they may cunningly turn all their works to folly. For (they hearken) not (to) Thy (voice), nor do they give ear (Lo'[šam*e**û*...]) to Thy word.[49]

Further references to the passage in Isaiah may appear in CD 1:14; 4:19-20 and 5:11-12.[50]

---

[47]Cf. n. 28.

[48]IQH 2:18bf., in Vermes, *The Dead Sea Scrolls in English* (Penguin Books, 1966) 154.

[49]IQH 4:16 in *ibid.*, 162. In both instances, Eduard Lohse translates "fremde (r) Zunge," cf. *Die Texte Aus Qumran, Hebräisch und Deutsch* (Kösel-Verlag, 1964) 117, 127.

[50]Cf. Betz, *Bibel und Qumran* 23, and C. Rabin quoted in Menahem Mansoor, *The Thanksgiving Hymns* (Eerdmans, 1961) 125 n. 13.

The principal difference between the Massoretic text and the lines from the Thanksgiving Hymns is that in the former Yahweh is subject, whereas in the latter the "lying prophets" or "those who seek smooth things" speak with a foreign or alien tongue. This interpretation is all but identical with that of the Septuagint,[51] the text of which reads: διὰ φαυλισμὸν χειλέων διὰ γλώσσης ἑτέρας, ὅτι λαλήσουσι τῷ λαῷ τούτῳ[52] This alteration of subject in 1QH 2:18; 4:16 and in the Septuagint is in contrast to the Massoretic text; in contrast to the quotation in 1 Cor 14:21 as well as to the version of Aquila, all of which render Yahweh subject of the sentence. In only one respect does Aquila's version approximate the Septuagint translation of Isa 28, viz., in the use of γλῶσσα together with λαλεῖν and a modifier. In harmony with Paul, however, and in contrast to the Septuagint and the Lucianic reading.[53] Aquila joins the modifier to the noun to form the compound ἑτερόγλωσσος. As noted,[54] the same compound appears elsewhere in Aquila.[55] Further, Aquila's text, as Paul's, deviates from the Massoretic to the extent it inverts the word order, rendering the *bᵉlaʾ ʾăgê śāpāh* ("with stammering lips") with ἐν χειλεσιν ἑτέρων.

It appears to be a secure result of modern research that Aquila's revision (as Symmachus' and Theodotion's) represents a late stage in the assimilation of the Septuagint to the consonantal Massoretic text, more specifically, that it has as its *Vorlage* or exemplar a Babylonian local text,

---

[51]According to J. L. Teicher, IQH 4:16 actually constitutes an attack on glossolalia and prophecy, cf. "The Teaching Of The Pre-Pauline Church In The Dead Sea Scrolls, III," *JJS* 4 (1953) 10. J. P. M. Sweet writes that if Jews criticized Christian glossolalia, Isaiah's words could be used against them, an apologetic which Paul now turned against the Corinthians, cf., "A Sign for Unbelievers: Paul's Attitude to Glossolalia," *New Testament Studies* 13 (1967) 244.

[52]*Isaias (Septuaginta: Verus Testamentum Graecum Auctoritate Academiae Litterarum Gottingensis Editum* 14; edidit J. Ziegler, 2te Auflage; Göttingen: Vandenhoeck und Ruprecht, 1967) 217. In a twelfth c. Paris MS, the word δολιάς ("deceit") is substituted for ἑτέ ρας as in Ps 119(120):12. The Sahidic version makes an equivalent substitution, cf. Ziegler's apparatus.

[53]Cf. Ziegler, *ibid.*, 217.

[54]Cf. n. 30.

[55]In Ps 114:1, the Massoretic text reads *mēʿam lōʿēz*, the Septuagint ἐκ λαοῦ βαρβάρου in Isa 33:19 the MT reads *nilʿag lāšôn* and the LXX βαθύφωνον Cf. Joseph Reider, *An Index to Aquila*, completed and revised by Nigel Turner (E. J. Brill, 1966) 98.

reflected in the so-called καίγε Greek recension and reintroduced to Jerusalem in the first century B.C.[56] For this reason, Paul's use of γλῶσσα λαλεῖν, which antedates that of Aquila by a good one hundred years, suggests that the *terminus a quo* for such usage was furnished by the apostle himself, or perhaps, as Betz contends, by pre-Pauline, Palestinian Christianity.[57]

Still, it is a curious fact, of which Betz, e.g., takes no cognizance, that the earliest Qumran Isaiah scroll (1QIs[a]) renders the Isaiah phrase in precisely the same fashion as do the Massoretes, Paul and Aquila.[58] If this scroll serves as Hebrew counterpart if not parent to the earliest representative in the evolution of the Greek Bible,[59] which yields no evidence of the influence of the Massoretic text,[60] then its origin antedates the third century B.C.[61] From this it could be inferred that despite the fact that Aquila's Hebrew exemplar was a relatively late text, in this instance his and Paul's agreement with a reading representing an Egyptian text type at the

---

[56]Cf. Frank M. Cross, "The History of the Biblical Text in the Light of Discoveries in the Judaean Desert," *Harvard Theological Review* 57 (1964) 281, 283, 289, 295, 297; "The Contribution of the Qumran Discoveries to the Study of the Biblical Text," *IEJ* 16, 85f., and James Shenkel, *Chronology and Recensional Development in the Greek Text of Kings* (Harvard University Press, 1968) 11, 18.

[57]Cf. Betz, *Bibel und Qumran* 23.

[58]Cf. *Scrolls From Qumran Cave I*, From Photographs by John C. Trever (The Albright Institute of Archaeological Research and the Shrine of the Book, 1972) 58f. To my knowledge, Origen first called attention to the identity of readings in Paul and Aquila: "Εὗρον γὰρ τά ἰσοδυναμοῦντα τῇ λέξει ταύτῃ ἐν τῇ τοῦ Ἀκόλω ἑρμηνείᾳ κείμενα." *Philocalia*, LX. 2, cited in J. De Waard, *A Comparative Study Of The Old Testament Text In The Dead Sea Scrolls And In The New Testament* (Eerdmans, 1966) 64. Such disagreement as exists here between the Isaiah scroll and the LXX moved Ziegler, who described the two as betraying a common text, to protect his flank by adding that neither the Isaiah-translator, the editors of the LXX Hebrew exemplar nor the revisor of the Isaiah scroll were thorough-going, and by noting the fact that in numerous passages the LXX reading is opposed by the Massoretic text and the Isaiah scroll; cf. Joseph Ziegler, "Die Vorlage Der Isaias-Septuaginta (LXX) Und Die Erste Isaias Rolle Von Qumran," *JBL* 78 (1959) 59, cf. also Cross, "The History of the Biblical Text" 289.

[59]Cf. Shenkel, *Chronology* 5.

[60]Cf. Cross, "Qumran Discoveries" 82, 95.

[61]Cf. Shenkel, *Chronology* 7; Cross writes that in the book of Isaiah, the Egyptian is virtually identical with the Palestinian text, originating in the fifth c. B.C., cf., "Qumran Discoveries" 87.

base of the Old Greek translation[62] harks back to a period in which *lāšôn 'aheret* (γλῶσσα λαλεῖν) had become more or less fixed. Thus Paul's (and Aquila's) reading need not be explained as a "correction of the customary exegesis" of Isa 28, resting merely on the Massoretic text,[63] but as reflecting a dependence upon a Greek recension based on the ancient Egyptian text type. In that case, the deviation of the Septuagint and 1QH from that ancient reading would hardly constitute a majority interpretation, but rather reflect the use of Hebrew exemplars of later origin and provenience. As to the agreement of the Massoretic text with that of 1QIs[a], it may be due to that shifting of textual families which occurred with the Massoretes in the recension of the Latter Prophets and which resulted in the use of a non-Babylonian text for Isaiah.[64]

Of course, the identity of reading here might simply be regarded as one of those exceptions to prove the rule of the acknowledged development of Proto-Massoretic tradition.[65] But if something akin to glossolalia was practiced in Jewish circles,[66] particularly among those who nourished apocalyptic hopes,[67] the community at Qumran furnished an atmosphere congenial to the emergence of the technical terms under discussion. Further, the reading of the Isaiah scroll strongly suggests that the origin of such

---

[62]Cf. Shenkel, *Chronology* 7, 18.

[63]Betz, *Bibel und Qumran* 25f.

[64]Cf. Cross, "Qumran Discoveries" 94.

[65]Cf. Cross, "The History of the Biblical Text" 289, where he writes in reference to the Former Prophets that "the proto-Massoretic tradition at Qumran and underlying the καίγε Recension of Samuel-Kings is not identical with the official text now known from the era between the two Jewish Revolts, and from Aquila. Some recensional activity was involved." Cf. also Cross, "Qumran Discoveries" 85f., and Shenkel, *Chronology* 5, 21.

[66]Cf. Hermann Gunkel, *Die Wirkungen des Heiligen Geistes* (Erster Teil: Dieterich'sche Univ.-Buchdruckerei, 1888) 21; Feine, "Zungenreden" 758, Eddison Mosiman, *Das Zungenreden geschichtlich und psychologisch untersucht* (J. C. B. Mohr, 1911) 36; Wilhelm Bousset, *Der erste Brief an die Korinther, Die Schriften des Neuen Testaments* (3te. Auflage, Zweiter Bank: Vandenhoeck und Ruprecht, 1916) 138; *Die Religion Des Judentums Im Späthelienistischen Zeitalter* (3te. Auflage: J. C. B. Mohr, 1926) 396. Engelsen refers to the poetic, half-metaphorical speech of the OT as furnishing the most reasonable background for glossolalia, *Glossolalia* ii.

[67]Cf. Frank M. Cross, *Canaanite Myth and Hebrew Epic* (Harvard University Press, 1973): 332ff.

terms lay in exemplars which antedate the Hodayot,[68] but which, despite
the syntactical differences, have left their deposit there and in the otherwise conservative translation of the Septuagint.[69]

Thus, by the time Paul and the author of Acts had put pen to paper the
terms had become more or less fixed, a possibility which would also explain the combination of γλῶσσα with λαλεῖν, but never with λέγειν.
Such an hypothesis, of course, does not require the establishment of literary dependence between Paul, Acts and Qumran, but it does indicate a
common dependence upon a common, parent text. Nor does this hypothesis prejudice our understanding of definitions, since it does not deny that
phenomena parallel to those described by the NT occurred outside the Jewish or Christian communities. Finally, it does not detract from Paul's giving the term a nuance it had not earlier possessed.[70] It merely proposes that
the technical term had its birth in pre-Christian Judaism. If such is true,
then those scholars who elect for ἑτέραις γλώσσαις λαλεῖν or ἑτερ-
ογλώσσαις λαλεῖν as the more original, and the simpler γλῶσσα λαλεῖν as an ellipse, have the probabilities in their favor.[71]

The only other alternative to this hypothesis is to fix the origins of the
technical term with Jewish Christianity or with Paul, and regard its occurrence elsewhere as merely coincidental.[72] But even the "poetic" use of

---

[68]E.g., in the Egyptian text type which furnished the exemplar for the Old Greek recension Cross, "Qumran Discoveries," reckons with the possibility that a Palestinian Hebrew MS may have been used for the Old Greek translation of Isaiah, 88.

[69]Cf. Herbert Braun, *Qumran und das Neue Testament* (J. C. B. Mohr, 1966) 1, 40,
154, 252f., and Betz, *Bibel und Qumran* 26, who despite his main contention regarding
the origin of glossolalia in Jewish-Christian circles writes that it is conceivable from the
Qumran literature that the speech given by the Holy Spirit could be regarded as "the language of angels." Cf. the contrary arguments in Sherman E. Johnson, "The Dead Sea
Manual of Discipline and the Jerusalem Church of Acts," *The Scrolls and the New Testament*, ed. Krister Stendahl (Harper, 1957) 131; Armin Dietzel, "Beten im Geist," *TZ* 13
(1957) 19, 31, and Teicher, "Teaching of the Pre-Pauline Church" 10.

[70]Cf. Feine, "Zungenreden" 759, Engelsen writes that there is no immediate basis in
pre-Christian language for the specific Pauline use which denotes unintelligible speech, and
elsewhere states that Isa 28:11 and the term for the speech-gift which Paul has from tradition do not conform, *Glossolalia* ii, 165.

[71]Cf. p. 38f.

[72]Contra C. f. Nösgen, *Geschichte der Apostolischen Verkündigung* (C. H. Beck'sche

γλῶσσα in the conservative Septuagint text and other Greek literature leads in the other direction. For example, it is no great leap from Sirach's confession[73] that "the Lord gave me a tongue for my reward and with it I will praise Him,"[74] or even from the Septuagint rendering of the Psalms to which earlier reference was made,[75] to the more technical use of γλῶσσα λαλεῖν. As has occasionally been pointed out,[76] such poetic use in pre-Christian, Jewish literature is most strikingly illustrated in the Testament of Job (first century B.C.), highly reminiscent of the NT accounts. Of Job's enraptured daughters the narrator (brother of Job) writes:

> And she (i.e. Hemera) received another heart, no longer to mind the things of earth, but uttered (ἀπεφθέγξατο , cf. Acts 2:4) a hymn in the angelic language (διαλέκτω, cf. Acts 2:6, 8), having rendered (it) to God according to the angels' psalmody . . . And her (i.e. Cassia's) mouth took on the language of the Archons, she glorified and her poem (was) lofty in fashion . . . And she (i.e. Amaltheia) had a mouth speaking in the language of those in the heights, and her heart was changed, being drawn from earthly things; for she spoke (λελάληκεν) in the language of the Cherubim . . . And I wrote down the entire book of the most remarkable hymns by my brother's three daughters, that these are salvation, these are the mighty deeds (τὰ μεγαλεῖα, cf. Acts 2:11; 10:46) of God . . . And each blessed and glorified in her special language.[77]

Verlagsbuchhandlung, 1893) 12:14, n. 2; Adolf Schlatte, *Paulus Der Bote Jesu, Einer Deutung seiner Briefe an die Korinther* (Calwer Verlag, 1956) 25, 372; Rudolf Otto, *The Kingdom of God and the Son of Man* (tr. Floyd Filson and B. Lee-Woolf; Starr King Press, 1957) 343; T. W. Manson, *Studies in the Gospels and Epistles*, ed. M. Black (Manchester University Press, 1962) 203, 205; Betz, *Bibel und Qumran* 26, and Engelsen, *Glossolalia* 174f. On the other hand, Johannes Behm writes that the assumption that γλῶσσα emerged as a technical term on the basis of Acts 2:3f lacks all support in the sources: "Γλώσσα" *TWNT*, erster Band, 725.

[73]Greek translation from the second c. B.C.

[74]1:22.

[75]Cf. p. 38f., and the similarities noted there.

[76]Cf. e.g., Bousset, *Brief an die Korinther* 135ff.; Weiss *Korintherbrief* 513, 338; Schmithals, *Die Gnosis in Korinth* (Vandenhoeck und Ruprecht, 1956) 143, n. 1; Betz, *Bibel und Qumran* 26, n. 27; Engelsen, *Glossolalia* 52.

[77] 48:2-3a; 49:2; 50:1a-2; 51:4 and 52:7 in *Testamentum Iobi*, ed. S. P.Brock (E. J. Brill, 1967) 56-68 (Author's translation).

Similar parallels appear in *Jub* 25:14;[78] in the *Test. Judah* 25:3;[79] in *I Enoch, Similitudes* 40 and 71:11; in *4 Mac*, 10:21,[80] and in the *Martyrdom of Isaiah* 5:14[81] which from the standpoint of the history of forms at least belongs to the period of Antiochus. Taken as a whole, these parallels appear to support the contention that for the OT and Inter-Testamental Jewish community, glossolalic utterance was not regarded as a category separate from the ecstatic *per se*.[82] A reading of Philo, e.g., tends to reinforce this position.[83] On the other hand, with the exception of the parallels in *Jub* and the *Test. Judah* from which it may be inferred the inspired speech constituted intelligible utterance,[84] the remainder ranges from references to a modicum of intelligibility (*I Enoch, Similitudes* 40) to the unintelligible or inarticulate (*I Enoch* 71:11 and the *Martyrdom of Isaiah* 5:14), thus yielding soil for the development of a term exclusively applied to ecstatic speech.

All questions of definitions and parallel phenomena in pagan religion aside, our conclusion is that use of the technical term γλῶσσα (ἐν γλώσσῃ or γλώσσαις) λαλεῖν had its occasion and origin in pre-Christian, Jewish sources.

THE POST-NEW TESTAMENT PERIOD

Use of this technical terminology did not cease with the NT age. A host of references to speaking in tongues occurs in Origen, Chrysostom, Sev-

---

[78]Cf. R. H. Charles, *The Apocrypha And Pseudepigrapha of the Old Testament* (Clarendon Press, 1968) 11, 51.

[79]*Testamenta XII Patriarcharum* (With Short Notes by M. De Jonge: E. J. Brill, 1964) 35.

[80]Cf. Charles, *Apocrypha and Pseudepigrapha* 211f., 235f., and *The Third And Fourth Books Of Maccabees* (edited and Translated by Moses Hadas; Harper and Brothers, 1953) 202.

[81]Cf. Charles, *Apocrypha and Pseudepigrapha* 162.

[82]Cf. p. 41f., and Engelsen, *Glossolalia* 58.

[83]Cf. Quis Rerum Divinarum Haeres, LI, 249; LII 259; LIII 264-266 in *Philo, LCL* (tr. F. H. Colson and G. H. Whitaker) IV 408, 410, 416, 418; De Specialibus Legibus, I 65 in *Philo* (tr. F. Colson, 1950) VII 136; De Specialibus Legibus, IV 49 in *Philo* (tr. F. Colson, 1954) VIII 36, 38; De Vita Mosis, I 274 in *Philo* (tr. F. Colson, 1959) VI 416.

[84]Cf. De Decalogo, IX 32-33, 46 in *Philo* (tr. F. Colson, 1950) VII 20-22. On the modern debate surrounding the definition of glossolalia, cf. Roy A. Harrisville, "Speaking in Tongues—Proof of Transcendence?" *Dialog* 13 (1974) 11ff.

erian, Theodore, Cyril, Theodoret and Photius (i.e., from the late third to the ninth century A.D.), by far the greater number a mere recital of terms appearing in Acts and 1 Corinthians,[85] and with such minor differences as inversion of word order, substitution of the plural for the singular and vice versa, together with such changes of case as are required by the context.

At the same time, the fathers indicate some slight trend away from the use of the technical terminology, e.g., in the substitution of adjectives, nouns and verbs not used in biblical or para-biblical literature.[86] For the rest, the differences consist of inferences drawn from the biblical text,[87] the combining of passages[88] or epexegetical remarks.[89]

Since none of these changes suggests the reading of any known biblical texts, the conclusion may be drawn that this trend, far from disputing the persistence of the technical terms or their provenience, reflects attempts at coming to grips with a phenomenon which had become more or less unknown. What had occurred in Judaism and in primitive Christianity had to wait for other, later generations for its explication.[90]

---

[85]Cf. Origen in *Catenae Craecorum Patrum In Novum Testamentum*, ed. J. A. Cramer (Georg Olms Verlagsbuchhandlung, 1967) V 227, 255; Chrysostom in *ibid.*, 223, 243, 251, 260, 263ff., 268, 273f., 281; Severian in *ibid.*, 262, 272; Theodore in *ibid.*, 259; Cyril in *ibid.*, 232, 261, 267; Theodoret in *ibid.*, 255, 260, 262, 265, 275, and Photius in *ibid.*, 264f., 267f., 269.

[86]For example, Irenaeus uses the adjective παντοδαπαῖς; Chrysostom and Severian πολλαῖς; Severian and Theodoret διαφόροις (or the noun διαφοράν) and ἀσαφούς in apparent substitution for the ἑτέραις in Acts 2:4. The verb λέγομαι and its congeners appear together with γλῶσσα in Chrysostom, Cyril and Theodoret; likewise the verb χράομαι and its relatives in Cyril and Theodoret. In one instance, Cyril substitutes the noun ἐναργέστατα for τά μεγαλεία τοῦ θεοῦ in Acts. Cf. Irenaeus, *Contra Haereses* V. 6. 1, in *PG* VII 1137, and Cramer, *Catenae Graecorum Patrum* III 24; V 234, 248, 261ff., 267, 271f.

[87]E.g., τὸ τῶν γλωσσῶν χάρισμα or ἡ τῶν γλωσσῶν χάρις in Chrysostom, Severian, Theodore and Theodoret; cf. Cramer, *Catenae Graecorum Patrum* V 246, 259, 267, 273, 275, 281.

[88]Cf. the τὸ γὰρ πνεῦμα . . . μυστήρια φθέγγεται διὰ τῶν γλωσσῶν in Severian with Acts 2:4 and 1 Cor 12:3; cf. Cramer, *Catenae Graecorum Patrum* V 262.

[89]Cf. the ὁ λαλῶν λαλεῖ γλῶσσαν ἥν οὐκ οἶδεν of Severian with 1 Cor 14:14; the γλώσσαις ταῖς ἑτέρων λαλεῖν of Cyril with Acts 2:4; and the λαλεῖν τι ταῖς γλώσσαις καλόν καὶ σπουδαῖον of Photius with the arguments in 1 Cor 14; cf. Cramer, *Catenae Graecorum Patrum* V 262, 268f., 272.

[90]Cf. Chrysostom's remarks concerning 1 Cor 12:1-6: "This entire passage is most obscure. Ignorance and absence of the events taking place then but not occurring now makes for the obscurity," Cramer, *Catenae Graecorum Patrum* V 223 (Author's translation).

4

L. CARLYLE MAY

A Survey of Glossolalia
and Related Phenomena
in Non-Christian Religions

[Reproduced by permission of American Anthropological Association, from *American Anthropologist*, 58(1): 75-96, 1956.]

Ecstatic vocalization in the form of incoherent sounds and foreign words has long been of interest to students of religion. The books of Cutten (1927), Lombard (1919), and Mosiman (1911) analyze Christian glossolalia in both psychological and historical perspective but provide only brief treatment of its nature in other religions. This paper will show that glossolalia and similar speech-phenomena occur in various forms during shamanistic rites of the New, and especially of the Old, World.

The Christian tradition of speaking-in-tongues probably had its roots in the ancient religions of Asia Minor. Herodotus (Lombard 1910:90) speaks of an inspired priest in Greece who suddenly spoke in a barbarian language, and Virgil in the *Aeneid* (1953:vi. 44-49, 97-99) tells of a Cumaean sibyl who spoke strangely while possessed. The Old Testament (Lombard 1910:89) alludes to a form of ecstatic behavior similar to glossolalia. Guillaume (1938:144-45) states that in 853 B.C. four hundred prophets raved in ecstasy before the gate of Samaria, and in ancient Egypt (Erman 1894:352-55) necromancers uttered formulas, believed to be revelations from the gods, made up of foreign words and senseless noises. The more mysterious and incomprehensible these formulas were, the greater their power was thought to be. It is entirely probable, moreover, that sorcerers of India and China, contemporaneous to the Samaritans, spoke incoherently while divining, curing, and communing with the spirits. An example of glossolalia in the Later Han Dynasty will be cited subsequently to indicate the antiquity of the phenomenon in China.

Christian glossolalia apparently had its beginning in the Pentecost. St. Paul, himself a glossolalist, listed speaking-in-tongues among the divine gifts but deplored its excessive use. During the Middle Ages the incidence of glossolalia is not well known, although, according to biographies (Lombard 1910:106-7), St. Hildegarde is said to have possessed the gift of visions and prophecy and to have been able to speak and write in Latin without having learned the language. Guibert de Nogent in the twelfth century observed many female members of a Christian sect speaking strange words that were later interpreted.

During the Protestant Reformation members of revivalistic movements frequently spoke in tongues. For example, while in a state of religious excitement accentuated by persecution, Huguenot children of the late seventeenth century (Cutten 1927:48-66) are said to have spoken correct French which differed considerably from their native patois of the Cevennes Mountains. The Quakers at the time of Oliver Cromwell spoke in tongues, and the Methodists at the time of Whitefield and the Wesley brothers are said to have employed an alliterative form of glossolalia. In the 1840's the "preaching desire" or "calling voices" (Roestar's epidemic) was a characteristic of Christian revivals in Norway and Sweden. Glossolalia occurred frequently during these revivals. Joseph Smith instructed the early Mormons to rise upon their feet and to speak in tongues. Hawthornthwaite (1857:91), in describing the Mormons, states that the members, "instead of waiting for a suitable word to come to their memories," utter "the first sound their tongues can articulate no matter what it is."

Early in the present century a Christian religious revival (cf. Pratt 1928:186) began in Australia and swept around the world. During evangelical gatherings in Britain, India, China, continental Europe, and the United States, speaking-in-tongues was looked upon as one of the sure signs a person had received the "divine afflatus." Today Pentecostal churches in the United States practice glossolalia and quote the New Testament as a basis for it (cf. Clark 1949:85ff). The Shouters of Trinidad (Herskovits and Herskovits 1947:192-93) are among other cultic groups known to speak in tongues. In contrast, the larger, established Christian denominations tend to look upon glossolalia as a primitive trait to be discouraged in individual worship. In fact, the teachings of St. Paul are often interpreted to be in opposition to speaking-in-tongues rather than in favor of it. But, despite the disagreement (Brumback 1947) among Christian groups as to scriptural advocacy of glossolalia, the phenomenon occurs frequently—almost with regularity—in newer Christian bodies led by ministers who are skilled in the arts of creating and sustaining a high level of religious excitement among worshipers.

Among nonreligious examples of glossolalia is the famous case of Helène Smith (pseudonym). In 1892 this woman became acquainted with a group of spiritualists in Geneva and thereafter had frequent trances that gave rise to verboauditive, vocal, verbovisual, and graphic automatisms. The psychology of this case and the so-called Martian language Miss Smith spoke and wrote while in a trance have been studied and reported by Flournoy (1900). After he asserted that Martian depended syntactically and grammatically upon French and showed connection with Sanskrit, Miss Smith developed Ultra-Martian, Uranian, and Lunaire. A second case is that of Albert LeBaron (pseudonym), an American. Like Helène Smith he came in contact with spiritualists. During a meeting at a summer resort he had a vision followed by automatic movement and speech. Sometime later he involuntarily spoke an unknown language that he was unable to identify after extensive research (Cutten 1927:148-55). Other nonreligious instances of glossolalia have been reported.

Speaking-in-tongues has been analyzed in psychological terms by Lombard, Cutten, Mosiman, and others. The following represents a résumé of their more outstanding findings. The glossolalist speaks in tongues while in a state of ecstasy or emotional exaltation and shows symptoms, depending upon the individual and his social environment, associated with one or more of the following: somnambulism, hypnotism, catalepsy, or hysteria. It is difficult to say which form of nervous instability best typifies glossolalia. According to Cutten (1927:3), a person indulging in glosso-lalia is in an emotional state where the controlling part of his mind is not functioning, where "primitive reactions, which usually sleep in the sub-conscious, find their way to the surface." Cutten further states (1927:160-61) that automatisms occur when the subconsciousness has control. Sensory automatisms are in the form of visions, auditions, and other hallucinations while motor automatisms include writing (cf. Tyrrell 1947:134ff.), as in the case of Miss Smith, and speaking-in-tongues. The glossolalist's involuntary behavior is often sensory as well as motor.

Excitement hastens the cessation of thought, and, when speech continues after thought is exhausted, strange utterances are frequently heard ranging from mumbling to recognizable words. Mosiman (1911:101ff.) says that glossolalia occurs when the speech organs come under temporary control of the reflex centers. Psychosociologically, the interstimulation and response of a religious gathering encourages glossolalia and in Christianity is the setting for most cases of it. The subject is not fully aware of what he utters. His jaws move involuntarily, and his memory tends to be exalted. Some persons who at one time have studied or overheard foreign languages are able, when in ecstasy, to speak them with varying degrees of fluency, but are unable to do so when their logical thinking processes are in force (cf. Shirokogoroff 1935:257).

According to Lombard (1910:124), speaking-in-tongues is a form of regression in which infantile linguistic patterns come to the fore. In this connection it may be noted that there seems to be a tendency among monkeys toward continual vocal expression with presumably little effort to convey meaning. Cutten (1927:168) states that glossolalists are usually persons who are devout, ignorant, illiterate, and of low ability, but he apparently believes this is true mainly for Christians. Glossolalia is customarily an adult phenomenon but, as shown above, is not unknown among children. In Christian religions women speak in tongues more often than men. Seldom does the speaker remember what he utters.

Lombard recognizes four main types of glossolalia (1910:25ff.). The first type he calls *phonations frustes*, characterized by incomprehensible sounds such as mumbling, gurgling, groaning, and the like. These sounds usually precede complex forms of articulation but may be the subject's only vocalization during the entire period of his religious excitement. For example, there is little or no literary evidence that the ecstatic vocalizations of medicine men is South America and Australia go beyond this first level. The second form is called pseudo-language. Sounds fabricated by the subject are articulated and frequently can be recognized as fragments of words. The utterances are often alliterative and may conform to certain exterior aspects of ordinary language when grouped into a form simulating a sentence. The Martian language of Helène Smith is a good illustration of the third type, verbal fabrication. Words coined by the individual may contain particles of foreign and native phonemes and may be used according to identified grammatical rules. A fourth kind of glossolalia Lombard calls *xenoglossie*, or speaking foreign tongues. In most cases the subject has had previous contact with the languages even though he may be unable to speak them when he is fully rational and conscious. In addition to the four grades of glossolalia there is a related form of speech, that of interpreting what the speaker says. Unlike most glossolalists, the interpreter may or may not maintain all contact with reality while he performs.

The above types of speaking-in-tongues are not, of course, mutually exclusive. For instance, in specific cases it is difficult or even impossible to differentiate pseudo-language from verbal fabrication. During one period of excitement the subject's utterances, with initial mumbling and gurgling, may verge into the second and third types and finally into full-blown xenoglossia. If the person employs all four grades during the course of his glossolalic experience, the investigator may have trouble in determining which of them is dominant, longest in duration, and most typical; or, he may find it difficult to distinguish one form from another.

The phenomena we are dealing with are, to be sure, but part of a much larger picture: the behavior of religiomedical practitioners. In addition to studies of ceremonial life in individual cultures, there are works that describe one or several aspects of shamanism on an area- or world-wide scale. The study of Clements (1932) is valuable in its statistical view of concepts of disease as found in most parts of the world. Stewart (1946) analyzes the incidence of spirit possession in the Americas with reference to the contributions of Boas, Loeb, and others, while Charles (1953) has made a cross-cultural survey of drama in exorcism. The account of drama in voice in the latter work (pp. 108-10) is germane to the study of glossolalia.

Review of literature depicting shamanistic ceremonies indicates that ecstatic vocalization is infrequently described. Moreover, the descriptions that are available tend to be brief and rather vague, thus complicating the analysis and classification of the types of vocalic behavior presented. It is difficult to determine from the laconic description, "muttered unintelligible sounds," the exact nature of the vocalization. Were the sounds unintelligible to members of the shaman's own tribe or only to the ethnographer present? Were the sounds rapidly spoken words of the shaman's native dialect or were they nothing but meaningless gibberish? To avoid being overcautious and thereby discarding as unreliable and unusable 50 per cent or more of the descriptive data, it will be assumed that the reporter-ethnographers' accounts of shamanistic utterances are more accurate than inaccurate, and that they coincide for the most part with the native's interpretation, conveyed to the investigator in a great many cases by an informant or interpreter.

The forms of speech-phenomena to be analyzed include the language of spirits, sacerdotal language, the language of animals, *phonations frustes*, xenoglossia, and interpretation of tongues (*ermeneglossia*). It will be noted that the first three types and interpretation of tongues are not glossolalia as defined above. Xenoglossia and *phonations frustes* have been identified by Lombard in his classification of glossolalic behavior. To classify vocalic data from primitive and non-Western societies into all his categories was found to be unfeasible largely because of the brevity of most descriptive material. Some question could be raised as to the advisability of placing the examples to follow into the above six divisions. No claim is made that these types are conceptually as separate and distinct as may be desired or that the illustrations in each of them are entirely homogeneous, but it is believed that these types will serve, at least in a preliminary way, to bring together and distinguish for purposes of comparison and analysis diverse ethnographic materials dealing with shamanistic utterances. Furthermore, it would seem that there are enough cases of a similar nature in each category to warrant their being grouped separately under each of the six headings.

Language of spirits, an esoteric "dialect" known only to the spirits and to the shaman who speaks it, is difficult to define in terms of sound quality. Sacerdotal language similar to the jargon of spirits, is a vernacular containing obsolete or archaic words preserved through the years by a priestly class. Animal language is simply the reproduction of animal sounds. The category *phonations frustes* will contain a miscellany of examples describing mutterings that vary from gurgling to meaningless syllables; the cases found under this heading are perhaps less uniform than those placed in the other five divisions. Accounts of xenoglossia, animal language, and ermeneglossia tend to be more straightforward and amenable to classification than those of *phonations frustes*, language of spirits, and sacerdotal language. Psychologically, the six categories are related. The strange sounds in their various forms and settings are uttered in a majority of cases while the practitioner is in a state of religious excitement or ecstasy, but this is much less true for sacerdotal language and ermeneglossia than for the other four types. Considerable overlapping of material is unavoidable in the analysis of interpretation of tongues. That is to say, this category includes illustrations of strange utterances, including *phonations frustes*, explained to the laymen by an interpreter. The present study is cross-cultural in perspective, and the illustrations, unless otherwise noted, represent religions that had received little or no Christian influence at the time they were observed and described.

THE LANGUAGE OF SPIRITS

Speaking the language of supernatural beings while entranced or religiously exalted occurs frequently in divinatory and curing ceremonies (cf. Bouteillier 1950:126). Rasmussen (1921-24:39) reports that among the Hudson Bay Eskimos a shamaness spoke to the spirits in their own language amid sounds of trickling water, rushing wind, snuffing of a walrus, and the growling of a bear. A spirit language is also present in the shamanistic complexes of the Chukchee (Bogoras 1907:413), Northwest and Southeast Koryak, Asiatic Eskimo (Bogoras 1907:438), Lapps, Yakuts, Tungus (Lehtisalo 1936-37:11-13), and Samoyeds (Mikhailovskii 1895:67). Bogoras states that many words of the spirit language employed by Asiatic Eskimos are analogous to the spirit language of Eskimos in Alaska and in the Atlantic area. According to Lehtisalo, the Tungus shaman is supposed to learn the entire language of nature during his trance. Batchelor 81927:227-28), in his description of Ainu religion, reports that the self-hypnotized shaman becomes the mouthpiece of his inspiring gods but, as they "do not speak to him, but only through him, he often does not know himself what he is saying, and afterwards he does not remember (so he says) that he had spoken."

The *hala*, or shaman, of the Semang pygmies (Eliade 1951:100) speaks to the celestial spirits in their own language, and, among the Papar, Putatan, and Tuaran groups of North Borneo (Rutter 1929:241-43), the priestesses of the *Gusi* cult offer incantations to a *gusi* (sacred jar) in a language known only to the spirits and themselves. In the Mortlock Islands of Micronesia, Wallis asserts (1939:82) that following convulsive twitching of the hands, nodding of the head, and other dynamic stigmata frequently accompanying glossolalia, spirits open the priest's mouth and speak through him in a language very different from ordinary speech. In the Solomon Islands (Wallis 1939:82), the male or female religious medium falls into a trance and speaks with the voice of a ghost which declares itself in possession of the medium. The Tshi-speaking priests of the Gold Coast (Ellis 1887:135) during a religious performance frequently utter words or sentences spoken in a croaking or guttural voice. The words and the person's unnatural voice were said to be those of a god.

SACERDOTAL LANGUAGE

The special language of priests differs from spirit language to the extent that it contains obsolete words and is not clearly of supernatural origin. The Eskimo shaman of East Greenland speaks a mystic language that is identical for all *angakuks* in the area. According to Thalbitzer (1931:432), this language is a stereotyped argot preserved through many centuries by shamans; it is not mere abacadabra. Other instances of obsolete or archaic language employed by religious functionaries have been described. Dunn (1906:174-75) states that the Dyak *manang* (medicine man) chants a song with words that are partly obsolete and therefore unintelligible to most laymen. According to Roth (1896:269), the language used by the Dyak priest in his incantation is incomprehensible even to the Dyaks themseles and is called gibberish by the uninitiated. "Some profess to understand what is said, but if they really do it is because they have taken the pains to learn it with the view no doubt, of performing cures on their own account later on." Roth further states (1896:270) that the *timong* (a *manang*'s monotonous chant) is a mixture or prayer and invocation, cursing and imprecation. The chant contains "archaic forms and disused words; sense gives way to the exigencies of rhyme with jingling-like endings."

Wilken's description and analysis of Indonesian shamanism stands as perhaps the most definitive work of its kind. He reports (1887:461) that the Macassarese and Buginese priests of the southern Celebes speak a language of their own which in many respects is like the language of old Buginese as preserved in the epic, *La-galigo*. This is a clear instance of sacerdotal language containing obsolescent words. Among the Olo-Ngadju

Dyak of Borneo (1887:453) the male and female religionists chant during rites of exorcism a form of language containing words that are either obsolete or of Malayan origin. The chants are interspersed with shrill shrieking tones. In Bali (1887:469) the priest uses an oracle language different from ordinary speech, a dialect that is probably, in part at least, an archaic form of modern Balinese. Further investigation today may disclose that this language contains words of both Pali and Sanskrit.

The use of an obsolete, cabalistic language in religious ceremonies is not confined to the East Indies. In Haitian ritual (Deren 1953:196) a religiously excited priest speaks a special language as a medium of communication with the *loa* (deity). This medium, called *langage*, is believed to be a vestige of African speech. One author quoted by Deren (1953:315) believes that *langage* may even be oriental in origin; another writer asserts that the vernacular contains Spanish and Indian words as well as African. It is doubtful, according to Deren, if the Voudoun priest knows what the words mean. Only the *loa* is supposed to understand this language.

It will be noted that archaic speech in sacred rites is not glossolalia as defined above. However, it is conjectural if, in the case of the Olo-Ngadju Dyak, the language was entirely obsolete. That is, the priest may have been experiencing xenoglossia when uttering words Wilken suggests were of Malayan origin. Nevertheless, it appears that most cases of obsolete language in sacerdotal litany are on the whole learned by the practitioner from his elder colleagues. The words have become sacred through many years of use, but they are more in the nature of prayers and formulas than glossolalia. In this connection it may be noted that in Christendom the High Episcopal and Roman Catholic churches still recite prayers in Latin; the litanies of the Orthodox church are not in modern dialects.

THE LANGUAGE OF ANIMALS

Eliade (1951:99-102) and Lehtisalo (1936-37:23-34) have described the use of animal language by religiomedical functionaries and state that this medium of expression is widely adopted, especially among Siberian shamans. The practitioner imitates the cries and sounds of animals, birds, and natural phenomena as a sign that he can transform himself at will into a nonhuman embodiment and circulate freely among the three cosmic zones: hell, earth, and heaven. The Chukchee (Bogoras 1907:442) and Ainu (Pilsudski 1909:77) shamans employ the language of animals. Im Thurn

(1883:337) states that during a Macusi curing ceremony in Guiana the spirits of ocelots, deer, monkeys, birds and reptiles speak to the medicine man, each with a voice appropriate to its form. The Blackfoot (Catlin 1848:39-41) medicine man in curing and the Micmac (Corlett 1935:134) shaman during his initiation both employ animal sounds. The example of the Hudson Bay Eskimos has been cited above. Animal, spirit, and sacerdotal languages are uttered ecstatically or semi-ecstatically to communicate with the spirit world but differ fundamentally in their sound patterns, the latter two manifesting some articulation presumably lacking in animal cries.

PHONATIONS FRUSTES

The occurrence of *phonations frustes* in non-Christian religions is often accompanied by other sounds ranging from animal cries and ventriloquism to whistling and shrieking. The Chaco magical rites described by Métraux (1946:353) consist of a monotonous repetition of a melodious theme interspersed with meaningless words or syllables. On occasions the priest's conjuration includes a short sentence requesting the evil to go away. Among the modern Quillancinga and Pasto groups of the Andean region studies by Ortiz (1946:967), the *curanderos* or tribal doctors intermittently recite unintelligible prayers as they chew drugs and suck the area of the patient's affliction. No description of the prayer itself is given, but it was ostensibly delivered while the priest was in a semi- or unconscious state. In North America we may note Espinosa's descriptions of a Caddo harvest ceremony (Swanton 1942:229), during which an old man delivered "a harangue of pure jargon in a hasty, high-pitched voice without saying an intelligible word."

The curer among the Niue of south Polynesia (Loeb 1924:397) whistles incessantly while he is in a trance; the Visayan (Filipino) female shaman (Wilken 1887:463) mumbles incoherently between her teeth while she is entranced; in East Malaya (Wilken 1887:448-49) and among the Teleuts (Mikhailovskii 1895:98) the possessed shaman mumbles strange words. The shaman of the Kalmuk Kirghiz (Radlov 1885:54) sings a song, punctuated with drum beats, in a whimpering and gurgling tone. Tschubinow (1914:55) asserts that the Chukchee and Koryak shamans employ ventriloquism in their seances and that demons—through the shamans—utter incomprehensible word-like noises. During a theurgic ceremony of the Orochee tribe in eastern Siberia the shaman, according to Lopatin (1946-

49:367), cries out strange wordsds which the parents of the patient cannot understand. At times the shaman changes his voice as he carries on a conversation with the spirits.

Graham (1928:15) tells of a girl in Szechwan Province, China, who was possessed by demons and "began to utter words incoherently." Farther north in Korea, Akamatsu and Akiba (1938:56) provide an account of sorcerers who, as part of their initiation, sometimes suddenly run out of their houses and into the snow without any clothing. They rove aimlessly in the mountains, dance madly, speak strange words, and fall down into a faint. These shamans undoubtedly were experiencing a form of "Arctic hysteria," but so far as the author can determine from the works of Aberle (1952), Shirokogoroff (1935), and Czaplicka (1914:307-25), speaking-in-tongues is not a frequent concomitant either of *latah* of southern Asia or "Arctic hysteria" of northern Asia.

In a seance the Kurnai (Howitt 1904:391) medicine man's whistling is shrill and he talks in a very curious voice. Like the Kurnai and Niue priests, an entranced "witch woman" of New South Wales (Parker 1905:45) whistles as she invokes the spirits. In addition to employing ventriloquism, the above diviner mutters in an "unintelligible dialect." Spence (n.d.:111-12) quotes Father Burgoa's account of a Zapotecan ceremony at Mitla. At the time of a royal funeral the enrobed priest bowed low before the idols, renewed the incense, and then began to converse with the images in a murmuring, inarticulate way. His grimaces and writhings were hideous, and his murmuring was quite unintelligible.

Because the mysterious dialects and strange words of the above cases are not described in detail, it is difficult to determine exactly what forms of speech-phenomena they represent. It is believed, however, that the illustrations cited fit rather closely into the category of *phonations frustes* with the possible exception of the Andean and Malayan examples. Other cases of *phonations frustes* and simple word formation will be presented in connection with interpretation of ecstatic utterances by mediums or "speakers."

XENOGLOSSIA

Cases of xenoglossia are somewhat more numerous in the literature and more fully described than simpler types of vocalization. Examples of it will be shown to be widespread in their incidence and striking in their uniform-ity. Swanton (1905:38) states that during a Haida shamanistic performance a spirit directed the shaman's language. If the spirit was "from the Tlingit country, as was often the case, the shaman spoke Tlingit, although in his uninspired moments he might be totally ignorant of the language." The Eyak (Ugalakmiut Eskimo) of Alaska (Birket-Smith and De Laguna 1938:209-10) is said to be able to talk and understand Tlingit, English, "or any other language" when assisted by helping spirits. During a winter ceremonial observed by Boas (1807:544) at Fort Rupert, a Kwakiutl man arose and acted as though he were a Haida. "He delivered a speech during which he made violent gestures, imitating the sound of the Haida language." An interpreter who stood next to the man translated the speech into Kwakiutl.

Ethnography of the Wintu tribe (DuBois 1935-39:91ff.) also contains illustrations of glossolalia. The shaman, Albert Thomas, who was half Wintu and half Achomawi, sang in Wintu in the middle of the night but was said to be ignorant of this language when he was awake. DuBois tells of another Indian glossolalist, Nels Charles, who attended a white school. Charles is quoted as saying, "I can't even talk Wintu well, but when a spirit enters me the spirit talks and they say I talk Wintu perfectly well. It is just like talking with unknown tongues and getting the spirit in the Pentecostal church." Unlike the Haida, Eyak, and Kwakiutl examples, the case of Thomas and, especially, that of Charles show unmistakable Christian influence. If we assume that glossolalia, by no means a universal religious phenomenon, was a trait borrowed by the Northwest Coast peoples, to deduce a shamanistic and Siberian origin would appear to be as feasible as deducing a Christian origin for the trait.

Outside of the Northwest Coast, the sub-Arctic, and California, xenoglossia does not appear to be present in those Indian religions of North America that were observed and described prior to Christian proselytizing. In South America, however, there is one case that may be illustrative of xenoglossia. According to Corlett (1935:134), the Warraus medicine man of Guiana, after hours of shaking his rattle and addressing the spirits, finally converses with them in a language unintelligible to the Indians present. Furthermore, because of the Zapotecan illustration of rudimentary glossolalia, it is conceivable that speaking-in-tongues and interpretation of sacerdotal language were part of the elaborate ceremonial life of the Mayans, Incans, Toltecs, and Aztecs.

In African religions xenoglossia has a wide geographical distribution and is a rather frequent occurrence. Among the Thonga (Junod 1913:445), the patient being exorcized sings a curative song which he himself creates. "These songs are generally in Zulu, and it is asserted that, even if the patient does not know this language, he will be able to use it in his conversation, by a kind of miracle of tongues!" Langston (1954:30) quotes Danholz as saying that in East Africa many persons possessed by spirits speak in Swahili or English, although when normal they neither understand nor speak these languages. Marwick (1940:238-39) tells of an interesting case in which an army of Swazi men moving to Portugese East Africa was possessed by the *Mandzawe* spirit because they ate cattle they had been warned not to eat. When they returned home, this peculiar spirit made them talk in BaThonga until it was expelled by a witch doctor. Gā women on the Gold Coast, when possessed by the spirit, will talk in Twi, Adangme, or Ewe, which ordinarily they are unable to speak (Field 1937:107), but, as the observer points out, most Gold Coast people do, at some time or other, learn to speak languages of neighboring tribes. One Gā glossolalist, according to Field, claimed to be ignorant of Twi but showed every sign of comprehension when asked in this tongue if she wanted a shilling. In the witch society of Kpelle tribe (Welmers 1949:224-35) the members who come to meetings from distances as great as forty miles or more are said to speak Kpelle at one moment and, later on, Loma.

Those who observe *Diqr* ceremonies in Arabia may on first encounter believe the excited participants are speaking a foreign language. But it was reported to the author that, upon investigation, the language spoken by one dervish order in Iraq was found to be not Syrianic but rapidly spoken Arabic. However, it is believed that some form of ecstatic vocalization may be present in other dervish rites as well as in the conjurations of the little-known witches of the Middle East who continue to perform despite the influence of Islam (cf. Kissling 1954:26ff.).

Rivers (1906:252-55) gives a rather detailed analysis of glossolalia as observed among the Todas. One entranced functionary, while divining at a funeral, uttered broken sentences in a loud, almost chanting voice and spoke in Malayalam, a dialect he was unable to speak when normal. Among the Palaung peoples of Burma (Milne 1924:262) a person possessed by a Palé-speaking *bre*, or "black magician," is impelled to talk in the magician's tongue, although at ordinary times he is unable to speak it. In Kelantan (Cuisinier 1936:15) an entranced sorcerer would deliver entire passages in Javanese or Siamese, particularly in the former, and in Perak (Maxwell 1883:226) during a curing ceremony the Malayan shaman "spoke in a feigned voice, pronouncing Malay words with the peculiar intonation of the Sakai aborigines and introducing frequently Sakai words and phrases unintelligible to most of the Malays present.'' An Ifuguao priest (Parton 1946:121) spoke the Aiyangan dialect of his tribe while possessed by an ancestor and was said never to have had any acquaintance with this language before his seance.

During the closing years of the Later Han Dynasty, in approximately A.D. 196, Seng-yu, as recorded in the *Taishō Tripitaka* (1928:40b), states that the wife of Ting-in in Chi-yin would suddenly become ill and speak in foreign languages she apparently could not speak when normal. Like Helène Smith seventeen centuries later, she would ask for a writing instrument and paper to write down what she had spoken. Sometime after her experience a monk from either Central Asia or India saw what she wrote and said that it was a sutra. Unfortunately, Seng-yu, who lived in the early Liang Dynasty, A.D. 445-518, did not give a detailed narration of the above case probably due to the fact that the historical materials he worked with were similarly brief in their description. This rather complex type of glossolalia strongly suggests that the phenomenon in its various manifestations was a part of theurgic and priestly practice long before the Han, perhaps as far back as the Shang Dynasty when cracked tortoise shells were divined. In modern China there are also instances of glossolalia, exclusive of those having definite Christian inspiration.

In the Koko-nor area of central China a ''T'ou-jen'' shaman observed by Schröder (1952:29) often excites himself into a deep trance and murmurs deformed words later written down and explained by his assistant. While in the trance the shaman, a Lamaist Buddhist, is said to be able to speak ''all languages''—Tibetan, Chinese, and Mongolian—even if he has not learned them before. In passing, it is worthwhile to note a Buddhist explanation of glossolalia based on the doctrine of transmigration of souls. If, say, an entranced Korean is able to speak German without having learned the language, it is indicated that in one of his past lives he was a German.

Xenoglossia has been observed in shamanistic performances of Siberia. Jochelson (1905-1908:52) tells of a Tungus shaman whose spirits were Koryak in origin and spoke through him in the Koryak dialect. Like other glossolalists he did not remember after his trance what he uttered and claimed that he did not understand the language he had spoken. Jochelson states that he was convinced the man did not understand any Koryak and that he could only recite the Koryak incantations, previously learned, when in a state of genuine excitement. Some patients suffering from hysterical seizures ("Arctic hysteria") are also known to speak in tongues (Jochelson 1910:30), but, as previously noted, such an occurrence does not seem to be frequent. It appears that glossolalic shamans themselves seldom suffer from "Arctic hysteria" while performing as shamans and that symptoms of hysteria analyzed by Aberle (1952), such as *echolalia* (repeating what a person says) and *echopraxia* (repeating what a person does), do not invariably coexist with glossolalia or serve as its psychomotor foundation.

Mikhailovskii (1895:64-65) reports that during a Tungus exorcizing ceremony the language of the shaman was unknown. Shirokogoroff gives a more thorough picture of glossolalia among the Tungus (1935:256-57) both descriptively and analytically. There are those persons—not necessarily shamans—who sing while asleep. Others in this state speak for themselves or on behalf of certain spirits in Buriat, Russian, Manchu, or Chinese. Like the Haida, the Tungus believe that specific spirits speak in specific tongues. Some glossolalists speak foreign languages well, others haltingly. Many Tungus, according to Shirokogoroff, have some knowledge of a foreign language they are unable to speak readily when encountering mnemonic and other inhibitions of full consciousness. Of course, speaking in a foreign language while asleep is not characteristic of the Tungus alone. Shirokogoroff asserts that he knows of Europeans who were surprised to learn that they speak foreign languages better when dreaming than when awake.

In Japan glossolalia is known to occur in small cultic groups, during sorcerous seances in Hokkaidō and northern Honshū, and in the postwar sect known as the Dancing Religion. A full range of glossolalic phenomena is said to occur frequently during the ceremonies of the small cult led by a Genji Yanagida of Moji City, Fukuoka Prefecture, and in other groups similar to it. In the Dancing Religion (cf. May 1954:130) members when in a state of ecstasy are able to speak in foreign languages, especially English and Chinese. The devotee usually claims he has never *studied* the language before and that he is unable when conscious to recall what he has said. Similar to the Tungus and Haida cases, the motivating force of glossolalia in the Dancing Religion is said to be that of spirits. Mrs. Kitamura, the leader of the above sect, while not strongly concerned with the occurrence of ecstatic utterances during worship services, does recognize two kinds of "speaking spirits." The first kind she calls *gairei*, or "foreign" spirit. It is a wandering, troublesome spirit seeking salvation. If the spirit is that of a dead Spaniard, the glossolalist is persuaded to speak in Spanish; if it comes from England, the subject speaks English. If it is that of an animal or inanimate object, the person will make strange sounds identifiable as *phonations frustes* or verbal fabrication.

While in a state of ecstasy two worshipers possessed with kindred spirits may converse in the same foreign language, and, on occasions, other members while in ecstasy or fully conscious may interpret what the speakers have said. The other type of spirit, *futsu no rei*, or ordinary spirit, is a "foreign" spirit that has been saved by prayers of worshipers. The living person in whom the saved spirit resides talks only in his native tongue, whatever it might be. In an exact sense, the utterances of the ordinary spirits are not in the realm of glossolalia even though they may be impassioned and ecstatic. When malefic, the spirits are energetically exorcized, either by the glossolalist after he has spoken or by another member. Benign spirits thank members for having been saved. Like Helène Smith and the wife of Ting-in, one female devotee is said to have written while she was entranced. Her words were in the English language which she had studied in her childhood.

INTERPRETATION OF TONGUES

Shamanistic utterances in Hokkaidō and northern Honshū illustrate the sixth form of vocal behavior, interpretation of tongues or ermeneglossia. One type of sorcerer in northern Japan is usually a woman who has received no formal training in divinatory art. She puts her client in a trance or, failing to accomplish this, employs a medium who may also be a sorcerer. If the entranced patient or medium utters a sort of babble, it is promptly interpreted by the sorceress to assist her in diagnosing the patient's disease or misfortune. The spirit causing the trouble may be either an ancestral spirit or that of some animate or inanimate thing. Like the patient and medium, the sorceress herself may utter strange words later interpreted by her medium. The words are often said to be those of her guardian deity, either *Inari*, *Jizō*, or *Dainichi*. The second type of sorceress must be blind and must be trained before her first menses, but, according to a conversation with Professor Ishizu of Tōhoku University, these shamanesses never speak abnormally.

In his discussion of shamanism in Japanese religion, Oguchi (1953:90) tells of a man living in Hokkaidō who founded a new religion attaching importance to horses and water. While being anesthetized preparatory to an abdominal operation, this man, Yasui Juiji, experienced a curious form of interpretation of tongues. He avers that he could understand the German his surgeon was speaking, just as though it were Japanese. That the attendants laughed when he told them he could understand the doctor's words indicates that he was not unconscious at the time. Mr. Juiji claims that God's dwelling within him enabled him to understand German.

Harvey (1933:133-35) tells of a *chi-tung*, or divining youth, who performed in Hunan Province, China, in 1921. After invoking the gods, he shivers, yawns, shakes, and dances while in a semicataleptic state. "Questions are put to him and he mumbles incoherently in reply. His interpreter translates the babble into intelligible speech." The answer in this case consisted of a medical prescription which was filled to the letter and given to the patient.

Among the Bataks of Sumatra (Loeb 1935:81) a particular ghost descends into a new shamaness-medium, displaces her soul, and causes her to speak a ghost language which has to be interpreted. In Oceania ecstatic utterances are also interpreted. For example, in the Sandwich Islands (Tylor 1920:134) a priest's features became distorted, his limbs were convulsed, and his eyes were wild when the god Oro gave his oracles. While rolling on the ground, foaming at the mouth, the priest would reveal the will of the possessing god in violent and indistinct sounds, which attendants interpreted to the people. Handy (1927:163) tells of a Tahitian prophet who in a state of inspiration would utter shrill cries and violent, often indistinct, sounds later interpreted by priests. In Dobu (Fortune 1932:154) medical patients are said to make delirious or semidelirious statements about canoes at sea used by sea witches. The patient's ravings are apparently translated.

According to Park (1938), shamans of western North America are known to employ interpreters or speakers. In curing rites the Paviotso shaman mumbles and speaks rapidly in broken sentences (Park 1938:50) while his assistant interprets to the spectators what he has said. Speakers are also reported to perform among the Takelma (Sapir 1917:44) and Shoshoni (Steward 1933:315), among the Sanpoil, Nespelem (Ray 1933:190), and Okanagon (Cline 1938:149) of the Plateau, and in northern California among the Achomawi, Atsugewi, Modoc, and Wintu (Park 1938:128). However, with the possible exception of the Wintu (Cf. Dubois 1935-

39:107), it is apparent that the shamans do not speak in a truly incomprehensible language or use obsolescent words.

In the ethnography of Africa several examples of interpretation of tongues are forthcoming. Among the Loma peoples of West Africa (Welmers 1949:232) possessed persons speak Kpelle, and their words are interpreted into Loma. Pauwels (1951:355), in his description of the Nyabingi cult of Ruanda, reports that when a client presents himself to the witch doctor a female medium goes into a trance, rolls on the ground, and utters unintelligible words and incoherent phrases which are immediately explained by the priest. In northern Rhodesia those persons possessed by spirits of dead Awemba chiefs will, after arriving at a requisite state of religious exaltation, fall to the ground and burst forth into an almost inarticulate chant (Gouldsbury and Sheane 1911:83). At this point the spectators remain silent, and the medicine man and assistants gather round to interpret what the possessed medium has said. The Baganda and Bakitara also interpret the oracular words of entranced persons. Among the Baganda (Roscoe 1911:275) the medium or "mouthpiece of the gods" remains silent and stares steadily into the fire or upon the ground until the spirit comes to him. When the spirit enters him he becomes frenzied, and the attendant priest adroitly interprets the speech which only he can understand. In the Bakitara tribe (Roscoe 1923:26), if a divine message was desired, the priest might either act as a medium himself or employ an assistant. If the priest acted as the medium, the listeners had to interpret his words as best they could, but, if another person spoke, the priest himself would do the interpreting.

In the discussion of xenoglossia, interpretation of tongues was also noted in the Dancing Religion of Japan and in the ceremonies of the Kwakiutl and the Chinese semiprimitives of the Koko-nor area. It is apparent that ermeneglossia and ecstatic vocalization are closely related and that functionally the former depends to a large extent upon the latter. Cooperation takes place between priest, the medium and, in the Japanese case, even the patient, but the strange sounds uttered are not merely an impractical part of a priest's or medium's esthetic trappings. The gibberish is explained and put to use.

PROBLEMS AND CONCLUSIONS

In the above survey a number of questions have arisen as to the geographical distribution of glossolalia and related forms, their presence in some areas and absence in others, and their sociocultural explanation. Some of these questions can be answered with a fair amount of assurance, while others, for the time being at least, appear to be unanswerable.

Speaking-in-tongues and similar behavior have been seen to be highly variegated and widespread in their incidence, but with few exceptions they appear to be mainly Old World phenomena. In the western hemisphere cases of xenoglossia uninspired by Christianity are, so far as the author can ascertain, confined to the sub-Arctic area and the Northwest Coast. Animal and spirit languages characterize the Arctic area, and to the south *phonations frustes* and interpretation of tongues have been reported. The archaic *langage* of Haiti is in all probability an African rather than an American Indian trait. Other illustrations of glossolalia in the New World may have been overlooked, but on the whole it appears that the phenomenon and similar behavior are atypical of Indian religions.

In Africa examples of xenoglossia and interpretation of tongues are plentiful, while cases of *phonations frustes*, archaic sacerdotal language, and spirit language are relatively uncommon. No account could be found of an African priest or magician speaking the language of animals as it is known in Siberia and the Arctic. The Moslem areas of North Africa and Asia Minor have not been shown to be illustrative of modern cases of speaking-in-tongues, but farther east ecstatic vocalization is reported in Moslem Malaya and in many areas of the East Indies. Wilken's research in particular shows clearly that an archaic priestly language is spoken by religious practitioners in this general region. *Phonations frustes* are found in Malaya and Indonesia. Animal language and interpretation of tongues, on the other hand, are not reported, *per se*, in the ceremonies of these two areas.

China and Japan enter into the picture with examples of spirit language and especially xenoglossia and interpretation of tongues. Korean sorcerers are known to utter incoherent sounds, and to the north Siberian shamans employ all identified forms of vocalization but ermeneglossia and sacerdotal language. Languages of animals and spirits appear to be common as modes of shamanistic behavior, more so than xenoglossia. In literature describing the religious ceremonies of Oceania, interpretation of tongues and *phonations frustes* are noted. In Australia the latter form has been cited, and, in the Philippines, *phonations frustes* and xenoglossia.

From the above one can further generalize that there are three main regions of glossolalic vocalization, i.e., Africa with its xenoglossia and interpretation of tongues, Indonesia and Malaya with their archaic sacerdotal language and *phonations frustes*, and Siberia with all our categories but ermeneglossia and archaic sacerdotal language. With few exceptions other parts of the world, notably the western hemisphere and Australia, are areas where glossolalic and glossolalia-like utterances, especially the more complex forms, do not appear to be characteristic of native religious and magical behavior.

The Arctic and the Northwest Coast resemble Siberia with reference to spirit and animal languages and xenoglossia, respectively. Were xenoglossia, spirit language, and animal language introduced into North America by non-Europeans or were they already a part of Indian and Eskimo religions when these peoples first settled in the New World? In this regard we should not overlook the influence Ignace LaMousse and other Christianized Iroquois may have had upon religions of the Northwest early in the nineteenth century (cf. Spier 1935:30-39). Another problem is the occurrence of interpretation of tongues in the Plateau, California, and contiguous area but not demonstrably in other parts of the western hemisphere. If stimulus diffusion is proposed as a possible answer or solution, an Asiatic as opposed to an African origin of the trait is not inconceivable.

The geographical distribution of glossolalic and glossolalia-like traits raises the question as to whether or not they appear inevitably and as a matter of course in the behavior of entranced practitioners. Grunting, gurgling, mumbling, and the like do, of course, take place during periods of ecstasy, and there would seem to be little learning involved in this rudimentary form of glossolalia. But it is important to know if spectators allow their medicine man to carry on in this manner, or if they would ostracize him, after he mumbled uncannily, for behaving like a lunatic or devil. Religious mores determine to a great extent how the practitioner may act when he is entranced and whether or not he may become entranced at all while curing, divining, or convoking the spirits. Even if frenzied behavior is countenanced in a given society, as it is in Siberia and elsewhere, the shaman is not given absolute freedom of behavior: he must follow within certain bounds the customs of their shamans in his own clan or tribe. Consequently, there seems to be considerable truth in the assertion that people do not speak in tongues unless they have heard about speaking-in-tongues, and to this should be added that on the whole they become glossolalists only if their customs permit them to. For example, most of the Christian world looks with varying degrees of disdain upon glossolalia and related emotionality typical of revivalistic sects, biblical sanction to the contrary notwithstanding.

Spirit language, xenoglossia, and ermeneglossia are more the result of learning than *phonations frustes*, but this is only an a priori assumption. The former categories would seem to be more elaborate, more complex, and less apt to manifest themselves accidently or spontaneously without having a precedent somewhere in a tribe's religious and ceremonial history. Perhaps animal language is more a result of learning than *phonations frustes*.

The psychological explanation of glossolalia with especial reference to its Christian manifestation has been studied heretofore. Religious explanations include that of Buddhism and that of the Dancing Religion of Japan, the former being based on the idea of transmigration of souls, and the latter upon specific spirits possessing the glossolalist. Generally speaking, the Christian interpretation is that the gift of tongues is a gift of God. It is a spiritual charisma along with prophecy, healing, performing miracles, and interpretation of tongues. But none of these explanations tells why certain forms of vocalization are found in some areas and are absent in others, or to what extent or in what way culture and society determine the religiomagical milieu giving rise to glossolalia. Effort should therefore be made to identify and explain sociocultural factors accounting for ecstatic vocalizations. Such an explanation admittedly would be more suggestive than conclusive due to the brief and fragmentary nature of most relevant ethnographic data.

Glossolalia in one form or another is found in religions that are tolerant of highly emotional individualistic behavior on the part of medicine men and their assistants. The priest may seize upon exotic utterances to demonstrate the realness and variety of his powers and to maintain about himself an air of mysticism and otherworldliness (cf. Charles 1953). Laymen are inclined to accept his odd sounds as proof of his spiritual prowess. But speaking-in-tongues is not an inevitable derivative of spirit possession and ecstasy. The shaman may enter a cataleptic or hysterical state, writhe on the ground and gasp for air without uttering strange sounds or imitating animal cries. If he says anything, it may well be coherent and in his own language. Parsons (1939:711-12) tells of a Zuni medicine man who became violent and stiffened into a kind of catalepsy during a curing ceremony, but this man apparently did not utter strange words. It is probable that formalization of rites and symbolization of the supernatural discourage ecstatic vocalization.

On the whole, glossolalia occurs infrequently in both Christian and non-Christian religions. In the latter, speaking-in-tongues is generally the forte of shamans and their assistants, not of the laymen, while in certain Christian sects, the Dancing Religion, and a small number of other religions, anyone can speak in tongues if he is properly inspired. Only among the Palaung of Burma and the Thonga of Africa have laymen been shown to speak while in ecstasy. There is no clan- or tribe-wide speaking-in-tongues in religions unaffected by Christian revivalism. That is, whole groups of worshipers are not motivated by a few practicing glossolalists to utter strange sounds. A possible exception to the above assumption is Bogoras' description (1901-10:42) of shamanizing *en masse*, characterized by a strange pathological state of mind simultaneously seizing an entire group of Chukchee spectators and causing them to shout and dance savagely.

Loeb's study of shamans and seers (1921) is of value in analyzing the sociocultural basis of glossolalic behavior. The seer, according to Loeb, is usually a noninspirational religionist who, in contrast to the inspirational shaman, neither prophesies nor exorcizes. The noninspirational priest seeks guardian spirits and they speak *to* him; the true shaman as found in Siberia is possessed by spirits that speak *through* him. The main difference lies in whether or not the vision is sought for or comes voluntarily. Loeb states that inspirational shamans are found in Siberia, among the Ainu, everywhere in Africa, in India, Ceylon, Melanesia, Fiji, Polynesia, in the Arctic, and possibly in the Northwest Coast. Stewart (1946) has shown that spirit possession, closely correlated with inspirational shamanism, is found in the New World more widely than previously believed but that it is, nevertheless, uncommon outside of the Plateau, Northwest Coast, and Arctic culture spheres.

As a rule, speaking-in-tongues and kindred phenomena are confined to those areas where there is spirit possession and where inspirational shamans hold forth. Glossolalia can be and often is the result of spirit-induced ecstasy making it possible for the inspirational shaman to cure, exorcize, and prophesy. The shaman who is spoken through by spirits is more inclined to make strange sounds than one who is spoken to, the latter being more intent on listening than on speaking during his spirit-inspired moments.

One may ponder on the beginning of glossolalia and related speech-phenomena, on their having one place of origin or several. There may have been two zones of development, i.e., somewhere in the early settled areas of the Middle East and the Far East. It is doubtful if xenoglossia and interpretation of tongues arose independently in other regions of the world. The strong Christian tradition of glossolalia with its roots in the ancient religions of Asia Minor suggests a place of development somewhere in Arabia or Egypt. The illustration taken from the records of the Han Dynasty points to an early area of development in China, and, until we know to what extent China in pre-Han times was influenced by the West in matters ceremonial and religious, it would be hazardous to propose that glossolalia was introduced into East Asia from abroad.

This survey has shown that speaking-in-tongues is widespread and very ancient. Indeed, it is probably that as long as man has had divination, curing, sorcery, and propitiation of spirits he has had glossolalia. Other forms of speech-phenomena that have been discussed would also seem to be very old. With the exception of *phonations frustes* all forms of vocalization presented appear to be largely derived from learning, but this does not rule out independent invention of new ways to contact the supernatural. Since religion is a very conservative institution, borrowing of glossolalia and related forms and their integration into tribal rites must be a very slow process. Additional field work in folk religions is needed to show the extent to which ecstatic vocalization is learned, to answer questions related to its psychosociology, and to give a clearer picture of its history in specific cultures.

REFERENCES CITED

ABERLE, David F.
  1952   "Arctic hysteria" and latah in Mongolia. Transactions of the New York Academy of Sciences 14, Ser. 7:291-97.

AKAMATSU, Tomoshiro and Takashi Akiba
  1938   Chōsen Fuzoku no kenkyū. Vol. 1 of 2 vols. Osaka, Osakayagō shoten.

BARTON, R. F.
  1946   The religion of the Ifugaos. American Anthropological Association, Memoir No. 65.

BATCHELOR, John

1927   Ainu life and lore. Tokyo, Kyobunkwan.

BIRKET-SMITH, Kaj and Frederica de Laguna
1938   The Eyak Indians of the Copper-River Delta, Alaska. Copen-
        hagen, Levin and Munksgaard.

BOAS, Franz
1897   The social organization and secret societies of the Kwakiutl Indi-
        ans. Washington, D.C., Smithsonian Institution, Report of the
        National Museum.

BOGORAS, W. G.
1904-10 The Chukchee. Publications of the Jesup North Pacific Expedition
        8.

1907   The Chukchee—religion. Reprint from Vol. VII, Pt. II, of the Je-
        sup North Pacific Expedition. Memoirs of the American Museum
        of Natural History XI, Pt. II, New York, G. E. Stechert.

BOUTEILLIER, Marcelle
1950   Chamanisme et guérison magique. Paris, Presses Universitaires de
        France.

BRUMBACK, Carl
1947   "What meaneth this?" Springfield, Missouri, Gospel Publishing
        House.

CATLIN, George
1848   North American Indians. Vol. 1 of 2 vols. London.

CHARLES, Lucile H.
1953   Drama in shaman exorcism. Journal of American Folklore 66:95-
        122.

CLARK, Elmer T.
1949   The small sects in America. Rev. ed. New York, Abingdon-
        Cokesbury Press.

CLEMENTS, Forrest E.
1932   Primitive concepts of disease. University of California Publica-
        tions in American Archaeology and Ethnology 32:185-254.

CLINE, Walter
1938   Religion and world view in the Sinkaietk or Southern Okanagon of
        Washington, ed. Leslie Spier. Menasha, Wisconsin, George Banta
        Publishing Co.

CORLETT, William T.
1935

The medicine-man of the American Indian and his cultural background. Springfield, Illinois, C. C. Thomas.

CUISINIER, Jeanne
    1936   Danses magiques de Kelantan. Travaux et mémoires de l'Institut d' Ethnologie, University of Paris.

CUTTEN, George B.
    1927   Speaking with tongues, New Haven, Yale University Press.

CZAPLICKA, M. A.
    1914   Aboriginal Siberia. Oxford, Oxford University Press.

DEREN, Maya
    1953   Divine horsemen. New York, Thames and Hudson.

DeBOIS, Cora A.
    1935-39   Wintu ethnography. University of California Publications in American Archaeology and Ethnology 36, No. 1.

DUNN, Edm.
    1906   Religious rites and customs of the Iban or Dyaks of Sarawak, Borneo. Anthropos 1:11 ff.

ELIADE, Mircea
    1951   Le chamanisme et les techniques archaíques de l'extase. Paris, Payot.

ELLIS, A. G.
    1887   The Tshi-speaking peoples. London, Chapman and Hall.

ERMAN, Adolph.
    1894   Life in ancient Egypt. Trans. by H. M. Tirard. London, Macmillan.

FIELD, M. J.
    1937   Religion and medicine of the Gã people. London, Oxford University Press.

FLOURNOY, Th.
    1900   From India to the planet Mars. Trans. by. D. B. Vermilye. New York, Harper.

FORTUNE, R. F.
    1932   Sorcerers of Dobu. New York, E. P. Dutton.

GOULDSBURY, Cullen and Hubert Sheane
    1911   The great plateau of northern Rhodesia: being some impressions of the Tanganyika plateau. London, Edward Arnold.

GRAHAM, D. C.

1928   Religion in Szechwan Province China. Washington, D.C., Smithsonian Institution Collections 80.

GUILLAUME, Alfred
1938   Prophecy and divination among the Hebrews and other Semites. London, Hodder and Stoughton.

HANDY, E. S. Craighill
1927   Polynesian religion. Honolulu, Bernice P. Bishop Museum Bulletin, No. 34.

HARVEY, Edwin D.
1933   The mind of china. New Haven, Yale University Press.

HAWTHORNTHWAITE, Samuel
1857   Mr. Hawthornthwaite's adventures among the Mormons as an elder during the last eight years. Manchester, England.

HERSKOVITS, Melville J. and Frances S.
1947   Trinidad village. New York, Knopf.

HOWITT, A. W.
1904   The native tribes of south-east Australia. London, Macmillan.

IM THURN, Everard F.
1883   Among the Indians of Guiana. London, Kegan Paul.

JOCHELSON, Vladimir I.
1905-08 The Koryak. Publications of the Jesup North Pacific Expedition 6.

1910   The Yakughir and the Yakaghirized Tungus. Publications of the Jesup North Pacific Expedition 9.

JUNOD, Henri A.
1913   The life of a South African tribe. Vol. 2 of 2 vols. Neuchatel. Imprimerie Attinger Frères.

KISSLING, Hans J.
1954   The sociological and educational role of the dervish orders in the Ottoman empire. American Anthropological Association Memoir No. 76, pp. 23-35.

LANGSTON, Edward
1954   What are demons? The London Quarterly and Holborn Review (January), pp. 26-32.

LEHTISALO, T.
1936-37 Beobachtungen über die jodler. Suomalis-Ugrilainen Seura Aikakauskerja 48:1-35.

LOEB, E. M.
1921   Shaman and seer. American Anthropologist 31:60-84.
1924   The shaman of Niue. American Anthropologist 26:393-404.
1935   Sumatra its history and people. Published as Vol. III of Wiener Beiträge zur Kulturgeschichte und Linguistik des Institutes für Völkerkunde der Universität Wies, Vienna.

LOMBARD, Émile
1910   De la glossolalie chez les premiers chrétiens et des phénomènes similaires. Lausanne, Bridel.

LOPATIN, Ivan A.
1946-49   A shamanistic performance for a sick boy. Anthropos 41-44:365:68.

MARWICK, Brian Allan
1940   The Swazi. Cambridge, Cambridge University Press.

MAXWELL, W. E.
1883   Shamanism in Perak. Journal of the Straits Branch of the Royal Asiatic Society (December), pp. 222-32.

MAY, L. Carlyle
1954   The Dancing Religion: a Japanese messianic sect. The Southwestern Journal of Anthropology 10:119-37.

MÉTRAUX, Alfred
1946   Ethnography of the Chaco. In Handbook of South American Indians, ed. Julian H. Steward, Vol. 1, pp. 197-370. Washington, D.C., Bureau of American Ethnology.

MIKHAILOVSKII, V. M.
1895   Shamanism in Siberia and European Russia. Trans. by Oliver Wardrop. The Journal of the Anthropological Institute of Great Britain and Ireland 24:62-100.

MILNE, Leslie (Mrs.)
1924   The home of an eastern clan. Oxford, Oxford University Press.

MOSIMAN, Eddison
1911   Das zungenreden, geschichtlich und psychologisch untersucht. Tübingen, Mohr.

OGUCHI, Iichi
1953   Nippon shūkyō no shakaiteki seikaku. Tokyo, Tokyo University Press.

ORTÍZ, Sergio Elias
1946

The modern Quillancinga, Pasto, and Coaiquer. *In* Handbook of South American Indians, ed. Julian H. Steward, Vol. 2, pp. 961-68. Washington, D.C., Bureau of American Ethnology.

PARK, Willard Z.
1938   Shamanism in western North America. Evanston, Illinois, Northwestern University Press.

PARKER, K. Langloh
1905   The Euahlayi tribe. London, Archibald Constable.

PARSONS, Elsie Clews
1939   Pueblo Indian religion. Vol. 2 of 2 vols. Chicago, University of Chicago Press.

PAUWELS, Marcel
1951   Le culte de Nyabingi (Ruanda). Anthropos 46:337-57.

PILSUDSKI, B.
1909   Der schamanismus bei den Ainu-stämmen von Sachalin. Globus 95:72-78.

PRATT, James B.
1928   The religious consciousness a psychological study. New York, Macmillan.

RADLOV, Vasilii V.
1885   Das schamanenthum und sein kultus. Leipzig, Weigel.

RASMUSSEN, Knud
1921-24   Intellectual culture of the Hudson Bay Eskimos. Report of the Fifth Thule Expedition 7.

RAY, Verne F.
1933   The Sanpoil and the Nespelem. University of Washington Publications in Anthropology 5.

RIVERS, W. H. R.
1906   The Todas. London, Macmillan.

ROSCOE, John
1911   The Baganda. London, Macmillan.

1923   The Bakitara. Cambridge, Cambridge University Press.

ROTH, Henry L.
1896   The natives of Sarawak and British North Borneo. Vol. 1 of 2 vols. London, Truslove and Hanson.

RUTTER, Owen
1929   The pagans of North Borneo. London, Hutchinson.

SAPIR, Edward
    1907   Religious ideas of the Takelma Indians of southwestern Oregon.
            Journal of American Folklore 20:33-49.

SCHRODER, Dominik
    1952   Zur religion der Tujen [T'ou-jen] des Sininggebietes (Kukunor).
            Anthropos 47:1-79.

SENG-YU
    1928   Chu-san-tsang chi-chi. Taishō Tripitaka 55.

SHIROKOGOROFF, S. M.
    1935   Psychomental complex of the Tungus. London, Kegan Paul.

SPENCE, Lewis
    n.d.   The magic and mysteries of Mexico. London, Rider.

SPIER, Leslie
    1935   The prophet dance of the northwest and its derivatives: the source
            of the ghost dance. Menasha, Wisconsin, George Banta Publish-
            ing Co.

STEWARD, Julian H.
    1933   Ethnography of the Owens Valley Paiute. University of California
            Publications in American Archaeology and Ethnology 33.

STEWART, Kenneth M.
    1946   Spirit possession in native America. Southwestern Journal of An-
            thropology 2:323-39.

SWANTON, J. R.
    1905   The Haida. Publications of the Jesup North Pacific Expedition 8.

    1942   Source material on the history and ethnology of the Caddo Indians.
            Bull. 132. Washington, D.C., Bureau of American Ethnology.

THALBITZER, W.
    1931   Shamans of the East Greenland Eskimo. In Source Book in An-
            thropology, ed. A. L. Kroeber and T. T. Waterman, New York,
            Harcourt Brace.

TSCHUBINOW, Georg
    1914   Beiträge zum psychologischen verständnis des Sibirischen
            zauberers. Halle.

TYLOR, Edward B.
    1920 (1871)   Primitive culture. 4th ed. London, John Murray.

TYRELL, G. N. M.
    1947

The personality of man. London, Penguin Books.

VIRGIL (Publius Vergilius Maro)
   1953   The Aeneid of Virgil. Trans. by C. Day Lewis. New York, Dou-
           bleday.

WALLIS, Wilson D.
   1939   Religion in primitive society. New York, F. S. Crofts.

WELMERS, William E.
   1949   Secret medicines, magic, and rites of the Kpelle tribe in Liberia.
           The Southwestern Journal of Anthropology 5:208-43.

WILKEN, G. A.
   1887   Het shamanisme bij de volken van den Indischen archipel.
           Bijdragen tot de taallanden volkenkunde van nederlandsch-Indie,
           Ser. 2. The Hague.

5

STUART D. CURRIE

Speaking in Tongues:
Early Evidence Outside the New Testament
Bearing on Γλώσσαις Λαλεῖν

[Reprinted from *Interpretation*, XIX (1965): 274-94. Reprinted with permission from *Interpretation*.]

There are Christians today who say of an experience they share in common, "We speak in tongues." This statement implies several claims: first, that these Christian know what is meant by the New Testament expression γλώσσαις λαλεῖν, "to speak in tongues"; second, that what these Christians do is so similar to what some Christians did in the first century that the same name, γλώσσαις λαλεῖν, is appropriate both to the current phenomena and to those of which the New Testament speaks; and third, that, since γλώσσαις λαλεῖν is spoken of in the New Testament as a gift of the Spirit what these contemporary Christians are doing constitutes a manifestation, perceptible to the senses, of the presence of the Holy Spirit.

Each of these claims raises questions in the minds of other Christians today. Take the first claim. Is the exact meaning of γλώσσαις λαλεῖν in the New Testament really so clear and plain and simple? In some places it appears that γλώσσαις λαλεῖν means to speak in a human language one has not learned; in others it is possible to suppose that γλώσσαις λαλεῖν means to speak in a non-human langauge or to give utterance to sounds which are not language at all in the sense of connected discourse, even if the sounds are in some way meaningful.

In Acts 2:1-13 we read that once when some Christians spoke "in other tongues" as the Spirit gave them utterance, some persons present heard God being praised, each in his own native tongue. In Acts 10:46 and 19:6 no indication is given as to whether the tongues were intelligible or whether any present understood what was being uttered. In 1 Corinthians, Chapter 14, Paul implies that there were, or could be, occasions when no one present was able to understand what was spoken in tongues.

Are we to infer that there were occasions when Christians spoke tongues they had not learned and that these tongues were recognized by persons who heard what was being uttered? Or are we to infer that as Christians "spoke in tongues" it was given to some hearers to understand in their own native tongue a message uttered in (to use Ernst Haenchen's phrase) a "supernatural Esperanto?"[1]

Is the gift of "interpretation of tongues" a gift of the ability to translate into the common language of the hearers what is being uttered by one who is "speaking in tongues?" Or does "interpretation" here mean, rather, exegesis or explanation? For instance, what is "spoken in a tongue" might be enigmatic or oracular: the words might be intelligible but the meaning is obscure; the gift of interpretation would then be the gift of the ability to make plain the meaning of what was being uttered. Or, to consider a third possibility, does "interpretation" mean here what an art critic does when he reports on the message or meaning of a piece of music? In this case the interpreter would neither translate nor convey in plain language the gist of an enigmatic message; he would, rather explain the aim and the mood (praise, lament, thanksgiving, exultation) of the utterance.

Unless and until one has some fairly clear idea of what γλώσσαις λαλεῖν means in the New Testament, it would appear rash to use the

---

[1]Haenchen, *Die Apostelgeschichte* (Göttingen: Vandenhoeck & Ruprecht, 1961), p. 137.

expression to describe a contemporary phenomenon. Yet when Christians today say, "We speak in tongues," they clearly imply either that there is something so distinctive about γλώσσαις λαλεῖν that it is immediately recognizable wherever it occurs and that it cannot be confused with any other phenomenon; or they imply that there are some persons (themselves included) who are qualified to discern the genuine gift of the Spirit from any counterfeit, however specious.

The New Testament itself, as well as other writings of early Christians, shows that a possibility of confusion did exist and that it was a task both real and difficult to discern whether the gift was from the Holy Spirit or from some other source. In Acts 2:1-13 different inferences were drawn from what was observed. In 1 Corinthians 14:23 Paul says that an outsider coming upon an assembly of Christians all "speaking in tongues" would surely think they were raving. The observer might not be able to decide whether the utterances are lunatic or mantic, frenzied or oracular.

And even when the one who "speaks in tongues" is regarded as inspired, there remains the question of the source of the inspiration. Those who use the New Testament expression γλώσσαις λαλεῖν to describe what they are doing clearly imply that they regard what they are doing as a manifestation of the presence of the Holy Spirit. But this claim raises today the same problems of discipline and order which it raised in the first and second centuries. Not all of those who claim contact with the Holy Spirit are able to convince members of the Lord's Body that what they are doing is at the behest of his Spirit. Even in the New Testament (1 Thess. 5:19-22; 1 John 4:1) Christians are instructed to weigh and test whatever is presented to them as a manifestation of the power of the Holy Spirit; but it is easy to understand the delicacy of the situation. Suppose one were to misjudge, and thereby refuse to admit, what was prompted by the Holy Spirit? Had not the Lord said something about sins against the Holy spirit being unforgivable? In the case of "speaking in tongues," just what standards of judgment can be brought to bear as one tries to determine whether the utterance is in fact the gift of the Spirit of Christ?

As we try to deal fairly with the New Testament records, it is appropriate to consider whether there is any evidence from other early Christian writings and from more or less contemporary non-Christian sources which may throw light both on the question of what is meant by "speaking in tongues" and on the kinds of problems of order and discipline raised by this or kindred phenomena.

WHAT WAS Γλώσσαις Λαλεῖν?

As early as the fourth century, Chrysostom frankly confesses the difficulty presented by the expression γλώσσαις λαλεῖν. The great preacher thinks he knows what is meant: he believes it refers to the gift of speaking unlearned human languages, a gift he believes was given first to the Apostles and then quite generally among the Corinthian believers. But he admits that he has no firsthand acquaintance with the phenomenon. Here is how he begins his *Homily* (XXIX) on 1 Corinthians 12:1-11:

> This whole passage is exceedingly obscure; and what creates the obscurity is both ignorance of these matters and the cessation of things which happened then but do not now occur. And why do they not take place now? You see how the cause of the obscurity once again presents us with another problem, that is, 'Why indeed did they happen then, but do not happen any longer?' But this we must put off until another occasion, while we discuss now what it was which happened then. Well, what did happen then? If someone was baptized, right away he spoke in tongues; and not only spoke in tongues, but many also prophesied while others displayed many other powers. These converts from idolatry received the Spirit immediately upon their baptism. But they did not see the Spirit, for he is invisible. So since they had no clear knowledge and had not been nurtured in the ancient Scriptures, grace granted them some sensible proof of that energy. And so each began to speak, one in the tongue of the Persians, another in that of the Romans, another in that of the Indians, or some other language. And this disclosed to outsiders that it was the Spirit in the speaker.
>
> Hence he also mentions this, saying, 'To each one is given a manifestation of the Spirit for the common good'—designating the gifts a manifestation of the Spirit. For since the apostles first received this sign, the faithful also used to receive this [sign] of tongue, and not this alone, but many others as well.

The difficulty of ascertaining precisely the meaning of γλώσσαις λαλεῖν is owing in part to extreme rarity of the expression. Aside from its occurrences in Acts (2:3f., 11; 10:46; 19:6) and 1 Corinthians (12:10, 30; 13:1, 8; 14:2, 4, 5, 6, 9, 13, 14, 18, 19, 22, 23, 26, 27, 39) the only instances known to me which are earlier in date than the fourth century are found in Mark 16:17 and in Irenaeus, *Against Heresies* (V vi I). [The date of the so-called longer ending to Mark is not known to us, but Justin Martyr may have known it in Rome about A.D. 150. In his *First Apology* (45) he uses words reminiscent of Mark 16:20; *Irenaeus*, in *Against Heresies* (III x 6), explicitly quotes Mark 16:19f. as being written by Mark at the end of his Gospel.]

Irenaeus' comment on "speaking in tongues" reads:

> Propter quod et Apostolus ait: sapientiam loquimur inter perfectos; perfectos dicens eos qui perceperunt Spiritum Dei, et omnibus linguis loquuntur per Spiritum Dei, quemadmodum et ipse loquebatur. Quemadmodum et multos audivimus fratres in Ecclesia, prophetica habentes charismata, et per Spiritum universis linguis loquentes, et absconsa hominum in manifestum producentes ad utilitatem, et mysteria Dei enarrantes, quos et spiritales Apostolus vocat.

> Therefore the Apostle says, 'We speak wisdom among the perfect'; calling perfect those who have received the Spirit of God and speak in all tongues through the Spirit of God just as he himself used to speak. In the same way we have also heard many brethren in the Church having prophetic gifts and speaking through the spirit in all tongues and bringing to light men's secrets for the common good and explaining mysteries of God. Such persons the Apostle calls spiritual.

Although Irenaeus wrote in Greek, this Latin text is perhaps older than the oldest Greek text of the second sentence of this passage, which is preserved for us in Eusebius' *Ecclesiastical History* (V vii 6). The Greek text of Eusebius differs from the Latin only in having the present tense instead of the past tense at "we have heard many brethren. . . . "

Thus Irenaeus (about A.D. 200), like Chrysostom, thinks γλώσσαις λαλεῖν means to speak in human languages one has not learned. He indicates that he believes Paul was able to speak in many languages, and he says either that he hears, or that he has heard, brethren in the church speaking in all kinds of languages. But between the time of Luke and that of Irenaeus there is little to suggest that there were Christians acquainted at first hand with any incident in which the Spirit gave any of their number the power to speak in a language they had not learned in some ordinary way.

If the experience had been widespread, one would suppose it should have left some traces in the writings of the early Christians. But even the extravagant tales of this apocryphal acts of the various Apostles do not give instances of this sort of occurrence, and early tradition has no hesitation in speaking of Mark as Peter's interpreter. Eusebius (*Ecclesiastical History* III xxxix 15), preserving Papias' report of the opinion of an Elder older than himself, the Anti-Marcionite Prologue to the Gospel of Mark, Irenaeus (*Against Heresies* III i 2), and Tertullian (*Against Marcion* IV v 3), all speak of Mark as Peter's *interpres* or *hermēneutēs*—an assistant presumably unnecessary for a man who could speak in other human languages.

During the course of the second century several books were composed, purporting to recount the exploits of one or another of the Apostles. Tertullian tells us the Acts of Paul were written by an elder in Asia Minor who felt Paul's reputation needed bolstering. Some scholars judge that this writer was able to make use of the work of the author of the Acts of Peter. The Acts of John appear to be of second-century date; and, while the Acts of Thomas are now accessible only in forms which make it difficult to separate the original composition from later additions, the composition of the original of this work seems also to be as early as the second century. We may be interested, therefore, in seeing what light they can throw upon the question of "speaking in tongues."

The evidence of the Acts of Peter may be given quickly. In Chapter 9 the Apostle sends a dog to speak a message to his archenemy, Simon Magus, and in Chapter 15 when Peter learns that a woman holding a seven-months-old baby has been sent by Simon Magus, he sends her back to him and the baby delivers Peter's message. Neither in these Acts of Peter nor in the Clementine Recognitions and Homilies is Peter ever presented in any situation where communication seems to be a problem. These writings do not suggest that Peter needed an interpreter, nor do they suggest that he was able to speak in languages he had never learned. Of the Apostle's own private communion with Christ, the Greek text of the Martyrdom of Peter asserts that it was soundless. In Chapter 39 we read:

> Because you have made known and revealed these things to me, O Word, whom I now name Tree of Life, I give thanks to you not with these fixed lips nor with the tongue through which comes both truth and lie nor with this speech which proceeds by means of physical nature; but I give thanks to you, O King, with that voice [*phōnē*] known through silence and heard in secret, sent forth by no bodily organ, reaching no fleshly ear, heard by no corruptible being, which is not the world nor spread abroad in the earth, which is not written books, and which belongs neither to this man nor that. Herewith I give thanks to you, Jesus Christ, with the silence of

voice [*sigē phōnēs*] with which the spirit within me, loving you and speaking to you and seeing you, attains to you.

The Acts of John offers no instance of "speaking in tongues" even in a book whose wonders include the Apostle's ability to command the bedbugs to march out of an inn he has chosen for a night's lodging (Chs. 60 f.). In Chapter 98 he says, "I saw the Lord above the cross, having no shape but only a voice (*phōnēn*)—a voice not like familiar to us, but one that was sweet, gracious, and truly divine." In Chapter 103 John says we are to worship the Lord "not with fingers or mouths or tongue, not even with the entire bodily organ, but with a disposition of soul." And in Chapter 106 the gift of tongues is notably absent from a list of powers (*dynameis*) which names "wonders, healings, signs, charismata, teachings, governings, refreshments, services, knowledge, praises, graces, confidences, sharings" which they have seen before their very eyes as being given by the Lord— things which eye had not seen nor ear heard.

In 1936 Carl Schmidt published an ancient fragment of the Acts of Paul. On pages four and five of the papyrus we read of Paul's encounter with a lion in the arena. The lion is the one which Paul has met previously and baptized, and there on the floor of the arena the lion converses with Paul in human language. But neither here nor elsewhere in the Acts of Paul is the Apostle to the Gentiles said to have spoken in tongues he has never learned. But Peter and John and Paul (and, for that matter, Andrew, whose apocryphal Acts recounts episodes in Greece) may not have ventured into areas where any languages were necessary other than those they had learned. Let us turn, then, to the Acts of Thomas.

In the very beginning of the Acts of Thomas we are told that the Apostles cast lots to see who should go where, and Thomas was assigned to India. He protests that he is a Hebrew man; how could he go and preach the truth to the Indians? So the Savior appears to him by night and says, "Don't be afraid, Thomas. Go to India and preach the word there, for my grace is with you." The opening episode in India finds the Apostle at a wedding feast, declining to eat the food provided. A waiter slaps him, and the Apostle rebukes him in Hebrew, being understood by no one present except a Hebrew slave-girl who is playing the flute (see Chs. 4-9). But thereafter throughout the book no problem of communication arises. We are given no indication as to whether the Apostle had the "gift of tongues," or learned Indian, or was miraculously understood when he spoke, or had an interpreter.

We do meet talking animals again. In Chapter 31 a serpent speaks; in Chapter 39 a young ass which was descended from Balaam's prophetic beast speaks with the Apostle; and in the rather different latter half of the Act we read an episode in which the Apostle is riding in an ox-drawn wagon with an army officer when the oxen grow tired and refuse to move any farther. At Thomas' bidding the army officer goes to a herd of wild asses feeding alongside the road and says to them, "Judas Thomas the apostle of the Christ of the new God says to you 'Let four of you come, for we need you.' '' Thereupon the whole herd of wild asses comes to the Apostle, and four of them replace the oxen and draw the wagon. Later Thomas uses one of the asses to go as his spokesman to exorcise a demon from a sick woman (Chs. 68-81).[2]

It is evident, then, that "speaking in tongues" in the sense of *speaking in human languages which one has not learned* is not mentioned in the early, apocryphal "Acts." Neither is it found in the soberer works of the Apostolic Fathers and the Apologists. Once again, its absence is notable in

---

[2]In the much later Acts of Philip the animal wonders grow more marvelous. In Chapters 94-101 we read how a leopard runs out and kneels before Philip and opens the conversation in a rather halting voice. At the command of the Apostle he begins to speak perfectly in human speech and relates how he had seized a kid and was about to eat it when the kid spoke in human language, exhorting him in Jesus' name to change his fierce ways. The whole party goes off then to find the kid, and in answer to Philip's prayer the two animals are enabled to speak men's language and to eat men's food and to accompany the Apostle on his journey. "And in that hour the animals stood up, both the leopard and the kid, and raising their fore-paws they glorified God and said in a human voice, 'We glorify and bless you, who took note of us and remembered us in this wilderness and changed our fierce and wild nature into tameness, who granted us the divine word and put in us tongue and understanding to speak and confess your name, for great is your glory.' ''

Apollonious of Tyana was a non-Christian contemporary of Paul, whose exploits we may read in a biography written sometime between A.D. 217 and 240. He visited India and found there some who could speak Greek. Apollonius is represented as a most remarkable man. In Book I, Chapter xix, he is said to have claimed to know all human languages because he understood the secret of silence. He is said to have claimed also to have learned from the Arabians the language of birds: that is, how to understand their sounds, not to converse with them. But in Chapter xxvii an interpreter is specifically mentioned, and elsewhere throughout the narrative it is made plain that Apollonius actually conversed with foreigners either through an interpreter or because the foreigner was able to speak Greek. Eusebius draws attention to these same facts in his treatise against Apollonius, in Chapters x and xiv.

Justin Martyr's *Dialogue with Trypho* (xxxix 2), where Justin lists the manifestations of the Spirit being given to Jews who are becoming disciples of Christ and receiving *charismata*.

The argument from silence is always risky. It may be that Irenaeus is right and that the gift of tongues was the gift of the ability to speak unlearned human languages. It is possible that the gift ceased, or that no early Christian writer happened to recount an episode known at firsthand involving the exercise of this gift, or that all such writings have perished. Yet the fact remains that there is a dearth of early Christian evidence for any Christian's exercising the gift of ability to speak in human language he has not learned.

If the phenomenon at Corinth was not that of speaking unlearned human tongues, perhaps it was that of speaking some non-human language or of uttering some vocal cadences which had significance, even if they did not constitute discourse of any sort.

Paul speaks in 1 Corinthians 13:1 of "the tongues of men and of angels." The exegesis of this passage is a separate problem, and it is unnecessary to repeat here the evidence for opinions about the possible connection between angels and the various languages of the world.[3]

But whatever the supposed relation between the guardian angels of the nations and the languages of the world, some thought the angels had a lan-

---

[3]Origen's *Against Celsus* (V xxix and xxx) is a convenient summary of this sort of speculation, which had a long history behind it when he wrote, about A.D. 240, in answer to a treatise composed perhaps seventy years earlier. In these two chapters Origen combines Deuteronomy 32:8-9 (LXX) and the account of the confusion of tongues at Babel in Genesis 11, and says that when mankind was divided into nations it was according to the number of angels, each angel being assigned to a given group of men, and each angel implanting in his group a peculiar language. (So also Severian of Gabala.) Philo treats of this in his essay *On the Confusion of Tongues*, in the opening and closing sections. The number of groups (and languages) is generally put at seventy or seventy-two. Exodus 20:18 (LXX) reports that at Sinai the people *saw* the voice. Philo finds great significance in this, and comments on it in his treatises *On the Special Laws* (II 189) and *On the Decalogue* (32ff. and 46f.). His remarks are interesting to those who consider the passage in Acts about the tongues of fire. Strack-Billerbeck, in their comments on Acts 2 and Hans Leisegang in *Pneuma Hagion* (p. 127), draw attention to rabbinical speculation to the effect that the voice at Sinai was (a) heard to the end of the earth, (b) divided into seven voices and then into seventy languages, so that everyone heard the law in his own native tongue, and (c) that Psalm 68:11 may be construed to bear witness to this event in which the Lord gave the word, and the company of them that proclaimed it was great, like the sparks that fly when the anvil is struck.

guage of their own. After all, Psalm 148 invites all and sundry to praise the Lord, and it seemed fitting and to be expected that each group should have a "language" appropriate to it, even if not all the "speech" were audible (see Ps. 19:2-3). Perhaps the gift of tongues at Corinth was the gift of speaking in angelic language. In 2 Corinthians 12:3-4 Paul tells of a man who was caught up into Paradise and heard there "sayings which cannot be expressed, which are not for man to speak."

Before the birth of Christ the Book of Enoch attested the varied language of angelic beings. Chapter 40 relates part of the information. The *Apocalypse of Abraham* (XVII) tells of Abraham's being taught a song by an angel. The song is reported, and therefore it must be regarded as translatable discourse, not just musical cadences voiced by the angel. The date of the Apocalypse of Abraham is uncertain, but some suppose it to have been composed near the close of the first or the opening of the second century A.D. The Ascension of Isaiah is a composite work in which a Christian editor has supplemented an older Jewish work with Christian materials. R. H. Charles dates the composite work as being brought to completion before the close of the first century. Chapters VI-XI record the vision of Isaiah, and relate how he was carried from one heaven to another, and how each rank of angelic beings had its own appropriate voice and praise to offer the Almighty. (See also the Testament of Levi 3 and Testament of Judah 25.)

By far the most interesting passage pertinent to the discussion of angelic languages available to us is the Testament of Job, Chapters 45-50. This remarkable document is also of uncertain date. Kaufmann Kohler, who republished in 1897 the Greek text which had been first printed by Cardinal Mai in 1833, believes the book to have been a pre-Christian Jewish composition. M. R. James, who published a Greek text from a different manuscript in the same year, 1897, speaks ambiguously about the date and provenance of the work and of the text he publishes. James was struck by some turns of phrase in the Greek text which resembled the language of the Gospel of Matthew, and he therefore hesitated to speak decisively for the fact that the work as a whole is free from Christian interpolation. C. C. Torrey is of the opinion that the work as a whole has suffered no Christian interpolation, being originally an Aramaic work of the first century B.C., which was soon afterwards translated into Greek.[4]

---

⁴See C. C. Torrey, The *Apocryphal Literature* (New Haven: Yale University Press, 1945), pp. 140-45.

Since this ancient work is not readily accessible, and since it is of such interest, there is offered here a precis of part of sections 45-50 and a translation of the most immediately pertinent passages. Job is on his deathbed and has divided his property among his seven sons. His three daughters are distressed: "Dear Father, are we not also your children?" He replies that he has reserved for them something even more valuable than the property he has distributed among his sons. He sends his daughter Hemera to bring a small treasure chest from which he takes three girdles of such marvelous appearance as to defy human description, like nothing on earth or in heaven, radiating sparks of fire like the rays of the sun. The daughters are still puzzled, not seeing how these girdles will be able to provide them a means of livelihood. "What use are they?" the girls ask. "How shall we live by them?" Job tells them these are none other than the girdles God gave him when he said, "Rise, gird your loins like a man; then I shall question you, and do you answer me!" (see Job 38:3). When Job put on the girdles the worms and wounds vanished from his body, his health was restored, his griefs forgotten; " . . . and the Lord spoke to me in might, showing me all that is and shall be." He assures the girls they will be able not only to find a livelihood but also to enter into the greater age and to live in the heavens. He invites them to put on a girdle, so as to be able to see those who come to carry his soul away. Sections 48-50 read:

So then the girl, called Hemera, rose and took possession of her cord as her father had told her. And she received another heart[5] so as no longer to be earthly minded, and was given utterance in the angelic dialect [*tē aggelikē dialektō*], raising to God a hymn after the angelic hymnology. And the hymns she uttered the Spirit allowed to be inscribed upon her robe. And then Kasia girded herself and had her heart changed so as no longer to yearn for worldly things. And her mouth received the dialect of the principalities [*tēn dialekton tōn archōn*: see Romans 8:38] and she sang in praise the song of the Lofty Place. Therefore anyone who wishes to know the poem of the heavens can find it among The Hymns of Kasia. Then also the third daughter, the one called Amalthias-keras (Cornucopia) girded herself and her mouth gained utterance in the dialect of those On High [*tōn en hypsei*]. Then her heart was altered, rapt from worldly circumstance. For she had

---

[5]The reference to a changed heart finds an echo in a saying attributed to Montanus by Epiphanius; see page 280, note 2, of this article.

spoken in the dialect of the Cherubim, praising the Lord of Hosts,[6] showing forth their glory. And anyone wishing to grasp the trace remaining of the paternal splendor will find these things written among The Prayers of Amalthias-keras.

Then Nahor, Job's brother, tells us he wrote down a whole book of the most significant of the hymns the three daughters sang.

Unfortunately, Nahor does not tell us how those present knew that they were hearing angelic tongues, and the hymnals and devotional books he mentions do not exist. He has not left us directions for testing utterances to discern whether they are angelic language or something else.

If the "kinds of tongues" in Corinth were other human languages, we find no subsequent firsthand account of an episode in which their use by a Christian in the first or second century is described. If they included angelic languages, we find no evidence of their further use nor any guide as to how they might be recognized should they recur. (Indeed, Chrysostom regards angels as incorporeal and hence no more able to utter sounds humanly audible than they are literally "to bow the knee" when every tongue confesses that "Jesus Christ is Lord," to the glory of God.)

"SENSIBLE PROOFS" OF THE POWER OF THE SPIRIT

Chrysostom suggested, in the passage quoted at the start of this paper, that the gifts of the Spirit included sensible proofs of his presence among the believers. Doubtless the true fruit of the Spirit is love, joy, peace, patience, kindness, goodness, faithfulness, gentleness, and self-control; but, Chrysostom suggests, was there not some sign perceptible to the eye or ear by which the Spirit's presence was made known?

In the New Testament we find two related expressions: "speaking in the Spirit" and "the Spirit speaking in" someone. Mark 12:36 refers to

---

[6]"Lord of hosts" represents here τὸν δεσπότην τῶν ἀρετῶν—an expression to which I have found no parallel in my limited acquaintance with biblical and ecclesiastical Greek. In the Septuagint one finds κύριος τῶν δυνάμεων, which the Vulgate renders *Dominus virtutum*. δεσπότης τῶν ἀπετῶν would be a possible Greek retranslation of the Latin— but I have never seen the Greek expression elsewhere. What light this may cast on the question of the date and provenance of the Greek translation of the Testament of Job must be judged by those more competent than I. I have not been able to consult the Köhler edition, and I do not recall that James (whose edition is no longer at hand) discusses latinisms in his brief introduction.

David's speaking in the Spirit (compare 2 Sam. 23:2 in the Septuagint). Ignatius of Antioch reminds the Christians in Philadelphia how, when he was visiting them, he delivered a saying to them "in a great voice, in the voice of God" (*Philadelphians* 7, 1). The arresting officers, we are told in an old part of the Martyrdom of Polycarp (7, 3), gave the aged pastor permission to pray before they took him into town to the jail: "and he stood and prayed, so filled with the grace of God that he could not stop for two hours." In the *Ascension of Isaiah* (III 18-19) we read that Isaiah foresaw how the twelve disciples would "teach all the nations and every tongue about the resurrection of the Beloved, and those believing in his cross will be saved . . . and many of those believing in him will speak in the Holy Spirit."[7]

One could multiply examples of references to persons "speaking in the Spirit" messages which are quite intelligible in a fashion which impresses upon their hearers the conviction that the speaker is exalted by a power not his own.

We find reference also to those in whom the Spirit speaks. In Mark 13:11 we read, "And when they bring you to trial and deliver you up, do not be anxious beforehand what you are to say; but say whatever is given you in that hour, for it is not you who speak, but the Holy Spirit." Acts 4:31 reads: "And when they had prayed, the place in which they were gathered together was shaken; and they were all filled with the Holy Spirit and spoke the word of God with boldness."

"Speaking in tongues" in Corinth is mentioned alongside teaching, revelation, and prophecy. Exactly what is meant by teaching, revelation, and prophecy is not clear. Perhaps Acts 21:10-11 is an example of either revelation or prophecy. But apparently all three—revelation, teaching, and prophecy—represented intelligible discourse delivered in the presence of the congregation. One possibility we have not yet considered is that "speaking in tongues" may refer to the utterance of some enigmatic sentence, some dark saying, something oracular in character which needs to

---

[7]The whole passage, III 13-31, for which a Greek text more or less imperfectly survives, should be consulted. There is no word about "speaking in tongues"; but specific mention is made of the problems which will arise because of false prophets and others who wish to usurp positions of leadership. The situation described resembles that treated in Hermas, Mandates XI, and in Didache XI-XIII.

be interpreted, since its meaning is not plain even when the words have been understood quite clearly.

Let us suppose, then, that "speaking in tongues" refers to some sort of oracular utterance, a dark saying which requires interpretation. Even what is intelligible, like teaching, or prophecy, or revelation, may create problems of discipline and order. For while one may be impressed with the exalted bearing or inspired appearance of a speaker or with the portentousness of the words spoken, it is not always easy to discern whether the exaltation is genuinely inspired by the Holy Spirit or it is mere enthusiasm or even possession. And occasionally the words spoken, while intelligible, are enigmatic or bewildering or shocking. So the early Christians were warned that they must test what was presented to them as utterance inspired by the Spirit. Even what the prophets said must be weighed by the prophets.

The task of judging was delicate and perhaps even dangerous, as acknowledged before, for one might be found giving judgment against what the Spirit himself had inspired. So one is not surprised to find in early Christian writings some attempts to give directions for the discernment of true prophets from false prophets. Two of the best known of these instructions are in the Didache or Teaching of the Twelve (Chapters XI-XIII) and in the Shepherd of Hermas (Mandates XI). The latter is of special interest, and should be consulted.

Moreover, it is hard to define closely the borderline between the prophetic or revelatory, on the one hand, and the oracular, on the other. The famous oracles of the Hellenistic world often uttered enigmatic responses to the questions put to them—answers which they might not claim to understand or be able to construe. Some early Christians thought it might be possible to be guided by a simple test: Oracular *answers* are to be distrusted: the Holy spirit speaks of his own initiative, not in response to interrogation.[8]

---

[8]Chrysostom, in his *Homily* XXIX which we have already quoted, relates his version of how the oracle at Delphi operated. At any rate the priestess sat on a tripod over a fissure in the earth up from which came a *pneuma*, a spirit or wind or vapor. Receiving this divine influence into her own body, the priestess then uttered (often in a voice like a ventriloquist) a response which was judged to be the divinely given answer to a question posed by a hopeful interrogator. These statements were often so ambiguous or dark that an interpreter's aid was sought; but the interpretation often left the inquirer in doubt as to what course of behavior the god's answer indicated. Plutarch has a long essay, written near the end of the first century, *On the Obsolescense of Oracles*.

Even before the first century came to a close the church was confronted with many situations in which strange teachings and prophecies and revelations had to be judged as to whether they were conformable to the Spirit of Christ. These problems multiplied prodigiously in the second century. And then came Montanus. Some time not far from A.D. 160 this former priest of the goddess Cybele in Asia Minor was converted to Christianity and offered himself to the credulous as the prophet of the promised Paraclete. His followers declared that, yes, the apostles of old had received the *arrabōn*, the down payment of the Spirit; but it was only with Montanus that the Holy Spirit in all his fullness appeared. Montanus appears to have claimed that he was the instrument of the Holy Spirit, that he was a lyre which was struck as with a plectron.

Recognizing that we are not reading an impartial testimony, we may nevertheless find of interest the account composed probably before A.D. 200 by an author whose name we do not know, preserved for us in Eusebius:

> A recent convert called Montanus, when Gratus was proconsul of Asia, in the unbounded lust of his soul for leadership gave access to himself to the adversary, became obsessed, and suddenly fell into frenzy and convulsions. He began to be ecstatic and to speak and to talk strangely [*xenophōnein*], prophesying contrary to the custom which belongs to the tradition and succession of the church from the beginning. Of those who at that time heard these bastard utterances some were vexed, thinking that he was possessed by a devil and by a spirit of error, and was disturbing the populace; they rebuked him, and forbade him to speak, remembering the distinction made by the Lord, and his warning to keep watchful guard against the coming of the false prophets; but others, as though elevated by a holy spirit and a prophetic gift, and not a little conceited, forgot the Lord's distinction, and encouraged the mind-injuring and seducing and people-misleading spirit, being cheated and deceived by it so that he could not be kept silent. But by some art, or rather by such an evil scheme of artifice, the devil wrought destruction for the disobedient, and receiving unworthy honors from them stimulated and inflamed their understanding which was already dead to the true faith; so that he raised up two more women and filled them with the bastard spirit so that they spoke madly [*lalein ekphronōs*] and improperly and strangely, like Montanus. The spirit gave blessings to those who rejoiced and were proud in him, and puffed them up by the greatness of its promises. Yet sometimes it flatly condemned them completely, wisely, and faithfully, that it might seem to be critical, though

but few Phrygians were deceived. But when the arrogant spirit taught to blaspheme the whole catholic church throughout the world, because the spirit of false prophecy received from it neither honor nor entrance, for the Christians of Asia after assembling for this purpose many times and in many parts of the province, tested the recent utterances, pronounced them profane, and rejected the heresy,—then at last the Montanists were driven out of the church and excommunicated.[9]

It is important to remember that the real issue raised by Montanism was not that of doctrine. Montanus, to be sure, expected the second coming in the immediate future and that Jesus would appear not in Jerusalem but in a town of Asia Minor; the Montanists took a stronger stand than many second-century Christians on the question of second marriages and the discipline of penitents. But the real issue was the claim that the Holy Spirit was now speaking through a person who was in no sense in command of himself when the Spirit spoke. The claim to be the instrument of the Spirit while in a state of ecstasy was the pivotal issue presented to the faithful in Asia, who had to meet many times and in many places before finally coming to the decision that the spirit speaking in Montanus was not the Holy Spirit of Christ.[10]

The question arises: Does the person who "speaks in tongues," uttering a dark saying or a new prophecy, have command of himself, or does another control him? The situation was complicated for the participants in the second century by a feature of the Greek language. The same word *ekstasis*, "ecstasy," is the word used (1) for Adam's "deep sleep" in Gen-

---

[9]Eusebius, *Ecclesiastical History* V xvi 7-10, following the Kirsopp Lake translation, Loeb Library edition.

[10]It should not be supposed that the Montanist movement, which took rise from Montanus and persisted for many decades, was primarily known as an ecstatic movement, so that the church in rejecting Montanism was "quenching the Spirit." One of the two women who followed Montanus "prophesied" in the spirit that prophecy would cease after her death. And, as one can verify for himself by reading through the material assembled by Labriolle in his *Les sources de l'histoire du Montanisme*, this "prophecy" seems to have been fulfilled. The utterances of Montanus and Priscilla and Maximilla were treasured and regarded as authoritative; but successors to them in ecstatic utterance do not seem to have persisted long. Later discussions deal almost exclusively with differences of doctrine and order. See the remarks of Hans Freiherr von Campenhausen, *Kirchliches Amt und geistliche Vollmacht* (Tübingen: J. C. B. Mohr [Paul Siebeck], 1953), pp. 207ff., and of Kurt Aland, "Der Montanismus und die kleinasiatische Theologie," *Zeitschrift für die Neutestamentliche Wissenschaft*, Vol. 49 (1955), pp. 109-116.

esis 2:21; (2) for Abraham's "trance" in Genesis 15:12; (3) for "derangement of mind" in Deuteronomy 28:28; (4) for the psalmist's "astonishment" in Psalm 115:2 of the Septuagint (Revised Standard Version, 116:11); (5) for Peter's and Paul's state of mind in which they receive divinely sent visions in Acts 10:10 and 22:17; and (6) to describe the appearance of those seized by a powerful emotion, as the women at the tomb, in Mark 16:8, or Isaac when he is discovering Jacob's ruse, in Genesis 27:33. (The Vulgate varies among *stupor, furor,* and *excessus mentis* or *pauor*.)

One possibility, as some thought, was that God's Spirit simply took over and used the man who "spoke," as a musician uses an instrument. This was certainly the view of Montanus, as we learn from a saying of his reported by Epiphanius (*Panarion* XLVIII iv): "Behold, a man is like a lyre, and I strike like the plectron: the man sleeps, and I wake. Behold it is the Lord who sets men's hearts aside, and gives men hearts."[11]

Others might say, "Well, at Joppa Peter may have been in a trance, and also Paul in Jerusalem; but each was able to furnish a quite rational account of his experience and of its meaning. God indeed gives the message: but it is a man in full command of his faculties who reports the event and its meaning in plain words."

If, then, "speaking in tongues" in Corinth meant some kinds of utterance similar to prophecy or revelation but requiring interpretation, uttered ecstatically by one who might or might not be in command of his faculties, the problem the phenomenon posed was a compound problem of order and

---

[11]Before the Montanist crisis becomes acute even an orthodox writer can use this argument. Athenagoras, *Embassy* IX, speaks of Moses, Isaiah, Jeremiah, "and the other prophets who, rapt from their mental processes (*kat' ekstatin tōn en autois logismōn*) as the divine Spirit moved them, uttered what they were empowered to say—the Spirit using them as a flutist blows the flute." (Compare also Theophilus, *To Autolycus* II ix.) After this crisis becomes acute orthodox writers generally contend that genuine prophets are men in command of themselves. See Origen, *Against Celsus* VII i-x; Epiphanius, *Panarion* XLVIII iii-x; Didymus of Alexandria on Acts 10:10 and on 2 Corinthians 5:12; and Jerome's Prologue to his commentary on Habakkuk, to name a few. The only exceptions known to me are Tertullian (who after all did become a Montanist), e.g., *Against Marcion* IV xxii; Hippolytus (who also had his troubles with the orthodox), e.g., *On Christ and Anti-Christ* ii; and Pseudo-Justin, *Exhortation to the Greeks* viii. (Tertullian cites Luke's account of the Transfiguration, where Peter "did not know what he was saying." Tertullian reverts to the theme of speaking in ecstasy in his treatise *On the Soul* xxi and xlv. Unfortunately his lengthy work on ecstasy, at first six, then seven, books in length, has perished.)

of discipline. The value of "speaking in tongues" would appear questionable, its difficulties all too real. In this case the *form* of the utterance could give no final proof of the *validity* of what was intended. The question was double: "Is this the *way* in which the Spirit speaks?" and "Does this disclose *what* the Holy Spirit, who speaks only of Christ Jesus, might have to say to us?" Events of the second century taught the church a very deepseated mistrust of messages delivered by one in ecstasy.[12]

But perhaps "speaking in tongues" in Corinth had nothing to do with a message, nothing to do with any language, human or non-human. Perhaps it was just some more or less musical cadence of vocalizations or "lalling," as some call it. That something like this could take place we may learn from a report of Irenaeus.

In *Against Heresies* (III xiii) Irenaeus is describing the despicable machinations of a man named Marcus whom Irenaeus judges to be a heretic of the Valentinian school. Irenaeus describes him as "a man most adept at magical sleight of hand who has led astray many men and not a few women, converting them to himself as to one most wise who enjoys supreme power from invisible and unnameable regions—indeed he seems the precursor of the Antichrist." Irenaeus relates how Marcus takes a cup of mixed water and wine, prays over it at length and manages to change its color to deep purple or red, leading those present to believe that a supernatural being called Charis, or Grace, has caused drops of her own blood

---

[12]Tertullian, in his *Treatise on the Soul*, ix, has an interesting report: "There is among us today a sister who has been granted gifts of revelations which befall her in Church during the services of the Lord's day through ecstasy in the Spirit. She converses with angels, sometimes with the Lord, and sees and hears mysteries and reads the hearts of some and prescribes medicines for those who need them. During the reading of the Scripture, while Psalms are being sung, during the sermon, or while prayers are being offered occasions are furnished for her visions. Perhaps I have been making some remarks or other about the soul when this sister is in the Spirit. After the services end and the people have been dismissed she regularly reports to us what she has seen—for they are most diligently examined and tested; and among other things she said, 'A soul was shown me bodily, and a spirit appeared, but not empty or without sensible quality, rather it appears palpable through delicate, bright and airy, yet thoroughly human in shape.' This is the vision; God is witness, the Apostle an appropriate warrantor of the gifts that would come to the Church. . . . "

Among the correspondence of Cyprian (*Letters* LXXV x 74) one may read Firmilian's account of what he says took place around A.D. 230—just twenty-two years before his letter was written to Cyprian—when a woman who spoke in ecstasy and claimed to be inspired by the Holy Ghost made some remarkable predictions of earthquakes to come.

to fall into the cup and leading them to desire heartily to partake of that cup in order that Grace may be instilled in them. He also, Irenaeus goes on to say, performs some trick with two cups, in which finally a large cup appears to have been filled to overflowing from a smaller cup. Then Irenaeus writes:

> With many such wonders he has deceived many and drawn them in his train. It seems likely that he has some demon as a kind of medium through whom he appears to prophesy and to cause to prophesy as many as he deems worthy of sharing his Grace. He carefully cultivates women, especially those of rank who are well-dressed and wealthy, trying to enlist them and flattering them with words like these: 'I want you to enjoy a share of my Grace, for the Father of all continually beholds your angel before his face. Now the place of your angel is among us, and it is fitting that we should be joined together. First receive Grace, from me and through me. Adorn yourself as a bride who awaits her bridegroom, in order that you may be what I am, and I what you are. Set in the bridechamber the germ of light. Accept from me your groom, receive him and be received by him. Behold Grace has come upon you: open your mouth and prophesy.'
>
> But the woman replies, 'I never prophesied; I don't know how to prophesy.' Then he offers some invocations a second time, to the amazement of the deceived woman, and says to her, 'Open your mouth and say whatever comes, and you will be prophesying.'
>
> Made flighty and gulled by what has gone before, her soul overheated in the expectation of being about to prophesy, her heart beating wildly she dares to speak inanities, to say everything which comes to her, rashly and emptily, flushed with the warmth of that vain spirit; and henceforth she regards herself as a prophet and gives thanks to Marcus who has shared his Grace with her.

Irenaeus goes on to observe that it is God alone, not Marcus, who can give the power of prophesying; and that those who truly prophesy speak when God wills, and not at the command of Marcus. He says that in their meetings the followers of Marcus draw lots and command one another to prophesy.[13]

---

[13]Marcus also taught a second baptism. In Chapter xxi Irenaeus presents his account of Marcus' teaching and of the ceremony of baptism and of the pageant which sometimes took

In addition to Marcus, who practices a second baptism for the impartation of powers of redemption and who claims to be able to arrange for his followers to prophesy on cue, Irenaeus tells of others who make use of nonsense syllables and seek to induce dreams and mediumistic messages. In Book I, Chapter xxiv, he tells of the Basilideans, who "practise magic, using images (or drawings) and incantations and invocations and all the resources of magical art, composing names which they attribute to angels, saying some belong to the first heaven, some to the second, and so they undertake to set forth the names, principalities, angels, and powers of the 365 heavens they have invented." In his next chapter Irenaeus tells of another heretical group led by Carpocrates: "They also make use of magic and incantations, of philtres and drugs to win love, of familiar spirits and dream-senders, and of all other black arts, claiming to have power of mastery over the governing and shaping forces of this world, and not only of them, but of all that is made in this world. These men are sent by Satan to the gentiles to bring slander on the divine name of the Church, in order that as men hear, one way or another, of these activities and judge us all to be such as they, they will turn deaf ears to the preaching of the truth, beholding their misdeeds and blaspheming us all."[14]

---

place in connection therewith. This second baptism is a baptism of redemption (*apolytō-sis*), beyond the baptism of repentance. In the course of the ritual the officiant baptizes them, saying "In the name of the unknown Father of all, into Alētheia ('Truth') the mother of all, into Him who descended upon Jesus; for union and redemption and communication of the powers"; while others utter some Hebrew words, the more to amaze those being initiated. The Greek and Latin texts here differ in their attempts to reproduce the "Hebrew words." It is possible that the Marcosians originally used some meaningful Hebrew terms. But the intervening chapters show that Marcus was also addicted to alphabetical studies. Like others, he saw the possibility of some connection between the seven vowels of Greek and the seven planets whose influence many felt governed the affairs of men; and felt that the generative powers of letters, the building blocks of words, held some clues to the understanding of the universe. Letters also served the Greeks as numerals; and much could be made of correspondences of this sort. Alpha + Omega equals 801; and the numerical value of the letters in the Greek word for dove also equals 801. Jesus says, "I am Alpha and Omega"; the Spirit descends upon him as a dove. See what an elegant correspondence! Irenaeus makes fun of this kind of theologizing in Book I, Chapters xi and xiv.

[14]It is well to remember that during the course of the second century there were many groups of people who made some use or another of the name of Christ and of the gospel story or of Christian doctrines who from the point of view of subsequent history were clearly unorthodox or basically non-Christian. But during the second century there may well have been locales in which a majority of those who were then claiming the name of Christ were adherents of these heretical groups. Flavius Vopiscus was one of the *Scriptores historiae*

If "speaking in tongues" in Corinth was some kind of cadence of vocalizations (constituting no language, human or non-human, bearing no message, however darkly uttered) and if its interpretation required of the interpreter something like what a music critic undertakes to do, it raised not only problems of discipline and order but problems of "external relations" as well: it could easily be confused with the sort of charlatanry which Irenaeus describes or with the practice of sorcery and magic. And if "speaking in tongues" in Corinth was of this character, it is astonishing that there is absolute silence about its recurrence in the first or second century in any orthodox groups of Christians.

Celsus, whose strong criticism of Christianity (written in the last quarter of the second century) provoked Origen's extensive reply seventy years later, lets us see that there were persons who claimed to be Christians who did in fact utter nonsense syllables under pretended inspiration. In *Against Celsus* (VII ix) Origen reports Celsus' summary of some street-corner preaching which sounds rather like something Montanus might have said. Then Celsus adds this comment:

> After holding these threats over the heads of their hearers, they go on
> to add incomprehensible, frenzied, and totally opaque utterances the
> meaning of which no person with a brain is able to discover, for they are

---

Augustae. In his *Life of Saturninus*, Chapter viii, he prints what purports to be a letter of the Emperor Hadrian (A.D. 117-138) written to the Consul Servianus in Egypt and preserved among the correspondence of Hadrian's freedman Phlegon. The authenticity of the letter has been contested (see Walter Bauer, *Rechtgläubigkeit und Ketzerei im ältesten Christentum* [Tübingen: J. C. B. Mohr (Paul Siebeck), 1934], pp. 51f.); but even if it is not by Hadrian it is revealing as to the religious situation in Egypt and as showing that Irenaeus' fears were not groundless. The letter begins: "Hadrian the August to his Consul Servian: Greetings. Egypt, which you have praised to me, I regard as altogether giddy, always in suspense, ready to take wing at every impulse of rumor. There persons who worship Serapis are also Christians: and some who call themselves bishops of Christ are devotees of Serapis. There you will find no Jewish synagogue ruler, no Samaritan, no presbyter of the Christians who is not at the same time an astrologer, an interpreter of omens, a ringmaster."

For an illustration of the oracular use of nonsense syllables, sometimes mixed in with real words, see "Alexander the False Prophet," Chapters 51 and 53 in the works of Lucian of Samosata (a contemporary of the Emperor Marcus Aurelius) who writes about a pagan soothsayer, hostile to Christianity, with whom he claims to have been personally acquainted.

without form or meaning. But to a fool or a sorcerer they offer an opportunity to put upon the utterance any meaning that suits his fancy.[15]

---

[15]The second of the two so-called Clementine Homilies on Virginity, which Quasten dates as contemporaneous with Origen, has in Chapter iv a warning about how to behave when one goes to a town where there are no Christians. One must be as wise as serpents and as harmless as doves; and this means in part, "We do not sing to the heathen, nor do we read to them the Scriptures, that we may not be like common singers, either those who play on the lyre, or those who sing with the voice, or like soothsayers, as many are, who follow these practices and do these things, that they may sate themselves with a paltry mouthful of bread . . . " (M. B. Riddle's translation).

For the use of nonsense syllables, as well as the use of divine names resembling Jewish and Christian designations of God, in the practice of magic see the Paris Magical Papyrus, lines 3,007-3,085, now conveniently reprinted in *The New Testament Background: Selected Documents*, C. K. Barrett, editor (New York: Harper & Row, 1961), pp. 31-35.

Exorcism also presented the church with a "public relations" problem. The power of healing the possessed was surely one of those visible proofs of the presence of the Holy Spirit; and exorcisms were surely successfully undertaken by Christians throughout the second century. [For insight into the sensibly perceptible manifestations of the Spirit's presence in the exorcist, see Campbell Bonner, "Traces of Thaumaturgic Technique in the Miracles," *The Harvard Theological Review*, Vol. XX (1927), pp. 171-81; and S. Eitrem, *Some Notes on the Demonology in the New Testament* (Oslo: A. W. Brøgger, 1940), pp. 41-44. Bonner discusses ἐμβριμάομαι and στενάζειν along with ἀναβλέπω and ταράσσω. To his evidence one might add the almost certain occurrence of ἐμβρειμ (ησάμενος) in the Egerton Papyrus, Fragment II (*recto*) where it has its familiar Septuagintal meaning; and in support of Bonner's thesis the comment of Cyril of Alexandria on John 11:33: " 'Agitated by the spirit'—this means, he is struck some way by the power of the Holy Spirit in his very flesh; which not containing the force of the divinity united to it, trembles and undergoes a kind of shuddering." With this, one may compare the comment of Ammonius in Cramer's *Catenae*: Origen's explanation is different. One might also consider ἀλλεσθαι as it occurs in Judges 14:6, 19; 15:14; 1 Samuel 10:10; 16:13; John 4:14; and perhaps as Lightfoot suggests in Ignatius, Romans 7:2. See also the comments of Theodore of Mopsuestia on John 7:38.] One representative bit of evidence occurs in Justin's open letter to the Roman senate, Apology II vi 6, where we read: "For many demon-ridden persons throughout the whole world and in your city as well numbers of our men, the Christians, have healed and even now are healing, exorcising them in the name of Jesus Christ who was crucified under Pontius Pilate, disabling and expelling the demons who had possessed men who had not been healed by all other practitioners of exorcisms, incantations, and drugs."

Non-Christian exorcists met with some success as well; and some of them used the name of Jesus in their incantations. Christians used simple prayer in the name of Christ, without fumigations, incantations, charms, and complicated gestures; they made no parade of the power; they did not offer themselves for hire; they knew the power was not theirs to command, but came always as the gift of God. No formula guaranteed success; no secret words could force the Deity to act or the demon to leave.

Public relations problems persisted, nonetheless. See the fascinating chapter in E. C. Colwell's *John Defends the Gospel*: "Jesus Was Not A Magician" (Chicago: Willett, Clark,

Whether or not "speaking in tongues" in Corinth was the uttering of cadences of vocalization which required interpretation to be of any value to others present, it appears that the phenomenon is not mentioned in subsequent Christian writings of the first and second century. And if it did take place, it would have constituted continually a potential source of embarrassment to the church because of the ease with which it would be confused with charlatanry, sorcery, or the magical practice of exorcism.

SUMMARY OF EARLY EVIDENCE OUTSIDE THE NEW TESTAMENT BEARING ON Γλώσσαις Λαλεῖν

1. The evidence available does not permit formulation of a precise description of the phenomena indicated in the New Testament by the phrase γλώσσαις λαλεῖν.

2. It cannot be determined, therefore, whether the New Testament phrase can be used appropriately to describe current "speaking in tongues" phenomena.

3. There are four possible constructions of γλώσσαις λαλεῖν in the early Christian and non-Christian writings canvassed for evidence:

a. Speaking a human language one has not learned;

b. Speaking a non-human language;

c. Uttering a "dark saying," more enigmatic than "prophecy" or "revelation" and therefore requiring "interpretation"; *and*

d. Uttering cadences of vocalization which do not constitute discourse.

For (a), this study disclosed no early, firsthand account of the use of such a gift by a Christian.

For (b), no early firsthand account of the use of such a gift by a Christian and no set of criteria by which to discern whether an utterance is of this character were found.

For (c), the church's experience in the first and especially the second century led Christians to regard with great diffidence dark sayings uttered ecstatically; and if such a phenomenon occurred the crucial problem it pre-

---

1936). Colwell declares no exorcism is depicted in second- and third-century catacomb art. The *Apostolic Tradition* (II 16, 21f.) and *Apostolic Constitutions* (VII xxxii 11) forbid practicing magicians, sorcerers, and soothsayers membership in the church; and the first mention of a specific office of exorcist appears to come as late as the time when Cornelius sat on the Roman bishop's chair, about A.D. 250.

sented was not the meaning of the utterance but the spirit of the speaker and his orderly subjection to his brethren in the Lord.

For (d), there was found no early, firsthand account of the use of such a gift by a Christian; and if such a phenomenon occurred it could so easily be mistaken for charlatanry, sorcery, or some other magical practice (thus constituting a hindrance to the hearing of the preached Word and bringing ill repute upon the church) that its exercise was kept unpublicized and unrecorded.

6

FRANK W. BEARE

Speaking With Tongues:
A Critical Survey of the New
Testament Evidence

[Reprinted from *Journal of Biblical Literature*, 83 (September 1964): 229-46. Reprinted with permission of the Society of
Biblical Literature.]

THE GOSPELS

There is no reference in any of the canonical gospels to "speaking with
tongues." It is never attributed to Jesus and is never promised by him to
any of his followers. The saying which precedes the Lord's Prayer in the
Sermon on the Mount appears to deprecate the kind of unintelligible utterance in prayer: the rendering of the New English Bible, "Do not go babbling on like the heathen," conveys the sense better than most other
renderings. The verb used here is very rare in Greek; there appears to be
no more than one other instance in all known Greek literature. βατταλ-

ογέω is formed of a verb ending meaning "speak," with the prefix βαττα, which is not a meaningful word but an onomatopoetic suggestion of the sound made; the literal sense would be something like: "Do not go on saying, 'Batta, batta, batta.' " With it we may compare the noun βάταλος, meaning "stammerer," or "stutterer"; and the verb βατταρίζω, meaning "to stammer," or "to stutter," etc. In the context of the sermon, it clearly does not refer to a mere defect in speech, but to the repetition of meaningless sounds (abracadabra). Instead of this heathenish resort to magical formula, they are bidden to say, "Our Father" (Matt 6:7, 9ff.).

The passage usually printed at the end of the Gospel of Mark (16:9-20) is not an authentic part of this or any other gospel. The textual evidence here is decisive. The passage is not found in any Greek manuscript earlier than the fifth century, and is not mentioned by any writer earlier than Eusebius, the fourth-century bishop and church historian. It may have been composed and added to some manuscripts of the gospel some time in the second century, but is definitely not Markan in origin. It is in this spurious passage that we read the words: "These signs shall accompany those who believe: in my name they will cast out demons, they will speak in [new] tongues, they will pick up serpents, and if they drink any deadly thing it will not hurt them; they will lay their hands on the sick, and they will recover" (vss. 17-18). These words have no more claim to be treated as words of Jesus than any of the extravagances of the apocryphal gospels.

The word καιναῖς (new) is omitted in a very few witnesses; the phrase would then be "they shall speak with tongues"; but since the whole section is spurious, there is no need to debate the merits of variant readings within it.

In the synoptic gospels (Matthew, Mark, and Luke) very little is said about the gifts of the Spirit as endowments promised to the followers of Jesus. He himself receives the Spirit in baptism, and the story is undoubtedly meant to be understood as the prototype of Christian baptism; but it does not move him to speak in tongues. He attributed his own powers of exorcism to the Spirit of God, in rebuttal of his enemies' charge that he is given his powers by the prince of evil. "If it is by the Spirit of God (in Luke, 'By the finger of God') that I cast out demons, then the kingdom of God has come upon you" (Matt 12:28; Luke 11:20). The assistance of the Spirit is promised by Jesus to his disciples in only one context—he will speak through them when they are put on trial for their faith, and they need not prepare their defense: "When they bring you to trial and deliver you up, do not be anxious beforehand what you are to say; but say whatever is given you in that hour, for it is not you who speak, but the Holy Spirit" (Mark 13:11; cf. Matt 10:19-20, Luke 12:11-12).

At the close of the Gospel of Luke, the risen Jesus assures the disciples that he is sending "the promise of his Father" upon them, and charges them to stay in the city until they are "clothed with power from on high." The words are undoubtedly an anticipation of the bestowing of the Spirit, which will be described in the second chapter of Acts; but the Spirit is not explicitly mentioned, and the nature of the manifestation of the "power from on high" that is to "clothe" them is not explained. It is related to the assertion that the gospel of "repentance for the remission of sins is to be preached in his name to all nations," and that they are to be "witnesses of these things." The "power from on high" would appear to be envisaged, then, primarily as the power to bring conviction by their testimony, in preaching the gospel to the world.

Even here, it should be observed that the tradition is not uniform. In Mark (by implication) and in Matthew, the disciples do not remain in Jerusalem; and in Matthew, the vision of the risen Lord is given to them in a mountain in Galilee along with the commission to go and make disciples of all the nations; there is no promise of the spirit, but in place of that we have the assurance of Jesus that he himself is with them "all the days until the consummation of the ages" (Matt 28:18-20; there is no corresponding passage in Mark as it has come down to us). Luke appears to have reconstructed this more primitive tradition, to eliminate the return to Galilee and to concentrate all the significant incidents in the formation of the new community of faith in Jerusalem. Is there not some ground for suspecting that he has projected into the earliest days a conception of the operations of the Spirit which really belongs to a later development of Christian experience and thought?

In John, as we shall see, there is no period of waiting for the descent of the Spirit. Jesus communicated it directly to his disciples on the evening of the day of resurrection (John 20:19f.).

In the Gospel of John there is a rich body of teaching about the Holy Spirit in relation to the followers of Jesus, but there is still no suggestion that his presence will be manifested by "speaking with tongues." When Jesus is introduced, in the multiple testimonies of the first chapter, John the Baptist affirms that he has seen the Spirit descending as a dove from heaven and abiding on him; and this is the sign of recognition given to him by the One who sent him (that is, God—1:6); by this he knows that this is "he who baptizes with the Holy Spirit" (1:32f.). In the night scene of the dialogue with Nicodemus (ch. 3), Jesus himself proclaims the necessity of a birth "from above"—a birth "from water and spirit"—for anyone who is to see or to enter into the kingdom of God. The meaning of these phrases is not unfolded at this point; but the Christian reader could not fail to see them in an allusion to Christian baptism understood as the sacrament of regeneration through the bestowal of the Spirit.

At the scene by Jacob's well in Samaria (ch. 4), Jesus speaks of his gift of life under the symbolism of a fountain of "living water" continually leaping up within. In contrast with the water from the well dug by the revered patriarch Jacob—itself a symbol of the spiritual resources of the Israelite tradition—Jesus declares that "Whoever drinks of this water will thirst again; but whoever drinks of the water that I shall give him will never thirst. The water that I shall give him will become within him a fountain of water, leaping up for life eternal" (vss. 13f.). At this point, the Spirit is not explicitly mentioned, but the significance of the symbolism is transparent to the Christian reader. (To the uninitiated hellenistic reader, it would be apparent that more was meant than meets the eye, but he would not fully understand the nature of this inward, never-failing abundance.) Later in this chapter, we are told that "God is spirit"; and from this it follows that "those who worship him must worship in spirit and truth." Any communion with the God who is Spirit is real only when the worshiper shares in some sense the Spirit nature of God. The realm of truth, or reality, is the realm of spirit. So the thought builds up, not by formal exposition, but by symbolism and suggestion. We have now arrived at the complex association of thoughts, that the true worshiper of God is the man who has been born again of water and Spirit, and thus has within him the abundant resources of the eternal life which alone is "spiritual," and which can be compared to a fountain continually leaping up with fresh supplies.

In the discourse which follows, and unfolds the meaning of, the miracle of the loaves (ch. 6), Jesus affirms that he is the true bread, that comes down from heaven and gives life to the world. "If anyone eat of this bread," he declares, "he will live forever"; and he explains further that the bread which he will give is his flesh, given "for the life of the world" (6:51-52). But though this "flesh"—the human substance of Jesus the Word Incarnate—is the indispensable medium for the communication of "life" (again, the life eternal), this is not to be taken in a merely material sense. Flesh as mere material substance has no efficacy. "It is the spirit that gives life; the flesh avails nothing"; and with this is coupled the statement that the words which Jesus has spoke to them are spirit and life (vs. 63). The evangelist does not bring out for us explicitly how he conceives the relationship between "The flesh" of Jesus, given for the life of the world; "the spirit" without which the flesh is profitless; and "the words" which Jesus has spoken, which are themselves "spirit and life." The language is by no means self-explanatory. To any reader who had not been initiated into the Christian mystery, they would be in a large measure veiled, and the symbolism would probably baffle him. But to the Christian reader, interpreting them in the context of the eucharist, they would convey the thought that in the reception of the flesh and the blood of Christ he was nourishing with spiritual food the life of the Spirit that was communicated to him in his baptism.

In ch. 7, Jesus goes up to Jerusalem for the feast of Tabernacles, and finds himself met with debates over his origin, with controversy, and with overt hostility; he is threatened with arrest and with stoning. He teaches in the temple, as it would seem, throughout the feast; and on the last day he makes the mysterious proclamation:

> If any man is thirsty, let him come to me;
> Whoever believes on me, let him drink.

To this the evangelist attaches a saying of "Scripture"—not found in any Scripture known to us—that "Out of his belly shall flow rivers of living water." He adds the explanation that "Jesus was speaking of the Spirit which those who believe on him were to receive"; and reminds his readers that "the Spirit was not yet (given to men); for Jesus had not yet been glorified" (7:37-39). Here we have the promised gift of "living water" explicitly identified as the Spirit; with the further thought that the Spirit is the gift of Jesus, and will not be bestowed until Jesus has completed his earthly mission, having finished the work which the Father gave him to do, and has returned to his heavenly glory, which he had with the Father before the world was (17:2). The life-giving Spirit, which will be a fountain of life within, is the gift of the ascended Jesus in his glorified humanity.

All this teaching about the Spirit is so far from contact with any of the themes of teaching attributed to Jesus in the synoptic gospels that we can hardly regard it as a report of sayings and discourses actually delivered by

Jesus himself in his days upon earth. There is nothing in the other gospels at all akin, either, to this highly symbolic, allusive, sometimes cryptic presentation of thought. It seems best, accordingly, to think of this evangelist as making use of his account of the earthly ministry of Jesus as a literary framework for the exposition of a theology which has occupied itself with themes that cannot be traced back to the earlier tradition of the teaching of Jesus himself. No doubt he felt assured that he was unfolding things that had their roots in the teaching of Jesus, under the inspiration of the Holy Spirit. Of the concrete human experience of Jesus in history he has no doubt; his Jesus is not a phantom of divinity in human disguise, but a man of flesh and blood. But in his flesh and blood he is still the eternal Logos ("Word"), and he speaks as the Incarnate Logos, in words that go far beyond the actual frames of reference of his historical manifestation. John is not an historian, but a theologian, and the teaching which he attributes to Jesus represents not a strictly historical record of what Jesus once said, but a highly developed interpretation of his teaching in the light of the church's experience of life lived by faith in him. This makes it all the more remarkable that he makes no reference whatever to "speaking with tongues" as a manifestation of the gift of the Spirit to the followers of Jesus.

The teaching about the Holy Spirit is unfolded much more fully and clearly in the farewell discourses, which are set in the framework of the last supper of Jesus with his disciples. Here the concrete historical setting becomes very thin indeed. It is shot through with the sense of the presence of the transcendent Lord of glory in the community of his followers. From time to time the actual setting is recalled to us, but the discourses are spoken predominantly from the perspective of eternity. It is the Christ victorious, ascended, and glorified, who speaks to the faithful gathered about the mystic table.

In these discourses the Holy Spirit is given the new title of Paraclete. The word has very wide connotations—advocate, helper, consoler, instructor—and cannot be rendered by any single English word. He is "another" Paraclete, whom Jesus sends, or who is sent by the Father at the prayer of Jesus. The world cannot receive him, for it has no powers by which it could perceive his presence; but Christ's disciples know him because he abides among them and is in them (14:15-18). He will reveal further truth to them, which Jesus could not himself make known, because as yet they were unable to bear it (14:25f.; 16:12-15). For the evangelist, Christian truth is not a closed system, given complete in the words and deeds of the historical Jesus; it unfolds continually under the leading of the Spirit. "When He, the Spirit of truth, is come, he will lead you into all the truth" (16:13). And yet this further truth is never a departure from the truth that has been communicated by Jesus himself. The Spirit has no independent message; it is impossible to think of the teaching into which we are led by the Spirit and the teaching that has been already received from the lips of Jesus as essentially different systems. The Spirit glorifies Jesus, is wholly concerned with the things of Jesus. "He will glorify me, for he will receive of that which is mine and will make it known to you. All that the Father has is mine; therefore I have said that he takes of that which is mine and makes it known to you" (16:14f.). And he will be with the church in her witness to a hostile world: "he will confute the world, and show where wrong and right judgement lie" (16:8f., New English Bible).

After the Resurrection, Jesus appears to his disciples, entering the room though its doors have been shut "for fear of the Jews." He brings them his word of peace, commissions them for their apostolic task, and gives them authority to forgive or to withhold forgiveness; and for the exercise of this authority he communicates to them the Holy Spirit, his own spirit. The bestowal of the gift is expressed in symbol—a symbol borrowed from the Creation story. There we read that when God had formed man of the dust of the ground, he "breathed into his nostrils the breath of life, and man became a living soul" (Gen. 2:7). The very same verb (ἐνεφύσησεν) is used here: Jesus "breathed upon them and said to them. Receive the Holy Spirit" (20:22). There is no suggestion that they are to speak with tongues. They are to share the mission of Christ himself to the world: "As the Father sent me, so I send you": and they are given the authority to deal with sins: "If you forgive any man's sins, they stand forgiven; if you pronounce them unforgiven, unforgiven they remain."

THE BOOK OF ACTS

The Book of Acts repeatedly speaks of the Holy Spirit as the source of power in the church, and as directing the activities of individuals and of congregations. In three instances it makes mention of "speaking with tongues" as a manifestation of the presence of the Spirit.

In the opening chapter, the risen Jesus is said to have "presented himself alive after his passion" to his apostles, "Appearing to them during forty days, and speaking of the kingdom of God" (1:5). He charges them not to leave Jerusalem until they have received the promised gift of the Father, which was described at the end of the Gospel of Luke in terms of "power from on high" (Luke 24:49), and is now identified with the baptism with the Holy Spirit. "For John baptized with water, but before many days you shall be baptized with the Holy Spirit" (Acts 1:5). He adds: "You shall receive power when the Holy Spirit has come upon you, and you shall be my witnesses . . . unto the end of the earth" (1:8). The contrast of the water baptism of John and the spirit baptism of Jesus takes up again the message of John the Baptist concerning the greater one who was to come: "After me comes one who is mightier than I . . . I have baptized you with water, but he will baptize you with the Holy Spirit" (Mark 1:7f.). In the "Q" version of ths saying, reported by Matthew and Luke, the phrase is enlarged to read: "with the Holy Spirit and with fire" (Luke 3:16; Matt 3:11). In these "Q" passages, moreover, the work of the "mightier one" is then described in terms of a devastating judgment under the figure of the winnowing of the grain—the separation of the chaff from the wheat, and the burning of the chaff "with unquenchable fire." It is possible, even probable, that this addition reflects the sense in which John himself spoke of the "baptism" to be administered by the "mightier one"; it was to be a baptism "with wind and fire," far more searching than the baptism with water administered by John. In that case, his own words will have been "wind and fire" (πνεῦμα καὶ πῦρ; the word πνεῦμα means both "wind," or "breath," and "spirit"); and the addition of the adjective ἅγιον ("Holy"), will be regarded as an interpretative Christian addition, which interprets the saying of John in terms of the Christian experience and understanding of baptism as the sacrament of the Spirit. Whatever its original sense, it is used here by Luke in the specifically Christian sense, and points forward to the event which will be described in Acts 2, and more broadly to the operations of the Spirit in the church which will be a recurring theme throughout the remainder of the book.

The Pentecost scene in ch. 2 described the fulfillment of the promise that the Spirit will come upon them, and clothe them with power from on high. But the passage offers critical problems of exceptional difficulty.[1] It

---

[1]See the discussion of W. Grundmann, "Der Pfingstbericht der Apostelgeschichte in seinem theologischen Sinn," in *Studia Evangelica*, II, ed. F. L. Cross (Berlin: Akademie-Verlag, 1964), pp. 584-94. He notes that there is no other reference in the New Testament

cannot be regarded as a simple report of what actually took place. It is probable that an historical occurrence lies beneath the story—perhaps with a tradition of the first public preaching of Peter, perhaps combined with a remembrance of the first experience of "speaking with tongues" among the Christian believers. It may even be that the attachment of the incident to the first Pentecost after the Resurrection is historical, though this may well be an element in the symbolism. At all events, the story as we have it is heavily overlaid with symbolism, and has been shaped as a whole into the myth of the beginnings of the church as a missionary community. There are many confusing factors, and these may be the result of a conflating of sources which described the event from divergent points of view, or of the attempt of Luke himself to recast his original source in a sense which it did not carry.

The story begins with the statement that "when the day of Pentecost had come, they were all together in one place" (2:1). It is not clear who were included in the gathering—whether the company (about 120 persons, according to Acts 1:15) or the twelve apostles, their number restored to its full complement by the election of Matthias in the place of Judas, as described just before (Acts 1:15-20). Probably the author intends us to understand that the apostles alone are present, seeing that they alone of the Christian group are mentioned in the sequel. The "place" is described in vs. 2 as "the house where they were seated." Perhaps this means the house which contained the "upper room where they were staying" of 1:13; but it is more likely that the two passages represent independent, unconnected sources, and no attempt should be made to harmonize them. The descent of the Spirit is signalized by a loud sound "like the rush of a mighty wind" which fills the whole house. The sound is followed by a strange sight: tongues "as of fire" appeared, distributing themselves around and settling on each of them. The words seem to suggest a tongue of flame resting on each head. It is hardly necessary to insist that this is not matter-of-fact reporting, but poetic imagery. Wind and fire are symbols of the Spirit, and the presence of the Spirit now manifests itself in all the participants in the form of utterance. "They were all filled with the Holy Spirit and began to speak in other tongues, as the Spirit gave them utterance" (2:4). The scene

---

to this event: "Das urchristliche Schrifttum weiss um den engen Zusammenhang zwischen Passion und Auferweckung und spricht von der Gabe des heiligen Geistes; aber er spricht nicht von einem Pfingstereignis, das von Ostern deutlich unterscheidbar und datierbar wäre" (p. 593).

of the story now shifts from the house to the outdoors. The transition is somewhat awkward, as we are told that "at this sound the multitude came together," but it is not clear whether "this sound" (φωνή) is to be taken as the sound (ἦχος) of vs. 2, which filled the house; or the sound of the apostles as they burst forth into utterance "in other tongues" under the control of the Spirit. Are we to assume that the apostles have rushed outside, as they spoke, or that the crowd has heard the sound coming from within? Neither now nor later is anything said about the apostles leaving the house. The author probably thinks of them as having come out into the street first, so that their strange utterances cause a public commotion; it would seem unlikely that he imagines the noise within the house as being so great as to cause crowds to come running from all over Jerusalem. At all events, from this point on there is no further reference to the house, and it is assumed that everything else takes place in the open, in the midst of the throngs.

But this "multitude" also is symbolic. It is not made up of a chance collection, but of "Jews, devout men from every nation under heaven" who are resident in Jerusalem. The words suggest permanent residents, not pilgrims who have come for the festival and will return home shortly— they are κατοικοῦντες, not παροικοῦντες. But they are not native-born Jerusalemites—they speak a variety of native languages, and recognize them all in the utterances of the apostles. In vss. 9-11, they give us a catalogue of the regions in which they were born, with the implication that in each region they have been brought up with a different mother tongue. It need not be said that no crowd can be imagined as uniting to sing out such a list of origins. The list is representative, and it appears to be drawn from an astrological grouping of nations and countries according to the signs of the Zodiac. This multitude represents the Jewish communities of the diaspora. The ministry of Jesus has been confined to the homeland of Israel; the mission of his church is to them and to their children "and to all that are afar off, every one whom the Lord our God calls to him" (2:39). The world-wide mission of the church is inaugurated on this day of Pentecost. It is still a mission to *Jews*. The breaking of the barriers of Jewish privilege awaits a further leading of the Spirit.

In this part of the story, the "speaking with tongues" is understood to mean that they were speaking foreign languages. This is not at all in accord with what we read elsewhere about the "speaking with tongues," where it is taken to mean some kind of unintelligible utterance which does not involve the mind of the speaker at all and may even give outsiders the impression that he is mad. This feature of our story is also symbolical. It foreshadows the future proclamation of the gospel in all the languages of mankind and the gathering before the throne of God of "a great multitude, which no man could number, from every nation, from all tribes and peoples and tongues" (Rev. 7:9). Taken literally, there was no need for so many different languages; and Jews born abroad would not normally be taught the language of Elamites (if it still was spoken anywhere) or of Persians or Libyans and so forth. They would speak a dialect of Aramaic, or the common Greek, or perhaps both. Again, if we are to be literal-minded, how could such a multitude distinguish one language from another if so many were speaking different languages at the same time? Or are we to think that they took turns at different languages, all speaking Elamite for a time, then switching to Persian, and so forth? Such suggestions are patently absurd, and indicate only that it would be absurd to approach the story as a literal, matter-of-fact report.

A different notion of the "speaking with tongues" is reflected in the remark (at the very end of the story) that some of the crowd laughed at the apostles and said, "These men have been drinking new wine." Although this comes in almost as an afterthought, it is this, and not the supposed mastery of foreign languages, that is made the starting point of Peter's sermon: "These men are not drunk, as you suppose" (2:15). God has fulfilled his promise of pouring out his Spirit upon all. Peter makes no further reference to the speaking with tongues. At the end, he accompanies his appeal for repentance and his invitation to be baptized in the name of Jesus for the forgiveness of sins, with the promise that they too will receive the gift of the Holy Spirit (3:28).

The relation between the healing miracle of ch. 3 and the Pentecost story of ch. 2 is not at all clear. The healing itself is not attributed to the power of the Spirit but to the name of Jesus. In fact, the story as a whole does not presuppose in the slightest the events of ch. 2, and it is at least possible that it is in substance a second, independent account of how the apostles were led to begin their public ministry, and of how the group first came to experience the kind of ecstatic utterance that was taken as the sign of the presence of the Spirit. Peter heals in his Master's name. A crowd gathers in the portico, and the apostle proclaims that it is God who has restored soundness of limb to the lame man to glorify his Son Jesus, whom he has raised from the dead. Five thousand hearers are converted (4:4), but the temple authorities order the arrest of the apostles and have them put in jail. The following morning they are tried, and, after some debate, they are ordered to cease speaking or teaching in the name of Jesus. The prohibition is vain; they plead that they must obey God rather than men. They are released, and return to their company; and it is now, in this atmosphere of excitement generated by the clash with the authorities, that "the place in which they were gathered together was shaken, and they were all filled with the Holy Spirit and spoke the word of God with boldness" (4:31).

The phrase "speaking with tongues" is not used, but it is probable that the author thought of "speaking the word of God with boldness" (παρ-ρησία) as an equivalent expression. It has often been observed that there is a remarkable series of parallels between the two blocks of material found in (A) Acts 2:1-47, together with 5:17-42; and (B) Acts 3:1-5:16. This has led to the suggestion that these are not accounts of successive stages in the life of the primitive church, but parallel accounts of the same events derived from two independent sources (or channels of oral tradition). Where this position is adopted, the (B) account is regarded as the one that stands closer to the actual occurrences, and the (A) account, which centers in the Pentecost story, is a re-working under the influence of later experience and fancy. (See, for instance, Harnack's *Acts of the Apostles*; K. Lake and F. J. Foakes Jackson, *The Beginnings of Christianity*, II, pp. 145ff.; and G. H. C. MacGregor, Exegesis of Acts, in *Interpreter's Bible*, 9).

The remainder of Acts adds little to the picture. "Speaking with tongues" is mentioned again, but in only two places. After Peter has preached to the household of Cornelius, the Roman centurion at Caesarea, "the Holy Spirit fell on all who heard the word. And the believers from among the circumcised (i.e., Christian Jews) who came with Peter were amazed, because the gift of the Holy Spirit had been poured out even on the Gentiles. For they heard them speaking in tongues and extolling God" (10:44-46). The center of interest here is not the manner in which the presence of the Spirit is manifested, but the admission of gentiles to the community of God's people and to a share in all the blessings of the gospel of Christ. The whole story culminates in the report of Peter to the Jerusalem church, and the astonished comment: "Then to the Gentiles also God has granted repentance unto life" (11:18). Again, the remaining passage tells of a flying visit of Paul to Ephesus during which he encounters a group of twelve who have been baptized "into John's baptism" but have not so much as heard that there is a Holy Spirit. They are now baptized in the name of

Jesus, Paul lays his hands upon them, and "the Holy Spirit came on them; and they spoke with tongues and prophesied" (19:1-7). This little story offers many difficulties of explanation, but it may be said that it is concerned chiefly with the cardinal difference between the baptism of John and Christian baptism—the one being merely a baptism with water, the other a baptism with water and Spirit. It would appear that a Jewish sect professing allegiance to John the Baptist continued to exist for years after his death, and was regarded by the Christians not as a rival body but as one that neglected the most important part of its master's teaching. He had baptized with a baptism of repentance, but he had also told the people "to believe on the one who was to come after him, that is, Jesus" (19:4).

In the story of the mission of Philip in Samaria, the converts are baptized, and "signs and great wonders" are performed (by Philip?, or by the newly converted?), but they do not receive the Holy Spirit until the apostles Peter and John come down from Jerusalem and lay hands on them; but nothing is said of the way in which this was manifested. The interest of the story lies at first in the extension of the gospel to the Samaritans, thus overcoming the traditional Jewish prejudice against this neighboring people; and after that, in the conflict between Simon Peter the apostle and Simon of Samaria, the founder of a sect which was afterwards looked upon as the root of all the gnostic heresies. In any case, it throws no further light on the matter of "speaking in tongues."

THE PAULINE EPISTLES

St. Paul makes mention of "speaking with tongues" in only one of his letters—1 Corinthians. This fact is in itself significant, for he is the great theologian of the Holy Spirit, and the work of the Spirit in the life of the church and of the individual Christian believer occupies a great place in his thought. In Romans, for instance, there is a rich and varied exposition of the work of the Spirit, without the faintest suggestion that it includes any "speaking with tongues." It is "through the Holy Spirit which has been given to us" that "God's love has been poured into our hearts" (Rom. 5:5). [It will become evident that the Spirit is above all the Spirit of love.] We serve God "not under the old written code (the Law) but in the new life of the Spirit" (7:6). It is "the law of the Spirit of life in Christ Jesus" that has set us free from the Law that provoked sin in us and issued in death (8:2). "To set the mind on the flesh is death, but to set the mind on the

Spirit is life and peace. . . . But you are not in the flesh, you are in the Spirit, if the Spirit of God really dwells in you. Anyone who does not have the Spirit of Christ does not belong to him. . . . If you live according to the flesh you will die, but if by the Spirit you put to death the deeds of the body you will live. For all who are led by the Spirit of God are sons of God" (8:6-14). The Spirit aids us in our prayers, for we do not know how to pray as we ought; the Spirit intercedes for us (8:26-28). Later in the epistle, he will tell us that "the kingdom of God does not mean food and drink but righteousness and peace and joy in the Holy Spirit" (14:17).

In 2 Corinthians, again, he has much to say about the work of the Spirit. Once again, he speaks of the gospel as introducing the dispensation of the Spirit, in contrast with the old dispensation of law (ch. 3). It is the Spirit that molds Christian character, so that he can compare the lives of Christians to letters from Christ, "written not with ink, but with the Spirit of the living God; written not on tablets of stone (like the commandments of the Law), but on tablets of human hearts" (3:3). The ministers of Christ have no natural capacity for their high task; they are qualified by the powers that God has communicated to them by his Spirit; and the Spirit is constantly transforming them and all Christ's people. "We all, with unveiled face, mirroring the glory of the Lord, are being transformed into his likeness from one degree of glory to another; for this comes from the Lord who is the Spirit" (3:18). The Spirit that God has given is the guarantee, the earnest, the first fruits, of a blessed immortality, the assurance that "if the earthly tent we live in is destroyed, we have a building from God, a house not made with hands, eternal in the heavens" (5:1-5).

In the letter to the Galatians, he again contrasts the free life of the Christian under the governing and transforming power of the Spirit with the constraints of life under the Law. God has sent the Spirit of his Son into our hearts, and made us not his slaves, but his sons (Gal. 4:6f.). We are called to freedom, but freedom does not mean abandonment to the fulfillment of selfish desires. It means freedom to serve one another in love. We are called to live by the Spirit and the fruit of the Spirit is seen in "love, joy, peace, patience, kindness, goodness, faithfulness, gentleness, self-control" (5:22-23). There is not a hint that these virtues must be, or are normally, accompanied with any kind of ecstatic utterance. Similar evidence might be drawn from letter after letter.

If the apostle treats particularly of "speaking with tongues" in 1 Corinthians, it is because he has been asked for help by the leaders of the Corinthian church. At the beginning of ch. 7, he commences to deal with a number of questions that they have put to him, introducing his answers with the words: "Concerning the matters about which you wrote" (7:1). He deals with relations between the sexes (ch. 7); then with the problem of eating food which had been offered at the altar in a heathen temple (ch. 8); and after some other matters have been treated he comes to their question, "Concerning spiritual gifts" (12:1). The meaning of the phrase is not certain, for "spiritual gifts" are usually called χαρίσματα ("gifts of grace"), as in vs. 4 (Rom. 12:6; etc.). The word here is πνευματικῶν, a genitive, which by its form could be neuter ("spiritual things," "gifts"), or masculine ("spiritual people," or "Spirit-gifted people"). The next two verses are somewhat obscure, but the apostle appears to be giving a warning that men may be inspired by other spirits than the Spirit of God; he reminds the Corinthians that in their pagan days they were led astray under the influence of false gods. He gives them a test: "No one speaking by the Spirit of God every says, 'Jesus is accursed'; and no one can say, 'Jesus is Lord' except by the Holy Spirit." The words imply that the church had been shocked by some of the things that were actually said by "spirit-filled" people in an ecstasy; they had even blurted out, apparently under the inspiration of a spirit, "Jesus is accursed!" Outwardly, they seemed to be going through the same kind of experience as those who "spoke with tongues" or "prophesied." A spirit other than their own was prompting their utterance. Only it was certainly not the Spirit of God. The test lies in the intelligible content of the utterance. There is an implicit warning that unintelligible utterance has its real dangers; it may be prompted by an evil spirit. It is not peculiarly Christian, and may be prompted by spirits that curse Christ. (A modern teacher would perhaps think of such "spirits" as evidences of a subconscious hostility to Christ and the gospel breaking out in words when the controls of the conscious mind were removed in a state of ecstasy.)

St. Paul's first concern is to set the gifts of the Spirit in perspective, and to relate them to the *common* life in the church. There are diversities of gifts, diversities of services, diversities of activities; but one Spirit, one Lord, one God is served by them all. "To each is given the manifestation of the Spirit for the common good" (πρὸς τὸ συμφέρον—"for some useful purpose," New English Bible). He now mentions some of this variety of gifts—"a word of wisdom, a word of knowledge, faith, gifts of healings"; he repeats four times that it is one and the same Spirit that is active in all these gifts. His list goes on: "Workings of miracles, prophecy, ability to distinguish spirits (evil spirits from the Spirit of God), kinds of tongues (γένη γλωσσῶν), interpretation of tongues." And again he emphasizes that "all these things are the work of one and the same Spirit, who distributes them to each as he wills" (vss. 4-11).

His next thought is that the church lives by a unity in diversity, or diversity in unity, like that of the body with its different parts. The body is one, an organic unity, but it has many parts and all the parts have different functions which promote, each in its own way, the full and healthy life of the body. Every part is needed, and none is able to get along without the help of others. If the body were all eye, there would be no sense of smell; if it were all nose, it would have a highly developed sense of smell, but no organ of vision. So in the church, the different members have different gifts, and all are needed. All must recognize their dependence on one another. It is wrong to value one gift highly, and to look upon others as trifling or valueless; to think too highly of oneself because one possesses gifts that others do not, or to think oneself useless because one has not received the gifts which others are exercising. It is God who determines how the gifts are distributed, and he has not chosen to give them all to anyone. All are not apostles, prophets, or teachers; neither do all have the gift of working miracles, healing diseases, speaking with tongues, or interpreting the speech in tongues.

At this point he introduces the lyrical passage on love, which interrupts the main discussion of spiritual gifts (which will be resumed in ch. 14) to bring forward the teaching that all other gifts are worthless without love. Speaking with tongues, even though it were angelic rather than human sounds that were uttered, is nothing more than the clang of gongs or the clash of cymbals, if the speaker be not moved by love. There is a suggestion that speaking with tongues, and indeed other spiritual gifts as well, belong to a stage of spiritual immaturity, which will not be wholly overcome in this life. Prophecy, tongues, knowledge—gifts of the Spirit, indeed, yet transitory, and imperfect. Love alone belongs to the eternal order of that which is perfect.

> When that which is perfect comes, the imperfect passes away. When
> I was a child, I spoke like a child, I thought like a child, I reasoned like a
> child; when I became a man, I put away childish ways. For now we see as

it were reflections in a mirror; but then we shall see face to face. Now I know in part; then I shall know fully, just as I have been fully known.

Throughout these two chapters, Paul has been speaking of spiritual gifts in all their diverse forms, in great comprehensiveness. Among them, without any particular emphasis, he has twice mentioned "'kinds of tongues'" (γένη γλώσσαις—12:10, 28); "interpretation [of tongues—vs. 10]" (vss. 10, 30); and "speaking with tongues" (γλώσσαις λαλεῖν—12:30; 12:1). Once he has used the word "tongues" (γλῶσσαι) alone (13:8). He does not use the term *glossolalia*. In all this he has not said anything that shows clearly what the word "tongues" means in this context. The primary use of the word in Greek is to designate the physical organ that lies on the floor of the mouth. That is clearly not the meaning here, for in that primary sense all human speech is spoken "with tongues." Secondly, as in English, it is used to mean "language" or "dialect." This usage is reflected in the story of Acts 2, where it is taken to mean "foreign language(s)" and is actually replaced by διάλεκτος (in Acts 2:8; reverting to γλῶσσα—in 2:11). As we have noticed above, this cannot be taken literally, but is a part of the symbolism which marks the recasting the story. In any case, this meaning is not reflected in the words of Paul. There is still a third sense, which is not paralleled in the English use of the word "tongue," to mean a strange, unusual, unfamiliar word; one that has become obsolete or belongs to a peculiar dialect. Aristotle remarks that diction may be given a certain elevation and distinction by the use of such γλῶτται; but if the speaker uses nothing else, his speech will be barbaric (*Poetics* 22a). This is strongly suggestive of Paul's words in 14:9-11:

> If you in a tongue utter speech that is not intelligible, how will anyone know what is said? For you will be speaking into the air. There are doubtless many different languages in the world, and none is without meaning, but if I do not know the meaning of the language, I shall be a barbarian to the speaker, and the speaker a barbarian to me.

This does not suggest a formless babble, or "lalling," but a succession of words which give the impression of language, but are unintelligible to the hearers.

It is clear that Paul is seeking to discourage the practice of speaking with tongues, not by condemning it outright, but by diverting interest and attention to other and better channels of activity in the church. He is quite ready to admit that the speaking with tongues is in its own way a manifestation of the Spirit in the church, and he will even claim that he has himself had this experience ("I thank God that I speak with tongues more than you all"—vs. 18). The fact that he has had the experience lends all the more weight to the fact that he never mentions it without pointing out its inferior value, and comparing it unfavorably with speech that is intelligible. His main point is that speaking with tongues does not benefit the church. It may be a helpful spiritual experience for the speaker himself, but the Christian is called to think not of himself alone, but of the good of the community to which he belongs. "He who speaks in a tongue edifies himself, but he who prophesies edifies the church" (vs. 4). "Since you are eager for manifestations of the Spirit, strive to excel in building up the church" (vs. 12). He suggests that there is something childish about this fascination with "tongues," and he urges them: "Do not be children in your thinking; be babes in evil, but in thinking be mature" (vs. 20). Even when he makes his claim that he himself speaks with tongues more than any of them, he discounts this at once by adding: "Nevertheless, in church I had rather speak five words with my mind, in order to instruct others, than ten thousand words in a tongue" (vs. 19).

The apostle is insistent on the rights of the mind. "If I pray in a tongue, my spirit prays, but my mind is unfruitful. What then? I will pray with the spirit and I will pray with the mind also; I will sing with the spirit and I will sing with the mind also" (vss. 14-15). He would certainly not agree with any suggestion that intelligible speech, prayer, and song is in any way less spiritual, or gives any less evidence of the presence of the Holy Spirit within us, than the unintelligible utterances of "tongues" in which the mind of the speaker is not engaged. Quite the contrary.

There can be no doubt, then, that the main purpose of Paul is to discourage the practice of speaking with tongues among Christians. He does not suggest that it is an evil; for him, it is in its own way a manifestation of the Spirit; but he certainly directs his readers to seek other manifestations, and especially to seek gifts that will be helpful to the church at large. The "prophecy" of which he speaks, which he sets far above the "speaking with tongues," is likewise an utterance prompted by the Holy Spirit; but it is intelligible, it brings penitence to the hearer, and convinces him that God is present (vss. 24 f.). Paul will not ask that speaking with tongues be forbidden (vs. 39), but he certainly seeks to direct the energies of Christians into other channels and insists that there are other ways of serving

God in the power of his Spirit, which will be of far more benefit to the church.

OTHER NEW TESTAMENT WRITINGS

There is no reference to speaking with tongues in any other part of the NT, and there is seldom any mention of the operations of the Spirit within the individual believer. The author of the Pastoral Epistles, though he writes in the name of Paul, has nothing at all resembling the apostle's many-sided doctrine. He knows that God in his mercy has saved us "through the washing of regeneration and renewal by the Holy Spirit, which he poured out upon us richly through Jesus Christ our Savior, so that we might be justified by his grace and become heirs in hope of eternal life" (Tit. 3:5ff.). All this is given in baptism, and nothing is said of gifts bestowed severally on individuals in differing manifestations. Apart from this, we have one reference to the Spirit as revealing (presumably to the author) the nature of the heresy which he is now combating (1 Tim. 4:1-4); and the only mention of the Spirit as a continuing presence ("the Spirit which dwells within us") is related to the charge to "guard the noble deposit"—that is, the true doctrine of Christ as it has been received from Paul (2 Tim. 1:13f.). There is still no thought of diversities of gifts, and the function of the spirit is limited to the safeguarding of the tradition. The author of Hebrews likewise takes it for common knowledge that all Christians "have become partakers of the Holy Spirit" in their baptism, when they were "enlightened" and "tasted the heavenly gift" (Heb. 6:4), and he warns that those who sin deliberately after they have received the knowledge of the truth "treat with insolence the Spirit of grace" (10:26-29); but he does not develop the thought of how this presence of the Spirit is manifested. He knows of "distributions of the Holy Spirit" (πνεύματος ἁγίου μερισμοῖς), but he links them with the "signs and wonders and manifold miracles" by which God associated himself with the testimony of those who heard the gospel of salvation from the lips of the Lord (2:3-4). He appears to think of them as giving supernatural evidences of the truth of the gospel, vouchsafed exceptionally in the first days of the mission, rather than as continuing features of the church's life.

Among the Catholic Epistles, only 1 John makes any large use of the doctrine of the Spirit. Here again there is no thought of a diversity of gifts. The whole emphasis is laid upon what Christians have in common. The

Spirit is "an unction from the Holy One," which "abides" in Christian believers, and teaches them about everything (2:20, 27). The Spirit witnesses to the truth, because he is the truth (5:7). His presence in us is our evidence that God abides in us and we in him (4:13); it is significant that this is said in the context of the teaching on love (4:7-21). But he warns that men may be possessed by other spirits than the Spirit of God, and may be moved by them to utterances which deny the reality of the Incarnation. He therefore warns his readers to "test the spirits to see whether they are of God" (4:1). He does not mention the speaking with tongues, but he clearly has in mind utterances which are taken to be controlled by a supernatural Power, and (like Paul) he is concerned to impress upon his readers that such utterances are not always inspired by the spirit of God. They may in fact be expressions of "the spirit of antichrist" (4:3).

The Book of Revelation contains nothing that bears upon our theme. The Seer is himself "in the Spirit" (1:9f.) when he hears the voices and sees the visions, but he has no occasion to speak about manifestations of the Spirit in his fellow Christians, or about the gifts of others.

SUMMARY

The phenomenon of speaking with tongues is mentioned nowhere in the NT apart from the Book of Acts and 1 Corinthians. The evidence of Acts throws little if any light on the nature of the practice, and can be interpreted only with the aid of the relatively full discussion of Paul. The great apostle recognizes it as a manifestation of the Spirit of God, but he does not regard it as common to all Christians. It is one among many gifts, amid a great diversity, and is less highly valued than the gift of prophecy or prayer and praise "with the mind."

In this article, no effort has been made to evaluate the phenomenon or to compare it with ancient or modern patterns of behavior which might appear to be similar. It is perhaps sufficient to note that it is not regarded by any NT writer as a normal or invariable accompaniment of the life in grace, and there is no justification in the classical documents of the Christian faith for holding it to be a necessary element in the fullest spiritual development of the individual Christian or in the corporate life of the church.

7

WILLIAM G. MacDONALD

Glossolalia
in the
New Testament

[Reprinted from *Bulletin of Evangelical Theological Society*, 7 (1964): 59-68. Reprinted with permission from Evangelical Theological Society and author.]

DEFINITION OF GLOSSOLALIA

The *locus classicus* of glossolalia is found in Luke's account of the first Pentecost after Christ's resurrection: "And they were all filled with the Holy Spirit and began to speak in other tongues as the Spirit gave them utterance" (Acts 2:4). Glossolalia, the technical term used to describe this phenomenon, does not appear as one word in Greek. It has been coined as a descriptive expression of the phenomenon of speaking languages that one does not know by the enablement of the Spirit of God, from γλωσσαι (tongues) and λαλειν (to speak). A more precise term would be "heteroglossolalia,'' since it is distinctively "other (ετεραις) languages,'' which are specified in this foundational passage (cf. 14:21 also).

ANTECEDENTS OF GLOSSOLALIA

One feature of Spirit theology should be briefly delineated here as a background to glossolalic study. The work of the Spirit of God is not to be temporally limited to one occasion in the experience of an individual. Christ is unique in His experience of the Spirit (Jn. 3:34). However, Jesus, who was *conceived* of the Holy Spirit was later *anointed* with the Spirit at the Jordan. The significant point is that He was born by the spirit which was the basis of His holy life as the Incarnate Son of God, and yet the Spirit thirty years later is said and seen to descend upon Him at the outset of a ministry in the power of the Spirit. Yet Christ, with all the gifts and operations of the Spirit, never spoke in tongues. Why? His temporal ministry was only to "the lost sheep of the house of Israel," while His primary service was the universal act of offering himself to God to atone for man's sin. Thus because His manhood was lived under the old dispensation, the law (Gal 1:4), the Holy Spirit did not choose to operate through Him in any oral manner, other than that common to the Old Testament saints and prophets, i.e., by prophecy. Having ascended, He is linked with glossolalia, not as a recipient, but as the One who together with the Father is responsible for all that was seen and *heard* (Acts 2:33) on the day of Pentecost.

The Apostles likewise had several experiences chronologically of the Spirit. On Christ's first encounter with them subsequent to His resurrection He breathed out from Himself into them "Holy Spirit" (Jn. 20:22— anarthrous construction). Thus they became united with Christ in a new way in the experience of receiving Christ's Spirit; this may properly be called their Christian "regeneration" or "the renewing of the Holy Spirit" (Titus 3:5). Fifty days later these same men were "filled with Holy Spirit" (Acts 2:4) and began to speak in other languages in evidence of this "filling," and in response to prayer in a crisis they again were "all filled with the Holy Spirit" with the result that "they spoke the word of God with boldness," i.e., prophesied, in the sense of speaking God's message.

THE BIBLICAL INCIDENTS OF GLOSSOLALIA
IN ACTS EXEGETICALLY ANALYZED

In Acts 2:1-21 is found the initial "filling" with the Holy spirit of one hundred and twenty of the most faithful of Christ's disciples—those who had received and obeyed His post-resurrection order to wait in Jerusalem until they should be clothed with power from above (Luke 24:49). Upon these "first-fruit" Jewish believers assembled together the Holy spirit came in a mighty manifestation.

In verses one through six it is to be noted that there are four things that were filled: (1) The divinely ordained *time* for the Spirit to be manifested was fulfilled (συμπληροῦσθαι—2:1) on the day of the feast of the first harvest, fifty days after Passover. (2) The noise of a violently moving wind filled (επληρωσεν—2:2) all the building in which they were assembled. (3) Jerusalem had been providentially filled with a multitude (πληθος—2:6) of God-fearing Jews from "every nation under heaven." (4) The hundred and twenty were filled (επλησθησαν—2:4) with Holy Spirit.

To the audible whizzing of the wind was added the visual as an aid in the comprehension of the divine character of the manifestation. "Tongues (γλωσσαι) like fire" were seen distributed upon each one of them. Upon which part of their bodies they may have touched is not stated, only that the "tongues" sat upon each of them. One is reminded of the seraph who placed a coal of fire from the altar of God upon Isaiah's mouth and lips at the inception of his ministry.

Just as there are multiple applications of filling in this passage, there is a double use of γλωσσαι, tongues. First it is used phenomenally of the fiery projections upon each one present (2:3); also the term is used for the *languages* (2:4) they spoke. This was the first perceptible expression *from within* that the disciples had been filled with the Spirit. They who were mostly Galileans began to speak in what observers from Rome to Mesopotamia and Arabia individually recognized as their "own language" (ιδια διαλεκτω 2:6, 8). Reference to this fact is made a *third* time in 2:11 using "ημετεραις γλωσσαις" (our languages) in which γλωσσαι is manifestly used synonymously with διαλεκτοι.

It is important to observe that the filling was prior to the speaking, and the text insures that the glossolalia was consequent upon the Spirit's full possession of their faculties. These were not ecstatic sayings that were unintelligible, but were clearly discernible languages (γλωσσαι ιδιος διαλεκτος) that were recognized. (If anyone was "ecstatic" in the *disorganized* sense of that word, it was the observers as seen in one of the words descriptive of their reaction—εξισταντο—lit., "they stood outside themselves," i.e., "were amazed.")

The sound of the supernatural wind signified power: it reverberated through the house but was non-destructive. The apparition of the tongues "like fire," differed from ordinary fire in that it did not burn them. The wind and fire were external manifestations of the Holy Spirit's presence, first *with* them, in the case of the wind, and *upon* them, in the case of the fiery tongues. Consummately, the manifestation of glossolalia was the attestation that the holy spirit was dominant *within* them, having perfect control of the tongue which no man can tame (James 3:8).

Acts 2:38, 39 contains Peter's words to the congregation of at least 3,000 which had gathered because of the extraordinary happenings of the upper room. Those who repent and are baptized in the name of Jesus Christ are promised "the gift of the Holy Spirit. For the *promise* is to you and to your children and to all that are far off, everyone whom the Lord our God calls to him." That "the promise" refers to the outpouring of the Holy Spirit is reasonably clear because: (1) The preceding context in which in explanation of the current event Peter quotes Joel's prophecy (2:17) that sets forth God's promise to pour out the Holy Spirit upon "all flesh," (2) Peter's statement in 2:33 refers to "the *promise* of the Holy Spirit,"—a genitive of apposition, (3) The syntactical proximity of "the promise" to "the gift of the Holy Spirit" in 2:38, 39 implies apposition.

Indeed, Christ had kindled their expectation for being clothed with divine power by instructing His disciples to wait in Jerusalem for "the *promise* of my Father" (Lu. 24:49). Now if Pentecost is the fulfillment of Christ's promise of the Father's promise, and Peter's message about "the gift of the Holy Spirit" as the promise for all whom God calls is valid, then there must be something *normative* about Pentecost. There was no outward manifestation when Jesus breathed and the apostles received Holy Spirit (Jn. 20:22) after the resurrection. However, on the day of Pentecost there are two outward manifestations of the Spirit's work (wind and fire) and one manifestation from within (glossolalia), which demonstrated the finesse of the Spirit's power to articulate through their speech organs the "mighty works of God" in languages they had never learned.

It is probable that the sound of the wind that attracted the first crowd, and the fire had vanished before the mockers (2:13) had arrived on the scene, but the glossolalia remained as a "sign" (1 Cor. 14:22; Mk. 16:17) to them. Significantly glossolalia is repeated in other instances of the Spirit's outpouring throughout the book of Acts, whenever the writer tells in detail what happens when people initially receive the holy spirit, as this subsequent investigation will demonstrate.

The second account of people who experienced the Holy Spirit's falling upon them in the period of Acts concerns the Samaritans. Acts 8:5-25 records the events in this order: (1) Philip preached the Christian gospel to them. (2) They believed and were baptized in water. (3) The apostles Peter and John were sent to them to pray and lay their hands on them that they might receive the Holy Spirit (anarthrous). (4) Peter and John laid their hands on them and they received Holy Spirit. (5) Simon, the sorcerer, infatuated with the supernatural power accompanying the gospel, tried to buy the power to impart the Holy Spirit, thinking that the source of the power lay in the apostles themselves apart from God.

In this instance no mention is made of glossolalia, but it is beyond doubt that something *palpable* and *immediate* was manifested that motivated Simon to seek to be able to duplicate this power with others. He "*saw* (ιςων—aor. ptc. οραω) that the Spirit was given through the laying on of the apostles' hands" (8:18). By the use of ιδων—"saw" a hasty induction should not be reached that this means visual perception, and only that. For just a little later in the same context Peter says "I see" (ορω—the same verb, οραω) "that you are in the gall of bitterness . . . " Thus if Peter's "seeing" was perceptual rather than strictly visual, the same could be true of Simon's analysis of how the Holy Spirit was imparted by the apostles. It is interesting to note that "see (βλεπετε) and hear" are united in Acts 2:33 in connection with Pentecost, meaning the total perception of what was happening before their eyes and ears.

Now the question remains, what did Simon "see" that caused him to know immediately and in truth that those touched by Peter's and John's hands had received the Holy spirit? The external audio-visual phenomena of the first Pentecost—the wind and fire—are possible here, but nowhere in Acts is it ever stated that these introductory heavenly (2:2) signs are ever repeated. Some new sign is less likely still for such probably would have found mention in the record. Glossolalia would fit the occasion, for it would occur immediately and be recognized as a form of the Spirit's control. Yet the record is silent at this point because Luke's immediate interest is the attempted merchandising of spiritual things by Simon. But his silence is not surprising, especially if the Samaritans gave evidence to their having received the Holy Spirit in a manner common to all the other Lukan accounts of what actually happened when people received the Holy Spirit (2:4; 10:44-46; 19:6).

In Acts 10:34-11:18 there is the account of the Holy Spirit's being poured out on Gentiles, whereas before, only Jews and semi-Jews had been recipients. The order of events was: (1) By divine directive Peter preached the gospel of Christ at Cornelius' home in Caesarea. (2) The Holy Spirit was poured forth on Cornelius and his household of friends as Peter preached, being evidenced by glossolalia coupled with magnifying God. (3) Then they were commanded to be baptized in water.

The crucial factor in this episode was the glossolalia which made Peter and his six colleagues know with certainty that the Gentiles had received identically the same experience that he and the others had at the Pentecost feast. Peter calls it the ισην δωρεαν "same gift" (11:17) and states *three* times (10:47; 11:15; 11:17) that these men have received the Holy spirit just as he and his companions had. By asserting that the Spirit "fell on them just as on us at the beginning" he has reference to Pentecost and its promised power (Lu. 24:49; Acts 1:3) rather than the quiet experience of Jn. 20:22 in which Holy Spirit was breathed into them as their new principle of life in Christ.

Three further facts about the experience at Caesarea are noteworthy: (1) Water baptism and Spirit baptism are not to be confused. Peter "remembered the word of the Lord" that had promised baptism in the Holy Spirit in contradistinction of John's water baptism (11:16) and saw in the experience of Cornelius the fulfillment of that promise. This was especially apparent in that their water baptism did not synchronize with their baptism in the Spirit that was just as much a distinct experience as water baptism ever was for them. (2) Though the fiery tongues and the heavenly hurricane-like wind were missing, the net result was as Peter said "the same gift." This throws the weight of evidence, in Peter's analysis, upon glossolalia and magnifying God (10:46) as the index of Pentecostal experience. These were principal ingredients of the first Pentecost also (2:4, 11). (3) It took more than Peter's recounting of his vision to "the circumcision party" in Jerusalem to convince his critics. It was the fact that the Gentiles had received the "same gift" that silenced all the critics (11:18).

Even more remote from Jerusalem, Samaria, and Caesarea is the experience of a dozen or so Ephesians (Acts 19:1-7) who had this sequence of experiences: (1) Paul came to Ephesus and found those who had been baptized with John's baptism; they were "disciples," but had not heard of the Holy Spirit. (2) Paul instructed them further in the gospel of Christ. (3)

They were baptized with Christian baptism. (4) Paul laid his hands on them and the Holy Spirit came on them manifesting Himself in glossolalia and prophecy.

It is noteworthy that this experience was not only considerably removed in distance geographically from the original outpourings of the Spirit, but also occurred considerably later in time during Paul's second missionary journey. Glossolalia remains a recurring evidence of the Spirit-baptism. In Acts 10 it was glossolalia and praise; here it is glossolalia and prophecy. The one constant factor that takes precedence in both cases as at Pentecost is glossolalia. That the nucleus of the church at Ephesus should experience glossolalia was no surprise to Paul, for the Church at Corinth that he founded likewise experienced the same, evidently from itsbeginning, and by inference this may well have been the norm in all the churches that Paul founded. Had not Peter prophesied, " . . . the promise is unto you and to your children, and to all that are afar off, even as many as the Lord our God shall call" (Acts 2:39)? All that are afar off (μακραν) appears to be *terminus technicus* for the "Gentiles" as it is used here and in Eph. 2:13.

Paul's own experience could be taken as a case in point that glossolalia was such an uncommon thing that it had to be specified every time it occurred. In the three accounts in Acts of his conversion experience (chapters 9; 22; 26), the light from heaven and his resulting blindness and healing occupy the thought of the writer more than anything else. However, in 9:17b, mention is made of Ananias' intention to pray for him that he might "be filled with the Holy Spirit." Is one to assume that Paul failed to receive the experience into which he led the Ephesians and Corinthians, because glossolalia is not specifically mentioned in the Lukan accounts of Paul's experience? To the contrary, he informs the Corinthians (1 Cor. 14:14, 15) of his praying "in the Spirit" (i.e., glossolalia, because he says "my mind is unfruitful") and singing "in the Spirit" (i.e., melodic glossolalia, for the same reason) and made his revealing statement in 1 Cor. 14:18: "I thank God that I speak in tongues more than you all," *thanking* God that he exceeded the Corinthians in glossolalia, who were exercising glossolalia excessively in the local meetings.

THE DISTINCTION BETWEEN PERSONAL GLOSSOLALIA
AND THE GLOSSOLALIC GIFT
FOR THE EDIFICATION OF THE LOCAL CHURCH

Not understanding the distinction between the personal and the ecclesiological *function* of glossolalia it is possible for one to become perplexed by what would doubtless seem to be contradictions in Paul's teaching and with the data already explored in Acts. 1 Corinthians, chapters 12, 13, and 14 are a cohesive unit on the subject of spiritual gifts including their intended end—love. First note that the gift of "various kinds of tongues" (γενη γλωσσων—1 Cor. 12:10, 28) is one of the many "gifts" listed in 1 Cor. 12, which the Spirit distributes among the saints as He wills (12:11). The exercise of this gift, listed next to the last in apparently what appears to be a descending arrangement (first, second, third, then, then . . . 12:28-31), is distinctly to be limited to two or at most three manifestations in any one service (14:27), and that is expressly not expected that all should exercise this gift any more than that all should be apostles (12:29, 30) or that all the body were feet (12:18-21). Repeatedly it is stated that this is a gift to the Church for the edification of the whole local church (12:7, 14:5, 12), which function is defeated unless it be followed by the exercise of the gift of interpretation of tongues (ερμηνεια γλωσσων) for the edification of all (15:13, 16, 17, 28). But in Acts 2 where glossolalia is an evidence of the Spirit's anointing and not intended to edify the Church but the individuals speaking, being also a sign to the world, one sees one hundred and twenty speaking in other languages simultaneously, and in every case in Acts there are more than the two or three speaking, and on the day of Pentecost the interpretation of tongues is obviated since their auditors understood the languages that the speakers did not.

The analysis of 1 Cor. 13-14 in the following scheme distinguishes between the exercise of glossolalia on the individual and group levels, although in some instances the quote can apply equally as well to either category as indicated.

DISTINCTIONS IN THE PURPOSE
OF GLOSSOLALIA IN 1 COR. 12, 13, 14

Note: Where the statement applies equally to one category as the other, the quotation begins in the left column and extends into the right column.

Personal Edification	*Edification of the Church*
Identifying Characteristic Phrase:	*Identifying Characteristic Phrase:*
"He who speaks in a tongue edifies himself"—14:4	"The manifestation of the Spirit for common good"—12:7
	12:10—". . . to another various

kinds of tongues . . .
12:38—"And God has appointed
in the church . . . speakers
in various kinds of tongues."
12:30—". . . Do all speak with
tongues?"

13:1—"If I speak with the tongues of men and angels, but have not love
. . ."
13:8—". . . as for tongues they will cease . . ."
14:2—"For one who speaks in a tongue speaks not to men but to God; for
no one understands him, but he utters mysteries in the Spirit."
14:4—"He who speaks in a tongue edifies himself."
14:5—"Now I want you all to speak in tongues . . ."

14:5—". . . He who prophecies is
greater than he who speaks in
tongues, unless some one interprets
so that the church may be edified."

14:6—"Now, brethren, if I come to
you speaking in tongues, how shall
I benefit you unless I bring you some
revelation or knowledge or prophecy or teaching?"
14:9—". . . If you in a tongue utter
speech that is not intelligible, how
will anyone know what is said?"

14:13—"Therefore, he who speaks
in a tongue should pray for the
power to interpret."

14:14—"For if I pray in a tongue, my spirit prays but my mind is unfruitful."
14:15—". . . I will pray with the spirit . . . I will sing with the spirit . . ."
14:16—"Otherwise, if you bless
with the spirit, how can anyone in
the position of an outsider say the
'amen' to your thanksgiving when
he does not know what you are saying?"

14:18—"I thank God I speak in
tongues more than you all; nevertheless, in church I would rather
speak five words with my mind, in
order to instruct others, than ten
thousand words in a tongue."

14:22—"Thus tongues are a sign not for believers, but for unbelievers . . ."

14:23—"If, therefore, the whole
church assembles and all speak in
tongues, and outsiders or unbelievers enter, will they not say that you
are mad?"

14:26—"When you come together,
each one has . . . a tongue . . . ."

14:27—"If any speak in a tongue,
let there be only two or at most
three, and each in turn; and let one
interpret."

14:28—"But if there is no one to
interpret, let each of them keep silence in church and speak to himself and to God."

14:39—". . .and do not forbid
speaking in tongues."

   In drawing the Scriptural lines of demarcation between personal, "devotional," or evidential γλωσσαι and the gift of γενη γλωσσων to the
Church for a ministry of edification, it should be noted that there is no co-
gent exegetical ground for making any differences in the *essential character* of glossolalia in Corinthians from that in Acts. The distinction would
lie only in the *purpose* of the Spirit, on the one hand being individual communion with God, on the other hand being such speech as intended to minister edification to the gathered congregation. Both of these purposes are
alluded to in Corinthians, whereas in Acts the incidents are to initial experiences of glossolalia which fall into the former category as personal or
evidential.

SUMMARY OF TEACHING IN 1 COR. 12-14 ON GLOSSOLALIA

In a paper of this dimension one can only touch on the exegesis of the Corinthians material, because of the prior responsibility to understand the first instances of glossolalia as delineated in Acts. Therefore only the findings of exegesis will be presented in summary statements of the pertinent material in 1 Cor. 12-14.

1. Glossolalia is a lesser or subsidiary gift to such "office" gifts as "apostles . . . prophets . . . teacher" (12:27-30); it is also inferior to love (12:31-13:1) because glossolalia is temporal, but love never ends (13:8).

2. For congregational edification glossolalia is provisionally inferior to prophecy because glossolalia requires the operation of a second gift to complete it. These two gifts, tongues plus interpretation, are equivalent to prophecy, however (14:5).

3. *Uninterpreted* glossolalia in the public assembly contributes to confusion rather than edification (14:6-17, 23). Five words of prophecy are better than 10,000 words of glossolalia, without interpretation (14:19).

4. Glossolalia is edifying to the speaker (14:4) though his mind is not cognizant of what he is saying (14:13, 14, 19) and is desirable for *all*, though prophecy is even more desirable (14:5).

5. Glossolalia was prophesied in the Old Testament (14:21) and is said to be a sign for unbelievers (14:22), but prophecy is more effective for securing their repentance (14:22-25). Note the parallel on the day of Pentecost; the "tongues" spoke of God's great works, arrested attention, and created amazement, but Peter's "prophecy" divulged God's meaning in all God's mighty acts, beginning at the cross, and was the linguistic instrument for their finding the way of salvation.

6. The exercise of glossolalia (like that of prophecy) must be regulated in the local meeting. There should be no more than two or three who speak in a "tongue" during one service. Moreover, these cannot be simultaneous, but must be by turns and these followed respectively by the interpretation. Where there is no interpreter present, one must remain silent, speaking only to himself and to God (14:27, 28).

7. Prophecy is to be desired in the church more than glossolalia, but glossolalia is likewise the work of the Spirit (12:4, 6, 9) and must not be forbidden (14:39); these instructions are not merely apostolic "convictions" but are "a command of the Lord" (14:37).

PROBLEM PASSAGES

Three crucial passages on "tongues" are explored here.

1. " . . . as for tongues, they will cease . . ." (13:8).

The ceasing of tongues in this passage is grouped by the Apostle Paul with the passing away of prophecies and knowledge: " . . . as for prophecies they will pass away; as for tongues, they will cease; as for knowledge it will pass away." "Knowledge" here is probably to be taken to refer to the "utterance of knowledge" (λογος γνωσεως) of 1 Cor. 12:8. These three kinds of speech are all "gifts of the Spirit" which are spiritual *means* to a divine end—eternal love for God. These gifts have only a temporal existence, and "when that which is perfect is come," and we no longer see "in part" but "face to face" the necessity for the gifts will be eliminated. There is no hint here that tongues will cease before prophecies that were to be earnestly desired by all the laymen at Corinth (14:1,5, 24, 31, 39) or before "knowledge" passes away or that any of these should pass off the scene *before* the time "when that which is perfect is come."

1 Corinthians is considered by the Church generally to be a letter that is pertinent to the whole Church age, and being apostolic, is authoritative for it. Now this letter contains no less than eighteen direct references to glossolalia, plus many supporting and explanatory verses applicable to same. The Acts of the Apostles likewise gives abundant testimony to the normative status of glossolalia in the Church as it began and spread. It is therefore incumbent upon those who say that the Pauline prophecy that glossolalia "shall cease," has in fact, already "ceased" at some juncture in Church history, to prove that the Church has entered another, if somewhat anticlimactic Dispensation, in which it is impossible for believers any longer to speak under any kind of control by the spirit, whether in his own language (as prophecy, an utterance of wisdom, or an utterance of knowledge) or in another language (glossolalia).

Peter indicated at Pentecost through his quotation of Joel that the "last days" (Acts 2:17) were to be identified by the outpouring of the Spirit upon everybody, young and old, male and female, all the Lord's servants. The fulfillment of this prophecy he equated with the Pentecostal outpouring then received, but he hastened to add that the promise was for all whom the Lord shall call in the future (Acts 2:39). There is no hint that glossolalia will cease before the "last days" (Acts 2:17) are superseded by "the day of the

Lord,'' (Acts 2:20) or that the Church will move into a new dispensation making obsolete 1 Corinthians and its teaching about spiritual gifts.

2. "Do all speak with tongues?'' (1 Cor. 12:30).

From the context it is evident that here Paul was speaking of the gift in operation *in the Church* and not necessarily concerning that of which had reference in his statement: "I desire *all* of you to speak in tongues,'' 1 Cor. 14:5. Moreover, the Lucan account of glossolalia in Acts 2:4 and 10:44 expressly states that in each of these instances *all* were filled and spoke in tongues. Assuredly all do not exercise the gift of tongues in the local meeting any more than all are teachers or that all have gifts of healings, or that all the members of the body were speaking apparatuses.

This same objection sometimes takes other forms, by saying that God is not limited to only one initial evidence of the Spirit-baptism; any one of the ''gifts'' may be the evidence. But this is not what was found in the exegesis of the history of outpourings of the Spirit in Acts. The initial evidence of having received the *Spirit* was invariably glossolalia—''for they heard them speak with tongues.'' It is not a question of what God could have done, but what He actually chose to do.

In the same vein it is protested that God's love of variety would *a priori* rule out glossolalia as the only initial evidence of the Spirit's anointing. Yet there is variety within the unity of the glossolalic phenomenon; it is to be found in the variety of languages that the Spirit chooses, while not changing the one basic factor that the Spirit speaks through man in a new way.

3. " . . . if you in a tongue utter speech that is not intelligible, how will any one know what is said?'' (14:9)

Are the Corinthian ''tongues'' unintelligible babblings of nonsense syllables thrown together in meaningless combination by the subconscious working of man's mind? Note these factors:

(1) The context before (14:5) and after (14:13) that brackets this verse stresses the need for *interpretation* of tongues for edification. Thus the verse in question has to do with uninterpreted glossolalia, and ''not intelligible'' or not ''easily recognizable'' (ευσημον) means that it sounds foreign to those unacquainted with the sound (φωνη) of the strange language. This does not mean that the speech is unintelligible per se, or that it is not understood by God, but merely that it is unintelligible to speaker and hearer without interpretation.

(2) Paul used the same term, λογους, for both the five *words* he would speak in the common language and for the 10,000 words he might utter in glossolalia.

(3) If glossolalia is really the Holy Spirit speaking through man's speaking organs, then the source of the content is to be predicated to the Spirit and not man. "He utters mysteries in the Spirit" (14:2), but this does not imply that the γλωσσαι or φωναι (14:10) are non-linguistic, sound-harsh, because they contain mysteries spoken to God. On φωναι as languages compare Bauer-Arndt-Gingrich's lexicon, and the LXX, Gen. 11:1, where γλωσσαα and φωνη are used synonymously.

CONCLUSION

Glossolalia, signifying the international and supernatural character of the Gospel, can be ignored only at the peril of misunderstanding an important factor in the history of the church of the New Testament. Because true glossolalia is a work of the *Spirit of God* through a yielded human being, it remains just as incomprehensible as the Incarnation, the Atonement, the Resurrection to immortality, and other acts of God involving man. This unique way of speaking to God (14:2) by the power of His Spirit within is a part of the heritage of the church. Those who renounce this heritage will only be the poorer for it. The Corinthians had much to learn about the meaning and regulation of glossolalia in the local assembly, just as they did concerning the significance and proper observance of the Lord's supper. But in neither case does the Apostle throw out the baby with the bath water. His "command of the Lord"—*do not forbid glossolalia*, but do all things properly and in order—has never been revoked! The God who made man's tongue and made him an intelligent, speaking creature, capable of fellowship and communion with Himself, has never renounced His option to speak as He chooses to His own glory through the man whose body and soul have become the temple of the Holy Spirit.

8

J. P. M. SWEET

A Sign for Unbelievers: Paul's Attitude to Glossolalia

[Reprinted from *New Testament Studies*, 13 (April 1967): 240-57. Reprinted with permission from Cambridge University Press.]

In this paper there are three related concerns: first, to attempt an interpretation of 1 Corinthians 14:20-25 against the background of Peter's activity in Corinth; secondly, recognizing the polemical nature of this passage and of the whole of 1 Corinthians 12-14, to discuss the application of these chapters to modern Pentecostal phenomena; and, thirdly, to examine the conclusions of J. C. Hurd,[1] which in both respects tell against mine.

---

[1] In *The Origin of 1 Corinthians* (London, 1965).

I

Recently there has been within the traditional churches increasing experience of 'speaking with tongues.' Whether or not this phenomenon is the same as that dealt with by Paul in 1 Corinthians 12-14, it is certainly close enough for his discussion to be relevant. Today, on the one hand, it is claimed, or suggested, that tongues are the normal if not the exclusive sign of reception of the spirit, and that there is something lacking in any Christian who has not had this experience. This is precisely what Paul wished to deny in these chapters: they make up a unified polemic against such an over-valuation, in which 13 plays an integral part, and put a corrective emphasis on prophecy.[2] On the other hand, anti-Pentecostalists may be inclined to overemphasize Paul's disapproval. For example, it is said that he more or less forbids the public use of tongues. In fact he allows it under proper safeguards (14:27-28), and these safeguards are practically the same as those laid down for prophecy, which was evidently also liable to abuse (14:29-33). He allows it, but how much weight should be given to statements like 14:5, 18 and 39? Are these concessions merely diplomatic, in recognition of a state of affairs which cannot be changed all at once? Would he have *liked* to forbid tongues altogether?[3] Or, recognizing that he was engaged in polemic, should we not be on the lookout for overstatement and be ready to maximize his concessions and minimize his hostile statements and insinuations? The *Expository Times* in a recent editorial[4] sums up: "Is it possible that through our distaste for 'this highly emotional phenomenon' we have done less than justice to these words of the Apostle? One has the impression in re-reading these chapters, that Paul's objection was not so much to tongues in themselves, but tongues paraded in public." This seems just. But "paraded in public" is only part of the story. Paul's main objection was not to the practice but to their estimate of the prac-

---

[2]There is no need for my purposes to define "tongues" and "prophecy" closely. The former seems to have been a normally unintelligible form of praying and singing, the latter speaking intelligibly in the name of the Lord. Both were "enthusiastic," and probably had not been sharply distinguished up to this point (cf. Acts 2:17-18; 19:6).

[3]See I. J. Martin III, "Glossolalia in the Apostolic Church," *Journal of Biblical Literature*, 68 (1944): 123-30. He takes the restrictions on prophecy as part of the diplomacy, to soften Paul's strictures on tongues.

[4]May 1966, p. 227.

tice—and not only to the general overvaluation attacked in 13. 1 Corinthians 12-14 is a closely knit unity[5] and the beginning of the passage sets the tone. In 12:1-3 he asserts in effect that all Christians are πνευματικοί by virtue of their baptismal confession (cf. 12:13). 'Ανάθεμα 'Ιησοῦς is the hypothetical opposite of Κύριος 'Ιησοῦς: a Christian fails to be πνευματικός only if he ceases to be a Christian.[6] Chapter 12 as a whole asserts the diversity and the equal authenticity of the Spirit's gifts. In other words pneumatic status is being denied at Corinth to those who cannot produce the more showy manifestations like glossolalia, and claimed exclusively for those who do. In particular, 14:20-25 indicates a claim that tongues "serve as a sign[7] for Christians" (εἰς σημεῖον τοῖς πιστεύουσιν), a claim which Paul tries to reverse in favour of prophecy. It is unlikely that the sign-value of tongues is an original contribution of Paul's; his other references to signs are few and mostly critical.[8] Further, it is only in a backhanded sense that tongues are "a sign for unbelievers" (14:22). Therefore it is probable that Paul is taking up a Corinthian slogan (from their letter to him?): αἱ γλῶσσαι εἰς σημεῖόν εἰσι τοῖς πιστεύουσιν.

14:20-25 is at first sign a puzzle: the examples given in 23-25 are the reverse of what one would expect from 22. "Tongues serve as a sign forunbelievers"—but if unbelievers come in when all who speak speak in tongues, they will say you are mad. "Prophecy serves as a sign for believers" (if, as I think, εἰς σημεῖον is to be understood), but the example

---

[5]Cf. most recently Hurd, *op. cit.*, pp. 186-93.

[6]Cf. Hurd, *op. cit.*, p. 193: "It seems hardly likely that if cries of 'Jesus be cursed!' had filled either the church or the synagogue, the Corinthians would have been at a loss to know whether such an utterance were the work of the Holy Spirit." He is probably right to take πνευματικῶν in 12:1 as masculine (p. 194, note 1). I think 12:2, 3 is a sarcastic statement of what should be obvious; see below, pp. 251-52.

[7]There would be an easy slide from "*a* sign" to "*the* sign," then as now.

[8]Paul three times mentions the traditional category σημεῖα καὶ τέρατα. 2 Thessalonians 2:9 (σημείοις καὶ τέρασι ψεύδους) and 2 Corinthians 12:12 (where ἐν πάσῃ ὑπομονῇ are the operative words) show its ambivalence for him. Romans 15:19 stands in the shadow of 2 Corinthians 10-12. The only other reference is the highly critical 1 Corinthians 1:22, 'Ιουδαῖοι σημεῖον αἰτοῦσιν, except for 2 Thessalonians 3:17 and Romans 4:11, which are not relevant.

given in 24-25 concerns solely its effect on an unbeliever who might come in.[9]

The one and only reason which Paul gives for allowing the use of tongues in the presence of others is that they may serve to attract the attention of unbelievers, and even this seems to be curiously at variance with the later comment that 'outsiders' coming in will think people who talk in tongues are mad—unless verse 22 refers to one single person talking in tongues and verse 23 to the confusion when several speak together.[10]

But this suggestion does not cover the apparent discrepancy between verses 22 and 24-25, and ignores the quotation at verse 21 from Isaiah 28:11-12.

A more hopeful line is to start from this quotation, though it is not certain how the passage should be understood. Perhaps we can follow Robertson and Plummer.[11] Isaiah's opponents are supposed to have jeered at him for repeating the same simple message, "we are not children, requiring to be told the same thing over and over again." Then he threatens them with the terrible gibberish (like stammering) of foreign invaders.[12] That is, Paul warns the Corinthians that according to scripture tongues are meant as a sign for (= against!)[13] those who reject God's simple message, not, as the Corinthians assume, as a sign for the benefit of believers; whereas prophecy *is* a sign for believers in the effect it has on unbelievers. On this view he is deliberately exploiting the ambiguity of ἄπιστος ("disbeliever," verse 22; "unbeliever," verses 23-24) and of the dative, but such shifts of meaning are common enough in Paul.[14] There is no need to sup-

---

[9]Dr. J. M. Ford, in *Journal of Theological Studies*, 17 (1966): 71ff., argues that ἄπιστος is not generally used for "unbeliever" and in certain contexts may represent '*am ha-'aretz*. This is at first sight attractive for 1 Corinthians 15:24, since ἰδιώτης can also bear this meaning (S.-B. III, pp. 455-56), but 14:22 is decisive for "unbeliever" (cf. 2 Corinthians 4:4). The precise meaning of ἰδιώτης is not important for my argument.

[10]*Expository Times, loc. cit.*; cf. R. A. Knox's note in his translation of the N.T.

[11]*I.C.C. 1 Corinthians* (Edinburgh 1914): 317.

[12]Cf. Isaiah 33:19; Jeremiah 5:15; Deuteronomy 28:49.

[13]Cf. E.-B. Allo, *Première Épître aux Corinthiens* (Paris 1934): 365: "ici σημεῖον est simplement un signe de l'activité divine, prodigieux ou non, donné en faveur ou en défaveur de quelqu'un, avec datif *commodi* ou *incommodi*."

[14]Cf. νόμος, Romans 7:21-8:3. The Greek dative leaves much to the imagination; we could translate simply "with reference to." Luke 11:30 is similarly ambiguous; so is the dative after εἰς μαρτύριον.

pose he genuinely thinks that tongues are intended by God to harden un-believers. The case in verse 23 is hypothetical; his concern is with the Corinthians.

According to Allo,[15] they should recognize that they are in the same boat as the people of Jerusalem threatened by the Assyrian invaders. What they take as a sign of the divine presence and favour is a divine warning. Is it perhaps, he asks, the sign that God is abandoning the community and letting it return to paganism, to the state of ἄπιστος who is led astray by demons (cf. 12:3)?

However, it is hard to believe that even Paul could have expected his hearers to read so much out of two verses of Isaiah—unless they were al-ready familiar with the passage. In fact, just as it is unlikely that Paul is introducing the "sign" question of his own initiative, it is also unlikely that he is introducing this quotation out of the blue. But the context in which they are likely to have been familiar with it turns out to be rather different from the original context in Isaiah, and points to a rather different inter-pretation.[16]

---

[15]*Op. cit.*, pp. 365-66.

[16]Various interpretations, of course, have been suggested. One of the most attractive is to take Isaiah 28 strictly in context, as Dr. T. F. Glasson suggests in a letter: "The Cor-inthian Christians and the men of Isaiah 28 were alike in despising the plain word of preach-ing in their desire for something more advanced . . . it is the unbelieving among the community of God's people (as in Isaiah 28) who are intended; similarly 'the believers' could mean people like the hearer of 1 Corinthians 14:24-25 who comes to faith through the word of prophecy. Isaiah 28-29 is a passage referred to a number of times in the N.T. . . . the readers could be expected to know the context." But (*a*) this involves a proleptic sense for οἱ πιστεύοντες, which is as far as I know without parallel, and surely impos-sible—though it is supported by J. Héring, *La Première Épître de Saint Paul aux Corin-thiens* (Neuchâtel 1959): "ceux qui sont en train de devenir chrétiens." (*b*) The "prophecy" discussed in 12-14 is not "the plain word of preaching," or the simple message of 1-2, but an enthusiastic and rowdy phenomenon; cf. K. Lake, *The Earlier Epistles of St. Paul* (Lon-don 1914): 204, "The difference between glossolalia and prophecy was only that glosso-lalia was unintelligible." There is no hint that the Corinthians were overvaluing tongues at the *expense* of prophecy; those who despised prophecy would have despised tongues too (cf. 1 Thessalonians 5:19-20; 1 Corinthians 14:39). Paul was perhaps the first to distinguish sharply between them. (*c*) "Knowledge of context" in N.T. times is a doubtful quantity. It seems to be *selective*, related to the purpose for which the passage was used—in this case anti-Jewish apologetic. On the whole question see James Barr, *Old and New in Interpre-tation* (London 1966): 142-43. "It seems that we generally have to see the use of quotations not against the context from which the quotations were taken, which is the modern literary approach, but against the context of what the early Christians were doing with them" (143).

The text of the quotation is that neither of the LXX nor of the MT, though closer to the latter, which reads, "Nay but by men of strange lips and with an alien tongue the Lord will speak to this people, to whom he has said, 'This is rest; give rest to the weary; and this is repose'; yet they would not hear." Paul's version (1) gives "I will speak" for "the Lord will speak" (2) omits "to whom he has said . . . ," so that "yet they would not hear" now refers not to the Lord but the men of alien tongues, and (3) adds οὕτως—"not *even so* will they hear." This might look like his own translation, modified for the occasion, though Origen said he found it in Aquila and in the rest of the Greek editions, except the LXX.[17] However, Paul rounds it off with another addition, λέγει Κύριος, which according to E. Earle Ellis[18] may identify it as a "testimonium" from the Church's anti-Jewish apologetic. He points out that there are nine N.T. quotations, four of them Pauline, which contain the words λέγει Κύριος, and they have features in common:

(1) Their text differs from both LXX and MT.

(2) In some of them, including all four of Paul's, λέγει Κύριος is neither part of the O.T. citation nor an introductory formula.

(3) Their O.T. source is often within a "testimony" pattern evident elsewhere—Isaiah 28:16 and 29:9-14 were well used.[19]

(4) The subject matter fits the Church's anti-Jewish polemic. The majority are related to the "Temple" typology, in which the Christian community is viewed as God's new temple, cf. 2 Corinthians 6:16-18. Of Paul's three other instances, two are concerned with divine judgement—both moralized, but both suitable for earlier apologetic use[20]—and the third is

---

[17]*Philocalia* 9:2. The LXX has . . . διὰ φαυλισμὸν χειλέων διὰ γλώσσης ἑτέρας, ὅτι λαλήσουσιν τῷ λαῷ τούτῳ, λέγοντες αὐτῷ. Τοῦτο τὸ ἀνάπαυμα τῷ πεινῶντι καὶ τοῦτο τὸ σύντριμμα, καὶ οὐκ ἠθέλησαν ἀκούειν.

[18]*Paul's Use of the Old Testament* (Edinburgh 1957): 107-13.

[19]Cf. C. H. Dodd, *According to the Scriptures* (London 1952): 41-43, 83-84.

[20](a) Romans 12:19, = Deuteronomy 32:35: Ἐμοὶ ἐκδίκησις, ἐγὼ ἀνταποδώσω, λέγει Κύριος. This citation is closer to MT and Aramaic Targum than to LXX. It occurs also at Hebrews 10:30, which adds κρινεῖ Κύριος τὸν λαόν αὐτοῦ from the following verse. In context, verse 35 refers not to Israel but her enemies, and κρινεῖ in verse 36 means "vindicate." But taken out of context the five lines verses 35-36a make a very satisfactory warning of divine judgement impending on Israel (or later, as in Hebrews, the Church). (b) Romans 14:11 = Isaiah 45:23 + 49:18 or Deuteronomy 32:40: ὅτι ἐμοὶ

1 Corinthians 14:21, where the anti-Jewish application is obvious. If Jews criticized Christian glossolalia, then Isaiah's words, suitably modified, could be effectively turned against them: tongues are a sign of divine judgment on Jerusalem. This old apologetic, I suggest, is now deliberately turned against the Corinthian Christians by Paul.

We must ask later how such an apologetic might have become familiar at Corinth. Let us now expound 1 Corinthian 15:20-25 more fully.

Verse 20, μὴ παιδία γίνεσθε ταῖς φρεσίν, ἀλλὰ . . . τέλειοι. This picks up 2:6ff. and 3:1-3, with the contrast between πνευματικοί and τέλειοι, and σάρκινοι and νήπιοι; perhaps also 13:11, ὅτε ἤμην μήπιος, ἐλάλουν ὡς νήπιος. The Corinthians claim to be both πνευματικοί and τέλειοι, and count tongues as a sign of this.[21]

Verse 21. "Consider what scripture says about tongues." He quotes a text which has been used by Christians to justify glossolalia against Jewish aspersions and to turn the tables.

Verse 22. He then goes on to show that this text recoils on its Christian users if they go further and claim that tongues are "a sign for believers," as proof of pneumatic status and authority. Scripture shows that the only sign-value of tongues intended by God is for (or against) *un*believers. There

---

κάμψει πᾶν γόνυ, καὶ πᾶσα γλῶσσα ἐξομολογήσεται τῷ θεῷ—the LXX A text, apart from a change in word-order, used again christologically at Philemon 2:10-11. The citation is preceded by ζῶ ἐγώ, λέγει Κύριος, perhaps a conflation of 49:18, though the phrase is quite common—in which case λέγει Κύριος does belong to the O.T. text cited. The words may at one stage have been used in context, to justify the Gentile Mission as a sign of the eschatological glorification of Israel; this is the reference of 49:18 and of 45:14, alluded to at 1 Corinthians 14:25. On the other hand, ζῶ ἐγώ may have been conflated from Deuteronomy 32:40 and λέγει Κύριος added, as to Deuteronomy 32:35, under the conditions of Christian prophecy discussed by Ellis. The two passages are fairly similar in language and spirit, and were perhaps used together as announcing judgment on Israel—or rather misused: the Isaiah passage in context announces *salvation* to Israel even more obviously than Deuteronomy 32. It is interesting that they were both used by Paul so close together with so similar a purpose.

[21]R. M. Grant, in *Harvard Theological Review*, 39 (1946): 71ff., suggests that the enthusiasts at Corinth were using the saying of Jesus which lies behind Mark 10:15 and parallels to justify their emphasis on glossolalia. Jeremias interprets "unless you become like little children" as "unless you learn to say Abba," and many connect Galatians 4:6 and Romans 8:15 (κράζομεν Αββα ὁ Πατήρ) with glossolalia. But this "cry," however enthusiastic, is still intelligible, and Paul connects tongues not with childish babble but with foreign languages, in particular that of the angels (13:1), cf. J. G. Davies, *Journal of Theological Studies*, N.S. m (2962): 228-31.

is, however, sign-value for believers in prophecy.[22] Verses 23-25 show from hypothetical cases how this would work out in practice.

Verse 23. "So if the whole congregation is assembled"—party strife has not gone so far that this is unthinkable—"and all who speak speak in tongues, and ἰδιῶται[23] or ἄπιστοι come in, will they not say that you are mad?" In other words, unbelievers will be confirmed in their unbelief; tongues will have the effect of the σημεῖα καὶ τέρατα ψεύδους which will attend the coming of "that wicked man," according to 2 Thessalonians 2:9ff.; though, as we said, it is pressing Paul's argument ludicrously far to suggest he had the divine hardening of unbelievers in mind; his aim is simply to ridicule the Corinthian position.

Verses 24-25. On the other hand, if the meeting were given over wholly to prophecy, then the effect on the unbeliever would be conviction of sin (ἐλέγχεται), judicial examination (ἀνακρίνεται), and exposure of his inmost being (τὰ κρυπτὰ τῆς καρδίας αὐτοῦ φανερὰ γίνεται); "and so falling on his face, he will worship God and declare that God is really among you." Three comments may be made on this.

(1) "Examination" (ἀνακρίνειν) has already come up at 2:15: ὁ πνευματικὸς ἀνακρίνει μὲν πάντα, αὐτὸς δ' ὑπ' οὐδενὸς ἀνακρίνεται, and at 4:3, 4: "it is a very small thing that I should be examined by you or any human court. I do not even examine myself . . . it is the Lord who examines me"; cf. 9:3: "my reply to those who would examine me"—in a passage where Paul compares himself with the rest of the Apostles, including Cephas. Chapter 4:5 continues with some of the phrases of 14:24: "Therefore do not pronounce judgement before time, before the Lord comes, who will bring to light τὰ κρυπτὰ τοῦ σκότους, καὶ φανερώσει τὰς βουλὰς τῶν καρδιῶν" cf. 14:24; τὰ κρυπτὰ τῆς καρδίας αὐτοῦ φανερὰ γίνεται.

It looks as if some Corinthians were claiming, as πνευματικοί, the right of judging others, including Paul, and of not themselves being called to account (cf. 14:37-38), and were insisting that the sign for believers of

---

[22]It is beside the point to object that prophecy does have value for unbelievers also. Οὐ τοῖς ἀπίστοις is put in for rhetorical balance, and anyway the point is not value in general but sign-value.

[23]Ἰδιῶται are introduced simply to weave in the argument about "edification" from verse 16.

pneumatic status and authority was the ability to speak withtongues.[24] In reply Paul maintained that ἀναϰρίνειν was a function carried out by *prophets*, and his words in 4:5 show that he saw it as *God* acting in them, an anticipation of final Judgement.

(2) In the light of this, verse 24 can hardly refer to the practice of mind-reading, as many commentators suppose. Certainly mind-reading was part of a prophet's stock-in-trade,[25] but as Allo remarks, "quel profane aurait alors voulu se risquer en de telles réunions?"[26] Here surely it is much more what is described at Hebrews 4:12-13: the word of God, spoken by the prophets, sifts the purposes and thoughts of the heart, and cuts away the veils men put between themselves and God. "And so falling on his face, he will worship God and declare that God is really among you."

(3) Verse 25 is a clear allusion to Isaiah 45:14: "the Sabaeans . . . will bow down to you . . . saying 'God is with you only . . . ,' " LXX . . . προσϰυνήσουσίν σοι . . . ὅτι ἐω σοὶ ὁ θεός ἐστιν (cf. Zechariah 8:20-23). Here is a real "sign for believers" in the conversion of unbelievers, the fulfillment of the eschatological promises of scripture, rather than in showy performances which profit only the performer. The collection for Jerusalem, on which Paul was already engaged (16:1ff.), was intended at least partly as an acted sign in fulfillment of related Isaianic prophecies of the Gentiles flowing to Jerusalem with their tribute.[27]

II

I want now to ask how this overvaluation of tongues arose at Corinth, and who might have used this anti-Jewish "testimonium," which Paul naughtily twisted against the Corinthians. Apollos is described as ζέων τῷ πνεύματι (Acts 18:25), which may be a technical term for Christian en-

---

[24]It is possible that many were disposed to accept their claims. Chapter 12:15, "Because I am not a hand, I do not belong to the body," may indicate self-depreciation in those who had not received the gift—or, more likely, incontinent seeking of the gift. Does 14:12, ζηλωταί ἐστε πνευμάτων (cf. 12:31, 13:4, 14:1), point to rivalries about *charismata*?

[25]Cf., in addition to the O.T. examples, John 4:19 and 2:25; and Luke 7:39, 40, where Jesus reads the thoughts of the Pharisee, who said to himself that if Jesus were a prophet he would be able to "read" the woman who was touching him.

[26]*Op. cit.*, p. 367.

[27]Cf. J. Munck, *Paulus und die Heilsgeschichte*, E. T. *Paul and the Salvation of Mankind*, (London 1959): 301-305; K. Nickle, *The Collection*, (London 1966): 129-42.

thusiasm (cf. Romans 12:11), but from 1 Corinthians 3-4 and 16:12 he and
Paul seem to have seen eye to eye. The "Christ party" is to my mind an
error of translation.[28] What about Cephas?

T. W. Manson[29] argued that at the time 1 Corinthians was written Paul
was engaged in a struggle with the agents of Palestinian Jewish Christianity, either under the direct leadership or acting in the name of Peter; outwardly it was an attempt to correct various abuses or deficiencies in Corinth,
but beneath the surface it was an attack on Paul himself, a challenge to his
status and authority as an Apostle. In particular, he thought glossolalia was
introduced to Corinth by or in the name of Cephas. This and similar phenomena are Asiatic in origin, not Greek, though they find fertile soil in
Greece, and Paul treats it as something *new*—the fact that he can thank
God he outdoes them all suggests that the practice has not yet reached imposing proportions. Paul is dealing not with "a surfeit of glossolalia at
Corinth, but a demand which was being made on the Church to produce
this particular fruit of the Spirit. I suggest that the demand came from the
leaders of the Cephas party, and was part of the concerted move to instill
Palestinian piety and orthodoxy into the Corinthian Church. Paul's converts were being told that here was something most important, indeed absolutely essential to the Christian life" (perhaps also that this was the true
mark of a πνευματικός and a sign to believers of his authority?).

C. K. Barrett, in his article "Cephas in Corinth,"[30] strongly supported
this general approach, and showed good reason to suppose that Cephas had
actually taught and baptized in Corinth, but judged the particular suggestion about glossolalia, though attractive, to be open to question because it
is not certain whether it was practiced in the Palestinian Church—referring
to M. Goguel (p. 8). But Goguel's[31] arguments do not stand up. They are

[28]Cf. Hurd, *op. cit.*, pp. 103-106. He also regards Cephas as a red herring.

[29]In "The Corinthian Correspondence (1)," *Bulletin of the John Rylands University Library*, 46 (1941), reprinted in *Studies in the Gospels and Epistles* (Manchester 1962), esp.
pp. 197-207.

[30]In *Abraham Unser Vater*, Festschrift for O. Michael (Leiden 1963): 1-12; cf. his own
Rylands lecture of November 1963 (*Bulletin of the John Rylands University Library*), 46:
296-97, n. 3, where he mentioned Manson's suggestion without qualifying his approval.

[31]See *La Naissance du Christianisme* (Paris 1946): 112-15, and his essay in *Mélanges
Franz Cumong*, (Brussels 1936): 209-23.

based (a) on rejection of the Acts evidence, which, however justifiable the rejection, cannot *disprove* the practice (and it is not without weight that Luke thought it happened there); and (b) on the dogma of contemporary Judaism that prophecy and inspiration belonged to the past—an assumption which needs much qualification,[32] especially for Galilee. More positively, it seems clear that both the parties in the original Church—those who wished to continue within the framework of Judaism and the Torah, and those who felt the need to break away—were equally based on the Spirit. As E. Käsemann[33] has said, we can see "daß nicht der Enthusiasmus als solche beide Gruppen unterscheidet. Er ist (zum mindesten ursprünglich) beiden gemeinsam." Later James succeeded Peter and Nomismus replaced Enthusiasmus, but in the beginning glossolalia would surely have been at home in either camp.

What did distinguish the two groups was their attitude to a Gentile Mission. The one regarded the conversion of the Gentiles as God's own final act, for which the gathering of the lost sheep of the house of Israel was preparatory; a direct mission to Gentiles would therefore be premature. The other maintained that with Easter and the giving of the Spirit the end of the world had broken in, and the Gentile Mission to that extent bore the character of an eschatological sign.[34] That Paul should introduce this motif (1 Corinthians 14:25) in a critique of the sign-value of tongues is therefore fully consistent with Manson's thesis: the demand in Peter's name for a more Palestinian pattern, including glossolalia, at Corinth was going back on the agreement about the Gentile Mission described at Galatians 2:7-9.

One minor reservation, however, is necessary: it is hard to believe that there was no glossolalia in Corinth or other Pauline churches before Cephas appeared on the scene. We must briefly discuss the passages which may be relevant.

(1) Galatians 4:6, "God sent the Spirit of his Son into our hearts, κρᾶζον, Αββα ὁ Πατήρ," cf. Romans 8:15, ἐλάβετε πνεῦμα υἱοθεσίας, ἐν ᾧ κράζομεν, Αββα ὁ Πατήρ. Κράζειν indicates excitement,

---

[32]See, e.g., W. D. Davies, *Paul and Rabbinic Judaism* (London 1955): 204-17.

[33]"Die Anfänge christlicher Theologie," *Zeitschrift fuer Theologie und Kirche* (November 1960): 168.

[34]Käsemann, *op. cit.*, p. 167.

and Abba was a foreign word to Greeks—but not unintelligible surely.[35] Decisive, however, against a primary reference to tongues is the fact that in both passages Paul is writing of the basic experience common to *all* Christians. It is possible that in the early Palestinian days tongues were a general Christian endowment, and just possible that this was also the case in Galatia. But it is quite impossible that, if this phrase referred to glossolalia, Paul should have so used it writing from Corinth, after having written 1 Corinthians 12-14: Romans 8:15 refers, like 1 Corinthians 12, to the Spirit received by all Christians in baptism.

(2) The same consideration applies to Romans 8:26:[36] αθτὸ τὸ Πνεῦμα ὑπερεντυγχάνει στεναγμοῖς ἀλαλήτοις. At first sight this looks more like glossolalia, since it is *prayer* (cf. 1 Corinthians 14:14) and "to God" (cf. 1 Corinthians 14:2). But a closer look makes it less likely.

(*a*) The commentaries reveal several other possible interpretations of ἀλαλήτοις—an odd word to use of λαλεῖν γλώσσῃ.

(*b*) Ετεναγμοῖς refers back to 8:22-23: "the whole creation *groans* . . . even we who have the Spirit as ἀπαρχή groan,* as we wait . . . In the same way the Spirit helps us . . . he himself intercedes for us with wordless *groans.*" Cf. 2 Corinthians 5:2, 4, where the groaning certainly has nothing to do with glossolalia. So far as we can tell from 1 Corinthians 14 and Acts (2:11, 10:46) glossolalia was essentially praise, not groaning under the burden of mortality.

(*c*) Paul goes on to say (8:28) that the Spirit[37] πάντα συνεργεῖ for those who love God. The passage tells of the Spirit's general help and co-operation—though glossolalia could be in mind as a particular mode of helping.

But the conclusive point is that the whole of 8 is concerned with the Spirit which every Christian received (in baptism), and therefore glossolalia can at most be in the background.[38]

---

[35]See above, p. 244, n. 1.

[36]Not strictly relevant to my immediate inquiry, since the Church at Rome was not a Pauline foundation. But he appeals where he can to common ground, and if 16 is part of the letter to Rome a large number of Christians there came from his sphere.

[37]The *New English Bible* is surely right to take πνεῦμα as subject.

[38]The ᾠδαί πνευματικαί of Colossians 3:16 could be "in tongues" (cf. 1 Corin-

(3) There is, however, a much more probable reference to tongues at 1 Thessalonians 5:19-20: τὸ πνεῦμα μὴ σβέννυτε,[39] προφητείας μὴ ἐξουθενεῖτε. Tongues and prophecy are coupled at 1 Corinthians 14:39, ζηλοῦτε τὸ προφητεύειν, καὶ τὸ λαλεῖν μὴ κωλύετε γλώσσαις, and in Acts—at 19:6, and by implication in 2, where tongues are interpreted as the fulfillment of a promise of the pouring out of the Spirit, with special emphasis on prophesying; καὶ προφητεύσουσιν is added to the Joel quotation at 2:18.[40] There is no reason to suppose that the categories were clearly defined; in a state of general excitement and enthusiasm one could pass over into the other, the intelligible into the unintelligible. In an original Palestinian community everyone is likely to have been involved; only when Christianity moved to foreign soil where some were cool (1 Thessalonians 5:19) would glossolalia have become a controversial sign of the Spirit. Perhaps it was not specially singled out from other enthusiastic phenomena until elevated by or in the name of Cephas at Corinth, and in reply played down by Paul in favour of prophecy.

To sum up, it is not necessary to go as far as Manson in suggesting that Cephas *introduced* glossolalia at Corinth, or that "Paul had said little or nothing about it when he was with them."[41] Manson does not distinguish

---

thians 14:15)—provided we take them with ᾄδοντες, like the *New English Bible*, and not with διδάσκοντες καὶ νουθετοῦντες ἑαυτούς, like Lightfoot. At Ephesians 5:19 πνευματικαῖς is omitted by 𝔓⁴⁶ B d and by *New English Bible*. If it is retained, the Pentecostal flavour of verse 18 makes a reference to tongues possible. In neither case is there a necessary reference. At Ephesians 6:18 ἐν παντὶ καιρῷ makes a reference to "praying in tongues" (1 Corinthians 14:14) impossible.

[39]If this can be accepted, then Romans 12:11, τῷ πνεύματι ζέοντες, could be a reference too.

[40]It is hard to see how a sudden outburst of glossolalia, hitherto unexperienced, could have been at once interpreted as the fulfillment of Joel's prophecy. Passages about the unintelligible language of foreign invaders lay readier to hand (Isaiah 28:11, 33:19; Jeremiah 5:15; Deuteronomy 28:49, cf. above p. 242), and the original interpretation is more likely to have been as a warning of judgment against unrepentant Israel. But Peter's speech in Acts 2 is widely recognized to be a later construction—cf. Barnabas Lindars, *New Testament Apologetic* (London 1961): 36-59—and so the coupling of tongues and prophecy there is evidence only for Luke's view. But there is no reason why this should not have been a primitive, even if not the original, view. Πνεῦμα and πνευματικός may well for a time have carried a primary reference to tongues as the most obvious φανέρωσις of the Spirit; cf. 1 Corinthians 14:37, εἴ τις δοκεῖ προφήτης εἶναι ἢ πνευματικός: tongues and prophecy are the two activities which have just been regulated, so πνευματικός may be used by Paul here sarcastically as the self-designation of a tongue-speaker.

[41]*Op. cit.*, p. 105. Cf. Munck, *op. cit.*, p. 35, n. 1: "Did the Corinthians know, before Paul wrote those words (1 Corinthians 14:18ff.), that he had the gift of tongues?"

glossolalia and the problem of glossolalia. The practice may already have existed in a small and unpopular way (14:39, τὸ λαλεῖν μὴ κωλύετε, cf. 1 Thessalonians 5:19). The problem, as he rightly saw, was new, and lay not in a surfeit of, but in a demand for, glossolalia, and this cannot be accounted for simply by the Greek temperament. But before agreeing with Manson that Cephas was the source of the demand for glossolalia, we must come to terms with J. C. Hurd's contention that, paradoxically, it was Paul.

III

The argument of Hurd's *The Origin of 1 Corinthians* is so close-knit that it is unfair to isolate his treatment of 14, and although any brief statement of his position is likely to sound unconvincing, we must make the attempt. From a careful literary analysis he concludes that 7-16 is Paul's unified reply to a letter from Corinth (together with oral reports, which he deals with in 1-6 and 11)—a letter which was not politely asking for arbitration or advice but reacting with puzzled hostility to his own letter, mentioned at 5:9. In this "Previous Letter" he has executed a *volte-face*. On his first (and so far his only) visit to Corinth he had preached an enthusiastic gospel, about a Lord who would soon be revealed in glory, and against whose coming Christians were preserved from death by baptism and eucharist. On this basis he had taught a strenuous morality, combining asceticism in family life with emancipation from Jewish tabus, and encouraged an enthusiastic form of worship in which women, and glossolalia, played an unrestricted part; and naturally there had been no cause to work out any teaching about the bodily resurrection of believers. But now in the Previous Letter, he enjoined a normal married life, avoidance of association with immoral men, i.e., unbelievers,[42] abstinence from εἰδωλόθυτα, and a more sober and masculine conduct of worship; he outlined a doctrine of resurrection, on the same lines as 1 Thessalonians 4:13-18; finally he announced his collection for the poor of the Jerusalem Church.

Behind this *volte-face* Hurd sees, along with delay of the Parousia and the natural development of Paul's thought, the Apostolic Decrees of Acts 15. In order to buy recognition at Jerusalem of his apostolate and his Churches—perhaps also because he saw that Jewish-Christian criticism of

---

[42]On this view, the likelihood that 2 Corinthians 6:14-8:1 belongs to the "Previous Letter" is very strong; cf. Hurd, pp. 235-37.

the conduct of these Churches was not unfounded—he tried to impose by letter a more Jewish pattern of behaviour and of relationships with unbelievers, and agreed to organize a collection for the Jerusalem poor (cf. Galatians 2:1-10?—pp. 254-70).

The Corinthians not unnaturally asked him to explain himself in the light of his previous practice, and 1 Corinthians with all its bluster and demands for "maturity" was the result. There was neither a Hellenistic nor a Jewish "party" at Corinth, simply one all too Pauline Church.[43] With regard to tongues then, Cephas is irrelevant. Paul was trying to justify his new position without denying his previous practice (14:5, 18, 39); his concessions, and the variety, and varying weight, or the arguments employed show, as in 11:2-16, that he was under pressure.

On Hurd's analysis of 12-14, Paul's two main concerns were the need for maturity and the danger of idolatry.

(A) "The three chapters form one long attack upon the notion that speaking in tongues was the single or the best manifestation of the Spirit at work in the Church. On the contrary, Paul maintained, glossolalia is the least gift of all (12); the highest gift is love (13); and, moreover, love, when it is present, leads to the suppression of the public practice of speaking in tongues (14)."[44] Why did they take this gift as the real mark of the Spirit? Hurd points out that in all his long attack Paul never directly criticized it (pp. 188-89), and concludes that he did not wish to contradict himself. Paul himself said of his first visit to Corinth, "My speech and my message were not in plausible words of wisdom, but in demonstration of the Spirit and power" (2:4). The nature of this "demonstration of the Spirit" is indicated by his statement, "I thank God that I speak in tongues more than you all" (14:18). It appears therefore that Paul spoke with tongues, that he considered glossolalia a prime "demonstration of the Spirit," and that he

---

[43]Hurd can claim the support of Munck—*op. cit.*, chapter 5, "Die Gemeinde ohne Parteien"—and the parties must not be overemphasized: they could still meet and be addressed as one Church. But his treatment of Cephas and his party is unsatisfactory (pp. 99-101, 269-70). Barrett's articles were not available to him, and he barely mentions Manson's theory about the introduction of tongues (p. 101).

[44]P. 192. He shows brilliantly that the purpose of 12 is not to defend the unity of the Church but to encourage diversity, against the narrowness of the Corinthians' view of the operation of the Spirit (pp. 190-92). He is also very good on the fervour of Paul's denigration of tongues and the variety of his arguments in 14 (pp. 188-89).

encouraged the Corinthians to follow his example (p. 281). In the meantime Paul, but not the Corinthians, had matured. "Once he had preached
in simple terms; once he had relied on the 'demonstration of the Spirit and
power'; once he had spoken in tongues (13:11). Now, however, he sought
to communicate mature doctrine (2:6, 7; 15:51, 'mystery'); now he preferred to speak in tongues no longer (13:11, 'I gave up childish ways';
14:19, 'I would rather speak five words with my mind'; and 14:6)." However, they had failed to mature (3:2, 3), and he urged them to grow out of
their childishness (13:2, 4:16, 14:20: pp. 243-44).

(B) What was the context of his attack on tongues? Hurd thinks it was
the danger of idolatry, which lay behind 8-10 and 11:2-16 also (pp. 227-
28).

(a) 12:2, "You know that when you were heathen, you were led astray
to dumb idols." An explanation is needed why he should begin the whole
discussion in this way.

(b) "Paul's discussion of ideal worship appears set in contrast to a
background of the indecency, shamefulness and disorder which characterized pagan worship" (14:33, 40).

(c) Chapter 12 seems to answer some such question περὶ
πνευματικῶν[45] as "How is it possible to test for the Spirit or to distinguish between spiritual men? You yourself spoke freely in the Spirit without making such distinctions" (p. 293, cf. pp. 193-95). This suggests that
in the Previous Letter[46] he had denounced the similarity of their enthusiastic worship to that of idolaters and they had objected that this distinction between enthusiasms was an impossible one.

This is an attractive approach, and fatal to my argument: it disposes of
Cephas, and it makes clear that Paul had turned completely against glossolalia—the concessions he made were simply to soften his self-contra-
dictions. However it is open to serious question. Let us start with (B).

(B) 1. Hurd's reconstruction of the Corinthians' *question* does not fit
his reconstruction of their *position*, which he rightly states, on the basis of
12, as that "glossolalia is the main (or only) evidence of possession by the

---

[45]I think he is right to take πνευματικῶν as masculine (p. 194, n. 1).

[46]He reconstructs its gist as "Do not quench the Spirit, but test everything. Do not abandon yourselves to pagan enthusiasm" (p. 292). His theory that 1 Thessalonians had a special relationship to the Previous Letter (pp. 231-33) is very interesting.

Spirit . . . only those Christians who have this gift are to be classed as spiritual" (p. 193). This position requires a question not "How can we distinguish between spiritual men?" but "How can we tell who is spiritual?" It is not a matter of distinguishing between spiritual men, but between spiritual and non-spiritual men.

2. Chapter 12 is not really concerned with "testing." Πάντα δοκιμάζετε of 1 Thessalonians 5:21 is of dubious relevance; 1 Corinthians 12:1-3 provides no help for an inquiry such as is enjoined at 1 John 4:1. Although Hurd recognizes that ἀνάθεμα 'Ιησοῦς is simply the hypothetical opposite of Κύριος 'Ιησοῦς, not a real case (p. 193, cited above, note 2) he goes on: "Paul intended to emphasize to the Corinthians that before they became Christians they might have been deceived about spirits, but now they should know that the Spirit shows himself by the results he produces" (pp. 193-94). He fails to see that the criterion provided is hopelessly wide:[47] it covers every baptized Christian who does not renounce his Lord—and *that* must be the point. 12:3a is so painfully obvious that it can only be sarcastic; this impression is reinforced by γνωρίζω, which should mean "reveal"; cf. 15:1, where again he is telling them, not without sarcasm, something they know very well already. 12:3b *should* be obvious, on the Pauline view of baptism, and the rest of the chapter rubs it in.

3. Chapter 12:2, therefore cannot be a warning against idolatry. I accept gratefully from Hurd the veiled hostility of the Corinthians' question, but reconstruct it as "How are *we* to tell who is πνευματικός? God has given tongues as a (or the) sign for believers," or the like. Paul replies with heavy sarcasm, "About πνευματικοί, I don't want you to remain in ignorance. You know how you used to be dragged off to dumb idols in your heathen days [i.e. were liable to delusion, incapable of the simplest discrimination—N.B. *dumb* idols,[48] perhaps in contrast to the God who speaks]. Therefore I reveal to you that no one is πνευματικός who curses

---

[47]Cf. Héring, *op. cit.*, p. 108, "Il va sans dire que le critère indiqué n'est pas suffisant"; K. Lake, *The Earlier Epistles of St. Paul* (London, 1914) says "it is obvious that this simple test was likely to prove insufficient" (p. 205), without drawing the equally obvious conclusion that Paul's intention was different.

[48]Άφωνα is not merely *epitheton ornans* (in which case it would be ill chosen): Paul is consciously exercising his Jewish contempt for pagan stupidity.

Jesus,[49] and no one can confess Jesus in baptism without being πνευματικός.'' In the whole of 12-14 there is no other indication that *idolatrous*
enthusiasm is Paul's concern. Εὐσχημόνως (14:40) is much too general;
and 14:33 and 40 refer equally to prophecy—as Lake pointed out, the difference between the two was only that glossolalia was unintelligible.[50]
Certainly the question needs to be asked why Paul should begin the whole
discussion with a reference to idolatry (p. 227). The answer, I think, is not
so much fear of idolatry as disparagement of tongues by insinuation: the
practices they value so highly are no better than the weak and beggarly[51]
transports[52] of paganism. How much sharper the sarcasm if these practices
were being demanded by Jerusalem! The same hypothesis explains Paul's
careful avoidance of any direct attack on glossolalia—he was reluctant to
contradict not himself but Cephas.

But even if Hurd's position on idolatry (B) were destroyed, his position on maturity (A) could stand still. It is still possible that the cause of
the Corinthians' exclusive valuation of tongues was Paul's own original
behaviour, but the evidence for this is inevitably even more direct, and the
arguments are even less satisfactory.

(A) 1. ''Once he had preached in simple terms . . . Now, however, he
sought to communicate mature doctrine'' (2:6, 7; 15:51). It is extremely

---

[49]Is there a reference to a saying of Jesus like Mark 9:39? 1 Corinthians 14:39 indicates
there were some who would like to ''forbid'' tongues altogether. Paul's instructions are
ἐντολὴ Κυρίου (verse 37).

[50]*Op. cit.*, p. 204. It is worth noting for contemporary discussion that there is no objection to tongues on the grounds of ''ecstasy,'' or loss of control. Chapter 14 presupposes
that both tongues and prophecy are under control—verses 26-32. The objections are (1)
that tongues are unintelligible, and therefore unhelpful to others; (2) the νοῦς is ἄκαρπος—the man is therefore not making the most of himself.

[51]Robertson and Plummer compare Galatians 4:3. Paul may have in mind the poverty
as well as the blindness of the old situation, on contrast with the richness of the new (cf. 1
Corinthians 1:4-9). In Galatians 4:3-4 the danger is of *renouncing* the new, here of *limiting*
it.

[52]Héring's reading ὡς ἀνήγεσθε, ἀπαγόμενοι, is attractive: ''vous croyiez être trans-
portés au ciel (ἀνήγεσθε), mais en réalité vous étiez victimes des forces du mal (ἀπαγόμενοι) qui vous entraînaient'' (*op. cit.* p. 108). There are similar insinuations at 13:1 where
he compares tongues to the gong and cymbals of pagan worship; at 14:21-22, if εἰς σημεῖον
τοῖς ἀπίστοις refers to the delusion of unbelievers, as in 2 Thessalonians 2:9ff.; at 14:23,
where μαίνεσθε could suggest *demon*-possession (cf. John 10:20); and at 14:39 if, as Hurd
thinks, εὐσχημόνως hints at the indecency of pagan worship.

doubtful that Paul intended any such opposition. His "wisdom" was simply a deeper understanding of the original and only message—Christ crucified.[53]

2. "Once he had relied on the 'demonstration of the Spirit and power' (2:4).'' But these words can hardly be glossed by 14:18 to mean that Paul considered tongues a "prime" demonstration of the Spirit. (a) It is clear from 15 and Acts that tongues belong to the category of prayer and praise, not of preaching, which is the subject of 2:1-5, and are normally unintelligible, where λόγος and κήρυγμα (2:4) involve rational discourse. (b) Paul's contrast is not between intelligible human words and unintelligible Spirit-powered words, but between "the wisdom of this age" and the weakness and foolishness of "the word of the Cross," between human self-confidence and "fear and trembling." 'Απόδειξις πνεύματος καὶ δυνάμεως is better glossed by Romans 1:16—the gospel is δύναμις θεοῦ εἰς σωτηρίαν—and 15:19, ἐν δυνάμει σημείων καὶ τεράτων, ἐν δυνάμει Πνεύματος. The preaching for all its weakness, mediates the judging and saving presence of God. No doubt the σημεῖα in which this σωτηρία expressed itself included tongues, which to this extent would be a (but not a "prime") demonstration of the Spirit.[54] But this is very different from saying Paul's preaching was attested by his own speaking in tongues.

3. "Once he had spoken in tongues . . . now he preferred to do so no longer (13:11; 14:19 and 6).'' But

(a) 14:19 and 6 refer only to the *public* use of tongues. 15:15-18 show Paul still valued the private use, and there is no reason why 14:5, θέλω πάντας ὑμᾶς λαλεῖν γλώσσαις, should not be as sincere as 7:7. There is no evidence that Paul's own glossolalia was ever public, except 2:4, which we have seen is highly doubtful.

(b) 13:2 ὅτε ἤμην νήπιος, ἐλάλουν ὡς νήπιος is not making a statement about Paul's past and present practice as a Christian. It is using the relation between child and adult as a model for the relation between

---

[53]Cf. M. D. Hooker, *Theology*, 69 (January 1966): 19-22.

[54]It is worth noting that Hurd's view also requires considerable development in Paul's doctrine of *Baptism*, which by the time he wrote 1 Corinthians 12 was the one necessary and sufficient mark of being πνευματικός. This is by no means impossible (1 Corinthians 1:17?)—cf. J. Weiss, *History of Primitive Christianity* (London 1937): 2: 622-29.

"now" and "then," when not only tongues but also prophecy and knowledge will be left behind (13:8). There may also be a side-thrust at the Corinthians, if some of them were taking tongues as a sign of deification,[55] a sign that they had already arrived (cf. 4:8; Paul and his contemporaries seem to have thought tongues were the language of the angels, 12:1). If so, Paul would be hinting that such speaking belongs very much to *this* age (cf. 14:20, 3:1-3). But Hurd's reading of 13:11 makes Paul claim for himself already the status of τέλειος ἀνήρ,[56] which he castigates the Corinthians for claiming.

4. "The highest gift is love (13); and, moreover, love, when it is present, leads to the suppression of the public practice of speaking in tongues (14)."[57] But

(a) it is worth insisting that Paul does not call love a χάρισμα. Certainly it is *given* by God, and Paul expresses this by calling it καρπὸς τοῦ πνεύματος (Galatians 5:22). He uses the term χάρισμα τοῦ πνεύματος for activities and powers in which Christians may differ, not for qualities which all Christians should possess or at least cultivate. Love and glossolalia, like mercy and sacrifice, are words of different logical level, and it is misleading to treat them as alternatives.[58]

(b) What 14 in fact lays down is not suppression of public glossolalia but regulation, so that all may profit—and the same applies equally to prophecy (5b, 12, 26-33). The positive statements about tongues can be read as *merely* tactical only if it is certain on other grounds that Paul had completely turned his back on tongues. We have seen that this is not so.

---

[55]Cf. E. Schweizer, *The Body of Christ* (London 1965): 27.

[56]Contrast Philemon 3:12; Ephesians 4:13.

[57]*Op. cit.* p. 192.

[58]At Romans 12:9, ἡ ἀγάπη ἀνυπόκριτος does not refer back to χαρίσματα in verse 6, but begins a new section addressed to all, cf. C. E. B. Cranfield, *A Commentary on Romans 12-13* (*Scottish Journal of Theology*, Occasional Papers no. 12, Edinburgh, 1965), p. 38. At 1 Corinthians 14:1, διώκετε τὴν ἀγάπην καὶ ζηλοῦτε τὰ πνευματικά, the New English Bible blurs the sense by rendering: "Put love first; but there are other gifts of the Spirit at which you should also aim." Διώκειν and ζηλοῦν can be practically synonymous, but διώκειν is more suitable for cases of duty, ζηλοῦν for cases of desire. At 12:31b, ἔτι καθ᾽ ὑπεβολὴν ὁδόν must in the context be a different *kind* of way (cf. Matthew 5:20—a different *kind* of righteousness?). In 13 love is not alternative to tongues, prophecy, knowledge, etc., but a *sine qua non*. Love cannot exist unless expressed in activities, any more than faith can, cf. James 2:18.

If he was attacking not tongues but the Corinthians' estimate[59] of tongues, the positive statements can be allowed their natural weight. We must turn now to the evidence outside 1 Corinthians, which shows that Paul's attitude was reserved, but not negative.

IV

Paul's own attitude can perhaps be inferred from his attitude to the "visions and revelations" and "sign of an apostle" discussed in 2 Corinthians 12; here I follow E. Käsemann's article,[60] "'Die Legitimität des Apostles," especially section 3, "Die Apostelzeichen."

(1) Paul did not deny the authenticating value of σημεῖα καὶ τέρατα, and he reminded the Romans of what Christ had done through him ἐν δυνάμει σημείων καὶ τεράτων, ἐν δυνάμει πνεύματος (Romans 15:19).[61] But this passage must be read in light of 2 Corinthians 12:12, where he said, "In no respect did I fall short of these superlative apostles, even if I am a nobody. Τὰ μὲν σημεῖα τοῦ ἀποστόλου κατειργάσθη ἐν ὑμῖν ἐν πάσῃ ὑπομονῇ, τέρασιν καὶ δυνάμεσιν." The mighty works are all qualified by ὑπομονή[62] just as all the χαρίσματα, according to 1 Corinthians 13, must be qualified by ἀγάπη, of which the culminating mark is πάντα ὑπομένει (verse 7).

(2) His attitude to the particular χάρισμα of tongues is indicated by 2 Corinthians 5:13, εἴτε ἐξέστημεν, θεῷ—cf. 1 Corinthians 14:2 ὁ λαλῶν γλώσσῃ οὐκ ἀνθρώποις λαλεῖ, ἀλλὰ θεῷ . . . πνεύματι λαλεῖ μυστήρια, which Käsemann connects with the experience de-

---

[59]This exclusive valuation of tongues does need explanation. There is no reason to think it would happen naturally—certainly, to Greeks, tongues would be evidence of Spirit-control, but prophecy, for example, was just as "inspired." If it cannot be traced to Paul we must look elsewhere, and "Cephas" fits. Hurd's basic contention is that all the questions at issue in 1 Corinthians can be traced to Paul's original teaching and subsequent development: there is no need to postulate Hellenistic reinterpretation at Corinth, or the influence of Cephas or anyone else. Therefore, if my arguments with regard to glossolalia are sound, they undermine his whole position. But even if this be so, his book is still stimulating and instructive, with a great deal of acute and original perception, especially in the literary analysis.

[60]In Z.N.T.W., 41 (1942): 33-71.

[61]Cf. above, p. 253, on ἐν ἀποδείξει πνεύματος (1 Corinthians 2:4).

[62]Käsemann, op. cit. pp. 61-63; for ὑπομονή, cf. 11:23ff.

scribed at the beginning of 2 Corinthians 12.[63] This experience, though marvelous and significant, was something to keep quiet about, and one may suppose Paul felt the same about tongues.[64]

(3) While Paul recognizes tongues as a charisma, his concept of charisma is essentially different from the Corinthians'. To them it is something extraordinary and supernatural. To Paul it is something more. It includes that, but is essentially the concrete expression of the Church's διακονία[65] (1 Corinthians 12). If εἴτε ἐξέστημεν, θεῷ (2 Corinthians 5:13a) can be compared with 1 Corinthians 14:2, then the other half, εἴτε σωφρονοῦμεν, ὑμῖν, must be compared with 14:3, ὁ δὲ προφητεύων ἀνθρώποις λαλεῖ οἰκοδομήν. . . For the service of others σωφρονεῖν, νοῦς, is essential. Käsemann well says that Paul's insistence on νοῦς must not be taken over-rationalistically: it represents the whole man, in intelligent relationship with his world; without this there can be no opportunity for love.[66]

The "right mind" is emphasized in Romans 12, which was written, significantly, at Corinth: μὴ ὑπερφρονεῖν παρ' ὃ δεῖ φρονεῖν, ἀλλὰ φρονεῖν εἰς τὸ σωφρονεῖν (verse 3). As Cranfield[67] argues, λογικὴ λατρεία (verse 1) means not *spiritual* as opposed to external, but rational as opposed to irrational or ecstatic. Paul continues, "be transformed by the

---

[63]*Op. cit.* pp. 66-68, "Glossolalie und Ekstase . . . repräsentieren das noch nicht enthüllte göttliche Mysterium, sind Hinweise auf bisher nicht angebrochene eschatologische Ereignisse, die mit der Verborgenheit des Paradieses zusammenhängen" (p. 68).

[64]It is possible Paul had kept so quiet about his gift of tongues that his pneumatic status could be called in question—Manson and Munck both think 1 Corinthians 14:18 could be the first the Corinthians had heard of it (above, pp. 249, n. 1). H. J. Schoeps, *Paulus*, E.T. (London 1961): 81ff., thinks "it is just this spirit-derived character of his apostolic ministry—he calls it an office of the Holy Ghost (1 Corinthians 12:4)—which has made him so suspect in the eyes of his Judaizing opponents," and finds confirmation in the pseudo-Clementine literature. But Käsemann is surely right that both Jerusalem and Paul were equally based on the Spirit (above, p. 247). Paul did not parade his private experience till forced to do so in the Corinthian letters, and it is a *later* polemic, based on these letters, which the Pseudo-Clementines reflect.

[65]*Op. cit.* pp. 68-69.

[66]"Denn die Agape kann nicht ohne Einsicht, nicht ohne das σωφρονεῖν sein und nicht ohne den νοῦς, der sich aus der Bezogenheit auf den andern versteht" (p. 69). This is not to say that glossolalia is incompatible with agape, but that glossolalia *by itself* is.

[67]*Op. cit.* (above, p. 254, n. 2), p. 14.

renewal of your νοῦς'' (in glossolalia it is ἄκαρπος, 1 Corinthians 14:14), and the χαρίσματα mentioned (verses 6-8) are προφητεία, διακονία, and then a number of more specific jobs. At verse 9, ἡ ἀγάπη ἀνυπόκριτος introduces a series of qualities and attitudes[68] which can be demanded of all, as opposed to the χαρίσματα which can be expected only of some, and it is here that the only reference to "spiritual enthusiasm" (τῷ πνεύματι ζέοντες, verse 9) is found. It is preceded by "not slack in zeal" and followed by "serving the Lord," lest there should be "any misunderstanding on the part of those who tended to regard exciting and showy ecstasies as the most precious evidence of the Spirit."[69]

V

It remains to outline what can be said of Paul's attitude for guidance in the contemporary debate about Pentecostal phenomena, in particular speaking in tongues.

(1) We must reject any claim that tongues are the exclusive or even the normal sign that a Christian has received the Spirit. But we should beware of setting up Baptism as the criterion, unless we are sure our idea of Baptism is the same as his.

(2) Equally we must reject any claim that tongues are essentially devil-inspired. Any comparison in 1 Corinthians 12-14 with heathen false inspiration is purely a *canard*.

(3) We must recognize the polemical nature of 1 Corinthians 12-14; even if my interpretation of 14:20-25 is unacceptable, it is clear Paul was using arguments of doubtful weight; Hurd well compares 11:2-16. Paul was contesting an abuse of glossolalia, the more dangerous for its backing, which explains his rather indirect attack.

(4) His condemnation of glossolalia is not absolute, but in relation to other charismata. He valued it highly as a private experience, but insofar as it was private it could not effect οἰκοδομή, and he therefore regarded it as inferior to those activities that could. If the practice *were* to help the

---

[68]Cf. above, p. 254, n. 2. "Genuine love" is unfolded in what follows, as at 1 Corinthians 13:4-7.

[69]*Op. cit.* p. 43. I think he is right to read Πνεύματι, against *New English Bible*—cf. τὸ Πνεῦμα μὴ σβέννυτε (1 Thessalonians 5:19), which may well refer to tongues, cf. above, p. 248.

community, as is often reported to be the case today, his attitude might be different.

(5) He does not regard glossolalia, but the Corinthians' estimate and practice of it, as childish (except insofar as we are still in the age of the "child"). There is a certain kind of childlikeness which is necessary, and in an over-cerebral community his attitude might be different from that in one which valued the irrational.

(6) Paul has no notion of a Holy Spirit without concrete manifestations. He wrote to a Church which was rich in all the charismata (1 Corinthians 1:4-9), anxious that they should not narrow their idea of the spiritual, or let it be dominated by the least valuable gift. In less gifted Churches, where there is no such danger, the positive statements about tongues which he allowed himself may be given their natural weight.

(7) But having done all we can to minimize Paul's hostility to tongues, we must still admit that their absence in Romans 12, as compared with 1 Corinthians 12, is most significant. His authority cannot be claimed for regarding glossolalia as a necessary part of Christian life. The most we can say—but with the authority and emphasis of Jesus himself (cf. 15:37-39)— is μὴ κωλύετε. "Do not quench the Spirit, do not despise prophesying, but test everything; hold fast what is good, abstain from every form of evil" (1 Thessalonians 5:19-22).

9

JOHN T. BUNN

Glossolalia in Historical Perspective

QUESTION: What is the first recorded incidence of glossolalia? Most likely answer: The Pentecost account given in Acts 2:1-13.

Many Christians would no doubt be surprised to learn that instances of frenzied speech predate the account of glossolalia in Acts by several hundred years. Although masses of contemporary Christians have been exposed to tongue-speaking, they seem to have little appreciation either for its ancestral heritage or its relatively modern expression in non-Western cultures. In order to assess the validity of the current resurgence of glossolalia, one must have some knowledge of its origin. Even a brief historical review demonstrates its spotted acceptability as a legitimate means of religious expression.

While it is at times suspect to reduce religious phenomena and personalities to categories, this method offers the simpler approach to glossolalia. Where within the broad scope of religious personalities does the glossolalist fit? There is but one class, that order known as prophets. The history of religions is replete with testimony affirming the validity of the prophetic personality as a spokesman of deity. Generally speaking, the communication of deity to or through the prophetic personality occurs when the prophet is in a mental state defined as ecstasy. Literally the word *ecstasy* means "to be beside one's self" or "to be out of one's senses." Pathologically speaking it denotes the state of a person when consciousness is lost by absorption in an idea and as a result the person is insensible to his environment.

Ecstasy may manifest itself in one of two ways, lethargic or orgiastic. Lethargic ecstasy is quiet or contemplative as seen in Israelite classical prophets such as Isaiah or Hosea or in the guru of India. Orgiastic ecstasy is distinguished by heightened physical and emotional states and is to be observed in such religious figures as the Israelite ecstatic prophets and the Muslim dervish. Those who speak in unknown languages (that is, glossolalists) fall under the category of orgiastic prophetic personalities.

There is a well-delineated progression of events related to entrance into a state of orgiastic ecstasy. Ecstasy is seldom, if ever, identifiable in the history of religions as an instantaneous action. The normal process moves along the following lines: (1) quiet meditation, (2) audible or inaudible prayer, and (3) reflection upon deity. Slow rhythmic chants, dance, and/or music may be employed. Drugs or alcohol also may be utilized to assist in inducing the desired state. The state is advanced by an increased tempo in music, chants, and bodily movements accompanied by an increasing rate of respiration and heartbeat. As the state is identified and heightened, it reaches a climax. That climax may be defined as the state of ecstasy. It is in this state that the prophetic personality receives mental impressions. These impressions surface in the form of visions or auditions.[1]

Alfred Guillaume attempts an explanation of ecstasy by affirming that the state cannot be one of dreaming, for the person is in a state of inten-

---

[1]For a full discussion see I. M. Lewis, *Ecstatic Religion* (Baltimore: Penguin Books, 1971).

sified wakefulness. It cannot be defined as hallucination since it is temporary or even momentary enhancement without disintegration of mental capacities. In addition, it cannot be a type of poetical imagination since the state is passive mentally. Ecstasy is rather the enhancement of a state of inspiration.[2]

The practitioners of glossolalia are definitely prophetic. Simply put, wherever one finds religious man, he finds the prophetic personality. Additionally, wherever we find the prophetic personality, we find ecstatic experience. And, wherever we find ecstatic experience, we find evidences of enigmatic prophetic utterance.

MESOPOTAMIAN PRACTICES

In ancient Mesopotamian religion (c. 2000-1500 B.C.) at least three different ecstatic personalities are identifiable. Each is categorized by the media used to convey the message of deity. These were (1) oral pronouncement, (2) sleep revelations (that is, dreams), and (3) physical signs, such as jerking, facial contortions, and the like, unusual physical features or physical abnormalities. Categories one and two are most important to this study.

The first category is of particular interest to the student or devotee of glossolalia. This type of revelation is always associated with that which Leo Oppenheim describes as "prophetic ecstasis,"[3] which refers to a specific instance of ecstasy. Of growing interest, however is the second category of sleep revelations which are attested to in some ancient texts found at Mari, an Amonite state situated on the Euphrates in Mesopotamia. These texts date from the second millennium B.C.

The Mari documents refer to both men and women as givers of oracles. In certain texts the prophetic individual is designated by the term *Muhhum*. Basically, *Muhhum* means "to be beside one's self" or "to be put out of one's mind." Undoubtedly the name was given to this group due to their extraordinary physical and mental states. In Accadia the Mahhu group were actually priests, thus within the boundaries of an acceptable religious es-

---

[2]Alfred Guillaume, *Prophecy and Divination* (London: Hodder and Stoughton, 1938), p. 293.

[3]A. Leo Oppenheim, *Ancient Mesopotamia* (Chicago: University of Chicago Press, 1964), p. 221.

tablishment, who worked through the media of ecstatic inspiration to receive and convey messages from deity.[4] Many of the same texts refer to such priests as *'a mel-ili* (that is, godsmen) which may imply unique possession by the spirit of the god.

Herbert B. Huffman, in a most excellent study of prophetic materials from the Mari archives, has shown that some twenty of a group of one thousand letters are concerned with the ecstatic prophetic experience.[5] In these letters there is ample evidence to demonstrate that the ecstatic individual received messages from deity which he delivered orally to a specific person. Whereas most of the documents appear to refer to messages received in an ecstatic state and subsequently relayed to a recipient, one such message was delivered while in the state of ecstasy rather than subsequent to the seizure.

Accounts of ecstatic personalities who were not priests are recorded in other documents. These individuals were subject to ecstasy and spoke messages from deity. One such individual is referred to as "a certain wife of a citizen." Although the vast majority of the messages are related to a dream state or placed in the category of sleep revelations, one case refers to a dream which came during the day and apparently in a public place. Quite likely this implies a visionary ecstatic experience which was vocalized.

Another text relates a most intriguing situation. On a particular occasion in a sanctuary a "strange voice" (that is, one somewhat unintelligible) repeatedly spoke. This text does not clarify the situation as to whether the "strange voice" was from within or without the prophetic personality. It is, however, to my knowledge the earliest reference known of the possible use of some unintelligible tongue during an ecstatic experience.

Every indication is given in this body of Mari correspondences to indicate that communications emanating from an ecstatic state were considered to be outside the generally accepted boundaries of religious experience. The one exception is that of the Mahhu priests. Most letters relating this type of religious communication contain references to efforts to verify the

---

[4]Alfred O. Haldar, *Associations of Cult Prophets among the Ancient Semites* (Uppsala: Uppsala University, 1945), pp. 21 ff.

[5]Herbert B. Huffman, "Prophecy in the Mari Letters," *The Biblical Archaeologist*, 4 (December 1968): 101-24.

experience. Additionally, clarifications of the messages were sought. Divination was generally practiced by the Mesopotamians to determine the will of the gods. Thus, the verification or the authentication of ecstatic utterance was placed in the hands of a priest who was an expert in divination. Consequently the prophetic message was held to strict accountability by the established religion of the state.

Other texts seemingly imply an association between music, alcohol, and ecstaticism. Alcohol and music apparently were used as aids to ecstasy or as means of more quickly conditioning the individual to arrive at an intense state of inspiration.

As a general rule. Mesopotamian ecstaticism was associated with the lower economic and social classes. It was considered to be on the same level as sorcery or wizardry by official religious orders. There is enough reference to the phenomenon, however, to surmise that this type experience was at the center of Mesopotamian folk religion. It may also be assumed that ecstatic personalities occupied positions of prime religious influence among the farming and shepherd communities.

EGYPTIAN PRACTICES

While Mesopotamian evidences are fairly extensive, there is but scant evidence from Egypt. The most intriguing of these, however, is found in the document entitled "The Journey of Wen-Amon to Phoenicia" (c. 1117 B.C.).[6] The story is rather delightful as it records the misadventures of Wen-Amon on a trip to the coast of Syria. Wen-Amon was commissioned to obtain lumber for a ceremonial barge to be constructed in honor of the god, Amon. Upon arrival at Byblos, Wen-Amon fell into the hands of a designing local ruler, Zakar-Baal, who thwarted every attempt by Wen-Amon to conclude his assignment. During the period of Wen-Amon's forced internment, an Egyptian youth in his company, possibly a court page, was caught up in a violent state of ecstasy when he stood before Amon's sacred image. While the youth was in this state, the god, Amon, spoke through him. The young man's seizure was considered to be prophetic frenzy. The

---

[6]John A. Wilson, "The Journey of Wen-Amon to Phoenicia," *Ancient Near Eastern Texts*, ed. James B. Pritchard (Princeton: Princeton University Press, 1950), pp. 25-29.

text reads as follows: "Now while he was making offering to his gods, the god seized one of the youths and made him possessed."[7]

Wen-Amon accepts the situation without any undue anxiety as if this was an accustomed occurrence. Even when the god spoke through the young man, it produced no alarm. There is no evidence in this document of speaking in unknown tongues.

Herodotus, the father of history, does however refer to a religious ceremony associated with the Cult of Isis which culminated in an ecstatic frenzy. Under the influence of this strong emotional frame of mind, the worshipers frequently self-inflicted wounds upon their bodies while from their lips poured a veritable babel of voices.[8]

CANAANITE PRACTICES

The reaction of Zakar-Baal to the ecstatic seizure of one of Wen-Amon's company points to the typical Canaanite response to messages from deity spoken in the state of ecstasy. Immediately upon hearing the message, Zakar-Baal enters into serious negotiations with Wen-Amon. This ultimately resulted in a successfully concluded business agreement. Such an act on the part of Zakar-Baal, the Canaanite ruler, reflects a high regard for such messages from deity.

That messages from the gods delivered during ecstatic seizures were a part of Canaanite religious expression is clearly denoted in the biblical account of the contest on Mt. Carmel. The narrative, which focuses upon the prophet Elijah and the priest and prophets of Baal, is a classic in biblical literature (see 1 Kings 18).

As the story of the contest evolves, the prophets of Baal work themselves into an ecstatic frenzy. They are so translated beyond normal behavior that they slice their own flesh with ceremonial knives. Their dance is so violent under the impact of ecstasy that they are finally reduced to limping about the altar. The King James Version translates the words to indicate that in this state they "prophesied." In the Revised Standard Version, the same Hebrew term is translated "raving." What does the biblical

---

[7]Ibid., p. 26.

[8]George Rawlinson, trans., *The History of Herodotus* (New York: Tudor Publishing, 1947), p. 102.

terminology imply? A literal translation of the Hebrew means to "behave as a prophet"—or "to be in an ecstatic state."

The manner of behavior not only implies violent physical motion but vocal utterance. We would do no violence to the text to intimate this utterance was in the form of guttural expressions, a din of sound produced by the voicing of unintelligible syllables. This, to the Canaanites, denoted invasion of the person by the spirit of Baal. It was the voicing of dark and mysterious messages.

HITTITE PRACTICES

Although there are no specific Hittite documents which refer to a phenomenon closely allied to glossolalia, there is sufficient documentation to point out a possible relationship. Among the Hittites there were at least four types of official religious personalities: (1) prophets, (2) priests, (3) sibyls, and (4) private persons who were the recipients of dreams of a prophetic nature. These categories are quite similar to those of Mari, and we may suppose they fulfilled somewhat similar functions. In extant documents, the Hittite prophetic group is the one referred to as declaring messages. We can only ponder as to whether or not they were delivered in an ecstatic state. If they were and if they followed the contemporary pattern, then the messages may well have been delivered in some incomprehensible language.

ISRAELITE PRACTICES

Israelite ecstatic prophets appear for the first time in a clearly identifiable way in those narratives dealing with the elevation of Saul to tribal leadership. It is apparent that the ecstatic group arose in the religious and political vacuum created by the Philistine oppression.

Several remarkable features of the ecstatic prophets are revealed in the accounts. We find they used harp, tambourine, flute, and lyre as aids to achieve the state of ecstasy (see 1 Samuel 10:5-6). In other instances dance is employed (2 Samuel 6:16), and the use of wine is implied (1 Samuel 10:3). Whenever the Spirit of God invaded one of these men, the man was considered to be "turned into another man" (1 Samuel 10:6). One of the curious manifestations of this prophetic ecstasis was the act of dancing naked. Implications are that this was a customary act of one caught up in this particular religious fervor (1 Samuel 10:24; 2 Samuel 6:30). Once the state of ecstasis had been reached prophesying occurred, and we may well surmise that the utterances were not identifiable as any specific language system.

This primitive Israelite religious experience had three facets which are recognizable in modern glossolalia. (1) The religious ecstasy was contagious. Saul's messengers, Saul, and even David succumbed to the communicable nature of the act. As such, they were turned into different men (1 Samuel 10:3-8; 20:19-24; 2 Samuel 6:16-23). (2) Those who practiced ecstaticism were gregarious (1 Samuel 10:5, 10; 1 Kings 22:6ff.; 2 Kings 2.3ff., 7 ff.; 9.1ff.) Without exception they are referred to as being in groups or companies. Saul came into contact with one such band near Gibeah (1 Samuel 10: 8,10). Samuel appears to have found such a band at Ramah (1 Samuel 19:18). Second Kings indicates that companies were associated with the towns of Bethel (2 Kings 2:3), Jericho (2 Kings 2:5), and Gilgal (2 Kings 4:38). (3) The act of prophesying was considered to be an invasion of the individual by the Spirit of God, and the vocal message conveyed was considered to have issued from the impinging Spirit of God (1 Samuel 10:6, 10; 11:6).

As was the case with the Mari ecstatics, the Israelite ecstatics were looked upon as a marginal religious group. That is to say, they did not comply with the acceptable standards of religious conduct in their day. That their moral and social standing was dubious is evidenced by the amazement and dismay of Saul's friends when he succumbed to ecstaticism. They could scarcely believe his association with a disreputable group. The wording of the phrases "What has come over the son of Kish?" and "Is Saul also among the prophets?" denotes consternation and disbelief on their part (1 Samuel 10:11). Perhaps an even more incisive view of the low esteem of this Israelite group is found in 1 Samuel 6:20. Michal, daughter of Saul and wife of David, upbraided her husband for his involvement in ecstaticism and prophesying. According to Michal, her husband had acted as one of the wild, reckless, uncouth men! Reinforcing this position is the stance of an eighth-century classical prophet. Amos boldly repudiated the intimation that he was an ecstatic, and his words imply that they constituted, in his mind, an inferior class of prophets (Amos 7:14).

ARABIC PRACTICES

Steeped in the antiquity of Near Eastern tribal culture and hidden beneath the unknown canopy of history stand two ecstatic personages of tremendous powers: the *Kahin* and the dervish.

The *Kahin* was and is a tribal seer or soothsayer. His primary function was to communicate oracles and only as a subsidiary action did he divine the future. Remarkably, this religious individual stands in the center of a hoary line of ecstatic succession. The *Kahin* would enter a state of ecstasy and in this state become the spokesman of the *jinn* (that is, impersonal spirits). This indwelling of the *jinn*, clearly similar in nature to the concept of the indwelling of the Spirit of God, would result in the conveying of messages.

A pertinent case at point is presented by Alois Musil in the *Manners and Customs of the Rwala Bedouins*. A *Kahin* is called upon to bring healing to one who is sick. Through the use of music, especially that of heavy rhythmic drum beats accompanied by increasingly violent contortions of the body, the *Kahin* enters a state of ecstasy. He casts himself upon the body of the patient, mumbling unintelligible words. He speaks in voices! At times the sick are healed; at other times they die. All, however, who witness the event claim that the unintelligible message is the vocalized word of Allah.

The dervish constitutes a group which Johannes Lindblom feels arose within the context of Islam to provide an element of personal communion with Allah.[9] If this indeed is the case, then its similarity to the modern search for ecstasis which culminates in glossolalia is clearly affirmed.

A dervish utilizes certain conditioning agents to achieve a state in which he will become the spokesman of Allah. Contemplation, repetition of the divine name, recitation of creeds, religious formulas, prayers, and passages from the Quran are effectively used to induce a state of ecstasy. Vocalization of the literature is, at first, slow and deliberate, but then the momentum increases at an alarming rate. Suddenly the recitations are punctuated again and again with the explosive syllable *hu*. As the tempo increases, so does bodily movement, and the climax is an ecstatic delirium. In this state prophecies are given. These are considered to be messages from the realm of the spirit. Again there is the striking parallel to glossolalia, for the messages are quite often delivered in no known language. Rather, they seem to be little more than elongated dialogues composed of curious syllables emphasized with the explosive formula *hu*.

---

[9] Johannes Lindblom, *Prophecy in Ancient Israel* (Philadelphia: Muhlenberg Press, 1962), p. 9.

GREEK PRACTICES

The sophistication of the Greeks did not preclude their acceptance of a type of glossolalia. This was especially true in relationship to worship connected with the oracles and mystery religions.

At Delphi, for instance, when one consulted the sibyls, the communique from the gods was apt to be obscure. Therefore it was necessary for a priest to interpret the oracle. The oracles of the Delphi sibyl were delivered during a state of possession or ecstatic seizure. As such, the messages were very enigmatic and delivered in a language not akin to any known.

Aeschylus in his *Agamemnon* presents the case with excellent clarity in the speeches between Cassandra and the chorus. Cassandra is considered to be a prophetess and the chorus chants:

> Thou art crazed, on gusts of God-sent madness born!
> Thyself the theme of thy sad ecstasy!

Cassandra protests that the chorus does not understand what she says and speaks:

> And yet I speak good Greek, your tongue I know too well.

The chorus answers in reply:

> So doth the Pythian oracle,
> Yet are his divinations wondrous dark.

Cassandra in her replies says of herself:

> Why do I shrink? Why do I wail?

In essence, Cassandra is looked upon as one possessed by the gods, and as a result she speaks messages unknown to those about her. She is referred to as *prophētēs* and speaks good Greek; but when under the influence of the spirit, she speaks in an unknown tongue like those of the Pythian oracle.

An identical type of glossolalia is referred to in Virgil's *Aeneid* when he writes of the sibyl at Cumae, and something of the same type religious phenomenon is spoken of in Apuleius' *The Golden Ass*.

Plato also gives due recognition to this dimension of religious experience in his *Phaedrus*. Not only does Plato describe the state of ecstasy but apparently understands and condones the nature of such experience. He considers the state to be madness as a gift of the gods. For Plato the madness (that is, ecstasy) of the prophets of Pythia at Delphi which produced prophecy was not only superior to divination but above the insights of human sanity (that is, pure reason). Such religious figures were, to Plato, the vocal reproductions of deity who knew not what they spoke. Needless to say, when the prophetic word was spoken, it was often in a language so strange and unusual it needed interpretation.

The mystery religions present a variation on the theme of glossolalia. In the Dionysian mysteries the phenomenon is not unknown. Cultic rites were designed to move the devotee through a series of steps, each pyramiding emotion upon emotion. Frequently worshippers would move into a state of ecstasis and under the impact of the experience speak in a type of language understood only by other initiates. Thus a type of specialized glossolalia was practiced.

Euripides in his work *The Bacchantes* affirms that Bacchus possessed men and that among his worshipers there was a considerable element of prophesying. This occurred only when the full might of the god entered the human frame. Most frequently, the result was a message which foretold the future. We may surmise that such messages were equally as unintelligible as those issuing from the oracles since a drunken stupor was associated with possession by Bacchus.

WESTERN PRACTICES

In a band stretching from the Arctic through Russia. North Asia, and North America, there is another religious figure of formidable power. This is the *shaman* who may be traced through tribal history only to disappear in the mists of most ancient history. The shaman served primarily as a mediator between the realm of spirit and the realm of flesh. By the use of highly individualized rituals the shaman was considered to be capable of either entering the spirit world or bringing spirits into the human realm. Not only did he perform primitive acts of divination, but he delivered messages while in the state of ecstasy. Ordinarily the state of ecstasis was achieved through the use of artificial stimuli.

A shaman uses music as an ecstatic stimulant. He sings and accompanies himself with a tambourine drum. The songs begin quietly and have a plaintive quality, yet the words or syllables used are not akin to a known language. As the ecstatic experience heightens, the shaman changes the tempo and volume of musical sound, both vocal and instrumental. He is encouraged by onlookers, and suddenly from his lips there pours a confusion of sounds, some of an animal quality, others resembling strange foreign tongues. It is the contention of the shaman that while he is in the trance state spirits have spoken through him, and he claims to be unconscious of what he has said or done.

Three other widely scattered manifestations of similar nature should be mentioned. Among the Polynesians of the Pacific there is a religious figure, who for lack of better terminology, we shall call a medium. From time to time these mediums enter a state closely resembling a physical convulsion. While in the state they speak in shrill cries and unknown syllables. They, as well as the people, consider the action to denote possession by the gods and the words as messages from deity.

The two other examples are from ancient Indian and Persia. One of the Vedic deities of India was Soma. It appears that the name derived from a potent drink used in the Vedic ceremonies. This substance, when ingested, caused ecstasy and then visions. In Persian Zoroastrianism there was the use of *haoma*, identical with the Indian *soma*. Apparently the *soma* plant was a mushroom with hallucinogenic properties. Whether one under the influence of the "juice of the *soma*" spoke in unknown language is not known; however, such may have been the case.

CONCLUSIONS

What conclusions may we legitimately draw from these evidences, and what inferences are to be reasonably tolerated?

1. Glossolalia is actually a common religious phenomenon. Throughout history two distinct types of religion are to be observed. First, there is the officially sanctioned religion embraced by priests, scribes, rulers, the court, and the educated classes. Secondly, there is a religion of the rank and file, the masses. On the one hand, we might say, is official orthodoxy and on the other a practical or pragmatic lived-out folk religion. Throughout the world and history, there is to be seen in the second type of religion the ecstatic personality. And among such ecstatics, whether Mesopota-

mian. Egyptian, Israelite, Canaanite, Greek, or Muslim, there were those who, when possessed by the spirit of deity, delivered messages in strange tongues. No religion, ancient or modern, may claim exclusive rights to such a religious act.

2. Glossolalia has been associated with lower social and economic classes for four thousand years and has had full acceptance only in countercultures. It is quite apparent from the sources that the ecstatic incoherent messages of prophetic types in many cultures were a distinguishing characteristic of religious fervor among the lower classes. The Mesopotamians suspected messages from ecstatics. Their validity was dependent upon verification by an official religionist. Among Israelites, ecstatics were associated with the lower classes and were considered to be base or crude men. In these cultures, as well as the Islamic culture, the ecstatic was considered to be on the boundary of orthodox religious experience.

3. For centuries glossolalia has served as a device to denote the presence of deity in an acute personal dimension. There is a strange relationship, both in Mesopotamia and in Israel, between historical event and the rise of ecstaticism. At the time when such personalities arose in Mesopotamia and Israel there was a noticeable shift in religious influence.

Official Mesopotamian religion had become bogged down by the weight of official religion. The mechanics of official state religion had replaced the dimension of personal involvement by the populace. Primary emphasis was placed upon the sanctioned rituals, and priests stood solidly between deity and man. The people knew not if the gods spoke unless informed of such by a religious official following a narrow, rigid, and formal routine.

Israelite religion faced a much different historical situation. A religious vacuum had occurred. The Philistines had overrun the country. The central sanctuary, Shiloh, had been destroyed. Religious and political leadership was practically nonexistent. Into the religious vacuum there arose the ecstatic prophet who affirmed the presence of deity through possession by the spirit.

A somewhat similar illustration is to be found in Islam but is due to a different set of circumstances. The tribal Muslim of the hinterlands of Arabia was cut off from any vital relationship with the official religious centers. The mosque and the minaret were the province of the town and city dweller. They reinforced the concept of the presence of Allah, but what of the Bedouin whose life was filled with the wastelands of the desert? The tribal dervish filled the void and affirmed Allah's presence.

It is not trite to say that in any condition when for any reason, religious man by official act, condition of life, or unique circumstances feels alienated from deity, ecstaticism of one type or another enters the picture.

4. Aids to ecstasy were regularly employed with music and recitation (that is, prayer or repeating of sacred literature or formula) being most frequently referred to in the sources. These same devices are much in evidence in the modern phenomenon of glossolalia. It occasions no wonder as to why the disciples were spoken of in Acts 2:13 as being "filled with new wine." The world of the ancient Near East was accustomed to ecstatic utterance which had been preceded by aids to attain ecstasis. Suffice it to say wine was an aid to ecstasy peculiar to the ancient Near Eastern and Greek religions.

Part II
Historical Studies

10

E. GLENN HINSON

The Significance of
Glossolalia in the History
of Christianity

[Reprinted from *Speaking in Tongues: Let's Talk about It*, edited by Watson E. Mills, copyright © 1973, pp. 61-80; used by permission of Word Books, Publisher, Waco, Texas 76796.]

Evaluations of the role of tongue-speaking in the history of Christianity readily betray the perspectives (or should I say biases?) of their authors. Pentecostals obviously want to make the most of a phenomenon which they view as the axis around which the spiritual life of the Christian turns. Non-Pentecostals, especially conservatively oriented evangelicals, on the contrary, stress the insignificance of tongues during many centuries of Christian history and exaggerate the negative features which have accompanied it. If one views the matter from the extreme Pentecostal side, Christianity has only been Christianity when it has experienced tongues. If he views it from the extreme anti-Pentecostal side, tongues have been the devil's way of leading Christians astray or man's way of deceiving himself.

Looking at individual facts of the case in isolation you may find ammunition to support both points of view. Taking the historical evidence as a whole, however, you will likely conclude that tongues has been neither as significant as Pentecostals claim nor as insignificant or as bad as some non-Pentecostals claim. The question which Pentecostals have difficulty answering when they stress the significance of glossolalia is: If glossolalia is so significant, why has its history been so spotty, almost nonexistent from the apostolic age to about 1650? On the other hand, the question which non-Pentecostals have to wrestle with is: If the phenomenon is so insignificant, why is it now making such an impact on the church scene? As Pentecostals have argued, there does appear to be some connection between glossolalia and spiritual awakenings. If so, what is it? Does glossolalia contribute to the origin of such awakenings? Or is it itself a by-product of the emotional fervor produced by them?

In the interest of obtaining a balanced answer to these questions, I will seek to take an objective look at both sides of three major questions: First, how do we explain the spasmodic character of tongue-speaking in the history of the church until around 1900? Second, when tongue-speaking movements arose, what triggered them and what did they mean? Third, what is the relationship of glossolalia to spiritual revivals or renewals in different periods of history? You will note that I am giving only incidental attention to individual occurrences. This is because the historian is concerned with movements and institutions more than with isolated phenomena. Therefore, the latter will be explained only insofar as they help to explain the former.

WHY THE GLOSSOLALIA GAP?

Why did glossolalia occur so intermittently during many centuries? Pentecostals and their critics have raised two subsidiary questions here: (1) How much evidence is there? (2) Why is there limited evidence?

HOW MUCH EVIDENCE?

Those who have been sharply critical of glossolalia have made much of the paucity of evidence of tongue-speaking from about A.D. 100 to 1900. Professor George W. Dollar, Dallas Theological Seminary, has labeled the evidence "an almost complete silence." Both he and a colleague, C. L.

Rogers, Jr., have contested the significance of evidence for glossolalia during the patristic period and, to the contrary, have made much of the silence of most of the Fathers. Indeed, Rogers took great pains to argue for the significance of the silence of the apostolic fathers, the apologists, and others. He strongly doubted whether Justin Martyr was alluding to glossolalia in his *Dialogue with Trypho,* 82. On the contrary, he contended that the only real evidence for the practice is related to Montanism, an early Christian Pentecostal movement. Both Irenaeus and Tertullian had Montanist contacts. Tertullian became a Montanist, although Origen made no clear statement of firsthand contacts. Chrysostom[1] supplied negative evidence that tongues had "died out and were no longer needed to establish Christianity." Then, concluded Dollar, the gift of tongues was "neither widespread nor the normal Christian experience" in the period A.D. 100 to 400.[2]

The evidence for tongue-speaking does not increase until the seventeenth century. Whether tongues occurred at all during the Middle Ages, anti-Pentecostals argue, may be doubted. Dollar has insisted that tongue-speaking had no part in the Reformation, unless among heretical spiritualists. He denigrated the evidence of the Cevenols and Irvingites and queried whether tongues occurred in the Wesleyan revivals or "in the strenuous days of the Great Awakening and the days of spiritual heat of the frontier revivals." Instead, he argues that Pentecostalism began in the nineteenth century with the Mormons and the Shakers. It has had its heyday in the twentieth century.

Dollar's final judgment about the historical evidence allows no quarter for the Pentecostal position.

> The voice of church history, when read in its total ramifications, would indicate that God has been guiding His people and that He has been teaching them His Word down through the centuries. The voice of history also is that God has majored on those things which are given priority in His own Word and not on those things which men claim by experiences, however hectic or calm. The voice of church history, therefore, is against the

---

[1]Chrysostom, *Homilies on First Corinthians*, 29:1.

[2]G. W. Dollar, "Church History and the Tongues Movement", *Bibliotheca Sacra* 120:316-21; C. L. Rogers, Jr., "Gift of Tongues in the Post-Apostolic Church (A.D. 100-400)," *Bibliotheca Sacra*, 122:134-43.

modern tongues movement and would stigmatize it as being an unscriptural and unhistorical phenomenon arising out of the experiences, tempers, longings, desires, and emotional impulses so common in the last century.[3]

Pentecostals have questioned the accuracy of handling historical data in such a manner. In this endeavor they have received a substantial amount of support from church historians who, as a body, reject the sweeping generalizations found in the above quotation.

First, evidences for the continuance of glossolalia, among other charismatic gifts, are substantial for the second century. It is true that the evidence is connected largely with Montanism, but Montanism itself has recently been receiving a rather positive appraisal from historians. It appears to have aimed at a return to primitive, apostolic Christianity in an age when Christianity was perhaps moving too rapidly toward institutional lethargy and lukewarm discipleship. Therefore, it is possible to view Montanism as a kind of spiritual revival which was recalling the churches to their highest level of commitment.

Second, is it possible to connect all of the evidence with Montanism? Tertullian, yes. Origen, probably, for he was answering charges by the anti-Christian polemicist Celsus, who composed his *True Discourse* around A.D. 178 in the early days of Montanism. But what about Irenaeus and Mark 16:17, which is part of an ending added to Mark at a later date? If Irenaeus did have possible Montanist contacts in his earlier career, which originated in Asia Minor, would they have caused him to make as positive a judgment of charismatic gifts as he did in later years unless such phenomena occurred outside Montanist churches? Surely the bishop of Lyons was not reporting on Montanist churches when he wrote about his knowledge of such things, developing an argument for Christianity against paganism.

Admittedly there is some room to debate whether Irenaeus had firsthand or secondhand knowledge. Anti-Pentecostals have argued that the key passage in Irenaeus[4] implies secondhand rather than firsthand knowledge. The Greek, however, does not require and probably does not support this view. The report alludes to Paul's statement in 1 Corinthians 2:6 that "We

---

[3]Dollar, "Church History and the Tongues Movement," p. 321.

[4]Irenaeus, *Against Heresies*, 5.6.1.

speak wisdom among the perfect.'' Irenaeus goes on to say that the ''perfect'' are those ''who have perceived the Spirit of God and speak all languages through the Spirit of God, even as Paul himself used to speak.'' Then, for the benefit of his readers, he explains with a contemporary illustration: ''Just as we also hear many brethren in the Church, having prophetic gifts and speaking all sorts of tongues through the Spirit and leading human secrets into the open for the benefit [of others] and narrating the mysteries of God.'' In Greek the verb *hearing* takes the genitive as its object. The early Latin translator, therefore, rightly translated *multos adivimus fratres*, ''we have heard many brethren.''

The spurious ending to Mark 16 is of highly uncertain date and origin. My own conclusion is that it was probably composed during the second century, for it appears in the Latin version of Irenaeus' *Against Heresies*, which has been dated between A.D. 200 and A.D. 396.[5] There is no compelling reason to connect this document with Montanism.

To strengthen the argument that glossolalia could have occurred outside Montanist Churches, Pentecostals may cite extensive evidence for charismatic phenomena during the second and even later centuries. For the second century, Heinrich Weinel[6] has amassed copious references to Spirit-effected speaking, including tongues, writing, healings and other miracles, volitional acts, hearing, seeing, understanding, heightening of other senses, and feeling. When one takes into account such data as these, he cannot circumvent the likelihood that glossolalia was one of the charismatic gifts which flourished along with the others.

In the second and early third centuries, therefore, the evidences for glossolalia apart from Montanism are substantial. The subsequent story is less favorable, however, and debate waxes hot principally around which of the scattered bits of evidence may be applied to the history of tongue-speaking. In this debate it is clear that conservative evangelicals like Dollar have disallowed too much evidence in generalizing about almost complete absence of evidence until 1900.

---

[5]E. Glenn Hinson, ''A Brief History of Glossolalia,'' *Glossolalia: Tongue Speaking in Biblical, Historical, and Psychological Perspective*, Frank Stagg, E. Glenn Hinson, and Wayne Oates (Nashville: Abingdon, 1967), p. 53.

[6]Heinrich Weinel, *Die Wirkungen des Geistes und der Geister* (Leipzig: J. C. B. Mohr, 1899).

The problematic period is that from around A.D. 250 until the seventeenth century. The vague and allusive way in which Origen answered Celsus[7] suggests that the phenomenon was dying out by the middle of the third century as other charismatic phenomena also waned. By the fourth century it was unknown both to John Chrysostom[8] and Augustine,[9] except in apostolic references. The credulous Middle Ages, moreover, have left only a few highly debatable accounts, mostly related to the ability to speak foreign languages which had not been learned.[10] All of the medieval reports are so problematic that it is probably best not to try to evaluate them either pro or con.

Pentecostals have tried to enlist Luther among their number, but the grounds for this are highly tenuous, as even they admit.[11] On the contrary, Luther took some very hard swipes at the Zwickau Prophets because they questioned the sufficiency of the Scriptures. His answer to them reputedly was, "Nothing that you have advanced is based upon Holy Scripture, it is all a mere fable." When one of the zealous prophetists shouted back, "The spirit! The spirit!", Luther rejoined, "I slap your spirit on the snout."[12]

This means that, to all intents and purposes, tongue-speaking was not reintroduced until the seventeenth century after what has to be seen as "a long drought." It recurred then in connection with the English protest and revival movements (probably among the Ranters and the Quakers) and in the wake of the revocation of the Edict of Nantes in 1685 (among the French Huguenots). Then, contrary to G. W. Dollar, it accompanied the Wesleyan revivals, the Great Awakening of the 1740s, and the frontier revivals of the early 1800s. Both the Shakers and the Mormons assigned it an important place in their constitutions. Even the Jansenists of France, a Roman Catholic protest movement, experienced tongues in 1731.

---

[7]Origen, *Against Celsus* 7.9ff.

[8]Chrysostom, *Homilies on First Corinthians*, 29.1.

[9]Augustine, *On Baptism* 3.18.16-21.

[10]See Hinson, "A Brief History of Glossolalia," pp. 54-58.

[11]Carl Brumback, *"What Meaneth This?"* (Springfield MO: Gospel Publishing House, 1947), p. 92.

[12]Cited by H. J. Stolee, *Speaking in Tongues* (Minneapolis: Augsburg Publishing House, 1963), p. 17.

WHY LIMITED EVIDENCE?

Why is the evidence so limited for these centuries? Why did tongues not occur more often, especially between around A.D. 250 and 1650? Once more, Pentecostals and their detractors differ markedly in their responses.

Conservative evangelicals have elaborated upon an explanation given by Augustine and John Chrysostom for the absence of glossolalia in the fourth century. That is, tongues was an evidential sign for the apostolic age which was no longer needed to establish the truth of Christianity. In the infancy of the church the apostles needed and received this as a gift of God; now that church is established, the gift is no longer necessary. To quote Augustine:

> For the Holy Spirit is not only given by the laying on of hands amid the testimony of temporal sensible miracles, as He was given in former days to be the credential of the first beginnings of the Church. For who expects in these days that those on whom hands are laid that they may receive the Holy Spirit should forthwith begin to speak in tongues?[13]

The issue of tongues is a highly charged one among the more conservative (fundamentalist) Christians, for Pentecostal claims to contemporary inspiration tend to undercut the absoluteness of the scriptural revelation. God spoke his final word in the canonical Scriptures. Any further claim to hear his word apart from the Scriptures, therefore, is invalid. Tongues cannot be seen as a valid phenomenon derived from God either, for he has no other way of revealing himself. It may be, Lutheran H. J. Stolee[14] admitted, "a real religious experience," but this does not mean that it comes from God; it may be demonic.

The conservatives carry this argument further by noting that Scriptures themselves predicted the cessation of tongues (1 Cor. 13:8). If there were spasmodic outcroppings in later days, they had to originate from some other source than divine inspiration. Thus, according to Stolee,[15] "The very fact that certain tongues have appeared periodically after the days of Paul would

---

[13]Augustine, *On Baptism*, 3.18.16-21.

[14]Stolee, *Speaking in Tongues*, p. 85.

[15]Ibid., p. 99.

indicate that they were of another spirit, because they persist contrary to the Word.''

Stolee is willing to admit that supernatural signs, though not a further revelation, may occasionally occur even today. This may happen, for instance, in lands ''where the Gospel is just being introduced and where the ordinary use of the Word is so unheard of and so little understood that the Lord permits extraordinary signs to accompany His messengers.''[16] However, God works differently when he begins a work and after the work is underway. In the apostolic age he laid the foundation; we build on it. Foundation and building differ markedly. Therefore, ''After the completed revelation the special prophetic gift was discontinued; it was 'done away.' That special enduement is no longer required.''[17]

In response to these arguments, Pentecostals charge their critics with a misunderstanding. They do not claim that spiritual gifts such as tongues supplant the authority of Scriptures; rather, they are auxiliary to the Scriptures.

Further, it is claiming too much to say that glossolalia is no longer needed because of Christianity's success. The world has by no means been converted to Christianity. The churches have never shown themselves more powerless and in need of authentication.[18]

Finally, if one takes literally Paul's prediction that tongues shall cease, what will he do with his predictions in the same passage that ''prophecy'' and ''knowledge'' also will pass away. His prediction applies to ''when that which is perfect is come,'' not to the present.[19]

Pentecostals, however, cannot circumvent the fact that the evidence for tongues after the early period is patchy. Donald Gee, a distinguished British Pentecostal Bible scholar, has conceded that ''there was a great diminution of these gifts not only after the apostolic age, but probably even towards its close.'' But he argues that this was not because the Lord withdrew them. Instead, it was because men ''fell away.'' In support he quoted

---

[16]Ibid., p. 102.

[17]Ibid., p. 103.

[18]See Donald Gee, ''*Concerning Spiritual Gifts*'' (Springfield MO: Gospel Publishing House, n.d.), pp. 11-12.

[19]Ibid., pp. 9-10.

John Wesley: "Because the love of many, almost of all Christians so called, was waxed cold. . . . This was the real cause why the extraordinary gifts of the Holy Ghost were no longer to be found in the Christian church."[20] Along a slightly divergent track, Carl Brumback has posited the cause of decline in unbelief within the church.[21] Others have made the same point under the titles of formalism, secularism, modernism, and acculturation.[22]

To buttress their argument on the positive side, Pentecostals diligently cite the well-known references which invalidate the contention of those who minimize the evidence. These reports, they suggest, hint at wider occurrences which have not been recorded. As Brumback has put it, the appearances in the history of Christianity are "confined to certain spiritual awakenings in which the gift had not become so frequent and widespread as to cause much public comment."[23] Their day has come in the twentieth century when no one can doubt any longer that tongues have occurred since the apostolic age.

WHY GLOSSOLALIA?

Why these occurrences, however many or few they may have been? What gave rise to the outbursts of tongues? What do they mean? Once more the Pentecostal and the non-Pentecostal answers stand in stark opposition.

DEVILISH OR HUMAN INSPIRATION?

The stoutest opponents of Pentecostalism have ascribed outbursts of glossolalia in Christian history either to Satan and his demonic hosts or to human psychological factors. The latter, of course, sounds somewhat less severe and more scientific, but the two explanations are more closely related than they may appear to be at first glance. Belief in demons was the ancient man's psychology. It was his way of explaining both good and evil impulses which appeared to be beyond his control. Hence, many things which today we would explain psychologically were understood by him in terms of demonic influences. For example, the mentally sick were demon

---

[20]Ibid., p. 10.

[21]Brumback, *"What Meaneth This?"* pp. 83-87.

[22]See R. Leonard Carroll, "Glossolalia: Apostles to the Reformation," *The Glossolalia Phenomenon*, ed. Harold Horton (Cleveland TN: Pathway Press, 1966), p. 94.

[23]Brumback, *"What Meaneth This?"* p. 27.

possessed. Accordingly, critics of Pentecostalism who tend toward biblical literalism, accepting the biblical world view uncritically, still interpret
glossolalia in terms of demons while their more sophisticated contemporaries interpret it in terms of modern psychology.

The rationale for the critical understanding is as follows: There are three
possible ways of explaining glossolalia: (1) It is of God. (2) It is of the devil.
(3) It is psychologically induced.[24] Since the Scriptures do not allow for
its continuance within the church, it cannot be of God. Therefore, it must
be either of the devil or psychologically induced. Several factors confirm
that it originates in one or the other of these sources.

First, it is accompanied by wild and orgiastic enthusiasm which is out
of character for Christians. It was this which Apolinarius, the bishop of
Hierapolis, noted about Montanus and his prophetesses, Priscilla and
Maximilla. According to his interpretation, Montanus tried to seize leadership in the village church of Ardabau by claiming prophetic powers which
were really of demonic inspiration.

> And he became beside himself, and being suddenly in a sort of frenzy
> and ecstasy, he raved, and began to babble and utter strange things, proph-
> esying in a manner contrary to the constant custom of the Church handed
> down by tradition from the beginning.[25]

The judgment of those who witnessed this, Apolinarius went on to report,
was that he had gone mad. As a result,

> they rebuked him as one that was possessed, and that was under the control
> of a demon, and was led by a deceitful spirit, and was distracting the mul-
> titude; and they forbade him to talk, remembering the distinction drawn
> by the Lord and his warning to guard watchfully against the coming of false
> prophets.[26]

At about the same time the pagan critic Celsus registered a similar impression of certain Christian prophets who added to their enthusiastic procla-

---

[24]Cf. Anthony A. Hoekema, *What about Tongue-Speaking?* (Grand Rapids MI: Eerdmans, 1966); Russell T. Hitt, *The New Pentecostalism* (Philadelphia: Eternity Magazine,
n.d.).

[25]Eusebius, *Church History*, 5.16.7,8.

[26]Ibid.

mations "incomprehensible; incoherent, and utterly obscure utterances, the meaning of which no intelligent person could discover; for they are meaningless and nonsensical, and give a chance for any fool or sorcerer to take the words in whatever sense he likes."[27]

This kind of critique has been handed down through the centuries. With good reason non-Pentecostals have expressed concern about excesses. Indeed, what has impressed them most about modern Pentecostalism has been the lack of control exhibited in it. Thus H. J. Stolee, while conceding some faint glimmer of spirituality, concluded that "in the Tongues Movement it seems as if fanaticism, and sensuality and insanity are not the exception, but the rule!"[28]

Quite closely related to charges of emotional excesses are, in the second place, charges of immorality. Irenaeus hinted at moral abuses in one of his probable references to glossolalia. A certain Marcus, probably a Gnostic, evidently seduced gullible women by promising prophetic inspiration.[29] It was the moral danger especially which caused the early churches to put the lid on tongues and other charismatic phenomena.[30] And, unfortunately for Pentecostalism, this danger has hounded the revival movements with which glossolalia has been connected. The enthusiasm of the revivals was always balanced by the restraining influence of Puritanism, but non-Pentecostals have not remembered this side of the story. The Elmer Gantry image has regularly loomed large in their appraisals. Consequently, isolated stories become typical reports of the ugly side of Pentecostalism.

Another charge which has been used to sustain the demonic or human origins of Pentecostalism is that glossolalia has been divisive. Were it of divine origin, it has been argued, it would help to unite Christians and it would edify the churches. Paul saw this as the chief problem in Corinth (1 Cor. 12-14). New sects or churches have resulted from most of the charismatic revival movements: the Montanists, the Irvingites, the Ranters, the Quakers, the Shakers, the Mormons, and a multiplicity of modern Pente-

---

[27]Origen, *Contra Celsum*, 7.9.

[28]Stolee, *Speaking in Tongues*, p. 65.

[29]Irenaeus, *Against Heresies*, 1.13.3.

[30]See Hinson, "A Brief History of Glossolalia," p. 49.

costal churches. The Pentecostal revival which has invaded mainstream denominations in the past two decades has also resulted in division, bitterness, quarreling, and new churches.

Before taking up the Pentecostal reply to such charges, it will be appropriate to look more closely into contemporary psychological assessments. This more scientific appraisal is of twentieth-century origins, I believe, beginning in Europe in the wake of Freudian studies by E. Lombard[31] and E. Mosiman[32] and being popularized in America by George B. Cutten's well-known book, *Speaking in Tongues*.[33] It has been advanced further by recent studies of Morton T. Kelsey,[34] Wayne E. Oates,[35] and John P. Kildahl.[36] My purpose as a historian is not to assess these studies as applied to individual phenomena but as applied to movements. However, the latter will necessitate some assessment of psychological judgments regarding individuals.

The empirical study of John P. Kildahl, a psychotherapist, led to the framing of three hypotheses about those who have experienced tongues: (1) "That glossolalists are more submissive, suggestible, and dependent in the presence of authority figures than non-tongue-speakers." (2) That they "always thought about some benevolent authority person when they began to speak in tongues" or "initiate their speech in the presence of such a figure, whether in reality or fantasy." (3) That they "feel better about themselves after speaking in tongues" and that this feeling persisted.[37] Kildahl concluded that glossolalia was more or less a learned phenome-

---

[31]Émile Lombard, *De la glossolalie chez les premiers chrétiens et des phénomènes similaires* (Lausanne: Bridel, 1910).

[32]Eddison Mosiman, *Das Zungenreden, geschichtlich und psychologisch untersucht* (Tübingen: J. C. B. Mohr, 1911).

[33]George B. Cutten, *Speaking in Tongues* (New Haven: Yale University Press, 1927).

[34]Morton T. Kelsey, *Tongue Speaking* (Garden City NY: Doubleday, 1964).

[35]Wayne E. Oates, "A Socio-Psychological Study of Glossolalia," in Stagg, Hinson, Oates, *Glossolalia*, pp. 76-79.

[36]John P. Kildahl, *The Psychology of Speaking in Tongues* (New York: Harper & Row, 1972).

[37]Ibid., pp. 40-41.

non, the incidence of which was conditioned in 87 percent of the cases examined by some kind of personal crisis.[38]

Modern psychological interpretations of tongues have discerned among glossolalists a struggle for religious self-expression against a feeling of repression. There is some evidence that outbursts of tongues have been related at different periods to repression in religion. Repression may occur in a variety of ways. One is by *persecution*. In the second century, you will remember, Christians suffered persecution. The Montanists and other glossolalists possibly sought to authenticate their faith in the face of their critics and persecutors with proof. The Cevenol prophets were also reacting to intensive efforts at suppression. Another type of repression is *intellectual*. The heyday of Pentecostalism has also been the heyday of rationalism. The seventeenth and eighteenth centuries were the age of the Enlightenment of France and England, the very countries where the tongue movement broke out again. The twentieth century, the time of the "latter rain," has witnessed the consummation of the critical temperament.

Wayne Oates has called attention to a kind of taboo which the current era has been imposing upon us with reference to God-talk. Whereas Victorians repressed talk about sex, we repress talk about religion. Oates has concluded that this repression "may erupt into turbulent upheavals and expressions of pent-up feelings, such as we find in speaking in tongues. . . . The temper of our times has called forth the emergence of the phenomenon of speaking in tongues."[39] Although he is sympathetic with those who have had the experience, he regards it as a kind of infantilism, an attempt to break through the repressive shell imposed by the age.

DIVINE INSPIRATION AND REVIVAL

On the negative side, in response to charges of demonic inspiration, some Pentecostals readily admit the dangers into which the movement has fallen. Sometimes the experience is an illusion which the devil uses in order to lead the unwary astray. And there are instances of emotional excess, immorality, and divisiveness which mar the record.

However, they go on to argue, the devil may use many other good and properly spiritual things also. Is the danger of emotional excess any greater

---

[38]Ibid., p. 78.

[39]Oates, "A Socio-Psychological Study," p. 83.

than the danger of formalism? The fact is, highly institutionalized churches may be quite safe in their inertia, but this can hardly pass for inspiration of the Spirit. Better too much enthusiasm than none at all!

Further, although charges of immorality may be documented in connection with Pentecostalism, they may also be documented in connection with other Christian movements. Is this type of error, therefore, to be blamed on glossolalia? On the contrary, it can be documented that the experience often leads to moral renewal.

Moreover, where Pentecostalism has been divisive, were glossolalists alone responsible for the division? Or was it their critics, who could not tolerate tongues? Actually, this experience has tended to make people more loving and more devout.

On the positive side, against both demonic and psychological interpretations, Pentecostalists have argued the divine inspiration of the experience. In the main they have interpreted the outburst of tongues as the sign of a charismatic revival in periods when Christianity was lapsing into doctrinal error, formalism, and indifference. According to Harold Horton, it has been "God's unfailing answer to Modernism and Formalism—those 'two new cords' that have ever bound and humiliated the Spirit-filled Church of God."[40] Similarly, Leonard Carroll has connected tongues with release from deadening institutionalism in order to recover the essence of Christianity itself. Many times in history, glossolalia "has broken out of its institutional container—the church—and has reworked the landscape" in order to lay bare "some aspects of Christianity's inner struggle to be more than an extension of some social or secular movement."[41]

It is not possible, of course, to prove empirically whether something like tongues is prompted by the Holy Spirit or by some other external agency. Its validation rests, therefore, on manifest factors like improved moral behavior, churchmanship, personal demeanor, and the like. Pentecostals and Neo-Pentecostals cite an endless number of contemporary examples which confirm their contention. However, historical evidence is a bit harder to handle, and the main contention is that glossolalia has been a feature of great revival movements. How true is this argument?

---

[40]Harold Horton, *Gifts of the Spirit* (London: Assemblies of God), p. 223.

[41]Carroll, "Glossolalia," pp. 74, 94.

In part, as Hoekema has remarked, glossolalia ''has occurred sporadically, under unusual circumstances.''[42] If one lays aside the skimpy data for the period of ''the long drought'' (A.D. 250-1650), however, the Pentecostalist view possesses some substance. From this perspective Montanism represented the first Pentecostalist revival. Although Montanism was guilty of the kind of ecstaticism charged to Pentecostalism, there can be no charges of moral lapse placed against it. On the contrary, it was characterized by a moral rigorism which would not tolerate second marriages, even after the death of a spouse, and encouraged asceticism.

The glossolalia movement in the Cevennes mountains cannot be classified as a revival in the typical sense. It represented rather the frenzied reaction of the Huguenots to severe persecution. However, each of the other recorded occurrences was connected with a larger revival in religion: Both the Ranters and the Quakers arose around 1640 to 1650 in the context of the Puritan movement in England which called for a further reform of the Anglican church. The next outburst came in connection with the Wesleyan revivals in England, around 1740 and after, and the Great Awakening in America, which was itself related to the Wesleyan revivals. The next was related to the frontier revivals, the so-called Second Great Awakening, of the early 1800s. The Shakers originated in this same era and made some contribution to these revivals. However, their practice of glossolalia probably antedated the frontier revivals. A Baptist minister named Valentine Rathbun, Sr., gave an eyewitness report of a Shaker meeting held at Niskeyuna in Massachusetts, May 26, 1780, in which he noted that some sang ''without words, and some with an unknown tongue or mutter, and some with a mixture of English . . . ''[43] The Mormons came into existence in the 1820s, formally in 1830, in connection with the continuing revivalism of that period. In the 1830s also Edward Irving deliberately sought the experience. Finally, modern Pentecostalism originated in the early part of the twentieth century in the context of what J. Edwin Orr has documented as a worldwide revival of religion.[44]

---

[42]Hoekema, *What about Tongue-Speaking?*, p. 23.

[43]Quoted by Edward Deming Andrews, *The People Called Shakers* (New York: Dover, 1953), p. 27.

[44]Unpublished manuscript shown to me by Orr.

If we grant that glossolalia accompanied the revival movements, several questions arise: What contribution did it make to them? Did it have anything to do with their origin? Or, was it more a peripheral appendage?

I find no evidence to support the conclusion that glossolalia preceded any of the revivals. Actually, most, if not all, started rather conservatively and gathered steam as they went. What seems to have triggered most of them was prophetic preaching. There are insufficient grounds to question whether Montanists experienced glossolalia, but there is no doubt that they placed their chief emphasis upon prophecy. Indeed, they called the movement "the new prophecy,"[45] and quotations of Montanus, Priscilla, and Maximilla consist of intelligible prophetic statements. The Great Awakening is usually associated with a revival which broke out in the parish of Jonathan Edwards in Northampton, Massachusetts, around 1735, but it is probably better to see earlier antecedents in the evangelistic activities of Theodore Freylinghuysen and Gilbert and William Tennent in New Jersey. This revival was fanned further by its intersection with the English awakening under the preaching of the Wesleys and George Whitefield.[46] The revivals of the 1800s had a similar start. They usually are traced to a revival at Yale in 1795 with the inauguration of Timothy Dwight; actually, they had an earlier start in two Presbyterian colleges, Hampden-Sydney and Washington, both in Virginia, around 1786.

These three examples will perhaps suffice to illustrate the point. If the implications of it are accurate, glossolalia must be seen as a secondary feature of revivalism. It broke out as the larger revivals gathered momentum and increased in emotional fervor. There would appear to be some basis in history for the conclusion of Kildahl that tongues are learned. In most instances glossolalia has been part of an attempt to recapture apostolic Christianity literally in its entirety, above all the power of it, understood in terms of religious enthusiasm. The only quibble which we can have here with this restorationist philosophy is: How far do we go in imitating the primitive church?

---

[45]Tertullian, *Against Marcion*, 4.22; *On Fasting*, 1.

[46]See William Warren Sweet, *Revivalism in America* (New York: Scribner's, 1944), pp. 44ff.

A HISTORIAN'S POSTSCRIPT

Up to this point I have attempted to present the two sides of the Pentecostal debate. I should like now to draw some conclusions in response to the preceding arguments but based on a full assessment of the data. Basically these conclusions plow a furrow between the two sharply contrasting camps. For the sake of clarity the conclusions will be put in the form of answers to several questions.

First, how much evidence is there for glossolalia? Until the twentieth century there is limited evidence. I believe that by dividing the history into four segments this fact is obvious: (1) Early Showers (A.D. 100-250), (2) Long Drought (A.D. 250-1650), (3) Later Showers (1650-1900), and (4) Latter Rain (1900-). In all except the second period we can think in terms of Pentecostal movements and not simply isolated, spasmodic experiences of certain individuals. If we can trust any of the evidence for the second period, it was the one in which glossolalia occurred as a more or less individual phenomenon, if at all. In the other three periods tongues has probably played a more or less important role in the movements in which it occurred, but, until the twentieth century, these movements have not made a lasting or far-reaching impact on the church as a whole.

These facts pose a second question: Why has the history of glossolalia, especially in the Middle Ages, been so spasmodic? Here neither the Pentecostal nor the strong anti-Pentecostal answer seems to suffice. If, as the Pentecostals argue, this was due to a kind of "fall" of the church, then would there not have been all the more reason to expect more vigorous outbursts since tongues is supposed to accompany spiritual revival? On the other hand, if you say, as anti-Pentecostals do, that such phenomena were supposed to occur only in the apostolic age and then cease, what is to keep someone else from arguing the same about many other happenings in the life of the church? Furthermore, is it theologically acceptable to say that God works one way in one era and another way in another? And, along the same line, is it acceptable to interpret the same phenomena one way for the apostolic period and another way for our day? In other words, granted that tongues and related charismatic displays today may not have a divine origin, do you not have to ask the same of those which occurred in the apostolic age?

The historian probably cannot give a conclusive answer to the question: Why did tongues appear so spasmodically? For that reason it will be more illuminating to ask: Why did tongues die out during the third century, perhaps even among the Montanists, who continued until the fifth or sixth century?

This question, of course, has to be answered in connection with the contemporaneous decline of other individual charismata. During the second century and after, the early Christians were shifting the sphere in which they believed the Holy Spirit to operate. Rather than associating his operation with glossolalia, visions, auditories, healings, and other phenomenal occurrences, they began emphasizing his operation through the ordered life of the church—baptism, eucharist, ministry—and in proper faith, love, and morality. Why?

The answer is already evident in 1 Corinthians. Phenomenal displays did convince some pagans, for they lived in an era when they expected such things of the gods or demons. But the problem lay in determining where they originated. *Were they of the Holy Spirit or of the demonic spirits?* The ancients knew all sorts of miracle workers who claimed to receive their power from the gods of demons (the two words used almost interchangeably), who were believed to be both good and bad. There was Apollonius of Tyana, a Greek Neo-Pythagorean philosopher, magician, and miracle worker of the first century A.D. whom pagans cited as their answer to Jesus. Who was to say which wonder was valid and which was not when, on the surface, they appeared to be the same? About the only answer Christian apologists had to this was that Christians did not use the artifices pagans did in order to perform their wonders. Tatian, a late second-century apologist who could find little that was good in Hellenistic thought, even conceded that demons (the gods) could heal the sick. However, he went on to argue, they did so only to get the unwary in their power again. Whoever wishes real help should turn to God's power, and he will receive the Holy Spirit and be truly healed.[47]

Thus, whereas a few pagans were convinced that Christianity was the superior religion by virtue of its miraculous powers, many others were not. Those who could be convinced were people of more limited education. However, as early Christianity placed its appeals more and more before

---

[47]*Address to the Greeks*, 18, 20.

the better educated, it found itself rebuffed for its reliance upon phenomenal moods. The pagan Celsus' critique here is instructive. He ridiculed, you will recall, the (Montanist?) evangelist with his message of hellfire and brimstone followed by "incomprehensible, incoherent, and utterly obscure utterances, the meaning of which no intelligent person could discover; . . . " What he found particularly offensive was that, by using meaningless and nonsensical gibberish, they "give a chance for any fool or sorcerer to take the words in whatever sense he likes."[48] In ecstatic trances the Montanist prophets seem also to have made exaggerated claims about themselves, for example, "I am God [or a son of God, or a divine Spirit]. And I have come."[49] This is a claim which has sometimes occurred subsequently in charismatic revivals, for example, among the Ranters.[50]

If tongues and related phenomena could not be relied upon to authenticate Christianity, then the churches had to find something which could. Paul already pointed the direction here. The "fruit of the Spirit" is not visible in tongues, prophecies, healings, and so on as much as in "love, joy, peace, patience, kindness, goodness, faithfulness, gentleness, self-control," that is to say, in Christian behavior (Gal. 5:22-23). These are self-authenticating. They do not need to be validated before they can serve as proofs of the superiority of Christianity. This, likewise, was what Augustine was to argue in his treatise *On Baptism, Against the Donatists*. The Spirit is known in faith, love, and proper moral behavior. Heretics lack the Spirit because they lack love, as demonstrated by their schismatic nature. Evil Christians lack the Spirit because they do not behave as Christians.

The problem of validation, therefore, has been and will remain the fundamental problem of glossolalia and other experiential religious phenomena. Glossolalia may well be, as Paul would allow, "of the Spirit," but, except to the person who has the experience, it is not self-authenticating. It requires its own validation in faith, love, and morality. Consequently, it can provide at best only a secondary kind of witness to Christianity, one which helps to reinforce the basic witness.

---

[48]Origen, *Contra Celsum*, 7.9.

[49]Ibid., also Epiphanius, *Heresies*, 48.

[50]See Hinson, "A Brief History of Glossolalia," p. 63.

This brings us to a third question: If tongue-speaking has only secondary value, why has it occurred at all? As my discussion in the preceding section indicates, I am inclined to accept the contention of Pentecostals and Neo-Pentecostals that it has been related to larger charismatic revivals. As stated by Dennis Bennett, Episcopal rector in Van Nuys, California, who first reported the outbreak of Neo-Pentecostalism, the current revival of tongues in non-Pentecostal churches is part of a great charismatic revival which will sweep across America and the world and bring an end to the advance of secularism and restore vitality and unity to a weak and fragmented church. Bennett goes on to set the charismatic revival over against the rationalism of the day. Christianity, he insists, is ''not an intellectual matter at all. It is a purely personal and spiritual matter.''[51]

If we lay aside the highly debatable evidence for isolated instances of tongue-speaking, most of its history fits into the era of extreme rationalism, from the Enlightenment on. While rationalism has become the religion of vast numbers as Western science has registered more and more triumphs, revivalism has offered a more or less clear-cut alternative. As rationalism has gained converts, Pentecostalism has gained.

There is an interesting confirmation of this same point from the reverse side. There is the least evidence, hardly any at all, for the era in which rationalism made its poorest showing. The Middle Ages saw the ascension of belief, of the intuitive. It was ''the age of faith'' or ''the age of assent.'' Man's capacities or desires for the intuitive were being fulfilled. People looked at reality through the eyes of the mystics—Pseudo-Dionysius, Bernard of Clairvaux, Francis of Assisi. Art and architecture reminded them that an ethereal world lay in, around, and under the world of sensible realities. Their lives turned on the axis of the spiritual presided over by the church.

The Renaissance began to swing all of this around. It revived the rationalism of ancient Greece and Rome. People began to turn for guidance to the scientists—Copernicus, Galileo—away from the mystics. Art and architecture no longer pointed toward the ethereal. Rather, they depicted the real world as the best of all possible worlds. Temporal things became the focus of life.

---

[51]Dennis Bennett, *The New Pentecost Charismatic Revival Seminar Report*, Full Gospel Business Men's Fellowship International, 1963, p. 9.

The Protestant Reformation perhaps slowed down the momentum of rationalism. By the seventeenth century, however, the locomotive had gathered a full head of steam. The deists were proposing a rational religion to replace the religion of revelation. They pictured the universe as a clock which ticked along with unerring regularity. Everything operates according to clearly discernible natural laws. To be happy, man needs to act rationally, according to enlightened self-interest. Religion is a matter of morality.

It was in this context that Christianity began to feel the effects of indifference and criticism which led to the revival movements with which evidences of glossolalia are associated. These movements have sought to say, "Religion is not solely an affair of the mind. Indeed, it is not primarily an affair of the mind. It is, rather, an affair of the heart."

The argument that religion is primarily of the heart for a long time caught the ears mostly of the culturally and educationally deprived. The revivals—Ranters, Quakers, Wesleyan, and so on—began with the working classes, only occasionally attracting some of the cultured. Pentecostalism, coming out of Methodism, also gained its following among these. Neo-Pentecostalism, however, has not done so. It started and it has gained more and more adherents among the better educated and culturally advantaged. Why is this so? Is this not inconsistent with the argument that glossolalia is an answer to rationalism?

No, I do not think so. Quite the contrary. A series of crises in Western civilization has undermined a once limitless faith in science even among the culturally privileged. In America, the war in Vietnam, the violence in the great cities, problems of pollution, political problems, and many others have shown the inadequacy of a society based entirely upon the rational. And, as a consequence, hundreds of those who have depended most upon the rational have begun to trumpet the nonrational and intuitive. It is not surprising, then, that major outbursts of tongue-speaking have occurred at Yale, Princeton, Notre Dame, and other major campuses. It is not surprising that people of some prominence, like M. G. "Pat" Robertson, son of former Virginia senator A. Willis Robertson, have sought the experience and given their support to the movement. It is not surprising that glossolalia has occurred in mainstream denominations—Baptist, Presbyterian, Methodist, Episcopal, and even Roman Catholic. The popularity of tongue-speaking harmonizes perfectly with the widespread incidence of experiential religions of both secular and religious orientation:

the Hippies, the Jesus Movement, Campus Crusade for Christ, Satanism, witchcraft, and dozens more.

If glossolalia is related in this manner to revival movements, it is appropriate to inquire more specifically into the connection. Is it an integral feature of the experiential revival, or more peripheral? Does it really contribute to the revival?

The history of glossolalia, despite what the Pentecostalists say, suggests that glossolalia was more or less peripheral. At best it was a sign of the revival rather than an integral feature of it. There is no evidence to show, as stated earlier, that glossolalia preceded a revival. Instead, the outburst of tongues occurred after the revival movement had gathered its full momentum; then, it has tended to dwindle after the movement has passed its peak. This is true of the practice among Quakers, Methodists, Shakers, Mormons, and Irvingites. The early Quaker intensity of emotion in which the quakes occurred gave way quickly to reflective piety and social concern. During his lifetime, John Wesley struggled with the issue of the propriety of various charismatic displays and finally decided that glossolalia should be counted neither too significant nor too insignificant. Later, Methodism moved toward the rational as its constituency came increasingly from the upper classes. The Shakers continued to hold a place for glossolalia, but it never had the importance their sacred dances did. The Mormons have all but forbidden tongue-speaking in recent years.[52]

To some extent Pentecostals are the exception to the general pattern, and my contention requires some qualification in their case. Certainly it is to be conceded that most Pentecostals have kept glossolalia in the center. How have they done so when other groups have abandoned it or shoved it to the periphery? This is a difficult question to answer, but one or two factors may be cited:

For one thing, none of the other revival movements made the phenomenon so central. Pentecostals alone allotted glossolalia a central place in the credo. Many have insisted that only those who have had the baptism of the Spirit have had an authentic conversion.

For another, Pentecostals have sought to share the experience with evangelistic zeal. Pentecostalism has grown by leaps and bounds since its birth in the beginning of the twentieth century. Pentecostals have not stood

---

[52]See Hinson, "History of Glossolalia," p. 66.

by passively while this occurred. Their evangelists and missionaries have gone to the uttermost parts of the earth. Indeed, I am convinced, as I wrote earlier,[53] that Neo-Pentecostalism took its rise from the efforts of the Full Gospel Business Men's Fellowship International. This organization was founded by Pentecostals in 1953; only later did it incorporate others. All instances of persons who have recorded an experience of tongues which I have read report contact with Pentecostals or Neo-Pentecostals. So tongues initially seem to have been taught rather than caught.

CONCLUSION AND EPILOGUE

To sum up, glossolalia has been neither as significant as Pentecostalists contend nor as insignificant as anti-Pentecostals contend. It has accompanied a number of important revival or renewal movements in the history of Christianity, but it does not appear to have stood at the center of any save modern Pentecostalism. In the others it was a peripheral sign of the revival which faded as time passed. Pentecostals, however, have kept alive the experience of tongues by deliberately placing it in the center of the movement and ardently propagandizing for it. In recent years their evangelism has borne fruit in non-Pentecostal denominations.

As far as non-Pentecostals are concerned, there does not appear to me to be reason for the alarm which many have registered. If we do not make too much ado about it, there is a real likelihood, judging from history, that it will wither away, leaving only a small knot to remind us that it once started to sprout as a sign of spring. Attempts to tear off the sprout or to keep it from growing will do more harm than good in that they will produce divisions. It is perhaps best to keep in mind the counsel of Gamaliel with reference to the early disciples when they refused to stop preaching: " . . . if this idea or movement is of human origin, it will come to nought, but if it is from God, you will not be able to stop it. You may actually find yourselves fighting God!'' (Acts 5:38-38, Goodspeed).

----

[53]E. Glenn Hinson, "Why a Book on Glossolalia Today?'' in Frank Stagg, E. Glenn Hinson, and Wayne E. Oates, *Glossolalia: Tongue Speaking in Biblical, Historical, and Psychological Perspective* (Nashville: Abingdon Press, 1967), p. 12.

11

NATHAN L. GERRARD

The Holiness Movement
in Southern Appalachia

[Reprinted from *The Charismatic Movement*, edited by Michael P. Hamilton (Eerdmans, 1975), pp. 159-71. Reprinted with permission from Eerdmans Publishing Company.]

The term *Holiness movement* refers generically to dozens of sect-like groups with thousands of churches all over the nation and millions of members who strive to achieve spiritual perfection through strong emotional experience allegedly inspired by the beliefs and practices of primitive Christianity. Speaking in tongues is a frequent part of their religious experience. It has been estimated that there are approximately five million Holiness people in the United States alone.

There is much disagreement as to the most appropriate ways of achieving the state of holiness. The range is from the self-contained piety of the Adventists to the highly visible emotional fury of some "Jesus Only" churches. Although almost all Holiness churches originated as lower-class sects or as sects of newly ascending social classes in evangelical and scriptural opposition to the formalism of the dominant established churches, each social class develops a kind of Holiness church that is congenial to its lifestyle.

Southern Appalachian people, particularly small-town and open-country dwellers, take their religion seriously. A majority of Appalachians still adhere to Protestant fundamentalism; i.e., belief in the literal interpretation of the Scriptures, and Puritan morality, despite the social and economic changes embodying urban values that have taken place in the region during the twentieth century. Fundamentalism is still quite strong in religious groups that at one time evinced sectarian tendencies but are now the dominant churches of the lower and upper middle classes—Baptists, Methodists, and Presbyterians. The religious heritage of the region, however, is preserved in nearly pristine purity in the churches of the lower classes, particularly in remote valleys or hollows—pronounced "hollers," the communities of the nonfarm rural poor. This heritage is fundamentalistic, sectarian, and experiential. Originating in European religious dissent, it developed against a background of almost two centuries of subsistence agriculture, durable kinship ties, individualism, independence, and egalitarianism. It was shaped in large part and stimulated by the numerous and almost continuous revivals of the nineteenth century, and persisted in almost complete isolation from the urbanization which was going on in most of the rest of American society. The contemporary preservers of this heritage are indeed "Yesterday's People," and to an outsider, their religious beliefs and practices may very well appear strange.

I shall discuss the socioeconomic life-style of these "contemporary primitives," the religious beliefs, practices, and structure of their churches, and the social and psychological functions which account for the viability of these churches in the modern United States. I shall call these churches *Holiness churches of the stationary poor*.

A third of the families in Southern Appalachia can be called *poor* according to the standards of an affluent America. But the poor do not constitute a single homogeneous sociological group, and for our purposes we can distinguish two types of poor: the stationary poor and the upwardly mobile poor.

LIFE-STYLES—THE UPWARDLY MOBILE POOR

Among the upwardly mobile poor, the heads of the family are regularly employed at tedious and backbreaking jobs as laborers, service workers, and farmers. They themselves have little hope for advancement. They make strenuous efforts, however, to lead respectable lives according to the standards of the middle class of their community. The prospect of welfare assistance is looked upon with repugnance, and they feel humiliated when, because of severe illness or accidents, they are forced to accept aid. The homes in which our upwardly mobile poor live are painted, in good repair, well scrubbed, and tidy. Clothes are clean, although patched, and the family income is carefully budgeted. Children are taught to respect their elders, especially those in authority, such as teachers, and their activities and associates outside the home tend to be supervised. The father, acutely aware that his own upward strivings have been blocked by his meager education, advises the older children to postpone marriage, and encourages them to finish high school. Both mother and father expect their children to enjoy a better life, to have a higher standard of living and a higher social position, than they themselves have, and they raise their children accordingly. Some of the mothers attend PTA meetings, where they observe closely the ways of middle-class mothers.

Parents of the upwardly mobile poor attend church almost as regularly as do the middle classes. The churches they attend are the churches of the lower middle class, the class with which the members of the upwardly mobile poor identify, and to which they aspire. In the rural communities of Southern Appalachia, such churches are likely to be Methodist and Baptist, sometimes Presbyterian. If the need for respectability is accompanied by a nostalgic yearning for the strict fundamentalism and some of the fervor of old-fashioned religion, they may join such evangelical churches as the several Churches of God, the Adventists, Churches of Christ, various Pentecostal churches, the Church of the Nazarene, and the Assemblies of God. Or within the major denominations they may join the Wesleyan Methodist Church, the General Association of Regular Baptists, and the Orthodox Presbyterian churches.

We have called these poor people upwardly mobile because while not many of the parents, particularly those over forty, will manage to move out of the ranks of the poor, their children probably will.

LIFE-STYLES—THE STATIONARY POOR

The second group among the poor are those whose children probably will also be poor the rest of their lives. Working adults in these families are mostly unskilled and functionally illiterate. Their jobs tend to be seasonal or cyclical so that there are long periods of unemployment and underemployment. There are periods of hard times, and over the years the family income has to be supplemented by various kinds of welfare payments. Many of these families have been receiving public assistance for two or three generations. It is extremely difficult to save money even for necessities on their low, irregular incomes; getting cash involves a constant struggle. Frequently the family does not know where the next meal is coming from. Food is bought whenever anyone has cash or food stamps. During most of the month, purchases are made only for the day ahead. Members of the stationary poor are sick often and their medical care is poor.

The ceaseless struggle to make ends meet, to take care of the barest necessities, tends to foster a fatalistic outlook on life. This outlook can express itself in two sharply contrasting ways. The first is cynical and pessimistic. The sociologists sometimes call this "anomie." The attitude is: "Nothing good will ever happen to me." It is manifest in squalor, the failure to make the most of the little one has: dirty dishes in the sink; unrepaired, tattered furniture; litter in the rooms and around the unpainted shack; bugs and sometimes rats. It is also manifest in reckless hedonism, the conviction of those leading insecure, unpredictable lives that a pleasure postponed is a pleasure forever lost. A commonly encountered view is: "I'm going to live today. Who cares about tomorrow?" Reckless hedonism results in noisy drinking bouts, illegitimate births, incest, absenteeism or quitting jobs in order to go hunting or fishing, spur-of-the-moment purchases of luxuries when money is needed for necessities, and other kinds of behavior that are incomprehensible from a middle-class point of view.

Among the young adults of the stationary poor, a frequent manifestation of pessimistic fatalism is the attitude that too high a price should not be placed upon human life, not only upon the lives of others but also upon their own. A frequent response to the frictions and frustrations of their impoverished existence is physical violence, usually directed against friends or members of one's family. The bravery of southern Appalachians in war is well known.

Perhaps the most extreme manifestation of pessimistic fatalism is to be found among the elderly, who have discovered over the years that recklessness inevitably brings painful consequences. They feel that their only alternative is to search for apathy, a state of mind which while devoid of pleasure is also devoid of pain. The quest for apathy is manifest not only in soporific types of alcoholism but also in the very high rates of the type of psychosis loosely called schizophrenia, in which apathy and withdrawal from the external world are central. This apathy is usually accompanied by very low self-esteem. Such persons feel they are so worthless they don't even have a right to complain. The quest for apathy is to be found in its most extreme form in the quest for final oblivion, in suicide. Suicide rates are highest among the stationary poor.

The second way in which the fatalistic outlook can express itself is religious. Religious fatalism is the feeling that one's destiny is in God's hands. Since they conceive of God as loving and forgiving, as well as righteous, many of the religious poor achieve a psychological poise which enables them to carry on despite the trials and tribulations of their position at the bottom of the social and economic pyramids.

In the mine disaster at Hominy Falls, West Virginia, press coverage was extensive. Particular attention was paid to the six men, all but given up for dead, who were trapped in a thirty-six inch tunnel by rising water. One miner who was rescued after ten days was asked whether he would return to the mines. "I'll have to go over that with God," he said. "Whatever his plans are for me, that's what I'll do." The wife of another rescued man said she never doubted throughout the long wait that her husband would come out alive. "God told me he'd be all right," she said.

Unlike the upwardly mobile poor, the religious stationary poor do not hesitate very long before applying for welfare assistance when they are out of funds and out of work. They take their obligation to keep their families from going hungry more seriously than their worldly pride. I was present at a Holiness meeting when a member of the congregation voiced his opinion that welfare recipients were lazy and worthless. Although not more than one or two members of the congregation actually were receiving welfare, the response evoked was indignant and almost unanimous. The rugged individualist was castigated as unchristian.

As a matter of fact, religious fatalists are much less likely to be on welfare than are the pessimistic fatalists. Sober, scrupulous about money matters, and believing in giving an honest day's work in return for an honest day's pay, they are much less likely to be unemployed. I was informed by the manager of a chain of retail stores that quite a number of his cashiers are petty embezzlers, but that those who belong to Holiness churches are reliable and honest.

Although the women are far from compulsive housekeepers, the homes of the religious fatalists are almost as tidy as those of the upwardly mobile.

Children are taught to be courteous and well-mannered. In other respects, the style of life of the religious fatalists of the stationary poor resembles the style of life of the upwardly mobile poor. The central difference is that to the religious fatalists among the stationary poor, success in the pursuit of holiness is much more important than worldly success. Their children are not discouraged from marrying young or from dropping out of school. I know a bright young Holiness man who at the age of twenty-one already has three children. He married at the age of sixteen with the encouragement of his parents because he was marrying a Holiness girl. With an elementary school education and an ever increasing family, he will probably be poor the rest of his life. In the meantime, he and his nineteen-year-old wife attend Holiness church sessions at least three nights a week, taking their children with them, and the general picture is of an affectionate and harmonious family.

THE HOLINESS CHURCHES

The religious stationary poor spend a great deal of time listening to religious radio and television programs sponsored by the established evangelical churches. The elderly, particularly, enjoy the faith-healing of Oral Roberts, and anyone who turns on a radio in Appalachia is aware that there are dozens of radio programs of highly emotional religious content to be heard almost any time of the day.

The religious stationary poor find the rituals of the conventional middle-class churches formalistic and unsatisfying, and they feel ill-at-ease in the presence of the well-dressed and the conventionally polite who go to these churches. They look upon the tight scheduling and the role-stability[1] of the services as both unholy and absurd. They call such churches and their members ''stiff-necked.''

They do not feel at home even in the established evangelistic churches which allow the members of the congregation some freedom of emotional expression. A member of the stationary poor once attended a Church of God service in his community. While he was listening to the services, he felt he was being moved by the Holy Ghost. He asked the minister for per-

---

[1]By role-stability I am referring to the fact that in conventional churches, the same person delivers the sermon every Sunday, the same person plays the organ, the same people sing in the choir.

mission to testify. The minister, looking at his wrist watch, told him he could have five minutes whereupon this member of the stationary poor walked out in indignation, never to return. In telling me the story, he said: "Brother Gerrard, the Holy Ghost does not wear a wrist watch!"

The stationary poor prefer to seek religious fellowship in their own unpainted one-room frame churches, in abandoned school houses, in barns, in crudely constructed tabernacles, in tents, or in each other's homes. There are thousands of such churches in rural Southern Appalachia. They are to be found on secondary and tertiary roads where land values are very low. They are the equivalent of the storefront churches of the city poor. The stranger who passes one of these churches will not recognize it as a church unless he looks closely. Then he might observe a cross on the roof constructed of two-by-fours nailed together, or "Jesus Saves" crudely printed in whitewash on the front or the sides.

Many of these churches do not have names, but are identified by the community in which they are located, such as Camp Creek, Scrabble Creek or Frazier's Bottom. Of those churches which do have names, "Jesus Only" is probably most common. "Church of All Nations" is another frequent name. Or there will be a variety of names preceded by the word "Free."

Even where a church has a name, there frequently is no identifying sign on the building or in the yard. People in that area, when asked, will immediately identify it as "Ed Blankenship's church," or "Brother Homer's church."

These churches are not owned by their congregations but by individuals who built their own churches in order to worship as freely as they pleased. Sometimes the owner dominates the services and lets people in or keeps them out according to personal whim. One very strong personality, the "owner" of his church, changes congregations about every two years. He expels the old congregation and recruits a new one, the converse of middle-class churches in which ministers are sometimes expelled but congregations never. There is much variation, however. Some owners are self-effacing and welcome anyone who comes.

The services and beliefs of these privately owned, unaffiliated mountain churches have been standardized by the almost continuous religious revivals of the nineteenth century, the earliest being the great Kentucky Revival of 1800 to 1803, which spread rapidly to Tennessee and adjacent states.

RELIGIOUS BELIEFS AND PRACTICES
IN THE HOLINESS CHURCHES

In general, it can be said that the stationary poor carry individualism in religion to an extreme. Each man is indeed his own Pope. Since they lack the intellectual resources and will for doctrinal elaboration, the main emphasis is on emotional religious experience. Their theology is simple and concrete, and there is great variation in detail from local church to local church—and quite a bit from individual to individual within the same local church. Nevertheless, they all seem to share the belief that their religion represents a return to the purity of the Christians of the first century, and that the larger, more formalized churches are fallen and corrupt.

The theology, or foci of religious belief, of the churches serving the stationary poor can perhaps be best discussed under three headings: fundamentalism, other-worldliness, and perfectionism.

Fundamentalism. In these churches and among a large segment of the Appalachian poor, the Bible is seen as the sole justification of religious practices, with every word divinely inspired and literally true. Knowledge of the Bible is fragmentary, and passages are frequently cited out of context or in garbled form. Often there is no Bible in the church unless a member brings one, but this is not surprising since most members of the congregation, at least among the middle-aged and elderly, are functionally illiterate. Nevertheless, the members enjoy doctrinal disputes, and the older men in particular fancy themselves as biblical authorities. The issues argued, however, seldom involve conflicting interpretations of the same biblical passages, but are more likely to be a confrontation based upon apparently contradictory passages from different parts of the Bible. An outsider may sometimes get the impression that the cited "quotations" have been improvised in the heat of debate—chapter, verse, and all. The arguments in the disputes, like the testimonies and sermons, resemble streams of consciousness rather than logical discourse.

To the religious fatalists among the stationary poor, God is not a metaphysical abstraction but a real person. In fact, they often see him during vivid hallucinations, usually as a smiling, gentle Jesus. One Holiness church member, more literate than most in the congregation, remarked with a smile: "God isn't dead. He wasn't even sick when I talked to him this morning."

These people believe in the reality of the devil, who is hallucinated in various forms: sometimes with stereotyped horns and tail; sometimes as a loathsome insect; and sometimes, perhaps as a result of their economic deprivation, as a well-dressed man with white shirt, tie, and jacket. A Holiness church member once remarked in my presence: "When I think of the devil, I think of Mr. Mullins, the coal company's lawyer."

Other-worldliness. Not able to find luxuries, the stationary poor often make a virtue out of necessity, and view the pleasures and vanities of the world as incongruent with a way of life guided by the Holy Spirit. Subject to taboo are liquor, movies, athletic events, beauty parlors, jewelry, and makeup. They regard the use of cigarettes and chewing tobacco as "filth of the flesh." Sometimes even coffee and soft drinks are proscribed, but most Holiness people, like other members of the stationary poor, spend a disproportionate share of their income on soft drinks, as much as a dollar a day when they have the cash.

However, despite their strong feelings about the evils of the world, they are completely indifferent to the *social gospel* and take no interest in politics even when temperance is an issue at election time, as it is so often in Appalachia. They believe it is useless to reform the social order, so they concentrate on saving individual souls. Often stigmatized as "ignorant Holy Rollers," they do not participate in the few voluntary associations which exist in mountain communities.

The other-worldliness of these people is also manifest in the fact that many believe in the more or less imminent end of the world by means of a cosmic catastrophe, and what they hear about events in the real world tends to reinforce this belief. They look forward to the second coming of Christ and the establishment of the millennium.

Perfectionism. The stationary poor who are members of Holiness churches believe it is possible to attain in this life, despite man's original sin, a spiritual state of being which is free not only of sinful deeds, but— much more important—of sinful desires. This belief contrasts with the teaching of the Catholic Church, which stresses that a state of holiness can be gradually achieved by a very few through monastic asceticism and meditation, and the teaching of the established evangelical churches, which emphasize the holiness may begin with an experience of emotional regeneration, but that holiness requires a long spiritual growth. However, the stationary poor, it seems, cannot afford to wait. They believe that anyone who believes strongly enough can achieve holiness instantaneously and completely through the direct operation of the Holy Spirit in a violent emotional experience. This is frequently preceded by an emotional upheaval during which the individual, awakened from spiritual indifference, agonizingly repents of his sins.

The experience of *conversion* and *sanctification* are stimulated and encouraged by such familiar revival techniques as highly emotional sermons and testimonies, repeating and emphasizing the theme of damnation and salvation—especially salvation. Singing by the congregation, with hand-clapping and foot-stomping, is particularly effective. Even the smallest churches have members who play guitars, harmonicas, fiddles, and perhaps even cymbals, tambourines, and accordions. The pronounced beat and rhythm are contagious and create group rapport. The participant tends to lose self-consciousness and becomes highly suggestible to the central theme of the songs, sermons, and testimonies.

Subjective evidence of *sanctification* is the experience in feeling oneself in direct communion with God, the feeling that one has become a passive instrument of his will, and the attendant feeling of joy and rapture. External evidence is involuntary behavior that cannot be explained except in terms of control by the Holy Spirit: speaking in tongues, shrieking, convulsive dancing, rolling on the floor, jerking, jumping, and even passing into states of unconsciousness. Services in Holiness churches are noisy; the very walls and floors seem to rattle with the activity.

While roles in the church are culturally stereotyped, i.e., dancer, singer, faith-healer, testifier, etc., enactment is almost completely unstructured and spontaneous. Role-playing is very fluid, depending on the individual member's mood at the moment. Members who are passive on one occasion may dominate the meeting on another with their dancing and testifying. This constitutes an important appeal of the church, for if one feels the power of the Holy Spirit, there are almost no structural obstacles to immediate, untrammeled expression. In fact, such obstacles would be considered sacrilegious. This is one important reason why religious sessions are sometimes five or six hours long. No one would consider bringing the meeting to an end until every member who was so disposed had been given the opportunity to express his religious urges fully.

The fact that role-playing is fluid, that no distinction is made between ministry and laity, no record of membership is kept, no dues are collected, and that participants tend to sample other churches in the area indicates a social organization that is almost anarchical. I am not too happy with the terms *sect* or *church* to describe the religious fellowships of the stationary poor. Both terms connote a firmness of structure that does not exist. Perhaps the term *religious band* would be more precise.

The extreme individualism of the participants in the religious bands of the stationary poor frequently leads to religious innovations that most of us would label as queer or immoral or even pathological. The members of one Holiness church in Kanawha County, West Virginia, for example, believe in the immortality not only of the soul but of the body. To them the body is the temple of the soul, and if the soul is pure, the temple will last forever. Members of other Holiness churches refer to this group as the "Neverdies."

Members of another Holiness church in the same county practice a form of polygamy. If a married man talks to a married woman who is not his wife, and both feel the power of the Holy Ghost, they will leave their spouses and start a new "marriage" which they believe has been made in heaven. After the heavenly bliss has worn off, they will return to their spouses, to resume what they call the "marriages made in the world."

SOCIAL AND PSYCHOLOGICAL FUNCTIONS OF HOLINESS GROUPS

Although the evidence is inconclusive and indirect, Holiness churches of the stationary poor appear to be holding their own in rural Southern Appalachia, and are even springing up in Northern cities where there are substantial settlements of rural migrants from the Southern Appalachian region. The precarious nature of physical survival and the loneliness and emotional starvation of social life in the scattered settlements of the frontier explain, in important part, the appeal of revivalism in the past. The problem is to explain the viability of the Holiness churches of the stationary poor in the present, when the level of living has been raised considerably and isolation has been greatly reduced by paved roads, mass communication, consolidated schools, and other innovations embodying urban values.

It would seem that the rural Holiness churches are viable because they serve to alleviate anxieties gathered by status deprivation, guilt and illness, and last, but not unimportantly, because they supply recreation in areas of the region where recreational facilities are scarce.

It is not biological deprivation associated with low economic status that bothers the stationary poor so much as status deprivation. Increased contact with urban standards of achievement and success has developed a new awareness of social and cultural advantages they do not possess. Self-esteem based on the egalitarianism of their rural tradition is shaken, and strong feelings of social inadequacy emerge. In the religious fellowship of their church they experience an enhanced sense of personal worth and dignity. They enjoy status security as a member of God's elect.

They have been reared in a guilt culture and thus tend to interpret their present misfortunes and occasional moral lapses as signs of being unworthy of the affection and approval of their primary ''we'' group. In accordance with their religious beliefs, guilt means ''sin,'' the disapproval of a righteous God, the collective representation of the most important values of their group. The burden of sin is a very heavy one to bear, and unless relieved may lead to mental illness or other aberrations. But in the religious fellowship of the Holiness church they experience conversion and sanctification, they are reconciled with their group—their God—and they gain the psychological poise to carry on in the face of the trials and stresses of their existence at the bottom of the socioeconomic pyramid.

There is a great deal of illness among the poor, and medical facilities are scarce and inaccessible. Especially the older poor suffer from a wide variety of physical ailments. Participation in religious services of the Holiness churches, particularly the faith-healing rituals, enables them to ignore or to minimize their ailments.

Holiness church services are spontaneous, exciting, rhythmical, dramatic, and sometimes even humorous. Unlike many participants in conventional churches, the participants in Holiness churches are seldom bored. The general atmosphere is one of joy and pleasure despite the occasional exhibitions of agony attendant upon the conversion experience and the sober recital of ailments that precede faith-healing rituals. ''Jesus is fun'' is a cry that is sometimes heard during services, or a preacher might say: ''Let's all have a good time in Jesus tonight.''

It is well to keep in mind that unlike the pessimistic fatalists the religious fatalists are poor not because they are not thrifty—their religion forbids them to spend money on luxuries; not because they lack responsible work habits—their religion teaches them to be conscientious; not because they lack social skills—their religion teaches them to be loving toward others. They are poor because like the pessimistic fatalists they drop out of school early, work at relatively unskilled jobs, marry young, and have many children. They have many virtues which still have meaning and relevance for social life in the contemporary United States.

THE SNAKE HANDLERS

Perhaps the most numerous of the bizarre churches in Southern Appalachia are the serpent handlers. They are scorned by other Holiness churches as "possessed by the devil" and by the educated as emotionally disturbed. A service in one of these churches is likely to include tongue-speaking, hymn singing, healing prayers, and the other familiar expressions of Holiness worship. But in addition there is a period of ten or fifteen minutes when volunteers from the congregation come forward and pick up snakes as they continue to speak praises of God. The snakes used are rattlesnakes and copperheads. This dangerous ritual adds much to the excitement of the service, and indeed in the days preceding the occasion it is anticipated with some relish by members of the congregation.

The two or three dozen serpent-handling churches in Southern Appalachia justify the use of poisonous snakes in their religious services by quoting Mark 16:15-18:

> . . . And these signs shall follow them that believe: In my name shall they cast out devils; they shall speak with new tongues; *they shall take up serpents,* and if they drink any deadly thing it shall not hurt them; they shall lay hands on the sick and they shall recover.

Weston La Barre[2] believes that the founder of Christian serpent-handling was George Went Hensley, who initiated the ritual in rural Grasshopper Valley, Tennessee, during the first decade of the twentieth century. Hensley evangelized widely from Tennessee to Florida, particularly in Kentucky. Serpent-handling became widely diffused in the South, and in 1945 there occurred the first recorded death from snakebite suffered in a religious service.

Since then, about twenty-three more deaths have been reported in the press, taking place in Georgia, Alabama, Tennessee, Kentucky, and other Southern states. In 1955 Hensley himself, then seventy years old, died in

---

[2]The following paragraph uses La Barre's account from *They Shall Take Up Serpents: Psychology of the Southern Snake-Handling Cult* (Minneapolis, 1962).

Florida of snakebite. Five deaths have occurred in West Virginia since 1961, the most recent in 1974.

Serpent-handling has been outlawed by the state legislatures of Kentucky, Virginia, and Tennessee, and by municipal ordinance in North Carolina. Despite the law, however, serpent-handling persists. I am told that the Harlan, Kentucky, region has more serpent-handling groups than any other area in the country.

Serpent-handling is still legal in West Virginia. The two centers in the state are the Scrabble Creek Church of All Nations in Fayette County, about thirty-seven miles from Charleston, and the church of Jesus in Jolo, McDowell County, one of the most depressed sections of the state. Serpent-handling is also practiced sporadically elsewhere in the state, usually led by visitors from Scrabble Creek or Jolo.

The Jolo church, located close to the Virginia and Kentucky borders, attracts persons from both sides in addition to West Virginia. Members of the Scrabble Creek church speak with awe of the Jolo services, where members pick up large handsful of poisonous snakes, fling them to the ground, pick them up, and thrust them under their skirts or blouses and dance ecstatically. My wife and I were present at a church service in Scrabble Creek when visitors from Jolo covered their heads with clusters of snakes and wore them as crowns.

Serpent-handling was introduced to Scrabble Creek in 1941 by a coal miner from Harlan, Kentucky. The practice did not take hold in the area until 1946, when the present leader of the Scrabble Creek church, then a member of the Church of God, first took up serpents. The four or five original serpent-handlers in Fayette County met at one another's homes until given the use of an abandoned one-room schoolhouse in Big Creek. In 1959, when their number swelled several times over, they moved to the larger church in Scrabble Creek, two miles away.

About a dozen members of the church have suffered from snakebites in the seven years of our study (my wife and I were present on two of these occasions). Although there have been few deaths, each incident has been widely and unfavorably publicized in the area, particularly by members of other Holiness churches who abhor the practice. The serpent-handlers for their part say that the Lord causes a snake to strike in order to refute scoffers' claims that the fangs have been pulled to render the snake harmless. Each recovery from snakebite they see as a miracle wrought by the Lord, and each death a sign that the Lord "really had to show the scoffers how dangerous it is to obey his commandments, and how necessary it is to live with the Lord.'' Since adherents believe that death brings one to the throne of the Lord, some express an eagerness to die when God decides they are ready. Those who have been bitten seem to receive special deference from members of the church.

The social and psychological functions served by the Scrabble Creek church are probably very much the same as those served by the more conventional churches in the Holiness movement. In addition, the dangerous rituals probably help to validate the members' claims to holiness. The claim that one is a living saint on the same spiritual level as the early Apostles is, after all, extremely pretentious even in a sacred society, and particularly difficult to maintain in a secular society. The fact that one regularly risks his life for his religion is seen as a conclusive test. Serpent-handlers stress over and over: ''I'm afraid of snakes like anybody else, but when God anoints me, I handle them with joy.'' If one is not bitten, or if one is bitten and recovers through prayer, or even if one is bitten and dies—all serve to validate one's claim to holiness.

Our study of the serpent-handlers of Scrabble Creek left us with the definite impression that their worship and fellowship constituted a form of group psychotherapy for individuals who otherwise would be vulnerable to mental and behavioral aberrations because of the deprivations and frustrations associated with conditions of their existence as members of the stationary working class.

12

WILLIAM G. MacDONALD

The Place of
Glossolalia in
Neo-Pentecostalism

[Reprinted from *Speaking in Tongues: Let's Talk about It*, edited by Watson E. Mills, copyright © 1973, pp. 81-93; used by permission of Word Books, Publisher, Waco, Texas 76796.]

The single most characteristic feature of Neo-Pentecostalism is the mysterious—some would say mystical—form of communion with God known as glossolalia. No one who has spoken in tongues can explain the experience to another without resorting to terms of theological mystery. In all honesty he must confess that he does not know how he glorifies God in a language he did not learn. All he can say is this: God within me, who first entered my life when I believed in the lordship of the risen Christ, speaks now through my voice to God transcendent as I yield my inner being to the Holy Spirit's control. This spiritual yielding of oneself while he worships the Lord becomes the occasion of his being filled by the Lord with the power of his Spirit. His most human characteristic, his speech center, when fully surrendered to God, becomes flooded with the glory of the glorified Christ.

There is certainly no connection between a glossolalist and a ventriloquist, a linguist, or even an infant trying out his capabilities for making sounds. One who speaks in tongues resists the idea of his speech being classified as an instance of any of these phenomena. The reason is simple: In every case such speech is produced as a mental exercise dependent upon the person's creativity. But glossolalia requires no human skill as far as shaping the content of the speech itself. (If there is any skill involved, it is that of intimate submission to God.) Glossolalia must be classified and criticized by criteria that take no account of human ability. It is holy speech authored by and addressed to God (1 Corinthians 14:2).

THE THREEFOLD PARADOX

In at least three ways glossolalia is paradoxical. First, as I just mentioned, simultaneously both God and man are speaking in the same utterance. Man provides the speaking faculty (originally given to him by God), and God provides the content of what is said. Though this sounds like a theoretical statement, it nevertheless does not tell how man—to coin an expression—glossolalizes. The apostle Paul called such speaking a mystery (1 Corinthians 14:2). Glossolalia, therefore, is not amenable to how-to-do-it instruction and testing. Nor can it be reduced to a formula in which God becomes object rather than subject. How God so speaks in and through man is wholly hidden in God's inscrutable ways. Human instruction about this helps only so far as it points away from human ability and exhorts the believer to yield himself in rejoicing faith to God.

Glossolalia in Neo-Pentecostalism is paradoxical in another way. The Spirit (as holy Presence) is both the gift of God and a giver of gifts, glossolalia being one of them. When Jesus talked with the woman of Samaria about living water drawn not from a well, he was pointing her to God's intial spiritual gift (John 4:10, 14). Undoubtedly a person receives this first gift when he accepts God's grace by faith. It becomes the basis of his new life in Christ and effects his regeneration.

The Book of Acts recounts the occasion when the exalted Jesus together with the Father poured out gifts on his gathered church in a deluge of Holy Spirit. As a result, that believing remnant of Israel all spoke in tongues (Acts 2:4; compare Acts 10:44 and 1 Corinthians 14:23, 26 in reference to the gentiles).

Later that day when Peter offered salvation to the thousands gathered to hear what was going on, he promised that man's repentance and faith would be met by God's gift [Greek word: *dorēa*] of the Holy Spirit (Acts 2:38). This promise is none other than the Spirit himself whom all believers receive. But the gift of "kinds of tongues" (1 Corinthians 12:4, 10, 28) is a gift [Greek word: *charisma*] that the Spirit already present gives, that is, it is a "manifestation of the Spirit" (1 Corinthians 12:7). Paradoxically, the Spirit is received as a gift and manifested as a gift. The two different Greek words both meaning gift point to the paradox. One gift is the Giver of grace, life, and gifts; the other is one of those gifts—glossolalia.

A third paradoxical dimension implicit in glossolalia concerns its status as a spiritual gift. In popular terms it is "last and least" and also "first and foremost." On the surface this tension seems irreconcilable, but it is not. In the hierarchy of valuable gifts outlined by the apostle Paul for the church, the last gift in descending order of service was "kinds of tongues" (1 Corinthians 12:28, 30). When stacked up with office gifts (prophets, teachers, and so on) and gifts exclusively for the church, glossolalia is the least edifying. It functions far better as a means of self-renewal than for renewal of the church, though it can have some value for that purpose too.

Non-Pentecostals tend to accept the last character of this gift readily. but that it should in any way be the most significant of the Spirit's operational gifts to individuals raises the most horrendous consternation. Can such an assertion of being most significant be justified?

Before answering this question, it is necessary to establish firmly the gift's place as the least of the gifts. Glossolalia's lesser value can be assessed in terms of its limited and indirect function for edification of the gathered believers in a worship service. There are three reasons for this. First, time is seemingly wasted while one speaks publicly in a language unknown to the congregation. Second, another gift must be available and operative—the interpretation of tongues—in order to make the speech meaningful to those who hear the speaker. Third, the direction of glossolalia as speech to God temporarily bypasses the congregational presence as it speaks into the divine ear (1 Corinthians 14:2).

Now it becomes apparent that the glossolalic gift is wrapped in complexity. It is primarily meant to edify the individual speaker; on the other hand, it also can arrest the attention of the nonbeliever, and it can edify the church when interpreted. That is, in certain providentially arranged public gatherings, an utterance in tongues can be a sign to unbelievers who understand the language without interpretation (1 Corinthians 14:22; Acts 2:5-17). They will conclude that God is among these people and speaking through them. Furthermore, in reference to edification of the church, glossolalia will be as beneficial when interpreted as any other utterance of prayer or praise to God. Yet the interpretation will not be more important than ordinary prayer, praise, or prophecy. It is for this reason that Paul appealed for less glossolalia and more spiritual speech in the common language when the church was meeting for worship (1 Corinthians 14:1-40).

THE MOST SIGNIFICANT GIFT

It would be misunderstanding Neo-Pentecostal teaching to construe any form of spiritual gift as superior to the gift of the Spirit in salvation. The Giver is always to be preferred to his gifts, but how incongruous it would be to refuse spiritual gifts out of professed allegiance to the Giver! Likewise when the value of the glossolalia gift is held high, it is not that by so doing one is comparing this gift with the fruit of the Spirit—love, joy, peace, patience, and all the rest of the divine characteristics and states (Galatians 5:22). The fruit takes precedence over the gifts, certainly. But among the gifts there is a certain uniqueness about glossolalia. What constitutes this uniqueness, and why does Neo-Pentecostalism regard glossolalia as so highly significant?

(1) Glossolalia and its companion gift, the interpretation of tongues, are the only New Testament gifts not found already in the Old Testament. In speech gifts, prophecy was most characteristic of the Old Testament period although there were all the other non-office New Testament gifts operating then too. Whereas the divine confusion of languages at Babel disunited men of one language, the Pentecost experience in the New Testament was a blessing, not a judgment, and served to unite men of many linguistic traditions. The New Testament outpouring of the Spirit in new tongues was more than a novelty. This innovation symbolically expressed God's eternal purpose ultimately to have an international, polylinguistic people.

(2) Glossolalia allows a person to participate in the suprarational without compromising his rationality or mental integrity. The inability of phi-

losophy in our day to produce a totally integrated universal view and the failure of the rationalistic enterprise to produce a satisfactory knowledge of God have tended to intensify man's existential thirst for the reality that is beyond the reach of rational limitations and frustrations. For Neo-Pentecostals glossolalia becomes the spice in their spiritual diet of rational doctrine and behavior. This statement concedes nothing to irrationality, nonsensicality, and babbling. The Greek word *glossa* means "language" or by metonymy "tongue" (the language that comes over the speech organ). Not mouthing nonsense syllables, the glossolalist nevertheless speaks a *glossa* he knows not. He has the wholesome confidence that the one who speaks through him is the God of order. Therefore he has every reason to believe that the Spirit who speaks through him orders and shapes the speech according to intelligent patterns. Paul used the plural term *glossai* for both words spoken in tongues and for speech in the common language (1 Corinthians 14:19). There is a Greek word used in the New Testament meaning to babble (*battalogeō*), but it is never found in glossolalic contexts.

(3) Glossolalia is the most beautiful of the charismata (the plural form of gift). In sickness, a gift of healing restores the natural beauty of proper function to the body. The faith that moves mountains and works miracles is spectacular to behold in operation. Other gifts supply the mind with revelations about situations and courses of action one could not otherwise know. In all these gifts the recipient tends to be brought in contact with something that is being known or changed in the external world. Such knowledge, power, or speech comes to the church through an individual who uses the gift to bless the church and to confront the world with Christ's resurrection power. But when an individual speaks in tongues, he and God alone are communing. They deal in secrets (mysteries), and while this intimate communication may be shared with the church, it need not be if he is praying in private or within himself. Its beauty stems from the intimacy of the love-talk and the glory of God in transcending man's intellectually limited inventory of languages as a communicator. Seeing a person speaking in tongues is no more beautiful than seeing a foreigner speak. But the beauty described here is visible only inside the experience itself. It is not "the beauty of holiness" of which the psalmist wrote, but it is the next best thing—the beauty of holy speech, of vocal submission to God.

(4) Glossolalia affords a memento of authentic first-century, New Testament experience. Believers today want assurance that their Christian ex-

perience is identical with that of those first-century believers. All some Christians believe to be necessary for authenticity is to visit the Roman pontiff who presents himself as the last link in a human chain stretching all the way back to Jesus' right-hand man, Simon Peter. Some suppose that reverence for the relics of early saints that have been found will supply a sense of continuity with the early church. Some see a self-perpetuating priesthood as truly ancient, and that it is. But it tends to carry us back too far—on past the new to the old covenant without sensing the difference.

Some Protestant Christians seek to dismiss all tradition and live as if the twentieth century needed no links with the first century but the Bible. But while we may earnestly contend for the first-century doctrine and satisfy ourselves that we have it intellectually, there remains a sense of loss if the same signs that accompanied believers in the first century do not follow our faith as it did theirs. For many people baptism in water is just such a sign of genuine New Testament experience. Disputes, however, have centered on what form of baptism is most authentic. Whether one opts for immersion of confessing believers or sprinkling of infants, the rite is humanly performed. As such it is valid as a religious rite or symbol. But, even in case of those holding to baptismal regeneration, it lacks the divine answering power of the signs associated with the New Testament period. For charismatics today glossolalia gives not only a sense of community of experience with each other but a sense of oneness and continuity with the early, formative Christian period.

Neo-Pentecostalism sees the restoration of the gifts to the church as a valid sign of God's presence—the presence of the same God who lavishly poured out his Spirit in the first century. Glossolalia by itself is insufficient to provide a complete guarantee of authenticity for the church today; much more is needed. But where it accompanies a thoroughly biblical faith, it is a reliable benchmark of the fact that the God who worked mightily among his people then is no less at work today.

(5) Glossolalia revolutionizes the habits of prayer and praise for many Neo-Pentecostals. This gift enables one to speak to God in a special way. All speaking to God may be categorized loosely as prayer. The most important part of prayer is worship, that is, offering the praise due God's name and thanksgiving for the blessings of life. Glossolalia does not displace the prayer and praise one ordinarily voices in his customary language; rather it heightens the blessing and increases the desire to communicate with God. "What am I to do? I will pray with the Spirit [capital letter supplied] and

I will pray with the mind also; I will sing with the Spirit [capital letter supplied] and I will sing with the mind also'' (1 Corinthians 14:15, RSV). Instead of praying less in one's normal language, one finds himself praying more. A new level of intimacy has been opened to God, and one finds that he prays more because he shares much more in common with God, because of his love for the kingdom of God. Seldom, if ever, does a man pray in other tongues and then later bore God with stale petitions overcast by perfunctory devotion.

Two recent books by Merlin R. Carothers, *From Prison to Praise* and *The Power of Praise*, reveal the transforming power of praise and adoration of God. This surging human response is rising to God as a result of the Neo-Pentecostal emphasis on the presence of God being found where the praises of God abound. The more God is lauded for what he is, the more difficult it is to forget his faithfulness. Glossolalia works like a catalyst to heighten the reaction of one's entire outreach to God. The mystery of the utterance one makes humbles the mind, but at the same time its freshness and strangeness to the ear keep the one communing from getting bored by his own prayers. His spirit is praying in the Holy Spirit. Prayer, therefore, becomes less stereotyped and more spontaneous, less formal and more continual throughout the day.

Since talking to God is the most important activity the ordinary person will have during an average day in his life, how helpful it is for him to have the Spirit's gift of what is popularly known in Neo-Pentecostalism as a prayer language.

(6) Glossolalia serves as a sign of submission to God. Anyone who yields his speech to the Spirit's linguistic control will find it possible to be available to the Spirit's control—if God should so desire—for the operation of other gifts of the Spirit. This may include prophecy and the interpretation of tongues; power in faith, healing and miracles; and ability in special revelations of knowledge, wisdom, and identification of spirits. The first gift does not guarantee that the other gifts will follow, but it is an indication that the person has crossed the first hurdle of strangeness. For Peter and the church at Jerusalem, the glossolalia of the gentiles at Caesarea was a sure indication of their submission to God and their readiness to go on in the fullness of the Spirit as a participating church in the kingdom of God.

It is inevitable that Neo-Pentecostalists should recognize one another and value glossolalia as a unifying experience. This experience does not have to be divine. "The humble will hear thereof and be glad" (for them and with them). The poor in spirit will "rejoice with those who rejoice" (Romans 12:15, RSV). The recipient of the gift will be humbled before God. No human being ever truly experiences God without being brought low in his own eyes by God's stupendous majesty. Afterward he will be attracted, however, to those who have had similar experiences, for they will be those most likely to understand what is always an ineffable experience of God's glory. Because the fullness of the Spirit in power comes only to those with a deep spiritual thirst, when the means of satisfying the thirst is discovered, the one experiencing it feels instant community with all other charismatics. They will patiently hear him out in his attempt to describe the freedom and blessing this experience has brought to his life.[1]

(7) Glossolalia, while being an intimate, individual experience with God, nevertheless, is conducive to a feeling of unity with Christians of all languages. While glossolalia is in no sense a skill that can substitute for language study, it does have a conditioning effect on one's attitude toward people of other linguistic traditions. On numerous occasions tongues have confronted the unbeliever as signs of God's power and glory. When the hearer heard the speaker communicating with God in the hearer's national or provincial language, a language unknown to the speaker, God bridged the language gap.

Seeing that language differences can be overcome in the unity of the Spirit, charismatics view glossolalia as a type or promise of a united system of communication to be used by all those who are resurrected to participate in the New Creation. Assuredly, one day tongues will cease, but only when the perfect new order has arrived.

(8) Glossolalia has a way of uniting Christians who have been theologically deadlocked for centuries. This does not necessarily mean that the prospect of one new language in eternity has its counterpart in time in the prospect of one theology. The perfect balance found in Jesus' words "in spirit and in truth" must ever be our goal. If the spiritual unity can be achieved first as Christians everywhere join in the adoration of the risen

---

[1]See Don Basham, *A Handbook on Holy Spirit Baptism*, (Monroeville PA: Whitaker Books, Banner Publishing 1972): 85, 109-18, for wise counsel cautioning against overzealousness in sharing a testimony of experience with other Christians who are not charismatically conditioned.

Christ, then the truth side of the equation, "the unity of the faith," will have much better possibilities of realization.

The love of God, in truth, is ultimately the only power in the hearts of men that can overcome denominational pride and prejudice. Yet, among the gifts it appears that no gift has been so instrumental as glossolalia in bringing together spiritually responsive people of diverse and conflicting denominational traditions. When in the past four and a half centuries since the Reformation have so many denominational believers witnessed such a degree of unity as in charismatic prayer-and-share meetings? The union that ecclesiologists have not been able to engineer seems to be of no real concern to the charismatics. As they sincerely seek a gracious flood of God's Spirit in which the knowledge of the Lord will fill all the earth, they are discovering the deep sense of unity already existing in the will and spirit of Christ. Glossolalia is only a means and not an end in itself as is the fruit of the Spirit. Yet at this point in ecclesiastical history it is a means of appreciable importance. Who would have thought in the early 1900s that God would use the glossolalic experience of the despised and excluded Holy Rollers to unify Christ's body in the latter half of the twentieth century?

(9) Glossolalia is especially suited for self-edification in a manner the other gifts are not, "He who speaks in a tongue edifies himself" (1 Corinthians 14:4, RSV). When the Christian is unavoidably separated from the body of believers, he is not thereby completely cut off from spiritual ministries and gifts. He can minister (like a solitary Old Testament priest in the holy place) to the Lord. As he extols and magnifies his God, he is transported beyond himself into conscious communion with the Lord and thus is changed. Even though his one-thought-after-another conscious center is being transcended ("my spirit prays but my mind is unfruitful"— 1 Corinthians 14:14, RSV), he is being strengthened in the depths of his spirit.

One does not have to understand everything that benefits him. Christianity is not just a philosophical construct, nor is it merely the best of all philosophies. It has far more than philosophical congruence and integrity. In the words of Jesus, Christianity means "spirit and life" and, like worship, should be "in spirit and in truth." Moreover, for the theologian glossolalia is a constant reminder that now we "know in part" and "see in a mirror dimly" (1 Corinthians 13:12). The theologian has reason to know that the Spirit of God cannot be encapsulated in an airtight system that explains all mysteries to the point that it is not longer necessary to worship in order to know.

FIRST EXPERIENCE IN SPEAKING IN TONGUES

Differences in the older and newer charismatic viewpoint begin to emerge on the issue of how spiritual anointing is received. The basic reason for the new term *Neo-Pentecostalism*, however, is ecclesiological rather than methodological or theological. For the first five decades of this century it was generally customary for anyone who received a charismatic experience to be excluded from the good graces of his denomination. Some Pentecostal denominations, therefore were founded out of necessity.

Then in the sixties, as the century matured, there came about in non-Pentecostal churches a new tolerance for people coveting spiritual gifts. Receivers were by and large not excluded by social pressure or ecclesiastical interdict. To almost everyone's amazement, in the later sixties many Roman Catholics began having their Pentecost, too. Their growth as a renewal group has been phenomenal. It has surpassed the expansion of the Pentecostal experience in any one of the mainstream Protestant denominations. This whole new and changed picture should properly be called Neo-Pentecostalism or charismatic renewal, terms often employed synonymously.

In a typical older Pentecostal meeting where Christians are seeking to be filled with the Holy Spirit, at the conclusion of a public service, the seeker will be invited to an altar of prayer or to a prayer room where people are praying and seeking God for various reasons. Those with faith for the seeker's filling may lay hands upon him and offer prayers for him. The best help that they can give such a seeker is indirect rather than direct. That is, if they will seek the Lord by waiting upon him, they indirectly will be encouraging the one seeking the filling, and they too will be refreshed by the Lord and edified.

This is not the place to catalog all of the misunderstandings of God's ways that may have attended the so-called tarrying meetings. Too often helpers have hindered by getting the seeker's attention when it must be focused on the Lord. Some sincere people have thought that seeking the baptism in the Spirit was something other than ordinary seeking of the Lord. Some have become very loud, some athletically demonstrative, and some very tense in face and muscles of the upraised arms. Some have become physically and emotionally tired as if they thought they would receive the gifts through their efforts rather than by their faith.

A typical Neo-Pentecostal meeting where the baptism in the Spirit is sought takes a somewhat different form. After preliminaries of song and worship, there will be special instruction as to how to receive the Spirit's power and how to respond by yielding one's speech to the Lord. Instead of kneeling or lying on the floor, the seeker sits comfortably in a chair and relaxes. Then hands are laid on him buy those who are praying for and with him. It is expected that soon thereafter he will give expression to the Spirit within by speaking in another tongue as the Spirit enables him.

The most strategic difference introduced by the Neo-Pentecostal approach is the attempt to eliminate completely the process of tarrying, that is, waiting before the Lord. No one, of course, likes to wait for what he wants and especially not the now generation. But the reasons for the instant-baptism approach go much deeper than the temper of the times. These may be listed as follows:

(1) The old dispensational idea proposed that the approximately one hundred twenty disciples waited ten days before the Lord only because it was necessary for the symbolic fiftieth day (that is, Pentecost) after the Passover to arrive on the calendar. This view minimizes the fact that the believers spent a great deal of their time waiting in prayer that surely must have had some beneficent effect on them. Paul also spent three days in prayer, fasting, and contrition before he was filled with the Holy Spirit. It maximizes the fact that those first believers baptized in the Spirit at Caesarea and at Ephesus did not spend any long period engaged in prayer before they received their outpouring of the Spirit in powerful manifestation.

(2) The influence of the holiness-movement doctrine of a second definite work of sanctification was rejected for a baptism in the Spirit by faith alone without any requirements about faith's preparations of the vessel to be filled. The three-stage doctrine (justification, sanctification, enduement) was shortened by rejecting any prerequisites of sanctification, lest it introduce conditions that might be seen as grounds for meriting the gift. Older Pentecostals—even those who did not have an instant-sanctification tenet—taught that one must separate himself from all known sin before being filled. Neo-Pentecostals see sanctification as a less tangible factor and tend to stress the objective side of sanctification in Christ more than the subjective side.

(3) Since all believers have the Holy Spirit residing in them, all they have to do to be filled with the Spirit and speak in tongues is to start speaking in faith and the Holy Spirit will tune in at that juncture and direct what is said. This has become a primary point of Neo-Pentecostal emphasis, achieving for many the practical effect of a technique for coaching candidates.

One of the weaknesses in the older Pentecostal theology had to do with this matter of when the Spirit is received. It seems as though such a basic issue would have a simple answer, but seldom are spiritual realities that easy and well defined. Take Jesus' experience for instance. We have no reason to doubt the spiritual presence in him throughout his life from his conception by the Spirit forward. Yet at thirty years of age the Spirit descended upon him, symbolized by a dove. Did he only then receive the Spirit?

The older Pentecostal theology tended to equate receiving the Spirit with baptism in the Spirit accompanied by tongues. For the most part the first stage in the apostles' New Testament experience was overlooked. The apostles received the Spirit in connection with Jesus' resurrection (John 20:22), and later they received the experience of the power of the Spirit speaking through them in other languages (Acts 2:4). But they also had the Old Testament gift of prophecy prior to the crucifixion of Jesus. This complicated their condition, and the two-foldness of their post-Easter experience was largely ignored. But Neo-Pentecostalism has rightly recognized the fact—and proclaimed it boldy—that every New Testament believer received the Holy Spirit at the moment of regeneration.

Actually the instant-baptism concept did not originate the Neo-Pentecostalism but in a questioned strand of the earlier Pentecostalism. In the 1940s J. E. Stiles, concerned with the problem of chronic seekers for spiritual baptism, wrote a book entitled *The Gift of the Holy Spirit*.[2] His thesis has become the Neo-Pentecostal approach. To recapitulate, it goes like this: There need be no tarrying or making of preparations to receive the Spirit other than one's being a believer in Christ: one should have no fear of getting in the flesh, for speaking begins as a fleshly act and then the Holy Spirit takes over supernaturally directing that speech.

---

[2]J. E. Stiles, *The Gift of the Holy Spirit*, n.c., n.d., reprinted in 1970 by Mrs. J. E. Stiles, P.O. Box 3147, Burbank, California.

It is difficult to ascertain the originator of the Stiles style of receiving the Spirit. In England at about the same time, possibly earlier, this viewpoint was being advocated in some Pentecostal quarters by Harold Horton, who was noted for his book, *The Gifts of the Spirit*.[3] This view is spelled out in detail, however, in Horton's fifteen-page monograph, "Receiving without Tarrying."

In the main the Pentecostal movement was cool toward the Horton-Stiles methodology. The most troublesome aspect was the idea of beginning to speak in the flesh. For decades the solid principle, "*he* [the Christ] shall baptize you in the Holy Spirit," had been taken as axiomatic. It was unthinkable that the Lord needed any help. It was to be an experience of the Lord, engineered by the Lord, and for his glory. Sound counsel always had it this way: Seek the baptizer, not the baptism; you will know it when he is ready to speak through you. It is true that not all the older Pentecostals by any means have followed this ideal. Some glamorized the problematic King James rendering of "stammering lips" (Isaiah 28:11)[4] into an intermediate step between silence and glossolalia.

Generalizations are never safe when one is speaking in inclusive terms about such a dynamic movement as is Neo-Pentecostalism. However, it appears that a majority of the neocharismatics look favorably upon the self-starting method. One current illustration goes like this: Get the car in motion, and the Holy Spirit will then take over to steer. The use of meaningless sounds is encouraged, if necessary, to get the car under way.[5] Another charismatic coach was heard to advocate a relaxed singing of whole notes along with the one seeking to help the candidate get started.[6]

Originally and currently the idea of an instant baptism has held firm on the hope that all seekers will be filled, that no one will be disappointed in his desire for spiritual gifts. But the history of Neo-Pentecostalism records many instances in which seemingly sincere people go through the procedure, including the laying on of hands, and do not thereupon speak in

---

[3]Harold Horton, *The Gifts of the Spirit* (London: Assemblies of God Publishing House, 1934, 1960).

[4]The Revised Standard Version has "strange lips" in parallel with "an alien tongue."

[5]Stephen Clark, ed., "Praying for Baptism in the Spirit," *Team Manual*. 2d ed. (Notre Dame IN: Charismatic Renewal Services, 1972), p. 84.

[6]"The Presbyterian Charismatic Movement," *Presbyterian Life* 15 (April 1972):57.

tongues, whether a self-starter or not. This has led to what may be called the delayed-fuse doctrine that says the fullness was received concomitant with the act of reception and that tongues will come hours or perhaps days later. For many it does happen later; for others who did not initially receive there is little difference with them from the so-called chronic seeker of the older Pentecostalism.

Finally, the aspect of tarrying has been overcome more in name than in reality. In the typical charismatic service much time is consumed by preparations of the heart and mind before the candidate is given the laying on of hands or is exhorted to begin to speak. Sometimes many meetings are necessary before he feels ready. Then, for others, the delayed-fuse situation extends the time of waiting. Much more importantly, as Pentecostals of every vintage would agree, one must continue to "wait for the Lord" (Isaiah 40:31) all the days of his life if he is to maintain the power and glow of the Spirit's fullness.

My bias, you may easily detect, is one of critical loyalty to the Pentecostal and Neo-Pentecostal movements. Their similarities far outweigh their differences, and thus we can speak for one charismatic movement, not two. Both the historian and the theologian can demonstrate that they are blood relatives and that glossolalia is the characteristic family trait.

Paul charged the church to judge all prophecies that were publicly made in a meeting (1 Cor. 14:29), but with all his instruction on the restriction use of glossolalia in the assembly, he gave no command about similarly judging glossolalia. The motive behind glossolalia, however, is always open to review (1 Cor. 13:1), and where that motive is the pure love of God, God will continue to tame the tongue of man by speaking through him in the languages of men and angels.

13

RENÉ LAURENTIN

The Birth of
Catholic Pentecostalism

The Catholic Pentecostal movement, now to be found in almost a
hundred countries, came into existence at the beginning of 1967, at Duquesne University, a Pittsburgh foundation of the Holy Ghost Fathers. The
circumstances were as follows.

ORIGINS[1]

In August 1966, some lay professors of Duquesne University attended
the Congress of the Cursillo movement. They were looking for something

---

[1]The best account is by K. and D. Ranaghan, *Catholic Pentecostals* (New York, 1969).
For the "Notre Dame experience," cf. E. D. O'Connor, *The Pentecostal Movement in the
Catholic Church* (Notre Dame IN, 1971), pp. 39-110.

that would activate in them the full power of faith and evoke a total generosity, and they hoped to find it in this movement for spiritual formation that had started in Spain before the Council. They had already been involved in the liturgical, ecumenical, apostolic, and peace movements, and been disillusioned with all of them.

At the Cursillo Congress they met Steve Clark and Ralph Martin, who are now the leaders of the Ann Arbor community, and who at that time were coordinators of student activities in St. John's Parish, East Lansing, Michigan. Steve had just been reading a book that he found both moving and disconcerting: *The Cross and the Switchblade*, by David Wilkerson.[2] This is the autobiographical story of a Protestant pastor who was led by strong inner impulses to abandon the life of a salaried parish minister and embark on a dangerous mission to the delinquents and drug addicts of Brooklyn, in neighborhoods into which the average American would not venture at night, or even by day, for that matter.

Chapter 21 of the book penetrated to the heart of the pastor's, and others' experience: "The Holy Spirit is what you need." Here the professors found what they had been looking for and had failed to find, once again, in the Cursillo movement: the Bible, the Holy Spirit, the Spirit's charisms. For two months Wilkerson's book provided the basis for their prayer and discussions, while they tried to apply its lessons to their daily living. Then one of them, Ralph Keifer, came across another book on Pentecostalism: John Sherrill's *They Speak in Other Tongues*, which offered practical ways and means of attaining an experience of the Spirit.

In the fall, the group met for a period of deeper prayer, during which the recitation of the "Come, Holy Spirit," the Catholic hymn to the Holy Spirit, was given an important place.

These Catholic laymen asked themselves whether it might not be time to discuss matters with some Pentecostalists, despite the reputation of the latter for extremism and anti-Catholicism. W. Lewis, an Episcopalian priest, put them in touch with one of his women parishioners who was involved in the charismatic movement. The meeting on Epiphany, January 6, 1967, brought them an invitation to take part in a prayer meeting the following Friday, January 13. As the Catholics noted, this was the day when their Church's liturgy celebrated the baptism of Jesus by the Holy Spirit in

---

[2]D. Wilkerson, with J. and E. Sherrill, *The Cross and the Switchblade*.

the waters of the Jordan. Ralph was left somewhat confused by the prayer meeting, for he was convinced of the high level of sharing, prayer, and "lived theology" that he found there, but his university-trained mind was offended by the naïve approach to Scripture and the idea of a direct communication with God.

Of the four Catholics who had attended the first meeting, only Ralph returned the following week (January 20?), bringing with him Patrick Bourgeois, another professor on the faculty of theology. The prayer and discussion at this meeting centered on the Letter to the Romans. At the end, the two men asked to receive the "baptism in the Holy Spirit." One group prayed over Ralph and imposed hands on him; another group did the same for Patrick.

> They simply asked me to make an act of faith for the power of the Spirit to work in me. I prayed in tongues rather quickly. It was not a particularly soaring or spectacular thing at all. I felt a certain peace—and at least a little prayerful—and truthfully, rather curious as to where all this would lead.[3]

In the next week Ralph imposed hands on two other Duquesne colleagues. They had the same experience; an interior welling up of the Spirit, and a renewal without any revolutionary upheaval.

On February 18-19 about thirty students and professors gathered for a weekend at Duquesne University. On Saturday evening, at the time set aside for a birthday party celebration, the rhythm of things suddenly speeded up. Paul Grey and Maryanne Springle, an engaged couple, had heard about baptism in the Holy Spirit and now asked Ralph Keifer to pray with them that they might receive it. The little group went upstairs to do their praying; no one else was aware of what was going on. Paul and Maryanne experienced the same conversation and thanked God "in tongues."

At this very same time, another student, Patti Gallagher, had gone to the chapel to pray. She told me the story at New Orleans on June 21, 1974.

> We were all tired from our day of prayer and reflection, and somewhat distraught. No one was very eager about setting up the birthday party for that evening. The Lord was at work in us, but we were not aware of it.
>
> I wanted to shake off the feeling of apathy and to get something going, so I went to the chapel to see if any of the other students were there. I went

---

[3]Ranaghan, op. cit., p. 15.

in and knelt down, and began to tremble; I felt the presence of the Lord. I became afraid, yet I wanted nothing so much as to stay there and pray. But I said to myself: 'We've done enough praying today. It's time to celebrate our brother's birthday.'

One of the students in the chapel said to me: 'Patti, I don't understand it. Something's happening that we didn't plan.' I answered: 'I just want to pray.' Then I improvised: 'Lord, I don't know what you are asking, but I am ready.'

Then I could feel God's love for me; I experienced it. I was prostrate on the ground, overwhelmed by the 'foolishness' of this love. I knew no theology, I had never gone to Catholic schools, but as I lay prostrate there I understood Augustine's words: 'Lord, you made us for yourself; only in you will we find peace.' I realized that the others in the chapel were having the same experience.

Some of the students spoke in tongues, others did not. Patti received this gift a few days later.

SPREAD

Ralph Keifer telephoned the news to the University of Notre Dame, where at the beginning of the month he had begun his search.

A similar event took place at Notre Dame on the weekend of March 4-5; on Monday, March 13; and then elsewhere. It was like a series of independent explosions, rather than a spreading out from a center, because other people in other places were engaged in the same search for God.

In the fall of 1974 Edward O'Connor, professor of theology at Notre Dame, jotted down his first impressions:

Even for a priest who has seen some surprising things in the course of his ministry, it is not easy to take it in stride when a friend, a former student, tells you he has received the gift of tongues.

Things moved rapidly. Other students received the same gift. By March 14 I was almost the only one in the group who had not received it.

From this point on the movement spread by leaps and bounds, as is evident from the attendance figures for the annual meetings at the University of Notre Dame:

1967:	90	
1968:	100	plus
1969:	450	

1970:	1,300
1971:	4,500
1972:	11,000
1973:	25,000
1974:	30,000

What proportion of the whole do these figures represent? A little less than 10 per cent of the charismatics in the United States. The percentage can only be approximate, because there are no statistics; the movement is concerned with life, not with records, in the spirit of the Bible where the prophets blame the kings of Israel for having a census made. If you treat God's gifts as a form of wealth and try to keep an account of them, are you not turning away from God himself, and from men as well?

A lot of crosschecking gives grounds for thinking that the Catholic Neo-Pentecostal movement has somewhere from 2 million to 4 million participants throughout the world as May 1975. Two hundred thousand copies of the pamphlet *Pointing the Way* (an aid in preparing for the outpouring of the Spirit) have been distributed in English alone during the past four years. The international yearbook, which is intended to facilitate contact among groups, confirms us in thinking that the membership is doubling every year; the yearbook contained about 1,100 addresses in 1973, and 2,050 in 1974. But the yearbook lists are obviously quite incomplete. For example, forty groups, which form a single parish in an area that has no mail service and no such thing as an address (Khali), are not mentioned in the list, and this is not an isolated case.

The charismatic renewal has become a tidal wave in Puerto Rico, where whole parishes are involved in it; the warm and friendly style of this people is very congenial to the movement. A spontaneous meeting in Quebec in June 1974 brought together over 8,000 people.

The beginnings of the movement in France date from the end of 1971;[4] since the end of 1973 there is no important city in France that does not have one or more groups. The Emmanuel group in Paris quickly acquired 600 members and, like a hive that is too full, twice had to send out colonies.

---

[4]Father Regimbal, a Canadian, who came into very early contact with the movement in the United States, subsequently started it first in his own country and then in many others. On his international tour, he influenced two abbeys (especially the Abbey of Bec) and acted as catalyst for scattered individuals who likewise had come into contact with the movement on visits to the United States.

At Lyons the movement began with the visit of an American to Fourvière and the visit of two young Jesuits (Fathers Laurent Fabre and B. Lepesant) to America. In this city the movement developed and reached maturity under more propitious conditions than in Paris; in an atmosphere of tranquillity roots were sunk deep.

According to a recent statistic, 7 per cent of the 47 million Catholics in the United States (therefore more than 3 million) have been in contact with the movement. This would suggest from 1 million to 2 million convinced participants.

In Rome there are seven prayer groups. Three of these speak Italian, the others use French, German, Spanish, and English (this last is not listed in the yearbook). The Holy See has been favorably inclined toward the movement, even if in a discreet way.

WHAT SHOULD THE MOVEMENT BE CALLED?

We must return to the matter of vocabulary or nomenclature, for it can cause difficulty in a book geared to giving information.

1. Initially people spoke of the "Catholic Pentecostal movement," a name that provided the title for Edward O'Connor's first article in the summer of 1967.[5]

But "Pentecostal" is also the name of an organized Church in the United States. It could therefore cause confusion or imply competition, and it made Catholics uneasy. The report submitted to the National Conference of American Bishops (November 14, 1969) devoted the longest of its six paragraphs to this point; the name was thereafter dropped, and another adopted—"charismatic"—which the report mentions without voicing any reservations.[6]

---

[5] E. D. O'Connor, "A Catholic Pentecostal Movement," *Ave Maria* 105, No. 22 (June 3, 1967), pp. 6-10.

[6] Report submitted to the semiannual meeting of the United States Catholic Bishops in Washington, D.C., by Bishop Alexander M. Zaleski of Lansing, Michigan, chairman of the Committee on Doctrine of the National Conference of Catholic Bishops (United States Catholic Conference Documentary Service Press Release, Nov. 14, 1969). The report may be found in *Theology Digest*, 19 (1971), pp. 52-53; O'Connor, op. cit., pp. 291-93; K. McDonnell, "Catholic Pentecostalism: Problems in Evaluation," *Dialog*, 9 (1970), pp. 35-54 (repr. Pecos NM, 1970).

2. But the name "charismatic" was likewise challenged. It was said to be an "insufferable abuse" on two counts. First, it would limit the world "charism" to "its narrow sense of an extraordinary phenomenon, such as speaking in tongues, prophesying, or the gift of healing." Second, it would monopolize for a few Christians a name that belongs to the Church as a whole, since according to Vatican II the Church in its entirety is charismatic. Yves Congar concludes: "We are seeing the beginning of a very promising movement. We must find for it a name that is beyond reproach."[7]

3. The French leaders of the movement accepted the criticism and tried to introduce other names: "Renewal in the Spirit" or "Spiritual Renewal." But these names are vague and can be confusing. When I ask people, "What do you think of the spiritual renewal?" or "What do you think of spiritual prayer groups?" one out of every two answers is completely unrelated to the Catholic Pentecostal movement. "Renewal in the Spirit" may, strictly speaking, be a satisfactory name for the movement, but it does not enable us to describe the people who take part in it. "Catholic Pentecostals" is clear. "Charismatics" is ambiguous and aggressive. "Those renewed in the Spirit" or "Christians of the spiritual renewal" is impractical. The word "pneumatic," which the Greek Fathers use to signify what belongs to or is related to the Holy Spirit, has unfortunately been taken over by the automobile tire industry. As a result, we are left with a great verbal confusion.

The difficulties that have led to the downgrading of any viable descriptive name arise in fact not so much from the words themselves as from the irrational disquiet people feel when confronted by movements of an "enthusiastic" or "charismatic" type. In these circumstances any name whatsoever that proves evocative and meaningful arouses aggressive objections. We shall try to avoid this emotionally charged atmosphere without, however, failing to take into account people's reactions and the serious reasons behind them. Clarity will require us to use, as the context demands, the various names mentioned above. Frequently we shall be using the name that is clearest and most specific: Catholic Pentecostalism or Catholic Neo-Pentecostal movement. The next section will explain the sense of the prefix Neo-.

---

[7]In *La Croix* (Jan. 19, 1974).

THE FIRST FOUR CATHOLIC NEO-PENTECOSTALS
(January 13-20, 1967)

What are the names of the first four who were "baptized in the Spirit" in January 1967? The Ranaghans mention three of them: Ralph Keifer; his wife, Pat; and Patrick Bourgeois. They omit the name of the fourth: William Storey, professor of history, because Storey left the movement in 1969-70. At the end of the Charismatic Congress held in Rome at Pentecost 1975 (which he had tried in vain to prevent being held by sending reports of his own to the Holy See), Storey publicly announced his break from the movement, and so there is no reason now for concealing his name. Every renewal is marked by tensions and conflicts; we see these even at the very beginnings of Christianity, as reported in the Acts of the Apostles. Paul broke off from Barnabas, who had initiated him into the missionary apostolate (Acts 16:39). The important thing is that such conflicts are fruitful for the ongoing development of spiritual discernment. It is in this perspective that the Ranaghans dealt with the problem of Storey's defection.

14

LAWRENCE N. JONES

The Black
Pentecostals

[Reprinted from *The Charismatic Movement*, edited by Michael P. Hamilton (Eerdmans, 1975), pp. 145-58. Reprinted with permission from Eerdmans Publishing Company.]

The black communities in the United States have made two important contributions to the universal church; their religious music . . . and the Pentecostal spirituality which, since its beginning in a humble black church in Los Angeles in 1906, has swept across the world in a grandiose revival and numbers today somewhere between 25 and 35 millions.[1]

-Walter J. Hollenweger

---

[1]Hollenweger, "Black Pentecostal Concept: Interpretations and Variations," *Concept*, Special Issue, No. 30 (June 1970), 9.

THE AZUSA STREET REVIVAL

Professor Walter J. Hollenweger's assertion that Pentecostalism in its modern formulation had its beginning in a "Black Church in Los Angeles" has been vigorously debated among the historians of the movement.[2] But however that debate is decided, it is at least indisputable that the so-called "Azusa Street Revival" of 1906-1908 gave critical impetus to a religious phenomenon that has spread throughout the world. Similarly, it is generally conceded that W. J. Seymour, a Black Holiness preacher, was the initiator and principal leader of that revival in its earliest months. Black Pentecostals trace their lineage directly to Azusa Street. Seymour had been a sometime student in a Houston, Texas, Bible school founded by the Rev. C. F. Parham, whom some identify as the true founder of modern Pentecostalism. Parham, who was originally from Topeka, Kansas, taught that the "baptism of the Spirit" was validated in the gift of speaking in tongues. Seymour was convinced of the truth of the doctrine and stressed it in his preaching and conversation. A visitor to Houston, a Mrs. Terry, was impressed with Seymour's preaching and invited him to Los Angeles to become the associate minister of the Nazarene congregation of which she was a member.

The text of Seymour's first sermon was Acts 2:4, "and they were all filled with the Holy Spirit, and began to speak in other tongues, as the Spirit gave them utterance."[3] Though Seymour had not himself received the gift of the baptism of the Spirit and speaking in tongues, he believed that speaking in tongues was a work of grace beyond the holiness doctrine of sanctification. His first sermon was the last sermon he was to preach to this Nazarene congregation, for most of its members found his doctrinal stance offensive. Subsequently, Seymour was befriended by a Mr. and Mrs. Asbury, who were members of the church, and he began to hold services in their home. On April 9, 1906, "seven seekers were baptized by the Holy

---

[2]For a full discussion of this debate, see Leonard Lovett, "Perspective on the Black Origins of the Contemporary Pentecostal Movement," *The Journal of the Interdenominational Theological Center*, 1 (Fall, 1973): 36-49.

[3]All biblical references in this essay are to the King James version.

Spirit'' and began to speak in tongues.[4] So great was the impact of their experience that the meeting continued uninterruptedly for three days. These remarkable phenomena can be seen, in retrospect, as being the initial events in a religious revival which attracted such large crowds that Seymour and his followers were forced to seek larger quarters. They found a suitable auditorium in an abandoned Methodist Church in Azusa Street. The services in Azusa Street were virtually nonstop, often lasting as long as fifteen hours!

The nucleus of those persons who continued to meet in Azusa Street eventually called themselves the Apostolic Faith Mission and began to publish a modest newspaper called *Apostolic Faith*. For three years the revival at the Mission remained intense, and literally thousands of people from the United States and abroad flooded the services seeking the baptism of the Spirit and hoping to be graced by the gift of speaking in tongues. Many of these men and women became worldwide missionaries of the new doctrine.

FROM INTERRACIAL MOVEMENT
TO SEGREGATED INSTITUTIONS

An event of significant proportion for the future of Pentecostalism occurred when Elder C. H. Mason of the Church of God in Christ was, in his words, ''led by the Spirit to go to Los Angeles, California, where the great fire of the latter rain of the Holy Ghost had fallen on many. It was in March, 1907, when I received Him, Jesus, my Lord, in the Holy Ghost.''[5] Mason had been baptized at an early age in a Missionary Baptist Church in Arkansas and was ordained subsequently as a minister by that denomination. After an abortive three-month stay at Arkansas Baptist College (1893-1894), he became a traveling revivalist having been shown by ''the Lord . . . that there was no salvation in schools and colleges.''[6]

By 1896 Mason had joined forces with Elder C. P. Jones of Jackson, Mississippi, and in the next year they established a holiness congregation

---

[4]John T. Nichol, *The Pentecostals* (Plainfield NJ, 1966), pp. 32-33.

[5]Joseph Patterson, German R. Ross, and Julia M. Atkins, eds., *History and Formative Years of the Church of God in Christ with Excerpts from the Life and Works of Its Founder, Bishop C. H. Mason* (Memphis, 1969), p. 17.

[6]*Ibid.*, p. 16.

in Lexington, Mississippi, which they eventually named The Church of God. Shortly thereafter they added the words "in Christ" to distinguish themselves from the Church of God. The seed of his work was a revival conducted by Jones and Mason in Jackson in 1896 where many persons who received the gift of the Holy Spirit were "converted, sanctified and healed by the power of faith."[7] The holiness doctrine, in its main tenets, holds that the believer is converted or regenerated, receives the gift of the Holy Spirit, and is sanctified, i.e., empowered to live a sinless life. Holiness groups may differ as to whether sanctification is an immediate, complete gift of grace or is a more gradual process of growth. A clue to the posture of this church toward other Christians who were "not of its fold" was its watchword, "no salvation without holiness."

In the earliest phase of the Pentecostal revival one of its distinctive aspects was its interracial character. In marked contrast to mainline Protestantism, the Pentecostals fellowshipped together without respect to race. A. A. Boddy, commenting in 1912 upon this phenomenon, wrote:

> It was something very extraordinary, that white pastors from the South were eagerly prepared to go to Los Angeles to the Negroes, to have fellowship with them and to receive through their prayers and intercessions the blessings of the Spirit. And it is still more wonderful that these white pastors went back to the south and reported to the members of their congregations that they had been together with Negroes, that they had prayed in one spirit and received the same blessings as they.[8]

Elder C. H. Mason was to perform an important service to the movement, for he appears to have been the only early convert who came from a legally incorporated church and who could ordain persons whose status as clergymen was recognized by civil authorities. This official recognition was crucial to clergy who wished to perform marriages and other ministerial functions having legal consequences. There also were certain economic disabilities which accrued to clergy who were not identified with officially recognized church bodies, a typical one of which was the failure to qualify for reduced clergy rates on railroads. As a consequence

---

[7]*Ibid.*

[8]Quoted in Hollenweger, p. 15. Boddy was a longtime leader of British Pentecostalism.

. . . scores of white ministers sought ordination at the hands of Mason. Large numbers of white ministers, therefore, were to obtain ministerial credentials carrying the name of the Church of God in Christ. One group in Alabama and Texas eventually made an agreement with Mason in 1912 to use the name of his church but to issue ministerial credentials signed by their own leaders.[9]

This agreement lasted until 1914, when some of the white clergymen who were principals to it called a convention in Hot Springs, Arkansas, which resulted in the establishment of the Assembly of God. Apparently no Blacks, with the possible exception of G. T. Hayward, attended this organizing convention, though the invitation had been extended to all "Pentecostal Saints and Churches of God in Christ." With the founding of the Assembly of God it became clear that as Pentecostals moved toward institutionalizing the movement they would follow the prevailing cultural practice of segregating the races structurally. Thus, a movement which began in a shared religious experience and which was rooted in a theological consensus succumbed early to the acids of racist thinking. However, it should be pointed out that even today several of the predominantly white Pentecostal bodies have Black members.

The so-called interracial period in Pentecostalism did not come to an abrupt end with the establishment of the Assembly of God. Even within the Assembly, Blacks were members of local congregations. In 1916 a controversy developed in the Assembly of God which culminated in the withdrawal of a group popularly denoted as the "Jesus Name" ministers. These clergy dissented from the strongly worded trinitarian statement which the 1916 General Council of the Assemblies of God had adopted. The dissidents organized themselves into a body which they named the General Assembly of the Apostolic Churches. This group failed in its effort to gain official recognition from the federal government, which meant that its clergymen were vulnerable to the military service and similarly had no credentials permitting them to function as clergy with respect to the armed forces. As a consequence of this disability the General Assembly of the Apostolic Churches merged with a West Coast group which did have official standing with the federal government and became known as the Pen-

---

[9]Vinson Synan, *The Holiness-Pentecostal Movement in the United States* (Grand Rapids MI, 1971), p. 169.

tecostal Assemblies of the World, with G. T. Hayward, a Black Indianapolis evangelist, as its secretary.[10] Approximately 50 percent of the officers and members of the Pentecostal Assemblies group were Black. But this honeymoon in race relations did not continue for long. At the general conference of the Pentecostal Assemblies in 1924, the white clergy withdrew and left the organization to Hayward and his colleagues. Subsequently the whites organized The Pentecostal Ministerial Alliance in Jackson, Tennessee, in 1925.

During this period (1908-1924) the numerical strength of Pentecostalism was in the South, and it was perhaps inevitable that the regional racial patterns and prejudices would dictate the division of the churches into segregated structures. It should be remembered, however, that segregated structures have been characteristic of the religious establishment in America since the founding of the nation. One of the earliest organizational strategies employed by predominantly white bodies was to place Blacks into separate congregations of judicatories under the supervision of white leadership. The Church of God employed this strategy in a 1926 action when provision was made for its Negro members to have their own General Assembly with the stipulation that the "General Overseer" must always be white. This arrangement was continued until 1966. Similarly, the interracial Fire-Baptized Holiness Church, which had a sizable Black constituency from its founding in 1898, was split ten years later when the minority congregations voted, in the face of pressure from Southern whites, to form their own organization. In 1926 this Black group adopted its present name, The Fire-Baptized Holiness Church of God of the Americas.[11]

BLACK PENTECOSTALISM:
FAITH AND ORDER, LIFE AND WORK

Most Blacks first encountered Christianity under the aegis of Baptist or Methodist churches and the majority of Black Christians maintain this affiliation. It follows that the early Pentecostal movement, like the earlier Holiness gatherings, consisted of persons who had severed their initial de-

---

[10]*Ibid.*, pp. 170-172. Synan provides a quite detailed discussion of this formative period in the Pentecostal movement.

[11]Nichol, pp. 104-108. Cf. Synan, pp. 170-173.

nominational ties. They were, and are, often referred to as "come-out-ers." Holiness and Pentecostal evangelists and missionaries frequently encountered suspicion and sometimes violent resistance from both the established churches and civil authorities. C. H. Mason, for example, reports that he was shot at, personally assaulted, or hailed before the courts on more than one occasion.[12] Persons who were persuaded by the teaching of Pentecostal preachers usually withdrew from their churches and formed small congregations, meeting in houses or other temporary accommodations. In contrast to the mainline churches, some Holiness bodies became Pentecostal in doctrine through accepting tongue-speaking as a sign of the baptism of the Spirit. This was the case with the Church of God in Christ. Elder C. P. Jones, who was a cofounder with C. H. Mason of the church in 1896, was averse to the new doctrine which Mason brought from Azusa Street, and he and those who shared his convictions withdrew the right hand of fellowship from the members holding Pentecostal convictions.[13] Mason and thirteen clergymen who were persuaded by his teaching met shortly thereafter in what is referred to as the First Assembly of the Church of God in Christ.

During the eleven-year existence of the Jones-Mason body a dozen or so churches had been established in Tennessee, Oklahoma, Arkansas, and Mississippi. Following the Jones-Mason break, lawsuits were instituted to determine whether the earlier Church of God in Christ (Holiness) or its schismatic wing could exercise jurisdiction over congregations and their properties. When the litigation was completed, Mason and his followers were given authority over the churches in Tennessee, but their petitions were denied in Arkansas. By 1910 Mason had consolidated his leadership of the Church of God in Christ (Pentecostal) and Elder C. P. Jones continued his leadership in the Holiness body.[14]

To this point we have focused our attention primarily upon the God in Christ because it was so pivotal in the early days of American Pentecostalism and was the first Black Pentecostal denomination, and because it continues to be the largest among the more than two hundred Pentecostal

---

[12]Patterson, *History*, pp. 23-24.

[13]Charles H. Pleas, *Fifty Years of Achievement: Church of God in Christ* (Memphis, 1957), p. 7.

[14]*Ibid.*

bodies in the nation. The Church of God in Christ asserts that it has a worldwide constituency estimated to be as large as three million. In 1970 the church claimed a membership of one million in the United States alone.

W. J. Hollenweger, in his useful survey of Black Pentecostal bodies in the United States,[15] divides them into five categories as to doctrine: (1) those teaching the three-crisis experience; (2) those teaching the two-crisis experience; (3) the oneness of "Jesus Only" groups; (4) the "Father Only" organization; and (5) those groups which do not fit neatly into any of the above categories. The largest group by far are those that teach the three-crisis experience—i.e., conversion, or regeneration, or justification; sanctification; baptism of the Spirit with tongue-speaking. The two-crisis experience groups are distinguished from the three-crisis experience churches by their insistence that sanctification is a lifelong process which only begins at conversion. The "Jesus Only" groups find biblical proof for their distinctiveness in the baptismal formula "in the Name of Jesus" and in Jesus' statement, "I and my Father are One." The School of the Prophets, which is the only church body identified by Hollenweger as a "Father Only" organization, baptizes in the "Name of the Father."

Whatever differences in doctrine may distinguish major Black Pentecostal bodies from each other, they have certain characteristics in common. As has been pointed out, Pentecostalism among Blacks was a Southern, rural phenomenon in its early years. This fact is reflected in the decision of the Church of God in Christ to set its annual convocations in the period November 25-December 15 so as to conform to the agricultural calendar when "crops were all harvested and enough finances and other provisions were available which would enable them to attend and support a national meeting."[16] Similarly, their membership, like that of their white counterparts, has usually been drawn from the less privileged socioeconomic segment of the population.

The polity of Black Pentecostals is episcopal, although the title denominating the person exercising highest authority may be variously that of bishop, superintendent, apostle, or general overseer. Episcopal jurisdictions may be defined by state lines or may encompass larger or smaller

---

[15]Hollenweger, "Black Pentecostal Concept." See also his larger work, *The Pentecostals* (Minneapolis, 1972).

[16]Pleas, p. 19.

geographical areas. Frequently bishops will exercise jurisdictions in territories that overlap. This latter circumstance is due to the fact that most Pentecostal churches have sprung up at the initiative of individual clergy and episcopal jurisdiction is exercised by the prelate to whom that founding clergyman attaches himself. It is also the case that many Pentecostal churches are "free-standing" and are not affiliated with any larger body— thus they are Pentecostal as to doctrine but congregational as to polity.

The worship in Black Pentecostal churches is not distinctive save with respect to tongue-speaking and an emphasis upon healing. The singing, the praying, the dancing, the instrumental music, including horns and percussion, the testimonies, and the vigorous homiletical style of the preachers are also characteristic of other small churches in urban areas. Indeed, the Black Pentecostals continue a worship tradition that developed, in its main features, in Black congregations as far back as the eighteenth century. It is a fact that as Black Christians in the major Protestant denominations began more and more to conform to the worship style of the established white churches, this historic worship tradition was exiled to the unaffiliated, if not alienated, church groups, many of whom were Pentecostal or Holiness in doctrine. In the rural South, however, the historic worship tradition has tended to persist in all churches. While caveats are being noted, it should be observed that this style of worship is not "peculiarly Black" in any essential sense, since it emerged in the course of the evangelical revivals in the first half of the nineteenth century. One distinguishing aspect of worship in Black churches has to do not so much with the content of worship as with the consciousness of the worshippers. This consciousness is informed by the fact that the worshippers are members of an oppressed minority with all the social, economic, and political encumbrances that inhere in that status. This consciousness informs the way in which the worship is carried out, and the way in which its content is appropriated by the believers.

Pentecostalism has grown among the Blacks not because of central direction from a denominational bureaucracy, but because of the zeal and conviction of individual clergymen who have literally built their congregations from nothing save perhaps a few relatives and "folks from down home." Often a church meets in a building which is provided by the pastor and may survive in its initial months and years because of his willingness to sacrifice his own salary in order to have the enterprise succeed. As a consequence, Pentecostal churches tend to be dominated by their clergy, who after all have the largest investment of time and funds in their corporate life. The question may be legitimately asked why Pentecostalism has such persuasive appeal—particularly among Blacks, who formerly counted themselves to be Baptists or Methodists. There is, of course, the theological answer: God willed it. But without wishing to limit the freedom of God, one discovers other reasons which may be offered in partial explanation. The movement was born in a time when the civil and social situation of Blacks in America had bottomed out in what Rayford Logan called the "nadir" of the race.[17] Mob violence and lynching were on an upward curve in the South, and Blacks lived on the thin edge of terror. It was also a time of economic dislocation in which survival in the economy of Southern agriculture was very tenuous indeed. The period was marked by a farm-to-city and South-to-North migration which began as a trickle in the 1890's and reached a flood tide during and immediately following World War I. That migration continues, somewhat abated, to the present day. This highly mobile population inundated urban areas of the Northeast, West and Midwest that were totally unprepared to absorb them. These rural Blacks sometimes transferred their church memberships to the established religious bodies in the cities, but many found the churches as little attuned to their needs as were the social, economic, and political sectors of the larger society. Many abandoned the church and were lost, but still others turned to Pentecostalism, which was peculiarly suited to provide a kind of spiritual and religious structure in the midst of a bewildering new environment.

In a religious sense Pentecostalism was an antidote to and a critique of the failure of established church bodies adequately to minister to the personal and religious needs of the new urban dwellers. Though one can point to a number of large Black Pentecostal congregations, they tend to be the exception rather than the rule. The bulk of them have remained comparatively small and have thus retained an intimate character which lends identity, dignity, and a sense of self-affirmation to the "victims" of the impersonal urban culture. Moreover, since most of these congregations have been "preached out," i.e., they were organized and grew under the

---

[17]Rayford W. Logan, *The Betrayal of the Negro: From Rutherford B. Hayes to Woodrow Wilson* (New York, 1965). This book was originally published under the title *The Negro in American Life and Thought: The Nadir, 1877-1901*.

aegis of their founder-pastor, the personal attention which the members received was reenforcing and provided an institutional benchmark to persons who might not otherwise belong to anything. This ministry to individuals reflects both a pastoral concern on the part of the pastor and a prudential, political stratagem calculated to insure the financial health and stability of the congregation. Of course, this latter observation may be made of non-Pentecostal small churches as well.

Churches are the only institutions in Black communities belonging to and controlled by the people to which access is not proscribed on the basis of social, economic, or political considerations. As such they have always been the primary arena in which leadership, charisma, or other talents, gifts, ambitions, and graces could find expression. Pentecostal churches, like most other Black denominations, have not insisted upon an educated clergy and have rather placed greater emphasis upon doctrinal correctness and a demonstrated capacity for leadership. Familiarity with the Scriptures, firm doctrinal conviction, and experiential testimony are the indispensable credentials for access to clergy leadership in a Pentecostal congregation. These and the conviction that one has received a divine call to preach. It is conventional wisdom that, in addition to its religious function within a given community, the church functions as an important outlet for the various potentials for lay and clerical leadership within the community. This is true in any community, but it is especially crucial in Black communities, where the social fabric affords few other opportunities for service and self-expression.

The steady movement to cities both within and without the South is dramatically illustrated in the fact that whereas in 1900 26.6 percent of Blacks lived in metropolitan areas, by 1970 the percentage had risen to 70 percent. Pentecostalism, like the older Protestant churches among Blacks, has grown mainly in the cities and is not properly classified as a rural church body. I have already referred to social and economic elements in the urban environment which have contributed to the attractive intimacy of the Pentecostal churches. There are religious reasons as well. Pentecostalism as belief, as pietistic life-style, and as moral teaching tends to function as a barrier against the erosion of long-held beliefs and also as a protective communal shield against the acids of liberal (rationalistic) or non-spiritual thought.

From the beginning, Pentecostals knew themselves to be under strong discipline insofar as life style was concerned. Pentecostal churches have usually prohibited their members from smoking, drinking, seeking divorce, dancing (outside of the church), and indulging in so-called "worldly pleasures," which may or may not include attending or participating in athletic contests. The degree of strictness with which these demands are enforced varies from group to group, or indeed from congregation to congregation. Some Pentecostal bodies prohibit using cosmetics or wearing such popular dress styles as shorts and mini-skirts. On the other hand, I heard a Pentecostal radio preacher on a New York station encouraging his listeners to attend a fashion show sponsored by his "temple" for the benefit of the building fund. Similarly, it is becoming more and more evident that some more affluent Pentecostal clergy are beginning to outdo their counterparts in some other Black churches with their status-symbol cars, their commodious suburban homes, and the formal "appreciation banquets" they now sponsor. It is this seeming exploitation of the poor as reflected in the dress and life-style of the clergy that makes some churches in the Black communities vulnerable to the commonly heard criticism that they are parasitic upon rather than contributing to the upbuilding of the community.

The focus of Pentecostal doctrine and life-style is on the assurance of salvation for the individual believer. As a consequence, congregations tend not be actively involved in the struggle for racial justice. The formal posture of the Church of God in Christ illustrates this point. The preamble to the 1972 version of its Amended Charter, Constitution and By-Laws contains the following statements:

> We believe that Governments are God-Given Institutions for the benefit of mankind. We admonish and exhort our members to honor magistrates and civil authorities and to respect and obey civil laws.
>
> We declare our loyalty to the President of the United States and to the Constitution of the United States of America. We pledge allegiance and fidelity to the Republic for which it stands
>
> However, as God-fearing, peace-loving, and law-abiding people, we claim our heritage and natural right to worship God according to the dictates of our own conscience. Therefore, we abhor war, for we believe that the shedding of human blood or the taking of human life is contrary to the teachings of our Lord and Saviour Jesus Christ. And as a body of Christian

believers, we are adverse to war in all its forms and believe in the peaceful settlement of all international disputes.[18]

This declaration of the church's attitude towards the nation and towards civil authorities was issued at a time when the Black community was becoming increasingly suspicious that the institutions which this preamble affirms were in actual opposition to the best interests of the race. It is also remarkable that this statement duplicates in its essentials similar affirmations made in 1952 without taking cognizance of the momentous changes which took place in the intervening years. One would have supposed that some minimal notice might have been taken of the accelerated quest for social justice even if the liberation rhetoric of the Black nationalists was deemed to be unacceptable. While excessive weight should not be given to the formal principles, their reiteration in 1972 defines the continuing conservative outlook at the highest levels of leadership in the Church.[19] Though we have referred here to the Church of God in Christ, there is no evidence that other Pentecostal denominations have pioneered in these matters either. Nevertheless, numerous instances can be documented in which local churches have engaged in aggressive ministries aimed at improving the quality of life for their members and for the communities in which they are located. I know personally a number of outstanding clergy in the New York metropolitan area who are leading their congregations in community programs including day-care centers, prison ministries, head-start schools, and employment services, and in programs designed to feed the poor, to rehabilitate the drug addict or alcoholic, and to bring the Gospel to everyone. The names of some Pentecostal ministers are notable in the political arena and their support is solicited by candidates for public office. Similarly, some Pentecostal clergy participated conspicuously in the nonviolent movement headed by Martin Luther King, Jr., and are con-

---

[18]"Declaration of Faith and Preamble," *Amendment to the Charter, Constitution, and By-Laws of the Church of God in Christ, Inc.* (unpublished offset copy, Church of God in Christ, 1972). Cf. "The Creed, Discipline, Rules of Order and Doctrine of the Pentecostal Assemblies of the World," quoted in Hollenweger, "Black Pentecostal Concept," p. 63.

[19]It is noteworthy that the garbage collectors' strike in Memphis, which Martin Luther King was supporting at the time of his assassination, held its major mass meetings at the Mason Temple, which houses the headquarters of the Church of God in Christ.

tinuing to engage locally in the quest for social and economic justice.[20] One observes also a growing concern for the education of clergy and for the continuing education of clergy and lay persons as well. Bible schools and lay institutes have sprung up throughout the nation sponsored by various Pentecostal groupings.[21] And whatever may be said about the failures of these churches to engage the social, economic, and political inequities in this world with a view towards changing them, their distinctive doctrines are, in the view of their committed adherents, biblically warranted and experientially validated truths of ultimate consequences for one's eternal salvation.

POWER AND POLITICS

The posture of Pentecostal churches toward their Protestant counterparts has traditionally been highly critical and characterized by an arrogance derived from the belief that they, the Pentecostals, have discovered "the truth" and that outside of their circle there is no salvation. This feeling of exclusiveness is still the attitude of some church bodies. Nevertheless, there is evidence that Pentecostal congregations are becoming more ecumenical at the local level. It is not unusual to see denominational officers joining their counterparts in the mainline churches at state or local ecumenical gatherings. There are also signs that "Black consciousness" has had the effect of uniting clergy across denominational lines in causes and projects affecting the community. In this respect it should be noted that despite the nominal power of the bishops in the overall church structure, at the level of the local congregations the pastors and the people are virtually autonomous. Indeed the struggle within some Pentecostal bodies today arises out of the effort of national officials to exert control over property and pulpits which bear the name of the national church. It is the problem of bringing under the hierarchical yoke churches which have been created by the energy and sometimes by the personal funds of individual pastors.

---

[20]In the House of the Lord Congregation of the Reverend Herbert D. Daughtry in Brooklyn, New York, there are groups whose purpose it is to participate in marches and demonstrations as a witness of the church and its concern for the world.

[21]Pentecostalists have been slow in developing institutions of higher education. The Church of God in Christ supports Saints Junior college in Lexington, Mississippi, a school begun at the instigation of elders in Mississippi in 1917. In addition, the church established the C. H. Mason School of Theology in 1968 as a constituent part of the Interdenominational Theological Center in Atlanta, Georgia.

The weakness of the episcopacy within some of these groups has also contributed to the excessive proliferation of congregations within given geographical areas. This in turn has had the effect of keeping individual congregations small and impotent. One reason for the limited community impact of these churches is their limited human and fiscal resources. Many pastors work at secular occupations in order to be able to maintain their pulpits. These latter comments would be equally applicable to churches in the Black community where the polity is congregational, as in the case of the Baptist churches, or where the central authority is unable to enforce standards for ordination. There is a sense in which it is valid to observe that the Pentecostal churches mirror the situation of the majority of Black churches in the urban scene. The small size which is conducive to intimacy and in which access to leadership is fairly easy also helps to make them impotent as a social force. The ease with which one can become a leader, fed by the absence of rigorous, enforceable educational prerequisites, means that clergy are generally poorly prepared to cope with the complex problems of urban life. Conversely, it is a tribute to the native ability and charismatic gifts of these men and women that so many do sustain their posts in a highly competitive environment.

The Pentecostal movement has been an arena in which many Black women have been able to rise to positions of congregational leadership. In the more fully organized and centralized church bodies, women tend to fill leadership roles traditionally considered to be ''women's work,'' i.e., as head of women's auxiliaries, as evangelists, and as church ''mothers'' at both local and national levels. But in many unaffiliated Pentecostal congregations and in some loosely organized national bodies, it is not exceptional to find women clergy as pastors.[22] The best example is in the United Holy Church in America, where women have been ordained and have pastored churches since its organization in 1900.

PROSPECTS: PENTECOSTALISM
AND LIBERATION

For all its distinctiveness of doctrine, Black Pentecostalism faces the same future as other Black churches. There are new currents flowing in

---

[22]For a statement defining the place of women in Church of God in Christ, see Bishop O. T. Jones, ''Dedicated to the National Women's Convention of the Church of God in Christ,'' quoted in Pleas, *Fifty Years of Achievement*, pp. 35-37.

these communities, and these currents, powered by a renewed ethnic consciousness, are forcing new questions upon Black institutions. In some respects Black churches are just beginning to feel tremors forecasting changes
that have reached urgent proportions in white religious bodies. Langdon
Gilkey has summarized them very nicely:

> . . . The central axis of religion has shifted from matters of ultimate sal-
> vation, of judgment and justification before God in eternity, and of heaven
> and hell, to questions of the meaning, necessity and usefulness of religion
> for this life—be it self-fulfillment and self-integration, for ethical norms
> and moral efficacy, for "meaning in life," self-affirmation, or for what
> the existentialists call "authenic-existence."[23]

While these religious questions are being asked from within the major
white groupings, they are being asked in more strident political terms by
persons from outside the Black churches. Moreover, the Black secular
community has developed alternative institutions and ideologies which are
self-consciously in competition with the churches. The Black Muslims
(Nation of Islam) are an outstanding example of both of these phenomena.
The questions that one hears being addressed to the churches time and again
are: How can you purge yourself of the religion of your oppressors, which
is itself anti-liberation? When will you get on board in the liberation struggle, or does your religion cause you to be satisfied with the status quo?
What, concretely, is your institution or your ideology contributing to the
struggle? It is no defense to argue that the questions themselves arise out
of ignorance of Black religion and its institutions. The mood of the communities is increasingly pragmatic and is notable for its expectation that
the end of the world is imminent, brought on not by the activity of God,
but through the revoluntionary struggle of oppressed people. Neither Pentecostal bodies nor their constituencies have felt the full force of these
questions, but in the years ahead such issues will be a factor in determining
the strength and shape of the churches. It will be no easy task for these
churches whose basic posture is individual and eschatological to accom-
modate a corporate and temporal perspective. The outcome will depend
very much upon the ability of the second and third generation of leaders to

---

[23]Langdon Gilkey, "Sources of Protestant Theology in America," *Daedalus* XCVI
(Winter, 1967), 73.

sustain a creative tension between the emphasis upon a particular religious experience and the demand for the concrete embodiment of faith in actions directed towards the pressing problems of the community.

Part III
Theological Studies

15

J. MASSYNGBAERDE FORD

Toward a Theology of "Speaking in Tongues"

[Reprinted from *Theological Studies*, 32
(1971): 3-29. Reprinted with permission from
Theological Studies and author.]

The increasing frequency of the phenomenon of "speaking in tongues,"
in the Roman Catholic and other Christian denominations, challenges one
to outline a "theology" of this spiritual gift. Morton Kelsey has made an
important contribution in the field of psychology.[1] However, while psychological investigations are valid and interesting, they can hardly throw
adequate light on supernatural phenomena. One may compare 1 Corinthians 2:14-16: "The unspiritual man does not receive the gifts of the Spirit

---

[1]Morton T. Kelsey, *Speaking with Tongues: An Experiment in Spiritual Experience*
(London 1965), examines the biblical, patristic, and contemporary evidence concerning
"speaking with tongues," but emphasizes especially the association with certain aspects
of Jungian psychology (pp. 169-233). His book will be translated into German.

of God, for they are folly to him, and he is not able to understand them because they are spiritually discerned. The spiritual man judges all things, but is himself to be judged by no one. 'For who has known the mind of the Lord so as to instruct Him?' But we have the mind of Christ.''[2] The present essay will be approached purely from the biblical point of view.

First, it might be useful to give a brief survey of representative exegetical expositions of the pertinent scriptural texts. After this we shall discuss "tongues" from (a) the individual's and (b) the community's point of view. It is becoming impossible to assemble all the articles relating to glossolalia. Our main interest, however, lies in the fact that there is a general tendency among more recent exegetes to accept to some degree the validity of this spiritual experience, to interpret "tongues" as genuine languages uttered in nonecstatic state rather than "gibberish" in ecstatic or frenzied state.

REPRESENTATIVE EXEGETICAL EXPOSITIONS

In the main, exegetes may be divided into four classes: (1) those who regard "tongues" as unintelligible sounds produced in an emotional state; (2) those who admit some intelligibility; (3) those who view tongues as a real language; (4) articles written in the last decade. In the first class one may place Clemens (1898), Dewar (1924), Thomson (1926), Synge (1934), and Martin (1944).

Carl Clemens[3] reviews the second- and third-century references found in Origen and Irenaeus[4] and concedes that they interpret "tongues" as

---

[2]Cf. also Kilian McDonnell, "Holy Spirit and Pentecostalism," *Commonweal* 89:6 (November 8, 1968): 198-204.

[3]Carl Clemens, "The 'Speaking with Tongues' of the Early Christians," *Expository Times*, 10 (1898-99): 344-52.

[4]Clemens does not give the reference to either source. He would appear to refer to Origen, *Contra Celsum*, 5, 29-30. Origen refers to Deuteronomy 32:8-9 and Wis 10:5 (*LXX*) and Genesis 11 (the Tower of Babel). He states that each nation possessed a language peculiar to its guardian angel. Chapter 30 begins "all the people upon the earth are to be regarded as having one divine language and so long as they lived harmoniously together were preserved in the use of this divine language. . . . " The reference to Irenaeus is probably *Adv. haer.* 5, 6, 1, which reads: "For this reason does the apostle declare 'We speak wisdom among them that are perfect,' terming those persons 'perfect' who have received the Spirit of God and who through the Spirit of God do speak in all languages, as He used Himself also to speak. In like manner we do also hear [the old Latin has *audivimus*, 'have heard']

speaking in "foreign languages." He admits that Irenaeus appears to equate the "speaking of tongues" in his day with the "tongues" at Pentecost, but he avers that Irenaeus had no firsthand experience of this.[5] However, Clemens doubts whether this means an absolutely new language. In Acts 10:46 and 19:6 the word "tongues" is used without reference to foreign languages. If one compares these texts with the narrative of Pentecost, the phrase used is "tongues," not "other tongues." He asks, therefore, if the phenomenon of Pentecost was a miracle of speaking in "other" tongues. Perhaps this speaking in "other" tongues was a later addition in limitation of the midrash according to which seven voices changed into seventy tongues at Sinai. Before this addition the text read "tongues" like Acts 10:46 and 19:6. He remarks that the end of Mark is not clear.

Clemens feels that Tertullian is in a different position. Tertullian challenges Marcion to produce psalms, visions, prayers, and tongues.[6] "Tongues" seem to be understood as prayer in ecstasy. However, Clemens asserts that Tertullian was probably speaking about the Montanist idea of speaking in tongues and one cannot draw inferences from this about the early Christians.[7] Clemens then proceeds to compare prophecy and tongues and finds the distinguishing feature to be that prophecy is "universally intelligible" while tongues are not. However, Clemens would not think that one can go so far as to say that it consisted of inarticulate sounds. Romans

---

many brethren in the Church who possess prophetic gifts and who through the Spirit speak all kinds of languages and bring to light for the general benefit the hidden things of men . . '' (*ANF* translation).

[5]See below for the alternative reading in Irenaeus.

[6]Tertullian, *Adv. Marc.* 5, 8, where Tertullian refers to Isaiah 11:2-5 and accommodates it to 1 Corinthians 12:4-11. Concerning faith he says: " 'To another, faith by the same Spirit': this will be the 'the spirit of religion and the fear of the Lord.' " He makes healing and miracles equate the spirit of might. Prophecy, discerning of spirits, tongues, and interpretation comprise the spirit of knowledge. Another interesting note is Tertullian's remark: "When he [Marcion] mentions the fact that 'it is written in the law' how that the Creator would speak with other tongues and other lips, whilst confirming indeed the gift of tongues by such a mention, he yet cannot be thought to have confirmed that the gift was of another god by his reference to the Creator's prediction" (1 Corinthians 14:21). The *OT* passage to which he refers appears to be Isaiah 28:11.

[7]Yet if Tertullian is referring to "unfrenzied ecstasy," tongues might be equivalent to *ebrietas spiritalis* or *iubilum mysticum*. It is regrettable that Tertullian's books on ecstasy are lost. On the other hand, *glossais lalein* is not used with regard to the Montanists. They were criticized for para-ecstasy and passivity and speaking strange sounds. The word is *xenophōneō* (Eusebius, *Hist. eccl.* 5, 26, 7).

8:26 appears to be different and 12:3 would suggest that one can hear intelligible utterance. But in general they are not intelligible, even if some words were understood.

Clemens then turns to "interpretation." He asserts: "Perhaps the practice and familiarity with the matter enabled some to interpret simultaneously the speaker's face expressions and gestures." He feels that those who spoke in tongues were in ecstasy, so that they could not interpret their own tongues, but perhaps some remained conscious a little longer and were able to interpret some of their speech.[8]

His conclusions, therefore, are: (1) the speaking in tongues occurred in ecstasy, and was in general unintelligible; (2) there were differences in the case of different individuals, and even of the same individual at different times. Sometimes a man was conscious to such an extent that he afterwards remembered his utterances; but at other times he had so entirely lost control of his senses that he gave to his feelings an expression exactly contrary to their content. If, in addition to this, we may suppose that with these unconnected words and sentences meaningless sound combinations alternated, then some additional light will be thrown upon the Apostle's expression "kind of tongues" (Romans 12:10).[9] However, Clemens does contrast these New Testament tongues with pagan ecstatic speech, with Gnostic prayers consisting largely of names of gods, with the speech of the Camisards at the end of the seventeenth and eighteenth century, which consisted of inarticulate sounds and newly created words, and with the fanatical movement of the Jansenists in 1731 who believed that the organs of speech were controlled by another power. He also contrasts the forties, when there was "sermon-sickness" in Sweden, which consisted of inarticulate sounds, unconscious singing of hymns, sometimes horrible oaths. Least of all can it be compared with the speaking in tongues among the Irvingites, "for this phenomenon was from the very beginning artificial." Clemens asserts that the speaking in tongues at Corinth was "thoroughly natural." Perhaps the tongues at Pentecost, at the Cornelian Pentecost, and at Ephesus were a wonderful inspiration, though unconnected words and

---

[8]These statements show that Clemens had no firsthand experience of tongues; contrast Gundry's article (n. 41 below).

[9]But this is a wholly arbitrary "exegesis," for different "kinds of languages" cannot be subject to this interpretation.

sentences. Moreover, the apostles were masters of themselves when Peter asked for silence. Further, Paul forbade anyone to stop speaking in tongues (1 Corinthians 14:39). Clemens concludes that speaking with tongues soon died out and must not be confounded with speaking in foreign languages, but that there is an association because of their similarity. Thus arose the concept of Pentecost which we have now.

Clemens' article leaves an air of uncertainty. He seems to vacillate between accepting the validity of the experience and regarding it as ecstatic, inarticulate, and emotional; yet there is not the wholesale condemnation of tongues found in so many writers' work.

Lindsay Dewar takes a different approach.[10] He proposes that only the apostles spoke in other tongues, that Acts 2:9-11 are an editorial and so they cannot be used as a guide to suggest which languages were heard. He feels that the speaking in tongues was due to "sudden breaking down of a repression in the unconscious minds of the Apostles." This repression was due to the shock which they had sustained owing to the Crucifixion. He tries to support his point by referring to St. Peter's speech where the cross is spoken of, not with horror, but as a divine plan. Therefore the apostles, through emotion, broke into meaningless syllables which were probably learnt from the polyglot community in Jerusalem or may have been fragments of Hebrew texts. He notes that Jesus' attention was given to Old Testament texts when speaking of His approaching death. Dewar would suggest that some parts of the apostles' speech would appear as "gibberish" but other parts proclaimed the wonderful works of God. For the Jews, Hebrew could be regarded as "the tongues in which they were born." For once the Galileans may have spoken without the distinctive impediment to which their speech usually succumbed, that is, the confusion of gutterals in their dialect. Dewar compares the Camisards who spoke exhortations in good French from the Huguenot Bible.

When Dewar turns to the Cornelian episode, he claims repression once again. Cornelius felt this repression because as a proselyte he was unable to participate fully in the synagogue services. He would have heard the Hebrew or Greek text of the Bible and therefore spoke in fragments of passages. But the Holy Spirit did dwell in the community after Pentecost and His outpouring was a deepening of the receptive powers of men.

---

[10]Lindsay Dewar, "The Problem of Pentecost," *Theology* 9 (1924): 249-59.

Dewar, therefore, does not really regard tongues as "natural" but rather as abnormal behavior. His article would suggest that he sees little genuine spirituality in the experience.

W. S. Thomson regards "speaking in tongues" as a state of religious exaltation.[11] "It begins with a sense of being uplifted or *above oneself*, strengthens and then passes on through ecstasy and frenzy to a state of complete trance. . . . "[12] The frenzied and trance state produces the inarticulate ejaculations, moanings, and mutterings described by the Apostle in 1 Corinthians 12-14.[13] Thomson declares these to be bedlam, incoherent, childish; they may be of spiritual value to the speaker but are useless without an interpreter. When he examines Acts 2, he speaks of the emotional effects of the Crucifixion, of the enormous crowds of pilgrims (he states that the census of Nero gives two and a half million Passover pilgrims, and Pentecost was a more important feast);[14] the accusation of drunkenness suggests a disorderly scene. He declares that the theory that these tongues were languages has been "long abandoned." The text lists eighteen provinces or states. As the foreign pilgrims arrived, the apostles changed their praise to foreign words which they recalled at the sight of the pilgrims.

Thomson's view, therefore, appears more disparaging than Dewar's. It might be noted that no one who has ever heard the exquisitely beautiful choral singing in tongues at a quiet prayer meeting could ever declare this to be "bedlam." In a most inexplicable way the singing harmonizes, although different languages, tunes, and keys appear to be present.

F. C. Synge sees Acts 2 as a fulfilment of Isaiah 59:21 and Joel 2:28-30.[15] He cites examples of the Spirit's work in the Old Testament and says:

---

[11]W. S. Thomson, "Tongues in Pentecost, Acts ii.," *Expository Times*, 38 (1926-27): 284-86.

[12]Again Thomson cannot have experienced "tongues."

[13]But Thomson does not give the specific verses. Romans 8:23, 26 might have been more appropriate for his thesis, although the present writer would see even those texts in a different light.

[14]On the contrary, Pentecost does not seem to have been so important in mainline Judaism until at least the second century A.D. It was more important among the sectarians, e.g., Qumran.

[15]F. C. Synge, "The Spirit in the Pauline Epistles," *Church Quarterly Review*, 119 (1934): 79-93.

the examples cited are all connected with abnormalities of behavior, and probably a strain of animism lies behind the language. Such phrases as the spirit of a deep sleep, Isaiah 29:10 or of perverseness, 19:4, are due to the same diagnosis of abnormal behavior as are the explanations of prophecy and Saul's fits. Partial hypostatisation, as in 1 Samuel 16:14-23, is due partly to the old animistic ways of thinking and partly to a new philosophy, an attempt to solve the problem of evil which culminated in the personification of Satan.

He suggests that the outpouring of the Spirit in the New Testament produces similar abnormal or supernormal manifestation.[16] He attempts to translate such texts as Galatians 4:6; Thessalonians 5:19; and 2 Thessalonians 2:2 as ecstatic utterance and pronounces that this is "the key-word, so to speak, for the interpretation of Acts 2:10-14." In the same category he places Romans 8:26, 27; Ephesians 5:18.

Thus Synge, too, attributes tongues to psychological abnormality.

Ira Jay Martin wrote his article in 1944, but he seems to list bibliography mainly ranging from 1913-21.[17] Martin asserts that in Acts 2:1-42 the glossolalia was coincidental with being possessed by the Spirit and that Peter quoted Joel to prove this association: "ecstatic speech became the chief evidence of this [the Spirit's] possession—at least in some Christian circles."

Of Acts 4:31 he notes (with Harnack) that this is probably a doublet; glossolalia is not specifically mentioned "but we may assume that some of the speaking was ecstatic." Speaking of Acts 8:14-24, he says that Peter regarded glossolalia as a proof that the Spirit had come and that in Acts 10:44-48 and 11:15-17 he says that the Spirit has descended "even as on us at the beginning" (Acts 11:15), that is, he equates the Cornelian episode with Pentecost. In Acts 19:2-7 the converts spoke with tongues and prophesied. Approximately twenty-five years later, speaking in tongues is

---

[16]W. R. Shoemaker, in a very interesting article entitled "The Use of *Ruah* in the Old Testament and of *pneuma* in the New Testament: A Lexicographical Study," *Journal of Biblical Literature* 23 (1904) 13-67, demonstrates that the concept of the Spirit of Yahweh did not become, as it were, acceptable until the prophets became nonecstatic. One would date Isaiah 11:2:5 as exilic.

[17]Ira Jay Martin, "Glossolalia in the Apostolic Church," *Journal of Biblical Literature*, 63 (1944): 123-30.

found as one of the charismata but 1 Corinthians 13, on love, is a "poetic characterization of the true Christian, contrasted to a mere ecstatic speaker."

Martin then proceeds to claim that glossolalia is not confined to Christianity; it is found, e.g., in the episode of Eldad and Medad (Numbers 11-12), in the Baal prophets (1 Kings 18:16-46), in the case of Aaron (Numbers 12:1-2), in the Greek poets, the Cumean Sibyl, the *Aeneid* of Virgil, the Gerasene demoniac (Luke 8:26-39); but his references do not seem to refer to glossolalia. He continues by saying that "it might appear at any time and place under proper motivation," for example, the Irvingites of England, the Little Prophets of Cevennes, the Holy Rollers and the Pentecostal sects today. "There are also ample illustrations of uncontrolled speaking in delirium and in insanity."

Martin thinks that glossolalia arose from a desire to have an objective sign of the possession of the Holy Spirit, and he avers that this "speaking may have been occasionally intelligible and coherent, but for the most part it consisted of frenzied, inarticulate, incoherent, ecstatic speech"; the converts gained prestige and hoped to secure divine power and favor among men.[18]

Martin's article presents the theses of Dewar, Thomson, and Synge in a more exaggerated form, but his arguments are hardly compelling owing to his indiscriminate references and lack of linguistic analysis.

All these articles appear to speak from the standpoint of persons who have no empirical experience of the phenomenon which they wish to evaluate. The contention that tongues are due to psychological abnormality is contradicted by Kelsey and others who have made clinic experiments or acquired empirical evidence. It is not to be doubted that there are some cases of abnormality, but contemporary firsthand experience would seem to be analogous, for example, to archeological empirical evidence which confirms certain hypotheses in Scripture. Moreover, viewed objectively, the biblical text does not witness to the ecstasy or intense emotion of which these writers speak. *Ekstasis* in the sense of "trance" occurs only in Acts 11:5 and 22:17 but not in the texts concerning glossolalia.

---

[18]I have been unable to procure I. J. Martin's book *Glossolalia in the Apostolic Church: A Survey of Tongue-Speech* (Berea KY, 1960).

In the second class one may place Edwards (1928), Taylor (1928) and Stoll (1943).

Hubert E. Edwards recalls that Greek was the lingua franca of the Roman Empire and that it could be understood anywhere from Syria to Spain.[19] Most of the countries listed in Acts 2 would have understood this language. Why, then, would the Holy Spirit speak in "other tongues"? He says that there is nothing to suggest that St. Peter's speech was not spoken in either Greek or Aramaic; probably "tongues" were not used for addressing the crowds. It is not said that the crowd itself came to Jerusalem recently but that they were dwellers in Jerusalem. In the *LXX* and papyri, *katoikein* is used in a technical sense to distinguish permanent residents in the towns from those "dwelling as strangers" or "sojourners" (*paroikountes*). St. Peter seems to stress that they were local people from Judea and Jerusalem. Why, then, does the text say that they came from "every nation under the sun"? Edwards suggests that the Roman peace brought many Diaspora Jews back to their country to live (cf. Acts 23:6 and Paul brought up in Jerusalem) and that the miracle was hearing dialects from homes left some time ago. Dialects would occur in the praises of God uttered by the apostles.

Edwards' article appears much more tenable, but more evidence would be needed to show that these were dialects in languages.

R. O. P. Taylor does not agree with those who say that the miracle was one of hearing (interpretation) only, not of speech.[20] The text militates against this, but the obstacle overcome might be that of dialect rather than language (cf. Edwards above). There is a gap of time between the speaking in tongues and the hearing of the crowd, and one need not prolong it into the second part of the narrative. However, he adds: "we have to remember that in all other cases where the phrase speaking with tongues occurs, it appears to mean uttering inarticulate cries under the stress of great emotion. The speaker, through the very intensity of his feelings, was unable to put them into articulate words, and this had to be done by some other person who was capable of discerning the cause of his emotion." He quotes

---

[19]Hubert E. Edwards, "The Tongues at Pentecost: A Suggestion," *Theology* 16 (1928) 248-52.

[20]R. O. P. Taylor, "The Tongues at Pentecost," *Expository Times*, 40 (1928-9) 300-303.

Canon Raven, who speaks of interpretation as thought-transference. Taylor cannot accept the meaning of foreign languages for "other tongues" in the first part of Acts 2. The proclamation may have consisted largely of quotations from Scripture, probably Messianic texts, so that people would understand the meaning.

R. F. Stoll[21] refers to the appearance of tongues which had the form and color of fire,[22] and says that they symbolized the speech and preaching by which the New Law was given through the Spirit. Stoll gives the modern names for the tribes listed in Acts 2 and calculates that about five or six distinct languages were represented, but each had different dialects: there seem to have been about fifteen different dialects. In the New Testament, *dialektos* is used only in Acts 1:19 (of the Jerusalemites), 21:40, 21:2, and 26:14, each time with reference to a language spoken by the Hebrews. Stoll takes the view that the speaker was in control of himself, that the language could be understood by those who knew it, and that it was not a meaningless jumble of muttered sounds.

Stoll would, therefore, seem to support Edwards' and Taylor's contention that tongues comprise dialects rather than languages. On the whole, these three scholars take a more realistic and spiritual view of tongues: their opinions (save for Taylor's reference to inarticulate cries and great emotion) are consonant with the biblical text.

In the third class fall Brown (1875), Beel (1935), Lyonnet (1944), and Sirks (1957).

David Brown argues that the languages in Acts were "real articulate tongues" unknown to the apostles, but he thinks that the tongues in the Corinthian community differed to some degree from those in Acts.[23] He notes,[24] however, that the verb *apophtheggomai* is used in the *LXX* both

---

[21]R. F. Stoll, "The First Christian Pentecost," *Ecclesiastical Review* 108 (1943) 337-47.

[22]The Hebrew for flame is "tongue of fire"; I do not know whence Stoll derives the "color."

[23]David Brown, "The Acts of the Apostles, Chapter 2: The Day of Pentecost," *Expositor*, 1 (1875): 392-408.

[24]*Ibid.*, p. 339, n. 2.

of inspired utterances (1 Chronicles 25:1[25]) and of those falsely claiming inspiration (Ezekiel 13:19, Micah 5:12, Zechariah 10:2), and also that the gifts of tongues came to all Christians irrespective of sex, age, or rank.

A. Beel writes about the nature of the charism and notes that the speech was distinct from the apostles' native tongues.[26] It was not a miracle of hearing but of speaking, and was not incoherent or unintelligible. However, although it was articulate and audible, the accusation of drunkenness was made because there were 120 people speaking with religious fervor. He discusses also the object and scope of the gift of tongues and states that it was not preaching the word (cf. Acts 14:11ff.) but for the praise of God. He asserts that it was not a habitual or permanent gift.[27]

S. Lyonnet gives a summary of the opinions of various exegetes,[28] but his main point of interest is the fact that he refers to *ebrietas spiritalis* or *iubilum systicum* and quotes St. Teresa of Avila (*Life* 16), St. Bernard of Clairvaux (*In Cant.* 67,3), and St. Alphonsus Liguori (*Homo apostolicus*, Appendix 1, 15). This seems to be a phenomenon akin to tongues.[29]

G. J. Sirks claims that tongues are interpretations of glosses on the text of Scripture, that *lalien* can mean "ordered recitation of *pericopae*," that

---

[25]This reference is to the selection of certain sons of Asaph etc., "who should prophesy with lyres, with harps, and with cymbals." One wonders whether "prophesy" is a very apt translation.

[26]A. Beel, "Donum linguarum juxta Act. Apost. ii. 1-13," *Collationes Brugenses* 35 (1935) 417-20.

[27]The present writer's firsthand and secondhand information would seem to prove him incorrect.

[28]S. Lyonnet, "De glossolalia Pentecostes eusique significatione," *Verbum domini* 24 (1944) 66-75.

[29]St. Teresa: "Then the soul does not know what it should do, whether to speak or to be silent, laugh or cry . . . then many words are pronounced in praise of God, yet without order, unless God Himself gives them order; however, the human mind can do nothing." St. Bernard: "Thus love, especially divine [love], is strong and burning; when it is not able to restrain itself within itself, it does not wait for any order . . . it overflows because of poverty of words, while it feels no loss to itself through this. Meanwhile it requires neither words nor voice, content alone with sighs." St. Alphonsus: "Spiritual intoxication causes the soul to break forth in, as it were, delirium, such as songs, cries, immoderate weeping, leaping, etc., as it used to happen to St. Mary Magdalene of Pazzi." Yet I do not think these symptoms are always found with the gift of tongues. Tongues may be used even in a state of deep aridity, although an effort is required.

"other tongues" may mean offering Scripture interpretations contrary to those commonly accepted.[30] The Diaspora Jews were astonished at the variance of pericopes and interpretation in a new fashion, especially because they pointed to Jesus as Messiah. C. S. Mann remarks: "Sirks rightly observes that not only is there quite another word for 'languages' in Acts 2 than *glossae* (*dialektoi*), but also that the behavior of Peter was anything but that of a man possessed."[31]

These four writers seem to grasp the key to the gift of tongues, namely, that it is an inspired gift, a gift of prayer or praise, and associated with Scripture and possibly instruction. Their articles treat the text with an empathy not always discovered in the writers discussed previously. It might be remarked that the classical prophets and concept of the Spirit arose after the disappearance of the ecstatic prophets; a similar observation may be made with regard to classical Pentecostalism and neo-Pentecostalism.

Scholars who have written on the gift of tongues during the last decade include Beare (1964), Currie (1965), Gundry (1966), and Sweet (1967). It is in the first quarter of this decade that the gift of tongues was bestowed more profusely upon the historical churches—that is, neo-Pentecostalism was born.

Beare makes several important observations.[32] First, he rightly draws attention to the injunction in Matthew that one should not repeat meaningless sounds. Secondly, he recalls that we find no reference to "speaking in tongues" in the canonical Gospels (if one accepts Mark 16:9ff. as an addition); it is never attributed to Jesus or His followers.[33] Thirdly, although there is much about the Spirit in John's Gospel, there is no mention of tongues. Fourthly, he remarks that there is much symbolism in Acts 2 and that tongues in Acts appear to be different from tongues elsewhere, "where it is taken to mean some kind of unintelligible utterance which does not involve the mind of the speaker at all and may even give outsiders the

---

[30]G. J. Sirks, "The Cinderella of Theology," *Harvard Theological Review*, 50 (1957): 77-89.

[31]C. S. Mann, "Pentecost, the Spirit and John," *Theology*, 62 (1959): 188-90.

[32]F. W. Beare, "Speaking with Tongues: A Critical Survey of the New Testament Evidence," *Journal of Biblical Literature* 83 (1964): 229-52.

[33]But this would be to exempt Acts.

impression that he is mad." Acts 2 foreshadows such a scene as Ap 7:9. Fifthly, he adds a remark on those who say "Jesus cursed" (1 Corinthians 12:3: *anathema Jesus*): "A modern teacher would perhaps think of such 'spirits' as evidence of a subconscious hostility to Christ and the gospels breaking out in words when the controls of the conscious mind were removed in a state of ecstasy."[34] Beare appears to take a psychological approach with regard to 1 Corinthians, but his reservations with regard to the rest of the New Testament are important in the light of the Pentecostal stress on tongues.

S. D. Currie states that the phrase "to speak in tongues" might mean either a nonhuman language or utterance, which may not be languages at all "in the sense of connected discourse, even if the sounds are in some way meaningful."[35] However, the phrase may mean human language. He refers to Chrysostom, who believes that the phrase means unlearned human languages,[36] and to Irenaeus, who says: "many brethren in the Church having prophetic gifts and speaking through the Spirit in all tongues and bringing to light men's secrets for the common good and explaining mysteries of God. . . . "[37] Irenaeus' statement is found also in Eusebius' *Church History* (5, 7, 6), but probably the Latin text is older. The Greek text differs only in having the present tense instead of the past at "we have heard many brethren. . . . " Irenaeus also thinks that *glossais lalein* is a human language which one has not learned. However, between Luke and Irenaeus there is little suggestion of speaking in tongues. Even the apocryphal Gospels do not refer to the phenomenon, although they do refer to animals speaking human language. In the Acts of John (chap. 106) the gift of tongues is noticeably absent from the list of powers of the spirit: "wonders, healings, signs, charismata, teachings, governing, refreshments, services, knowledge, praises, graces, confidences, sharings." Tongues are not

---

[34]Beare, *op. cit.*, pp. 241-42. I would like to add that obsession or possession by an evil spirit would certainly produce a "tongue" which cursed Jesus. The writer has some experience in the mission field and elsewhere, and finds it difficult to argue against the existence of evil powers.

[35]S. D. Currie, " 'Speaking in Tongues': Early Evidence outside the New Testament bearing on 'glossais lalein,' " *Interpretation* 19 (1965): 274-94.

[36]Chrysostom, *Homily 29*, on 1 Corinthians 12:1-11,

[37]Irenaeus, *Adv. haer.* 5, 6, 1.

mentioned in Justin's *Dialogue with Trypho* 39, 2, where charismata are listed.[38]

Currie considers whether the "tongues" at Corinth could be angelic languages (cf. 2 Corinthians 12:3-4, where Paul heard "sayings which cannot be expressed, which are not for man to speak"). Enoch 40 refers to the various languages of angelic beings; in the *Apocalypse of Abraham* 17, Abraham is taught the song of an angel and the song is reported.[39] In the *Ascension of Isaiah* 6-11, each rank of angelic beings has its own voice; with this text one may compare also the *Testament of Levi* 3 and the *Testament of Judah* 25. But the most interesting document which Currie quotes is the *Testament of Job* 45-50. The daughters of Job receive the ability to speak in angelic voices: Hemera is given a change of heart and "the utterance of the angelic dialect"; Kasia, "the dialect of principalities"; the third daughter, "the dialect of those on high"—she spoke in the language of Cherubim.[40] Nahor wrote down these hymns.

Currie concludes that speaking in tongues may be "some sort of oracular utterance, a dark saying which requires interpretation." But if speaking with tongues were some kind of cadence of vocalization, it could be confused with charlatanry; but if so, then the silence of the first and second century is surprising. The aberrations of Montanism may have quenched the charismatic gifts.

This is an interesting and important article, but it is surprising that he does not refer to Qumran, especially to the seven words of blessing by the chief princes, the liturgy of the three tongues of fire, and the passage based on Ezekiel 1:10.

A great turning point in the theology of tongues is reached with R. H. Gundry's article.[41] Gundry takes his thesis further than J. D. Davies.[42] He

---

[38]Justin, *Dialogue with Trypho* 39, 2: "For one receives the spirit of understanding, another of counsel, another of strength, another of healing, another of foreknowledge, another of teaching, and another of the fear of God." One notes the blending of the "Isaian" and "Corinthian" gifts.

[39]The *Apocalypse of Abraham* is first or second century A.D.

[40]Currie does not compare the liturgy of angels at Qumran; see A. Dupont-Sommer, *The Essene Writings from Qumran* (New York 1962): 329-36.

[41]R. H. Gundry, "Ecstatic Utterance," *Journal of Theological Studies*, n.s. 17 (1966) 299-307.

[42]J. D. Davies, "Pentecost and Glossolalia," *ibid.*, n.s. 3 (1952): 228-31.

questions the New English Bible's translation "ecstatic utterance" for this phrase: this suggests that it means "the broken speech of persons in religious ecstasy," either in "antiquated, foreign, unintelligible, mysterious utterances" or in "marvelous, heavenly languages" (Bauer-Arndt-Gingrich, *glossa* 3a). He produces the following arguments for regarding tongues as human speech:

1. *Glossa* through the New Testament is used for human speech. "The use of the term for understandable language far exceeds its use for obscure speech, especially biblical Greek." There are only two cases where it is used of unintelligible speech and these are not in ecstasy but in stammering, Isaiah 29:24 and 32:4 (*LXX*); nevertheless, it does refer to language.

2. As regards the word *hermēneia* (interpretation), normally this means translating a language (except for the seven occurrences in 1 Corinthians 12:14); one case refers to satire, two to explanation, eighteen to translation.

3. In Acts 2:6-11 *glossais lalein* must mean languages.

4. As regards the "tongues of angels" in this context, Paul does speak of the tongues of men as well. Further, *ean* with subjunctive, "if I speak in the tongues of angels," would not necessarily suggest factual reality; the supposition is that Paul does not speak in the tongue of angels, just as he has not all the powers to prophesy, etc.

5. In verse 28b neither "mystery" nor "in the Spirit" denotes ecstasy. It is the absence of an interpreter which causes the tongue to be unintelligible, not the ecstatic nature of the tongues. Indeed, the "effectiveness of glossolalia as an authenticating sign (as well as its effectiveness in conveying a divine message—see 14, 6-12, 16-18, and especially 23) depended on its *difference* from the ecstatic gobbledegook in Hellenistic religion."

6. "Tongues" seems to be a convincing miracle but not a means of overcoming a communication barrier.

7. St. Paul's use of *lalein* does not militate against the argument that tongues are a human language. *Lalein* can mean incoherent speech but does not mean so ordinarily. In 1 Corinthians 14:6 Paul uses *legō*, and he uses *lalein* when speaking-with-the-mind is the subject in 1 Corinthians 14:9. In 1 Corinthians 14:29 *lalein* is used in association with the prohibition of wives speaking in the church (14:34f.). It is probably the use of *lalein* in Isaiah 28:11f. in the *LXX* which caused its use for glossolalia.

8. The accusation of intoxication does not necessarily imply that the speech was unintelligible; it was the "others," the non-Palestinians, who were the accusers.

9. In 1 Corinthians 14:5 Paul says that tongues with interpretation are just as valuable as prophecy.

10. The precepts for order to be observed with reference to tongues are the same as the precepts for prophecy and for wives asking questions: neither of the last two mentioned is concerned with incoherent speech.

11. The fact that Paul rules that only two or three should speak in tongues and that there should be no tongues if there is no interpreter implies that the speaker was in control.

12. Paul in 1 Corinthians 14:10f. must be speaking of tongues as a gift of language.

Gundry's article leaves little doubt that Corinthian speaking in tongues is not ecstatic and that the gift is one of language.

Gundry's article is complemented by an article of larger compass in which Sweet discussed 1 Corinthians 12-14 in the light of the modern Pentecostal phenomena.[43] Anti-Pentecostals may wish to overstress Paul's disapproval of tongues, but he merely wished to deny that tongues were the *exclusive* sign of the Spirit. He did not object to glossolalia itself, but to glossolalia paraded in public. He affirmed that all Christians are spiritual people (*pneumatikoi*) through sacramental baptism and lose this quality only if they deny Christ. 1 Corinthians 12 stresses the diversity and the "equal authenticity" of the charismata. The Apostle, through an adaptation of Isaiah 28:11-12, warns the recipients of the letter that tongues are meant as a sign "for (= against)" people who reject God's message, not as a sign for the benefit of the faithful. Thus, as in the Old Testament, it was a sign for the faithless Jew. Sweet may be right on the last point; but while concurring with the rest of his thesis, I am a little exercised about this part.

Sweet feels that the Cephas party in Corinth may have been too insistent on this manifestation of the Spirit; "the demand came from the leaders of the Cephas party, and was part of the concerted move to instill Palestinian piety and orthodoxy into the Corinthian Church" (p. 146). Sweet,

---

[43]J. P. M. Sweet, "A Sign for Unbelievers: Paul's Attitude to Glossolalia," *New Testament Studies*, 13 (1967): 240-57.

however, recognizes that the practice of glossolalia was not introduced by Peter into Corinth and that it did exist elsewhere. Sweet concludes his important article by offering seven "Pauline points" for guidance with reference to the contemporary Pentecostal phenomena:

1. Baptism, not tongues, is the criterion of a Christian.

2. Tongues are not devil-inspired.

3. One must recognize the polemical character of 1 Corinthians 12-14 and understand that Paul does not condemn tongues.

4. Paul valued tongues highly as a private gift but ranked it lower than the other gifts because it did not contribute so much to the community.

5. Paul does not see glossolalia as childish but as childlike.

6. Paul did not conceive of the Holy Spirit without concrete manifestations. I would add that he may not have had a clear view of the Spirit as the Third Person of the Trinity in distinction from the spirit of Jesus.[44]

7. However, the absence of a reference to tongues in Romans 12 is significant. Paul's authority cannot be claimed for viewing tongues as an essential element of the Christian life, and yet he would not quench a manifestation of the Spirit (cf. 1 Thessalonians 5:19-22).

The result of the survey would seem to suggest that the question of tongues is complex, but the most recent exegesis, guided by the contemporary experience of those who possess or have witnessed the gift, would favor the interpretation of nonecstatic utterance of one or more languages not learnt by human means.[45] Our next consideration will be the utility of this charism (1) for the individual and (2) for the community.

RELATIONSHIP TO THE INDIVIDUAL

To understand the importance of "tongues," we must consider the gift's relationship to Pentecost as "new creation."[46] An examination of certain

---

[44]See my article "Holy Spirit in the New Testament," *Commonweal*, 89 (1968): 173-79.

[45]Some books which may be of interest are: F. Stagg, E. Glenn Hinson, and W. E. Oates, *Glossolalia: Tongue Speaking in Biblical, Historical and Psychological Perspective*, (Nashville 1967), a symposium on these different aspects; John L. Sherrill, *They Speak with Other Tongues*, (New York 1964), describing his search to discover the genuineness and meaning of "tongues"; Howard M. Ervin, *These Are Not Drunken As Ye Suppose*, (Plainfield NJ, 1968).

[46]For Pentecost as a new creation, see, e.g., J. Goettmann, "La Pentecôte premices de la nouvelle création," *Bible et vie chrétienne* 27 (1959) 59-69.

traditions about the reaction of man suggests that a certain emphasis was placed upon man as a speaking being. This is seen, for example, in the targums. The Onkelos Targum reads: "And the Lord God created Adam from the dust of the ground, and breathed upon his face the breath of lives, and it became in Adam a *Discoursing Spirit*. . . . " The Palestinian Targum reads: "and there was in the body of Adam the inspiration of a speaking spirit, unto the illumination of the eyes and the hearing of the ears . . . " (the Jerusalem Targum adds "and Adam became a soul of life").[47]

Speech or language, to the ancients, was a mysterious science. "God knew words and determined their meaning even before there were any men to speak them."[48] Speech, therefore, might be regarded as the result of the direct inspiration of the Spirit of Yahweh; in fact, "revelation" or "divine inspiration" is sometimes called "speech."[49] Thus it is man's speech which distinguishes him from the animals and places him partly in the category of intellectual spirits or angels, because he is able to utter some of the wisdom of God and pronounce His praise.[50] However, the Palestinian text quoted above appears to imply that the divine inspiration not only affected speech but was "unto the illumination of the eyes and the hearing of the ears. . . . " This would seem to refer not merely to the organs of the physical senses, but to the employment of the spiritual senses;[51] for animals, too, possess eyes and ears and indeed a tongue, but not for speech. For

---

[47]The English translation is from J. W. Ethridge, *The Targums* (New York 1968).

[48]Cf., e.g., A. Dupont-Sommer, *The Essene Writings from Qumran*, tr. G. Vermes, (New York 1962): 204, n. 1.

[49]See the interesting article by Herbert Parzen, "The Ruah Hakodesh in Tannaitic Literature," *Jewish Quarterly Review*, n.s. 20 (1929-30): 51-76. For this point cf. pp. 53 and 75; the ten synonyms of the Holy Spirit are proverb, metaphor, riddle, word (revelation), speech, glory, command, burden of prophecy, prophecy, vision (only two are not associated with speaking).

[50]It is praise which constitutes the most exalted use of the faculties of the mind and speech. It is the lament of the Psalmist (Psy 115) that the dead cannot praise God and that idols are dumb (*ibid.*). For the association of angels with priests who minister at the alter, see A. R. C. Leaney, *The Rule of Qumran and Its Meaning* (London 1966): 95.

[51]For an account of the spiritual senses (sight, hearing, touch, taste, and smell), cf. e.g., A. Poulain, *The Graces of Interior Prayer*, tr. Leonora L. Yorke (London, 1957): 88-113. For a similar thought in Judaism, see J. Abelson, *The Immanence of God in Rabbinical Literature*, (London 1912): 94, 82-115, 212-23. See also my *The Spirit and the Human Person*, (Dayton 1969).

further reference to the spiritual senses, one might compare the text of Sir 17 concerning the creation of mankind. The relevant verses are as follows:

> He [God] endowed them with strength like His own, and made them in His own image (3). He made for them [Syr., Gk.: inclination and] tongue[52] and eyes; He gave them ears and a mind for thinking. He filled them with knowledge and understanding, and showed them good and evil (6-7). Their eyes saw His glorious majesty[53] and their ears heard the glory of His voice (13).

This text may refer to the theophany on Mount Sinai, but in the context of a creation story it is more likely that it refers to man's intimacy with God before the Fall, when probably it was believed that he possessed the full use of his spiritual senses. The idea of the spiritual blindness and deafness caused by rebellion or sin is a fairly constant theme in the Old Testament and rabbinic sources and recurs in the literature of Qumran. The most notable Old Testament text is Isaiah 6:9-10:

> And he said, "Go, and say to this people: Hear and hear, but do not understand; see and see, but do not perceive." Make the heart[54] of this people fat, and their ears heavy, and shut their eyes; lest they see with their

---

[52]For the association of the gift of tongues with the fact that mankind was created in the image and likeness of God, see Irenaeus, *Adv. haer*, 5, 6, 1: "Now God shall be glorified in His handiwork, fitting it so as to be conformable to, and modeled after, His own Son. For by the hands of the Father, that is, by the Son and the Holy Spirit, man, and not [merely] a part of man, was made in the likeness of God. Now the soul and the spirit are certainly a *part* of man, but certainly not *the* man; for the perfect man consists in the commingling and the union of the soul receiving the spirit of the Father, and the admixture of that fleshly nature which was molded after the image of God. For this reason does the Apostle declare, 'We speak wisdom among them that are perfect,' terming those persons 'perfect' who have received the Spirit of God, and who through the Spirit of God do speak in all languages, as He used Himself also to speak. In like manner we do also hear many brethren in the Church who possess prophetic gifts, and through the Spirit speak all kinds of languages, and bring to light for the general benefit the hidden things of men, and declare the mysteries of God, whom also the Apostle terms 'spiritual,' they being spiritual because they partake of the Spirit, and not because their flesh has been stripped off and taken away, and because they have become purely animal."

[53]A similar phrase occurs frequently in the targums and appears to be almost identical with the Shekinah, whose presence was frequently experienced as radiance or light (the *ziv*) of the Shekinah.

[54]For the Hebrew, "heart" is the seat of the intelligence and the innermost life of man.

eyes, and hear with their ears and understand with their hearts, and turn and be healed.

While the targum on this text does not give further light upon these two verses, a rather remarkable alternation is made in verses 6-8:

> And there flew unto me one of the *ministering* angels, and his mouth was the *speech* which he had received from before him, whose Shekinah is on the throne of glory in the highest heaven, high above the altar; and he placed *it* in my mouth, and said, Behold, I have set the words of my prophecy in thy mouth, and thy transgressions shall be taken away, and thy sins expiated. And I heard the voice of the Memra of the Lord which said, Whom shall I send to prophesy, and who will go to teach? Then I said, Here am I; send me.[55]

Divine inspiration to prophesy is here described as speech, but unfortunately the speech of the prophet will not be "unto the illumination of the eyes and hearing of the ears" of the sinful people.

The same Isaiah theme appears at Qumran. For example, in the *Rule*, in the section concerning the doctrine of the two spirits, the evil spirit, or spirit of perversity, brings in its train numerous vices, but among them are "a *blaspheming tongue, blindness of eye* and *hardness of ear*, stiffness of neck and *heaviness of heart* causing a man to walk in all the ways of darkness, and malignant cunning" (*Rule* 4, 11). One may also compare "Moreover, they [those who follow Belial, i.e., Satan] have defiled their Holy Spirit, and *with a blaspheming tongue* have opened their mouth against the precepts of the covenant of God, saying, They are not true" (*CD* 5, 11-12).

Rebellion, therefore, causes a "sacrilegious speech," but those who adhere faithfully to the covenant are a people "learned in the precept" . . . with intelligent under[standing . . .] who *hear the voice of the venerated (Being)* [either God or the Teacher of Righteousness] and see the angels of holiness; . . . *whose ear is opened and who hear profound things . . .* " (*M* 10, 10-11; cf. Sir 17).

Moreover, the faithful recognize the divine origin of speech and music:

---

[55]Text and translation from J. F. Stenning, *The Targum of Isaiah* (Oxford 1949).

It is thou who hast created breath on tongue and known the words of the tongue and determined the fruit of the lips before ever they were. And thou hast set out words on a measuring cord and measured the breathing of breath from the lips and hast sent out sounds according to their mysterious (laws) and breathings of breath according to their harmony, that thy glory might be made known . . . (*Hymn Scroll* 1, 28-30).

Further, to the Teacher of Righteousness God gave the special office opening "the fountain of knowledge to all the understanding" (*Hymns*, 2, 18), but the unworthy "bartered it for uncircumcision of the lips and for the foreign tongue of a people without understanding, that they might be lost in their straying" (*Hymns* 2, 18-19), and the false prophets deceived the people by speaking to them "with bar[bar]ian lips and in a foreign tongue" (*Hymns* 4, 16). On the other hand, the good reply of the tongue is associated with the Spirit or good spirits, e.g., in *Hymns* 17, 17: "[I give Thee thanks, O Adona]i, because of the spirits which thou hast put in me! I will [utt]er a reply of the tongue. . . . " In *Hymns* 18, 10 f. a similar thought is found: "[For] thou hast opened a [fount]ain in the mouth of thy servant and upon his tongue thou hast graven [thy precepts] on a measuring cord, [that he] may proclaim them unto creatures because of his understanding, and be an interpreter of these things unto that which is dust like myself."

But one of the most interesting references is found in *CD* 14, 10, where it is provided that the overseer who is in charge of all the camps should have mastered all "the secrets of men and all the tongues which their various clans speak." Dupont-Sommer thinks that this means "insight into the mind of men and gift of 'speaking in tongues.' "[56] He makes a reference to Acts 2:1-15. I would not wholly concur with this interpretation, but certainly it is worth consideration. Perhaps it would be better to see this skill as the gift of interpretation of languages of even a natural (i.e., learned) knowledge of languages. However, a late midrashic collection (*Agadat Bereshit* 14) attributes to Isaiah, the greatest prophet, and Obadiah, the least of prophets, the knowledge of all spoken languages. Further, certain renowned individuals such as Joseph and Mordecai are said to have known seventy languages of all the languages of the world. This is obviously a gross exaggeration. However, one may ask whether there is a similarity with the duty of the Instructor at Qumran. Does it mean that the overseer

---

[56]Dupont-Sommer, *op. cit.*, p. 157.

is classed with the prophets and personages alluded to above and that he must have perfectly adequate knowledge of the languages spoken in the community?[57]

To sum up, one may say that the members of Qumran strove to purify themselves in order to receive the spirit of God and thereby to cultivate spiritual sight, hearing, and understanding; their tongue then spoke of the wisdom of God and the Torah and sung the praise of God; evil men blasphemed and were spiritually blind and deaf. Yet, although wise speech, prophecy, and interpreting the Torah are attributed to "divine inspiration," one may see a preparation for, but not the actual possession of, the gift of tongues. Yet this is not to deny the existence of esoteric or mystical traditions at Qumran or among the Essenes and Pharisees of the first century A.D.

The theme of spiritual blindness and deafness runs through the four Gospels and is also present in the Acts of the Apostles.[58] However, with the resurrection of Christ the eyes of the disciples and their followers were opened, so that they understood the Scriptures and the events of salvation history (cf. Luke 24:31). After the coming of the Holy Spirit they were re-created and entered a different spiritual dimension, so that they adopted a role similar to the Teacher of Righteousness, declaring the wonders of God and His praise and by bold teaching through the Holy Spirit bringing people into the Christian community. It is against this background that one may place the gift of tongues: it is one more spiritual "sense" which has been revived. Seen in this light, the gift of tongues might be the restoration or re-creation of the organ necessary for giving vocal praise to God and communicating divine inspiration to others (cf. the *utterance* of wisdom and *utterance* of knowledge in 1 Corinthians 12:8). A new language is given as proof of divine intervention. Pentecost recapitulates Genesis and Sir 17. Indeed, in the Johannine Pentecost, where Jesus breathes on His disciples

---

[57]There are numerous references to seventy languages, and the most convenient source of reference is Louis Ginzberg, *The Legends of the Jews*, tr. H. Szold (Philadephia 1964), Vol. 1, 62: Adam invented seventy languages; vol. 2, 68-69: Gabriel taught Joseph seventy languages so that he might be viceroy of Egypt; 214: Michael and the angels taught the sons of Noah seventy different languages; vol. 3, 360: Mordecai, "being a member of the great Sanhedrin, understood all the seventy languages spoken in the world" and the language of deaf-mutes.

[58]E.G., Mark 4:11ff.; the healing of the blind man in John 9 and Acts 28:25ff.

saying "Receive the Holy Spirit," the author uses the same word (*emphysan*) as Genesis 2:7 (*LXX*),[59] and John 3:1-15 may have the same creation narrative in view. The gift of tongues could be regarded as a concrete sign, by the giving of an unlearnt language, that thus the function of speech is recreated, a symbol of divine inspiration given again to man. F. C. Synge speaks of Luke's interest in speeches and the fact that "the sign of the spirit which he most frequently records in Acts is in some way connected with speech. Twenty-three times in Acts and five times in the Gospels [*sic*] he uses *pneuma hagion* in connection with speech."[60] The gift of new speech, then, may be regarded as one of the basic charismatic gifts. "Tongues" is the least gift but it will be "expanded" into others, such as poetry and music and prophecy.

In addition to the Scrolls, other nonbiblical traditions attribute not only speech but also poetry and music to the inspiration of the Holy Spirit. The Holy Spirit (*Ruah Hakodesh*) was "God's representative," "the Greek Logos,"[61] and the effects of the possession of the *Ruah Hakodesh* are that some recipients "become prophets, others sages, still other poets and musicians. . . . "[62] One reads in *Sukk.* 5, 4 that the water libation of the Feast of Tabernacles brought jubilation to the pious men and was the occasion of the outpouring of songs, dancing, and other manifestations of rejoicing[63] (cf. the songs which Luke places in the mouths of his "saints" and the number of times jubilation is associated with the Spirit, e.g., Matthew

---

[59]The only other texts which use this work are 1 Kings 17:21 (Elijah raises the dead child); two questionable texts in Tobit (7:8 and 11:11 A.B. *al*); Job 4:21; Wis 15:11: "because he failed to know the one who formed him and inspired him with an active soul and *breathed* into him a living spirit"; Sir 43:4: "but the sun burns the mountains three times as much; it *breathes* out fiery vapors"; Na 2:2, of the opponent breathing against Israel; Ezekiel 21:31: "I will *blow* upon you with the fire of my wrath": 22:20: "As men gather silver and bronze . . . into a furnace, to *blow* the fire upon it in order to melt it"; Ezekiel 37:9: "*breathe* upon these slain, that they may live." These references suggest a strong or vehement breathing which will result in "resurrection" or "destruction"; the association with fire is interesting.

[60]F. C. Synge, "The Holy Spirit in the Gospels and Acts" *Church Quarterly Review*, (July 1935): 205-17, at 209.

[61]Parzen, *art. cit.*, p. 57.

[62]*Ibid.*, p. 66.

[63]Cf. also *Jer Sukk.* 5, 55a: *Sukk.* 50-51, with reference to Isaiah 12:3—though the Holy Spirit is not explicitly mentioned.

11:15-30). Artistic work was also inspired by the Holy Spirit (cf. Exodus 31:3; 35:31).

The greatest gift of the Holy Spirit, however, was prophecy (cf. 1 Corinthians 14:1). Prophecy is not necessarily prediction but rather a speaking forth a word or message from God. Parzen states: "examination of the texts in which the *Ruah Hakodesh* is defined as prophecy, we believe, will show that by prophecy is understood the power to foretell events, the ability to foresee occurrences as well as the faculty to know what is in another person's mind."[64] According to some Jewish traditions every good and wise man has the gift of prophecy,[65] but according to the Talmud only the physically strong, mentally wise, and rich have the gift (*Shab.* 92a, *Ned.* 38a), which also depended upon the worthiness of the generation: if the generation were not worthy, the Holy Spirit could not come.[66] However, in the future all men and women will be under divine inspiration (cf. Joel 2:28; 3:1 f.; Isaiah 44:3; 59:19-21).

So the gift of speech inspired by God is the organ of much "spiritual cultural activity"; it is something which makes the spiritual man, as it were, a "well-rounded" person. The use of the gift of tongues realizes many of these activities, as we shall see below, but often when it is used one is able to experience the presence of God and occasionally to experience the use of other spiritual senses. Why should it be instrumental in this kind of thing?

The gift of tongues is essentially a gift of prayer, especially of praise and love. Usually the mind is not active but the prayer is one of simple, loving regard—often accompanied by the experience of God's presence.

---

[64]Cf. Parzen, *art. cit.*, pp. 51-56; he discusses the conditions for the experience of the *Ruah Hakodesh*. He summarizes this section of his article as follows: "The Ruah Hakodesh is experienced only by saintly, godly men in a holy, virtuous environment, preferably Palestine. The Biblical centuries supply the necessary favorable background because of Israel's perfection. With the decrease of Israel's perfection, the Ruah Hakodesh diminished its activity. The climax was reached at the end of the Biblical era, with the death of the last three prophets, when the Ruah Hakodesh completely ceased to function." We should, however, be obliged to modify significantly this last statement in view of the findings at Qumran. However, the condition of ritual purity makes one acutely aware of the difficulty experienced by St. Peter and others in realizing that the Holy Spirit could indeed fall upon uncircumcised Gentiles.

[65]See *Jewish Encyclopedia*, *s.v.* "Inspiration."

[66]*Sanh.* 11a; *Ber.* 57a; *Sukk.* 28a; *B.B.* 134a.

To see why the gift of tongues may be productive of "touches of infused contemplation"[67] and contribute to the building up of spiritual characteristics, one may measure the constructive power of love in the gift of tongues against the destructive, demolishing power of the tongue. The "uncircumcised" tongue or perverse tongue is the source of great danger not only to the individual but also to the community. This is well illustrated in James 3:1-12:

> Let not many of you become teachers, my brethren, for you know that we who teach shall be judged with greater strictness. For we all make many mistakes, and if anyone makes no mistakes in what he says he is a perfect man, able to bridle the whole body also. If we put bits into the mouths of horses that they may obey us, we guide their whole bodies. Look at the ships also; though they are so great and are driven by strong winds, they are guided by a very small rudder wherever the will of the pilot directs. So the tongue is a little member and boasts of great things. How great a forest is set ablaze by a small fire!

> And the tongue is a fire. The tongue is an unrighteous world among our members, staining the whole body, setting on fire the cycle of nature, and set on fire by hell. For every kind of beast and bird, of reptile and sea creature, can be tamed and has been tamed by humankind, but no human being can tame the tongue—a restless evil, full of deadly poison. With it we bless the Lord and Father, and with it we curse men, who are made in the likeness of God. From the same mouth come blessing and cursing. My brethren, this ought not to be so. Does a spring pour forth from the same opening fresh water and brackish? Can a fig tree, my brethren, yield olives, or a grapevine figs? No more can salt water yield fresh.

This fact is also referred to in the Gospel, where Jesus speaks of the heart as the source of "uncleanness" (Mark 7:21). If one reflects upon it, one sees that the tongue is the instrument of realizing many sins: falsehood, slander, uncharity, anger, flattery, pride, quarreling, unchastity, blasphemy and sacrilege, etc. It has a disruptive effect on the individual

---

[67]When God gives an experimental intellectual knowledge of His presence rather than our mere thinking of or recalling His presence, then we may say that there is a touch of infused contemplation or incipient contemplation. See Poulain, *op. cit.*, pp. 64-87; R. Garrigou-Lagrange, *The Three Ages of the Interior Life*, tr. M. Timothea Doyle, (London 1951): 279-349.

and on the community. As Proverbs 18:21 says, "death and life are in the power of the tongues," but contrariwise Proverbs 15:4 states that the "wholesome tongue is a tree of life" and Proverbs 12:18 that "the tongue of the wise is health." Proverbs 10:20 further declares that the tongue of the just is a choice silver. These are no mere metaphorical statements; for the tongue is the instrument of righteousness (Psalms 35:28) and for teaching wisdom (Psalms 37:30), expressing kindness (Proverbs 31:26), proclaiming justice, establishing peace and pardon—in short, for building up the community and indirectly building up the individual, since goodness expressed by the tongue is goodness expressive of the whole personality. One knows the demoralizing effect of the wrong use of the tongue, and contrariwise the moral impetus in the right use; how much more, then, a use divinely inspired?

This type of thought may be in St. Paul's mind when he says that "tongues" edify or build up the individual (1 Corinthians 14:4). Indeed, "tongues" are a very useful gift. They can be used when one feels inadequate to praise God in one's own language, can be used to restore joy, peace, and love of soul and to kindle one's desire to serve God and neighbor. They are also a useful weapon against sin, e.g., anger, and against the influence of "evil spirits," even those troubling other people, not the speaker. "Tongues" are often accompanied by the sudden realization of some spiritual truth, especially if the one who prays allows silence to intervene at intervals during the prayer; sometimes these thoughts are "interpretation." Further, they appear to be especially efficacious in intercessory prayer. The spiritual tongue, therefore, does "build up." However, the recipient has a responsibility to use this gift in these ways. Initially, exaltation is experienced in the use of the "tongues"; later it is not necessarily so. If one perseveres in faith, however, good does result and this is very helpful in aridity in prayer.[68]

Further, in the employment of "tongues" one often enters into the realm of poetry and music. Singing in "tongues," especially in chorus, is very beautiful and peace-provoking. Even those who are unable to sing in tune in the natural way or to compose poetry or music often can do so with the

---

[68]Incidentally, deaf-and-dumb people have received both the gift of tongues and interpretation. Naturally, the "interpretation" must be transmitted to the rest of the congregation in deaf-and-dumb language.

gift; interpretations are sometimes given in verse. Some Spirit-inspired songs have been written and printed.

St. Paul says clearly that one should pray for interpretation (1 Corinthians 14:13-19). This is important, because it would seem spiritually immature to continue to speak without understanding, and it may well be that the first exuberance of tongues is removed so that one conceives the desire for interpretation. Interpretation of one's private tongue can be instructive, e.g., in encouraging one to accept suffering or accomplish charity. Interpretation is close to prophecy. To receive interpretation privately is like receiving an exhortative prophecy.[69]

Thus we may say that for the individual the gift of tongues can be the gateway towards another spiritual dimension.

RELATIONSHIP TO THE COMMUNITY

The community aspect of the gift of tongues is seen in Acts and in 1 Corinthians. It is clear that Luke intended the account of the first Christian Pentecost in Acts to appear as the reversal of the Tower of Babel (Genesis 2). This "parable" relates that God created diversity of languages (according to the Targum, seventy in number) to divide mankind and prevent the world from becoming man-made instead of God-made. At Pentecost the gift of tongues is given to restore international unity. Davies has shown the verbal similarity between the LXX account and Pentecost.[70] He writes as follows:

> God said, "Go to, let us go down, and there confound (*sugcheōmen*) their language (*glōssan*), that they may not understand one another's speech (*phōnēn*)." Representatives of every nation under heaven, according to the account in Acts, were at Jerusalem when the disciples "began to speak with other tongues (*glōssais*) as the Spirit gave them utterance," whereupon "when this sound (*phōnēs*) was heard, the multitude came together, and were confounded (*synechythē*)." The parallel use of words in the two passages is obvious, but at the same time there is a contrast between the two. . . . This is the work of the Holy Spirit, who reverses the previous disrup-

---

[69]I have not heard a prophecy giving a specific prediction. If one did occur, the utmost prudence, prayer, and counsel should be used before acting on it.

[70]J. D. Davies, "Pentecost and Glossolalia," *Journal of Theological Studies*, n.s. 3 (1952): 228-31.

tion in the unity of creation "when the Most High parted the nations asunder (*diemerizen*) by Himself manifesting His coming to the Church under the form of tongues of fire 'parting asunder' (*diamerizomenai*)."[71] Men were scattered (*diespeiren*) from Babel and later the Christians were scattered (*diesparēsan*) from Jerusalem.[72]

Further, M.D. Goulder has demonstrated that the tribes in Genesis 10 are parallel to the list of peoples in Acts 2:8-11.[73] These two articles, as well as others, indicate that "tongues" symbolize international unity.

However, "tongues" also indicate "international revelation." This is suggested by the correspondence between the Lucan Pentecost and the traditions about the giving of the Law on Mount Sinai. There was a popular tradition that all nature stood still while the Law was proclaimed[74] and that the divine voice divided itself into the seventy languages of the world so that all might understand it. The pertinent references are found in Ginzberg.[75] He reports that in all these sources[76] " 'the seven voices' (i.e. sounds or tunes) which were heard on Sinai are referred to, whereas in *Berakot* 6b and *BHM* 5:33 mention is made of only five voices, and in *BHM* 6:41 . . .the number is still further reduced to four. The seven sounds of the trumpet at the resurrection referred to in *BHM* 6:58 are modeled after the seven sounds on Sinai. The seventy tongues stand for all the languages of the world. . . . "

---

[71]*Ibid.*, pp. 228-29.

[72]*Ibid.*, p. 229.

[73]M. D. Goulder, *Type and History in Acts* (London 1964): 152-58. Cf. p. 157: "the peoples of pentecost are a one-for-one translation of the grandsons of Noah. What we have done is to show that the world of Acts 2 is the world of Genesis 10, and that it is probable that St. Luke selected and ordered the names of the pentecostal peoples in the way that we have suggested."

[74]Ginzberg, *op. cit.* 3, 97.

[75]*Ibid.* 4, 39; *ShR* 5, 9 and 28:6; *Shabb.* 88b; *Tehillim* 68, 317 and 92: 403; *Tan B.* 2, 13-14; *Tan. Shemot* 25; *Midr. Shir* 2b; *BHM* 39 and 45; *Yelammedenu in Yalkut* 2, 709 and 843, on Psalms 91 and 92 respectively. I have been unable to check all these references. The idea does not seem to appear in the targums.

[76]The references from *Midrash Rabbah* and *Talmud* are probably the earliest; however, one must always allow for this tradition being post-Christian. Cf. also Goulder, *op. cit.*, p. 152.

Philo says that the Law was produced with flames and did not grow less distinct because of distance as a human voice would:

> But the new miraculous voice was set in action, and kept in flame by the power of God which breathed upon it and spread it abroad on every side and made it more illuminating in its ending than in its beginning by creating in the souls of each and all another kind of hearing far superior to the hearing of the ears. For that is but a sluggish sense, inactive until aroused by the impact of the air, but the hearing of the mind possessed by God makes the first advance and goes out to meet the spoken words with keenest rapidity.[77]

In *Spec. leg.* 2, 189 he refers again to the fact that the voice reached the extremities of the earth, and speaks about the general laws which came from the mouth of God, "not like the particular laws, through an interpreter. This is significance peculiar to the nation. What follows is *common to all mankind*" (italics mine).

Whatever the correct tradition is, the symbolism is evident; the idea which the Jewish teachers wished to convey was that the Law or revelation from Sinai was universal; however, only Israel accepted it, the other nations rejected it.[78] There is also a certain historical or linear continuity, for it was believed that every prophet and prophetess or wise man or woman derived their authority from Sinai:

> . . . AND GOD SPOKE ALL THESE WORDS. . . . The prophets received from Sinai the messages they were to prophesy to subsequent generations. . . . Not only did all the prophets receive their prophecy from Sinai, but also each of the Sages that arose in every generation received his [wisdom] from Sinai. . . . (*Exodus Rabbah* 28, 6; one may compare Joel 2:28-29 and Acts 2:16-21).

What is suggested both at Sinai and at Pentecost is not so much the overcoming of a communication barrier as a prophetic *ōth* (dynamic symbol) predicting or producing international unity. When speech is not understood, there is disunity; when speech is understood, communication and action are possible, and after this one Torah could be the essence of

---

[77]Philo, *De decal.* 33, 35; translation from Loeb edition of the text.

[78]Ginzberg, *op. cit.*, 3, 80-82 etc.

unity or, in the New Testament, the preaching of Christ and baptism was the foundation of unity (Galatians 3:23-29).

Moreover, we are not certain whether "tongues" were used for preaching; rather, we might incline towards those who confine "tongues" to the praises uttered by the apostles and which were a "sign" to "unbelievers" rather than a medium of communication. Yet this does not mean that "tongues" in Acts are in a different dimension from 1 Corinthians. The linking concept is *apistos*. I have argued elsewhere[79] that *apistos* does not necessarily mean "unbeliever," *pace* Sweet;[80] it refers to one who is weak in faith or who is nonkosher. The same meaning might be apposite to 1 Corinthians 14:22; to those who are lacking in full faith in Jesus, probably Jews or proselytes, tongues are a sign as they were in Acts and in Isaiah 28:11-12.[81] It is a sign that the fullness of the Jewish-Christian faith is for them (either Jews or those formerly nonkosher). It is not otherwise in the Cornelian Pentecost (Acts 10) or the Samaritan Pentecost (Acts 8).[82] There again tongues were a prophetic sign that the Holy Spirit finds no distinction between Jew, half-bred Jew, or Gentile. In these cases, however, the sign is efficacious to Peter and the apostles as well as to the recipients of the gift.[83]

I have used the term "prophetic sign" because I see no sharp distinction between tongues and prophecy. The biblical data and our existential experience teach us that prophecy is often given in tongues. The value or edification of "tongue-prophecy" lies in the interpretation given either by

---

[79]"Hast Thou Tithed Thy Meal" and "Is Thy Child Kosher?" *Journal of Theological Studies*, n.s. 17 (1966): 72-79.

[80]Sweet, *art. cit.*, p. 241.

[81]From contemporary "oral tradition" I have gleaned a story illustrative of 1 Corinthians 14: 24-25. A woman spoke in tongues to a pagan; she did not receive the interpretation herself, but the pagan knew the language and realized that she was speaking about certain sins or impediments which kept him from the Christian faith. On another occasion a member of the audience at a Pentecostal rally asked God to give him a sign that these experiences were genuine. Not long afterwards a woman spoke in a rather rare Italian-German dialect known to him and his father; this set the seal on his conviction.

[82]Tongues are not recorded here, but there must have been some external sign because of the reaction of Simon Magus.

[83]Acts 19:1-7 might fall into the same category. Here the sign may have been needed to fulfill the faith of those who did not yet believe beyond what John the Baptist taught.

the speaker or by a second party (one or more persons) or the simple fact that a hearer might know the language in a human way.[84]

However, there is a further aspect to the prophetic sign. When two people or more are involved in the sign, that is, a prophet and interpreter, this would seem to signify the interrelationship between the different parts of Christ's Body. In a prayer meeting or the liturgy there is an act of "community contemplation." The congregation is dependent on the dual action for the hearing of the message, for no one save Christ is sufficient for himself or herself.

> When everyone plays his or her part, one with spontaneous prayer, another with a reading, a tongue, prophecy, image, testimony, the Holy Spirit seems to work a kind of mosaic or tapestry until the whole picture or theme is built up for the edification and encouragement of the whole community . . . this interdependence makes one realize community in the deepest sense of the word, but it is also a safeguard. The community . . . has the duty to judge the authenticity of the parts played by several members, to keep charity and to see that there are no excesses.[85]

It is not without great significance that Paul's teaching about the Church as the Body of Christ occurs in this section of 1 Corinthians. So "tongues" continue their prophetic symbolism on the existential level.

I should, therefore, summarize this section by saying that in Acts and 1 Corinthians "tongues" are a prophetic sign with the dynamism to re-create faith, either (1) to bring the Jew to the realization of the fulfillment of Sinai, or (2) as a sign that the *apistos* is entitled to the plenitude of Jewish-Christianity; (3) as a sign to apostles etc. that the latter may be received into full membership of the Church; (4) as a general dynamic sign to build up the faith of the individual or the community; (5) as a sign of international unity, a sign that Babel wrought by God has been reversed by God.

---

[84]E.g., the Catholic Hail Mary has been recognized. A Catholic was "detected" praying it in Greek by two different hearers on separate occasions, and once a group of people heard a non-Catholic pray this prayer in Latin—the translation was unknown to himself.

[85]I have written simply but more at length on this point in *The Pentecost Experience* (New York, 1970).

We may add one further point on which I propose to enlarge in a second article.[86] In biblical times "tongues" were a sign of international unity and a sign of the extension of the Christian message to all peoples. Today it may be the same profound and dynamic prophetic symbol—a prophetic ōth of interdenominational unity. It may be a sign to Christian denominations that they have much to give to and receive from each other, but also much in common. It is not without significance that the charismatic renewal began shortly after Pope Leo XIII's Encyclical on the Holy Spirit, the non-Roman Catholic prayers for unity, and then Vatican Council II, which was preceded by the earnest prayer of the Church for a New Pentecost.

---

[86]I hope to follow this essay with another examining the Jewish and early Christian traditions about Pentecost and the application of this to the contemporary situation. Pertinent material from early Jewish material is also found in my *The Spirit and the Human Person* (Dayton, 1969).

16

ERNEST BEST

The Interpretation
of Tongues

[Reprinted from *Scottish Journal of Theology*, 28:1 (1975): 45-62. Reprinted with permission of Scottish Academic Press, Ltd.]

We do not possess a large amount of information about the worship of Christians in the early days of the church and most of what we do comes from First Corinthians. In it Paul answers various questions raised by the Corinthians, among them one about spiritual gifts. We ought probably to envisage a small group meeting in a house (cf. 1 Corinthians 16:19; there would have been a number of such 'house-churches' in Corinth). In these meetings the Christians present made various contributions to the worship according to their abilities, or, more correctly, their spiritual gifts, *charismata*.

The Corinthians ask for Paul's guidance in their exercise. Probably he himself had introduced the concept of spiritual endowment to the Corinthians when he first brought the gospel and remained some time to build them up in the faith, for he has no hesitation in accepting the idea and it is found again in his letter to the Roman church (12:5ff). In his answer to the Corinthians he attempts to clarify what these charismata are, to indicate their manifold nature and to show their relationship to one another. The Corinthians themselves have been concerned principally with the gift of speaking in tongues—glossolalia. In chapter 12 Paul begins by expounding the origin in God of these gifts (12:4-11) and points to their great variety (12:4-11, 28-30). They are to be exercised not only in the worship of the church but also in its administration and daily life ('helpers, administrators', 12:28), and those who exercise these charismata of whatever kind are to use them in such a way that the whole community is benefited (12:12-27). It is here that for the first time in his extant writings Paul introduces the concept of the church as the body of Christ. If the body is to be an organic and harmonious unity, then each gift is necessary and no gift has precedence over any other; so he emphasises that those gifts which appear to attract less attention should be honoured as much as those which everyone can see and admire. There is no gift which every Christian will possess by the simple fact that he is a Christian, nor can it be said that because a Christian does not exercise some particular gift, e.g. prophecy or tongues, that he is not therefore a Christian; nor is it to be expected that a true Christian will manifest them all.

At this point in 1 Corinthians we find the hymn to love; whether Paul wrote it at this time for this precise context, or wrote it earlier and takes it up now, or borrows it with or without adaptation from some earlier Christian does not matter to us. Love is not itself one of the charismata; it belongs to another, probably higher, category, though it resembles the charismata in being a gift of the Spirit. The hymn is used here to drive home the lesson that while different members of the community may have different gifts no gift can be exercised by a Christian without love, otherwise the church is injured and not aided. Unlike the charismata of which different ones are exercised by different believers, love is freely imparted to all (cf. Romans 5:5) and should be displayed by all in their conduct towards one another, and of course towards the world outside the community.

Paul then goes on in chapter 14 to deal more directly with the gift of tongues; this he does by comparing its place in worship with the gift of prophecy. The latter is often taken to be the equivalent of modern-day preaching. This is an inadequate understanding. It is better to relate it to revelation; the prophet discloses God's will for man now and in relation to the future; the element of prediction cannot be excluded, and the prophets of the NT regularly predict future events.[1] Because of its revelatory nature the value of prophecy in building up the community is not in dispute between Paul and the Corinthians. Paul's criterion in estimating the relative importance of tongues and prophecy thus becomes their ability to 'build up' the community. Tongues do not achieve this purpose. Since they are addressed to God and not man (14:2, 6, 9) and are in a language which man cannot understand without an interpreter (14:27), they cannot benefit him. This might seem a totally adverse judgment but Paul's view is not so simple. Tongues are addressed to God and therefore they may help the speaker himself (14:4); Paul acknowledges that he himself has the gift (14:18), though he thinks it much better to speak five words that people will understand than to pour forth a torrent of tongues. Again, Paul lays down regulations for the use of tongues in worship, as he does for prophecy, and so acknowledges their value (14:27-32). He also apparently refers to them when in chapter 13 he speaks of the tongues of angels; probably the Corinthians have used this phrase to describe glossolalia and Paul picks it up as he often picks up the terms of others; it is not then clear whether he regards it as a correct description; the point of his argument is to drive home the necessity of love. Paul's own position is probably summed up best in the concluding words of the chapter: 'So, my brethren, earnestly desire to prophesy, and do not forbid speaking in tongues; but all things should be done decently and in order' (14:39, 40).

We have not yet identified what this gift of tongues actually is. That it cannot be understood by fellow worshippers, that it is spoken apart from mental processes (v. 14), that an interpreter is necessary if others are to understand—all this suggests that it corresponds to what we today know as speaking in tongues, a phenomenon which has appeared in all denominations and not merely in the so-called Pentecostal. At times, however, the glossolalia of 1 Corinthians 14 has been taken to be the same as what appears to be intended in Acts 2 where the disciples are depicted as speaking in foreign languages. But if this is what it had been Paul would hardly then have criticized it since it would have been so useful in evangelism and certainly could not have been described as speech to God alone. (A great

---

[1] cf. Best, 'Prophets and Preachers', S.F.T. 12 (1959), 129ff.

part of the importance of the gift of Pentecost in Acts 2 was its usefulness in the proclamation of the Gospel.) It is proper to say here that in modern glossolalia there are two types, private and public; the latter since it occurs in worship requires interpretation; the former does not. The difficulty in understanding Paul may come partly from his failure to make this distinction clear.

To the listener the gift of tongues will have appeared strange; the speaker obviously uses sounds, the sounds appear to fall into some kind of grammatical structure, yet nothing can be understood. At times the speaker may appear to be in a trance, though this is by no means necessarily always true. To the speaker, and here the author depends for information at second-hand, there is something of importance in what he says, he believes he is talking sense, and through his experience he receives release of mind and soul and is filled with a deep sense of abiding joy.

So far so good, but what is to be said about all of this? The report of a special committee of the United Presbyterian Church in the U.S.A. to their General Assembly of 1970 provides a carefully balanced conclusion:

> We therefore conclude, on the basis of Scripture, that the practice of glossolalia should be neither despised nor forbidden; on the other hand it should not be emphasised nor made normative for the Christian experience. Generally the experience should be private, and those who have experienced a genuine renewal of their faith in this way should be on their guard against divisiveness within the congregation. At the same time those who have received no unusual experiences of the Holy Spirit should be alert to the possibility of a deeper understanding of the gospel and a fuller participation in the gifts of the Spirit—of which love is the greatest.

Attention needs to be given to the opening words: 'We therefore conclude, *on the basis of Scripture. . . .*' Underlying this is the assumption that whatever can be shown to have been a practice found in, and at any rate commended to some extent by Scripture, cannot be dismissed. It is well known that there are many Christians who look down on glossolalia, describe it as gibberish proceeding from unbalanced and uncultured minds and therefore consider it ought to be rejected by all intelligent Christians. Clearly they have a different attitude to Scripture. It may not be so well known but the Reformers, who can hardly be regarded as not paying sufficient respect to Scripture, also dismissed glossolalia.[2] This too is the verdict of many conservative scholars today.[3] They regard it as a genuine gift of the Spirit but one which was intended only for the founding period of the church, i.e. they do not deny its existence but regard it as so firmly placed in the first century that we cannot expect to see it reproduced today; indeed some of those who take this position regard the modern manifestations of glosso-lalia as induced by the devil.[4] These differing conclusions on the place of glossolalia really depend on different theories of how Scripture is to be in-terpreted, i.e. they employ different hermeneutical keys to unlock Scrip-ture.

The title of this paper was deliberately intended to be ambiguous. Paul mentions the interpretation of tongues and argues for its necessity where tongues are used in public worship, but there is another sense in which tongues have to be interpreted: How are we to interpret glossolalia for our-selves? The point can be brought home with an illustration: strict conser-vatives who deny glossolalia as relevant to us today probably also argue that women should wear hats in church and should not be ministers; ardent advocates of glossolalia rarely deny to women the right to use this spiritual gift and probably are quite happy to see them in church whether they have hats on or not. How do we know which prescriptions in Scripture are to form the basis of our conduct? In what way are they to do so? There are in fact two related questions here: one asks after the authority of Scripture, and the other after its interpretation in the modern situation.

We do not intend to attack these questions directly but to come at them in a roundabout way. Whenever Protestant interpretation of Scripture has been carried out seriously it has been governed by two principles; (1) Scripture is its own interpreter; (2) the meaning of Scripture is the literal meaning.[5] Catholic interpretation has tended traditionally to add a third principle which in practice came to control the other two: interpretation must follow the line which the magisterium says is true. Tradition was therefore

---

[2]See Calvin on Mark 16:17, which of course he took to be canonical. Calvin's state-ment is somewhat qualified. Later Reformers were more absolute in their expressions.

[3]Cf. M. F. Unger, *New Testament Teaching on Tongues* (Grand Rapids MI, 1972), 23f.

[4]Unger, op. cit., 1ff.

[5]E.g., cf. R. M. Grant, *The Interpreter of the Bible* (London, 1965), 102ff.

given a very high place. Despite their official rejection of such a principle Protestants have in fact allowed it to influence them, and so there has emerged in the course of exegetical history since the Reformation recognisable Lutheran, Reformed, Anglican, Baptist, Methodist traditions of interpretation. But we need not concern ourselves with these traditions but take up only the official principles of Protestant exegesis.

Quite clearly there has been a considerable change in the understanding of Scripture since the time of the Reformers, so if we work with these two principles we must allow for this change as we interpret. The development of the historical critical method from the nineteenth century onwards has made us see clearly what the Reformers only dimly glimpsed—the situational orientation of Scripture: all that is written in Scripture was directed to a precise historical situation and must be understood in the light of that historical context. This seems perfectly natural to all biblical scholars today though it is doubtful if its full consequences have yet been drawn for our understanding of the authority of Scripture and its interpretation. That it was not so obvious to the Reformers can be seen at once in the way in which in scholastic Protestantism Scripture came to be regarded as divine truth revealed in propositional form. Propositions have universal validity and therefore can be divorced not merely from their written context but also from their historical context—their situation—and applied to every situation. Hence, though wearing hats in church for women was originally anchored to a precise situation in Greece in the first century, it could easily become a proposition, and therefore applicable to every situation.

We take up first the principle of the plain meaning of Scripture. We can quickly dispose of certain false ideas. We must distinguish between poetic expression, parabolic expression and the plain meaning; such distinctions had already been drawn in the medieval period, worked out in response to the extremes of allegorical interpretation which had plagued exegesis from early days. Allegorical meaning was still accepted but only under certain restraints (e.g. it must be used only to confirm and not to establish doctrine). The literal meaning was always the primary meaning, and the literal meaning is the meaning intended by the author. If the author uses poetic imagery it is not to be taken literally because he did not intend it literally.

Now if we relate this literal meaning to the situational orientation of Scripture the procedure of interpretation is not so straightforward as it might appear. When Paul ordered women in Corinth to keep their heads covered what was his intention? The interpretation of the passage in 1 Corinthians 11 about women having their heads covered in church is very much disputed by scholars. Did Paul think only prostitutes went with uncovered head and was therefore zealous to preserve the good name of the church? Was Paul seeking to introduce the Jewish custom by which women were always veiled in public, and presumably he did this because he had been brought up to see this as God's way? Is it because in worship glory must be given only to God, and woman's hair, if it was seen, might distract man or the angels from this primary objective? Is it because the veil on her head represents her authority from God which allows her to take part in worship, and therefore again she wears it to fulfill God's will? When any of these interpretations is pushed we end by coming back to some primary intention: to do God's will, to further God's worship, to follow God's way. Within a concrete situation this primary intention is crystallised in a particular way—it is this crystallisation which is Scripture. What then was the intention of Paul? Surely it is the ultimate intention, an intention which can only be expressed in a very general way. What Scripture does is to provide examples of how this intention was worked out in a particular situation— and often to supply us with what, drawing on another context, may be termed 'middle axioms'. In Paul's description of worship the middle axiom would be the need for orderly worship. But worship can become over-orderly and lack spontaneity. This can never therefore be more than a middle axiom.

We have therefore now to ask about the Corinthian situation. Is it the same situation as ours? If so we can easily transfer Paul's instruction to our case. There are in a general kind of way situations which are the same then as they are now. If the situation is my position before God's justifying grace, then it is the same as a Christian in Corinth because we are both sinners— though our sins are very different in actual content. But there are few situations that are as general as that, especially when we ask the question: What ought we to do? A personal anecdote may illustrate this: I was crossing the sea of Galilee with some friends. One was eating toffees and throwing the papers overboard. I said to him, 'Would Jesus have done that?' He didn't really answer me but the reply could have been—'Jesus never had any toffee papers'! The world has changed so much in twenty centuries that to take as a method of guidance, 'What would Jesus have done?', 'What would Paul have said?', simply will not work. There are other difficulties as we shall see later.

If Scripture is situationally oriented nothing, absolutely nothing, can forbid us asking after its situation. But how far can we go? We may say that these Christians in Corinth were young converts, that the church was not yet a stable community, that it was mostly composed of the poor and uneducated, that many of its members were slaves. But we need to be careful here for we cannot move from statements of that type to statements such as: 'For such a kind of people the emotional release which glossolalia brought was valuable': and then write tongues off. It is impossible to go back to first-century Corinth and examine individually the converts, but we can see what psychologists and sociologists have to say about glosso-laliacs today, and, lacking any other information, assume that those in Corinth were psychologically similar. Some psychologists at any rate tell us that psychiatric tests do not show present-day glossolaliacs to be mentally unstable, but that in many cases they are the more mentally stable within congregations (though whether this was true of them before they became glossolaliacs or not cannot be determined, nor can it be shown that their stability comes from their being able to speak in tongues since there are present with tongues usually other gifts of the Spirit). The sociologists will tell us that glossolaliacs do not belong necessarily today only to the poorer classes: as a phenomenon glossolalia broke out first recently in the U.S.A. in Episcopalian and Presbyterian churches whose members have the highest 'wealth' rating. Nor do they belong to the uneducated; their main centres of activity in the U.S.A. are university campuses. Nor are they just young converts: many ministers of twenty and more years standing are glossolaliacs. Nor are they people lacking liturgical interest: the movement has spread widely in the Roman Catholic Church. Nor are they necessarily fundamentalists, though there is, it appears, a tendency among them to accept Scripture as true (that would not have applied to the Corinthians converts because they did not possess Scripture with the same fullness we do). If then the individual makeup of the believer is a part of the situation and we cannot interview individual believers of Paul's time and have to infer what they were like from people who do similar things today, then certainly we cannot attribute glossolalia only to those with weaker characters, and in that way dismiss it.

But the total situation is not that of the character of the individual. There is the general cultural pattern of the time. Here we can only speak in broad terms: the old religious ways were disappearing; new religions, the mystery cults, were coming in from the east; gnostic ideas were beginning to manifest themselves. Corinth was a great centre of trade where this ferment had probably proceeded further than in many places. Society as a whole was probably unstable in its religion. Where religion existed it tended to centre on ritual and on experience rather than on morality. Ritual has obviously no bearing on our problem but experience has. Various forms of ecstasy were known in ancient religion; people were believed to be possessed; sometimes something very like glossolalia appeared;[6] prophecy was known; spiritual healing took place. It was therefore probable that something like these should appear in any new religion. This is not to say that glossolalia only appeared among the first converts in Corinth because they saw it in the world around them; it may have begun spontaneously with them independently of its appearance elsewhere. But because of the cultural situation in Corinth there was a strong likelihood that religion would be manifested in forms which we would term ecstatic or possessed. (We should note that in many religions untouched by Christianity such forms still appear.[7]) Presumably Christians then would have ascribed these phenomena outside Christianity to the work of evil spirits and disposed of them in that way (cf. 1 Corinthians 12.3); it is more difficult for us to do so.

We turn now to the other principle of interpretation—Scripture is its own interpreter—that is to say that where we come on a difficult passage we look for easier passages within Scripture by which we may interpret it. No one doubts there are passages whose plain meaning is difficult to determine, and no one doubts that there are passages which are relatively easy to understand. While this is a principle which obviously applies to the interpretation of any author the Reformers saw it as having special reference to Scripture. To them Scripture was no ordinary book; its ultimate author was God. Therefore if a believer could not easily understand him at one place he might understand that place with the help of others where the same God was speaking. This clearly depends on a view of all Scripture as equally inspired by God. The principle, however, is not as straight-

---

[6]Cf. E. R. Dodds' essay, 'Supernormal Phenomena in Classical Antiquity', in his *The Ancient Concept of Progress and Other Essays* (Oxford, 1973), pp. 202f and the literature quoted there. See also *Theological Dictionary of the New Testament*, ed. G. Kittel trans. G. W. Bromiley. (Grand Rapids MI, 1964), vol. 1, pp. 722ff.

[7]Cf. I. M. Lewis, *Ecstatic Religion* (London, 1971).

forward as it appears to be. If we possess a writing in an unknown language, then we have to discover its meaning from an internal discussion of the writing itself. This is how codes are broken; in this way also Minoan Linear B was deciphered (if it was deciphered). But the New Testament is not in that position. It is written in a language in which many other books have been written. We can therefore find out the meaning of most of the words in it from literature outside it—and Calvin was a good secular Greek scholar. The discovery of the Greek papyri at the end of last century led to the elucidation of some passages previously regarded as obscure. Thus the circle is not and cannot be complete. This is not to say that words like *charis* do not take on a special meaning within certain parts of the NT, but that as an absolute rule the principle that Scripture is its own interpreter is not rigid. An additional qualification is necessary. One of the advances of the historical-critical method has been the realisation that each of the writers of Scripture is an author in his own right; the way in which he uses a word or a concept may not be the same as the way in which another NT writer uses it.[8]

These criticisms of the principle do not mean we discard it; clearly those who wrote the NT wrote out of an experience which had common elements—the experience of Jesus as Lord—though they will have expressed this experience in different ways because of the differing situations in which and to which they wrote. On the other hand, the fact that the Reformers drew on the general knowledge of Greek in the Renaissance period to interpret the NT must itself be widened into the area of experience; in order to understand an experience or an idea in the NT we may have to look to see if light can be thrown on it by similar or parallel experiences or ideas in the ancient world, recognising also that just as *charis* has a special NT meaning so there may also be special NT experiences and ideas. This would then bring us back to looking at experiences of ecstasy and possession in relation to healing, prophecy and tongues. We have already seen that these existed and we need not go back on this now.

If we applied the principle in its original sense we would probably move directly from the tongues of Corinth to the tongues of Pentecost. Do either

---

[8]One of the faults of a certain type of biblical scholarship is its failure to recognise this and therefore its easy paralleling of texts from different NT writings. This is another aspect of the situational view of Scripture; a writer's language is a part of his situation.

throw light on each other? At the time of the Reformation Acts 2 was used to interpret 1 Corinthians 14—i.e. tongues was regarded as speaking in another existing language which could be understood by people. Because it was given this character it was regarded as appropriate only to the first days of the church. But few scholars today regard the underlying experience in Acts 2 as foreign language speaking, though they do not dispute that Luke understood it in that way. Today it is Acts 2 which is the difficult passage and 1 Corinthians 14 is used to explain it. 1 Peter 4.10 throws little light; 1 Thessalonians 5.19-21 implies the existence of charismata, in particular of prophecy, but does not allow us to draw any conclusion about tongues. But in Romans 12.5ff Paul again refers to charismata and relates them to the image of the church. The list of charismata is different, but the fact that Paul writes to a church he had not visited about these charismata suggests that this subject appeared normally in his teaching and in that of other early Christian missionaries. Though prophecy is present in Romans 12 tongues is missing. Thus writing to Rome where Paul knows less about the situation he does not mention the gift of tongues, and this accords with the relatively unimportant position he gives it in Corinth. He refers to them in Corinth because he knew that they had appeared in that city and is prepared to list them among the charismata, though he may not have taught about them on his original mission (probably they manifested themselves while he was present and he himself shared in the gift, hence his allusion in 1 Corinthians 14.18 to speaking in tongues himself more than the Corinthians do). Acts 2 does, however, allow us to infer that tongues were known in areas other than Corinth, probably at least in Jerusalem. We may fairly conclude that for Paul charismata were a necessary part of Christian experience, though an individual or a whole community could well exist without any particular charisma.

Our principles have brought us some distance on our way, but not all we need to go. We require to return now more directly to the situationally oriented nature of Scripture. Our situation is not the same as that of the Corinthians. It is unnecessary to drive this home. Anyone who has worked with biblical material knows that there are presuppositions in Scripture about the world of its time which no one would hold today; man himself is regarded in a different way. Apart from all that there is a formal difference; we know of their situation but they knew nothing of ours. What is written in the Bible about the Corinthians, or any other group, is itself a factor in our situation, and the more authority we give to it, the more powerful a factor is it in our situation. The existence of tongues in the early church is part of our situation.

Now we need to look at the remainder of our situation. We have already seen that the kind of people who speak in tongues in our situation are not exceptional in any way; we cannot conjecture any actual difference in their psychological makeup. We looked at the social situation then; what then about or own?

There is a certain superficial similarity in that now as then there is a rapidly changing religious situation in which traditional patterns are disappearing and in which strange sects, magic, astrology and witchcraft are beginning to flourish. We shall not dwell on this though it resembles the first century since situations are never really the same, but instead point out what appears to be one relevant factor in our total cultural situation. If we read Milton, we can follow his imagery because it is almost entirely drawn from the Bible or from classical Greece and Rome. A knowledge of this common cultural fount of imagery can no longer be depended on in readers nor is it used by writers. For their imagery the poets and artists of today more often draw from within themselves than from what in the normally accepted sense is common to all men. In a paper this can be more easily illustrated from literature than from art; it is also more relevant since in tongues we deal with words. We begin with a short quotation from Joyce's *Ulysses*:

> What other infantile memories had he of her?
> 15 June 1889. A querulous newborn female infant crying to cause and lessen congestion. A child renamed Padney Socks she shook with shocks her moneybox: counted his three free moneypenny buttons one, tloo, tlee: a doll, a boy, a sailor she cast away: blond, born of two dark, she had blond ancestry, remote, a violation, Herr Hauptmann Hainau, Austrian army, proximate, a hallucination, lieutenant Mulvey, British navy.[9]

The connexions by which we move from one phrase to another are not those of normal rational speech which anyone can understand but depend on the inner consciousness of the character (Bloom is meditating on Millicent's

---

[9]Penguin edition, pp. 613f.

mind). They are those of a stream of consciousness which is peculiar to one person.

It is necessary to introduce two technical terms. A *dialect* is a language in which people can communicate with one another; an *idiolect* is a language which is peculiar to one person, a language which in some cases he may deliberately invent.

> 'Twas brillig, and the slithy toves
> did gyre and gimble in the wabe:
> All mimsy were the borogoves,
> and the mome raths outgrabe.

Everyone knows that this comes from *Alice Through the Looking Glass*. It sounds pleasant but it really has no meaning. It is an idiolect. The same kind of thing is found in Tolkien's *Lord of the Rings*. Two lines are sufficient to demonstrate it:

> Annon edhellen, edro hi ammen!
> Fennas nogothrim, lasto beth lammen!
> (Part I, The Fellowship of the Ring, Bk 2, Ch. 4)
> (cf. the long elvish song in Part I, Bk 2, Ch. 8)

It would not be right to suggest that this is the same as glossolalia, but the books mentioned are all widely read and widely admired, the last two especially among young people. There are many other ways in which idiolects appear: the nonsense talk and rhymes of children; the meaningless syllables uttered by people who have lost their temper and who do not have a sufficient reserve of profanity to express themselves; the nonsensical words of refrains to many songs (and the lyrics of pop music).[10] The implication is that we should not be surprised to find idiolects appearing in religious contexts. Young people are used to them—and if we enjoy *Alice* let us not be too hard on glossolaliacs![11]

---

[10]See W. J. Samarin, *Tongues of Men and of Angels* (New York, 1972).

[11]Since the first draft of this paper was compiled the writer has met a well-known NT scholar who has taught himself the technique of speaking in tongues. He can speak in several 'languages'; he regards this as a purely natural phenomenon and can exercise the technique at will.

This means that we live in a situation today in which idiolects are likely to appear; this is a way in which people have begun to express themselves. And since this type of literature and art finds as ready an acceptance, if not a readier, among college and university students than anywhere else we should not be surprised to find glossolalia among the well-educated. When you add to this the hermeneutical principle accepted by most ordinary Christians that because it happened then it ought to happen now we can see that the ground for the appearance of glossolalia stands ready fertilised.

If it is not surprising that tongues should appear in our present culture and their exercise be found beneficial by many Christians, there is still the all-important question: Are they in our situation a good thing? Many people object to modern art and find it incomprehensible; some people are turned on by some modern art and left cold by large parts of it. Again it is not surprising that some Christians should find in tongues a way of expressing themselves in prayer and worship which brings them joy and release. That still does not answer the question as to its value, for drugs can bring release and joy to some people. There is, however, a more fundamental question than the one we have asked: Are tongues really a manifestation of the Spirit?

Here we must go back to almost the beginning of what has been said about exegesis. If the literal meaning of Scripture is the meaning intended by the author, it was presumably Paul's intention when he was writing about charismata to say that in the activities of Christians when they administered charity, when they governed the church, when they taught, prophesied, healed or spoke in tongues, they were not doing this wholly of themselves but that the Spirit was at work in them. Since he gives lists of charismata and these lists vary between Romans and 1 Corinthians we should not take either of them individually or both together as stating all the charismata that might exist, or as defining all those that ought to exist in every situation. (Some Neo-Pentecostalists refer to the 'nine' gifts of 1 Corinthians 12:8-10; others do not make this restriction.) What Paul is doing is to list charismata appropriate to certain situations. Should we expect to see the same charismata today? If we look at his lists we see they relate to the internal life of the community except insofar as teaching, prophesying, healing may be regarded as also missionary activities directed outwards from the community. Today because of our situation we expect the church to be engaged in activities in the world which are less directly related to evangelism and we expect individual members of the church to take their place in the general activities of mankind, in politics, in industry, in the media, in the arts. Ought we not then to expect that there should be charismata in respect of these activities—the charisma of the trade unionist, the charisma of the politician, the charisma of the journalist? It is true that some of those who are leaders in these fields are said to have a 'charisma'—but that is not what Paul would have meant by the word.

An example will perhaps help. In certain cities in Ireland, both Protestant and Catholic, the neo-Pentecostalist movement has made considerable progress. Those who have been affected have been largely politically neutral, i.e. they have not adhered to violent policies; in their pulpits, if ministers, they have spoken of law and order; they have ministered to those who have suffered whether belonging to their side or not; they have prayed with one another across sectarian boundaries; yet they have not been active to seek a political solution. It would be wrong to say that their glossolaliac activities have been an escape from the real and terrible political problems which face Ireland and to the solution of which the church for years has failed to give adequate and clear guidance, but if Paul were to list the charismata necessary for the Church in Ireland today it is probable that right at the top of the list would come a political charisma. We cannot deny that there are some with this gift of God, but they are few and far between, and it is necessary also to say that there are those in the neo-Pentecostalist movement who would allow that such gifts should be desired by some Pentecostalists. It is in the light of this need for wider charismatic gifts and of the individual joy and heightened sense of God of glossolaliacs in Scotland that we must judge the usefulness of this particular gift here. No final judgment will be made in this paper.

At this point we can see that wider issues are involved, and the decision anyone makes on these will determine his decision on the present relevance of tongues to God's work. The first of these issues relates to the nature of charismata. Is a charisma a gift of the Spirit to a Christian which enables him to do something new which he could not do at all before? Or is it an inborn ability which is heightened because the man has become a Christian? The preacher will suffice as an example. It does not seem likely that on becoming a Christian his ability to put words together so as to prove persuasive should suddenly appear, but he would receive an insight into the gospel which he clearly did not previously possess and this coupled with his inborn persuasive ability, or ability gained through training in the use of words, would enable him to preach so that men would be converted and nurtured in the gospel. In the case of the charisma of administration the recipient does not suddenly attain an ability to administer but he attains a new way of doing it—in love. But it may not quite have appeared like that in Paul's day. Remembering the nature of those who became Christians, we can see that their recently gained ability to preach and administer seemed entirely new because they had never previously been in situations where their ability to speak or administer had been able to develop. In the Christian church they were now doing these things and this must have seemed a miracle. The gift of tongues also would not have been exercised by any of them in their pre-Christian days, and its sudden appearance would have seemed miraculous. Yet if we attribute some of the 'miracle' of the preacher and administrator to the Spirit must we not do the same for the glossolaliac? We can see what we attribute to the Spirit in the case of the administrator and preacher, but what in the case of the glossolaliac, especially if idiolects are not miraculous but natural? Tongues do not appear to be continuous with any previous ability.

A second wider issue must also be faced. Where does the Spirit operate? Only within the church (and this is the general answer of Scripture), or does the Spirit operate also outside the Christian community? Those who hold that the true sphere for the activity of the Spirit is the church will not exclude the prevenient activity of the Spirit in turning the hearts of sinners to God, but this is not what is at stake here. The question at issue is seen rather when we ask: Has the Spirit a share in the creative work of the artist? The church has never faced up to this question and those related to it; different Christians will offer varying answers.

But now we need to return to glossolalia. A number of options are open in the light of the views we take on the nature of charismata and the sphere of operation of the Spirit. We may decide that glossolalia is a natural phenomenon and not a charisma; it certainly brings joy and release from tension to some Christians, but to others the same will come through weeding the garden. We may decide that glossolalia is an activity of the Spirit whether it is found inside or outside the Christian community and so should be encouraged in both spheres. We may decide that glossolalia is a natural phenomenon outside the church but within the church there is an activity of the Spirit heightening the natural phenomenon. We may decide that it is a charisma within the church but where we find it outside then it is due to demonic influences. We may decide that Christian love is supernatural but glossolalia is natural. There are only a few of the options. It is important to realise that when we make our decisions we are bringing into play our theories, probably unconsciously held, on the nature of charisma and of the area of activity of the Spirit—in the end we bring into play our whole theology of the Spirit.

But this is not all that comes into play. Our reading of the sociological situation today will affect our view of tongues. Even more fundamentally there will be some who would argue that the sociological situation today has nothing to do with the matter and that in fact it is wrong to explore it.

If the argument of this paper has been followed up to now the reader will have realised that no answer to the question of the value of tongues is going to be provided. The purpose of the paper has not been to provide this but to do two other things; (i) to show the factors, often unconscious, which come into play when we try to make a decision about tongues; (ii) in a more general way to try and see how we unlock the Scriptures so that they speak to us today. How do we get from what Paul says about tongues to what the church should be saying today? Briefly what we have done is to look at a passage in Scripture and see how it is set in a particular situation; we have then tried to see what this has to do with us. Because of the situational nature of Scripture we have rejected a simple transference of what happened then to what ought to happen now. We have been forced to build up a picture of our situation. But our situation is not just a certain cultural situation; it is also a situation in which we already hold certain views about Scripture and its authority and about the Spirit and his activity in relation to the church and the world. When we attempt to move from Scripture to today we are inextricably involved in our own interpretation; there is no neutral way of making this movement. Even if we use a key to unlock Scripture that what is advocated in it should always govern Christian thought and conduct, this itself involves the holding of a total theological position, and one which is not itself derived from Scripture but brought in from outside.

There is one further and very necessary qualification. To speak of each one making his own decision in the light of the total view he holds omits all reference to the church. Part of the frame of reference in which the individual Christian makes decisions about his own conduct and evaluates the conduct of others is the structure of the whole Christian community of which he is a member. To deny this would be to deny that Christian experience is corporate experience. The scholar may work at what Paul says, what the ancient world was like and what the world of today is like, yet the resolution of the problem cannot be left to him alone. The Reformation rejected rule by priests; rule by scholars would be a thousand times worse. What the scholar can do is to make us aware of the hidden presuppositions of our own cultural and ecclesiastical situation which come into play when we try to make up our minds, and of the more individual views that we have on theological, philosophical, aesthetic, political . . . . matters and of which we are probably never aware (they may not even be consistent) but which determine the way in which our minds and wills work. This negative function is important and it is this which this paper has attempted to carry out.

17

RICHARD A. BAER, JR.

Quaker Silence, Catholic Liturgy, and Pentecostal Glossolalia: Some Functional Similarities

[Reprinted from *Perspectives on the New Pentecostalism*, edited by Russell Spittler. Copyright 1976 by Baker Book House and used by permission.]

Among non-Pentecostals, much of the recent discussion of glossolalia or speaking in tongues focuses on the strangeness of the phenomenon. Many leaders in mainline denominations see the current charismatic movement as a clear threat to the peace of the Christian community and the integrity of the church's witness. Scholarly papers raise the question, Are tongues basically a pathological religious practice? In not a few churches pastors have been dismissed when it was learned that glossolalia had become part of their personal religious experience.

Whereas even ten years ago it was possible for most Christian leaders to dispose of glossolalia with a few condescending remarks about "religious fanatics'' and ''lower class fringe sects,'' the explosion of the charismatic movement in the past few years among Catholics and mainline Protestants rules this out today. In a paper entitled ''Personal and Situational Determinants of Glossolalia'' presented at the September 1973 Los Angeles conference on *Religion and the Humanizing of Man*, H. Newton Malony of Fuller Theological Seminary argued that what little evidence there is regarding personality characteristics of glossolalics not only tends to rule out psychopathology but may even suggest that as a group ''glossolalics [are] better adjusted than members of a conventional denomination.''[1]

I would argue that the ''strangeness'' of glossolalia to most people, not least of all ministers and seminary professors, has blinded them to a fundamental functional similarity between speaking in tongues and two other widespread and generally accepted religious practices, namely Quaker silent worship and the liturgical worship of the Catholic and Episcopal churches. My thesis is that each of these three practices permits the analytical mind—the focused, objectifying dimension of man's intellect—to rest, thus freeing other dimensions of the person, what we might loosely refer to as man's spirit, for a deeper openness to divine reality. In their own distinctive ways I believe that tongues, Quaker silence, and the liturgy of the church all contribute powerfully to this goal.

Significantly, this goal is not achieved by a deliberate concentration on the emotions as over against the analytical mind. Neither the silent worship of the Quakers, the practice of glossolalia, nor the liturgical worship of the Catholic or Episcopal church seeks to stimulate the emotions as such in the manner of some revival meetings or some of the more contrived celebrations in certain avant-garde Protestant and Catholic congregations. Rather, in each of the three traditions I have mentioned, the desire is to free man in the depth of his spirit to respond to the immediate reality of the living God. The intent is not to play on the emotions either as an end in itself or as a means to some other desired end—for example, deeper commitment to the beliefs and practices of the church.

---

[1]H. Newton Malony, Nelson Zwaanstra, and James W. Ramsey, ''Personal and Situational Determinants of Glossolalia: A Literature Review and a Report of Ongoing Research,'' (paper presented at the International Congress of Learned Societies in the Field of Religion, Los Angeles, September 1-5, 1972). p. 1.

SPEAKING IN TONGUES

My thesis will become clearer as we examine in some detail these three practices which on the surface appear so very much dissimilar. Contrary to uninformed speculation and opinion, speaking in tongues is not a form of religious hysteria or spirit possession. Nor is it, except occasionally and quite incidentally, uncontrolled expression of emotion. Not only is the glossolalic fully aware of what he is doing when he begins to speak in a tongue but he also can stop at will. Although the glossolalic may be moved by deep emotion—as indeed he often is in non-glossolalic experiences of prayer and worship—the act of speaking in tongues itself is not best characterized as emotional in contrast to intellectual. The actual speech can be only a quiet whisper or even subvocal; or, on the other hand, it can be loud and boisterous. At times the glossolalic feels a singular *lack* of emotion while speaking in tongues.

For the most part, the glossolalic makes use of tongues for praising God. But three other uses are also common: (1) the expression of deep anguish or inner sorrow, (2) intercession, and (3) petition. In each instance there may be something deep inside the individual which he simply is unable to express in words. For some people, and occasionally for almost everyone, silence seems appropriate at such moments. But others find that unpremeditated glossolalic speech best permits them to express their joy or sorrow. The use of tongues in such a case is similar to the fulfillment a person may find in spontaneous dancing; and, of course, the use of the dance for the expression of religious ecstasy is a well-known and virtually universal phenomenon.

In petition and intercession one may not really know *what* to pray for. Even though there may be a deep sense of need or an acute awareness of distress, the one praying may possess little intellectual understanding of what is wrong, of what needs changing, or of what "solution" or healing would be appropriate. In such cases praying in a tongue may well be the most satisfying religious response available. Recall Paul's words in Romans 8:26 about the Spirit helping us in our weakness as He "intercedes for us with sighs too deep for words." Glossolalic prayer is felt by many to be of particular value in relation to the healing of early childhood traumas which have become submerged in the depths of the unconscious. Frequently an individual will know that something from his early childhood is sabotaging his behavior in the present but he will neither know what the trauma was nor how to pray for deliverance. In such cases praying in a tongue for the "healing of the memories" may be thoroughly appropriate.

It should be noted that I am describing glossolalia mainly as it occurs in the context of a person's private devotions. Much of what I have written is also relevant to the employment of glossolalia in the gathered worship of the church, but I should prefer not to discuss this controversial topic in this paper. Suffice it to say that such a public manifestation of tongues as group singing "in the Spirit" can be an exquisitely beautiful and joyful experience for the participants and even for observers.

QUAKER SILENT WORSHIP

Striking parallels exist between Quaker silent worship and the practice of glossolalia. At its best Quaker silent worship involves a kind of letting go, a lack of strain or effortful attention, a willingness to "flow" with the leading of the Spirit and with the larger movement of the entire meeting. In the course of the worship an individual may be led to speak to the gathering, but he retains the freedom either to yield to this urge or to fight it. In either case, however, it would seem quite inappropriate to describe this experience as hysterical or label it a form of spirit-possession in the classical mystical sense. The individual is quite aware of what he is about and retains definite control over his speech.

However, it is not a strained or forced control but rather more like that of the skillful dancer or lover. What is said will, to be sure, have intellectual content—but intellectual content is not the main element. One does not plan ahead of time what he will say, just as one does not invent a tongue in which to speak. There is rather a sharing out of the depths of one's self, or differently described, a speaking that is prompted by the leading of the Spirit. It is almost universally felt in Quaker circles that rational analysis and argument over what is spoken "out of the silence" is inappropriate. One is not to analyze or judge but rather to listen and obey.

As in the case of glossolalia, the process of speaking out of the silence and of listening in the silence involves a resting of the analytical mind, a refusal to let deliberative, objective thinking dominate the meeting. Rather, one tries to "center down" and become open to the "inner light" within himself, to "that of God in every man," to the "leading of the spirit."

Silence is common among Quakers both in private devotions and in public worship. Although what one speaks out of the silence in the meeting needs no interpretation as such, others, as led by the spirit, may add to what has been said, often in a manner not dissimilar to the Mishnaic commentary of the rabbis on the Torah. I find a rough parallel here to what is common practice among Pentecostals. The use of tongues in one's private devotions needs no interpretation. But in the public worship one should not speak in a tongue unless someone who can interpret is present (1 Corinthians 14:28). Significantly, the interpretation usually appears to be less a word-for-word translation of what has been said than a kind of paraphrase of the tongue with particular emphasis on reproducing its spiritual tone and general direction.

The phenomenon of quaking or shaking is still found among some Friends and would seem to be religiously and psychologically similar to glossolalia. A significant difference, however, is that one seems to have less control over the quaking than one does over speaking in a tongue and cannot necessarily terminate the practice at will. Actually, quaking is extremely rare today among Friends, but there are other stylized physical manifestations which typically accompany speaking out of the silence. For example, one often speaks with a slightly lowered head and with little or no direct eye contact with fellow worshipers. Frequently the tone of voice has a decidedly subdued quality, probably reflecting what is the deep inner conviction among Friends that one does not try to persuade or convince others of the truth of what is said by human emotion, logic, or eloquence. Rather one speaks ''out of the depth of silence'' by the leading of the inner light, the divine Spirit. It is only this divine Spirit that can bring true conviction and response on the part to the hearer. In other words, the communication or revelation is immediately self-authenticating. It is a word spoken not primarily in order to change the ideas of the hearer or rouse his emotions but rather to confront him in the inner depths of his spirit.

It is noteworthy by comparison that in public Pentecostal-type worship what is spoken in a tongue, although usually more animated than the word spoken by Quakers out of the silence, nonetheless possess something of the same quality. The speaker does not attempt to convince, persuade, or rouse people to action, perhaps in part because he is not himself rationally aware of the content of his speech. Also there is frequently a marked degree of inwardness on the part of the speaker, often reflected in the avoid-

ance of direct eye contact (or closed eyes) and a tone of voice different from
what he would employ in ordinary affairs.

THE LITURGY

Similarities between glossolalia and the liturgical worship of the church
are less obvious than those we have noted in relation to Quaker silent worship. But they are also significant. I shall refer mainly to the liturgical worship of the Episcopal Church, since this is the tradition I know best. Just
as glossolalia and silent Quaker worship may at first be puzzling, frustrating, even irritating to the non-initiate, so to many outsiders the practice
of liturgical worship sometimes appears to be little more than a mechanical
exercise in futility. What good can possibly come of the repetition week
after week of the same prayer of confession, word of absolution, interces-
sions, and petitions? And how can one even focus on what is being said
when most of his attention is directed to turning pages and deciding whether
to stand or kneel? Even though he remembers the advice "when in doubt
kneel!" the noninitiate is so preoccupied with physical motions and the
proper sequence and enunciation of prayers and other responses that it is
almost beside the point to talk of the resting of the analytical mind and an
encounter with God in the depths of the human spirit.

But all of this is not really surprising and is not unlike the experience
of the person first learning to dance. At that point even walking seems far
more graceful than those awkward, contrived motions. But when one has
mastered the dance steps, a kind of "wisdom of the body" takes over which
indeed permits the analytical mind, the focused attention, to rest. One begins to "flow" with the beat of the music, the rhythm of the dance.

So with the liturgy. The very repetition Sunday after Sunday of the same
prayers, responses, and creeds frees the individual from needing to focus
consciously on what is being said. To be sure, his mind and heart are frequently stimulated by the theological content and the aesthetic movement
of the liturgy. Also the total aesthetic impact of the environment—stained
glass, wood carvings, Christian symbols, singing, organ music, incense,
candles—helps produce a sense of awe and mystery.[2]

---

[2]It is at this point that Quakers remain understandably cautious and choose for themselves utterly simple surroundings for worship. Their fear is that one can be so captivated

But as beautiful and moving as all of these elements are, there is yet a deeper movement of the human spirit as it encounters the spirit of God, the presence of the risen Christ, the reality of the Holy Spirit. The analytical, objectifying mind is permitted to rest and thus the spirit of man is free to experience reality on a new level. Moreover, although feelings are often heightened by liturgical worship, there is no conscious attempt to manipulate the emotions to achieve some desired effect. It is on the level of spirit that liturgical worship becomes most significant.[3]

Furthermore, the very formality of the liturgy and the fixed nature of the responses may save the worshiper from undue introspection and thus help him to center more fully on the presence of God. Nor does he need to fear revealing more of himself than is appropriate in public. Romano Guardini writes that "the liturgy has perfected a masterly instrument which has made it possible for us to express our inner life in all of its fullness and depth without divulging our secrets. . . . We can pour out our hearts and still feel that nothing has been dragged to light that should remain hidden."[4]

As has been frequently noted, a high level of sound, insofar as it insulates a person from ordinary auditory stimuli, has an effect in some ways similar to a complete absence of sound. There is a rough analogy here to the interrelationship between Quaker silence and liturgical worship. Also the fact that one knows the prayers and responses by heart (not, *by head!*) frees one to be open to ever-new and ever-changing leadings of the Spirit

---

by external form and beauty that worship will remain on the level of the aesthetic. This has been perhaps a necessary corrective within the total life of the church and reflects an austerity not unlike the Old Testament prohibition against making graven images. At its worst, however, Quaker worship sometimes reflects a Gnostic-like repudiation of the rich beauty and vitality of creation and man's somatic existence.

[3]Although I have been greatly helped by Romano Guardini, *The Spirit of the Liturgy* (London and New York: Sheed and Ward, 1935), I cannot fully agree with him that thought is dominant over feeling in the liturgy. To be sure, as he argues, emotion in the liturgy is generally "controlled and subdued" (p. 129), but I have difficulty with his statement: "The heart speaks powerfully, but thought at once takes the lead" (p. 129). The more accurate contrast, I believe, is that between thought and feeling, on the one hand, and man's spirit (the dimension of depth or self-transcendence) on the other. Thus neither feelings nor the analytical mind is the dominant or controlling factor but rather the reality of the Spirit of God addressing man's spirit.

[4]Guardini, *The Spirit of the Liturgy*, p. 131.

during the very act of repeating fixed prayers and predetermined responses.[5]

This same dynamic probably explains much of the value of Father Zossima's famous Jesus-prayer in *The Brothers Karamazov* and of the repetition of the Catholic Rosary. In some evangelical Protestant circles the repetition of a single-stanza chorus five or six times in a row would seem to have a similar effect. Even highly intellectual people frequently discover as much (or more) fulfillment in the singing of such choruses as they do in some of the great theological-doctrinal hymns of the church. Compilers of hymnals would do well to note this fact, for often they have reflected a kind of Calvinistic, ascetic, theological snobbishness in making up their collections.

The argument can still be heard that the mass would be more effective in its religious impact if it were left in Latin. Authentic religious sensitivity, it is said, is reflected in the considerable resistance which many people—both young and old and from almost all social, national, and intellectual backgrounds—have shown to changing the mass into the vernacular. One could also point to the distress many Episcopalians today feel about "updating" the language of the liturgy.

It is too easy to dismiss these reactions with such labels as "conservative" or "reactionary." Perhaps the fact that one does not understand much of the Latin of the mass makes it easier for him to be open to God on the level of spirit, just as in the case of glossolalia and Quaker silent worship. In the latter the silence is experienced—or, more accurately, facilitates the experience of God—but is not as such "understood."

My own position is that to leave the mass in Latin rules out for most people an important element of ethical and theological content. In Pentecostal churches this dimension is achieved through the interpretation of the glossolalic speech, and in Quaker silent worship what is spoken out of the

---

[5]But, on the other hand, the fixed quality of the liturgy can be used by the individual to insulate himself from real change. In this case the regularity of the liturgy imprisons rather than frees the person. But it could be argued that roughly the same insulating effect can take place in Quaker silent worship and in glossolalic worship. Rather than using the silence to center down into a creative openness to the leading of the spirit, the Quaker worshiper may simply become drowsy or retreat into a kind of numb withdrawal from reality. Likewise, glossolalic speech may be employed in a given situation to escape from a more reflective understanding of God's will or a specific decision of the will to be obedient to God's leading.

silence has ethical and theological content, even thought it is not presented in a critical or analytical fashion.

PLAYFULNESS IN WORSHIP

So much for my basic thesis. It is an analysis which suggests or illuminates several subsidiary issues, to which I now turn in the second part of this paper.

People frequently ask me: But what is the value of speaking in tongues? I have already addressed myself to this question above, but here I am tempted simply to add: "Because it is a lot of fun." More and more I am impressed with the element of playfulness in glossolalia, the sheer child-like delight in praising God in this manner. It is a contagious delight, and in many charismatic prayer groups people will infrequently break out in a childlike, spontaneous, almost irrepressible (but not hysterical) laughter right in the midst of prayers. Such laughter suggests an absence of a heavy, super-seriousness about oneself and one's worship. It is the freedom a child has to burst into laughter even at an important family gathering. It reflects a lack of pomposity, an ability to see oneself (even one's serious praying) in perspective. My experience is that such laughter has almost always had about it a releasing quality; and although it may sometimes be occasioned by some slight awkwardness of speech or action on the part of someone in the group, it is almost always a sympathetic and joyful laughter, thus ultimately healing and redemptive.

How fascinating then that Romano Guardini refers to the "playfulness of the liturgy." In his book *The Spirit of the Liturgy* he contends that the liturgy, formally analyzed, is more like play than work. The liturgy, he writes,

> is life pouring itself forth without an aim, seizing upon riches from its own abundant store, significant through the fact of its existence. . . . It unites art and reality in a supernatural childhood before God. . . . It has no purpose, but it is full of divine meaning. . . . It is in the highest sense the life of a child, in which everything is picture, melody and song.[6]

Of all human activities such worship is the least goal-oriented. "The soul," Guardini concludes, "must learn to abandon, at least in prayer, the

---

[6]Guardini, *The Spirit of the Liturgy*, pp. 179-81.

restlessness of purposeful activity; it must learn to waste time for the sake of God.''[7] One is immediately reminded of the beginning sentence of the great Westminster confession: ''The chief end of man is to glorify God *and to enjoy him forever.*''

If it is not too presumptuous for a non-Friend to venture a judgment, I would suggest that present-day silent Quaker worship often manifests a kind of heaviness which comes from taking itself too seriously. The way of simplicity has in some instances become a life of drabness, and one could only wish that out of the silence laughter and playfulness might emerge as well as reverence and heightened moral sensitivity.

THE PROMISE OF FOLLY

It is noteworthy that each of the three phenomena we have examined— glossolalia, Quaker silence, and the liturgy of the church—exhibits a kind of strangeness or peculiar style as over against man's more usual religious and secular activities. This is perhaps most often felt in the case of glossolalia, but it is not absent from the other two.

Of particular interest to me is the resistance which the noninitiate often exhibits when confronted with this strangeness. Various faith healers point to the resistance often encountered by one who is seeking for healing. And John Sherrill, author of *They Speak with Other Tongues*, writes that ''there seems to be a strange link between taking a seemingly foolish step—which God specifies—and receiving spiritual power.''[8] Billy Graham refers to the same phenomenon and sees the value of the altar call at revival meetings as linked to it.[9] John Sherrill describes his own considerable resistance to the seemingly foolish step of raising his hands to God in praise. Only when he risked his middle-class decorum and respectability through actually praising God in this way did he break through to a deeper experience of the Holy Spirit.[10]

Paul's experience of coming to faith in Jesus as the Christ is, on a theological level, analogous. As a sensitive, educated Pharisee with all the

---

[7]Ibid., p. 183.

[8]John L. Sherrill, *They Speak with Other Tongues*, (Pyramid Books, 1964), 116.

[9]Ibid.

[10]Ibid., pp. 116f., 123.

proper credentials, he simply could not grasp how God's promises could have been fulfilled through a simple Galilean who was put to death on a cross as a common criminal. Indeed, the gospel was a scandal to him as it was foolishness to the Greeks. But after his encounter with Christ on the road to Damascus, Paul was able to write that:

> God chose what is foolish in the world to shame the wise, God chose what is weak in the world to shame the strong, God chose what is low and despised in the world, even things that are not, to bring to nothing things that are, *so that no human being might boast in the presence of God. He is the source of your life in Christ Jesus.* . . . (1 Corinthians 1:27-30, italics supplied).

There appears to be a principle of the spiritual life that as long as man insists on keeping full control of himself he cuts himself off from a deeper relationship with God. I am reminded of Jesus' saying in Mark 10:15 (and parallels): "Truly, I say to you, whoever does not receive the kingdom of God like a child shall not enter it." Or we could point to the account in 2 Kings 5 of Naaman the Syrian, who was required to wash in the muddy waters of the Jordan in order to receive healing. Apparently many individuals are required to perform a seemingly foolish or ridiculous action in order to be released for a genuine spiritual breakthrough. Parenthetically I would want to add, however, that not every foolish act or belief is valuable. Perhaps it is just foolish!

It seems plausible to me that the attitude of the conservative evangelical towards the Bible also reflects a certain setting aside of the arguments of the analytical mind. Even though intellectually he may feel the force of evidence against the plenary or verbal inspiration of the biblical autographs, nonetheless experientially he has discovered that in submission to what he holds to be a verbally inerrant Bible, growth and renewal have taken place in his spiritual pilgrimage. He may be willing to live with intellectual difficulties for the sake of the positive religious experience. So too with many Roman Catholics in relation to the doctrine of papal infallibility. One would need to ask in these instances, however, whether the intellectual price is not too high.

One final question on this subject: If my basic thesis is correct that there is an underlying functional similarity between glossolalia, Quaker silence, and the liturgy of the church, why then have so many Episcopalians and some Quakers sought and experienced glossolalia? I am not sure this question really can be answered. It may well be that these three types of religious practice complement and build upon each other, as indeed has been my own experience. Or, it could be the case that glossolalia for many people in our culture represents a more decisive break with the hegemony of the analytical mind than either Quaker silence or the liturgy of the church and thus opens the way to spiritual growth beyond what the individual has previously experienced.

LIFE AS THE PRAISE OF GOD

Let me examine in somewhat greater detail a religious practice closely related to the phenomena we have just described, namely the discipline of praising and thanking God for all things that happen in one's life—for pain as well as joy, darkness as well as light, evil as well as good. This is an old theme in Christian piety. Eighteenth century English clergyman William Law, for example, writes:

> If anyone could tell you the shortest, surest way to all happiness and perfection, he must tell you to make it a rule to yourself to thank and praise God for everything that happens to you. For it is certain that whatever seeming calamity happens to you, if you thank and praise God for it, you turn it into a blessing.[11]

More recently, in our own century, the German poet Rainer Maria Rilke picks up the theme when he writes:

Tell us, poet, what is it you do?
  I praise.
But the deadly and the monstrous things, how can you bear them?
  I praise.
But even what is nameless, what is anonymous, how can you call upon it?
  I praise.
What right have you to be true in every disguise, beneath every mask?
  I praise.
And how is it that both calm and violent things, like star and storm, know you for their own?

---

[11]Quoted by Merlin R. Carothers, *Power in Praise*, (Logos International, 1972), p. v.

Because I praise.[12]

In our own day, in the book *Prison to Praise* (1970), which has sold close to half a million copies in two brief years and has been lauded by people of widely divergent backgrounds, Army Chaplain Merlin Carothers develops this theme of praise for all things. He is careful to avoid blurring distinctions between good and evil or denying the reality of evil altogether, as is the case in Christian Science. Also, he recognizes the danger of repressing anger, hurt, and disappointment. One should not pretend that he likes everything that happens in his life. Nonetheless, Chaplain Carothers presents a powerful statement in favor of the discipline of praising not only *in* all circumstances but *for* all circumstances. He describes dozens of case histories in this and in two more recent books,[13] where learning to praise God for all circumstances in life has resulted in major personality change and spiritual development.

My immediate interest in this practice of praising God for all things is that it represents a kind of relaxing of the hegemony of the analytical mind which is analogous to what happens in glossolalia, Quaker silence, and liturgical worship. It involves the confession: "Lord, I do not really understand *why* you have permitted these things to happen, but I will submit to your will and the realities of the world you have created nonetheless. I do not believe you sent or caused this hurt or darkness of evil, yet I accept the fact that you permitted it."

Many who practice the discipline of praise for all things witness to the fact that they had previously found it quite impossible fully to accept certain experiences and realities in their own lives and circumstances. They simply found the dynamics of full acceptance beyond their ability. But in praising God for those very circumstances which they could not accept, they frequently discovered that they were able to accept and come to peace with the reality itself.

---

[12]I cannot locate the source of this particular translation. For another translation of this poem, which in the original is entitled "Für Leonie Zacharias," see Rainer Maria Rilke, *Poems, 1906 to 1926*, trans. J. B. Leishman (New Directions, 1957), 258.

[13]*Answers to Praise* (Logos International, 1972); *Power in Praise* (Logos International, 1972).

The one theme that consistently runs through this paper is that the individual who insists on being fully in control of his own self insulates himself from divine reality.[14] To experience the presence and power of the Spirit of God necessitates a letting go, a being open to. The saints and mystics have witnessed to this from time immemorial. Such a letting go is not easy for modern Western man, not least of all because of an intellectual tradition dating back to Francis Bacon, Descartes, Leibnitz and others, which sees knowledge primarily as the ability to gain power over, to control, one's environment. Moreover, as Western man increasingly lost faith in a transcendent God and in the reality of the resurrection of the dead, death no longer was seen as a rite of passage to fuller life, but rather as a confrontation with nothingness, the abyss, and the final loss of self-control. To "let go" in a world without God was to risk chaos and the destruction of self.[15]

It is not surprising that the church has been influenced by this cultural framework and has also come to be wary of the loss of control, especially as this occurs in religious ecstasy. Tillich argues that the church "must avoid the secular profanization of contemporary Protestantism which occurs when it replaces ecstasy with doctrinal or moral structure."[16] How-

---

[14]See Reinhold Niebuhr's discussion of this theme in *The Nature and Destiny of Man* 2 (Scribners, 1949): 107-17. Man's self is shattered at the very center of its being "whenever it is confronted by the power and holiness of God and becomes genuinely conscious of the real source and center of all life" (p. 109). Niebuhr points to the Pauline dialectic, which makes clear that the self is not obliterated but rather for the first time finds true fulfillment when it is possessed by the Holy Spirit. "Yet such possession of the self is destructive," he concludes, "if the possessing spirit is anything less than the 'Holy Spirit' " (pp. 111-12).

[15]In the secular context of psychotherapy and psychoanalysis the "letting go" motif is basic. If the client insists on censoring his thoughts and his speech, the therapist has little access to his repressed experiences and the realm of the unconscious. The therapist often encourages the client to "let go" and discover the powers of life emerging within him. The operative assumption is that reality is of such a nature that it tends towards integration and wholeness. By trying too hard to become whole the client may only impede the healing process. Some therapists and sensitivity group trainers, however, have perhaps over-reacted to our cultural bias in favor of control and exhibit in their work a prejudice against clear ideas, conscience, will, and the analytical mind. My own position is that the individual must discover a balance between head and heart, mind and body, objectivity and subjectivity. Significantly, orthodox Christian theology has consistently held that the balancing, harmonizing, or centering of one's life is found outside of the self. It is realized only in the entrusting of oneself to God.

[16]Paul Tillich, *Systematic Theology*, 3 (University of Chicago Press, 1963): 117.

ever, both structure and ecstasy are needed in the church, according to Tillich, and "the church must prevent the confusion of ecstasy with chaos."[17]

In a statement which J. Rodman Williams quotes in his book *The Era of the Spirit*, Tillich writes:

> This whole part of the present system [Part IV: 'Life and Spirit'] is a defense of the ecstatic manifestations of the Spiritual Presence against its ecclesiastical critics; in this defense, the whole New Testament is the most powerful weapon. Yet, this weapon can be used legitimately only if the other partner in the alliance—the psychological critics—is also rejected or at least put into proper perspective.[18]

Such words cannot, of course, be used to validate glossolalia or other charismatic phenomena in the church. At the very least, however, they might encourage greater openness to such experiences among non-Pentecostals, and by God's grace a deeper experience of the richness of life God wants us to realize in our commitment to Jesus Christ as Lord and Savior.

---

[17]Ibid.

[18]Ibid., p. 118. See the excellent discussion of Tillich's position in J. Rodman Williams, *The Era of the Spirit* (Logos International, 1971), 85-91.

18

WATSON E. MILLS

Reconstruction and Reappraisal

[Reprinted from *Understanding Speaking in Tongues*, edited by Watson E. Mills (Eerdmans, 1972), pp. 61-76. Used by permission from Eerdmans Publishing Company.]

God is trying to get through into the Church, staid and stuffy and self-centered as it often is, with a kind of power that will make it radiant and exciting and self-giving. We should seek to understand and be reverent toward this phenomenon, rather than to ignore or scorn it.

Samuel M. Shoemaker

Much of the disagreement concerning glossolalia today would subside if there could be a distinction drawn between the meaning of the form and the symbolism of the phenomenon. Many non-Pentecostal scholars who totally reject speaking in tongues would not hesitate to insist that the Holy Spirit can play a meaningful role in the lives of contemporary Christians. Similarly, by focusing upon the totality of the phenomena which attest to the Spirit's presence, and by viewing glossolalia as only one of these, some Pentecostals who possess the gift of tongue-speech might refrain from regarding their gift as superior to all others. A contemporary Christian with a modern, twentieth-century world hypothesis might "stumble" at the *form* of glossolalia as it is presented in the New Testament, but this same Christian might well concede that this outmoded structure once represented the power and presence of God to the early Christians. While he would not accept the form, he might well share a similar belief about the availability of God's power and presence in the world today. As Lester Cleveland observes:

> When glossolalia first appeared in Christian circles, men of other religious persuasions commonly accepted it as the mark of possession by the gods. It undoubtedly made a profound impression on these people and a strong witness for Christianity.
>
> Our worldview is so different today most people look upon it as a sign of insanity or fanaticism, if not both. Love is hardly increased by these reactions.[1]

But having said this, Cleveland cautions that we must still recognize the value in a demythologized glossolalia. That is, somehow there must be a way to strip tongue-speech of its repulsive outer appearance and see it beneath its veneer. To put it another way, is it possible for the nonparticipating Christian to "get inside" his glossolaliac brother and see firsthand what's going on? How does the world look? The church? If the movement is to be understood, it seems that we must first listen to *him*—not to his often loud and random speech sounds, but to him. We must listen to him in order to discover what all this "noise" really signifies.

Thus in attempting to survey the overall relevance of glossolalia for the church today, we will explore both the formal and the symbolic avenues of meaning.

THE FORMAL STRUCTURE OF GLOSSOLALIA

THE REALITY OF GLOSSOLALIA

That glossolalia occurred among the early Christians cannot be denied. Further, instances of the phenomenon can be documented outside Chris-

---

[1] Lester D. Cleveland, "Let's Demythologize Glossolalia," *The Baptist Program*, 45 (June 1967): 11.

tendom, as well as in the history of the Christian church. Obviously, while apparent in the first century, glossolalia was not unique to that age. Yet it appears that neither the Pentecostal event itself nor any of the subsequent manifestations of the phenomenon has had any significant apologetic thrust along the nonparticipants. At Pentecost at least part of the crowd scoffed at this manifestation of the Spirit, linking it with the "babbling" of drunkards. Luke represents Peter as the one who shrewdly proceeded to defend the actions of the disciples who uttered these strange sounds. Peter evidently spoke in his ordinary tongue, and, judging from the results of his preaching, was highly effective (Acts 2:41).

At Corinth the *charismata* were made ends in themselves and were sought after as signs of superiority to be used superciliously over other Christians. The Christians there were "eager for manifestations of the Spirit," but apparently did not use them to build up the church (1 Corinthians 14:12). Those who excelled in extraordinary gifts, particularly glossolalia, paraded them (1 Corinthians 12:4-5) and looked down upon the less gifted Christians (1 Corinthians 12:21); they also produced intolerable confusion in the services of worship (1 Corinthians 14:33). In time, those who sought the various *charismata* for their own sake began to counterfeit these gifts. Thus, the gift of distinguishing the true from the false was necessary within the context of the church. At the close of the first century, the problem had become acute:

> Beloved, do not believe every spirit, but test the spirits to see whether they are of God; for many false prophets have gone out into the world. By this you know the Spirit of God: every spirit which confesses that Jesus Christ has come in the flesh is of God. (1 John 4:1-2)

Thus, the writer of 1 John indicates that the Christian could no longer trust what appeared to be the working of the Spirit. Rather, he had to carefully examine "every spirit."

(*a.*) *Values.* While Paul saw no value in glossolalia for the church as a whole (1 Corinthians 14:2; 14:4; 14:5; 14:19; 14:28), he evidently recognized some personal reward for the individual who spoke in tongues. Also, Paul realized that glossolalia could potentially serve as a sign to convince an unbeliever that God existed and exerted his power upon men. Perhaps Paul best expresses his estimate of glossolalia when he writes:". . . in church I would rather speak five words with my mind, in order to instruct others, than ten thousand words in a tongue" (1 Corinthians 14:19). Thus, while Paul did not deny that glossolalia was a valid *charisma*, he did deny that it was to be exalted to first place as the sole evidence of the indwelling of God's Spirit. In fact, the apostle noted that it was inferior to prophecy (1 Corinthians 14:5), and in his list of gifts in 1 Corinthians 12, tongue-speaking comes last. Yet Paul was unwilling to write off the phenomenon completely, indicating that it could be a meaningful part of the worship service provided certain regulations were adhered to: (1) there should not be more than three glossolaliacs speaking during a single service (1 Corinthians 14:27); (2) of those allowed to speak, only one should speak at a time (1 Corinthians 14:27); (3) and this one should speak only when someone who can interpret is present, either the glossolaliac himself or someone else (1 Corinthians 14:27).

Luke, on the other hand, does not assess the value of the gift per se; however, his writings presuppose belief in a God whose Spirit is active in the proclamation of the gospel—a God who vindicates the work of the apostles by demonstrating through some sign his presence and power.

(*b.*) *Dangers.* According to Paul's own teaching (Galatians 5:16-26), a demonstration of the indwelling of the Spirit was requisite to the Christian life; however, because glossolalia had become the standard whereby all charismatic gifts were to be judged, Paul advocated strict controls for its use. Glossolalia demonstrated the presence of the Spirit as an external sign which of itself had no value. But at Corinth this sign had degenerated into the sensational, the showy, the gaudy. The Corinthians Christians appeared to have overlooked the fact that a demonstration of the Spirit's presence ought to reflect to some degree the character of that Spirit itself. Indeed, Paul emphasized this when he developed love as the greatest of all the *charismata* (1 Corinthians 13:13).

A CRITICAL EVALUATION OF THE FORM STRUCTURE OF GLOSSOLALIA

It is understandable that the Christians of the first century chose glossolalia as the proof that the Holy Spirit had come upon them. The early church was born and grew in a hostile environment, and a clear, outward sign of the Spirit's presence was necessary to indicate to the unbelievers that the work of the gospel was legitimate.

Today, for the mainstream of Protestantism, public instances of glossolalia bring confusion, disunity, and disillusionment. From the perspective of many non-Pentecostals, glossolalia is a weird, esoteric phenomenon that belongs to immature Christians who come from a low socio-economic background and who possess a fundamentalist understanding of life and the faith. On the other hand, viewed through the eyes of their Pentecostal brothers, these same "mainstream" Protestants lack the "baptism of the Spirit." While the non-Pentecostals point to the whole context of glossolalia as a highly charged atmosphere," the glossolaliacs note that the phenomenon "can also occur in quiet surroundings, and the unleashing of emotionalism is simply not a necessary part of speaking in tongues."[2] While some critics of the tongues movement often dismiss it as "praying in gibberish," its defenders point to the results of the study done by Morton T. Kelsey, a disciple of Jung:

> It seems to be a physical impossibility to duplicate tongue-speech by deliberate imitation; when gibberish is produced by conscious effort, this also produces muscular tension which soon differentiates the sounds from the effortless flow of glossolalia.[3]

These observations point to the mounting difficulties separating those pro and con. Obviously, both the defenders of glossolalia and the remainder of Christendom must share the burden of compromise if these difficulties are to be overcome.

(a.) *A reconstructed non-Pentecostal position.* The apostle Paul wrote this: "So, my brethren, earnestly desire to prophesy, and do not forbid speaking in tongues; but all things should be done decently and in order" (1 Corinthians 14:39-40). Thus, while Paul does advocate certain legislative controls for the exercise of glossolalia, he does not forbid the phenomenon among the Corinthian Christians. Can the church today have a different attitude? Paul does, however, recommend that the Christians at Corinth seek a more important gift—prophesying (1 Corinthians 14:39). Here, Paul probably meant the intelligent expression of the reality and power of God and of his redemptive work and purposes among men. Even though Paul ranks glossolalia low among spiritual gifts, he nonetheless does not consider it a gift. It would appear, therefore, that the task of the non-

---

[2]Morton T. Kelsey, *Tongue Speaking: An Experiment in Spiritual Experience* (Doubleday 1964), p. 145.

[3]*Ibid.*, p. 6.

Pentecostal Christian with respect to his Pentecostal brother is threefold: (1) Accept glossolalia as a legitimate, nonnormative experience which attests to the presence of God's Spirit. (2) More importantly, accept the brother who speaks in tongues, even if he is unwilling to search elsewhere for a more meaningful symbol through which to express his conviction that God's Spirit is working in and through him. The person who clings to this traditional symbol needs as much to be accepted as any other Christian. (3) Admit that important lessons and insights can be learned from the Pentecostals. The structure of glossolalia is a loud protest to the sometimes cold, impersonal form which institutional worship may acquire. Indeed, some regard the movement as a rebellion against overintellectualized and overorganized Christianity. Further, the Pentecostals have demonstrated a zeal and commitment to the Christian faith that is matched only by a small minority of denominations. This may be because they have set definite spiritual goals and have worked out highly developed methods by which to reach these goals. Regardless of how nonparticipants view the outward manifestations of glossolalia, only the most narrow-minded Christian would proceed to write off the Pentecostal denominations as insignificant and irrelevant.

(b.) A reconstructed Pentecostal position. Alternatively, the Pentecostal advocates of glossolalia as an objective phenomenon must lend a sympathetic ear to those who are skeptical of the worth of random speech sounds as a valid symbol of the presence of God's Spirit. The serious glossolaliac who is concerned about meaningful dialog with his non-Pentecostal brother might consider the following suggestions: (1) Recognize that while glossolalia is *a* legitimate symbol it is not the only symbol of the presence of God's Spirit, and consequently it is not normative for all Christendom. The Christian whose worldview requires him to reject the symbol of speaking in tongues may not be passing a judgment upon his Pentecostal brother at all; rather, he may be honestly searching elsewhere for what to him is a more meaningful symbol through which to express his belief that God is dwelling in him. The Pentecostal must not view as a threat the estimate of glossolalia that relegates it to the place of irrationalism. One individual who spoke in tongues described the experience as follows:

> I heard of a group of people . . . who had a dynamic experience of the Spirit and manifested the gifts of tongues. I was filled with question, being a rather conservative person and of a rather intellectual bent, but I was more

filled with an awareness that these people really had something vital in their Christian living that I needed and wanted. So I took the leap and joined their group . . . earnestly seeking the Holy Spirit and whatever gifts he might want to give me. [The] willingness to receive the gift of tongues was a real turning point, because that willingness—to be a fool for Christ— involved a new degree of surrender, which made it possible for the Spirit to come. Needless to say, he did come in great overwhelming power and joy. . . . [4]

In this case history, as in many others, the symbol is relatively unimportant, while the total surrender is absolutely necessary and all-important. Thus, the glossolaliac should allow his non-Pentecostal brother a certain degree of freedom in choosing other symbols that will be as meaningful for him as glossolalia is for the Pentecostal. What symbols are there from which the non-Pentecostal can choose? Perhaps this total surrender could be symbolized through specific involvement with minority groups who seek equal housing and job opportunities; through commitment to the cause of Christian unity around the world; or through leadership in the Christian understanding of war, of sex, or of leisure time.

(2) Not only must the glossolaliac recognize that tongue-speaking is not the only evidence of the indwelling of God's Spirit, but he must avoid stating or implying that glossolalia is superior to all other gifts. The words of Paul are clear:

Now there are varieties of gifts, but the same Spirit; and there are varieties of service, but the same Lord; and there are varieties of working, but it is the same God who inspires them all in every one. To each is given the manifestation of the Spirit for the common good. To one is given through the spirit the utterance of wisdom, and to another the utterance of knowledge according to the same Spirit, to another faith by the same Spirit, to another gifts of healing by the one Spirit, to another the working of miracles, to another prophecy, to another the ability to distinguish between spirits, to another various kinds of tongues, to another the interpretation of tongues (1 Corinthians 12:4-10).

Larry Christenson, pastor of the Trinity Lutheran Church in San Pedro, California, has had extensive experience with tongue-speech, and he

---

[4]Quoted in Fred B. Morris, ''Now I Want You All to Speak in Tongues . . . '' *The Christian Advocate*, 7 (July 4, 1963): 9-10.

maintains that the experience of glossolalia is only *one* gift of the Spirit. In fact, Christenson continues, the Pentecostal does not pray for the gift of tongues, but rather for the gift of the Holy Spirit. Those who have not received this specific gift, therefore, should not be regarded as inferior by the glossolaliacs, nor should the former reject the latter because they have found meaning in tongue-speech. His central conclusion for the church today is that glossolalia is a valuable experience—one that should not be forbidden. He asks Christian love and understanding from those who have not had this experience as well as from those who have, as each seeks to relate to the other.

Finally (3) a glossolaliac must realize that to reject glossolalia is not perforce to reject the belief that the Holy Spirit has a place in the life of an individual. Many non-Pentecostals know that the Holy Spirit is active and powerful, but expect the Spirit to manifest himself not in spectacular demonstrations but rather in the Christian graces mentioned in Galatians 5:22-23a.

Pentecostals and non-Pentecostals alike must exercise Christian love as they seek to examine the other's estimate of the external form of glossolalia. Each group has its differing estimates of the significance of this outward manifestation of the Spirit's presence. Perhaps more light can be shed upon the problem by moving to a discussion of the *meaning* of this phenomenon.

THE SYMBOLISM OF GLOSSOLALIA

In terms of its objective form, glossolalia cannot be said to be a religious phenomenon per se, since phenomena identical in sound and psychological effect can occur in a nonreligious context; therefore, the inherent meaning of the phenomenon must transcend its formal structure. What, then, did this symbol *mean*, and what should it signify in the church today?

THE MEANING OF BIBLICAL GLOSSOLALIA

The Pentecost event very definitely made a tremendous impression upon all those present, as well as those who later heard of the tradition and those who read of it after Luke wrote Acts. In fact, the records seem to indicate that the Pentecost experience was simulated in other instances (Acts 4:31; 10:44-48; 19:2-7). At Pentecost, a soul-stirring experience dynamically affected the lives of those converts who were sensitized to and expectant of some great revelation from God. Consequently a number of those present broke forth spontaneously into ecstatic, involuntary speech. Something so greatly impressed them that it called forth an ecstasy of joy which took the form of "speaking in tongues." Peter attributed this demonstration to the action of the Holy Spirit (Acts 2:33; 2:28). Evidently, glossolalia was accepted as unquestionable evidence of possession by the Spirit of God. For the converts it was a manifestation of the inflowing of the divine Spirit—the Spirit of power. While the phenomenon was not mechanical or induced, a significant religious realization lay behind it. This experience was evidently so impressive that others, encouraged by Peter's promise of a share in such an experience, began to seek it so that they might share in the power which lay behind it.

There is little question that Luke intended his reader to understand that the converts of the Jesus-faith received the Spirit, and that this Spirit came in *power*. This indwelling of God's Spirit became the *sine qua non* of their teaching and practice (Acts 2:38). For Paul it may well have become an essential requirement—a standard for conversion and religious experience of all the followers of Jesus. His letters seem to indicate that converts not only must have the Spirit, but must also *demonstrate* their possession of it (see Galatians 5:16; 5:22; 5:23). He maintained that the Spirit was supposed to reveal his presence in the believers by special gifts, that is, the development of particular powers, gifts, and graces which could be accounted for only by the presence of God's Spirit of power. Paul offers specific lists of these gifts (1 Corinthians 12:10; 12:28-31). Among these is glossolalia.

Seen in this context—*a* gift of the Spirit—what did this glossolalia in Acts signify? One evident feature of the phenomenon is that the vocal sounds were addressed to God. This point should not be neglected, as it helps to indicate the meaning of glossolalia. Luke indicates that "they heard them speaking in tongues and extolling God" (Acts 10:46a). Paul points out to the Corinthians that "one who speaks in a tongue speaks not to men but to God" (1 Corinthians 14:2a). Probably glossolalia was not intended to convey a message to men; rather, it was a form of prayer (1 Corinthians 14:14; 14:16). It was an effort to express to God the inexpressible indwelling of the Spirit of God. When the truth of the *kerygma* sank home to a responsive heart, ordinary human language was too restrictive to express the depth of the emotions that were aroused; therefore, the convert broke forth in ecstatic speech. It was an objective witness to the reality of the *kerygma*. The gifts, then, are to be studied as a part of the Spirit's witness to the gospel.

A CRITICAL EVALUATION OF THE SYMBOLIC MEANING
OF GLOSSOLALIA

All Christians ought to recognize that there is a relevant place for the Spirit of God in the church today. The various Pentecostal sects and others who manifest glossolalia have chosen not to suppress "speech about God." They are seeking to give meaning and content to their belief that God's Spirit moves spontaneously in the church and in individual lives. In terms of the individual, the Spirit's unique work is the endowing of the individual with specific gifts. Luke maintains, for example, that Agabus prophesied at the bidding of the Holy Spirit (Acts 11:28; 21:11). Similarly, in the context of the church, the Holy Spirit is that power which enables the church to carry out her mission. In summarizing the work of the church in Jerusalem, Luke notes that "with great power the apostles gave their testimony to the resurrection of the Lord Jesus" (Acts 4:33). This, then, was a community of power because its constituents possessed the Holy Spirit which empowered them to witness to the gospel.

Thus, the various Pentecostal groups have forced the more "respectable" denominations to take a hard look at their doctrine of the Holy Spirit. Wayne Oates feels that religion is the "delicate" subject of this generation, and that there is a certain shyness and inarticulateness when it comes to talking about God. For this reason—and others—he defends the glossolaliac:

> The person who speaks in tongues cannot be "written off" as a fanatic, a sick person, or a fool. We do not know how to pray as we ought. Therefore, these tongue speakings may be the "sighs too deep for words." On the other hand, they may become extremely meaningful to us personally whether they mean anything else to anyone else at all notwithstanding.[5]

Moreover, in general there is a feeling among many Christians that charismatic behavior is not "respectable." Some say that the church has

---

[5]Wayne E. Oates, "A Socio-Psychological Study of Glossolalia," in Frank Stagg, E. Glenn Hinson and Wayne E. Oates, *Glossolalia: Tongue Speaking in Biblical, Historical, and Psychological Perspective* (Abingdon, 1967), p. 77.

lost its "charisma," that men look back to it as a thing of the past. Into this spiritual vacuum the Pentecostal sects bring a needed emphasis upon the role of the Holy Spirit. Apart from affording the individual and the community meaningful channels through which to express the conviction that God's Spirit is working, the organized, institutional church with its "busyness" is irrelevant to the needs of mankind. The late James Pike was correct in his analysis:

> Proponents of this [glossolalic] movement are indubitably right that our Church is in need of a greater sense of the activity of the Holy Spirit in the here and now and a greater resultant zeal of the Mission of the Church, for a change in lives and for personal testimony to Christ.[6]

By the same token, the Pentecostal groups need to be more creative in developing and articulating a theology of glossolalia, that is, what the phenomenon *means* for the Christian life. I have suggested here that the apostles understood its significance to be that it indicated the presence of God's Spirit in the individual. A telling weakness of most Pentecostal material is that it says little or nothing about the relevance of glossolalia for the Christian life. Rather, one gets the impression that the experience per se is what is being sought. *Eternity* magazine describes how a group will gather about a seeker and lay hands on his head. The seeker will be urged to use some foreign words he knows to start the flow. In addition he might be advised to let his jaw become loose and his tongue limp. Or he might be asked to repeat the name of Jesus over and over with great rapidity until he begins to stammer. "Now you are getting it," the group will tell the seeker.

It would appear that some Pentecostals assume that a spiritual blessing *must* be attested to by means of a physical phenomenon. This is a difficult position to defend, especially when some prominent Pentecostal writers concede that the tongue-speaking which occurred at Corinth had nothing directly to do with being filled with the Spirit. Paul took a different stance in Galatians: "But the fruit of the Spirit is love, joy, peace, patience, kindness, goodness, faithfulness, gentleness, self-control" (Galatians 5:22-23a. Cf. Matt. 7:22-23).

---

[6]James A. Pike, "Pastoral Letter Regarding 'Speaking in Tongues,' " *Pastoral Psychology*, 15 (May 1964): 57.

When one demands any specific physical sign as proof for any subjective experience, there will evolve an implicit standard that will rigidly separate those who possess the sign and those who do not. Such a position could be a real stumbling block to Christian unity. Explicit in some Pentecostal writers is the view that Spirit-baptism—as objectified by glossolalia—is a prerequisite to sanctification.[7]

In Christian worship there ought to be more room for spontaneity in worship—more opportunity for the worshippers to participate. Bishop Pike's remarks do not render invalid the practice of glossolalia; rather, he forbids its practice in public worship:

> While there is no inhibition whatsoever as to devotional use of speaking in tongues, I urge that there be no services or meetings in our Churches or in homes or elsewhere for which the expression or promotion of this activity is the purpose, or of which it is a part.[8]

His statement presupposes a certain rigidity in the order of service *from which there will be no deviation*. Henry P. Van Dusen has concluded:

> I have come to feel . . . that the Pentecostal Movement, with its emphasis upon the Holy Spirit, is more than just another revival. It is a revolution in our day. It is a revolution comparable in importance with the establishment of the original Apostolic Church and with the Protestant Reformation.[9]

It may well be that one of the greatest needs of the modern church is to rediscover the tremendous resources of the Holy Spirit. All of Christendom needs to experience the joy and vigor of the Spirit's presence. Indeed, as James McCord, president of Princeton Seminary, has said:

> Ours must become the Age of the Spirit, of God active in the world, shaking and shattering all our forms and structures, and bringing forth responses consonant with the Gospel and the world's needs.[10]

---

[7]See P. C. Nelson, *Bible Doctrine* (Gospel Publishing House, 1948), p. 94 and Ralph M. Riggs, *The Spirit Himself* (Gospel Publishing House, 1949), p. 73.

[8]Pike, p. 59.

[9]Quoted in John L. Sherrill, *They Speak with Other Tongues* (Revell, 1964), p. 27.

[10]*Ibid.*, p. 68.

Again, John Newport asks reflectively:

> Could it be that God is using the Pentecostal movement and the so-called
> Neo-Pentecostal or charismatic revival to summon us not to quench the
> Spirit and to earnestly desire and appropriate the power and resources of
> the Holy Spirit?[11]

Could it be that through this "strange stirring in the church" God may be
calling Christians to a higher level of faith and service?

Finally, let there be constructive dialogue between the glossolaliacs and
non-glossolaliacs. Let us all affirm that every Christian needs both order
and freedom. Out of constructive debate could come a resolution of differences that would be profitable to all. There is a Presbyterian church in
Pennsylvania, for example, where a "pray and praise" service on Saturday night precedes the more formal, liturgical worship service on Sunday
morning. This pattern of worship is intended to maintain a proper balance
between order and freedom. This calendar of worship does not "quench"
the Spirit.

CONCLUSION

Admittedly, glossolalia often arises out of a highly emotional atmosphere. Often those who speak in tongues are ultra-conservative, and consequently the usual reaction is to write off the entire movement as the
product of some kind of psychosis which comes to the surface during high-
pitched revivalist meetings. Such a cursory dismissal of the challenge of
the Pentecostals, however, does not settle the question of what this new
outburst of tongues means for the rest of Christendom.

Those who reject tongue-speaking as no longer relevant for the church
ought to be secure enough to concede that these random speech sounds may
attest to a genuine experience; namely, that God's Spirit is dwelling in the
individual in power. This means that Christendom generally is obligated
to accept the glossolaliac brother who is convinced that this particular
symbol is adequate for him. Moreover, the non-glossolaliac—admitting
that the symbol originally attested to the power and presence of God—must

---

[11]John P. Newport, "Speaking in Tongues," *Home Missions*, 36 (May 1965):25.

now search elsewhere for a relevant symbol to indicate his commitment to a belief in the Spirit's presence.

The proponents of glossolalia ought to recognize that the phenomenon had been abused in the Corinthian congregation. Paul consequently set down some rules and limits for its future use. Among the Pentecostals in this century there have been similar abuses. The former General Secretary of the Pentecostal World Conference is reported to have said:

> There is not much in church services that is more distressing than the shocking ignorance about, and the lamentable absence of the gifts of the Holy Spirit. Even in our Pentecostal Churches, where there is evidence of more liberty in the Spirit, we find far more physical and emotional "reactions" to the presence of the Spirit. . . . I consider it heresy to speak of shaking, trembling, falling, dancing, clapping, shouting, and such like actions as "manifestations" of the Holy Spirit. These are purely human reactions to the power of the Holy Spirit and frequently hinder, more than help, to bring forth genuine manifestations.[12]

Consequently, those who speak in tongues must recognize that these objections and fears are ever present and real. On the other hand, non-Pentecostals must recognize that abuses are neither necessary nor inevitable.

Likewise, the glossolaliac must not expect all Christians to speak in tongues; neither must the Pentecostal deny his brother in Christ the right to search for yet another symbol to express the indwelling of God's Spirit, if that symbol would give concrete meaning to the conviction that God is dwelling in the individual.

The most important question about glossolalia for the church is this: Is glossolalia a legitimate expression of the presence of the Spirit? Paul's answer is that it is a legitimate expression if the time and place are right. Whether this is so is determined by whether love is increased or, at the very least, not harmed in any way whatsoever. This will mean that Pentecostals and non-Pentecostals alike will have to recognize that, though their methods are different, their goal is the same: to demonstrate the presence of God's Spirit.

---

[12]Tod W. Ewald, "Aspects of Tongues," *The Living Church*, 146 (June 2, 1963): 13.

Truly, then, the way for both those with and those without the experience to keep the phenomenon in perspective is neither to forbid nor force tongues, but rather to exercise mutual tolerance, understanding and Christian love.

Part IV
Psychological Studies

19

JOHN P. KILDAHL

Psychological Observations

[Reprinted with permission from *The Charismatic Movement*, edited by Michael P. Hamilton (Eerdmans, 1975), pp. 124-42. Reprinted with permission from Eerdmans Publishing Company.]

In the past twelve years, hundreds of letters have been sent to me by persons who speak in tongues. I have been helped enormously in my research into glossolalia by these letters, and am grateful for the persons who have shared their experiences with me. For this chapter, I have collated the common denominators of these letters into one composite letter which will form the introduction to this chapter. The chapter will consist of nine psychological observations about speaking in tongues. Each of those observations is illustrated in the following letter:

It was with a great deal of interest that I read the findings of your research on glossolalia.[1]

"It is of particular interest to me since I received the baptism of (by, in, or with) the Holy Spirit when I was eighteen years old (I am now twenty-eight) after fasting and praying during my school lunch period for about ten days. Those ten days had been a time of serious struggle for me, both spiritually and in every other way. I had been seeking for answers to the great turmoil and uncertainty in my life. I was having trouble sleeping, studying, getting along with people, and even eating. I was a religious person, thoroughly grounded in Scripture, and had been seeking guidance and answers in my struggle. During the preceding ten days I had gone to prayer meetings at one of the local churches in which speaking in tongues and the gifts of the Spirit were much in evidence. I was greatly taken by the warmth and Christian spirit of the group, particularly by the minister, who seemed to be positively Christ-like. Finally I received the baptism, during my lunch period when I was sitting alone in an empty classroom. I had been prayed for fervently the night before, with the laying on of hands, and had felt strange urgings inside me, but it was not until the next day that I received the baptism. The evidence to me of his incoming was speaking in tongues. This gift of tongues I have continued to use through the years, primarily in private prayers and praise, particularly praise.

I had earlier accepted Christ as my personal Savior but I had not had the baptism of the Holy Spirit. This came only through travail and prayer and worship, and finally when the Holy Spirit entered in for the first time, it was an experience of burning all through me. I felt chills and great beads of perspiration. And yet for me, it was a very quiet experience. But a change had taken place all through me and I became the temple of God's Spirit, which was evidenced by the speaking of an unknown tongue. There was no need for me to know what I was saying—the Spirit knew what I was in

---

[1]The writer of the letter is referring to the final progress report, "Glossolalia and Mental Health," a research project supported by the Behavioral Sciences Branch, National Institute of Mental Health, No. MH-10514-01, principal investigator John P. Kildahl, co-investigator Paul A. Qualben. The results of the five hypotheses investigated in this research are the following: (1) glossolalists are more submissive, suggestible, and dependent in the presence of authority figures than non-tongue-speakers; (2) glossolalists initiate their speech in the presence of a benevolent authority figure, either in reality or fantasy; (3) glossolalists are less depressed than non-glossolalists; (4) glossolalists continued their sense of well-being following a year's interval as they continued the practice of glossolalia; (5) the spoken utterances of glossolalia do not meet the criteria of what constitutes a human language. These findings are further explained in John P. Kildahl, *The Psychology of Speaking in Tongues* (New York, 1972).

need of and he gave me utterance when I was thanking and worshiping the Lord. I felt that I could take all the joy, love, thrills, and lusts of the flesh that the world could offer and roll it up and it couldn't compare to the joy, the thrill, the peace, and the excitement of that experience.

You have mentioned in your writing the importance of the leader, but I say to you the only leader was Christ and the Holy Spirit. The group of Christians in that church where I found the baptism were only weak instruments of the Holy Spirit. I could recognize that they were crude channels of the Holy Spirit but all glory belongs to Christ himself. I came to love and trust them, not for what they were as individuals, but because I knew the Lord spoke through them.

This gift was tremendously helpful to my spiritual life, since the physical evidence of God's presence this way made a serious lack of faith in him impossible. I had that which, to me, was irrefutable evidence of God's power and concern for me, and I felt that his wishes influenced my actions in the many times I asked him to guide me.

I left home after graduating from high school and was in the service. Later, my work called for me to travel a great deal. I moved about a lot, and during months and sometimes years of carelessness, I would not pray, so naturally I did not pray in tongues. I suppose that I could have prayed in tongues if I had wanted to, but the thought never occurred to me. But in times of need I would come back to the Lord, and when I moved close enough to God to speak to him, I again started praying in tongues. I might add that praying, or, as was the general rule, praising, in tongues was practically always accompanied by a definite lifting of my spirit and a deep feeling of thankfulness for his care for me and for his goodness to me.

During the time when I strayed from the Lord, I was almost continuously among strangers for months at a time. From time to time during those years I would find myself troubled in spirit and would make my way to a church where I could find Bible-believing Christians. I might add that I had had a solid foundation in the Bible in my youth and knew from that what God expected of me. I only accepted as God's revelations to me what was consistent with conservative Bible doctrine. I felt most at home in those churches where the pastor preached the Bible and believed in the baptism of the Spirit.

Believe me, doctor, while I know nothing of the depth and strength of your own faith in a personal God or your consciousness of the indwelling Holy Spirit I can testify to you that knowing that his Spirit lives in you, and orders, with love, your comings and goings, is not to be described— it can only be experienced. Let me point out as strongly as I am able that speaking in tongues to me, and to most others so gifted, is merely an outward evidence of something infinitely greater within.

Other outward evidences of what is within me are expressed in the movements of my hands when I pray. Sometimes I touch my forehead with my fingertips, and at other times the palms of my hands turn upward and my arms spread. Also, sometimes I raise my face, and other times I lower it. All these movements, and others, as with the words I speak in tongues, are instinctive, though I am as conscious of what I am doing as if it were a formal liturgical action. At those moments, I know that God is directing my whole being, not just my tongue.

Since I use my gift of tongues primarily in private, I do not have much experience with the interpretation of tongues, and I myself do not have that gift. I feel that a tongue is the language of God and not for man. It is the Spirit of God speaking to God directly through me. There is no need for me to know what is said. I am, of course, curious about exactly what it is that is being spoken and how it happens. I have wondered about the possibility of not merely recording the messages on a tape recorder, but of measuring the source of the message, just as radio and TV waves can be identified. However, this may not be permitted because 'His ways are past finding out,' and this might not be of faith. I can add that a number of interpretations that I have heard in the past ten years have concerned warnings and rebukes to God's people as well as instruction and comfort. In all cases, the genuine message was appropriate to the immediate need or situation. I also think that you can't take a supernatural blessing bestowed from God and bring it down to a common denominator or natural level. The Gospel of John says 'The wind bloweth where it listeth, and thou hearest the sound thereof but canst not tell whence it cometh and whither it goeth: so is everyone that is born of the Spirit.'

As I said, I do not know what my own tongue means, and I do not know if it is a language spoken anywhere in the world. Maybe I would have found out more if I had used my gift more publicly. But here is an example of the language I most often speak:

> Un te a tiki, un se;
> un se, un se;
> te a tiki un se.

I pronounce the *t* with my tongue pressed hard against the roof of the mouth just behind the teeth, similar to the sounding of *th*, except the tongue is forced forward while the breath is expelled with enough force that it makes a slight sound. I hope you will find this example of my own speech useful in your work. If you do have any information about whether this is a true language, please let me know.

I think you may also be interested in knowing that having the baptism of the Holy Spirit and the gift of tongues has never made me successful in business, but it has cast out fear of people and has made me a strong leader and salesman—a person who loves God and tries seriously to put him first and tell others about his wonderful Son, Jesus Christ. For me, the indwelling of the Holy Spirit can be considered *bona fide* only if the person shows a deep love for Christ in that which he promotes. By the same token a person who doesn't show a profound love for Christ very possibly does not have the Holy Spirit in him.

As a psychologist, it should be easy for you to see that a person who has experienced, or regularly experiences (as in the matter of speaking in tongues), a miracle within himself should be more convinced and convincing than one who has not had any such experience with God.

My own experience of the baptism has tended to make me a poor follower, since I generally feel that I know what God wants and expects of me; and I trust my judgment more than that of many who would presume to tell me what I should do. When I am subject to authority it is generally with well-defined reservations—usually expressed, so there is no misunderstanding. In order that you may better understand my attitude toward my pastor and other church leaders, I might say that I think of myself as an apostle, subject first to God, and to people only when there is no conflict of interest. Normally, there isn't. Nevertheless, this attitude has caused me to change churches a number of times. But while I had never entertained the thought of being an Episcopalian[2] before last year, I find that I have had more freedom and opportunity to work in my Episcopalian church than I have had for over twenty years. My present project, which I undertook with the church's blessing, is to try to activate inactive members. I find that my hours of visiting, writing, and phoning are paying off and that I am more effective than someone who does not have the Holy Spirit in him, even though that person may be a true Christian. The chances are that evangelism for that person is work, rather than a source of deep satisfaction.

As an example of how strongly I feel about my opinions, I have always felt that it was God's will that I marry my Presbyterian wife. Furthermore, I feel that it was his will that I take my two children out of the Presbyterian

---

[2]The denominations mentioned here are not necessarily the ones mentioned in the letter actually being quoted.

church and prevent them from getting enmeshed in it at all. As a matter of fact I am quite sure that my Presbyterian wife will soon learn to depend on Christ instead of the Presbyterian church, if she doesn't already.

In closing, may I caution you to be at least neutral in this investigation, since it is easy for a person to feel that 'if he doesn't have it, it can't be important'; or worse, take a pharisaical attitude toward it, assuming that if it isn't approved 'by the Board of Trustees' it can't be of God.

The fact remains, whatever conclusions you come up with, that through the centuries God has blessed people—sometimes few and sometimes, as now, many—with this gift of tongues, and he will continue to do so.

I hope you will excuse the length of this letter, but I recognize that you are in a position to do a great deal of harm, especially since reason is much more popular than faith—although it alone has little value before God. Many people continue to go to hell, we can be sure, because faith isn't recognized by the common senses, so these people will have none of it. Let me urge you to remember that you will stand before God much longer than you will stand before men. So please be careful.

Truly yours,
John Doe

P.S. Doctor, this letter is an example of my doing what I felt God would have me do. The results or your attitude toward it are no concern of mine. I feel I have contributed my bit under his direction, and that is all I am expected to do. I am merely a small cog in an intricate machine, a cog which doesn't even know what product is being produced, except that it is something for the glory of God. Truly, JD.

P.P.S. I hope this has helped you. I am enclosing a card of our church, where I guarantee you will witness the manifestations of the Spirit. Truly, JD.''

This composite letter, then, reflects the common features in the autobiographical statements of tongue-speakers. I would like now to develop nine observations from the letter.

Observation one: There are five steps in the process of one's coming to speak in tongues. Each of these five steps may be seen in the testimony of John Doe. First, the person who is about to speak in tongues has a great sense of personal distress, often called an existential crisis. In his distress, he is openly seeking and is open for someone who will tell him what to do and provide relief from his suffering. Second, he is generally drawn to a person who is a leader whom he trusts or eventually comes to trust. In his sense of weakness and dependency, he looks for a person with certainty, for someone who has a sense of definiteness and strength. Third, the charismatic leader is surrounded by a supporting group of fellow believers. The credibility of the leader is enhanced by the presence of this group of followers, who are almost equally firm in their convictions that a solution and an end to suffering lies in following their own path. Fourth, a comprehensive rationale is offered to the initiate to explain what tongue-speaking is, and how it may be understood. Fifth, there is an intense emotional atmosphere at some point in what I have come to call the induction process.

Let us now explore each of these five steps. Again, it is well to remember that the danger of oversimplification is great, and that there surely must be some exceptions to every rule.

Persons who begin to speak in tongues have suffered before they began to speak with the strange sounds that appear to be a language. This suffering and distress is usually intense, with feelings of confusion or estrangement or isolation. The distress may be environmental, physical, or emotional in origin. Or more likely, it is caused by a combination of circumstances. Marital difficulties, financial concern, ill health, feelings of depression are common. At times the crisis is ethical or religious in nature and involves concerns about spiritual values, a sense of guilt, or questions about the ultimate meaning and purpose of life. Preoccupation with one's internal psychology seems to create the atmosphere in which a person is open to finding answers for one's problems. Persons who are generally anxiety-free or who are not feeling any particular distress are less likely to seek answers to existential questions, and are therefore less susceptible to the induction of a glossolalia experience. Note that John Doe turned to speaking in tongues during his travels whenever he fell into periods of profound emotional distress.

One of the common features of a person in distress is that he has a powerful sense of dependency. When a swimmer tires, he looks about for someone to lean on or to clutch for safety. A dependent and distressed person can be likened to a tired swimmer. He wants to find someone or something who can do for him what he feels he cannot do for himself. What he generally looks for at those moments is a perfect parent. While John Doe says that his only leader was the Holy Spirit, it is possible to see that he had a great admiration for the leader of his group who served as the channel for the Holy Spirit. He came to trust this leader, which is the second precondition for beginning to speak in tongues.

Doe also presents an interesting variant on the usual pattern, inasmuch as he reports that he very rarely took advice from other persons who offered it. He reports that he trusted his own thinking more than that of others. This is a case that might be described psychologically as counterdependence. Mr. Doe appears to be a man who is quite fearful of being dependent upon others, and bends over backward not to be influenced by others. And yet, under situations of extreme distress he did return to a church fellowship where he found support. Some people who are independent seem to go 180 degrees in the opposite direction intermittently, and become what appears to be the opposite of independent. One example of this behavior is the case of a minister who was actually in the middle of preaching a sermon against tongue-speaking when he suddenly broke out into speaking in tongues himself. A belligerent skeptic may in fact be quite susceptible to the experience—which is an example of the psychological mechanism called reaction formation. In Shakespeare's words, "Me thinks he protesteth too much," may well indicate an underlying desire to conform.

The comradeship of the group is the third factor in the induction process. The warmth of the group provides acceptance. Enthusiastic members of the group promise relief from turmoil. It appears to me that once having begun to speak in tongues, relatively few persons continue it with any degree of importance unless they keep in touch with an ongoing group of fellow believers. This is a consistent finding with other groups, including members of Alcoholics Anonymous, who derive great support from their fellow members. Without follow-up group support, it seems that many psychological changes will dissipate.

The fourth feature in the induction process is providing a rationale so that making these strange sounds appears to be part of some comprehensible plan. Perhaps no one would make the strange sounds of tongue-speaking without having a rationale to explain that these sounds are indeed a special gift and not just nonsensical babble. I do not know of any persons who have begun to speak in tongues without knowing that there was such a thing described in religious literature. It appears that no one begins speaking in tongues until he or she has some grasp of the New Testament explanation of what it is.

A heightened emotional atmosphere is the fifth element in the induction process. Some leaders are more effective than others at preparing the emotional atmosphere which is optimally effective in inducing the experience. A skilled leader may have a number of effective rituals which he feels are beneficial for the initiate. This systematic activity may generate a great deal of emotional feeling, sometimes even to the point of fatigue or exhaustion. In these instances the advent of tongue-speaking is all the more euphoric or dramatic. One noted tongue-speaker now reports that he is able to preach a sermon during which he never mentions the gifts of the Spirit, or even the Holy Spirit, and nonetheless at the end of his sermon, or even during it, initiates begin to speak in tongues for the first time. This leader's reputation is so great that persons come to his meeting already aware that indeed they may be seized with the impulse to speak in tongues. His reputation has preceded him, so that he needs to make very little conscious effort to induce people to speak in tongues. Nonetheless, the overall rule holds true, that a heightened emotional atmosphere is what has brought the onset of glossolalia.

I am therefore advancing the hypothesis that glossolalia is a learned experience, and that these five factors constitute the steps in the learning process. These five steps closely parallel the essential steps for religious healing to take place.[3] James Hanson agrees that speaking in tongues rarely develops spontaneously without some kind of coaching. He himself reports that he would not have received this gift if someone had not coached him.[4]

It is not my purpose in this chapter to make a value judgment on the induction process or on the hypothesis that glossolalia is a learned experience. Rather, my purpose here is simply to observe that the evidence is strong that one may learn to speak in tongues under certain prescribed conditions.

Observation two: The capability of being hypnotized and the capability of speaking in tongues are closely related.

Tongue-speakers begin to speak in tongues through the help and direction of a leader who actively initiates the neophyte into the experience. It appears essential that the initiate develop a deeply trusting and even submissive relationship to the person who is his or her mentor. If the initiate

---

[3]The reader will find a number of fascinating parallels between the atmosphere for healing and for glossolalia in the excellent work by Jerome Frank, *Persuasion and Healing* (Baltimore, 1961).

[4]*The Holy Spirit in Today's Church*, ed. Erling Jorstad (Nashville, 1973), p. 46. This book contains a number of firsthand accounts of people's reactions—both pro and con— to the charismatic movement.

holds back, if he is only partly involved in the experience or has strong reservations about the credibility of the leader, then he or she will not begin to speak in tongues. If, for example, a group of twenty persons are exposed to a charismatic leader, those persons in the group who trust the leader the most have the best chance of becoming glossolalists. In subordinating one's own ego to that of the authority figure, the initiate is able to regress psychologically to a level of childlike openness, dependency, and suggestibility.

The ability to submit oneself to a mentor appears to be a precondition for speaking in tongues. This capacity to regress exhibits the same general traits as the trait of hypnotizability. Hypnotizability requires that one be trusting enough to turn himself rather fully over to someone else and to place one's momentary destiny in the hands of the other person. Some persons tend to hang on to their own psychological controls and do not develop the trusting relationship which is the precondition for hypnosis. However, many persons who at first cannot give themselves up will gradually come to trust the mentor and in time will allow themselves to regress enough to be hypnotized.

Hypnotizability constitutes the *sine qua non* of a glossolalia experience. If one can be hypnotized, then one is able under proper conditions to learn to speak in tongues. While people who speak in tongues are not hypnotized, the induction of glossolalia is very similar to the induction into hypnosis. There is a further connection. After a person has been hypnotized for the first time, it becomes increasingly easy for him to be hypnotized on repeated occasions. This holds true also for the tongue-speaker. Once he has begun to speak in tongues under the conditions of a trusting dependence and regression in the face of the mentor, then the tongue-speaker himself is able to repeat the tongue-speech without repeated induction efforts by the mentor. Once the tongue-speaker has been able to regress and let go of the conscious controls so that glossolalia is produced, then it is easy for him to repeat the same or similar sounds under a wide variety of conditions, whether kneeling in the quiet of a church or driving along the freeway.

Observation three: The feelings of well-being experienced by the new tongue-speaker are caused by his or her feeling of acceptance by the leader and the group of fellow tongue-speakers. The feeling of euphoria is not caused by the actual making of the sounds of glossolalia itself.

The feelings of well-being are caused by the belief, as reinforced by the group, that this is an act of God's intervention in one's speech. The actual verbalizing is a neutral experience. It is one's belief that this is a gift of God which brings an experience of euphoria.

The new tongue-speaker has been told for days or weeks or months or years that once he begins to speak in tongues there will be a variety of benefits. It is a sign of God's approval, physical evidence that the speaker has been singled out for a special blessing. Many new tongue-speakers have been striving with a great deal of energy, curiosity, and perseverance to experience this phenomenon. When one has striven diligently to reach a goal, and that goal is seen as one which will produce tremendous benefits in one's life, then a feeling of relief and elation will occur when one reaches the goal.

It is known that when a person has been hypnotized and been given post-hypnotic suggestions that he will feel more relaxed or more confident, these benefits will actually occur, at least for a time. The hypnotized person begins to experience the mood which has been suggested to him. This is precisely what happens with the new tongue-speaker. He exhibits those results in his life which he has been led to expect.

Whether or not these suggested benefits will persist appears to depend upon whether or not the experience is reinforced by one's fellow practitioners, and whether or not these persons continue their support and encouragement. Psychologically, there is a common experience of feeling let down after a major experience in one's life. We are familiar, for example, with post-graduation letdown. This may also happen with tongue-speakers who are not surrounded by a group of fellow believers who buoy each other up. If they continue to feel that they are a company of special people, the subjective feelings of euphoria seem to continue. But the new tongue-speaker who is soon cut off from a supportive group or who has conflicts with his group so that he comes to put less stock in their comradeship seems to derive relatively less psychological benefits from the experience. He may have felt special at the moment, but he needs continuing reinforcement from his fellow believers if he is to continue to feel that he is one of a select fellowship. Otherwise glossolalia becomes relatively less meaningful for him.

The actual making of the sounds is not what makes a person feel good. It is rather the belief that God Almighty is moving his tongue. It is a physical experience, but it is confirmed by one's intellectual understanding that it is a gift of the Spirit, and is combined with emotional support from one's fellow believers. When all these factors are present, it is understandable that tongue-speakers are less depressed as they continue to believe in the special gift of God that is given to them.

Four examples will illustrate my point here. While being interviewed on a television program, I was surprised to hear the master of ceremonies begin to speak in tongues. He did so to give the television audience an example of what glossolalia sounded like. He explained that he had not made those sounds for twenty years. As an adolescent he had belonged to a religious fellowship in which he spoke in tongues, but had discarded the practice as he moved away from home and left the fellowship of his church. Twenty years later he could still demonstrate the ability to make the sounds, but they had no emotional or spiritual impact for him. Twenty years previously, he had felt a warm, inner glow when he made those sounds, believing that this was God speaking through him.

Speaking in tongues is practiced in non-Christian religions, particularly among the Hindus in India.[5] The physical manifestations appear to be analogous to what happens in a Christian context, though the belief system connected with the experience is quite different. Similarly, the subjective experience is correlated with what each religious group teaches will be the results of what happens subjectively when one speaks in tongues.

A linguist has reported that he has been able to teach members of his linguistics class how to speak in tongues.[6] This experience was developed outside any religious beliefs about the practice. And as would be expected, no particular feelings of euphoria developed as a result of the linguistics class members learning to speak in tongues.

Acting classes encourage students to develop a type of glossolalia called "turkey talk" as part of training in acting. Class members are encouraged to use verbal expression without using a known language. Actors and actresses under these conditions are able to speak a "language" which sounds like glossolalia, but is simply an exercise in the free flow of emotion and verbal expression without intellectual content. Actors and actresses will

---

[5]L. Carlyle May, "A Survey of Glossolalia and Related Phenomena in Non-Christian Religions," *American Anthropologist*, 58 (May, 1956), 75-96.

[6]William J. Samarin, "The Linguisticality of Glossolalia," *Hartford Quarterly*, 8 (Summer, 1968), 49-75.

speak somewhat different "languages" when they are asked to talk a language that conveys joy, warmth, sadness, etc.

In summary, it is not the speech itself, but rather the belief about what the speech is, that makes glossolalists feel good.

Observation four: Subjective experience alone cannot determine the value of an experience. Tongue-speakers, especially beginning tongue-speakers, report very positive subjective feelings. However, positive subjective feelings can be produced in a wide variety of ways. And the subjective feelings can be equally euphoric, even when produced by very difficult kinds of stimuli.

LSD users, for example, have said that nothing can compare with the heights of ecstasy which they feel when they are on a good trip. They often say that if one hasn't tried it, one should not knock the experience. Nothing can compare with the unfathomable beauty of a leaf rustling in the wind when on an LSD trip, someone has said. And the true inner nature of a Beethoven symphony can best be grasped when using LSD, someone else has said.

An Oxford University professor of English literature once told the story of having been hypnotized by Adolf Hitler during a mass meeting in Nazi Germany during the 1930s. This professor was a British citizen on a visit to Berlin, when he decided to observe at first hand a Nazi rally. Before the meeting was over he found himself standing on his seat (along with thousands of others), cheering wildly for Hitler, waving his arms, stamping his feet and shouting Nazi slogans.

Hours later in his hotel room he wondered what had possessed him to act in a way so totally out of character. He thought not only that he was an undemonstrative man temperamentally, but that he had also been and continued to be opposed to the Hitler movement. In fact, a year later he was no longer allowed to enter Germany because of his opposition to Nazism. But that night, he said, during Hitler's speech he had felt a wonderful kind of wholeness and enthusiasm. He later said that he felt completely convinced about the rightness of what he was doing, and would have sworn that he was fully in possession of all his faculties, and was psychologically "together." He said later that during the Nazi rally perhaps nothing could have convinced him that he was not doing the right thing. For the moment, he became convinced intellectually, he was emotionally supported by thousands of others at the rally, and he was caught up in the subjective sense of euphoria.

LSD users and those hypnotized at Hitler rallies illustrate that different kinds of experience can produce the same euphoria. The spiritual validity of glossolalia, therefore, cannot be proved by how good it makes one feel subjectively. Tongue-speakers often report how marvelous they have felt since they began speaking in tongues. Someone else could report the same feelings after having successfully dieted and lost sixty pounds. Therefore, it is wise to discount the glowing accounts of subjective feelings as determinative of the spiritual value of glossolalia.

Glossolalists will occasionally say that if one has not experienced the phenomenon, one is not in a position to evaluate it. It may be said with equal validity that the person who has experienced the phenomenon may tend to place undue significance on the feelings of well-being that accompany speaking in tongues. To repeat, subjective experience cannot alone determine the value of any phenomenon.

Observation five: The interpretation of tongues raises many questions.

The interpretation of tongues is numbered among the gifts of the Spirit in 1 Corinthians 12:10. Often when someone speaks in tongues during a religious meeting, someone else gets up to report to the group what he understands the tongue-speaker to be saying. The interpreter has a strong conviction that he knows at least the substance of what is being said by the tongue-speaker.

Fewer people claim the gift of interpreting tongues than there are persons who are able to speak in tongues. Only a few persons report that they have the ability both to speak in tongues and to interpret what one's own tongue-speech means, as well as the meaning of some other person's tongue-speaking.

St. Paul in 1 Corinthians 14:26 advises that there be only two or three persons at a meeting who speak in tongues, and that one person interpret the tongue-speaking. He goes on to say that if no one is there to interpret, then the tongue-speakers should keep silence in the church and speak in tongues only to themselves. This pattern is generally followed in neo-Pentecostal meetings. However, there are occasional mass meetings where dozens or even hundreds of persons may speak in tongues all at the same time, and there is no attempt to make individual interpretations of the individual tongue-speaker's words.

Most persons who interpret glossolalia offer interpretations which are quite general. After a tongue-speaker has spoken for several minutes, a typical interpretation might summarize what the tongue-speaker has said in just a few sentences. Most of the interpretations offer the view that the tongue-speaker has been praising and thanking God. Another general theme is that the tongue-speaker has been asking for help, guidance, and strength.

But sometimes—and it may be about one-third of the time—an interpreter will offer very specific interpretations of what the tongue-speaker has been saying. More rarely, the interpreter will translate phrase by phrase what the tongue-speaker has been saying. My colleagues and I have witnessed occasions when the interpreter interspersed his interpretation as the tongue-speaker paused for a comma or a period. It is a remarkable experience to witness this kind of interpretation, because the interpreter implies that he or she knows exactly what is being said, and does not appear to be confused or uncertain about the meaning of each individual word or phrase. We have witnessed occasions when the interpreter's own emotion appeared to reflect the emotion of the tongue-speaker. When we asked how the interpreter knew exactly what each syllable or word meant, we received only general answers about how the interpreter viewed his ability to interpret as he was doing. He simply had a conviction that such and such a phrase meant a certain thing.

Because of our curiosity about these literal translations of tongue-speaking, we wanted to investigate the accuracy of these interpretations. We therefore played taped examples of tongue-speech privately for several different interpreters of tongues. In no instance was there any similarity in the several interpretations given by the interpreters who claimed to do a literal translation of the tongue-speech. For example, a tape recorded sample of Mr. Jones' glossolalia was taken to three different persons who claimed the gift of interpretation of tongues. One interpreter was convinced that the tongue-speaker was seeking guidance about a new job offer, and another interpreter reported that the same speech was a prayer of thanksgiving for one's recent return to health after a serious illness.

We explained to the different interpreters that someone else had offered a different interpretation of the same example of glossolalia. Without hesitation or defensiveness, the interpreter said that God gave to one interpreter one interpretation, and gave to another interpreter another interpretation. We then asked the tongue-speaker himself what he felt that he was saying, and as is usually the case the tongue-speaker reported that he himself did not know what he was saying. He was uttering things beyond his own understanding; God was giving him a blessing that was beyond his own intellectual understanding of what was happening.

I have gained the impression that interpreters who translate tongue-speech literally are often poorly integrated psychologically. Their view of their gift of interpretation borders on the grandiose. This impression has not been tested clinically, and I offer it to the reader simply to see whether it coincides with the general impression left by this type of interpretation of tongues.

The following example, which I have reported elsewhere,[7] sheds further light on the nature of the interpretation of tongues. We know a man who was raised in Africa, the son of missionary parents, who decided to test the interpretation of tongues. He attended a tongue-speaking meeting where he was a complete stranger. At the appropriate moment, he rose and spoke the Lord's Prayer in the African dialect he had learned in his youth. When he sat down, an interpreter of tongues offered the meaning of what he had said. The interpreter reported that it was a message about the imminent second coming of Christ.

Observation six: Glossolalic speech is not a natural, human language.

Two important questions may be asked in reference to whether tongue-speaking is an actual human language. First, are there examples of tongue-speech which can be translated by a person who knows the language that the person is speaking? Second, do linguists report that tongue-speech has the qualities of human language?

When a person speaks in tongues, it generally sounds like a foreign language to a person who is not familiar with what is being said. The speaker's fluency gives the impression that he is speaking with certainty and with feeling. The sounds appear to a nonlinguist to have the rhythm and the other qualities of a language. And it does not appear possible for the average person consciously to duplicate the fluency and the structure of tongue-speaking. No two persons sound exactly alike when they speak in tongues. It is as if each person were speaking a different language.

Because it sounds so much like a language, there are many reports that glossolalic speech must indeed be a language spoken, say, in Africa, or in some other remote area of the world. Most people who have contact with glossolalia have heard reports that a tongue-speaker had been speaking in

---

[7]*The Psychology of Speaking in Tongues*, p. 63.

Egyptian, or in some Hindu dialect, etc. The story usually goes something like this: A visitor from abroad dropped in on a religious service where tongue-speaking was in progress, and reported hearing his own language spoken by a person who had spent all his or her life in the United States and had never had any contact with the visitor's native language. The report develops that the tongue-speaker was indeed speaking the visitor's language.

Such stories are numerous. However, to the best of our knowledge, these reports are always thirdhand. Someone tells the story about someone else having heard that this was indeed the case. There are no reported instances of a glossolalist speaking a language which was then literally translated by an expert in that language. Of the hundreds of thousands of occasions on which glossolalia has been uttered, there is no tape recording that can be translated from a language spoken somewhere in the world. My point is this: If glossolalic utterances were somehow real languages, it would seem that there would exist somewhere in the world evidence that the speaking in tongues was in fact in such a foreign language.

The second question that concerns us here is whether or not tape recorded examples of glossolalia resemble a natural language. This is a technical linguistic question and the reader is encouraged to refer to the Nida and Samarin material in the bibliography.

Linguists begin with a definition of a natural human language and then see how tongue-speech does or does not meet the criteria implied in the definition of a natural human language. One of the basic methods for characterizing a language is that of Charles F. Hockett.[8] He has suggested sixteen defining features as the universals of a language. He calls them design features of a language, and reports that these sixteen features exist in every language on which we have reliable information. Without describing here what those features are, we may observe that by these standards tongue-speech is not human language. The absence of many of these sixteen features is sufficient to demonstrate the non-linguisticality of glossolalia. The evidence indicates that tongue-speech is not a language spoken anywhere in the world. Some tongue-speakers have countered that perhaps glosso-

---

[8]See Hockett, "The Problem of Universals in Language," *Universals of Language*, ed. J. H. Greenberg (Cambridge, 1963).

lalia is an example of the speech spoken by the angels. We have no answer for that.

Observation seven: Tongue-speakers reported the following positive results:

One of the positive results reported by tongue-speakers was personal happiness. Almost invariably, they said they were more cheerful, more joyful and more optimistic as a result of speaking in tongues. They were less depressed and less pessimistic and had a pervading sense of God's presence and strength within themselves.

In addition to happiness, most tongue-speakers reported a sense of greater personal power. They were more self-confident in interpersonal relationships. They felt bolder and took more risks, whether in their business dealings, or in their marriage relationships, or in witnessing to their faith. Tongue-speakers reported a sense of purposefulness in their lives which provided a feeling of security about who they were and about what they were doing. Often they expressed a sense that God had touched them significantly and they were therefore sure that they were significant people and were doing significant things in the world.

Religious convictions were held more firmly and played a larger part in their lives. They reported a maturing of their own religious and spiritual insights. This was expressed through an intense desire that their friends and fellow church members pursue the same experience. The presence of God in their lives seemed to be a central reality in their existence. Spiritual factors played a large role in almost every conversation with them. Life was most often viewed in spiritual terms, and the jargon of religion was almost always a part of any conversation, regardless of the subject under discussion.

The personal fellowship among tongue-speakers seemed to be joyful and warm. Their sense of community with each other appeared to be genuine and intense. Persons of different intellectual capacities or socio-economic background seemed to be at home with each other. It appeared that their common overwhelming spiritual experience surmounted other barriers of background or class.

However difficult it may be to survey or measure, it seemed that glossolalists had tremendous love and concern and care for one another. According to their own reports, their ways of dealing with life had indeed changed significantly since their experience with glossolalia. They all seemed to report that being filled with the Spirit had made them better able

to cope with frustration, and better able to show greater patience and stability in dealing with others.

Observation eight: The following negative results have often been observed in persons who speak in tongues:

Dependency on the leader who introduced the person to tongue-speaking is a prominent factor. Submission to the leader is a necessary factor in
the induction in tongue-speaking, and often that dependency continues. The
dependence on the leader is then often extended or transferred to a dependence on a group of fellow tongue-speakers. This dependency produces a
provincialism among tongue-speakers which isolates them from influences that might give them a more balanced perspective. Many members
of tongue-speaking groups are reluctant to make life decisions without getting the permission of their leader or of fellow members of the group. This
dependency may often be a form of immaturity in which one is unable to
see oneself as an independent and autonomous person. At times, mutual
dependency seems to be a mark of the personal insecurity of tongue-speakers.

A special problem is presented by the fact that most tongue-speakers
are initiated to this experience after a severe identity crisis. After a profound crisis in which one has nearly lost his moorings in life, the onset of
tongue-speaking often is experienced as the rescue from an abyss. One's
whole life may begin to revolve around this experience, often with a mil-
itant defensiveness against any self-examination. A few seriously upset
persons have sought to keep their personal and professional heads above
water by clinging to tongue-speaking. In my opinion, this is the situation
among some clergy who have been impervious to the counseling of their
fellow clergy. Some clergy seem to prefer masochistically to split congregations and terminate their own pastorates rather than cooperate with the
guidance or proposals made by their bishops. Such extreme instances are
few, but it should be noted that this may be a sign of emotional instability.
It is an evidence of how a religious context can be used in the service of
one's neurotic or even psychotic needs.

Some tongue-speakers view the way in which God directs their lives
as almost magical. Viewed from the standpoint of science, glossolalists give
an "irrational" explanation for what they are doing. That is, the explanation offered is that the Holy Spirit is giving the movement to the tongue
and the sounds to the speech. This explanation is unverifiable from a scientific point of view. Because of this private type of explanation, it is often

difficult to communicate with tongue-speakers. When they say, for example, that God gave them the message, or God spoke to them through glossolalia and it was interpreted by someone else as meaning that they should follow a certain course of action, this is difficult to discuss. There is an exclusiveness to the glossolalia experience that tends to alienate tongue-speakers from discourse with a wider community.

Tongue-speaking is a divisive influence in many congregations. In fact, one bishop of a mainline Protestant denomination, who has asked to remain anonymous, has said that it is the unanimous view of bishops in his church that tongue-speaking has been a divisive influence in every congregation where it has been introduced. The charismatic movement has not made for easy compromise or impartiality. More often it has polarized congregations. In many congregations, those persons who began to speak in tongues left their congregation and went to another or formed a new congregation. The great visibility of the charismatic movement has caused battle lines to be quickly formed. The tongue-speakers' experiences were so overwhelmingly powerful in most cases that they could not keep the experience to themselves. Causes for the divisiveness are the seemingly irrational nature of the act, and the specialness with which the tongue-speakers regard themselves and their gift.

It is easier to be tolerant of one's neighbor if he exhibits behavior that is commonplace and understandable. Tongue-speech is not commonplace, nor is it readily understandable. This makes for suspicion and distance.

Further, the language of the glossolalist serves to alienate him from others. Phrases such as "I have been filled with the Spirit," "I have a special gift from God," "I have had a new experience with God," imply that the listener perhaps is not filled with the Spirit or has not had an experience with God which is special. However careful tongue-speakers are to watch the way in which they describe themselves and others, they often nonetheless betray a subtle disrespect for non-tongue-speakers and towards those who show no interest in joining their group. Non-glossolalists usually report that they are made to feel somewhat inferior in the presence of a tongue-speaker.

Histrionic display is another negative feature of the glossolalia experience. It is evident in only a minority of the situations in which glossolalia is practiced. When speaking in tongues is followed by interpretation of tongues and then by prophecy, three experiences of a basically irrational nature are following one upon another. One cannot critique the value of the sounds glossolalists make; one cannot criticize the interpreter of tongues; and when someone offers a sentence or a paragraph of prophecy, again the speaker will offer the explanation that this is indeed a gift of the Spirit, and the gift was just given to him to say what he just said.

The critic of the movement may offer the explanation that things are not being done decently and in order, nor do the events seem to be edifying the church as a whole. But the person who feels that he has the gift of the Spirit may be impervious to these critiques.

Observation nine: What are the criteria by which glossolalia should be evaluated? A minor criterion is whether it has an upbuilding and uplifting effect on oneself. The major criterion is whether it edifies the community as a whole.

While the fact that tongue-speakers feel good is important, it must be kept in mind that many experiences in life can make one feel good. A religious experience should measure itself by its fruit, and not simply by how it makes one feel. Because of the subjective nature of glossolalia, it is important that other observers contribute their evaluation of the experience and make an attempt objectively to evaluate both its positive and negative effects.

There is some truth to the claim that no one can truly evaluate an experience which he has not had himself. However, the converse is equally true: the person who has had the experience is often in a poor position to evaluate the very experience which he has had.

It is my personal opinion that the experience of glossolalia has the effect of being a security operation, as understood in the way in which Dr. Harry Stack Sullivan, the psychiatrist, used that term.[9] A security operation is a behavior that enables one to cope with anxiety and thus to feel more secure. Speaking in tongues often works as an effective security operation for people; when they do it, their fears and their feelings of worthlessness diminish and they feel much better.

In my opinion the obsessive use of glossolalia is an evidence of an underlying emotional disequilibrium. Those persons who use their tongue-speaking in a more responsible way are emotionally less needy in the first place. They are less likely to use their tongue-speech in the service of their own emotional problems.

---

[9]Sullivan, *The Interpersonal Theory of Psychiatry* (New York, 1953), p. 346.

It appears to me that the reason tongue-speakers feel so much better after they begin to do it is precisely that they have been going through a fundamental life-crisis and have found a security operation which makes them feel better by helping them to cope with their inner feelings of desperate loneliness or meaninglessness. If they become very dependent on tongue-speaking and the comradeship of a tongue-speaking community, this may indicate their great need for external sources of support by which they compensate for their own inner weaknesses.

In summary: My glossolalia research has convinced me that it is a learned behavior which can bring a sense of power and well-being. It may also lead to excesses resulting in community disruption. It is the use of glossolalia which determines whether or not it is constructive.

Micah said that true religion was to do justice, love kindness, and to walk humbly with God. If the practice of glossolalia produces these fruits, then it appears to me to be a responsible use of the experience.

20

JAMES T. RICHARDSON

Psychological Interpretations of Glossolalia: A Reexamination of Research

[Reprinted from *Journal for the Scientific Study of Religion* 12 (1973): 199-207. Reprinted with permission from Society of Scientific Study of Religion and the author.]

This paper reexamines a great deal of research that has dealt with psychological maladjustment and glossolalia, including more recent studies of tongue-speaking in middle- and upper-class groups. Issue is taken with the conclusion of some recent research that there is no relationship between psychological or personality factors and glossolalia. Some data commonly used to substantiate this conclusion is reexamined and found to support rather different conclusions, though many of the studies looked at are faulted on methodological grounds. Special attention is given to the much-cited but unpublished work of Lincoln Vivier. It is argued that misleading conclusions may have been drawn from this important study. Suggestions are made for further research on glossolalia that would allow more definitive conclusions to be reached.

Within the last few years much research has been conducted on the recent upsurge of tongue speaking or glossolalia.[1] This phenomenon, when it occurs among higher status groups, is referred to as the Charismatic Renewal or the Neo-Pentecostal movement. The research of Gerlach and Hine (Gerlach and Hine, 1968; Hine, 1970; Hine, 1969; Gerlach and Hine, 1970) and that of Kildahl (1972) and Samarin (1972) are examples of this increased interest in glossolalia. Close examination of some of this research reveals that there are some important differences of opinion about glossolalia. One important area of difference concerns the relationship of glossolalia to psychological maladjustment. The major task here will be to reexamine some evidence for psychologically related theories concerning glossolalia. It should be made explicit that this effort is not intended to discredit the research just cited; it is instead an attempt to build on this work.

PSYCHOLOGICAL INTERPRETATIONS

There is ample evidence that Cutten (1927) was wrong in his conclusions concerning the association of glossolalia with hysteria and schizophrenia, and Hine (1969) is apparently justified in stating this fact. Hine's assessment of the research of Alland (1967); Boisen (1939); Kiev (1964); Vivier (1960); Wood (1965); Plog (1965); Gerrard and Gerrard (1966), is that " . . . available evidence requires that an explanation of glossolalia as pathological must be discarded" (1969: 217).[2] This also seems to be the judgment of most of those such as Lapsley and Simpson (1964); Kelsey

---

[1]This paper is an attempt to review research that may help explain the causes of the Pentecostal (and especially the Neo-Pentecostal) movement. Therefore, much theological and historical writing on the subject of glossolalia will not be directly referenced. Impetus for this literature review came from research and unsystematic observation over several years of several groups practicing glossolalia. See Harder, Richardson, and Simmonds (1972) and Simmonds, Richardson and Harder (1972) for one such group. Research on other groups is in progress.

[2]Noting the tenacity of the notion of pathology as a correlate of glossolalia, Hine (1969: 218) suggests that "future studies of [glossolalia] might usefully include an examination of possible bias on the part of nonglossolalic observers." This point is similar to the comment by Stark (1971: 172) that " . . . . many social scientists are inclined to regard conservative religious beliefs as abnormal," because " . . . they find it difficult to imagine that a normal person could believe them." Stark does not mention glossolalia in his provocative paper, and one wonders whether he would include tongue-speaking as a conventional form of religious commitment.

(1968); Oates (1967); Plog (1965); Samarin (1972); and Hine who have investigated the more contemporary manifestations of tongue-speaking in middle- and upper-class groups.

It should be noted, however, that most researchers who reported *prior* to recent work such as Hine's, while discounting psychosis as associated with glossolalia, have certainly emphasized *psychological considerations* in attempting to explain why the phenomenon of speaking in tongues occurs. Kelsey (1968) has made an important contribution in this regard by presenting the largely unknown views of Jung on glossolalia. He indicates that Jung considered the experience of glossolalia to be " . . . a positive preparation for integration of personality" (1968: 199). After surveying the work of Jung and others, including Sargant (1949) and Vivier (1960), Kelsey (1968: 207-208) adds "Tongue speaking may well be an unconscious resolution to neurosis." He does, however, discount ties of glossolalia with hysteria, a form of neurosis. Oates (1967), in an analysis that focuses more directly on the verbalizing involved in glossolalia, seems to feel that the phenomenon of tongue-speaking may arise from deep-felt personality needs resulting from aspects of the cultural milieu.

Lapsley and Simpson (1964: 20-21), in an earlier report *not* cited by Hine, also stress the psychological aspects of the glossolalia experience. They believe on the basis of some research and an examination of other work such as Vivier (1960), that

> Glossolalia is understood to be a regression in the service of the ego. . . . That is, regression controlled by the ego and for the purpose of maintaining personality, rather than a disintegration of personality. It is a genuine escape from inner conflict . . . [glossolalia] is likely to be of benefit to emotionally labile, disturbed persons who have internalized their emotional conflicts, in that it provides a unique kind of release.

Pattison (1968: 76), in another prior report not cited by Hine, admitted that his research is not systematic, but nevertheless claimed to have found a general tendency in lower- and lower-middle class persons in both rural and urban areas for such glossolalists to demonstrate "overt psychopathology of a sociopathic, hysterical, or hypochondriacal nature." He claimed, however, that his interviews with middle- and upper-class glossolalists "demonstrated no psychopathology. They were well integrated, highly functional individuals who were clinically 'normal.' " His report tells us too little about his research for a thorough evaluation. However, it does in part seem contrary to the view of Hine.

One study reported *after* Hine wrote also concluded that glossolalia has psychological implications. Kildahl (1972: 58), who focused on Neo-Pentecostalism, says, "Preoccupation with internal psychological factors seemed to create the necessary atmosphere in which a person was ready to speak in tongues." His research revealed that glossolalics tended to be submissive, suggestible, and dependent on authority figures.

Because of the ostensible differences of opinion between researchers concerning the relationship between glossolalia and mental health, a reexamination of some of the research cited by Hine and others may be fruitful. First, we will examine the research cited by Hine.

Most of the research cited by Hine can be criticized because the study designs were inadequate for the gathering of definite evidence.[3] No piece of the research cited incorporated a time-series design, with control groups, that would be required to establish sound findings (cf. Campbell and Stanley [1963] for a discussion of this and other study designs). More simply stated, no research to date has assessed the personality characteristics of a set of potential converts to a tongue-speaking group, and then followed them up after conversion in order to assess (1) whether or not psychological changes had taken place, and (2) what types of changes had occurred.

Alland's work (1967) utilizes a "one-shot" design (cf. Campbell and Stanley, 1963: 6) with no control group, and while the findings are interesting and probably largely true, they do not represent strong evidence for Hine's conclusion. Alland says, "Receptivity to trance is most certainly influenced by personality differences" (1967: 92), and he earlier had made reference to "neurotic patterns emerging from guilt and anxiety in the Negro church community" which serve as a basis for personality traits associated with susceptibility to trance (1967: 90). Thus, although Alland emphasizes the fact that a simple learning model explains *how* the members of the Negro church participate in "possession," he seems to assume a psychological explanation to explain *why* the members participate.

Boisen (1939) also does not employ a complete design, although his research involves some comparisons with persons (all mental patients)

---

[3]This is not to imply that the research designs of other researchers not cited by Hine are better. Sound research in such an area as this is rare.

outside the church group studied. His research does not allow personality assessment of participants *previous to affiliation*, or any changes that might have occurred in the participants' personalities. Wood (1965: 107) says that "Boisen . . . believes that all deep religious experiences spring from the drive to reintegrate the personality and the personality's relationships with people and values." Thus, we are forced to reconsider the meaning of the finding of Boisen that there was no evidence of mental illness in the tongue-speakers from the church. This finding says nothing about the mental health of the tongue-speakers *prior* to their tongue-speaking experience that led to entrance into the church. In fact, implied in Boisen's approach is the understanding that entrance into the church, with its accompanying experiences, did effect changes in the personality structures of the participants. Hine (1969: 213) states that Boisen " . . . found that for the most part the experience was therapeutic . . . ," which may imply some changes in the psychological structure of the participants.

The study of Kiev (1964b) that Hine cites also involves a comparison of "normal" Pentecostals with mental patients. His study does not allow definitive statements about the effect of conversion and participation on the immigrants who are his population of study. In another paper dealing with West Indian immigrants in England (Kiev, 1964a), he apparently allows for and assumes that participation can and does serve a therapeutic function, although he admits explicitly that he has no evidence that speaks to the question. A lengthy quote will illustrate the point.

> Although there is no evidence that emotional instability is a necessary ingredient for participation in the services, behavioral patterns institutionalized in the meetings are sufficiently broad as to provide suitable channels for the expression of a variety of needs and personality traits. For the depressed and guilt-ridden the sin-cathartic basis of the ideology and services provides a useful guilt-reducing device; for the hysteric a socially acceptable model for acting out; and for the obsessional the encouragement of a reduction of inhibitions and increased emotionality. For the accompaniments of neurotic and real suffering as feelings of inferiority, self-consciousness, suspiciousness and anxiety, the social aspects of the movement would seem of value. [Kiev, 1964a:135]

Kiev adds (1964a:136) that since most of the West Indian immigrants involved had been exposed to fundamentalist beliefs from early childhood, their participation "seems likely to play a role in the reduction of anxieties." Thus, Kiev seems to assume some psychological reasons for participation by the West Indian immigrants in the Pentecostals sects.

The largely unreported research of Plog (1965), while representing perhaps the largest single study of Pentecostals (and one of the few focusing primarily on Neo-Pentecostals) that has been done to date (over 800 subjects), also does not allow a longitudinal analysis because his respondents all answered the questions only once—after they were participants in a Pentecostal group. He relies on retrospection (as do several others in this area), which is thought by some to be a weak method of gathering information with which to test hypotheses. Reliance on this method may be especially problematic in this instance because the ideology of the tongue-speakers constrains them to believe that they have undergone change through their affiliation experience. This constraint would probably compound the usual kind of selective perception error into a full-blown case of what Berger (1963: 54-65) calls the "reconstruction of biography." As it is, Plog does find some evidence for improved interpersonal relationships in the lives of group members, a finding with intriguing possibilities.

Wood (1965), who is given credit by Hine (1969:215) for making ". . . . an important and little-reorganized point that his study provides no information about whether the 'Pentecostal type' is attracted to or developed by participation in the (Pentecostal) movement," raised some interesting questions with his research. He compared, using Rorschach techniques, members of a Pentecostal group with members of a non-Pentecostal group. He finds several differences between his Pentecostal group and the non-Pentecostal group members from the same general geographical area and same cultural milieu. Realizing the tentativeness of his results, Wood (1965:92-96) states his findings in the form of hypotheses, some of which will be quoted.

H1   Pentecostal people lack an adequately structured value-attitude system.

H2   Pentecostal people are mobilizing their inner resources to meet the strongly felt threat of instability in their value-attitude systems and their social relationships; they are in the process of reorganizing their basic perceptual patterns.

H4   Pentecostal people have an uncommon degree of uncertainty concerning interpersonal relationships.

H6   Pentecostal people have a strong drive to feel close fellowship with others but they are uncertain that these interpersonal involvements will be satisfactory.

H7   Pentecostalism attracts uncertain, threatened, inadequately organized persons with strong motivation to reach a state of satisfactory interpersonal relatedness and personal integrity.

H8   Pentecostalism provides patterns of behavior leading to personality integration, interpersonal relatedness and certainty.

H13   Religious enthusiasm is one solution to sociocultural situations in which cases of personality disorganization are widespread.

H14   It would be possible to predict from Rorschach protocols those people who would respond favorably to a Pentecostal campaign conducted in a socially disorganized, lower-class, southern, Protestant neighborhood.

H15   Adherents of a sedate, legalistic Christian sect will reveal a Rorschach protocol different from the protocols found for Pentecostal adherents.

These tentative statements do not, of course, indicate that adherents suffer from severe mental disorders. However, it is plain that Wood does believe that there may be psychologically-based reasons for the participation of individuals in a movement such as Pentecostalism.

The work of Vivier (1960), which is also discussed by Kelsey (1968) and by several others, appears to be some of the best research done on glossolalia to date. However, the full potential of the study has not been taken advantage of by the author and others and what has been reported has been somewhat misinterpreted. Vivier uses two control groups: "... . twenty non-tongue speaking Pentecostals (or pre-tongue speakers) and twenty members of a Christian church who did not approve of or practice glossolalia" (Hine, 1969:214). Results for these two groups on a great number of psychological and other tests are compared to those of an "experimental group" made up of twenty-four glossolalics. What Hine, Lapsley and Simpson, Samarian and Kelsey fail to report in their discussion of Vivier's work is that the control and experimental groups are *not independent* of one another. In fact, Vivier (whose research is an unpublished dissertation and must be obtained on microfilm) points out that *fifteen of the twenty-four glossolalics were originally members of the non-Pentecostal church which furnished subjects for the non-tongue-speaking control group. Also, eleven of the members of the control group of pre-tongue speakers were originally members of the non-Pentecostal church.* Thus, twenty-six of the forty-four pre- and postglossolalics studied came from one church, a church which was doctrinally opposed to speaking in tongues. This information causes a complete reconsideration of Vivier's results and the interpretations of them that have been presented by Hine and Kelsey. Vivier has, either by design or accident, completed the beginnings of a possibly classic study. He has gathered information (a great deal of it) on persons that are in various stages of the *process* of moving from one religious community to another that sanctions an activity (glossolalia) which was precluded in the original group. This interpretation is given some support by Vivier's statement that the control group made up of pre-glossolalics is significantly younger than the glossolalic group itself.

A number of questions arise with this realization. Why did certain persons select themselves out to start the movement from one group to the other? Which persons now members of the non-Pentecostal church will move into the Pentecostal church in the future? What factors are associated with this movement? What effect does movement from one group to the other have in terms of changing the lives of the participants? These and many other questions will have to await a possible follow-up report from Vivier—a report which this writer hopes will be forthcoming.

Some tentative answers to a few such questions can be garnered from the original study report, especially if one assumes the new perspective that would interpret the research from the "process" point of view, which would suggest that the glossolalics have completed the process of moving from the traditional non-Pentecostal church into regular tongue speaking (Vivier reports that eighteen of the glossolalics report speaking in tongues daily). These tentative answers can best be presented by material taken directly from Vivier. It should be noted that the material will appear somewhat at odds with the interpretations given by some reporters.

First, Vivier indicates that the Test Group (glossolalics) are from a home atmosphere which was more "disturbed," and in which there was more psychopathology present (he specifically mentions alcohol, epilepsy, nervous breakdowns, and admission to mental hospitals). He also notes that members of the Test Group had more initial problems in marriage, but that these problems were obviated by the joint conversion to Pentecostalism of the spouses. The Test Group was more anxious, had more difficulty in nervous control, was more superstitious, and, along with Group A (pre-glossolalics), was more instable. Contrary to the impression of the Hine report, the Test Group and Group A scored much higher on the Willoughby neuroticism test than did the members of Group B (nonglossolalics). The Test Group and Group a were ". . . . more likely to use the mechanism of repression in frustrating situations" and "the factor of repression is associated with those people who 'Speak in Tongues' " (1960: 343-344).

Vivier, who analyzed his data according to frequency of glossolalia in the Test Group, says regarding the results of the TAT test that, "the 'frequency group' (daily) of glossolalics reflect a poorer frustration tolerance and a tendency to cling to objects in the environment for emotional support" (1960: 382). A lengthy quote from the conclusions section of Vivier's report will give the reader an overall feeling for the results of the research (1960: 432-433):

> Dynamically (glossolalics) can be considered as a group of people who, psychologically speaking, have had a poor beginning in life. This has been reflected by their difficulty in adjustment in the home situation in infancy and later adulthood. It can therefore be seen that they have been torn by insecurity, conflict, tension and emotional difficulties.
>
> Being troubled by doubt and fear, anxiety and stress, they have turned from the culturally accepted traditional, orthodox and formalized, to something that held out for them the unorthodox, the supernatural; to an environment of sensitiveness for emotional feelings and a group of people bound with the same purpose and clinging to each other for support.

Implicitly, Vivier seems to be assuming that certain factors have led to the self-selection of persons from the non-Pentecostal church who chose to move into the Pentecostal group. There is evidence for this view in the data, but only more thorough follow-up work (particularly on those of Group B—non-glossolalics—who might decide to "switch") will disallow an alternative explanation that the movement into Pentecostalism may have contributed to some of the difficulties discerned through testing procedures employed by Vivier.

The study of Gerrard and Gerrard (1966) is not readily accessible, but a brief description of their results appeared later (Gerrard, 1968). It appears as most thorough, and exceptional care was taken in the analysis of the results. However, the point must be made that the study did not incorporate a thorough analysis of the possible changes of personality occurring in persons as they became associated with the group and over time became complete converts to the group. What the group members were like *before* they joined the cult is an unanswered question that looms large for anyone attempting to explain the etiology of such groups and movements.

The criticisms of the research cited by Hine can also be made of most other research in the area. Many of the reports of research do not contain enough information about design and data gathering to allow evaluation, or they appear so subjective that conclusions drawn are questionable.

Without going into detail on specific studies, we would mention in this regard Lapsley and Simpson (1964); Kelsey (1968); Oates (1967); and Pattison (1968).

The work of Kildahl (1972) is somewhat better, in that two groups (one glossolalic and the other not) are compared on several standardized tests and through clinical interviews. However, the conclusions of the study, while intriguing, are based on a comparison of only the two groups (matched on some characteristics) of twenty people per group. This small data base, plus the fact that no time series data was used detracts greatly from the value of the study.

CONCLUSIONS ABOUT PSYCHOLOGICAL INTERPRETATIONS

Our examination of the research dealing with psychological interpretations of glossolalia has shown that little of it is sound enough to allow conclusions to be drawn concerning the issues involved. Apparently the weight of *opinion* (and some evidence such as Vivier's) seems to be in favor of some sort of psychologically-based explanation for the phenomenon, although most reject the idea that serious mental health deficiencies are always present with glossolalia.[4] Thus, Hine's statement about the nonpathological nature of glossolalia seems acceptable, but we would not agree with what may be an implied lack of connection between the occurrence of glossolalia and certain psychological states in individuals.[5]

One major hindrance to resolving the question is the tremendous conceptual difficulty in this area. Stark's (1971: 167) comment to this effect is worth noting: "There are perhaps no more elusive and value-laden concepts in social science than mental illness, insanity, neurosis, inadequacy, and other terms referring to various forms and degrees of psychopathology." We would add that the line between some areas of what are usually

---

[4]It should also be understood, of course, that even if definite ties between psychological conditions and glossolalia were established, this would not constitute a complete explanation of the phenomenon of glossolalia. A fuller explanation would probably require moving to another level of abstraction—that is, to structural analysis. This we plan to do in a future paper.

[5]Our conclusions are quite similar to those of Lewis (1971), who presents a comparative study of spirit possession and shamanism among "primitive" groups. His chapter entitled "Possession and Psychiatry" is insightful for the purposes of this paper, particularly if glossolalia is treated as one form of spirit possession.

termed psychopathology and simple psychological needs and drives that might serve as motivating factors for individuals is sometimes difficult to discern. The question of the part played by specifically psychological states in gathering and sustaining the tongues movement is still an open one.

IDEAS FOR FURTHER RESEARCH

Throughout this paper we have criticized previous research in the area of glossolalia. Implicit in the criticism has been a call for sound research which would allow more definitive conclusions to be drawn about the phenomenon. Now we would like to be specific about what we feel would be the best ways to proceed with the research. Plainly the "one-shot" study design is deficient, and we must move far beyond it for more understanding. We thus strongly recommend longitudinal research designs that allow some assessment of change over time. Long-term studies would be preferred, but even follow-up work of several months' duration might yield valuable knowledge. Adequate instruments about which there is intersubjective agreement concerning validity would, of course, be essential to any such project. The administration of such instruments even over a period of months might allow researchers to "catch" persons as they move from the "pre-glossolalic" stage to the "glossolalic," and from the "infrequent glossolalic" to the "frequent glossolalic." Personality changes associated with these significant movements deeper into tongue-speaking would thus be more readily ascertained.

An even more valuable way of proceeding would be to find a situation similar to that used (but not fully appreciated) by Vivier (1960) in his research. If a research could document that most of the glossolalics in a population of study were coming from one source, then this would allow the possibility of going to the source and administering instruments in anticipation of further movement into the glossolalic group. This type of research where potential glossolalics are isolated and studied could yield the most information about psychological variables associated with this type of movement. Perhaps Vivier will take advantage of the remarkable situation that he has uncovered, and do follow-up work on the groups involved. If he does not, then such a task will be left to others to accomplish.

21

RICHARD A. HUTCH

The Personal Ritual of Glossolalia

[Reprinted with permission from *Journal for the Scientific Study of Religion*, 19 (1980): 255-66. Reprinted with permission from Society for the Scientific Study of Religion and the author.]

Research on tongue-speaking is surveyed, and its methodological assumptions are suggested. These assumptions are threefold, concerning how psychologists, sociologists, and anthropologists believe glossolalia functions: Some believe it to be aberrant behaviour; others think of it as extraordinary behaviour; and still others regard it as anomalous behaviour. Examples of these positions are given, their shortcomings are presented, and a fourth methodological paradigm is offered as a corrective: Glossolalia is seen as ritual behaviour which aims, first, to amalgamate the sounds of crying and laughing, which are symbols of hurt and joy in life, and, second, it thereby points to conditions of existence, that is, to death and birth in life. Thus, tongue-speaking is a ritual process wherein a "scanning" of one's phenomenal world takes place, useful in facilitating the biological survival of the individual.

Three major studies of religious tongue-speaking were published in 1972, each representing a dominant and persistent style of research for analyzing the phenomenon of glossolalia. These publications were, *The Psychology of Speaking in Tongues* by John Kildahl; *Speaking in Tongues: A Cross-Cultural Study of Glossolalia* by Felicitas Goodman; and *Tongues of Men and Angels* by William Samarin. Kildahl's work, focusing on the personal experiences of individuals, suggests that tongue-speaking is most usefully studied when compared with varieties of aberrant behaviour, like neuroses and other psychogenic disorders of different kinds. Goodman says that tongue-speaking is extraordinary behaviour, usually associated with altered states of consciousness which are culturally patterned and beneficial to society. The third publication lays emphasis neither on the aberrant aspects of glossolalic behaviour, nor on its extraordinary features. Rather, Samarin views tongue-speaking as anomalous behavior because it departs from run-of-the-mill speech by being nonlinguistic in nature. He believes that glossolalic utterances are neither abnormal, pathological, nor always an expression of an altered state of consciousness. This paper argues that the work of each representative researcher fails to come to grips directly with the experience of tongue-speaking as a patently personal religious phenomenon. The three research foci have precluded an exploration of the religious function of glossolalia in the life of the individual.

Put more positively, this paper presents the view that glossolalia functions symbolically in the very same way as religious rituals like the Christian eucharist. Rituals not only describe a person's relationship to the sacred, but they also aim at eliciting some experiential sense of confirmation about the nature of one's religious beliefs. Thus, ritual behavior becomes valuable, normative. On the basis of a review of the works cited above and subsequent research spawned by them, shortcomings of regarding tongue-speaking as aberrant, extraordinary, and anomalous behavior will be pointed out. After such a review and critique, a consideration of the ritual nature of tongue-speaking will be posed. This involves a descriptive understanding of the sound of tongues as a ritualized amalgamation of crying and laughing, which are non-linguistic expressions of two very basic modes of human feeling and relating to the world. I shall argue that glossolalia functions as an exploratory rehearsal of the experiential parameters which give rise to abstract, cognitive efforts to make sense out of a wide range of situations of extreme hurt and intense joy. Overall, the argument is that the charismatic and the non-charismatic Christian and non-Christian function alike in response to a shared existential condition symbolized by the sounds of glossolalia.

ABERRANT BEHAVIOUR

The bulk of research on tongue-speaking centers around the aberrant behaviour focus and can be placed into two groups. The first is related to the depth-psychological tradition, and is usually expressed in terms of recent theories of American egopsychology, especially theories of regression and narcissism. The second kind of research is concerned with empirical investigation into kinds of tongue-speaking experiences and whether such experiences serve to disintegrate or integrate the personality. Both types of work stem from assumptions associated with aberrant, or socially useless (and, often, antisocial) behaviour about which consideration of the possible attenuation of mature ego-control is the predominant feature.

John Kildahl's work exemplifies the ego-psychological viewpoint, which assumes that temporary regressions serve the growth of the ego. The key assumption is that ego control is somehow suspended, and the speaker is led to assume he has been seized by an agency totally other than himself. Kildahl offers an example of a thirty-one-year-old man named Bill. At the start, the charismatic leader "lays hands" on Bill and says to him, "Say after me what I say, and then go on speaking in the tongue that the Lord will give you. . . . Aish, nay gum nay tayo . . . " (Kildahl, 1972:3). Bill proceeds to follow the instructions in a deliberate, self-conscious manner, imitating the leader's utterances until, as Kildahl puts it, "he simply uttered the strange sounds as they came to him *without knowing how they came*" (Kildahl, 1972:3). The most noteworthy point is that the subject was in control of the process at the outset but, according to Kildahl, somehow became less in control of the event of speaking as, evidently, he claimed to have no knowledge of how the sounds came to him. In spite of the possibility that such phrasing (e.g., "aish, nay, gum, tayo. . . .") may be a routine and inherited verbal formula derived or fabricated on the spot from the subject's social and cultural circumstances, a distinct kind of psychological analysis holds sway. By assuming that at some point in the process of tongue-speaking a person loses all or part of the control of his speech to the unconscious, a correlation with aberrant behaviour becomes possible. In this sense tongue-speaking is likened to psychopathology, abnormality. Now we can turn to consider empirical studies which imply a research paradigm of aberrant behaviour.

Perhaps the latest definitive survey of psychological aspects of glossolalia and how they have been studied is by James Richardson (1973). He acknowledges that much empirical research on tongue-speaking reveals important differences of opinion, one of which concerns the relationship of glossolalia to psychological maladjustment. He points out, however, that in recent studies the growing tendency is toward explanations of health, not pathology. For example, Morton Kelsey, a Jungian, suggests that tongue-speaking may well be ''an unconscious resolution to neurosis'' (Kelsey, 1968: 207-208). Healthy glossolalia also is thought to be ''a genuine escape from inner conflict. . . . likely to be of benefit to emotionally labile, disturbed persons who have internalized their emotional conflicts, in that it provides a unique kind of release'' (Lapsley & Simpson, 1964: 20-21). The intensity of such a release can be defined as pathological only in lower-middle class persons in urban and rural areas, but the same label would be inapplicable for upper class glossolaliacs (Pattison, 1968: 73-78). Richardson, however, is less concerned with deciding whether glossolaliacs are suffering from clinical psychopathology or enhanced mental health than he is with weighing the adequacy of researchers' experimental designs and subsequent findings.

Richardson concludes that most of the studies he surveyed were plainly of the ''one-shot study design'' in that they emphasized a synchronic analysis of data accumulated from questionnaire responses of glossolaliacs. Richardson called for more diachronic studies, ''longitudinal designs that allow some assessment of change over time'' (Richardson, 1973: 206). Diachronic studies would facilitate a deeper ascertainment of possible personality changes as one moved from being pre-glossolaliac to glossolaliac, even to post-glossolaliac. In 1977 Richardson's recommendation was taken seriously by other researchers who reported diachronic findings (Lovekin & Malony, 1977). Recent empirical studies of glossolalia are summarized and reach their high water mark with the appearance of this work. Lovekin and Malony found little support for asserting that becoming glossolaliac significantly integrates the personality, or that it resolves neurosis and re-establishes ego control. Where group rather than individual experience was gauged, however, the group experience, not the individual act of becoming glossolaliac itself, proved to cause changes in personality integration and, thus, to lead to greater mental health. Group interaction fosters ''greater ego strength, and fewer reported problems'' for participants (Lovekin & Malony, 1977: 391). An interesting additional finding was that those of the pre-glossolalic group who did *not* eventually become glossolalic evidenced higher ratings on state anxiety, hostility, and depression scales. Lovekin and Malony have improved the scope of studies of glossolalia. But even with a more sophisticated research design, which involves a longitudinal framework, their data also turn on the assumption that tongue-speaking is associated with degrees of aberrant behaviour, or at least with less than maximal psychological functioning.

EXTRAORDINARY BEHAVIOUR

Two factors distinguish studies of glossolalia which understand tongue-speaking as a kind of altered state of consciousness, or what some refer to as extraordinary behaviour, from studies in which the aberrant behaviour paradigm is predominant. First, whilst the aberrant behaviour paradigm focuses on individual and intrapsychic regression, the extraordinary behaviour paradigm dwells almost exclusively on society and broad cultural meanings associated with the practice of tongue-speaking in Christian as well as in non-Christian religious traditions. The study by Lovekin and Malony cited above indicates that the charismatic group, not the individual's act of becoming glossolaliac, is the key to the so-called healthy aspect of the practice. The experiential quality of tongue-speaking for the individual is down-played. The extraordinary behaviour paradigm assumes that the production of glossolalia is due largely to various groups in the process of ritualizing (e.g., praying together), institutionalizing (e.g., continuing prayer fellowships), and, thus, culturally elaborating upon the experiences of individuals. The locus of action is not intrapsychic processes in an individual tongue-speaker, but the interaction between the tongue-speaker, others, and the social and cultural forms according to which the group stylizes the practice. Moreover, Goodman suggests that ''the glossolalist speaks the way he does because his speech behaviour is modified by the way the body acts in the particular mental state, often termed trance, into which he places himself'' (Goodman, 1972: 8). Such states are traditionally defined dispositional elements of one's cultural legacy, to be used or not; for example, frenzy, delirium, drunkenness, guilt, work ethic, and so on. In spite of the experiential quality of these altered states of consciousness, Goodman stresses the social approbation received by those states associated with glossolalic practice.

The second factor which makes the paradigm of extraordinary behaviour unique is the implication that full ego-control is maintained during tongue-speaking. The culturally defined trance or altered state of mind which Goodman considers essential for glossolalia is a condition into which the glossolaliac, she says, "places himself." She suggests that a deliberate choice occurs from within a framework of ordinary consciousness. One may raise an eyebrow of doubt or consternation about the self-conscious control with which glossolalia may be experienced, especially since, as Goodman would have it, glossolalia is "an artifact . . . of the altered state of consciousness" (Goodman, 1972: 8). How can ego-control be maintained if one is in a trance? Does not an altered state of consciousness preclude self-conscious choice or, at least, deliberate structuring of perception? In other words, how can it be that although "seized" by the "Spirit," a charismatic, nonetheless, is fully in control of the experience of glossolalia? In order to consider these questions we must temporarily turn from Goodman's work to a subsidiary consideration of altered states of consciousness in themselves, viewed from an allied field of research.

According to recent work on the nature of human consciousness, all experience has been found to be "statebound" (Tart, 1973, 1975, 1975a; Ornstein, 1972). This means that consciousness, including what researchers labouring under the assumptions of the aberrant behaviour paradigm would call the "unconscious," arises from two things: First, subcortical arousal; either an increase ("ecstasy") or a decrease ("tranquility") in the sensory and electrical-chemical stimulation of one's sympathetic nervous system and overall psychic state is necessary. Second, also required is cortical (cognitive) interpretation of that arousal, which involves various degrees of conceptual and abstract thought under the control of prevailing cultural forms and symbols and their variations. Experience is essentially symbolic and necessarily state-bound—it can be invoked in its specific instances only by inducing a particular level of arousal, or by presenting some symbol of its interpretation such as an image, a melody, or a taste. The coupling together of arousal levels and interpretations articulates various levels of human consciousness (Fischer, 1971, 1975; Goodwin, 1969). Hence, when I bite into a peach on a warm summer day I allow myself to be bound in a state of consciousness significantly altered by imagery which floods from the past, when I placed myself in the same situation as a young boy in my father's orchard.

Goodman and others who labour with the paradigm of extraordinary behaviour are saying that a tongue-speaker controls his ego-state by the deliberate induction of levels of subcortical arousal, and by self-consciously employing formal cortical (social and cultural) interpretations of arousal levels so as to ''expand,'' as it were, ''consciousness.'' Cast in the glossolaliac's own words, the following description of such cognitive coupling is apt.

> I had heard about the gift of tongues, and my first reaction was that this was meaningless sound, like word-salad or syllable-salad. The more I thought about it, the more real God became, the more a real possibility it seemed. It became very plausible. When I was prayed over (for the Baptism), I asked for the gift of tongues. I didn't speak in tongues at that time. A couple of people were confident that I had the gift but just hadn't used it. I was attending a concert four or five days later—one of the Requiem Mass at Hill Auditorium. During the concert I became bored and went outside. I had been advised that if I wanted tongues, I ought to try to make sounds, so I did, thinking how stupid I would look later on; so I made a sound, and gift was there, fullblown. I began immediately praying in tongues. It was for me a specific proof that I had received the Holy Spirit. It was detached from any emotionalism. It was something I knew I would be incapable of. Just to make a lot of syllables and make it seem like it were a language. The pace was too rapid and it did sound like sentences. It is a continuing proof that regardless (of) what my own situation happens to be—that God is still operating in me (Harrison, 1974: 405-406).

Here an arousal level of boredom is shifted and focused by means of deliberate attempts to speak in tongues. Therefore, antecedent interpretations, like knowledge about Christian charismatic gifts and the assurance of advisors that he could receive them, become coupled with the new level of arousal induced outside the auditorium. The result is an articulation of a level of consciousness in which ''God is still operating in me.'' In other words, the symbolic utterances of one's prayer language give rise to more abstract expressions which are culture-bound and, as such, also socially shared. What appears to an outsider as a word- or syllable-salad is a vital method of activating the potential immediacy of shared religious meanings associated with an expanded awareness of the meanings of personal experience (Goodman, 1972: 153-161).

ANOMALOUS BEHAVIOUR

The last of the three research paradigms emphasizes language structure and assumes that glossolalia is anomalous behaviour because, although it is like the regular process of speaking, it departs from run-of-the-mill speech in a significant way. Such is the stated position of William Samarin (1972: 228). However, one should note that while Samarin stresses the linguistic nature of tongue-speaking, I shall employ the anomalous behaviour paradigm more broadly, as a point of departure for considering glossolalia as religious ritual behaviour *per se*. Samarin says that all the glossolalic specimens he studied produced no features that would even hint at the existence of some kind of communication system. As he bluntly puts it, "glossolalia is fundamentally *not* language" (Samarin, 1972: 227). This includes those utterances which are claimed to be xenoglossolalic, or speech in a real but unknown language (Samarin, 1972: 109-115). Glossolalia really is "a linguistic symbol of the sacred . . . a precious possession, a divine gift" (Samarin, 1972: 221). Unlike Goodman, Samarin considers symbols in themselves, not merely as expressions of an altered awareness. The implications of such a view raise issues of a comparative nature, issues familiar to studies by religion scholars.

A distinction needs to be made between the view of the non-believer that tongues are not miraculous, just anomalous in regard to ordinary speech, and the believer's staunch conviction and felt sense that God is present in such utterances. The bridge between these two views is to say that tongue-speaking *symbolizes* the presence of the sacred, God. Two major functions are thereby performed: First, glossolalia functions linguistically, with no mystery, to distinguish the sacred from the profane. Second, glossolalia activates the affective existential dimension of religion in the individual life. Recognition of the nonlinguistic symbolic communication capacity of glossolalia leads to a comparison of the strengths and weaknesses of each of the three research paradigms.

The nonlinguistic symbolic communication capacity of glossolalia precludes a consideration of the aberrant behaviour paradigm because no longer is loss of ego-control thought to be a necessary prelude to speaking in tongues. Also, the anomalous behaviour paradigm goes beyond the extraordinary behaviour paradigm by its insistence that altered states of consciousness are only marginal to glossolalic utterances. As Samarin so clearly puts it, ". . . we would agree that the acquisition of charismatic or Pentecostal glossolalia is *sometimes* associated with *some* degree of altered state of consciousness, that this occasionally involves motor activity that is involuntary or, rarely, a complete loss of consciousness, and that in any case subsequent use of glossolalia (that is, after the initial experience) is *most often independent* of dissociative phenomena" (Samarin, 1972: 33, 1972a). In order to speak in tongues, ego-control is considered necessary by researchers working within the anomalous behaviour paradigm. Regression to a less than mature level of psychological functioning, whether as a defensive strategy toward some external threat or "in the service of the ego," is not essential to the experience from their point of view, as it would be for workers within the aberrant behaviour paradigm. And, too, unlike Goodman's emphasis on glossolalic communications in social settings, the third paradigm also insists that the sounds produced hardly give rise to more abstract expressions of extraordinary behaviour which can be considered to be culture-bound and, as such, socially shared. The overall gist of my criticisms of the three paradigms is shared in part by Nils Holm (1978), who, like Samarin, focuses on sound structure and people's ability to produce pseudo-language. Therefore, a linguistic analysis of glossolalia not only poses an alternative to other research methods. It also points beyond them, and paves the way for a consideration of the strictly religious functions of tongue-speaking. These functions are quite different from either psychological or sociocultural functions, which are the respective touchstones of the aberrant and extraordinary behaviour paradigms. And they are different from, or go beyond, the strict linguistic emphasis of the paradigm of anomalous behaviour.

PERSONAL RITUALIZATION IN TONGUE-SPEAKING

The avowals of glossolaliacs imply that most tongue-speaking involves little loss of ego-control and a minimum of altered states of awareness. My thesis is that praying in tongues is a deliberate act, purposely undertaken for religious benefit just as one would enter into any other sort of religious ritual process. This view, we noted, was stated by Goodman, who believes one "places himself" in a situation in which glossolalia makes sense or communicates meaning to others. Moreover, Goodman also intimates this position when she says that her study pointed to some possibilities of "ritualizing" aspects of culturally defined trance experiences (Goodman, 1972: 160). Such a thrust into a consideration of glossolalia as religious ritual behaviour *per se* also is reinforced by the work of Gordon Stanley, *et al.* (1978). The authors tell us not only that their results "appear to support Samarin's (1972) assertion that glossolalia occurs in a fairly normal state of consciousness," but also that glossolalia "functions primarily as a ritual, confirming experience" (Stanley, *et al.*, 1978: 277). Let us, then, move on to consider this emerging new paradigm for research on tongue-speaking, that which can be referred to as the paradigm of ritual behaviour.

Like most religious rituals functioning as primitive forms of technology, glossolalia is a technique for surveying and reckoning with the conditions of existence. Glossolalia represents what may be called (borrowing one of Goodman's points) a "placing," or a repetitive activity aimed at accentuating and directing attention to the intransigent, existential parameters of ordinary, everyday life and responsibilities. In his most recent work on religion as a system of communication within the process of human evolutionary development, John Bowker, scholar of comparative religion and the social sciences, gets even closer to the mark. He suggests that what comes to be referred to as religion in all cultures "appears as a part and consequence of the general attempts of men to scan their environment, to discern the limitations which circumscribe a projected action (or the continuity of their life-way as such), and to engage whatever resources they accept (whether consciously or not) as appropriate to the penetration or understanding of any particular compound of limitation" (Bowker, 1978: 15-16).

Placings are personal processes of scanning in the manner suggested by Bowker. During placings, one attempts to discern limitations in life, and to engage resources to find a way through such constraints. Scanning is a self-conscious activity of paying attention to the fragility of life, to existence itself. Reckoning with such intransigent powers in life is a strategy for gaining personal power in the form of new meaning. Not only are such embedded meanings largely intuitive and pre-semantic (and almost pre-verbal), but they give rise to abstract, cognitive thought in other contexts. Therefore glossolalia is one technique that mediates or builds a bridge between subcortical arousal and cortical (cognitive) interpretation. It takes the statebound limitations of various levels of arousal and seeks (and finds) a way through them, toward a resolution of human intransigencies, at least for a moment.

If glossolalia represents such a placing, we can ask, how do the underlying dynamics of such placings operate so as to focus the individual tongue-speaker on basic modes of religious meaning implicit in his everyday experience? For an answer to this question, we must consider, first, how a person relates to perceptual and existential experience, or generally to the phenomenal world. This task will depend on an understanding of a basic process of cognitive psychological functioning. The second requirement for an answer to our question is to relate this psychological process to the phenomenal world of glossolalic practice, that is, to the perceptual and existential qualities of tongue-speaking themselves. This task will depend on the nature of the phenomenal world of glossolalic practice which has to do with localizing and controlling auditory and, to a lesser degree, tactile sensations, the latter of which are associated with the tongue, larynx, lungs, and lips. To these two tasks we now turn.

Recent work in cognitive psychology has placed emphasis on the dynamic process by which human senses like touching, hearing, and so on, permit an awareness of the empirical world (Deikman, 1972; Ornstein, 1972: 1-47). Such studies dwell on the objects and modulations of human attention. The central idea is that our senses are data reduction systems, which not only screen out various ranges of energy, but also habituate or, as Arthur Deikman puts it, "automatize" what sensory input they do in fact pick up and recover. For example, the human auditory sense is incapable of picking up frequencies above 20,000 cycles per second. When compared with the same sense in most dogs, which can easily process cycles above that frequency, the human sense of hearing is clearly seen as reducing all auditory data to a limited range. Says Deikman, "Automatization normally accomplishes the transfer of attention from a percept or action to abstract thought activity" (Deikman, 1972: 221). We tend to ignore sensory constancies like the elevated railway train rushing past my flat in Chicago day after day, hour after hour, minute after minute until we do not notice the roar at all, unless, of course, we have cause to direct attention to it (e.g., the deafening silence caused when the rail workers strike and stop trains). This process of habituation or automatization is biologically valuable insofar as it facilitates neurophysiological efficiency. It enhances the survival activity of the organism by freeing enough energy for use in responding to more random alterations in one's personal environment, alterations which could spell life or death. This selecting, patterning, and valuing of the perceptual and existential dimensions of one's phenomenal world helps conserve attentional energy for maximum efficiency in reaching the basic biological goal of survival as an organism, and this same process serves the psychological goal of survival as personality. Constancies, thus, function to construct the ordinary world of everyday living. However, automatization can be a very fragile process indeed.

The practical systems of habituated attention can be set aside and often modified by what may be referred to as conditions of dysfunction. Not only may personal crises serve to disrupt the structure of attention, but controlled situations like meditating, rhythmic chanting and drum-beating, blowing a didgeridoo, singing, and hyperventilating (to name but a few) also may create conditions of dysfunction. The practical effect of controlling the process of breaking down or setting aside perceptual and existential "blinders," so to speak, is this: alternate or "deautomatized" modes of attention, whose stimulus processing may be less efficient from a biological point of view may, nevertheless, permit the experience of aspects of the real world formerly ignored or selectively excluded. How the brain processes sensory input is the key. The overall point is that ritual behaviour is synonymous with controlled situations of dysfunction. This is why rituals take on so much importance in religious life. By means of the religious ritualization of all experiencing, one is able to focus on fundamental modes of meaning implicit in everyday experience. These are meanings associated with the biology and economy of survival. Thus rituals allow "placings" to occur. If one is able to "replace" oneself over and over within one's phenomenal world, then such rituals succeed and operate as primitive technologies for manipulating the environment to maximum biological and economic advantage (Rappaport, 1971). Rituals are the symbolic equivalents of what goes on at the level of our cognitive psychological considerations above. Moreover, while the senses build up perceptual constancies, culture, which carries one's religious and symbolic structures, builds up existential constancies. In Christian theology, for example, these take the form of theodicies. Thus, ritual behaviour aims at temporarily setting aside the existential constancy which places most of a person's attention on maintaining without disruption the ongoingness of ordinary, everyday life and the usual responsibilities within it. Existence is regarded not only as an ordinary constancy to be taken for granted during ritualization, but also precarious and subject to collapse.

The deautomatization of existential constancies in personal religious ritual is analogous to the "liminal" phase of collective ritual behaviour as specified by Arnold Van Gennep and Victor Turner. Van Gennep (1960) has shown that all rites of passage are marked by three phases—separation, margin, and aggregation. During phase one, the individual or group is detached from some earlier fixed point in the social structure, or from some set of cultural conditions. In the second phase, the liminal (*limen:* "threshold" in Latin), the features of the ritual are ambiguous, not constant, not automatized. The ritual actor has few of the attributes of the past or coming state. In the last phase, the passage is completed. The ritual actor finds himself once again in a relatively stable niche in the social structure, with clearly defined rights and obligations vis-a-vis others in the society. Turner (1969) singles out Van Gennep's second, liminal phase for his special treatment of the ritual process. The liminal phase is important because it is with the ambiguous condition of being on a threshold that a major juxtaposed alternative to built-up social and cultural constancies is established (Turner, 1969:94f). While Turner sees this alternative in relation to hierarchical secular social structures, like governmental and economic systems in societies, his notion of a juxtaposed alternative to ordinary social and cultural arrangements, which is not unlike conditions of cognitive dysfunction in the individual, is a helpful analogy for understanding the ritual of tongue-speaking. Liminality is to the collective order as placings are to the more personal process of praying in tongues. At any rate, we now turn to a consideration of tongue-speaking not only as an illustration of the process involved in all ritual behaviour, but also as a practice with its own inherent and unique features.

Having considered how a person relates to his phenomenal world through the ritualization of experience, we now must ask how all this relates to the localization and self-conscious control of auditory and, to a lesser degree, tactile sensations associated with speaking in tongues. For indeed, glossolalia, like mantras in some eastern religious ritual practice, is composed of sounds modulated by movements of the tongue, larynx, lungs, and lips. It is surprising that to my knowledge no researcher, especially no researcher from the methodological tradition of phenomenology, where one might reasonably expect it, has pointed out the similarity between the sounds of glossolalic utterances and other very evident pre-semantic (and pre-verbal) human sounds. I refer to the sounds of crying and laughing. Both of these sounds not only express strong feelings; they

also serve to demarcate where language proper ends and non-linguistic utterances begin. In other words, crying and laughing are strategic psychological responses by which an alteration and juxtaposition of a new world
of meaning is made to stand over and against a more rigidly structured,
cognitively organized and controlled world of meaning, in which those two
affective processes would usually appear as anomalies and be of little use.
However, in themselves, crying and laughing are essential liminal aspects
intrinsic to the ritualization of all human experience. The ritual dimension
of the practice of tongue-speaking would appear to capitalize on this fact.

The ritual dimension of such praying would appear to imply that glossolalic utterances are amalgamations of the sounds of crying and laughing.
This description of the sound of tongue-speaking indicates that conditions
of dysfunction are activated by the deliberate act of praying. Organized,
semantic communication and seemingly disorganized non-semantic word-
or syllable-salads or amalgamations of crying and laughing thus become
altered and juxtaposed. For example, this may account for the particular
style of Christian charismatic prayer meetings: tongue-speaking is usually
juxtaposed to scripture reading, which itself is based upon semantic communications of the religious meanings of the Old and New Testaments. It
also may be followed with whispered semantic utterances like, "Praise Jesus, praise the Lord. Thank you Jesus. . . ." So from scripture reading to
post-glossolalic praises, the entire ritual process gets carried through: semantic structure yields to liminal non-semantic utterances, and finally the
personal, social, and cultural meanings of one's faith are reinforced. In effect, the tongue-speaker learns to shift his attention from ordinary, everyday concerns (for example, as stated in "give us this day our daily bread,"
and so on) to basic questions of existence. He or she becomes an explorer
of the meaning of the linguistic symbol of the sacred one's "prayer language." The paths the glossolaliac follows are staked out by the quality of
the sounds of his prayer language itself, even though such behaviour is
learned. Therefore, glossolalia is a ritual process whereby the meanings
associated with two ideal types or modes of non-semantic utterances—
crying and laughing—are contained and entered into over and over again.

But why is it that crying and laughing are specifically cited rather than
some other sort of human sound or referent? Crying and laughing are taken
as the most basic of expressive utterances. This is because each points to
the intransigent parameters of the biological baseline of the life of the spe-
cies, namely, to the life cycle and to the symbolic marks related to the flow

of birth, death, and symbolic immortality of rebirth. Other non-semantic utterances like yelling, coughing, belching, and so forth, hardly carry the personal significance that crying and laughing do. Pushed to the outer limits of its symbolic breadth, crying (and deep sobbing) points, first, to the possibility of extreme hurt being activated at any time and being made to reverberate throughout one's phenomenal world. Screaming is like crying in that it too expresses extreme hurt or, at least, threat, but differs insofar as it usually is a spontaneous response to a moment of sudden painful dysfunction, rather than the protracted response to an abiding condition of existence. If crying is the physical element of extreme hurt, then the emotional element usually pertains to some sense of evil in the world, or the "demonic" aspect of sacred power. But crying points, second, beyond situations of hurt to their source, namely to the end of the life cycle and to the inevitability of one's own death, however disguised. Similarly, laughing suggest the ever-present possibility of intense joy, which itself is but one reflection of its source, namely, recurrent birth in life and the possibility of moments of symbolic rebirth. Shouting for joy, as spectators may do during athletic contests, is to laughing as screaming is to crying, namely, a spontaneous response to a moment of sudden, but now pleasant, dysfunction. If laughing is a physical response to intense joy, then a sense of goodness in the world, or the "holy" aspect of sacred power, is the corresponding emotional element.

Thus, glossolalic sounds activate a range of possible painful or pleasant conditions of dysfunction which point to the existential meanings conditioned by human biology and actively rehearsed in terms of ritualized sounds, which are their symbols. Tongue-speaking is a personal ritual which can bring about a deepening of the spiritual dimension of human existence.

22

JESSE E. COULSON
and RAY W. JOHNSON

Glossolalia and
Internal-External Locus of Control

[Reprinted from *Journal of Psychology and Theology*, 5:4 (1977): 312-17. Reprinted with permission of *Journal of Psychology and Theology* and J. E. Coulson.]

A group of glossolalics was compared with a group of non-glossolalics on Rotter's Internal-External Locus of Control Scale. The sample of glossolalics was drawn from Foursquare Gospel and Assembly of God churches, the non-glossolalics were Methodists. There were 95 glossolalics and 79 non-glossolalics. A two-way analysis of variance (sex by glossolalic status) was applied to the data to determine if there was a difference between the groups. Non-glossolalics were found to be significantly more external than glossolalics.

The religious experience of "speaking in tongues" has a long history in both non-Christian (Flournoy, 1900; May, 1956) and Christian (Kelsey,

1964) religions. Within the Christian communities, attitudes toward glossolalia have varied from acceptance to toleration to condemnation. The practice of glossolalia as religious expression has waxed and waned with the position church leaders have taken toward it. At the present time, despite a generally skeptical and cool attitude on the part of traditional clergy, the number of glossolalists associated with traditional denominations seems to be increasing (DuPlessis, 1961; Ranaghan & Ranaghan, 1969; Rosage, 1971). While it is virtually impossible to get statistical data on the number of glossolalists in the United States even in churches which accept glossolalia as evidence of " . . . the reception of the fullness of Spirit . . . " (Mead, 1970), the membership in such churches is reportedly increasing at a more rapid rate than all other churches in the United States (Gerlich & Hines, 1970; Nichol, 1966).

Psychological descriptions of members of Pentecostal-type churches including glossolalists have been uncomplimentary, despite the fact that there is little empirical data available concerning glossolalists. They have been described as, in some sense, childish or infantile, egocentric, mentally ill (paranoid schizophrenic type reaction), anxious, unstable, suspicious, grandiose, guilt-repressing, illiterate and ignorant, projecting, having few formalized thought processes, punitive, uncertain in their relations with other people, and as having threatened, inadequately organized personalities (Cutten, 1927; Oman, 1963; Stagg, Hinson, & Oats, 1967; Wood, 1965).

Not all writers have been so negative in their evaluations of glossolalics. Osser, Ostwald, MacWhinney, and Casey (1973) are of the opinion that glossolalic behavior is pathological only if used in a nonreligious context and for purposes of annoying or confounding the listener. Goodman (1969), while considering glossolalia a dissociative phenomenon, believes it to have favorable aftereffects, a view shared in part by Hine (1960). He concludes that assumptions that glossolalia is linked to hysteria and schizophrenia have not been supported empirically and that glossolalia, when experienced in the proper social context, may result in positive behavioral results. Within the Pentecostal movement, he sees it as a powerful, motivating force for individual attitudinal and behavioral changes in the direction of group ideals. Samarin (1972) sees no evidence that glossolalics are abnormal, and Goodman (1969) cites Vivier (1968) to support the view that the glossolalist is in better psychological health than his traditional counterpart. Thus, while some view glossolalia as a form of psychopathology, others, with an eye to the dearth of empirical data, deny the pathology; a few argue for the beneficial effects of the experience. The purpose of this article is to compare a group of glossolalics with a group of non-glossolalics on a single psychological dimension, internal-external locus of control.

Relevant work, not directly concerning glossolalia but dealing with internal-external locus of control as a factor in religious behavior, has been conducted by several researchers. Tolor and Reznikoff (1967) found a relationship between death anxiety and external locus of control. Bernan and Hays (1973), however, did not find such a relationship nor did they find a relationship between locus of control and a belief in life after death. Scheidt (1973) and Jahoda (1970) found relationships between superstition, supernatural beliefs, and externality. Benson and Spilka (1973), however, found that there was no relationship between locus of control and one's belief about God's control over the believer's fate. They and Schrauger and Silverman (1971) found a relationship between internal locus of control and frequency of participation in religious activities. Strickland and Schaeffer (1971) reported that people to whom religion was highly personal and meaningful were also likely to have intense religious belief and to be internal. Javillonor (1971), in the study most relevant to this article, found no significant differences between a group of Pentecostal-type church members and a group composed of members with other religious orientations. It is highly likely that her Pentecostal group would have contained tongue-speakers. She did report that new members of Pentecostal-Holiness sects (less than six months) had substantially higher externality scores than those who had been in the church six to ten years.

The Strickland and Shaeffer (1971) study cited above probably provides the basis for reconciling the apparent contradictions in the locus of control and religion research. Individuals with highly personal and intense religious beliefs are not so likely to suffer death anxiety to the same degree as nonreligious individuals. Nor are they likely to view their religion in the same class of beliefs as superstitions or supernatural phenomena. In short, they are likely to believe that they can approach life with a greater certainty than they can cope, and thus, they are more internal.

If one were to generate hypotheses simply on the basis of locus of control studies of religious groups and practices, the most reasonable hypothesis would be that glossolalics would be internal in orientation. One cannot, however, ignore the suggestion that psychopathology or at least psychopathological processes are involved in this particular practice and the research relating locus of control to psychopathology points to externality and psychopathology as being related. Anxiety and depressive states have been found to be related to externality (Hersch & Schribe, 1967; Watson, 1967; Lottman, Davis, & Gustafson, 1973; Powell & Vega, 1972). Schizophrenics have been found to be more external than nonschizophrenics (Harrow & Ferrante, 1969; Lottman & DeWolfe, 1972; Duke & Mullens, 1973). Cash and Stack (1973) found psychotics more external than neurotics and stated that most of the differences were accounted for by a paranoid group.

A third possible source of hypotheses lies in the religious practices and stated beliefs of persons affiliated with churches in which glossolalia is believed to be a "Gift of the Holy Ghost." It seems clear that it is believed that " . . . a divine power is controlling the person . . . " (Williams, 1953), that " . . . every baptized believer will speak with tongues . . . " (Van Cleave, 1950), and that by submitting to the Lord a need for greater power would be fulfilled. The power is gained for the purpose of working in God's service (Van Cleave, 1949).

In addition to a belief that the faithful are literally filled with the Spirit and, therefore, directed by it, the conduct of the services in the Pentecostal-Holiness type churches is such as to bring the considerable external influence of the minister and congregation to the individual member. Public glossolalia, public confession of sin, public prophecies, loud "divinely inspired" staccato-style preaching, impassioned public prayer, and emotional congregational participation in the music and dancing are all part of these services and could lead to an hysterical state of suggestibility resulting in the glossolalia phenomenon. It might be supposed that glossolalics are more suggestible than non-glossolalics and, therefore, more external.

From this brief review of the literature, it is apparent that, because of the conflicting nature of the research and theorizing, any hypotheses regarding differences between glossolalics and non-glossolalics on internal-external locus of control will be rather arbitrary. However, because of the suggestion of psychopathology in glossolalics, the relationship between psychopathology and internal-external locus of control, the suggestion of the need to overcome feelings of powerlessness among Pentecostals. and religious practices which presumably would be most effective with persons more than ordinarily susceptible to influence from the environment, it was expected that glossolalics would be more external. Nonetheless, it was simply hypothesized that there would be a significant difference between glossolalics and non-glossolalics on internal-external locus of control.

METHOD

SUBJECTS

The sample for this study included 80 males (38 glossolalics and 42 non-glossolalics) and 94 females (57 glossolalics and 37 non-glossolalics) drawn from four churches. The glossolalics had a slightly lower level of educational attainment, but there were no differences in income level. The age range of the subjects was 16 to 87 years. The sample was drawn from Foursquare Gospel, Assembly of God, and United Methodist churches in Texas and a Foursquare Gospel church in California.

INSTRUMENTS

A religious survey questionnaire was designed to investigate the relationship between the practice of glossolalia and locus of control and to solicit information about other aspects of religious practices and beliefs. The questionnaire also asked for information about the subject's educational level, income level, sex, marital status, and age.

Rotter's (1966) Internal-External Locus of Control Scale was used to measure locus of control. The scale purports to measure the degree to which one believes that positive or negative events of his life are the result of his own behavior and under his personal control (internal locus of control), or that such events are unrelated to his behavior and beyond his control (external locus of control).

PROCEDURE

The Rotter scale and the religious questionnaire were distributed to all attenders of every adult class at each church. Instructions were given that they should fill out each form completely. Those who chose not to participate had their forms marked to indicate "nonparticipant." All questionnaires were completed in class. Groups were formed on the basis of sex and status as glossolalic or non-glossolalic; a 2 x 2 analysis of variance was applied to the data to determine if there was a difference between these groups. A difference at the .05 level of significance was required for accepting these hypotheses.

RESULTS AND DISCUSSION

The results of the statistical analysis supported the hypothesis (Table 1), but the differences were in a direction opposite than expected (Table 2). Glossolalics, regardless of their sex, tended to be more internal than non-glossolalics.

Table 1

Summary of Analysis of Variance

Variable	Ss	df	Ms	
Sex (A)	26.3890	1	26.3890	2.2454
Glossolalia (B)	97.6913	1	97.6913	8.3124*
Interaction (A x B)	.2706	1	.2706	ns
Within	1997.9434	170	11.7526	

$*p < - .01$

Table 2

Means, SDs, and t-values for Glossolalics and Nonglossolalics

Group	N	X	o	t
Glossolalics	95	6.18	3.26	
Male	38	5.66	2.97	
Female	57	6.53	3.42	
Nonglossolalics	79	7.60	3.55	2.74**
Male	42	7.26	3.66	2.14*
Female	37	7.97	3.42	2.00*

$*MG < MNG, p < .05$
$**FG < FNG, p < .05$
$**G < NG, p < .01$

The differences are admittedly small but are in agreement with research, previously cited, indicating that people to whom religion was highly personal were more internal (Strickland & Schaffer, 1971). It also, in a sense, supports the findings of Benson and Spilka (1973) and Shrauger and Silverman (1971), who reported that frequency of church activities and devotions were related to internality. In short, people who are involved in religious activity and to whom religion is personal and of intrinsic value seem to perceive themselves as having more control over what is happening to them.

When combined with the relationships previously described, between locus of control and psychopathology, the present results suggest that while the behavior of some members of Pentecostal-Holiness sects may, in a statistical sense, be deviant, it probably does not, when displayed within the context of this religion, represent psychopathology. On the basis of present data, it should not be construed to be such. Indeed, the self-descriptions of internals presented by Hersch and Scheibe (1967) suggest that they feel highly competent and capable of dealing with the environment. It may be that the fact that the glossolalics chose to associate themselves with non-traditional religions is evidence of their internal orientation.

Benson and Spilka (1973), who found that locus of control was not related to controlling beliefs about God, suggested another possible explanation for the results of this report. They pointed out that the Rotter Scale might not be an accurate measure of the truly religious person, who may see things as being under divine control but not as controlled by chance, fate, or luck, which are key words on the Rotter scale.

A part of the lack of research on glossolalia may be due to a lack of interest on the part of psychologists. It is very likely, however, that much of the lack of empirical data may be attributed to a perhaps justifiable suspicion of psychologists on the part of people who are glossolalists and the members of their churches. Psychologists have been too eager to assign pathological significance to the phenomenon on the basis of extremely limited data. It is hoped that the results of the present study might allay some of the suspicion and encourage further research on this phenomenon.

23

MARVIN K. MAYERS

The Behavior
of Tongues

[Reprinted with permission from *Speaking in Tongues: Let's Talk about It*, edited by Watson E. Mills, copyright © 1973, pp. 112-27; used by permission of Word Books, Publisher, Waco, Texas 76796.]

American society is disenamored with the church. The disenchanted are looking to other movements, to other programs, and to new leadership for their spiritual stimulation. Some are looking to the drug subcultures. Others are investigating Far Eastern religions—sitting at the feet of the Indian guru, practicing the body postures of yoga, and so on. Many while remaining nominally within the established church are, in fact, turning to the small group movement. These people find the major part of their spiritual development growing out of such a fellowship. Still others are looking to the charismatic movements which stress healing and tongues, that is, glossolalia, as valid manifestations of the Holy Spirit.

One observer of the contemporary scene has put it this way:

> In the United States today, glossolalia is practiced by over two million people. Among the lower social classes, particularly in the primitive, remote regions of the South, glossolalia is only part of a full range of snake handling, convulsionary, hysterical behavior. On the other hand, among urban middle- and upper-class churches, glossolalia is practiced as an isolated phenomenon by physicians, college professors, captains of industry, even psychologists, who sit in full composure and dignity while speaking in tongues.[1]

Much has been written about glossolalia. Historic theological debates concerning this phenomenon centered on its divine or devilish origin. The purpose of this chapter, however, is not to review the theological positions of the respective points of view. Nor is it to go back through the history of the church and deal with the various movements which stressed glossolalia. Rather, from the point of view of an anthropologist and linguist, I will examine the human behavior associated with such movements.

THE LINGUISTIC BEHAVIOR OF TONGUES

Language is learned behavior. Any form of language, either actual language or partial language, is learned through the process of socialization. A child is born and immediately comes under the influence of the speech community represented by his mother. The ohs and ahs, even the cooing, that go on in admiration of the baby are all elements of the speech of the larger community the baby will enter. The sounds, the order of the words, the various idiomatic expressions are being heard, internalized, and responded to during the early period of learning. By the time the child is ready to begin talking, he has already begun practicing all the elements of speech which he has heard. He will continue practicing these throughout the early stages of his life until he achieves complete fluency in the language.

Those about him will encourage the child to practice by uttering sounds correctly and in keeping with the standards and expectations of the speech community and by ordering various elements of speech so that sense is made and not nonsense. Such encouragement takes the form of informal drill

---

[1] E. Mansell Pattison, "Behavioral Science Research on the Nature of Glossolalia," *Journal of the American Scientific Affiliation*, 20 (September 1968): 74.

sessions, such as the mother correcting the child. It grows to include formal sessions when the child is placed in the classroom and required to write themes in correct English.

E. Mansell Pattison relates such a process of socialization to the experience of glossolalia by suggesting that, "When the glossolalic phrases which have been heard and stored in memory are brought into awareness, they are practiced over and over again in inner speech until an acceptable form of glossolalia is mastered. With its mastery, the inner speech is reproduced externally and the spontaneous glossolalic utterance may be heard for the first time." When an outsider observes a tongues experience, he sees this reflected in the behavior of respect involving the various participants. The more experienced tongue-speaker receives the greater respect and is looked up to because of his greater expertise. The novice receives a minimum of respect and a maximum of encouragement so that in time he will become as proficient as the others. This is further evidenced by the type and intensity of the encouragement given the novice, the self-imposed feelings of inadequacy that cause the novice to rely more and more on God to give him the total experience of tongues, and finally by the attitudes expressed toward those without the tongues experience.

Even the individual who enters a group and speaks in tongues for the first time provides no exception or contradiction to the experience of tongues as learned behavior. Every individual is part of such a complex network of interpersonal relations that the learning experience as it relates to any part of the network is in operation long before there is actual utterance. It is not at all necessary, therefore, for one to be part of an immediate speech community to be able to express oneself in a way that is acceptable to members of that speech community.

One can learn all the elements of speech he will need in a charismatic speech community by participating in many other communities. These elements simply become combined in a new way for the new speech community. For example, a member of the American speech community who has become proficient in American English finds acceptance in Great Britain where British English is spoken, or in Australia, or even in the English-speaking Philippine community because of the range of acceptable speech behavior recognized in each of the other English speech communities. There are differences in pronunciation as well as differences in the selection of words and word order, but the visitor can do the necessary recombination of the parts and become a member of the community without too much strain.

Tongues, among English-speaking subjects, is composed of the basic speech elements of English. A person raised in an English-speaking setting would find his English influencing every new language he would learn as well as every recombination of speech forms he might produce. The learning or socialization process is so powerful that the most brilliant linguists and the most fluent multilingual speakers find the characteristics of the first language or languages they spoke influencing the later ones.

This comes as a surprise to some since glossolalic utterances by English speakers do not sound like English. There is a lack of organization of the basic phonemes (speech sounds) into the syntactical (grammatical) elements necessary for fully intelligible speech. Further the elements of speech involving pauses, breaths, intonations, and so on are markedly reduced and modified. They resemble the early speech qualities of young children prior to the organization of all the variables associated with adult language. These changes and modifications will sound to others like a foreign language and may even impress the hearer as a language they have spoken or heard spoken. This would not be at all unexpected since language is an extremely complex form of behavior. In fact, it is so complex that professionals have been unable to program computers either for correct language usage or for effective translation from one language to another.

Describing tongues as learned behavior in no way invalidates the experience of tongues nor does it limit, in any way, the power of the Holy Spirit of God. It simply suggests, rather, that we are human and subject to human limitations and that the Holy Spirit chooses to work within the context of human strengths and frailties. This involves dealing within the complexities of verbal culture, even as it involves dealing within the complexities of nonverbal culture which I will discuss later.[2]

---

[2]"The structural linguistic data suggest that glossolalia has specific linguistic structure based on the language tongue of the speaker, that the linguistic organization is limited, and that the capacity to speak in this type of semiorganized language can be replicated under experimental conditions. Thus, glossolalia does not appear to be a 'strange language,' but rather, the aborted formation of familiar language.'' Pattison, "Behavioral Science Research on the Nature of Glossolalia," p. 73.

As a speech form, glossolalia can be classed with other disordered patterns of language and/or speech. The final production of glossolalic speech is vocalizations in the form of words or segments of words which have no denotative or referential sense. They appear to be like the jargon aphasia of a person with a brain dysfunction, the schizophasia (split speech) of the mental patient, the speech of the sleep talker, and the neologistic stage of speech development in children. This does not mean that they are necessarily disordered patterns of language or speech; rather, they are classed with this kind of speech. In no way does a classification negate the validity of a speech form or the experience of using the speech form. Such classification aids in understanding the phenomenon as well as gives valuable clues in working with it, both for the sake of the participant as well as the observer.

Language is a system of reciprocating statements and responses. Language is part of the communicating process, perhaps a major part or the key to communication. The speaker intends that he be heard precisely as he spoke. The hearer responds in a way that indicates to the original speaker that he was heard and that he was comprehended in the precise way intended. Anything more or less than this reciprocal communication process is either not language or it is only partial language.

Certain biblical scholars disclaim a distinction between the tongues experience of the Book of Acts and that of 1 Corinthians. Within the linguistic context, however, it becomes clear that in the New Testament period, there were two kinds of "tongues." The first met the requirements of language within the communicative process. There was a certain reciprocal relationship between speaker and hearer. The hearer comprehended that which the speaker intended whether the speaker knew precisely what he was saying or not. There was no need for an intermediary to explain to the hearers what was being said. As many as spoke that tongue or language heard and comprehended precisely what each of the other hearers was comprehending. The speaker was aware that they were getting the precise message intended.

The Book of Acts has no less than six references to tongues as language. The clearest and most complete account is on the day of Pentecost when the disciples spoke to people whom they did not know, in a language that they probably had not learned previously.

An interesting theory that tantalizes the linguist is the possibility that the disciples had had extensive ethnic experience prior to the day of Pen-

410 Speaking in Tongues

tecost. In other words, their cultural backgrounds were varied and mixed so that the Holy Spirit needed only to bring the languages of these ethnic contacts to mind and let the men speak. To many, this would negate the power of the Holy Spirit, but to a linguist, this would enhance the Spirit's working in the normal processes of speech and thus be grounds for greater respect of the Holy Spirit's power than would otherwise be true.

Rather, the kind of experience spoken of during the day of Pentecost likely came from some kind of Spirit impulse within the lives of the disciples. They were thus able to speak directly to men of different languages and be understood by them in precisely the way that they each intended. Each disciple could also ascertain that he was being fully understood. Such an experience of reciprocal communication is being shared today by any missionary in a true language learning and scientific translation setting. The speed with which the disciples and the contemporary missionary learned the language differ, but the impact on the audience is the same, and the sense of accomplishment in the speaker is the same.

A second type of tongues is not a two-way phenomenon, rather it is one way—directed out from the speaker irrespective of the reciprocating response of the hearer. The person speaking does not need to know what he has said and is likely not to. Nor does anyone in his audience need to know what he has said. It is enough that it is uttered. If no one in the audience knows what has been uttered, the speaker himself will turn to the interpretation. If someone else knows, then he will interpret. The one interpreting is not ''the one speaking intending a specific response to the message.'' Rather he is fulfilling the function of an intermediary who communicates the sense of the message. *There is never more than one person who can respond ''correctly'' to the stimulus of the primary utterance.* No one else can validate the message or the intent of the message as is possible with reciprocating communication. This is true even when there is a second or third interpreter.

One-way tongues are therefore not true language. They are based on partial language in the sense that only one person at a time has a chance to comprehend and interpret. There are numerous indications in the Bible that it was this second kind of tongues experienced within the Corinthian church. We, therefore, have an interesting division linguistically between the tongues experience of the Corinthian Christians and the Christians referred to in the Book of Acts who shared in the two-way tongues or languages.

Tongues results in a new dialect or language. Besides certain manifestations of tongues resulting in partial language, the partial language forms a system that becomes in itself a dialect or language. This is a dialect of glossolalic speech which has its own sound system, grammatical system, semantic reference system, and paralinguistic system (stress, breath, intonation, and so on). Even as any language may have numerous acceptable dialects, so glossolalists produce a language dialect and develop it into polished glossolalic speech. Further, each person has his own unique dialect which is called an idiolect. There need not be many speech distinctives to give one's speech individual quality; but if you listen closely to another person, his speech distinctives will become apparent. So it is within the experience of glossolalia. Each participant has his own distinctives, and we can begin to speak of idiolects as well as dialects of glossolalic speech.

The question is not, therefore, Is glossolalic speech real language or not? but rather, Is glossolalic speech *a* language? It should not be compared with other languages to see if it is in reality that particular language. It should be studied by analytic or descriptive linguists to find the patterned regularities of the language itself. The sound system would be described with special attention being given to patterns of stress, pitch, and duration. The grammatical system would be investigated with the order and arrangement of the parts in mind. Concern would be given to the function the various grammatical units play within the whole, that is, are there clauses and phrases of different types? And finally, the semantic system would be looked at to see if certain parts of utterance have some correlation with meaningful expressions in the interpretation of tongues. Thus we await a full linguistic description of a glossolalic tongue, and, for that matter, of the various tongues, to see if there are dialects of glossolalic speech. Until this is done, no claim that a certain utterance or speech is or is not language can be substantiated. Further, there is no indication that glossolalia is in fact language or partial language or just gibberish.

During any discussion of the linguistic and cultural considerations of tongues, it is necessary to keep in mind that a linguistic or cultural description of tongues has nothing to do with the validity of the tongues experience. Just because someone can produce a linguistic description of a glossolalic utterance does not invalidate the experience. It simply tells us the cultural aspects of the experience. It allows us to look on an experience with that objectivity man was endowed with but seldom practices.

THE SOCIOCULTURAL BEHAVIOR OF TONGUES

Another important aspect of human behavior that is involved in the experience of tongues is the need source for such manifestations within society and the ways tongues fills such needs. Society is essentially a structure designed to meet the needs of its members. The structural elements thus designed are termed culture or life way. Culture is therefore the map or program or series of guidelines by which an individual member can expect to live adequately within his society. Once he has internalized these guidelines, he comes to a point of peace within it. He is able to cope effectively with all its demands, expectations, and challenges.

Sometimes society lets its members down. Sometimes members do not live up to the fullness of opportunity they have within the society. In either case a variety of responses and reactions can be expected. Speaking in tongues becomes a medium for these reactions. When this occurs, it may represent a means of protest, an expression of a people with a marginal socioeconimic position in the larger society, a technique of recruitment for a group, a method for organization of people, and a means of demonstrating the effect of behavior change. To these could be added other reactions including the validation of new leadership with qualities of leadership not called for in the established church, a means of escape from unpleasantness if not tension as well, and an expression of people in conflict with their sociocultural backgrounds and present situations.

The behavior of extremism is clearly noted in the biblical account of the Corinthian church. It is easy to be impressed with their enthusiasm. Here was a hard-hitting, hard-living group that seemed to go to extremes in almost every aspect of life. Their enthusiastic eating habits carried over into the communion. Their enthusiastic sexual practices violated the incest taboo that was designed to keep relatives from cohabiting. Their enthusiasm in discussion propelled them into debate and argumentation which in turn fragmented them into cliques or factions. Their enthusiastic development of a self-image brought Paul's response: "You're puffed up." Their enthusiasm in worshiping God expressed itself in ecstatic utterance or tongues.

Paul was forever saying, "Cool it! Why are you forever arguing and debating?" or, "Cool it! I have spoken in tongues more than you all, but you go beyond anything that I, a normal person, hope to experience. And not only are you doing it in public, but you are doing it in a way that lends itself to oddness and strangeness. You are doing it without interpretation. How can anyone be expected to comprehend, to be part of the experience if he does not understand'' (personal interpretation of portions of 1 Corinthians 14).

And so in a variety of ways, Paul was saying to an enthusiastic group, ''Listen, you Corinthian characters, you are just going whole hog! You're way out! You're extremists! Hold back a bit! Cool it! Relax a bit! Many of the things you are doing are uncalled for.'' A more biblical term that Paul uses is *carnal*.

People in our contemporary world live in extremes of sociocultural conflict. Conflict arises because of the multiplicity of cultures and subcultures existing in our world. Every time a person has difficulty moving from one to another he is thrown into conflict. Alvin Toffler relates one such area of conflict in his provocative book, *Future Shock.* One moving into the future is disturbed because he is unable to cope adequately with the vast amount of change he encounters, even within the context of his own sociocultural setting. Any time a person seeks to instill one aspect of a given culture or subculture in another, he can throw someone in that second culture into conflict.

Conflicts can arise in any aspect of life, and conflict in one aspect can serve to reinforce conflict in another. Mate conflict can reinforce family conflict which in turn can reinforce employment conflict. People in conflict tend to have numerous conflicts each in its own way interacting with and reinforcing other conflicts.

In the lives of many people today conflict exists between facets of one's own personal interests, between personal interests and the interests of others, among individual interests with the family, and among various interests expressed within the context of the church. Today's church has become part of the establishment or system. It seems to be traditional in its own ways, impersonal in its approach to outsiders, and often impersonal toward its own members. As people become disgruntled with the church and its practices, they seek out more personal organizations, leaders who relate to them individually.

I am not suggesting by this that these people are emotionally disturbed. Varying stages of conflict may or may not result in emotional disturbances. But these people are ready for a new experience, one that promises them vitality, involvement, and participation. They are ready to flee from some bad experience or some bad situation.

To what degree are the tongues groups attracting unbelievers? To what degree are they attracting dissatisfied Christians? My own impression, based upon informal research techniques of participant observation and interviewing, rather than on formal techniques, is that these groups attract other Christians. Tongues becomes the equivalent of prophesying in the New Testament church for edification of believers rather than a sign to the unbeliever. This means that the contemporary tongues movements must rely on existential proof for their validity rather than biblical proof. They can thus only be proven biblically if the biblical material is taken out of context.

I do not object, either as an anthropologist or as a theologian, to the existential validation of the contemporary practice of tongues. It is clear that the movement is with us for very good social and religious reasons. The church has been praying for revival. Revival comes; sometimes it occurs outside the doors of the established church, for example, in the small group movement or the tongues movement. The success claimed by such groups indicates that they are meeting needs expressed within our contemporary society. These movements are not small. They pervade our entire society, irrespective of age, sex, spiritual or social maturity. They are needed because people are healthy and want to go deeper into the experience of God. They are also needed because people are in conflict and need resolution of such conflict.

Resolution of some conflict can come through encounter with the Holy Spirit movements. There is healing in the Bible. This healing is both physical and emotional. There is resolution of conflict in the Bible. This involves both spiritual peace, "We have peace with God through our Lord Jesus Christ" (Romans 5:16, RSV), as well as social peace, "Let patience have her perfect work, that ye may be perfect and entire, wanting nothing" (James 1:4). There is also acceptance in the Bible. God takes us just as we are. Too frequently in the impersonal established church, the individual feels unwanted, rejected, and alienated. Holy Spirit movements tend to reverse this process. The key is involvement and participation which bring the individual into the total experience.

Holy Spirit movements tend to be dogmatic and authoritarian. North American society has moved away from authoritarianism and dogmatic pronouncements toward a certain permissiveness. It has moved from assured self-confidence to uncertainty regarding what to do in certain situations and with certain problems. In these areas of concern, the Holy Spirit movement comes with a fresh air of authority. Many of its leaders are de facto dictators. Even though they claim to rely on the Holy Spirit, much of the development within the group is through their whim.

Even though the Bible teaches release from conflict, not all of the release from conflict is made available through these groups. In fact, in certain cases, the group, though helping to resolve some of the conflict in the life of the adherent, will tend to introduce a new conflict as well. In one such group, young people were aided for a period of time. Certain conflicts within their lives were resolved. Then the emphasis of the group turned toward giving oneself wholly to God. This resulted in a number of students leaving their college programs, determined to spend much time in prayer and Bible reading. This was fine as long as the leader was with them to encourage them in their flight from formal education which had been a lifelong expectation for many of them. When the leader left, however, the young people realized that they had been living below their potential. They realized that in reality they had taken the easy out from their tension involvement that had developed from a demand to study and to think. They returned to school and have come into a whole new awareness of Christ in their lives in keeping with what they actually are and in keeping with themselves as whole people.

The Holy Spirit never leads toward irresponsibility in life; rather, toward responsibility. The Holy Spirit never leads one to abandon one's obligations, rather, to fulfill them. The Holy Spirit never leads one to destroy trust. Our society more and more, through some malfunctioning of the system, is training youth to cop out on life, to shirk responsibility, to abandon one's obligations. When a youth under the so-called leadership of the Holy Spirit leaves a responsibility unfulfilled, he is more than likely yielding to the training of his culture rather than to the Spirit of God.

The North American utilizes three main means of resolving his conflict: withdrawal from unpleasantness, conformity just to get along, and the formation of a new group—a counterculture. The person withdrawing from society may be seeking release from some problem too great for him to handle. He may be fleeing one set of problems and find himself in another. The person conforming just to get along with another person or group may risk losing his self-respect, for he may readily abandon principles upon which his life is based. Again he compounds his problems. The person who forms a new group to get out from under his conflicts is well off so long as that group turns outward from itself. If it turns inward, reinforcing its boundaries by ritual practices and other forms of group identification, developing an in-group feeling bordering on an unhealthy ethnocentrism, the person involved may very quickly find himself cut off from all those groups of which he had formerly been a part. The person might turn from family, from mature Christian friends outside the charismatic movement, from his church however sound it might be, and from his school or place of otherwise suitable employment.

When the resolution of conflict lies in the way of inward peace or peace with man and God, there is biblical evidence for the working of the Holy Spirit. When the end result is only more conflict, there is serious reason to suspect some other movement than that of the Spirit of God.

The behavior of tongues grows out of underlying values. Every individual lives his life valuing one thing more highly than another. One's values are ranked according to his priorities. Such ranking controls how the person applies his value orientation in specific situations. When a choice between values is involved, one becomes more important than another. Decisions are made on the basis of this choice.

Values placed in such an order generally include social, political, economic, and religious choices. Underlying these values are other more basic values that in effect motivate our everyday behavior. A person may wish to worship God; insofar as he is concerned, this is a very high-level religious value. But a more basic value controls the total experience of worship. If a worship experience is designed to fit into an hour period with each part being timed so as to take only a part of the total experience yet not all of it, then a time-oriented person can worship God fully and completely. The experience is responded to positively; the person is refreshed, and he even looks forward to the next opportunity to worship.

On the other hand, someone who values the lived experience above the time schedule may be frustrated by such a restricting worship experience. He may be unable to worship because his mind is distracted. He may find himself far from the place of worship—if not in body, at least in mind. Though it would be quite easy to say that this person is not seeking God fully, or that he is fallen from grace, such does not need to be the case. He may be seeking with all his heart to worship God, and his life may evidence a consistent maturity toward God in every way, and yet he could find an attitude of worship eluding him. The timed schedule, foreign to his life-style to some degree, is intruding in the experience of worship in ways that another person may not even be aware. A more basic value than the religious urging to worship God has intervened in the experience and has thwarted worship.[3]

A person can wish to praise God with tongues. This value may be controlled by a more basic value. If a person tends to be dichotomistic, he divides reality into two parts—here-there, right-wrong, for-against, and so on—and it is unlikely that he will be led of the Spirit to praise God with tongues. Tongues grow out of a holistic world and life view in which one object is not set off definitively from another object; rather each object is seen as part of a larger whole. Upon asking a dichotomist a question, one would anticipate a two- or three-point answer. The same question asked of a holist would tend to elicit a one-point response with various aspects of the whole pointed out, but these would be somewhat lost in the larger concern of the question. The difference between the dichotomist and the holist is no problem whatsoever as long as each accepts and respects the other. The moment one tries to make over the other through some kind of pressure, the other becomes forced to abandon the principle upon which his life is based and in effect become an ethical relativist proceeding toward antinomianism.

In his approach to language, the dichotomist seeks for clear distinction of sound from sound; he also looks for a clear distinction of order and arrangement of the parts of speech so that one knows exactly what is spoken. Further he is concerned with semantic definition so that what is being talked about is clearly distinguished from everything else; there need be no ambiguity in this world and life view. In their attempt to be precise some dichotomists become overprecise in definition and overly careful in their pronunciation and grammatical usage. Such people are a real drag in conversation because more attention is focused on how something is said than to what is actually communicated. However much you try to listen to the message, the form of the speech demands your sole attention.

At the opposite end of the spectrum is the holistic approach to language which is not concerned with precision of sound or correctness of order. In

---

[3]For a more complete discussion of such basic values, consult Mayers, Richards, and Webber, *Reshaping Evangelical Higher Education* (Zondervan 1972).

its most extreme form the holistic approach has the potential for total lack of comprehension to the speech uttered. Aphasia victims thus would be classified as holist, in this case due to some illness. Tongues participants would also but for totally different reasons. The average person uses speech more as a dichotomist would use it, speech and the communication process almost demanding a degree of clarity in utterance. Written systems symbolizing speech are not under quite the same restrictions and range from the sharply defined phonetic script known in the Western world all the way to pictorial or hieroglyphic writing known in the ancient world and used to some degree holistically in the Far Eastern world as functioning writing systems.

With this background in mind, it is possible to take a new look at the New Testament experience of tongues. Paul appears to be a dichotomist who tends a degree toward holism. A number of biblical narratives concerning his life indicate this. He makes use of numerous paired concepts, dividing the totality of reality into two parts, for example, spitirual vs. carnal. He also divides reality into a multiplicity of parts (see his listing of the fruit of the Spirit). Paul seems to take a step toward holism as he moves toward his climactic experience at Mars Hill. He did not attempt to distinguish the image to the unknown God from some other idol or idols as a thoroughgoing dichotomist might do. Instead, he says, "I perceive that along with all of your worship experience you have established something in relation to the whole" (personal interpretation).

First Corinthians 14 may possibly refer to Paul's life-style. A paraphrase of his words might be, "I may at times use speech more as a holist does. I'm then concerned with what I say in terms of the whole. There are times when I move even further away from sharper definition of speech to a more blurred speech. I do this only in private, and I don't do it very much. You Corinthians do it a great deal, not only in private, as I do it, but in public as well. In fact, you've gone so far along the continuum of blurring of speech that no one can distinguish what you are saying. Now, when you go this far, it is absolutely necessary that you have an interpreter to tell others and yourselves what you are saying." Here, the responsibility of the interpreter is not to translate from one language to another, as we commented earlier, but to get the general impression of what the person is communicating and to indicate this impression to the audience.

Tongues is an expression of a subculture which tends toward the holist end of the dichotomist-holistic continuum of behavior, perhaps, at times even to an extreme along this end of the continuum. Tongues people would thus tend to have a holist life-style that gives them a freedom of identity in worshiping God most effectively by means of speech blurring. A dichotomist is not likely to be attracted by tongues unless certain aspects of his life tend to be holistic.[4]

It is now possible to ask a number of questions. In what areas of behavior is a person dichotomistic or holistic or some combination of the two? If the higher value areas of one's life tend to be dichotomistic, will a person yield to a tongues movement? Which religious traditions are dichotomistic and which are holistic? What does this say about their acceptance or resistance to tongues? If certain traditions are perceived as dichotomistic in their pronouncements and worldview and yet have a tendency to embrace tongues, does it follow that tongues are then in reality a feature of dichotomism, or rather, is there an element of holism within the otherwise dichotomistic tradition? Further, are these holists or holistic trends compatible or incompatible with the tradition itself? Such questions take us beyond the scope of our discussion but become quite promising once further research and research-based considerations are made.

The Reformed church is perceived, in light of the dichotomism-holism continuum, as primarily dichotomistic. A study of its major pronouncements reveals attention paid to paired considerations, to a miminum division of reality, and to sharpness of definition. The tongues movement has had a minimum impact on the Reformed tradition, and a hypothesis could be formed and tested suggesting that holists within the larger dichotomistic tradition, in achieving a sense of their true identity, have begun realizing and practicing tongues as a vital expression of this identity. Non-Reformed traditions stemming from Arminius rather than Calvin are perceived to be holistic—at least to a degree more than the Reformed tradition. The tongues movement seems to dominate these movements or at least lies very close to the heart of these particular groups. The Pentecostal movements trend even farther from dichotomism, however, than do the Armin-

---

[4]Many holists living in an extremely dichotomistic society such as North America will find themselves socialized in that area of their lives involving school, work, and so on as dichotomists. Examinations of the objective type tend to reinforce such learning, demanding extreme focus on the proscribed material of the course, sharpness of definition, and so on. Yet these same people will reflect holism in areas of their lives they have been able to control more completely, such as in recreational pursuits, week-end activities, and so on.

ian background groups, and the Holy Spirit groups trend even further than do the Pentecostals.

	Reformed	
Dichotomism	Arminian	Holism
	Pentecostal	

"Holy Spirit"
Movements

Tongues and tongues movements can be used of God for holistic people allowing them to open up more fully to God than they would otherwise find possible. Such people are often, due to the larger cultural design, in conflict within the dichotomistic structures of the larger society. Such conflict may be due to spiritual problems and concerns but can also be due to social and psychological concerns. On the other hand, those who tend to be dichotomistic can open up to God in other ways than through glossolalia. These people find ways to worship God fully through timed devotions, through precision in utterance that comes from praying, preaching, or Bible study. Their praise takes the form of order, control, and organization. Unless each can accept the other in Christian love, the message of the love of God will be lost.

TONGUES AS MISSION

Tongues groups are needed among people who are oriented toward supernatural powers and who see their spirits more powerful than the spirits of the Christian. Since certain youth subcultures are seeking the power of the devil, of the spirit world, and of representatives of Far Eastern religions, perhaps they should be encouraged toward tongues groups.

On the island of Mindanao in the Southern Philippines a tribal group resisted the missionaries and their message. They saw no power in the new religion or in the lives of the messengers. Later the missionaries came under the influence of a Holy Spirit movement and began practicing healing and tongues. When they returned to their people, there was enthusiastic response to the evident demonstration of power in the Christian faith.

It is not known just how influential the Holy Spirit movements could be in such settings since no research is available on the subject and also since, by their very nature, Holy Spirit movements have not made contact with such tribal groups. The contemporary tongues movement is young and characteristically does not work through established missions. This means that their influence is not felt much beyond the boundaries of the so-called civilized world. Certain holiness and Pentecostal groups have had some degree of success in Christian outreach but again mainly where some Western religion has gone previously as in Chile and South America.

Even though tongues movements might be useful on the mission field, a second problem blocks their impact. Tongues groups not only do not work through established missions, they do not feel that these missions are really of the Lord. Whenever someone goes into a second culture, he must do specific things to have a measure of success. He needs to tune into the leadership of the other culture so that he can have the necessary legitimacy to be within the nation's boundaries. He further must adapt to the culture else the people will constantly be suspicious of him and his motives. Such preparation comes to the person via studies in the behavioral sciences of anthropology, sociology, and psychology as well as through theological and biblical studies. Holy Spirit movements are characteristically suspicious of these disciplines and of the way Christians in these fields of learning speak and deal with problems. Further, the established missions have gradually tuned in to many principles from these fields that give them a degree of effectiveness, organization, and ministry in their respective areas of responsibility. The tongues movements are thus suspicious of the approach of the established mission, not seeing it as truly from the Spirit of God. This prevents them from benefiting from the types of studies and kinds of training that can help them in the cross-cultural communication process. Thus these movements fail to achieve an impact within the settings in which their influence is so badly needed.

The Holy Spirit of God works through responsible members of society in keeping with their linguistic and sociocultural backgrounds. An understanding of these various social and linguistic forces can help us understand ourselves in keeping with our true identities and permit us to open up to God in full keeping with our unique identities. Further, such an understanding can aid us in our relationships with others, encouraging those who can best profit from a tongues experience to enter and at least see if this is what God has for them. But more significantly, since the power manifest by these movements is so crucial in missions in the world today, such an understanding and an acceptance of the variety of worldviews involved will enable the Spirit to place strategically in the world those who can have most effective impact on the peoples of the world.

Part V
Sociocultural Studies

24

WATSON E. MILLS

Glossolalia as a
Sociopsychological Experience

[Reprinted from *Search*, Winter 1973. ©
Copyright 1972 The Sunday School Board of
the Southern Baptist Convention. All rights
reserved. Used by permission.]

The recent, rapid rise of speaking in tongues—or glossolalia—in the
ranks of Christendom has been phenomenal. Stanley Plog, a psychologist
at the University of California, questioned more than 350 glossolaliacs, and
concluded that there are over forty denominations involved in the new outbreak of the tongues movement.[1] He believes that the largest groups are
Episcopalian, Baptist, and Presbyterian, asserting that about 11 percent of
the memberships of each of these groups are experiencing the phenomenon. Morton Kelsey claims that during "this century some two or three

---

[1]Quoted in McCandish Philips, "And There Appeared to Them Tongues of Fire," *The
Saturday Evening Post*, 237 (May 16, 1964): 38.

million, and perhaps a great many more, Americans have had a strange personal experience of religion known as speaking in tongues."[2] These figures may well be exaggerated, but nevertheless there is mounting evidence that the Neo-Pentecostal movement is making a significant infiltration into the main stream of Protestantism.

This rapid spread of the phenomenon has produced many books and articles dealing with the subject, most of which reflect one of the several views held by the writers. Some feel that glossolalia is a sign of church renewal and that it is an experience that all Christians should strive for. Others see it as a sectarian and clannish phenomenon which leaves disunity and bitterness in its path. Still others feel it can be nothing more than an escape from the more exacting demands of the Christian life.

A survey of the available material on the subject of glossolalia portrays a threefold pattern into which the vast majority of the writings readily fit: (1) exegetical studies,[3] dealing with the Old Testament, with the inter-biblical and Greek parallels, as well as with the several New Testament references; (2) historical studies,[4] examining the phenomenon as it has occurred throughout the ages of the church; (3) psychological,[5] including actual clinical research and firsthand accounts by involved persons.

It is this last avenue which is being increasingly explored by the researchers. This is due in part to the growth and application of psychological and behavioral research methodology to various religious phenomena. Indeed, since the time of William James, who suggested that a psychopathic temperament is often present in religious leaders, students of psy-

---

[2]Morton Kelsey, *Tongue Speaking: An Experiment in Spiritual Experience* (Doubleday & Co., 1964), 1.

[3]*Cf.* Merrill F. Unger, *New Testament Teaching on Tongues* (Kregel Publications, 1971); Anthony A. Hoekema, *What About Tongue-Speaking?* (William B. Eerdmans Publishing Company, 1966); William G. MacDonald, *Glossolalia in the New Testament* (Gospel Publishing House, 1963).

[4]*Cf.* George B. Cutten, *Speaking with Tongues: Historically and Psychologically Considered* (Yale University Press, 1927) or Robert C. Dalton, *Tongues Like as of Fire: A Critical Study of the Modern Tongue Movement in the Light of Apostolic and Patristic Times* (Gospel Publishing House, 1945).

[5]*Cf.* Kelsey, *op. cit.*; John P. Kildahl, *The Psychology of Speaking in Tongues* (Harper & Row Publishers, 1972); John L. Sherrill, *They Speak with Other Tongues* (McGraw-Hill Book Co., 1964).

chology of religion have not hesitated to consider the possibility of a psychopathic involvement in the religious experience itself.[6] But even though great religious movements may be accompanied by strong emotion, and despite the fact that glossolalia under religious auspices is itself an emotional experience, the presence of emotion alone neither accredits nor discredits the actual experience.

This paper will survey some of the experimental studies of the phenomenon from several perspectives, paying particular attention to the sociopsychological dimensions of glossolalia.

ECSTATICISM IN NON-WESTERN CULTURES

The subject of keen interest among anthropologists, ecstaticism is obviously a phenomenon which predates the beginnings of the Judeo-Christian tradition. Carlyle May[7] has published a study of the various ethnographic data on glossolalia and related phenomena. Practices which seem to resemble glossolalia as it is known today have been documented in ancient India and China, as well as in many other parts of the world. Some researchers point to the fact that speaking in tongues and related phenomena are usually found in those areas where spirit possession is commonplace.

The phenomenon itself can be, and often is, the result of a kind of induced ecstasy. May concludes that as long as mankind has known divination, curing, sorcery, etc., he has been practicing glossolalia.

In both Western and non-Western cultures, it is interesting that the "interpreter" who often volunteers from the audience to interpret the message into human language has never been venerated by empirical research. In fact, the investigations that have been carried on have never verified the claim of speaking in an actual foreign language unknown to the glossolalist. Moreover, actual linguistic comparisons of tongue speech and the "interpretation" have revealed that the interpretation is not in fact a translation. Thus, the role of "interpreter," rather than that of translator, is one

---

[6]William James, *The Varieties of Religious Experience* (Longmans & Green, 1902), 23, 478.

[7]Carlyle L. May, "A Survey of Glossolalia and Related Phenomena in Non-Christian Religions," *American Anthropologist*, 58 (February 1956): 75-96.

of "verifier" in which he serves to insure to the audience the genuineness of the experience.

Mansell Pattison concludes: "We can at least suggest that the reports of audience observers 'verifying' the foreign language of glossolalists is not an indication of either malingering or pretense, but an honest report of *subjective* auditory perceptions, which, of course, may be quite different from the objective linguistic patterns spoken."[8]

THE SOCIOCULTURAL DIMENSIONS OF TONGUES

Both the social and psychological significance of speaking in tongues varies with the particular social movement of which the phenomenon is a part. R. A. Knox,[9] for example, has surveyed the occurrences of glossolalia in the eighteenth and nineteenth centuries in traditional Christian groups. He noted that the experimental aspect of the religious experience had been replaced chiefly by a new kind of intellectual sophistication. Thus, speaking in tongues was a vehicle used to establish again an experimental base for the faith. At the same time, during this age, the enlightenment, with its rationalistic criticism of the faith, was in vogue; and glossolalia quickly became a proof for the presence of God in the believer's life. It served to validate one's Christian experience in certain circles.

By and large the main practice of glossolalia has been limited to the Pentecostal and Holiness groups. These groups may generally be characterized by their marginal socioeconomic position in society as well as by a lower degree of intellectual sophistication. There have been many studies which have sought to show that the various forms of ecstatic behavior, including glossolalia, served as both an outlet for repressed conflicts and as a means of demonstrating that, despite one's position in society, one does have a certain possession of truth and righteousness.[10]

---

[8]E. Mansell Pattison, "Behavioral Science Research on the Nature of Glossolalia," *Journal of the American Scientific Affiliation*, 20 (September 1968): 75.

[9]R. A. Knox, *Enthusiasm: A Chapter in the History of Religion* (Oxford University Press, 1950).

[10]A. T. Boisen, "Economic Distress and Religious Experience: A Study of the Holy Rollers," *Psychiatry*, 2 (1939): 185-94 and *Religion in Crisis and Custom* (Harper & Bros., 1955); V. Lanternari, *The Religions of the Oppressed* (Alfred A. Knopf, 1963).

Recently in American Protestantism, glossolalia has made significant inroads into the middle-class Pentecostal groups who do not occupy a marginal social position at all. This group, according to some researchers, employs glossolalia as a function in the sense of a *rite de passage*, that is, a technique of recruitment and demonstration of behavioral change.[11] Thus, in this stratum of society, speaking in tongues functions not to serve personal needs so much as it provides a mechanism for nurturance of the social movement itself.

PERSONALITY STABILITY OF THE GLOSSOLALIST

One of the major concerns as the psychologist looks at glossolalia is the exact nature of the psychological makeup of the person who speaks in tongues. There have been obviously many contradictory claims and reports, depending on the population samples and other sociocultural variables.

In the early part of the twentieth century, there were numerous psychological and psychiatric studies of glossolalia. Among the most extensive studies were those of George Cutten,[12] Émile Lombard,[13] and Eddison Mosiman.[14] In general, these researchers concluded that tongues speakers were probably emotionally unstable and that the experience of glossolalia itself was a regressive pathological experience.

In more recent years, clinical studies have been based on much larger and very diverse samples. William Sargant,[15] for example, alludes to tongue speech as a form of regressive abreactive behavior, while Weston LaBarre[16] reports an extensive case history of Southern snake handlers who,

---

[11]L. P. Gerlach and V. H. Hine, "The Charismatic Revival: Process and Recruitment, Conversion, and Behavioral Change in Modern Religious Movement." Unpublished paper, University of Minnesota, 1966.

[12]Cutten, *op. cit.*

[13]Émile Lombard, *De la Glossolalie chez les premiers chretiens et des phenomenes sililaires* (Bridel, 1910).

[14]Eddison Mosiman, *Das Zungenreden Geschichtlich und psychologisch untersucht* (Mohr, 1911).

[15]William Sargant, *Battle for the Mind* (Doubleday & Co., 1957).

[16]Weston LaBarre, *They Shall Take Up Serpents: Psychology of the Southern Snake-Handling Cult* (University of Minnesota Press, 1962).

in addition, engaged in the practice of glossolalia. In his view, these were examples of the externalization of characterological conflict.

One fascinating study conducted as a doctoral dissertation in Johannesburg, South Africa compared a group of glossolalists with a comparable group of controls. The researcher, Lincoln Vivier, found more histories of developmental conflict and life disturbances among those who spoke in tongues. He concluded, however, that personalitywise the tongues groups were not significantly different from the controls groups.[17] Similar conclusions have been drawn by John Kildahl and Paul Qualben in a study done on a grant from the Behavioral Sciences Research Branch of the National Institute of Mental Health.[18]

A study conducted in 1966 by a psychiatrist in Berkeley, Dr. Paul Morentz,[19] showed that the glossolaliac tended to assume a different position when he functioned in Pentecostal churches where glossolalia was a part of the expected religious ritual in comparison to its appearance among staid, mainline churches where it is usually considered to be deviant behavior. Based on interviews of some sixty glossolalists, Morentz found several dominant personality patterns. Among these were (1) hostility to authority, (2) a consuming wish to compensate for feelings of inadequacy, (3) the desire to rationalize feelings of isolation, (4) strong feelings of dependency and suggestibility mixed with a strong tendency to dominate.

Stanley Plog[20] employed a battery of tests to a group of glossolaliacs and concluded that there were no atypical personality patterns among the group. Also he did not find a higher than expected rate of psychopathology. A similar conclusion was reached by L. P. Gerlach and his associates,[21] who sampled a wide population. These researchers, likewise, found no evidence of unusual psychopathology among Pentecostal adherents. They conclude: ''Most Pentecostals, though they are different in some be-

---

[17]L. M. Van Eetveldt Vivier, "Glossolalia." Unpublished doctor's dissertation, University of Witwatersand, Johannesburg, South Africa, 1960.

[18]Kildahl, *op. cit.*, pp. 57ff.

[19]Paul Morentz, "Lecture on Glossolalia." Unpublished paper, University of Southern California, Berkeley, 1966.

[20]Stanley Plog, "Preliminary Analysis of Group Questionnaires on Glossolalia." Unpublished data, University of Southern California, Los Angeles, 1966.

[21]Gerlach and Hine, *op. cit.*

havior, are not 'sick'. . . . They function effectively and cope adequately.'' These researchers admit the possibility that some church groups do attract more troubled individuals than do others and concede that it is entirely possible that some groups in more depressed areas attract more deprived persons or persons who are aged or lonely.

GLOSSOLALIA AS A PSYCHOLINGUISTIC PHENOMENON

The glossolalia movement has created considerable interest among linguists. In general, these researchers maintain that "tongues" does not represent any language known to mankind. Eugene A. Nida, of the American Bible Society, conducted an analysis of "tongues" which was recorded on tape.[22] He was assisted in the project by linguists who represented more than 150 aboriginal languages in more than twenty-five countries. Nida concluded: "The types of inventory and distribution would indicate clearly that this recording bears no resemblance to any actual language which has ever been treated by linguists."[23]

The linguistic evaluations of glossolalia as a language vary considerably since the speech itself varies in degree of organization. Some glossolalia, for example, is poorly organized and consists of nothing more than grunts and barely formed sounds, while other instances of tongue speech are highly organized into systematic series of phonemes.

It appears that in most instances glossolalia from the linguistic standpoint is composed of the basic speech elements of English, the major difference consisting in the lack of organization of these basic phonemes into any meaningful syntactical elements necessary for intelligible speech. Pattison has concluded that glossolalia resembles the early speech qualities of a child prior to the time when he would organize many variables associated with adult language.[24] Many linguistic researchers point to the fact that among the glossolalists studied there seems to be a limited phonemic catalogue utilized. The conclusions reached generally seemed to indicate that those who speak in tongues use a language, the characteristics of which

---

[22]*Cf.* ''The Report of the Toronto Institute of Linguistics'' cited in V. Raymond Edman, ''Divine or Devilish?'' *Christian Herald*, 87 (May 1964): 16.

[23]*Ibid.*

[24]Pattison, *op. cit.*, p. 77.

resemble those of a partially formed language rather than one which has formal characteristics.

George Devereaux[25] has discovered a striking comparison between the speech of a child and that of the glossolaliac. In fact, some researchers have concluded that tongue speech may be nothing more than a regression to an earlier mode of speech in which vocalization serves a purpose other than that of just communication of rational thought. Al Carlson at the University of California recorded "genuine" glossolalia in a religious context and also recorded some "contrived" glossolalia outside of a religious context. These speech samples were then rated by confessed glossolalists. His research indicated that the two types of glossolalia were not distinguishable from each other. Moreover, the "contrived" glossolalia actually received a higher rating than the "genuine" glossolalia.[26]

So it is that the structural linguist suggests that glossolalia, though it does have specific linguistic structure based on the language tongue of the speaker, is limited in organization; and the capacity to speak in this type of semiorganized language can be replicated under experimental conditions. Perhaps, then, tongue speech is not at all a "strange language" but nothing more than an aborted form of "familiar language."

Frank Farrell, however, cites competent linguists who believe that the glossolalia which they heard did sound structurally like a language.[27] Farrell's view has been challenged by William E. Welmers, professor of African languages at the University of California and an ordained minister of the Orthodox Presbyterian Church. He confesses that he has had his own private spiritual experience which cannot fully be explained and which he considers "precarious."[28] He concludes: "When Christians publicize, propagate, and endeavor to perpetuate an apparent manifestation of psychological instability and an obvious blasphemy as a special 'gift of the Holy Spirit,' I cannot refuse to apply my knowledge and training to the

---

[25]George Devereaux, "The Voices of Children," *American Journal of Psychotherapy*, 19 (1965): 4-19.

[26]Al Carlson, "Tongues of Fire Revisited." Unpublished paper, University of Southern California, Berkeley, 1967.

[27]Frank Farrell, "Outburst of Tongues: the New Penetration," *Christianity Today*, 7 (September 13, 1963): 6.

[28]William E. Welmers, "Glossolalia," *Christianity Today*, 7 (November 8, 1963): 20.

problem. So far, I can only conclude, with all sympathetic Scripture-centered scholarship I know how to apply, that modern glossolalia is a sad deception."[29]

The glossolaliac knows his "tongue" well because it is a familiar subjective experience for him. Because of this and because of his own preconceptions, as a result of tongue speech, he may indeed be brought "closer to God." Speaking in tongues serves to give him a security when and if he needs it. The restricted linguistic nature of glossolalia, the predominance of vowel sounds, the "playful" quality of the utterance, the calypso-type rhythm all suggest that glossolalia may, in fact, be a vocal thought-speech regression that could be restricted to the various specific functions of the ego.

The question of "communication," if asked in a strict linguistic context, is a moot one. Obviously, once the qualification of nonverbal communication is opened, the researchers will have to be content to await the findings of additional psycholinguistic research.

SOME PSYCHOLOGICAL THEORIES

E. Mansell Pattison believes that glossolalia may occur as part of a larger syndrome of hysterical, dissociative, or trance states, or may occur as a discreet piece of behavior.[30] He further suggests that glossolalia may be deviant psychopathological behavior or it may be normal expected behavior, depending on the sociocultural context. Pattison claims that glossolalia is a form of partially developed speech in which the thought-speech apparatus of the glossolaliac is employed for a variety of intrapsychic functions and may accompany psychopathological regression or it may be a form of healthy regression in the service of the ego leading to more creative modes of life.

Dr. Pattison, a medical doctor, points out that the most important distinction that should be made is between cause and consequence. Glossolalia, avers Pattison, is not caused by supernatural forces, but tongue-speech may be a consequence of involvement in deep and meaningful spiritual worship.

---

[29]*Ibid.*

[30]Pattison, *op. cit.*, p. 85.

Tying the meaning and function of glossolalia to its sociocultural context, Dr. Pattison insists that it may serve various psychodynamic functions. He concludes that glossolalia per se is not a spiritual phenomenon, but it may be a consequence of a deep and meaningful spiritual experience. Thus, speaking in tongues, according to Dr. Pattison, does not miraculously change people in a supernatural sense; but participating in glossolalia as part of a larger social and personal commitment may play an important role in the change of direction in a glossolaliacs's life.

Professor John P. Kildahl is director of the program in pastoral psychology at New York Theological Seminary and is a member of the faculty in the postgraduate center for mental health. He has recently conducted a study and published a book[31] in which he has sought to demonstrate that glossolalia can be learned, almost as other human abilities are learned. So it is academic whether one refers to the practice as a gift of the Spirit. Since glossolalia does make the individual feel better, it is perhaps theologically possible to claim that anything that makes one more at home with himself is beneficial and could be referred to as a gift of God.

Kildahl concludes that it is the use of tongues that determines whether it is constructive or divisive.

Professor Ira J. Martin has written extensively on the subject of glossolalia and conceives that tongues appear "to be an ecstatic form of speech, seeking to give vent to the joy of new life of spiritual redemption."[32] He believes that glossolalia is one form of psychic catharsis, "a genuine but not universal concomitant of the Christian conversion experience."[33] Furthermore, Martin differentiates two types of glossolalia: the genuine and the synthetic. The former represents a "psychic catharsis." He suggests that in the deep, basic reintegration of the individual's personality the psychological upheaval is often too great to control; therefore, the resulting joy of release from suppressed guilt feelings is similarly too thrilling to repress and that the eager desire which one has to express the joys of the new life of inner peace and the fresh outlook will not be subjected to constrainment.

---

[31]Kildahl, *op. cit.*

[32]Ira J. Martin, *Glossolalia in the Apostolic Church: A Survey of Tongue Speech* (Berea College Press, 1960), 100.

[33]*Ibid.*

In Martin's view, "synthetic" glossolalia represents that tongue speech which occurs when other factors are operating, for example, autohypnosis, normal hypnosis, or the laws of autosuggestion.

Professor Émile Lombard suggests a threefold classification of "automatic speech."[34] These types represent degrees of progression from the remote forms to the nearer and the more familiar forms of organized language. First, there are inarticulate sounds such as hiccups, cries, sighs, and wailings. These simple vocal sounds are especially apparent in glossolaliacs at the beginning of their automatism. The second classification, avers Lombard, encompasses the most common type of glossolalia—a pseudo-language or speech composed of articulate sounds which resemble words. There is actually a phonic differentiation, and a person appears to be speaking and expressing specific ideas. In reality, however, the language is meaningless and has no content. Finally, Lombard suggests that there are "manufactured" or "coined" words (neologisms) which emerge on a base of well-characterized pseudo-language and have a constant representative value of meaning.

Having more than a passing interest in the phenomenon known as glossolalia, C. G. Jung's first reference to the phenomenon occurs in the published dissertation for his medical degree "On the Psychology and Pathology of So-Called Occult Phenomena." This was the first work Jung published. In it he describes his single observation of tongue speech and classifies the phenomenon as a kind of somnambulism or multiple personality in which some center other than the ego takes possession of the motor centers which control personality. He is not suggesting that somnambulism is necessarily pathological or otherwise damaging to the personality. In fact, he suggests that the experience may have "an eminently teleological significance" if it provides the individual, who might otherwise inevitably succumb, with a sense of victory.[35]

Almost fifty yeas later, Jung again referred to the phenomenon of speaking in tongues. He seemed to suggest that the more inhibited and out of touch with the unconscious, the more likely a person is to be a glossolalist. In his view, this is preferable to neurotic forms of behavior, which all serve to release tension and inhibition.

---

[34]Lombard, *op. cit.*, pp. 25-34.

[35]Carl G. Jung, "Psychiatric Studies," *Collected Works* 1 (Pantheon Books, 1957): 79.

Most of the interpreters of Jung have sustained the view that tongues is a genuine invasion into consciousness of content from the deepest level of the collective unconscious.

SOME THEOLOGICAL IMPLICATIONS

Since most of the discussions about glossolalia have been strongly polarized, perhaps what is needed more than anything else is sympathetic listening. There is much more research that will have to be done before the whole story can be known. Research is needed not only from the psychological point of view but also from the historical and biblical perspectives.

In the meantime, those of us who do not speak in tongues must be patient and understanding of our brother who is caught up in this experience. Sometimes beyond the repugnant external form of glossolalia, significant and abiding questions are being raised.

Beneath the external furor, the genuine glossolaliac may be deeply committed to the reality of the presence of God in his life. He may be desperately searching for a symbol which will adequately express his sincerity. But, alas, much of Christendom rejects both him and his symbol; and he may become withdrawn, defensive, and hostile. Yet he makes his point: every Christian is obligated to give a significant place to the concept of the Holy Spirit in his life. The nonspeaking brother may denounce the symbol, but how can he attack the reality?

Thus the glossolaliac forces the remainder of Christendom to elaborate its concept of the Holy Spirit since tongue-speech is rejected. At present, many of those both pro and con glossolalia need to think through the question of the relevancy for the Holy Spirit in the Christian life. What does it mean morally and socially to talk about God's presence through his Spirit?

Also, the resurgence of glossolalia may divulge a need in man to talk about God. The twentieth century "man come of age" is taught by his culture to suppress such unscientific or illogical speech. Glossolaliacs have chosen to vent this basic need, apparently disregarding the culturally imposed consequences. Again, how many "orthodox" Christians are willing to go this far in some other area to demonstrate that "the old creature has passed away"?

Glossolalia may be, in fact, a loud protest to the often cold, impersonal form which institutional worship sometimes acquires. Some regard the movement as basically a rebellion against overintellectualized and overorganized Christianity. Regardless of how the nonparticipants respond, glossolaliacs are saying that there must be more room for spontaneity in worship—more opportunity for the worshipers themselves to get involved. John Sherrill believes that every Christian needs a measure of order and freedom in worship, and he thinks that here the glossolaliac and the nonglossolaliac in dialogue can make a significant contribution to Christian life. Out of constructive debate can come a resolution of differences which would be profitable for all Christians.

What needs to be debated is not what tongues means so much as the form in which this meaning is couched. Many nonparticipants in the tongues movement would not hesitate to posit a meaningful role for the Holy Spirit in the Christian life. The real point of their stumbling is the actual manner in which glossolalia is practiced: it is both repulsive and repugnant.

It is obvious that mainstream Christians can learn much from their brother who speaks in tongues. Coming to accept him as he is may be itself a sign of approaching Christian maturity. Every effort must be made to understand the deepest needs of those persons involved—an effort to hear them and understand. This will require a sustained, sympathetic, nonjudgmental effort on the part of the total Christian community.

25

VIRGINIA H. HINE

Pentecostal Glossolalia: Toward a Functional Interpretation

[Reprinted with permission from *Journal for the Scientific Study of Religion*, 8 (1965): 161-64. Reprinted with permission from the Society for the Scientific Study of Religion.]

Theories which explain glossolalia as indicative of psychological pathology, suggestibility, or hypnosis, or as a result of social disorganization and deprivation are reviewed and found inadequate to explain recent data on the Pentecostal movement. Concepts of glossolalia as learned behavior and as part of a process of personality reorganization are found more useful. Data are presented to support a functional interpretation of glossolalia as one component in the process of commitment to a movement with important implications for both personal and social change.

Glossolalia, translated literally from the Greek, means "tongue speech." It is a form of unintelligible vocalization which has non-semantic meaning to the speaker, and is interpreted in the Bible as a divinely inspired spiritual gift. Glossolalia was well known among the early Christians, has been associated with almost all of the revivalistic movements that have punctuated the history of the church, and characterizes the modern Pentecostal movement. From the beginning it has occasioned controversy, not only between practitioners and their critics, but more recently among social scientists attempting to interpret or explain the phenomenon.

The purpose of this article is to review current psychological literature on glossolalia, to note sociological concepts of predisposing conditions, and to suggest a functional explanation of its role in the spread of the Pentecostal movement.

The research reported here is based on an anthropological study of the Pentecostal movement in the United States, Mexico, Haiti, and Colombia. Data on glossolalia among American Pentecostals were collected by means of 45 case histories, 239 self-administered questionnaires, informal interviews with leaders and members of more than 30 Pentecostal groups, and participant-observation in seven churches and prayer groups. Participants who cooperated with the study included members of traditional Pentecostal sects, as well as so-called "neo-Pentecostals" in independent churches, and groups of tongue speakers in non-Pentecostal Protestant and Catholic churches.[1]

DESCRIPTION OF THE PHENOMENON

The phenomenon of glossolalia, it should be noted, is not limited to a Christian or even a religious context. The term has been used to refer to a wide range of sounds from animal-like grunts and "gibberish" to well-patterned articulations (May, 1956). Glossolalia, as observed among participants in the modern Pentecostal movement, involves utterances of varying lengths, lasting from a few seconds to an hour or more. Though unintelligible, they are usually patterned sufficiently so that the tongue speech of one individual may be distinguished from that of another. Often

[1]The research was directed by Dr. Luther Gerlach, Department of Anthropology, University of Minnesota, and supported by grants from the Hill Family Foundation, the University of Minnesota Graduate School, the McKnight Family Foundation, and the Ferndale Foundation. The author served as research assistant.

one tongue speaker uses two or more different patternings or "languages." The experience is interpreted by Pentecostals as control of the speech organs by the Holy Spirit who is praying through the believer in "a heavenly language." It is felt to be more often praise than petition, and is usually accompanied by sensations of great freedom, tranquility, and joy. These emotions often continue long after the glossolalic utterance itself. Glossolalics frequently refer to the experience as one of being "in another dimension," "beyond oneself," or "truly out of this world."

Glossolalia in the Pentecostal context is sometimes associated with an altered mental state, with some degree of dissociation or trance. It occasionally involves involuntary motor activity or, rarely, complete loss of consciousness. These behaviors are most common during the initial experience of glossolalia which usually is associated with the Baptism of the Holy Spirit, a subjective experience of being filled with or possessed by the Holy Spirit. Subsequent use of the "gift of tongues" is most often independent of any altered mental state or trance behavior. Speaking with tongues may even occur without the usual emotional rewards. Particularly is this likely to be true in a clinical setting where the Pentecostal is cooperating with a scientific observer.

Linguists who have studied Pentecostal glossolalia stress the fact that the linguistic event can and should be distinguished from religious behaviors or from particular psychological and emotional states. It has even been suggested that the word "glossolalia" be reserved for a type of vocalization that can be produced without an altered mental or emotional state and which can occur in contexts other than religious ones (Jaquith, 1967; Samarin, 1968a). For the purposes of linguistic analysis, this is clearly a useful approach and has contributed much to our understanding of the whole phenomenon.

An anthropological analysis, however, requires contextualization of the linguistic phenomenon, an attempt to identify possible psychological and sociological correlates, and an interpretation of its function in the cross-cultural spread of Pentecostalism as a movement.

PSYCHOLOGICAL INTERPRETATIONS

GLOSSOLALIA AS PATHOLOGICAL

During the nineteenth and early twentieth century, glossolalia in revivalistic religion was often associated with an energetic form of religious

enthusiasm which inspired such labels as "Holy Rollers." Scholarly interpretations of these verbal and motor "automatisms" tended to assume some
form of psychological pathology. The classic and most oft-quoted source,
even by modern psychologists, is *Speaking With Tongues*, written in 1927
by George Cutten, a Baptist minister and educator. He illustrates his analysis with descriptive accounts of tongue speaking, and draws very unflat-
tering conclusions as to the psychological and sociological correlates. He
makes fairly extravagant statements about the gift of tongues being received only by nonverbal individuals of low mental ability in whom the
capacity for rational thought, a comparatively recent human achievement
according to Cutten, was underdeveloped.

Members of our research team can only wish that Dr. Cutten had been
able to join us in interviewing modern Pentecostals. A more verbal group
of people would be difficult to imagine. One of the remarkable things about
tongue speakers is the degree to which they can communicate both the
quality and the effect of their subjective religious experiences. Were it not
so, they would have been much less disruptive in their churches of origin.
This fact, indeed, is basic to the ability to Pentecostals to recruit, and is
therefore crucial to the successful spread of the movement.

As for "low mental ability" and "underdeveloped rational capacity,"
even those who began with very little formal education bring to their study
of the scriptures an intensity of mentation that would stand any college student in good stead.

Cutten's contentions concerning psychopathology, quoted and re-
quoted through the years, have taken on an aura of fact among non-Pentecostal churchmen who are critical of the movement. His assumption that
glossolalia is linked to schizophrenia and hysteria has not been supported
by any empirical evidence. Studies had been made of psychotic individuals in mental institutions who spoke in tongues, and the temptation to
generalize from these cases to otherwise normal glossolalics was seldom
resisted. More recent studies have clarified the difference between schizophrenic and non-pathological religious behavior.

NON-PATHOLOGICAL GLOSSOLALIA

Alexander Alland (1961) found that older psychological explanations
of glossolalia as schizophrenia or hysteria are no longer acceptable in view
of recent sociocultural data. Tongue speaking members of the Negro Pentecostal church he studied were well adjusted to their social environment

and behaved normally except for the glossolalic experiences. According to Alland, this weakens the interpretation of glossolalia as indicative of schizophrenia since schizophrenics are unable to limit their problems to one segment of behavior.

He also considers hysteria an inadequate explanation of the "religious trance states" which he found associated with glossolalia among his informants. This, he contends, is learned behavior, and not necessarily a result of personality disorder.

Anton Boisen (1939) interviewed and observed members of a Holy Rollers church and compared them to certain of his psychiatric patients who displayed superficially similar behaviors. He noted a conceptual similarity between the Pentecostals' interpretation of tongue speaking as possession by the Holy Spirit and the psychiatric patients' feeling that they are controlled by a power external to themselves. But he could find no evidence of mental illness in the tongue speakers from the church. A crucial difference, he believed, were the social influences brought into play when the glossolalic experience occurred within the matrix of church life.

Boisen had previously treated several cases of mentally disordered individuals who also experienced the Baptism of the Holy Spirit and tongues within the church context. He found that for the most part the experience was therapeutic for them. According to Boisen, glossolalia within a social matrix in which it is structured, and in which pressure for constructive behavioral results is exerted by group expectations, tends to be a constructive experience for both mentally disordered and for normal individuals.

Ari Kiev (1964) made a comparative study of ten West Indian schizophrenics in English mental hospitals and a group of normal West Indian immigrants who were Pentecostals. He found that:

> unlike nonpsychotic individuals who participate in various religious cults and in the revivalist sects in which dissociative phenomena and possession are permitted and encouraged, the schizophrenic patients could not maintain sufficient control of autistic and regressive behavior to fit into the prescribed ritual patterns.

The difference between the glossolalic behavior of psychotic individuals and that of nonpsychotic individuals was perfectly clear to the normal Pentecostals in Kiev's study.

Our interview data support this observation. Pentecostals of a wide range of socioeconomic and educational backgrounds are aware of the different results of glossolalic experience for normal as compared with emotionally unstable individuals. Many Pentecostal leaders have pragmatically developed ways of evaluating potential converts, and do not encourage the glossolalic experience in persons they consider to be in questionable mental or emotional health.

PSYCHOLOGICAL TESTING OF MODERN GLOSSOLALICS

Four recent studies, using reliable and widely accepted psychological tests have been conducted, three with long-established traditional Pentecostal groups and one with neo-Pentecostals. In none of these studies has it been shown that Pentecostal glossolalics as a group are more psychotic or even neurotic than the control groups or the societal norms.

L. M. Van Eetvelt Vivier (1960) used a battery of tests which included the Cattell Personality Test, the Willoughby test for general level of neuroticism, the Rosenzweig Picture Frustration test, a biographical background questionnaire, and a religious belief and activity questionnaire. The experimental group consisted of twenty-four tongue speaking Pentecostals. The control groups were twenty non-tongue speaking Pentecostals (or pre-tongue speakers) and twenty members of a Christian church who did not approve of or practice glossolalia. The three groups were matched as closely as possible for age, sex, education, occupation and religious convictions.

Vivier's findings reveal no significant differences between the test and the control groups except for two factors on the Cattell inventory. These are "desurgence" and "shrewdness-naiveté." On desurgence—defined by Vivier as the tendency to renounce immediate satisfactions for long-range goals and to accept moral restrictions and goals of higher achievement—glossolalics, although not far from the median, appeared to be more "long-circuiting" and renunciative in their habits than the control groups. Glossolalics were also found to be significantly different from the control groups in that they were "less realistic and practical, more concerned with feeling than thought or action, and more tolerant and humane in their interests."

Vivier found no significant difference between the glossolalics and the control groups (or between the pre-glossolalics and the anti-glossolalics) on the Willoughby test for general level of neuroticism. According to this finding there is no more evidence of persistent, unadaptive anxiety reactions in tongue speakers, or in Pentecostals who have not yet spoken in tongues, than in non-Pentecostals of the same socioeconomic and educational backgrounds. Vivier also specifically concludes that his findings did *not* substantiate theories of dissociation as a result of Freudian repression.

Another of Vivier's findings is interesting in view of the fact that faith healings, which are widely associated with Pentecostal glossolalia in all groups, are sometimes assumed to involve only psychosomatic illnesses which are symptoms of conversion hysteria (in the clinical sense of psychic tensions "converted" into physical dysfunction). Vivier found that glossolalics scored low on the three factors of the Cattell Personality inventory which are associated with conversion hysteria, and were not significantly different from the control groups.

Vivier characterized the glossolalics he studied as generally more sensitive, less bound by traditional or orthodox through processes, less depressed, having less generalized fear, but more need for emotional catharsis.

William Wood (1965) approached the subject with the hypothesis that personality types participating in highly emotional religions will vary in some regular way from types participating in more sedate religions. He used the Rorschach technique because he felt it reflected perceptual processes, and that these were essentially what religious emotion was. Wood conducted field observations in two Southern rural communities in an economically marginal area, and administered the Rorschach test to two socioeconomically similar groups, one Pentecostal and one non-Pentecostal.

The most significant differences between the Pentecostal and non-Pentecostal Rorschach records were in the area of shading. Unfortunately, according to Wood, this is the chief "area of dispute" among Rorschach authorities concerning the scoring of responses. The frequency of shading responses were the same for the test as for the control group, but the groups differed significantly in that Pentecostals were more likely to produce perspective, depth, and distance responses.

A second difference between the groups was in the area of movement responses. Pentecostals tended to use animal or inanimate forms more frequently, and to formulate their human percepts only partially or vaguely.

Wood feels that these findings establish regular differences between Pentecostal and non-Pentecostal Rorschach responses, and that this indicates, if not a difference in personality type, at least a difference in basic habits of perception.

Wood interprets the differences in personality type in the form of fifteen hypotheses rather than conclusions because of the "degree of doubt concerning Rorschach interpretive principles.'' Several of these hypotheses suggest that Pentecostals have inadequately structured value-attitude systems. Another suggests that Pentecostals have an uncommon degree of uncertainty regarding personal relationships, but are highly motivated to establish close interpersonal involvements. This hypothesis appears to be inconsistent with the following one which states that Pentecostals are able to canalize their emotions normally into interpersonal relationships, and have an emotional organization which makes positive and satisfying interpersonal relationships possible. The next hypothesis suggests that Pentecostalism attracts uncertain, threatened, inadequately organized people who are strongly motivated to reach a state of personal integrity. Several following hypotheses suggest that Pentecostal religious experiences lead to personality integration.

Apparent inconsistencies between hypotheses may be due to Wood's view that Pentecostals are in the process of restructuring attitude systems and social relationships. He makes an important and little-recognized point that his study provides no information about whether the "Pentecostal type" is attracted to or is developed by participation in the movement.

Wood's study provides no evidence, nor does he suggest, that the differences he found indicate abnormality or psychological pathology of any kind.

Stanley Plog conducted a study of neo-Pentecostal groups in Los Angeles and Seattle using two questionnaire forms, one for samples taken at regular meetings of three different groups and the other for interviews in depth. Over eight hundred group questionnaires were tabulated and two hundred individual interviews. Plog also used the California Psychological Inventory. He reported (personal communication) that individuals who were entering into the tongues experience were "very responsible and normally well-controlled individuals." He noted that the one dimension of the test in which they tended to fall low was that of interpersonal relationships. Plog considers this significant since this is the area in which he received "consistent responses [during interviews] as to the benefits participants have derived from tongues." Most report that they get along better with others after having received the gift. This supports Wood's hypothesis concerning changes in interpersonal relationships.

Our own observations, made during interviews and as participant-observers, are also consistent with Wood's and Plog's. Pentecostals as a group appear to be normally adjusted and productive members of society. In observing family interaction of participants, we noted that when both husband and wife participate actively in the "tongues movement," family life tends to be more than normally well-integrated. On our written questionnaire, responses to a question about specific changes in behavior patterns, habits, or ways of acting toward others could be grouped into three general categories, all of which had implications for interpersonal relationships. Forty-four per cent mentioned increased capacity for love toward, sensitivity to, or concern for others. Thirty-seven per cent mentioned the "fruits of the Spirit," such as love, patience, kindness, gentleness, etc. The remaining nineteen per cent described an increase in self-confidence and the "power to witness," an active attempt to influence others.

Nathan Gerrard. One of the most conclusive studies of the psychological correlates of glossolalia and related phenomena is that of Nathan Gerrard. Over a period of several years, he conducted a sociological-anthropological study of a serpent-handler cult in West Virginia. Although serpent handling is an independent outgrowth of nineteenth century Holiness movements, and thus only indirectly related to modern Pentecostalism, glossolalia is an important part of the religious behavioral complex.

Gerrard's field work included a thorough sociological study of the rural area in which the serpent-handler church is located. He compared the serpent-handler with other religious groups in the community with respect to economic, social, and political variables.

Repeated observation in the snake handlers church and interviews with members in their homes led Gerrard to the hypothesis that snake handlers are not psychologically or emotionally disturbed people. To test this hypothesis, he administered the Minnesota Multiphasic Personality Inventory to the snake handlers group, and to members of a conventional church of a major Protestant denomination in the same rural area. Both experimental and control groups were similar in age and sex distribution.

The 96 MMPIs (46 from the snake handlers and 50 from the conventional church) were sent to the Department of Psychology of the University of Minnesota for analysis. The analysis consisted of (1) an analysis of variance of scores, using church membership, sex, and age group (old versus young) as the factorial design; (2) an interpretation of the MMPI profiles of the two groups by three clinical judges; and (3) a sorting of the individual profiles by four other clinical judges.

Results of the analysis of variance revealed significant differences between the two groups on three MMPI scales. The conventional church members scored higher on the K scale and scale 3 (Hysteria) than the serpent handlers. A significant age/church group interaction on scale 2 (Depression) indicated that old members of the conventional denomination show particularly high Depression scores. Serpent handlers scored higher on scales 4 (Psychopathic Deviate) and 9 (Hypomania) but not at a significant level.

The differences were interpreted by the consultant from the Department of Psychology at the University of Minnesota as follows:

> The conventional denomination, compared to the serpent handlers, are on the average more defensive, less inclined to admit undesirable traits, more ready to use mechanisms of denial and repression. The older members of the conventional denomination, in addition, show indications of marked depressive symptomology. The serpent handlers appear less defensive and restrained. On the contrary, they seem to be more exhibitionistic, excitable, and pleasure-oriented . . . and are less controlled by considerations of conformity to the general culture, particularly middle class culture. There is no evidence for systematic differences between the two groups on dimensions of thought disorder (psychoticism). (Gerrard and Gerrard, 1966:56).

Clinical interpretation of the findings was done by three psychologists for whom the two church groups were identified only as church A and church B. They were provided with a brief description of the sociological background common to the two groups. Gerrard summarized their findings as follows: The serpent handlers, like the members of the conventional denomination, are essentially within the "normal limits" established by wide use of the MMPI. With respect to neuroticism, the clinicians found a higher incidence among the conventional denomination than among the serpent handlers although it was not statistically significant. Members of the conventional denomination presented a "somewhat more repressive and dysphoric picture" and were also found to be "more likely to present more symptoms of psychological distress" than were the snake-handling glossolalics. In general, the comparison of all serpent handlers with all members of the conventional denomination showed no marked differences with respect to mental health. What differences there were, were in the direction of the serpent handlers being more "normal" than members of the conventional denomination (Gerrard and Gerrard, 1966:65-67).

The sorting of the MMPI profiles was done by four other clinicians who were told that one of the groups was a snake handlers church and one a conventional church, but were not told which profiles came from which group. They were asked to categorize the profiles diagnostically and then to sort out the profiles they thought belonged to the snake handlers. The four clinicians assigned most of the profiles they judged to be "abnormal" to the serpent handlers and most "normal" profiles to the conventional denomination. The actual distribution showed that the reverse was true. According to the consultant who directed the analysis, "analysis of the data makes it clear that the clinicians did have rather definite ideas as to how serpent handlers' and conventional denomination members' profiles ought to look. These ideas, however, were quite erroneous."

The obvious bias revealed here is not uncommon. Informal interviews with four psychotherapists about our Pentecostal data revealed a remarkable readiness to assume pathology in glossolalics without adequate knowledge of the groups involved. This tendency to evaluate unusual religious behavior negatively has been noted by other students of glossolalia (McDonnell 1968) and religious trance (Bourguignon and Pettay 1964).

Quite clearly, available evidence requires that an explanation of glossolalia as pathological must be discarded. Even among those who accept this position, however, there often remains a sort of nonspecific suspicion of emotional immaturity, of subclinical anxiety, or of some form of personal inadequacy. This is particularly true of churchmen in whose denominations the ranks of Spirit-filled Christians are swelling (Martin 1960, Lapsley and Simpson 1964 a and b, Hoekema 1966, Protestant Episcopal Church 1963, American Lutheran Church 1964). As yet there is no empirical, scientific evidence for this interpretation of glossolalia. Future studies of it might usefully include an examination of possible bias on the part of non-glossolalic observers.

SUGGESTIBILITY AND HYPNOSIS

Another psychological theory that is commonly used to explain the occurrence of glossolalia, but which assumes no pathology, is that of suggestibility or predisposition to hypnosis. One of the problems with this theory is the definitional difficulty. According to social psychologist Hans Toch, suggestibility is characteristic of those who join movements, and is created by a strong increase in susceptibility (1956:12). It involves an awareness of a problem and a readiness to jump at promising solutions.

Hadley Cantril, in his study of social movements (1941), had defined the conditions of suggestibility as either (1) lack of adequate mental context, or frame of reference within which to interpret experience, or (2) a fixed mental context which, in its simplest form, is conditioned response. Presumably there is some area between these two states which is inhabited by individuals who have an adequate but not fixed mental context, and who would therefore not be likely to join movements or get caught up in revivalistic fervor.

Suggestibility is often poised against critical ability, sometimes with the connotations of the former as a more "primitive" type of mental functioning (Meares 1963). Several students of Pentecostal glossolalia suggest that it results from "a regression in the service of the ego" in a form of group hypnosis, and that glossolalics tend to be submissive as well as suggestible (Alland 1961, Kildahl 1966).

Our data pose a problem with regard to the hypnosis theory, as we have found that tongue speaking occurs frequently in solitary situations. After the initial experience of glossolalia, most Pentecostals speak with tongues as frequently, if not more frequently, alone in private prayer as in group situations where hypnosis could be practiced. Auto-suggestion and self-hypnosis are commonly used to explain this fact. Twenty-three per cent of our questionnaire respondents, however, experienced the Baptism of the Holy Spirit and spoke with tongues for the first time when they were alone.

This would suggest a sophisticated and calculated use of posthypnotic suggestion during previous group meetings, and this we did not observe.

Vivier, in the study discussed above, provides empirical data with respect to the suggestibility theory. He specifically challenges the notion of tongue speakers as highly susceptible to suggestion since his test group scored lower, though not significantly, than the control group on this factor of the personality inventory.

The problem of viewing suggestibility as a predisposing characteristic for experiencing glossolalia is complicated by the fact that suggestibility is also the basis for normal processes of socialization, education, and successful psychotherapy, and that the only truly non-suggestible person is the psychopath (Frank 1961, Kimball 1966, Sargant 1957). Cantril argues that suggestibility is a function of the situation in which any individual might find himself rather than a characteristic of the individual. Toch also stresses the specificity of susceptibility in different individuals, and in the same individual at different points in his life. Until we know more about the relationship between suggestibility and type of group interaction, and can measure the degree of suggestibility more accurately, generalizations about glossolalics as suggestible individuals do not seem either very useful or supported by available data.

SOCIOLOGICAL INTERPRETATIONS

DEPRIVATION AND DISORGANIZATION THEORIES

Two sociological theories which have been used to explain Pentecostal religious behavior should be mentioned, even if only in passing. One is the view that Pentecostalism spreads where there is social disorganization: the other is that it flourishes primarily among economically or socially deprived classes.

Disorganization theory. Our cross-cultural survey of the movement does not support the social disorganization theory either in this country or in others. While many Pentecostal congregations are located in socially disorganized communities, neither Pentecostal churches nor the practice of tongue speaking is limited to groups suffering from these conditions. In non-Western societies, the movement is successful in rural areas where traditional tribal or village social structures have not been disrupted or disorganized.

Deprivation theory. The same is true of the deprivation theory. Not only are members of the long-established Pentecostal sects, such as the Assemblies of God, moving up the socioeconomic scale into the middle class, the movement itself is spreading into Catholic, Episcopalian, Presbyterian, Baptist, Lutheran, and other denominational groups. Converts are being drawn from a wide range of socioeconomic and educational backgrounds.

The disorganization and deprivation models are analyzed in more detail in other reports and publications (Gerlach and Hine 1968, Hine 1967).

CONCEPTUAL PREDISPOSITIONS

Finding the psychological maladjustment, social disorganization and deprivation theories inadequate to explain the spread of glossolalic behavior as we had observed it, we turn to those characteristics which were common to the glossolalics in our study as potentially explanatory. In the analysis of our data collected by interviews and questionnaires, we found that in spite of wide differences in socioeconomic, educational, or church backgrounds, our respondents were strikingly similar in the area of pre-conversion conceptual orientation.

71% of our respondents considered their religious training to have been conservative or fundamentalist.

74% were brought up to consider smoking and drinking were wrong.

83% were trained to accept the scriptures as authoritative.

91% attended church regularly every week even before conversion to Pentecostalism.

54% were involved as officers or committee members of the organization of their churches (non-Pentecostal in three-fourths of the cases) *before* receiving the Baptism of the Holy Spirit.

Only 16% reported that they were experiencing any sort of crisis just prior to their Spirit Baptism and glossolalic experience, with 84% describing their pre-conversion situation as one of gradual spiritual growth.

Although these percentages must not be extrapolated to the movement as a whole, field observation and available historical accounts of case histories tend to support this general characterization of Christian glossolalics.

The picture that emerges from these data is one of individuals trained to orient their lives around a church organization and to interpret experiences and events in a religious context. J. M. Yinger points out that it is a serious mistake to identify religious interests and "needs" with the more anxious or insecure members of a society. The need for and interest in religion is largely, though not entirely, a result of training and variations in the socialization process (1957: 91-94). Thus a possible predisposition to glossolalia would be what Clifford Geertz (1965) would call the "religious perspective"—a mode of seeing, a way of construing the world, a conceptual framework by which experience is ordered into what we know as "meaning." The religious perspective, according to Geertz, is one of several equally workable ways of looking at life. The scientific perspective is another, the "common sensical" a third. As Geertz defines it, the religious perspective differs from the common sensical because "it moves beyond the realities of everyday life to wider ones which correct and complement them," and from the scientific because "it questions the realities of everyday life not out of institutionalized skepticism which dissolves the world's givenness into a swirl of probablistic hypotheses, but in terms of what it takes to be wider, non-hypothetical truths." Rather than detachment, the religious perspective demands commitment; rather than analysis, encounter. Such a perspective is generated out of habitual, concrete acts of religious observances.

LEARNED BEHAVIOR THEORY

Clearly an orientation to which an individual is socialized does not produce a specific behavior; otherwise all those who have acquired a religious perspective would practice glossolalia. Several students of the phenomenon would go beyond what might be called the socialization theory and view glossolalia as learned behavior. E. Mansell Pattison, studying the glossolalia of a group of neo-Pentecostals from the point of view of speech pathology, also rejects the theory that glossolalics are socioeconomically deprived or emotionally disturbed. His thesis is rather that glossolalia is an experience available to any normal person who is willing to "adopt a passive attitude about controlling speech," and who is supplied with the "appropriate motivation, group setting and examples" (1964). He concludes that glossolalia is an accompaniment of an intense and meaningful spiritual experience for normal, devoutly religious people, but that it must be seen as incidental to the attainment of spiritual goals and that it can be achieved as an end in itself. He emphasizes the fact that glossolalia is produced by natural speech mechanisms, and defines it as "a stereotyped pattern of unconsciously controlled vocal behavior."

Recent linguistic studies of glossolalic utterances have been used to support a "learned behavior" theory. James Jaquith (1967) compared the glossolalic and casual speech of his informants, and found that the phones, the distribution patterns of phones, the syllable types, and even the stress patterns of glossolalia were similar to those either in the natural speech of the individual or in familiar preaching patterns and intonations. William Samarin (1968a) also found that glossolalic utterances, analyzed linguistically, were derivative from casual speech patterns. But he observed in addition several innovative features, such as simplified syllabic structure, repetition of both phones and syllables, and the use of sound units not found in the native speech. Samarin suggests that further study of glossolalia might reveal much about the nature of man's language-creating ability, and about the unconventional use of speech "as an expression of the ineffable."

In his attention to the means by which a "tongue" is acquired, Samarin's observations parallel our own. The two studies were conducted independently in different cities, and neither principal investigator was aware of the other's work until later. Samarin records several instances of individuals for whom the first experience of glossolalia occurred with no previous knowledge of the phenomenon and no acquaintance with another glossolalic (1968b). Our records also include several such incontestable cases. There is no question that glossolalic utterances of length and fluency can be generated quite spontaneously. We have observed, however, as has Samarin, that the vast majority of Pentecostal tongue speakers "received the gift" in the context of a religious group, as part of a larger set of behavioral patterns and ideological formulations. One cannot learn to speak with tongues in the same sense that natural semantic languages are learned. Each glossolalic utterance is produced *de novo*. In a very much more general sense, however, glossolalia may be considered learned behavior.

Most candidates for the Baptism of the Holy Spirit have heard tongues at one time or another. Although they may or may not expect glossolalia to accompany the subjective experience they are seeking, most have received minimal instructions concerning such facilitating mechanics as bodily posture, relaxation, vocalized exhalations, and "turning your tongue over to the Lord." Some are instructed to praise God in their own language until another is given to them by the Spirit. Others are told just to start to speak, but not in English, and to let the Holy Spirit take over. In a few cases, a candidate may be instructed to "repeat after me" and copy the glossolalic utterances of the person who is helping him "pray through" to the Baptism of the Holy Spirit. Many candidates, on the other hand, have received no instructions concerning glossolalic vocalizations and concentrate only on the subjective experience of the Baptism. For these, glossolalia may be considered learned behavior only in that they are aware of a model. Expectations have been structured through study of New Testament references to the phenomenon, through discussion, or through witnessing others' glossolalic behavior.

Even if it is true that a certain "cognitive set" is a predisposing condition and that glossolalia is learned behavior, the phenomenon is still not explained or even interpreted adequately. Not all individuals with the same cognitive set become glossolalics. Furthermore, almost all human behavior may be considered learned behavior. Evidence of glossolalia as learned behavior or as a result of variations in the socialization process merely clears the ground for more questions.

FUNCTIONAL INTERPRETATION:
GLOSSOLALIA AS A FACTOR IN MOVEMENT DYNAMICS

PERSONAL CHANGES
ASSOCIATED WITH PENTECOSTAL GLOSSOLALIA

Conversion. An analysis of variance on our data revealed several significant correlations between glossolalia and other variables which support a functional interpretation of glossolalia in terms of movement dynamics. The sample of 239 was classified according to frequency of glossolalic experience. Those who reported that they speak with tongues daily or more than once a week were defined as frequent tongue speakers. All others were classified as non-frequent.

We found that the second generation Pentecostals in our sample (those who had been socialized to accept glossolalia as a valued experience) spoke with tongues less frequently than those who had been converted from denominations where the practice was either ignored or devalued. Furthermore, frequent tongue speakers were more often those who reported that their religious education had been "liberal" rather than "conservative" or "fundamentalist." (These differences were significant at the .001 level.) It would appear, then, that although the glossolalics in our study shared the common background of a generally religious orientation, the most frequent glossolalics were those who had been least socialized to accept the practice.

Fundamentalist ideology. Another and related observation concerns the ideology commonly associated with the practice of Pentecostal glossolalia. Sixty-six per cent of our respondents had always accepted the Bible as authoritative. Seventeen per cent had been trained as children to accept the authority of the scriptures, but had come to doubt it as adults. The Pentecostal experience brought them back to acceptance of Biblical authority. Of the remaining seventeen per cent, whose religious upbringing was liberal and who had not been trained to accept the scriptures as authoritative, all but one per cent became "fundamentalist" on this score before or just after the Baptism of the Holy Spirit and the initial experiences of glossolalia. Within the broad category of religiously oriented individuals, changes in the belief system in a defined direction appear to be associated with Pentecostal glossolalia.

Personal attitudes and social behavior. Other changes, of even more importance to glossolalics, were reported by all informants. Case histories invariably include a "before and after" statement describing changes in attitudes, behavior, and often social situations. These changes were traced by our informants not to glossolalia *per se*, but to the experiential complex of which the linguistic behavior is one component. The perception of themselves as being different after the glossolalic experience was characteristic. Attitudinal changes were generally described in terms of greater capacity for love toward others, a sense of tranquility and joy, and more confidence in their beliefs.

Frequent tongue speakers perceived themselves as better off physically since the Baptism and the onset of glossolalic experience, as compared with non-frequent tongue speakers (at the .003 level of significance).

Frequent tongue speakers also reported changes in the friends they see socially more often than non-frequent (.05 level). In the context of Pentecostalism, glossolalia appears to be associated with changes in both personal attitudes and social behavior.

COGNITIVE REORGANIZATION
ASSOCIATED WITH PENTECOSTAL GLOSSOLALIA

This interpretation of Pentecostal glossolalia as functional in processes of personal change is supported by four psychological analyses of conversion phenomena.

William Sargant (1949, 1957) points to functional similarities in the processes of religious conversion, thought reform, and psychotherapy. He notes that all three of these processes involve extensive cognitive reorganization, and contends that there are physiological mechanisms which produce such reorganization. His argument is built on an analysis of the most extreme forms of these phenomena. His examples of religious conversion are drawn from accounts of nineteenth century revival movements involving not only glossolalia, but various forms of trance behavior, violent motor "automatisms," and visual and auditory hallucinations. He quotes from the extended verbal assaults on the part of evangelists which seemed calculated to heighten guilt and anxiety, and producing a type of nervous exhaustion. He points to the similarities between this and the induced physical stress and carefully manipulated disruption of expectations and used in brainwashing or thought reform methods. His data on psychotherapeutic processes are based on his own treatment of victims of war neurosis. The functionally similar event here was drug-induced physical collapse which allowed therapeutic recall of incidents and subsequent cognitive reorganization eliminating neurotic patterns.

Sargant uses Pavlov's findings concerning physiological breakdown and the cessation, alteration, and even reversal of normal brain function in dogs. He suggests that permanent behavioral, as well as attitudinal changes, can result from a physiological state of the brain during which cognitive restructuring, even complete reversal of beliefs or cognitive patterns can occur. In order to explain this cognitive restructuring, Sargant postulates a temporary, but dramatic interruption of normal brain functioning. He suggests that experiences such as revivalistic conversions, snake handling and glossolalia can produce an effect similar to that of electro-shock therapy—temporary cortical inhibition that breaks up previous mental and emotional patterns and frees the individual to develop new ones.

It is difficult to find evidence for this degree of physiological breakdown in most of the Baptism or glossolalic experiences we have observed, even though cognitive changes were reported by participants. However, it is not impossible that this process involves a greater or lesser degree of interruption of normal functioning, and that there are physiological correlates of lesser intensity. In discussing the physiological aspects of the experience with Pentecostals, we found some support for this theory. Most could describe definite physical changes during the infilling of the Holy Spirit and certain experiences of glossolalia. Even those who experienced no involuntary motor activity reported release of muscular tension and pricklings or sensations of electric currents coursing through the body.

Jerome Frank (1961), expanding on Sargant's theory, compares the nature of revivalistic religious experiences with the process of psychotherapy, and suggested that such experiences serve as a mechanism through which attitudes toward God, the self, and those in significant relationships can shift in such a way as to lead to permanent attitude and behavior changes. These changes stem from a reorganization of the ''assumptive system'' or worldview that is possible during such experiences. Similar results can be obtained through the process of successful psychotherapy.

Both Sargant and Frank stress that the dynamics of revivalism and conversion are such that predisposing personality characteristics, emotional or sociological maladjustments are not required to explain participation. They offer evidence of successful involvement on the part of normal individuals, not only in religious conversion including glossolalia, but also in processes of thought reform and brainwashing. They emphasize that, contrary to popular belief, resistance to such processes if one is exposed to them can be maintained only by a condition of emotional detachment, by pathological immunity to suggestion, or by a counter-commitment to some other belief system or way of life that is as obsessive. According to Frank and Sargant, the common denominator in the changes wrought by psychotherapy, religious conversion, or brainwashing is not a psychological state, but a physiological state which can be brought about in any individual.

Abraham Maslow has also noted the relationship between intense emotional experiences and personality changes, in his observation of "peak experiences." Maslow has found that peak experiences may involve disorientation in time and space, and a type of cognition very different from that of normal states. Visual and auditory perception may also be different. The perceptions of his "peakers" are similar to those reported by Pentecostals during their glossolalic or Baptism experiences. Maslow considers such experiences contributive to personality growth and self-actualization, and notes that permanent changes are sometimes effected:

> To have a clear perception (rather than a purely abstract and verbal philosophical acceptance) that the universe is all of a piece and that one has a place in it . . . can be so profound and shaking an experience that it can change the person's character and his *Weltanschaung* forever after. (1964:59)

William Wood (1965) found that his data supported the hypothesis that emotionally intense religious experience is connected in an important way with the process of perceptual reorientation. He feels that his Rorschach results indicate that Pentecostals are in the process of personality reorganization, changing value and belief systems, and restructuring of interpersonal relationships. The Pentecostals in Wood's study were drawn from a low status group in a community where there was a widespread social disorganization. Assuming a correlation between social disruption and personality disorganization, Wood views the personal changes which he found correlated with Pentecostal religious practices as necessary because of preexisting personality disorganization.

PENTECOSTAL GLOSSOLALIA AS COMMITMENT ACT

Observations in a wider range of types of Pentecostal groups make it clear that not only glossolalia, but attitudinal and behavioral changes associated with it, occur also among well-educated, socially successful, and well-adjusted personality types. This can be understood only if the phenomenon of glossolalia and characteristic personal changes are set in the context of the movement as a whole. As we have shown in other articles (Gerlach and Hine 1968, 1969) there are five factors crucial to the growth and success of a movement. One of these is personal commitment on the part of participants. We found that glossolalia was significantly related to commitment in Pentecostalism as a movement.

As an indicator of involvement in the movement, we used frequency of interaction with other "Spirit-filled" Christians (tongue speakers in non-Pentecostal churches, as well as members of Pentecostal sects or independent groups of glossolalics). Individuals were assigned a score from one to seven based on whether they reported meeting with other participants daily, four times a week, twice a week, once a week, once or twice a month, a few times a year, or never. We found that frequent glossolalics were indeed significantly more involved in movement activities (at the .04 level).

The two components of commitment which we have been able to identify in Pentecostalism, Black Power, and other movements are: first, an experience through which an individual's image of himself is altered and some degree of cognitive reorganization in the direction of movement ideology takes place; and second, the performance of an objectively observable act. This must be what we have called a "bridge-burning" act which sets the individual apart from the larger society to some degree, identifies him with the group in which he experienced it, and commits him to certain changes in attitudinal or behavioral patterns.

It has already been suggested that glossolalia is part of an experiential complex through which cognitive changes occur. For American Pentecostals, glossolalia can also constitute a bridge-burning act. In a society where public display of intense emotion is reserved for spectator sports, and where the appropriate background for spontaneous and uninhibited self-expression is the cocktail party, the abandonment of one's self to a joyous flow of unintelligible vocalizations and possibly some non-consciously controlled physical behavior is considered indecent if not insane. The enthusiastic "witnessing" or recruitment activities that seem to be an irresistible after-effect are thought by many outsiders to be equally unseemly. The type of criticism that tongue-speakers in non-Pentecostal churches are subject to, the many instances of removal of ministers who become involved, the economic pressures for "recanting," etc., make it quite clear that glossolalia can and does function to set its practioners apart from the rest of churchgoing America in a significant way.

FUNCTIONAL ALTERNATIVES

We found in our survey of the movement in Haiti, Mexico, and Colombia that there are functional alternatives for the bridge-burning act in other cultural settings.

In Mexico and other Latin American countries, particularly in rural areas, the break with the Catholic church often results in social and sometimes economic cleavages. In some cases just walking into an *Evangelico* church constitutes a bridge-burning act. We noted that those who were converted to Pentecostalism from other Protestant denominations—i.e. those who were not making the break with Catholicism and thus for whom attendance at the Pentecostal church would seem less radical—tended to put more emphasis on glossolalia as an important part of the Spirit-filled life.

In Haiti, where spirit possession is characteristic of Voodoo, the majority religion, and where glossolalia is a socially acceptable form of behavior, commitment to Pentecostalism was reinforced by a ritual burning of Voodoo objects. This was an act which involved risk and separation from the larger community.

SUMMARY

Cross-cultural studies of religious behavior support the assumption accepted by most anthropologists that the capacity for ecstatic experience and trance, or other associated behaviors is panhuman. Only the interpretation of it, the techniques designed to facilitate or inhibit it, and the form it takes differ cross-culturally. When such states and behaviors are valued in a society (as they are in many non-Western societies), this capacity can be systematically encouraged in some or all of its members. When they are devalued, they can be culturally inhibited, and appear only as deviant behavior. If such "deviant" behavior functions to set practitioners apart from the larger society through specific and desired personal changes, these extraordinary experiences may be institutionalized to make what David Aberle would call "religious virtuosi of the ordinary worshippers" (1966).

Through a functional approach to the phenomenon, we have come to assess glossolalia as a non-pathological linguistic behavior which functions in the context of the Pentecostal movement as one component in the generation of commitment. As such, it operates in social change, facilitating the spread of the Pentecostal movement affecting nearly every denomination within organized Christianity, and in personal change, providing powerful motivation for attitudinal and behavioral changes in the direction of group ideals.

26

SUSAN K. GILMORE

Personality Differences Between
High and Low Dogmatism Groups
of Pentecostal Believers

[Reprinted from *Journal for the Scientific Study of Religion*, 8 (1965): 161-64. Reprinted with permission of the Society for the Scientific Study of Religion and the author.]

Fundamentalist believers in general, and especially Pentecostal believers, are frequently stereotyped as being rigid, dogmatic, anxious, prejudiced, rejecting of themselves and others, etc. Such overgeneralized descriptions are often the results of inappropriate comparisons between different denominational groups which fail to take into account (1) that there are numerous factors (e.g., socioeconomic status and educational level) that influence denominational affiliation and are also related to personality, but may be only tangentially related to religious *beliefs*, such as fundamentalism and (2) that there is a distinction between the *content* of religious beliefs and the manner in which such beliefs are held (Adorno, *et al.*, 1950, p. 218).

The present study sought to correct both the above flaws by comparing the personality patterns of people who vary only in the manner in which they hold their religious beliefs, and are homogeneous on content of belief and on educational and socioeconomic levels.

It is the general hypothesis of this study that *within a highly homogeneous group of Pentecostals* (known to hold the same fundamental religious beliefs) *those who are identified as holding their beliefs in a dogmatic manner will have predictably different personality patterns from those who are identified as holding their beliefs in a nondogmatic manner.*

From Rokeach's (1960) description of the nondogmatic or open believer as being able to "receive, evaluate, and act on relevant information from the outside," one would expect that such persons, compared with more dogmatic or closed believers, would be more accepting and tolerant of themselves and others, more flexible and sensitive, more outgoing and sociable, more trusting of reason and intellect, and more independent.

Therefore, it was hypothesized that low dogmatism Pentecostal believers would score significantly higher than high dogmatism Pentecostal believers on the following CPI scales: dominance, capacity for status, sociability, self-acceptance, sense of well-being, tolerance,, intellectual efficiency, psychological-mindedness, flexibility and achievement via independence. It was hypothesized that the high dogmatism believers would score higher on the achievement via conformance scale of the CPI. No hypotheses were offered for the remainder of the CPI scales.

INSTRUMENTS AND PROCEDURES

The Rokeach (1960) *Dogmatism Scale* (Form E), Gough's (1957) *California Psychological Inventory* (CPI), and Broen's (1957) *Religious Attitude Inventory* (RAI), were administered to 62 Pentecostal subjects in groups at their churches. In addition, the subjects were asked questions concerning their degree of identification with their present denomination, their personal religious practices, and the amount of time spent in church-related activities.

High and low dogmatism groups were identified by selecting the upper and lower 25 per cent of all dogmatism scores (N = 15 in each group).

The CPI profiles of these two groups (high and low dogmatism) were then compared.

SUBJECTS

The 62 subjects participating in this study were drawn from three Pentecostal churches in a large Northwestern city. Although the three churches represented three independent denominations, their doctrinal positions were highly similar. The instruments were administered to those attending a Sunday morning class at one church and Wednesday evening prayer meeting groups in the other two churches. (A code was used to maintain anonymity.) The total sample included 21 males and 41 females, a typical male/ female ratio among Pentecostal groups. The occupations reported most frequently were: housekeeping, secretary, truck driver, salesman, mechanic, laborer, custodian, and bakery worker. Only two out of the total group reported any college training; the majority had not completed high school. Characteristically for Pentecostals, these subjects would be described as belonging to a lower socioeconomic level.

MATCHED GROUPS

In order for the hypothesized differences in personality patterns between high and low dogmatism groups to be meaningful, it was imperative that the two groups be homogeneous on all other relevant variables, particularly in the content of their religious beliefs. This homogeneity is demonstrated in Table 1. In addition, the two groups scored less than one point apart on both the RAI scales ("Fundamentalism" and "Nearness of God"). In fact, nearly 100 per cent of all subjects concurred on such RAI[1] items as:

> God is constantly with us. (Agree)
> Christ died for sinners. (Agree)
> There is really no place such as Hell. (Disagree)
> It is through the righteousness of Jesus Christ and not because of our own works that we are made righteous before God. (Agree)
> The Bible is the Word of God and must be believed in its entirety. (Agree)

---

[1] Originally the RAI was administered in order to test its usefulness in differentiating religious attitude dimensions among subjects holding doctrinally similar positions. In general it was found to be inadequate for this purpose; however, it did help in establishing the high degree of homogeneity of religious belief content for the subjects in this study.

When in doubt it's best to stop and ask God what to do. (Agree)
Because of his terrible sinfulness, man has been eternally damned unless he accepts Christ as his Savior. (Agree)

The two groups not only matched one another on the dimensions of educational and socioeconomic level, nature and extent of personal religious
practices, and content of religious beliefs, but they also appeared to be
highly representative of Pentecostals in general. The only way in which
the high and low dogmatism groups differed significantly was on their degree of dogmatism, which was assumed to be an index of the openness or
closedness with which they held their fundamental religious beliefs.

RESULTS

The differences between high and low dogmatism groups on the hypothesized CPI scales were tested by one-tailed t-tests (see Table 2). Low
dogmatism Pentecostals scored higher on all CPI scales for which they were
predicted to score higher. Six of the twelve predicted differences between
the groups were statistically significant. (On the remaining CPI scales, there
were no differences between the groups that even approached statistical
significance; none was hypothesized nor expected.)

TABLE 1

GENERAL DESCRIPTION OF THE TOTAL

PENTECOSTAL GROUP AND THE HIGH AND LOW DOGMATISM GROUPS

	Total Group (N = 62)	High Dogmatism (N = 15)	Low Dogmatism (N = 15)
Age:			
29 and under	9	2	3
30-64	40	11	11
65 and over	13	2	1
Sex:			
Male	21	4	6
Female	41	11	9

Church Member:

Yes	59	15	15
No	3	0	0

Hours Per Week
in Church Activities: 8.5   8.3   9.2

Bible Reading:

Daily	37	11	9
Once or Twice a Week	14	3	3
Now and Then	11	1	3

Praying:

Daily	56	14	15
Once or Twice a Week	1	0	0
Now and Then	4	1	0
No Response	1	0	0

Witnessing:

Daily	21	5	4
Once or Twice a Week	9	2	4
Now and Then	30	8	7
No Response	2	0	0

If Moved to Another City,
  would:

Attend Church of Same Denomination, if Possible	55	15	15
Attend Nearest Protestant Church	1	0	0
Let Circumstances Determine Choice of Church	6	0	0

Dogmatism Scale:

Mean	174.0	201.2	142.9
S.D.	28.9	18.6	15.7

When the high and low dogmatism groups were compared with several college student groups reported by Rokeach (1960, p. 90), the low dogmatism group mean was not different from the means of college students, whereas the high dogmatism group mean was significantly different. Similarly, the high dogmatism group's CPI profile extended beyond one standard deviation below the CPI profile mean on several of the scales, whereas

Difference on CPI Scales Between High and Low Dominance Groups

CPI Scale	High Dogmatism (N = 15)	Low Dogmatism (N = 15)	p
Dominance	23.53	26.20	n.s.
Capacity for Status	14.33	16.47	< .10
Sociability	17.47	22.53	< .01
Social Presence	24.27	29.67	< .02
Self-acceptance	16.73	19.93	<075
Sense of Well-being	34.93	35.73	n.s.
Tolerance	19.60	23.00	< .05
Intellectual Efficiency	32.93	38.00	< .02
Psychological-mindedness	9.53	11.33	.05
Flexibility	6.40	8.00	n.s.
Achievement via Independence	16.13	19.33	<.025
Achievement via Conformance	25.13	26.93	n.s.

the low dogmatism group's CPI profile was quite close to the CPI profile mean on most scales and was within one standard deviation of it in every case.

CONCLUSIONS

This study provides clear support for the general hypothesis that within a group of Pentecostal believers known to hold highly fundamental religious beliefs, it is possible to identify individuals who hold their beliefs in an open or nondogmatic manner, and, further, that these nondogmatic Pentecostals score significantly higher on measures of personal adjustment and interpersonal skill (*i.e.*, the CPI) than do closed or dogmatic Pentecostals. When compared with other groups, such as college students and the normative samples of the CPI, the open or nondogmatic Pentecostal believers appear as well-adjusted and interpersonally skillful as do people in general.

27

VERN S. POYTHRESS

Linguistic and Sociological Analyses of Modern Tongues-Speaking: Their Contributions and Limitations

[Reprinted from *Westminster Theological Journal*, 42:2 (Spring 1980): 367-88. Used by permission of Westminster Theological Seminary.]

A significant body of professional linguistic, psychological, and sociological analysis of modern tongues-speaking (glossolalia) has now accumulated.[1] Some of it attributes a generally positive value to speaking in

---

[1]The most comprehensive and balanced scientific summary that I know of is William J. Samarin, *Tongues of Men and Angels: The Religious Language of Pentecostalism* (Macmillan 1972). Bibliography can be found in E. Mansel Pattison, "Behavioral Science Research on the Nature of Glossolalia," *Journal of the American Scientific Affiliation*, 20 (1968): 73-86; George J. Jennings, "An Ethnological Study of Glossalalia [sic]," *JASA*, 20 (1968): 5-16; Watson E. Mills, "Literature on Glossolalia," *JASA*, 26 (1974): 169-73; Ira J. Martin, *Glossolalia, The Gift of Tongues—A Bibliography* (Pathway Press, 1970); Kilian McDonnell, *Charismatic Renewal and the Churches* (The Seabury Press, 1976): 187-95.

tongues; some of it is quite negative. All of it agrees in treating glossolalia as at root a nonmiraculous phenomenon. The work of these social scientists has a valuable contribution to make in the formation of our pastoral approach to the ecclesiastical problems of tongues. We may know the Bible very well, but we cannot address ourselves effectively to an ecclesiastical problem unless we are well acquainted with the actual dimensions of the problem. The Reformed churches have typically been quite strong in theology but less strong in understanding full-bloodedly what is going on.

On the other hand, I believe that the linguistic and sociological approaches have distinct limitations, not always recognized by the practitioners. Scientists have sometimes drawn conclusions beyond the bounds of their presuppositions and their methods. My exploration of tongues-speaking will point out some of these limitations.

First, we might ask whether appeal to scientific research on tongues is legitimate. Some might feel that, if tongues-speaking is a "supernatural" phenomenon of some kind, research into it is illicit. However, God invites inspection of and meditation on his miraculous works (John 10:32, 10:37-38, 202:20, 202:27; Matthew 28:6; Luke 24:39). Such inspection is wrong only when it occurs with a disrespectful or unbelieving attitude. Modern tongues, of course, might be "supernatural" in some broader sense, without being on the same exalted level as the miraculous works of Jesus' earthly life. But, by analogy, we could still argue that similar principles would apply to inspection of tongues as would apply to the "more exalted miracles." It is then easy to conclude that scientific research on tongues is legitimate. We should also note that much of the research on tongues-speaking has been made possible by the cooperation of charismatics who consent to be observed, to have their speech recorded, and otherwise to participate in behavioral science experiments.[2]

To say that scientific research is legitimate is one thing. To say that it will be able to penetrate into the heart of the matter is another. Many are convinced on other grounds that tongues is at heart a spiritual phenomenon, requiring spiritual discernment. From their point of view, tongues speaking is properly validated and weighed by spiritual means. It is to be

---

[2]Samarin, *Tongues*, p. xiv. In this article I use "charismatic" to include both traditional Pentecostal and neo-Pentecostal proponents of tongues.

appreciated in the context of the accompanying gifts of interpretation, prophecy, and discernment of spirits. These gifts in turn are exercised in the framework of the total life of the Christian community ordered by the word of God in Scripture. The scientific approach, insofar as it demands results and evidence acceptable to and reproducible by non-Christians, can rise no higher than the position of the "natural man," who is unable to penetrate the things of the Spirit of God (1 Corinthians 2:10-16). Hence, the scientific approach is condemned to inconclusive results at the outset. Below, I will point out some specific areas of limitation in the scientific results.

Next, we must have some grasp of what is to count as a case of modern "speaking in tongues." What is the boundary line between "speaking in tongues" and other phenomena? Answering this question is not as easy as one might think. Non-Christian religions,[3] psychotics,[4] and small children[5] sometimes produce phenomena that might or might not be similar to "speaking in tongues." As working definitions, I propose the following:

Free vocalization (glossolalia) occurs when (1) a human being produces a connected sequence of speech sounds, (2) he cannot identify the sound-sequence as belonging to any natural language that he already knows how to speak, (3) he cannot identify and give the meaning of words or morphemes (minimal lexical units),[6] (4) in the case of utterances of more than a few syllables, he typically cannot repeat the same sound-sequence on demand, (5) a naive listener might suppose that it was an unknown language.

In this definition, features (1), (2), and (5) are the really essential features that we tend to associate with speaking in tongues (glossolalia). Features (3) and (4) are expected implications of (1) and (2).

---

[3]*Cf.* L. C. May, "A Survey of Glossolalia and Related Phenomena in Non-Christian Religions," *American Anthropologist*, 58 (1956): 75-96.

[4]Pattison, *JASA*, 20: 75-76.

[5]G. Devereaux, "The Voices of Children," *American Journal of Psycho-Therapy*, 19 (1965): 4-19. *Cf.* William J. Samarin, "The Forms and Functions of Nonsense Language," *Linguistics*, 50 (1969): 73.

[6]But Samarin reports cases where glossolalists have attempted to assign meaning to a few of their "words" and utterances (*Tongues*, pp. 91-92, 167).

Free vocalization still includes some infant speech and some phenomena outside the Christian religion. Hence it is a broader concept than what we usually call "speaking in tongues." To exclude infants, I propose the following:

Competent free vocalization is free vocalization by a person who already knows at least one natural language reasonably well. I intend thereby to include normal children older than four or five, but not infants.

Christian free vocalization is free vocalization by a Christian. This is intended to exclude cases of "tongues" appearing among non-Christians.

Religious free vocalization is free vocalization for the purposes of public or private worship or in the context of worship, in cases when the speaker wishes to speak to a spirit, or wishes that the spirit would speak to others through him, or both. (In the case of Christian religious free vocalization, it is understood that the "spirit" in question is God.)

Finally, *T-speech* (tongues) is Christian religious competent free vocalization.

This proposed definition counts as T-speech only those instances which meet several intersecting criteria. T-speech must be "free," and it must be by a Christian who is not an infant. Moreover, it must be used in the context of worship.

The advantage of this rather elaborate definition is that it does not demand from us an immediate decision as to whether T-speech in the modern church is from God, from the human psyche, from demons, or from some combination of these. Neither does it make any decision about the similarities or dissimilarities between T-speech and the "speaking in tongues" referred to in Acts and 1 Corinthians. Finally, it does not specify whether the speaker is in an altered state of consciousness (for example, trance). In fact, there are cases of T-speech both in trance and in otherwise completely normal state.[7]

The main results of modern social-scientific research can be summarized in terms of answers to a few selected questions.

1. Can the average person be taught to produce free vocalization?

Yes. Learning to free vocalize is easier than learning to ride a bicycle. As with the bicycle, the practitioner may feel foolish and awkward at first. But practice makes perfect. Moreover, though at first a person may feel

---

[7]Pointed out by Samarin, *Tongues*, pp. 26-34.

self-conscious, after he has learned he may sometimes forget that he is doing it. It is something that he can start or stop at will without difficulty.[8]

One easy way for a person to learn is to pretend that he is speaking a foreign language. He starts speaking, slowly and deliberately producing syllables. Then he speeds up, consciously trying to make it sound like a language would sound. Once he is doing well, he just relaxes and does not worry any longer about what comes out.

2. Is free vocalization likely to lead to a state of trance?

No, no more than reading a book. A person *can* become so engrossed in reading a book that he is oblivious to his surroundings.[9] Technically speaking, this being-engrossed is an altered state of consciousness, as are day-dreaming, dozing, sleep-walking, and being drunk. Free vocalization is sometimes associated with such altered states of consciousness, but by itself it does not cause them.

3. Is there any psychological danger in free vocalization?

As far as we know, no more than in reading a book. Many people have been free-vocalizing for years with no ill effects. A person's beliefs may lead to associating free vocalization with other practices that are questionable.

In short, it seems that the capacity for free vocalization is a normal, God-given human capacity. The person who was unable to do it would be unusual. We regard free vocalization as abnormal only because, in our modern Western cultural milieu, people usually cease to do it after childhood. Hence, in our society free vocalization among adults, as a socially "deviant" activity, may sometimes be a symptom (though certainly not the cause) of psychological or social abnormality.[10] This accounts, I believe, for some of the early negative conclusions about "tongues" by psychologists. Their evaluations measured, not what free vocalization is in itself, but their own perception of social deviance involved in the phenomenon.[11] But free vocalization *is* deviant only from the standpoint of the social norms of the majority, not from some absolute biological standpoint.

---

[8]*Cf. ibid.*, pp. 44-149; Pattison, *JASA*, 20: 78.

[9]*Ibid.*, p. 27.

[10]Pattison, *JASA*, 20: 75-77.

[11]*Cf.* McDonnell, *Charismatic Renewal*, pp. 13-16.

Now it is time to pay some attention to the question of how modern-T-speech (glossolalia with its specifically Christian associations) differs from other instances of free vocalization.

4. How does nonreligious free vocalization differ *linguistically* from T-speech?

Most of the time, we cannot distinguish the two linguistically. At least two experiments have shown this.[12] In one, Al Carlson of the University of California recorded speech samples from T-speakers and from volunteers told to speak unknown language. The samples were then rated by T-speakers. The nonreligious free vocalization actually received better ratings. In a second experiment, Werner Cohn at the University of British Columbia took students to Pentecostal meeting, asked them to imitate T-speakers in the laboratory, and received approving evaluations of the recorded samples from T-speakers.

5. Does religious free vocalization occur in other religions?

Yes, religious free vocalization and related phenomena occur among some non-Western religions.[13] This is natural, since free vocalization is so easy to produce.

6. How does competent free vocalization differ from known human languages?

The degree of differences varies with the speaker, and to some extent even from utterance to utterance by the same speaker. The sound system (phonology) of the utterances tends to be closely associated with the speaker's language background. For English speakers, frequently the proportion of vowels is higher than in English (open syllables predominate). The vowel /a/ is frequent. The number of distinct words and consonants is usually smaller than in English, and their distribution is more restricted. In a longer utterance, certain groups of two or three syllables ("pseudo-morphemes") tend to recur (sometimes with slight alterations).[14]

In almost all instances, linguists are confident that the samples of T-speech represent no known natural language and in fact no language that

---

[12]Pattison, *JASA*, 20: 78.

[13]May, *American Anthropologist*, 58: 75-96; Jennings, *JASA*, 20: 5-16; Samarin, *Tongues*, pp. 130-38. But Samarin expresses caution about whether much of this sounds like natural language (p. 222).

[14]Pattison, *JASA*, 20: 79; Samarin, *Tongues*, pp. 73-102.

was ever spoken or ever will be spoken by human beings as their native tongue. The phonological structure is untypical of natural languages. Some samples of T-speech, however, are more complex and cannot be clearly distinguished from a natural language on these grounds.[15]

These facts—especially the fact that free vocalization is so easy to produce and that most T-speech is not a natural language—have become one of the main grounds for a certain amount of debunking on the part of social social scientists. To them, it appears that T-speech has nothing to do with the Holy Spirit. But, as I hope to show, this conclusion will follow only if one makes certain nontrivial *theological* assumptions about the work of the Holy Spirit. What the research does show is that free vocalization is not an intrinsically miraculous and therefore infallible sign of the working of the Holy Spirit.

7. Are there any instances when modern T-speech has been identified as a known human language?

Yes. However, modern linguists do not usually think that these instances are "miraculous." In a number of cases, it appears that T-speech consisted of fragments or sentences from a language that the speaker had heard some time in his past, and had since forgotten. This phenomenon of recall of foreign language occurs occasionally in non-Christian contexts as well as in T-speech. Hence, even though it represents an unusual psychological process, it is deemed nonmiraculous.

But many of the reported instances of T-speech in foreign languages are not even this exciting. They are found, upon closer investigation, to be cases where a naive listener heard something that "sounded like German" or "sounded like Arabic," but where the listener had insufficient competence in German or Arabic to know the truth.[16] Hence linguists search for more thorough documentation.

Are there any modern documented cases of T-speech in a *non*recalled identifiable human language? Linguists who have investigated firsthand say, "No." But we must realize what kind of documentation they require. Ideally, (1) there should be a tape-recorded sample of the alleged foreign

---

[15]M. T. Motley reports one such case in "Glossolalia: Analyses of Selected Aspects of Phonology and Morphology," unpublished master's thesis, University of Texas, 1967, p. 95.

[16]Samarin, *Tongues*, pp. 109-15.

speech, of reasonable quality and length. (2) There should be living authorities (for example, native speakers) who recognize the language. (3) There should be documentation as to the identity of the speaker. (4) There should be a reasonably complete life history of the speaker, excluding the possibility that he was earlier in contact with the language.

The number of cases in which linguists have endeavored to obtain documentation is considerable. But of course it is far less than the total number of instances of T-speech. The truth is, then, that the possibility of T-speech in a nonrecalled foreign language can never be *conclusively* excluded by these methods. Moreover, it could be argued that the Holy Spirit is unlikely to work a miracle in controlled conditions for the convenience of the linguists, just as Jesus did not work a miracle in "controlled conditions" for the convenience of the Pharisaical seekers after signs (Mark 8:11-12).[17]

The literature from the charismatic movement does report a number of cases of T-speech in nonrecalled foreign languages.[18] But these cases do not display the completeness of documentation that linguists would like. In many cases the reports are vague and other explanations are possible. But in a few cases the evidence is difficult to evade. These cases will be rejected only by those whose theological or philosophical presuppositions require them to exclude such a possibility.[19]

Nevertheless, even if cases of T-speech in foreign languages occur, they are quite rare. We must still reckon with the great majority of T-speech which is not a foreign language.

8. Is it possible that T-speech might be language of some other kind, perhaps angelic language (1 Corinthians 13:1)?

Modern linguistics cannot tell us. Those linguists who believe in angels might suspect that "angelic" language would either be *more* like hu-

---

[17]Pointed out by Charles E. Hummel, *Fire in the Fireplace: Contemporary Charismatic Renewal* (Inter-Varsity Press, 1978): 202; Dennis J. Bennett, "The Gifts of the Holy Spirit," in *The Charismatic Movement*, Michael Hamilton, editor. Eerdmans, 1975. P. 29. This need not be construed as any criticism of the linguists' attitudes within their proper sphere. Rather it would be an attempt to point out the limitations of that sphere.

[18]*Ibid.*, pp. 22-30; Ralph W. Harris, *Spoken By the Spirit* (Gospel Publishing House, 1973); and Don Basham, *The Miracle of Tongues* (Revell, 1973); Harald Bredesen and Pat King, *Yes, Lord* (Logos International, 1973): 76-77.

[19]*Cf.* the caution in Kilian McDonnell, *Charismatic Renewal*, p. 10.

man language than is most T-speech, or else much *less* like it. For instance, angelic language could contain sounds that the human vocal apparatus is incapable of producing. Or it might be a "pure thought-language" with no sound at all. But we cannot be certain because we just have no idea what an "angelic" language might be.

What about other kinds of "language"? The biggest difficulty is that something that looks like nonsense can make perfect "sense" once one knows the "code" for interpreting it. Consider the following sample speech:

Bara ashayata. Bara-a. Alahayama. Ata hashamayama. Va ata ha-aratsa. This looks like nonsense. But it is actually the consonantal Hebrew text of Genesis 1:1, with the vowel *a* inserted between consonants.

Thus the problem of finding "sense" is the problem of breaking the "code" which a given communication may use. Moreover, it is easy to construct codes that are in a certain sense unbreakable. Suppose that one wants to communicate the phrase "in the beginning." Assign to each letter of the alphabet a number from 1 to 26, and assign to the space between words the number 0. One obtains the sequence:

9, 14, 0, 20, 8, 5, 0, 2, 5, 7, 9, 14, 14, 9, 14, 7.

Now take a random series of numbers from 0-26:

20, 22, 19, 23, 23, 21, 0, 23, 8, 8, 21, 16, 6, 26, 15, 0.

Add the two together, subtracting 27 when necessary:

2, 9, 19, 16, 4, 26, 0, 25, 13, 15, 3, 3, 20, 8, 2, 7.

Now reconvert to letter values:

bispdz ymoccthbg.

This is the coded message. The original message can be recovered only by someone who has the "key," namely the random series 20, 22, 19, 23, 23, 21, 0, 23, 8, 8, 21, 16, 6, 26, 15, 0. For someone without the key, there is no way of knowing whether or not the coded message is nonsense.

Thus it is always possible for the charismatic person to claim that T-speech is *coded* language, and that only the interpreter of tongues is given the supernatural "key" for deciphering it. It is impossible not only in practice, but even in *theory*, for a linguist to devise a means of testing this claim.[20]

---

[20]Samarin, *Tongues*, p.. 122n7.

It is more important, then, to determine whether T-speech can "function like" a language than to determine whether it *is* an identifiable foreign language. Since one important function of natural languages is to carry information, the following question is important:

9. Is there any indication that T-speech carries information?

The answer is yes. The information in T-speech is of at least two kinds: suprasegmental and associational-lexical. Suprasegmental or prosodic features of an utterance include voice quality, pitch, rate of articulation, and the structure of larger and longer patterns of speech (e.g., the position and length of pauses). These features, at least in English, may convey the feelings of the speaker about his audience or about himself or about a problem he is thinking about. In some cases, the message may be quite specific. E. M. Pattison reports,

> One subject, whose glossolalic speech became pleading and quite serious, made it clear that she was simultaneously wishing to herself that the interviewer might accept glossolalia for himself.[21]

The second kind of information in T-speech is associational-lexical. That is, it is information bound up with the associations that a speaker makes between ideas on the one hand and small relatively isolatable chunks of speech on the other. Now, of course, the small chunks of free vocalization have no lexical (dictionary) meaning in the native tongue of the speaker. But the speaker may build *associations* in his mind between his "nonsense" words and languages that he knows. A German psychiatrist, Oskar Pfister, attempted to explore this possibility by recording phonetically some utterances of a T-speaker named Simon.[22] He then pronounced small segments to Simon, asking what came into his mind. In every case Simon responded with an incident from his past (usually childhood) structurally related to his present emotional difficulties. Unfortunately, it is not always clear how much the interpretations were already "in" the T-speech in the first place, and how much they were "read in" by Simon's subsequent free associations. If we believe Pfister's analysis, T-speech may at least some-

---

[21]Pattison, *JASA*, 20:81.

[22]Oskar Pfister, "Die psychologische Enträtselung der religiösen Glossolalie und der automatischen Kryptographie," *Jarbuch Für Psycho-Analytische und Psychopathologische Forschungen*, 3 (1912): 427-66.

times carry information like the information in those dreams which symbolize or act out some emotional conflict in a person's life.[23] The dreams have meaning, even though that meaning is "coded" into apparently nonsensical symbolic form. In view of the fact that word-association phenomena are common both to Christians and non-Christians, there is reason to assume that forms of competent free vocalization *other* than T-speech have the same capabilities of carrying information.

The psychological value of these observations should not be overlooked. A speaker might use free vocalization to articulate and release emotions that he cannot express clearly, or that are too personal or intimate to share directly with others. This is presumably one reason (but not the only one or the most significant one) why T-speech is valued by the charismatic movement.

10. Does the linguistic and psychological evidence lead to the conclusion that almost all, if not all, instances of modern T-speech are not miraculous or divine?

Here is the crucial question. Some linguists and social scientists have indeed pronounced T-speech nonmiraculous. But I think that they can give such a clear-cut answer only by exceeding their competence. Social science does provide a plausible naturalistic explanation for T-speech. but I suspect it could also provide a plausible naturalistic "explanation" for some biblical miracles. Israel enjoyed quails in the wilderness because a wind brought them from the sea (Numbers 11:31). Peter's hunger, it might be claimed, excited in his mind the vision of unclean animals (Acts 10:9ff). Other biblical "miracles" are coincidences (1 Kings 22:34, 2 Kings 3:22-23, 7:17-20). Thus, the existence of natural "means" in a given incident does not exclude the working of God's power.

Consider also a case of healing. Suppose that Christians pray for a fellow Christian who is sick, and God answers by healing him. This healing

---

[23]Pattison, *JASA* 20: 78-85. *Cf.* also Kilian McDonnell's analysis: ". ... in the vast majority of cases the one who is speaking in tongues is not speaking a real language, but a prayer language or an art language. Speaking or praying in tongues is to prayer what abstract painting is to art. Just as good abstract art is not color and form without order or discipline, but is a non-objective expression of deep feelings and convictions, so also tongues. Those who are praying in tongues are expressing in a non-objective manner deep religious convictions and sentiments which they might have a difficult time expressing in their own native language" (McDonnell, *Charismatic Renewal*, p. 9).

is, in a broad sense, a sign of God's presence and his promises. It is so whether or not doctors are instrumental in the healing, whether or not doctors can "explain" the healing afterwards in naturalistic terms. But, our awe and wonder are most likely to be aroused when the case is an "impossible" one and when there is no "explanation."

Now compare this with T-speech. Because of its unusual character and because of the theological explanations attached to it, it tends to arouse awe and wonder—or fear and perplexity—quite often. People are likely to say that it is "miraculous." But linguistic and psychological investigation gives us a better understanding of some of the regularities involved, providing us with a rather satisfying naturalistic "explanation." That may take away much of the fascination and excitement of T-speech. By itself, however, this does not provide an answer to the question, "Is this (or some cases of it) from God? Is it a sign of God's presence and promises?"[24] Social scientific research does not bring us any farther than the doctor's putative explanation of a case of healing. To answer such theological questions we have to be able to assess God's intention in and behind T-speech. Such an assessment must be grounded in biblical teaching.

Hence, it is more important to know what the Bible says about these things than what the modern analysts say. Only so can we reach firm conclusions. But the modern scientific analysis is not profitless. It can help us not to blind our eyes to some of the ways that T-speech functions in charismatic communities. It can, moreover, push us away from the extremes of totally negative or totally positive evaluation of modern T-speech. The remainder of this article is devoted to arguing against the extremes.

People in one extreme evaluate modern T-speech in totally negative terms. According to this view, T-speech is a psychological delusion having nothing to do with the Spirit of God. Hence it ought to be forbidden. I will assume for the sake of argument that these people are basically correct in their reading of the biblical data. Assume, then, that the "speaking in tongues" mentioned in the Bible ceased with the death of the apostles.[25]

---

[24]*Cf.* Samarin, *Tongues*, p. 235.

[25]In fact, the church fathers continue to report prophesyings, tongues, and other "miraculous" phenomena down to the fourth century and beyond [*cf.* Hummel, *Fire*, pp. 164-66, 192-93, 210-12; George H. Williams and Edith Waldvogel, "A History of Speaking in Tongues and Related Gifts," *The Charismatic Movement*, Michael Hamilton, editor.

Assume further that modern T-speech is not of itself a special sign of God's presence and blessing.[26]

Even making these assumptions, we must still reckon with the fact that free vocalization can have psychological value in some circumstances. We must reckon with the fact that T-speakers are attached to free vocalization partly because of benefits that they sense they receive. I can illustrate most clearly by describing the experiences of someone who enters the charismatic movement. My particular example is, of course, hypothetical, but the various elements can be found documented in both social-scientific literature and in literature by charismatics themselves.

Our exemplary charismatic, then, receives benefits of three main kinds from T-speech. First, his T-speech reinforces belief in the power and presence of the Holy Spirit. The T-speaker believes that in T-speech God the Holy Spirit is speaking through him. When uttering a T-speech, or when reflecting on the fact that he has done this in the past, he may marvel at the fact that the Holy Spirit could thus speak through him. He is convinced more thoroughly than ever, and more deeply than ever, how wonderful and powerful God the Holy Spirit is. He also has a peace and assurance that the Holy Spirit is dwelling in him and can help him to do God's will. God's will no longer seems burdensome, but something that God himself will cause him to fulfill with joy. What a marvelous blessing!

Now, what is happening? Our T-speaker is being taught by God the biblical doctrine of the indwelling of the Holy Spirit in believers. He is being taught the power of the resurrected Christ who comes to dwell in him and give him joy and victory in the Holy Spirit. No wonder he is filled with joy!

Of course, there is also a danger here. Does the T-speaker base his convictions about the Holy Spirit first of all on his experience or first of all on what the Bible says (vividly brought to his attention by his experience)? If the former, he has developed a bad attitude concerning the grounds for his

---

(Eerdmans, 1975), pp. 64-70; Benjamin B. Warfield, *Counterfeit Miracles*, (The Banner of Truth Trust, 1972): 3-69]. Hence it is difficult to formulate satisfactorily a statement about the chronological point of cessation of "extraordinary" gifts. Warfield argues that such gifts extended only to the Apostles and those on whom the Apostles laid hands (*ibid.*, pp. 22-25). This provides a firm cut-off point. Of course, Warfield must then explain the post-Apostolic reports on other bases.

[26]One of the ablest defenses of this view is found in Anthony A. Hoekema, *What about Tongues-Speaking?* (Eerdmans, 1966).

beliefs. If his experience seems later on to be no longer so fresh or so deep, he will not have stability. Moreover, the habit of leaning on experience may leave open the door for false teaching (Ephesians 4:14). But let us suppose the best. Let us suppose that the T-speaker does not regard his experience as an ultimate basis for belief, but a reminder of the basis provided in the Bible.

Secondly, suppose a T-speaker is troubled by a deep problem or concern, and does not know how to pray (Romans 8:26-27). He pours out his heart to God in a T-speech, believing that God understands perfectly what his concern is, and that God is helping him to pray rightly. As we have observed, the T-speech can carry information—exactly how much, the linguist can not say—about the speaker's emotional state and about buried thoughts or associations. Even if it carried no information, we could still be assured that God does indeed understand the desires of his child, and answers those desires in accord with his will (1 John 5:14-15). Hence many times the T-speaker may find that those hidden desires and concerns of his are answered by God. Even when he does not receive an obvious or immediate answer, he is comforted by the assurance that God has understood. As a result, he may grow to express himself more deeply when he prays in his mother tongue.

What is happening here is again basically biblical (though the T-speaker may misunderstand the role of T-speech in it). The T-speaker is being taught confidence in a prayer-answering God who knows our inmost thoughts and desires (Philippians 4:6-7; Romans 8:26; Psalms 139).

A third kind of effect may occur to a Christian who in the past had never really believed that, in our day, God heals people (Deuteronomy 32:39; Psalms 103:3) and orders the details of Christians' lives for their benefit (Romans 8:28). Then, he has the experience of uttering a T-speech. He says to himself, "Why, God is still doing remarkable things as he did in the days of the apostles. And he is doing something remarkable with *me*. Little *me*. I never thought I was important to God. It must be that God can still heal and can still direct my life in both ordinary and remarkable ways for his glory. I will start praying for God to do those things, and expect that sometimes he will." Moreover, our T-speaker turns to the Bible, and says, "Why, the Bible is a book that speaks to me and my time too. God is still speaking when I read it. All his promises are true today!"

Once again, this Christian is learning something biblical. He is learning that God is still alive, God is still the same God, and the building of his church still goes on. It would become dangerous only if he started looking for modern apostles and additional commands to add to the Bible. Then he would not be seeing that God has completed the Bible and provided it for us so that, by reading it, we still hear the voice of the "old" apostles, Paul and Peter and John.

Finally, let us see how his "charismatic experience" as a whole may look to the T-speaker. He may have become interested in T-speech because he felt dissatisfaction with his own Christian life. He felt an emptiness, a lack of power, a lack of vital and fresh communion with God. He wanted to be filled with the Holy Spirit. So he began to pray, to seek God, to repent, and to seek instruction from the Bible about the Holy Spirit. He found that he was holding back certain things in his life. He found areas that he was keeping to himself rather than surrendering to God. So he began saying to God, "Yes, I will follow you in this and that area too." Earlier he had thought to himself, "If I surrender everything, God may ask me to do something foolish or humiliating." He was afraid. Perhaps for him the area of the use of language was one such area. So tongues symbolized for him the question of whether everything was given to God. Finally, he said, "All right, I *am* willing to speak in tongues if that is what God wants for me." We will suppose that he in some way misunderstood the meaning of modern T-speech. Still, many of his prayers and desires were genuine, and God answered them.

Since his first experience with T-speech, his life has been transformed. He has awakened to the reality of the work of the Spirit in his life. He has started to believe that God still does remarkable things today. He has come to trust that God knows and understands his deepest concerns. He has started to look to the Bible for answers to his daily problems. He finds now that the Bible is a living book where God speaks. The intensive fellowship that he has experienced with other charismatics has further strengthened his Christian life.[27]

Then our friend looks at others. Others too have had the same experience with T-speech. Many of *their* lives have been transformed. He turns to Acts 2. "It happened in the Bible, too," he says. "The church was set on fire after they experienced tongues. It is the sign of baptism with the Holy Spirit. It must be the key to revival."

---

[27]*Ibid.*, pp. 132-36.

What has happened? Good things, biblical things, things that God himself is doing in loose connection with T-speech, have now been linked tightly, inexorably, and *exclusively* to T-speech.

Now suppose an opponent tells our T-speaker that modern tongues are a delusion, and that the charismatic movement is unbiblical. What will the reaction be? The reaction is likely to be simply anger, incomprehension, and pity. The T-speaker has *seen*, has *experienced* these things. He has seen the Bible come alive to him. He says to himself, "my opponent wants to take it all away from me." The opponent says, "Doctrine cannot be based on experience, but only on the Bible." He will say, "If that is where the emphasis on cold doctrine leads, I'll have no more to do with doctrine."

There are lessons for us here. First, doctrine is indeed based on the Bible, not on experience. An experience valid in many ways can all too easily be misinterpreted and lead to bad doctrine. But the sword cuts two ways. We cannot base our doctrine of modern tongues on an experience of *not* having tongues.

Second, no one can dismiss or condemn the charismatic movement *as a whole* without becoming unbiblical. The easy, blunt, self-confident answer, "It is a delusion," is unbiblical because it is unloving, undiscriminating, unwise, and unhelpful. There is no substitute for patient, sympathetic listening as well as to speaking (James 1:19), trying to find the real rather than simply the apparent sources of disagreement.

Third, let no one remove the speck from his brother's eye before he has removed the log from his own (Luke 6:41-42). This applies to one's manner of argument. Charismatics are frequently more gracious in argument than their opponents. They will seldom be convinced unless they see the love that is so important to them manifested in those with different convictions.

The principle also applies to the areas which T-speech has sometimes affected: appreciation for the indwelling of the Holy Spirit, belief in God's presence and reality today, experiencing of the Bible as a living book, and so on. Let the opponent examine himself, repent, and ask God for his own renewal in these areas before he ventures to criticize. If necessary, let him say to his charismatic brother, "I have failed in these areas, and I need your help and encouragement—even though I disagree with you."

So far, we have looked at the practical conclusions for those who do *not* believe that modern T-speech is a special divine sign. Now, what about the people who *do* believe that, at least sometimes, modern T-speech is a special sign of God's presence and blessing? Are there some implications for them? For the sake of argument, I will assume that they are right in thinking that the gift of tongues continues beyond the apostolic age.[28]

First, we must reckon with the fact that competent free vocalization, by itself, is not a sign of anything *but* itself. It occurs even among non-Christians in both religious and secular contexts.

Second, it seems reasonably clear that T-speech, by itself, is not always a reliable demonstration of God's inward work in a person. True, Christians are united with Christ, and that means that they are radically different from unbelievers. But it does not mean that they cannot sin. They can free vocalize as easily as a non-Christian. And it seems inevitable that in some cases they will try to use free vocalization in worship, and yet still be sinning. In other words, they may practice T-speech "in the flesh." More thoughtful leaders in the charismatic movement recognize this.[29] They are even ready occasionally to say, "Be quiet, you're speaking in the flesh," to someone who uses free vocalization just to "sound off" or make an exhibition in church. 1 Corinthians 14 demonstrates well enough that similar problems arose even an apostolic times.

Third, T-speech may occur "in the flesh" not only here and there in the lives of T-speakers, but even the *first* time they use T-speech. If it is possible at other times, why not the first time?

As the diametrical opposite of my earlier example, of an ideal charismatic person, I will construct a bad example, a "worst case," to show how T-speech could be perverted. Fortunately, many charismatic groups in the United States have grown in maturity over the years. Even from the beginning they were aware of certain dangers. But in the last few years they have eliminated some remaining problems. Hence my "worst case" never did occur in most places, and could not occur now. But it will illustrate in the abstract what abuses might occur.

---

[28]One of the ablest defenses of this viewpoint is in Wayne Grudem, "The Gift of Prophecy in 1 Corinthians 12-14," doctoral dissertation, University of Cambridge, 1976. Grudem discusses only prophecy, but his arguments could be extended to embrace tongues and healing.

[29]*Cf.*, *e.g.*, Carl Brumback, *What Meaneth This?* (Gospel Publishing House, 1947): 259; McDonnell, *Charismatic Renewal*, pp. 145-46.

Let us imagine a Christian who, like Simon the sorcerer in Acts, desires to be looked upon as someone "great" (Acts 8:9-10). He wants to be able to perform miracles and have power (*cf.* Acts 8:19). He is told that these things are to be sought through the baptism of the Holy Spirit marked by tongues. He is told at the same time that not all Christians have received this baptism. Hence the baptism of the Holy Spirit seems to him to be something that will make him "greater" than those Christians who do not have it. He is eager to receive this baptism.

Hence others pray for him. He is told to open his mouth and let the "tongue" come out. Or perhaps he is told to begin by imitating a few lines spoken by a T-speaker. When he utters a few sounds, he is encouraged to do more.[30] So in a little while he learns to free vocalize fluidly. (The social scientist tells us that that is to be expected.) He is told, "Yes, that's it. You have received the baptism of the Holy Spirit." If he says, "I seem to be doing it myself," the "coach" replies, "That's the devil trying to make you doubt the gift that God has given you." And so he swells with pride in himself and thinks to himself, "I have become somebody great. I am no longer in the same category as ordinary Christians."

Would we say the Holy Spirit is at work blessing this man in a special way? When we are confronted with so blatant a case, most of us, I would hope, are willing to say, "No." But then the question arises, "How do we know that something like this never happens in subtler cases?"

Now consider what might happen to this Christian's prayers. He says, "Now the Holy Spirit prays in me when I pray in tongues. I pray so much better than people who don't pray in tongues. I don't have to worry about studying the Bible to find out what it teaches about prayer, because I can already pray perfectly and effortlessly. Think of the poor Christians who don't have tongues. According to Romans 8:26, they are weak in prayer and they don't have the Spirit to help them. I guess I don't need to pay attention to what they pray."

In this case, the Christian's presumption about tongues has led him to despise two things that he should not despise. First, he is despising the biblical teaching on prayer. But why was Paul so careful to say how he prayed

---

[30]"Coaching" people to speak in tongues in this way was a fairly common practice at an earlier date (Samarin, *Tongues*, p. 52). But I am told it no longer occurs in many contemporary groups.

(Ephesians 1:15-23, 3:14-21; Philippians 1:3-11; Colossians 1:3-14; 2 Thessalonians 1:3-12, *etc.*)? Why did God have so many prayers recorded in Scripture if not to instruct us (Matthew 6:5-15)?

Second, our hypothetical Christian has despised his brothers who do not use T-speech. That is because he has applied Romans 8:26-27 to T-speakers *only*. Paul, by contrast, applies it to the *whole* congregation at Rome. He had never visited Rome, so he could not know whether all spoke in tongues. Paul believed that the Spirit helps *all* true Christians to pray.

Consider now a third abuse, this time in connection with the issue of continuing revelations. Our Christian is told that it is important to respond to the impulse of the Spirit. He thinks, "If I get a noticeable urge to say or do something, it must be because the Holy Spirit wants me to." So he begins to criticize some of the brothers for things that he does not like about them. He says, "The Lord told me to do it." Then he begins to get some hunches about doctrine, and thinks, "These must be prophecies." He begins to say things like, "God has put the Holy Spirit within us so that eventually we can become gods."

Is this story of a hypothetical Christian a farfetched example? In some ways, it is. There are several constraints that keep this type of thing from happening. First, God has mercy on Christians and keeps them from wandering too far. Second, charismatic groups do hear and respect the bible, and the Bible's teaching keeps them from going astray (this is one of the *ways* in which God shows his mercy to us). Third, many charismatic groups do have conscious and unconscious safeguards to protect their members from these errors.

Nevertheless, we ought to be wise enough not to say, "It can't happen here." For one thing, something very like it has happened in the past. The Mormons claim to have their tongues,[31] their apostles, their prophets, and their modern revelations saying that we shall all become gods.[32] In other cases, "prophetic" teaching has not led this far, but has produced sectar-

---

[31]George B. Cutten, *Speaking with Tongues: Historically and Psychologically Considered* (Yale, 1927): 70-76; James H. Kennedy, *Early Days of Mormonism* (Reeves and Turner, 1888): 113-18; Samuel Hawthornthwaite, *Adventures Among the Mormons* (privately published, 1857): 88-95; Williams, in *The Charismatic Movement*, pp. 87-88.

[32]*Cf.* Hoekema, *The Four Major Cults* (Paternoster, 1969): 34-46.

ian movements like the Latter Rain Assemblies of South Africa, which consider the rest of Pentecostalism impure.[33]

Admittedly, the bad examples that I have mentioned are extreme cases. But I mention the extremes only to raise another question: can there also be cases of mixtures of good and bad? In our hypothetical case, the Christian wanted T-speech for the completely bad motive of desiring greatness. Is it possible that in some cases where a Christian's motives are basically good, this desire for "greatness" is mixed in?

For instance, in our hypothetical case, the Christian used his ability in T-speech to become puffed up about his own relationship to God (the bad side). In other cases a Christian is helped by T-speech to become much more thoroughly convinced of the Holy Spirit's power and presence (the good side). Are there cases where these two uses of T-speech are combined? Similarly, can we sometimes find mixtures of good and bad in Christians' attitude toward praying in tongues? 1 Corinthians 14 could seem to indicate the answer is "yes."

What protection, then, does the charismatic movement have against deviations, excesses and impure motives? Two kinds of protection come to mind. First, the gift of discernment of spirits (1 Corinthians 12:10). Paul does not tell exactly what kind of gift this is. But evidently it is a gift enabling one to sift the good from the bad in extraordinary manifestations of spirits. This gift is valuable, but it cannot be relied upon *exclusively*. Why not? First, this gift, like other gifts, could be corrupted. The sectarian movements like the Mormons and the Latter Rain Assemblies could claim to have *their* gift of discernment confirming the validity of their own prophecies. Second, the gift of discernment obviously did not rescue the Corinthian church from its manifold problems. It took the patience, the maturity, the well-constructed argument, and the divine authority of the Apostle Paul to deal with them—and even so his resources were strained to the limit. Third, Paul exhorts the *whole* church to exercise discernment, not just those with a special gift (1 Corinthians 14:29; 1 Thessalonians 5:20-22). If we ignore this command, we cannot expect to be protected from bad motives and errors.

Another source of protection is the Lord's general supervision of the church. We have the feeling, "If we remain faithful to the Lord, he will

---

[33]Walter J. Hollenweger, *The Pentecostals* (SCM Press, 1972): 140-46.

not let us go astray.'' That is true, and I think that it is the ultimate basis of security for all of us. But then we must ask, "What does it *mean* to remain faithful to the Lord? How do we know what kind of faithfulness he wants?'' For instance, does faithfulness mean simply obeying the voice of our modern prophets? But then the Mormon prophets will tell us that being a Mormon is being faithful to the Lord. The Latter Rain prophets will tell us that the Latter Rain Assemblies are alone fully faithful to the Lord. The only sound answer is Paul's answer to Timothy. Faithfulness to the Lord means faithfulness to the Old Testament and the Apostles. Timothy must continually nourish and reform his life on the basis of the Bible (2 Timothy 3:15-17). Listening to the Bible accurately requires that we exercise discernment.

And so we come full circle. The critics of the charismatic movement are tempted to be indiscriminating. But so are its advocates. The easy, blunt, self-confident answer, "The movement is *all* of God" is unbiblical, just as is its reverse, "It is all a delusion." Both charismatic and noncharismatic have something to learn from one another. On both sides this listening and learning process will, I hope, drive us back to a renewed and more discerning reading of the Bible. My hypothetical examples will have served their purpose if they help both sides to understand how to steer the opposite side away from extremes. This is possible, I believe, even when the opposite side cannot be completely won over.

Bibliography

28

WATSON E. MILLS

Bibliography

Adams, Moody P. *Jesus Never Spoke in Tongues*. Privately published, 1974.

"Against Glossolalia," *Time*, 81 (May 18, 1963): 84.

Agrimson, J. Elmo, ed. *Gifts of the Spirit and the Body of Christ: Perspectives on the Charismatic Movement*. Augsburg, 1974.

Aikman, Duncan. "The Holy Rollers," *American Mercury*, 15 (October 1928): 180-91.

Alland, Alexander. " 'Possession' in a Revivalistic Negro Church," *Journal for the Scientific Study of Religion*, 1 (1962): 204-13.

Allen, Jimmy. "The Corinthian Glossolalia: The Historical Setting, An Exegetical Examination, and a Contemporary Restatement." Unpublished doctor's dissertation, Southwestern Baptist Theological Seminary, 1967.

Allen, Stuart. *Tongue-Speaking Today: A Mark of Spirituality or Deception?* Berean Publishing Trust, 1971.

Alphandéry, Paul. "La glossolalie dans le prophétisme mediéval latin," *Revue de' histoire des religions*, 104 (November 1931): 417-36.

Alvarez de Linera, Antonio. "El glosolalo y su interprete," *Estudios Biblicos*, 9 (April June 1950): 193-208.

Amiot, F. "Glossolalie," *Catholicisme*, 5 (1962): 67-69.

Anderson, C. "Tongues of Men and Angels," *Lutheran Standard* (May 16, 1972): (

Anderson, Robert Mapes. *Vision of the Disinherited: The Making of American Pent costalism*. Oxford University Press, 1979.

Ansons, Gunars. "The Charismatics and Their Churches: Report on Two Confe ences," *Dialog*, 15:2 (1976): 142-44.

Archer, Antony. "Teach Yourself Tongue-Speaking," *New Blackfriars*, 55:651 (A gust 1974): 357-64.

Arnot, Arthur B. "The Modern 'Speaking with Tongues,' " *The Evangelical Christic* 46 (January 1950): 23-25, 59.

Arthur, William. *Tongues of Fire*. Harper and Brothers, 1856.

Ashcraft, Jessie Morris. "Glossolalia in the First Epistle to the Corinthians," in *Tongu* Luther B. Dyer, editor. LeRoi Publishers, 1971. Pp. 60-84.

Assemblies of God, USA: "Charismatic Study Report," 1972 in *Presence, Pow Praise: Documents on the Charismatic Renewal*, Kilian McDonnell, editor. 3 v(1 (The Liturgical Press, 1980): 318-20.

Atter, Gordon F. *The Third Force*. The College Press, 1962.

Axup, Edward J. *The Truth about Bible Tongues*. Privately published, 1933.

Bach, Marcus. *The Inner Ecstasy: The Power and Glory of Speaking in Tongt* Abingdon Press, 1969.

_____. "Whether There Be 'Tongues,' " *Christian Herald*, 87 (May 1964): 11, 20, 22.

Baer, Richard A. "Quaker Silence, Catholic Liturgy, and Pentecostal Glossolalia—S Functional Similarities," in *Perspectives on the New Pentecostalism*, Russe. Spittler, editor. Baker Book House, 1976. Pp. 150-64.

Baker, Cheryl Diane. "A Psycho-Political Comparison of Hallucinatory Phenon Amongst Schizophrenics, LSD Users and Glossolalics." Unpublished master's sis, University of Witwatersrand, 1983.

Baker, D. L. "An Interpretation of 1 Corinthians 12-14," *Evangelical Quarterl* (October-December 1974): 224-34.

Baker, J. B. "A Theological Look at the Charismatic Movement," *Churchma* (Winter 1972): 259-77.

Banks, R. J. and G. N. Moon. "Speaking in Tongues: A Survey of New Testa Evidence," *Churchman*, 80 (Winter 1966): 278-94.

Banks, William L. *Questions You Have Always Wanted to Ask about Tongues.* American Mission to Greeks, 1978.

Baptist General Conference, USA: "Biblical Charisma and the Contemporary New Testament Church," 1974 in *Presence, Power, Praise: Documents on the Charismatic Renewal*, Kilian McDonnell, editor. 3 vols. 1 (The Liturgical Press, 1980): 517-19.

Baptist Union, Great Britain and Ireland: "Working Group on the Charismatic Movement," 1978 in *Presence, Power, Praise: Documents on the Charismatic Renewal*, Kilian McDonnell, editor. 3 vols. 2 (The Liturgical Press, 1980): 379-90.

_____, New Zealand: "The Effects of Neo-Pentecostalism on New Zealand Baptist Churches," 1970 in *Presence, Power, Praise: Documents on the Charismatic Renewal*, Kilian McDonnell, editor. 3 vols. 1 (The Liturgical Press, 1980): 211-19.

Baptist World Alliance, International: "Summary Statement and Guidelines on the Charismatic Movement," 1978 in *Presence, Power, Praise: Documents on the Charismatic Renewal*, Kilian McDonnell, editor. 3 vols. 3 (The Liturgical Press, 1980): 79-81.

Barbarie, T. "Tongues, sí, Latin, no," *Triumph*, 4 (April 1969): 20-22.

Barber, Theodore X. "Multidimensional Analysis of 'Hypnotic Behavior,' " *Journal of Abnormal Psychology*, 74 (1969): 209-20.

_____. "Who Believes in Hypnosis?" *Psychology Today*, 4 (July 1970): 2-27, 84.

Barber, Theodore X. and David S. Calverley. " 'Hypnotic Behavior' and a Function of Task Motivation," *The Journal of Psychology*, 54 (1962): 363-89.

Barde, E. "La Glossolalie," *Revue de théologie et des questions religieuses*, 5 (1896): 125-38.

Barnes, Douglas. "Charisma and Religious Leadership: An Historical Analysis," *Journal for the Scientific Study of Religion*, 17 (March 1978): 1-18.

Barnett, Maurice. "The Gift of the Spirit in the New Testament, with Special Reference to Glossolalia." Unpublished master's thesis, University of Manchester, Manchester, England, 1946.

Barnhouse, Donald Grey. "Finding Fellowship with Pentecostals," *Eternity*, 9 (April 1958): 8-10.

Barratt, Thomas Ball. *In the Days of the Latter Rain.* Simpkin, Marshall, Hamilton, Kent, 1909.

Bartling, V. A. "Notes on Spirit-Baptism and Prophetic Utterance," *Concordia Theological Monthly*, 39 (November 1968): 708-14.

Bartling, W. J. "Congregation of Christ: A Charismatic Body: An Exegetical Study c 1 Corinthians 12," *Concordia Theological Monthly*, 40 (February 1969): 67-80.

Basham, Don. "Baptism in the Holy Spirit," in *The Holy Spirit in Today's Churc* Erling Jorstad, editor. Abingdon Press, 1973. Pp. 58-65.

──────. *A Handbook of Holy Spirit Baptism*. Whitaker Books, 1969.

──────. *A Handbook on Tongues, Interpretations and Prophecy*. Whitaker Book 1971.

──────. *A Manual for Spiritual Warfare*. Manna Books, 1974.

──────. "I Saw My Church Come to Life," *Christian Life*, 26 (March 1965): 3 39.

──────. "Speaking in Tongues," in *The Holy Spirit in Today's Church*, Erli Jorstad, editor. Abingdon Press, 1973. Pp. 77-87.

──────. "They Dared to Believe," *Christian Life*, 28 (April 1967): 28, 52-56.

Bauman, Louis S. *The Modern Tongues Movement*. Privately published, 1930.

──────. *The Tongues Movement*. Brethren Missionary Herald Company, 1963.

Baxter, Robert. *Narrative of Facts Characterizing the Supernatural Manifestations Members of Mr. Irving's Congregation*. Nisbet, 1833.

Beare, Frank W. "Speaking with Tongues: A Critical Survey of the New Testam Evidence," *Journal of Biblical Literature*, 83 (September 1964): 229-46.

Beasley-Murray, George R. "Tongues-Speaking in the Ancient World," *Biblical lustrator*, 5:3 (Spring 1979): 22-24.

Beckmann, David M. "Trance: From Africa to Pentecostalism," *Concordia Theol ical Monthly*, 45 (January 1974): 11-26.

Beeg, John Frederick. "Beliefs and Values of Charismatics: A Survey." Unpublis doctor's dissertation, Colgate Rochester Divinity School, 1978.

Beel, A. "Donum linguarum jukta Act. Apost. ii. 1-13," *Collationes*, 35 (1935): 4 20.

Belew, Pascal P. *Light on the Tongues Question*. Nazarene Publishing House, 192

Bell, Henry. "Speaking in Tongues." Unpublished doctor's dissertation, Evangel Theological College, 1930.

Bellshaw, William G. "The Confusion of Tongues," *Bibliotheca Sacra*, 120 (A| June 1963): 145-53.

Benner, P. D. "The Universality of Tongues," *The Japan Christian Quarterly* (Spring 1973): 101-107.

Bennett, Dennis J. "The Charismatic Renewal and Liturgy," *View*, 2:1 (1965): 1

_____. "The Gifts of the Holy Spirit," in *The Charismatic Movement*, Michael Hamilton, editor. Eerdmans, 1975. Pp. 15-32.

_____. "The New Pentecost: Charismatic Revival Seminar Report." Full Gospel Business Men's Fellowship International, 1963.

_____. *Nine O'Clock in the Morning*. Logos International, 1970.

_____. "Pentecost: When Episcopalians Start Speaking in Tongues," *The Living Church*, 142 (January 1, 1961): 12-13.

_____. "They Spake with Tongues and Magnified God!" *Full Gospel Business Men's Voice*, 8 (October 1960): 6-8.

_____. *When Episcopalians Start Speaking in Tongues*. Christian Retreat Center, n.d.

Bennett, Dennis and Rita Bennett. *The Holy Spirit and You*. Logos International, 1971.

Benson, Frank. "A Story of Division," in *The Charismatic Movement*, Michael Hamilton, editor. Eerdmans, 1975. Pp. 185-94.

Berger, Peter L. "Sectarianism and Religious Sociation," *The American Journal of Sociology*, 64 (1958): 41-44.

Bergquist, Susan L. "The Revival of Glossolalic Practices in the Catholic Church: Its Sociological Implications," *Perkins Journal*, 30 (1973): 256-65.

Bergsma, Stuart. *Speaking with Tongues: Some Physiological and Psychological Implications of Modern Glossolalia*. Baker Book House, 1965.

_____. "Speaking with Tongues," *Torch and Trumpet*, 14 (November 1964): 8-11.

_____. "Speaking with Tongues," *Torch and Trumpet*, 14 (December 1964): 9-13.

Bernstein, B. "Linguistic Codes, Hesitation Phenomena, and Intelligence," *Language and Speech*, 5 (1962): 31-46.

Bertrand, Philippe. "Expressions récentes du mouvement charismatique aux Etats-Unis," *Amitié*, 4 (1973): 33-35.

Bess, Donovan. "Speaking in Tongues: The High Church Heresy," *The Nation*, 197 (September 28, 1963): 173-77.

Bess, S. Herbert. "The Office of the Prophet in Old Testament Times," *Grace Journal*, 1 (Spring 1960): 7-12.

Best, Ernest. "The Interpretation of Tongues," *Scottish Journal of Theology*, 28:1 (1975): 45-62.

Beyreuther, Erich. *Der geschichtliche Auftrag des Pietismus in der Gegenwart*. Calwer Verlag, 1963.

Bird, Thomas. "Experience over Scripture in Charismatic Exegesis," *Catholic Thec logical Quarterly*, 45:1/2 (January-April 1981): 5-11.

Bittlinger, Arnold. *Die Bedeutung der Gnadengaben für die Gemeinde Jesu Christi.* Ede 1964.

_____. "Charismatic Renewal: An Opportunity for the Church," *The Ecumenice Review*, 31:3 (1979): 247-51.

_____. "Die charismatische Erneuerung der Kirchen: Aufbruch urchristlichen E fahrung," in *Erfahrung und Theologie des Heiligen, Geistes*, C. Heitmann and F Mühller, editors. Rauhen/Kössel, 1974. Pp. 19-35.

_____. *The Church is Charismatic*. World Council of Churches, 1981.

_____. "Disziplinierte Charismen," *Deutsches Pfarrerblatt*, 63 (1963): 333-3

_____. "Et ils prient en d'autres langues: le movement charismatique et la glc solalie," *Foi et Vie*, 72:4 (1973): 97-108.

_____. *Gemeinde ist Anders: Verwirklichung neutestamentliche Gemeindeor nung innerhalf der Volkskirche*. Calwer Verlag, 1966.

_____. "Gemeinde und Charisma," *Das nissionarische Wort*, 17 (1964): 231-3

_____. *Gifts and Graces: A Commentary on 1 Corinthians 12-14*. Eerdmans, 1967

_____. *Gifts and Ministries*. Trans. Clara K. Dyck. Eerdmans, 1973.

_____. *Gifts and Ministries*. Hodder and Stoughton, 1974.

_____. *Glossolalia: Wert und Problematik des Sprachenredens*. Kühne, 1969

_____. *Gottesdienst Heute*. Calwer Verlag, 1968.

_____. *Im Kraftfeld des Heiligen Geistes*. Edel, 1971.

_____. *Papst und Pfingstler. Der römisch katholisch pfingstliche Dialog und s ökumenische Relevanz*. Peter Lang, 1978.

_____. "Report on the Work of the WCC Consultant on Charismatic Renewa in *The Church is Charismatic: The World Council of Churches and the Charisme Renewal*, A. Bittlinger, editor. World Council of Churches, 1981.

Bittlinger, Arnold and Kilian McDonnell. *Baptism in the Holy Spirit as an Ecumen Problem*. Charismatic Renewal Services, 1972.

Blackwelder, Boyce W. "Thirty Errors of Modern Tongues Advocates," *Vital Ch tianity*, 94 (May 26, 1974): 9-10.

Blaney, H. J. S. "St. Paul's Posture on Speaking in Unknown Tongues," *Wesle Theological Journal*, 8 (1973): 52-60.

Blikstad, Vernon M. "Spiritual Renaissance," *Christian Life*, 26 (May 1964): 31.

Bloch-Hoell, Nils. "Der Heilige Geist in der Pfingstbewegung und in der charismatischen Bewegung," in *Taufe und Heiliger Geist*, Pertti Mäki, editor. Helsinki, 1979. Pp. 89-105.

_____. *The Pentecostal Movement: Its Origin, Development, and Distinctive Character*. Allen and Unwin, 1964.

Bloesch, Donald G. "The Charismatic Revival," *Religion in Life*, 35 (Summer 1966): 364-80.

Blossom, Willis W. *The Gift of the Holy Spirit*. Privately published, 1925.

Bobon, Jean. "Les Pseudo-Glossolalies Ludiques et Magiques," *Journal Belge de Neurologie et de Psychiatrie*, 47 (April 1947): 219ff.

Boer, Harry R. "The Spirit: Tongues and Message," *Christianity Today*, 7 (January 4, 1963): 6-7.

Boisen, Anton T. "Economic Distress and Religious Experience," *Psychiatry*, 2 (1939): 185-94.

_____. *The Exploration of the Inner World*. Harper & Row, 1936.

_____. "Religion and Hard Times: A Study of the Holy Rollers," *Social Action*, 5 (March 15, 1939): 8-35.

_____. *Religion in Crisis and Custom: A Sociological and Psychological Study*. Harper & Row, 1955.

Bord, Richard J. and Joseph E. Faulkner. "Religiosity and Secular Attitudes: The Case of Catholic Pentecostals," *Journal for the Scientific Study of Religion*, 14 (1975): 257-70.

Bosworth, Fred F. *Do All Speak with Tongues?* Christian Alliance Publishing Company, n.d.

Bourguignon, Erika. "The Self, the Behavioral Environment, and the Theory of Spirit Possession," in *Context and Meaning in Cultural Anthropology*, Melford E. Spiro, editor. Free Press, 1965.

_____. "World Distribution and Patterns of Possession States," in *Trance and Possession States*, Raymond Prince, editor. R. M. Bucke Memorial Society, 1968. Pp. 3-34.

Bourguignon, Erika and A. Haas. "Transcultural Research and Culture-Bound Psychiatry." Paper presented at the Western Division meeting of the American Psychiatric Association, Honolulu, 1965.

Bourguignon, Erika and Louanna Pettay. "Spirit Possession, Trance and Cross-Cultural Research." Unpublished paper, Ohio State University, 1966.

_____. "Spirit Possession, Trance and Cross-Cultural Research," *Proceedings of the Annual Meeting of the American Ethnological Society*, (1964): 38-49.

Bover, P. "Le parler en langues des premiers chrétiens," *Revue d'histoire des religions*, 63 (1911): 292-310.

Bradfield, Cecil David. *Neo-Pentecostalism: A Sociological Assessment*. University Press of America, 1979.

Bredesen, Harald. "Discovery at Hillside," *Christian Life*, 20 (January 1959): 16-18.

Brewster, Percy S. *The Spreading Flame of Pentecost*. Elim Publishing Company, 1970.

Bridge, Donald and David Phypers. *Spiritual Gifts and the Church*. InterVarsity Press, 1973.

Broadbent, W. G. *The Doctrine of Tongues*. Eldon Press, n.d.

Brown, Charles E. *The Confusion of Tongues*. Gospel Trumpet Company, 1949.

Brown, L. B. "Some Attitudes Surrounding Glossolalia," *Colloquium*, 2 (1967): 221-28.

Brumback, Carl. *Suddenly From Heaven*. Gospel Publishing House, 1961.

Bruner, Frederick Dale. *A Theology of the Holy Spirit: The Pentecostal Experience and the New Testament*. Eerdmans, 1970.

Bryant, Ernest and Daniel O'Connell. "A Phonemic Analysis of Nine Samples of Glossolalic Speech," *Psychonomic Speech*, 22 (1971): 81-83.

Buck, E. Parker. *The True Bible Teaching vs. the Unknown Tongue Theory*. Privately published, n.d.

Budd, William H. *The Bible Gift of Tongues*. Pentecostal Publishing House, 1909.

Bunn, John T. "Glossolalia in Historical Perspective," in *Speaking in Tongues: Let' Talk about It*, Watson E. Mills, editor. Word Books, 1973. Pp. 36-47.

Burgess, Stanley M. "Medieval Examples of Charismatic Piety in the Roman Catholic Church," in *Perspectives on the New Pentecostalism*, Russell P. Spittler, editor. Baker Book House, 1976. Pp. 14-26.

Burgess, W. J. *Glossolalia: Speaking in Tongues*. Baptist Publications Committee, 1968.

Burke, Kathryn L. and Merlin B. Brinkerhoff. "Capturing Charisma: Notes on an Elusive Concept," *Journal for the Scientific Study of Religion*, 20 (1981): 274-84.

Campbell, J. A. "A Speaking Acquaintance with Tongues." Unpublished paper, University of Pittsburgh, 1965.

Campbell, James M. *After Pentecost What?* Revell, 1897.

Campbell, Joseph E. *Warning! Do Not Seek for Tongues: A Sound Scriptural Appraisal of a Present-Day Trend in the Church*. World Outlook Publications, 1970.

Carlson, A. "Tongues of Fire Revisited." Unpublished paper, University of California, 1967.

Carroll, R. Leonard. "Glossolalia: Apostles to the Reformation," in *The Glossolalia Phenomenon*, Wade H. Horton, editor. Pathway Press, 1966. Pp. 69-94.

Carter, Charles W. "A Wesleyan View of the Spirit's Gift of Tongues in the Book of Acts," *Wesleyan Theological Journal*, 4 (Spring 1969): 39-68.

Carter, Herbert F. *The Spectacular Gifts: Prophecy, Tongues, Interpretations*. Privately published, n.d.

Cavanar, Jim. "Catholics: Pentecostal Movement," *Acts*, 1 (1968): 14-19.

Chafer, Lewis Sperry. "The Baptism of the Holy Spirit," *Bibliotheca Sacra*, 109 (1952): 199-216.

Cheshire, C. Linwood. "The Doctrine of the Holy Spirit in Acts." Unpublished master's thesis, Union Theological Seminary, 1953.

Christenson, Lawrence. *A Charismatic Approach to Social Action*. Bethany, 1974.

_____. *The Christian Family*. Bethany, 1971.

_____. *Der Dienst der Krankenheilung in der Kirche—Möglichkeit oder Verpflichtung?* Edel, 1964.

_____. *Die Gabe des Zungenredens in der Lutherischen Kirche*. Edel, 1963.

_____. "Pentecostalism's Forgotten Forerunner," in *Aspects of Pentecostal-Charismatic Origins*, Vinson Synan, editor. Logos International, 1975.

_____. *Social Action Jesus Style*. Dimension Books, 1976.

_____. *Speaking in Tongues and Its Significance for the Church*. Bethany, 1968.

_____, et al. "A Theological and Pastoral Perspective on the Charismatic Renewal in the Lutheran Church." Unpublished paper, 1975.

Clemens, Carl. "The 'Speaking with Tongues' of the Early Christians," *Expository Times*, 10 (1898): 344-52.

Clemens, J. S. "Pentecost," in *A Dictionary of the Apostolic Church*, James Hastings, editor. 2 vols. 2 (Scribner's Sons, 1908): 160-64.

Cleveland, Lester. "Let's Demythologize Glossolalia," *The Baptist Program*, 45 (June 1967): 8, 11.

Cocoris, G. Michael. "Speaking in Tongues: Then and Now," *Biblical Research Quarterly*, 46:6 (September 1981): 14-16.

Cohn, Werner. "A Movie of Experimentally-Produced Glossolalia," *Journal for the Scientific Study of Religion*, 6 (1967): 278.

_____. "The Paradoxes of Marginal Group—A Social-Psychological Suggestion." Unpublished paper, University of British Columbia, 1967.

_____. "Personality and Pentecostal Groups: A Research Note." Unpublished paper, University of British Columbia, 1967.

_____. "Personality, Pentecostalism, and Glossolalia: A Research Note on Some Unsuccessful Research," *The Canadian Review of Sociology and Anthropology*, 5 (1968): 36-39.

Conn, Charles W. "Glossolalia and the Scriptures," in *The Glossolalia Phenomenon*, Wade H. Horton, editor. Pathway Press, 1966. Pp. 23-65.

_____. *Pillars of Pentecost*. Pathway Press, 1956.

Coulson, Jesse E. and Ray W. Johnson. "Glossolalia and Internal-External Locus of Control," *Journal of Psychology and Theology*, 5:4 (1977): 312-17.

Cross, James A. "Glossolalia: Its Value to the Church," in *The Glossolalia Phenomenon*, Wade H. Horton, editor. Pathway Press, 1966. Pp. 181-213.

Currie, Stuart D. "Speaking in Tongues: Early Evidence Outside the New Testament Bearing on 'Glossais Lalein,' " *Interpretation*, 19 (1965): 274-94.

Cutten, George Barton. *The Psychological Phenomena of Christianity*. Scribner's Sons, 1908.

_____. *Speaking with Tongues: Historically and Psychologically Considered*. Yale University Press, 1927.

Dalton, Robert Chandler. *Tongues Like As of Fire*. Gospel Publishing House, 1945.

Daugherty, Bob. *New Testament Teaching on Tongues*. Privately published, n.d.

Davidson, W. D. "Psychiatric Significance of Trance Cults." Proceedings of the 121st Annual Meeting of the American Psychiatric Association, 1965.

Davies, Douglas. "Pentecostalism: Threat or Promise?" *Expository Times*, 76 (March 1963): 197-99.

_____. "Social Groups, Liturgy, and Glossolalia," *Churchman*, 90 (July-September 1976): 193-205.

Davies, J. G. "Pentecost and Glossolalia," *Journal of Theological Studies*, 3 (October 1952): 228-31.

Davies, John M. *Pentecost and Today: Tongues and Healing*. Walterick Publishing Company, n.d.

Day, Charles L. "Glossolalia in Biblical and Post-Biblical Perspective." Unpublished dissertation, Golden Gate Seminary, 1971.

Dean, Robert L. "Strange Tongues: A Psychologist Studies Glossolalia," *SK&F Psychiatric Reporter*, 14 (May-June 1964): 15-17.

Decker, Ralph Winefield. "The First Christian Pentecost." Unpublished doctor's dissertation, Boston University, 1941.

DeHaan, M. R. "Speaking in Tongues." Grand Rapids Radio Bible Class, 1964.

Dewar, Lindsay. "The Problem of Pentecost," *Theology*, 9 (1924): 249-59.

Dhorme, P. "L'emploi métaphorique des noms de parties du corps en hébreu et en akkadien," *Revue Biblique*, 30 (1921): 517-40.

Dirks, Lee E. "The Pentecostals: Speaking in Other Tongues," in *National Observer News Book: Religion in Action*. The National Observer, 1965. Pp. 168-76.

Dixon, Amzi C. *Speaking with Tongues*. Bible Institute Colportage Association, n.d.

Dollar, George W. "Church History and the Tongues Movement," *Bibliotheca Sacra*, 120 (October-December 1963): 316-21.

Dominy, Bert. "Paul and Spiritual Gifts: Reflections on 1 Corinthians 12-14," *Southwestern Journal of Theology*, 26:1 (Fall 1983): 49-68.

Douglas, J. D. "Tongues in Transition," *Christianity Today*, 10 (July 8, 1966): 34.

Duewel, Wesley L. *The Holy Spirit and Tongues*. Light and Life Press, 1974.

DuPlessis, David J. *Glossolalia*. Privately published, n.d.

_____. *Pentecost Outside "Pentecost."* Privately published, 1960.

_____. *The Spirit Bade Me Go*. Logos International, 1972.

_____. *The Spirit Bade Me Go*. Privately published, 1961.

Dupont, J. "La première Pentecôte chrètienne," *Assemblées du Seigneur*, 51 (1963): 39-62.

_____. "Le Salut des Gentils et la Significantion Theologigue du Livre des Actes," *New Testament Studies*, 6 (January 1960): 132-55.

Dyer, Luther B. *Tongues*. LeRoi Publishers, 1971.

Eason, Gerald M. "The Significance of Tongues." Unpublished master's thesis, Dallas Theological Seminary, 1959.

Edwards, Hubert E. "The Tongues at Pentecost: A Suggestion," *Theology*, 16 (1928): 248-52.

Edwards, O. C. "The Exegesis of Acts 8:4-25 and Its Implications for Confirmation and Glossolalia," *Anglican Theological Review*, supplementary series, number 2 (September 1973): 100-12.

Eggenberger, Oswald. "Die Geistestaufe in der gegenwärtigen Pfingstbewegung," *Theologische Zeitschrift*, 11 (1955): 272-95.

_____. "Die neue Zungenbewegung in Amerika," *Theologische Zeitschrift*, 21 (September-October 1965): 427-46.

Ehrenstein, Herbert Henry. "Glossolalia: First Century and Today," *The King's Business* (November 1964): 31-34.

van Elderen, Bastiaan. "Glossolalia in the New Testament," *Bulletin of the Evangelical Theological Society*, 7 (Spring 1964): 53-58.

Eliade, Mircea. *Le chamanisme et les techniques archaïques de l' extase*. Payot, 1951.

───────. *Shamanism: Archaic Techniques of Ecstasy*. Trans. Willard R. Trask. Pantheon Books, 1964.

Ellis, E. Earle. " 'Spiritual Gifts' in the Pauline Community," *New Testament Studies*, 20 (1974): 128-44.

Ellis, Paul N. "Concerning 'Tongues,' " *Light and Life*, (June 1972): 9.

Ellwood, Robert S., Jr. *One Way: The Jesus Movement and Its Meaning*. Prentice-Hall, 1973.

Engelsen, Nils Ivar Johan. "Glossolalia and Other Forms of Inspired Speech According to 1 Corinthians 12-14." Doctor's dissertation, Yale University, 1970.

Engelsviken, Tormod. "The Gift of the Spirit: An Analysis and Evaluation of the Charismatic Movement from a Lutheran Theological Perspective." Unpublished dissertation, Aquinas Institute, School of Theology, 1981.

Ennis, Philip H. "Ecstasy and Everyday Life," *Journal for the Scientific Study of Religion*, 6 (1967): 40-48.

Ensley, Eddie. *Sounds of Wonder: Speaking in Tongues in the Catholic Tradition*. Paulist Press, 1977.

Epp, Theodore A. and John Paton. "The Use and Abuse of Tongues." A sermon, Back to the Bible Broadcast, Lincoln, Nebraska, 1963.

Erasmus, D. J. "Enkele Gedagtes oor Glossolalie," *Nederlands Theologisch Tijdschrift*, 12 (April 1971): 247-61.

Ewald, Tod W. "Aspects of Tongues," *The Living Church*, 146 (June 2, 1963): 12-13, 19.

───────. "Aspects of Tongues," *View*, 2:1 (1965): 7-11.

Failing, George E. "Should I Speak with Tongues," *The Wesleyan Methodist*, 12 (January 20, 1965): 6.

Farrell, Frank. "Outburst of Tongues: The New Penetration," *Christianity Today*, (September 13, 1963): 3-7.

Fee, Gordon. "Tongues—Least of the Gifts: Some Exegetical Observations on 1 Corinthians 12-14," *Pneuma*, 2:2 (Fall 1980): 3-14.

Ferguson, Charles W. *The Confusion of Tongues: A Review of Modern Isms*. Doubleday, Doran and Company, 1928.

Finch, John G. "God-Inspired or Self-Induced," *Christian Herald*, 87 (May 1964): 13, 17, 19.

Fink, Paul R. "The Phenomenon of Tongues as Presented in Scripture." Unpublished research paper, Dallas Theological Seminary, 1960.

Fisher, J. Franklin. *Speaking with Tongues.* Privately published, n.d.

Fishman, Joshua A. "Some Contrasts Between Linguistically Homogeneous and Linguistically Heterogeneous Politics," in *Explorations in Sociolinguistics*, Stanley Liberson, editor. Mouton Publishers, 1966. Pp. 18-30.

Fisk, Samuel. *Speaking on Tongues in the Light of the Scripture.* The College Press, 1972.

Fleisch, D. Paul. *Die Pfingstbewegung in Deutschland.* Feesche Verlag, 1957.

Ford, J. Massyngberde. "The Theology of Tongues in Relationship to the Individual," *Bible Today*, 8 (April 1970): 3314-20.

_____. "Toward a Theology of 'Speaking in Tongues,' " *Theological Studies*, 32 (March 1971): 3-29.

Forest, Tom. "Tongues: A Gift of Roses," *New Covenant*, 11:1 (July 1981): 15-17.

Foster, Kenneth N. *I Believe in Tongues, but—.* Victory Press, 1976.

Fraikin, Daniel. " 'Charismes et Ministeres' a la Lumiere de 1 Corinthians 12-14," *Eglise et Theologie*, 9:3 (1978): 455-63.

Fuller, Reginald H. "Tongues in the New Testament," *American Church Quarterly*, 3 (Fall 1963): 162-68.

Gaddis, Merle E. "Christian Perfectionism in America." Unpublished doctor's dissertation, University of Chicago, 1928.

Gæbelein, Arno C. "The So-Called Gift of Tongues," *Our Hope*, 14 (July 1907): 13-16.

Gæbelein, A. C. and F. C. Jennings. *Pentecostalism, the Gift of Tongues and Demon Possession.* Our Hope Publication Office, n.d.

Gee, Donald. "Do 'Tongues' Matter?" *Pentecost*, 49 (September 1958): 17.

_____. *God's Great Gift.* Gospel Publishing House, n.d.

_____. "Wheat, Tares and 'Tongues,' " *Pentecost*, 67 (December 1963-February 1964): 17.

_____. "Why Is 'Pentecost' Opposed?" *Pentecostal Testimony*, 10 (November 1929): 16.

Gericke, P. *Christliche Vollkommenheit und Geisteserlebnisse.* Privately published, 1950.

Gerrard, Nathan L. "The Holiness Movement in Southern Appalachia," in *The Charismatic Movement*, Michael P. Hamilton, editor. Eerdmans, 1975. Pp. 159-71.

Gill, Merton and Margaret Brenman. *Hypnosis and Related States: Psychoanalytic Studies in Regression.* International Universities Press, 1959.

Gillespie, Thomas W. "Pattern of Prophetic Speech in 1 Corinthians," *Journal of Biblical Literature*, 97 (March 1978): 74-95.

Gilmore, Susan K. "Personality Differences Between High and Low Dogmatism Groups of Pentecostal Believers," *Journal for the Scientific Study of Religion*, 8 (1969): 161-64.

"Glossolalia," *The Living Church*, 146 (May 19, 1963): 11-12.

Glynne, W. "Psychology and Glossolalia: The Book of Acts," *Church Quarterly Review*, 106 (July 1928): 281-300.

Godin, André. "Moi Perdu on Moi Retrouré l'expérience Charismatique," *Archines de Sciences Sociales des Religion*, 20 (July-December 1975): 31-52.

Goettmann, J. "La Pentecôte premices de la nouvelle crètion," *Bible et vie chrètienne* 27 (1959): 59-69.

Goldingax, John. *The Church and the Gifts of the Spirit: A Practical Exposition of Corinthians 12-14*. Grove Books, 1972.

Gonsalvez, Emma. "A Psychological Interpretation of the Religious Behavior of Pentecostals and Charismatics," *Journal of Dharma*, 7 (October-December 1982): 408-29.

_____. "The Theology and Psychology of Glossolalia." Doctor's dissertation Northwestern University, 1978.

Goodman, Felicitas D. "The Acquisition of Glossolalia Behavior," *Semiotica*, 3 (1971) 77-82.

_____. "Altered Mental State vs. 'Style of Discourse': Reply to Samarin," *Journal for the Scientific Study of Religion*, 11 (1972): 297-99.

_____. "Disturbances in the Apostolic Church: Case Study of a Trance-Based Upheaval in Yucatan." Unpublished doctor's dissertation, Ohio State University 1971.

_____. "Glossolalia and Hallucination in Pentecostal Congregations." Paper presented to the annual meeting of the American Anthropological Association, New York, 1971.

_____. "Glossolalia and Single-Limb Trance: Some Parallels," *Psychotherapy and Psychosomatics*, 19 (1971): 92-103.

_____. "Glossolalia: Speaking in Tongues in Four Cultural Settings," *Confinia Psychiatrica*, 12 (1969): 113-29.

_____. "Phonetic Analysis of Glossolalia in Four Cultural Settings," *Journal of the Scientific Study of Religion*, 8 (1969): 227-39.

_____. *Speaking in Tongues: A Cross-Cultural Study of Glossolalia*. University of Chicago Press, 1972.

_____. *Trance, Healing and Hallucination*. John Wiley and Sons, 1974.

Goodwin, John W. *The Miracle of Pentecost: or The Evidence by Speaking in Tongues*. Nazarene Publishing House, n.d.

van Gorder, Paul. "Charismatic Confusion." Grand Rapids Radio Bible Class, 1972.

Gosnell, L. W. "The Gift of Tongues: The True and the False," *The Christian Workers Magazine*, 13 (November 1913): 1-11.

"Government and Glossolalia," *Christianity Today*, 8 (July 31, 1964): 44-45.

"Government Grant for Study of 'Speaking in Tongues,' " *Pastoral Psychology*, 15 (September 1964): 53-54.

Green, E. "Phonological and Grammatical Aspects of Jargon in an Aphasic Patient: A Case Study," *Language and Speech*, 12 (1969): 103-13.

Green, William M. "Glossolalia in the Second Century," *Restoration Quarterly*, 16 (1973): 231-39.

Greene, David. "The Gift of Tongues," *Bibliotheca Sacra*, 22 (January 1865): 99-126.

Griffiths, Michael F. *Three Men Filled with the Spirit: The Gift of Tongues*. Overseas Missionary Fellowship, 1969.

Gromacki, Robert Glenn. *The Modern Tongues Movement*. Presbyterian and Reformed Publishing Company, 1967.

Grudem, Wayne. "1 Corinthians 14:20-26: Prophecy and Tongues as Signs of God's Attitude," *Westminster Theological Journal*, 41 (Spring 1979): 381-96.

_____. *The Gift of Prophecy in 1 Corinthians*. University Press of America, 1983.

Grundmann, W. "Der Pfingstbericht der Apostelgeschichte in seinem theologischen Sinn," in *Studia Evangelica*, F. L. Cross, editor. Akademie Verlag, 1964. Pp. 584-94.

Guillaume, Alfred. "Prophecy and Divination," in *Bampton Lectures*. Hodder and Stoughton, 1938.

_____. *Prophecy and Divination Among the Hebrews and Other Semites*. Hodder and Stoughton, 1938.

Gulledge, Jack. "Jibberish Is Not A Gift!" *Western Recorder*, 145 (January 2, 1971): 11.

Gundry, Robert H. " 'Ecstatic Utterance' (N.E.B.)?" *Journal of Theological Studies*, 17 (October 1969): 299-307.

Gutierrez, Lalei Elizabeth. "The Effects of Enhancement of Right Brain Functions Through Glossolalic Training on Nonverbal Sensitivity." Unpublished doctor's dissertation, Kent State University, 1980.

Haavil, O. L. "Pentecostalism or the Tongues Movement," *Lutheran Herald* (Octobe 23 and 30, 1934): 935-37, 959-63.

Haldeman, I. M. *Holy Ghost Baptism and Speaking with Tongues.* C. C. Cook, n.d.

Hall, Robert B. *Receiving the Holy Spirit.* Privately published, n.d.

Hall, Thor. "A New Syntax for Religious Language," *Theology Today*, 24 (July 1967 172-84.

van Halsema, J. H. "Mededeling: de historische betrouwbaarheid van het pinkster erhaal," *Nederlands Theologisch Tijdschrift*, 20 (February 1966): 218.

Hamman, Adalbert. "La nouvelle Pentecôte," *Bible et vie chrètienne*, 14 (1956): 8 90.

Hanson, James H. "A Personal Experience," in "Symposium on Speaking in Tongues *Dialog*, 2 (Spring 1963): 152-53.

Hargrave, Vessie D. "Glossolalia: Reformation to the Twentieth Century," in *T Glossolalia Phenomenon*, Wade H. Horton, editor. Pathway Press, 1966. Pp. 9 139.

Harmon, George E. *The Gift of Tongues: What It Is and What It Is Not.* Faith Publishi House, n.d.

Harpur, T. W. "Gift of Tongues and Interpretation," *Canadian Journal of Theolo* 12 (July 1966): 164-71.

Harrison Michael I. "Sources of Recruitment to Catholic Pentecostalism," *Journal the Scientific Study of Religion*, 13 (1974): 49-64.

Harrisville, Roy A. "Speaking in Tongues," *Sisters Today*, 50 (June-July 1974): 5 609.

——————. "Speaking in Tongues: A Lexicographical Study," *Catholic Bibl Quarterly*, 38 (January 1976): 35-48.

——————. "Speaking in Tongues: Proof of Transcendence?" *Dialog*, 13:1 (19` 11-18.

Haskins, Dan D., Jr. "Glossolalia on Campus," *Collage*, 8 (1978): 4.

Hay, Donald and Ann Morisy. "Reports of Ecstatic, Paranormal, or Religious Ex rience in Great Britain and the United States," *Journal for the Scientific Stud Religion*, 17:3 (1978): 255-68.

Hayes, Doremus Almy. *The Gift of Tongues.* Jennings and Graham, 1913.

Haynes, Benjamin F. "Tongues," *Herald of Holiness*, 4 (June 23, 1915): 1-2.

Hendricks, William L. "Glossolalia in the New Testament," in *Speaking in Tong Let's Talk about It*, Watson E. Mills, editor. Word Books, 1973. Pp. 48-60.

Henke, Frederick G. "Gift of Tongues and Related Phenomena at the Present Day," *American Journal of Theology*, 13 (April 1909): 193-206.

Hilgenfeld, Adolf. *Die Glossolalie in der Alten Kirche*. Breitkopf und Härtel, 1850.

Hillis, Don W. *Tongues, Healing, and You*. Baker Book House, 1969.

_____. *What Can Tongues Do For You?* Moody Press, 1963.

Hinds, J. L. *The Modern Gift of Tongues Exposed*. Faith Publishing House, n.d.

Hine, Virginia H. "Non-Pathological Pentecostal Glossolalia—A Summary of Psychological Literature." Unpublished report of the Pentecostal movement research committee, Department of Anthropology, University of Minnesota, 1967.

_____. "Non-Pathological Pentecostal Glossolalia: A Summary of Relevant Psychological Literature," *Journal for the Scientific Study of Religion*, 8 (1969): 211-26.

_____. "Pentecostal Glossolalia: Toward a Functional Interpretation," *Journal for the Scientific Study of Religion*, 8 (Fall 1965): 211-26.

Hine, Virginia H. and James H. Olila. "Interim Report on the Study of the Pentecostal Movement Conducted by the Anthropology Department of the University of Minnesota." Research report, University of Minnesota, 1967.

Hinson, E. Glenn. "A Brief History of Glossolalia," in *Glossolalia: Tongue Speaking in Biblical, Historical, and Psychological Perspective*, Frank Stagg, E. Glenn Hinson, and Wayne E. Oates, editors. Abingdon Press, 1967. Pp. 45-75.

_____. "The Significance of Glossolalia in the History of Christianity," in *Speaking in Tongues: Let's Talk about It*, Watson E. Mills, editor. Word Books, 1973. Pp. 61-80.

Hobbs, Herschel H. "Tongues—Sign to Whom?" *Home Life*, 19 (1976): 1.

Hodges, Zane C. "The Purpose of Tongues," *Bibliotheca Sacra*, 120 (July-September 1963): 226-33.

Hoekema, Anthony. *Tongues and Spirit Baptism*. Baker Book House, 1970.

_____. *What About Tongue-Speaking?* Eerdmans, 1966.

Hoerschelmann, Werner. *Christliche Gurus. Darstellung von Selbstverständnis und Funktion idigenen Christseins durch unabhängige, charismatisch fegührte Gruppen in Südindien*. Peter Lang, 1977.

Hoffman, James W. "Speaking in Tongues, 1963" *Presbyterian Life*, 16 (September 1, 1963): 14-17.

Hollenweger, Walter. "Charismatische und pfingstlerische Bewegung als Frage an die Kirchen heute," in *Wiederentdeckung des Heiligen Geistes*, M. Lienhard and H. Meyer, editors. Lembeck, 1974. Pp. 53-76.

_____. *Enthusiastisches Christentum. Die Pfingstbewegung in Geschichte und Gegenwart.* Zwingli Verlag, 1969.

_____. "Literatur von und uber die Pfingstbewegung (Weltkonferenzen, Holland, Belgien)," *Nederlands Theologisch Tijdschrift,* 18 (1963): 289-306.

_____. *The Pentecostals: The Charismatic Movement in the Churches.* Trans. R A. Wilson. Augsburg, 1972.

_____. *Die Pfingskirchen: Selbstdarstellung Dokumente, Komentare.* Evange lisches Velagswerk, 1971.

Holm, Lewis. "Speaking in Tongues," *The Lutheran Standard,* 2 (September 11, 1962) 3ff.

Holm, Nils G. "Functions of Glossolalia in the Pentecostal Movement," in *Psycholog ical Studies on Religious Man,* Torvald Callstad, editor. Almqvist and Wiksell, 1978 Pp. 141-58.

_____, ed. *Religious Ecstasy: Based on Papers Read at the Symposium on Rel gious Ecstasy Held at Åbo, Finland, on the 26th-28th of August 1981.* Almqvist Wiksell International, 1982.

Horn, William M. "Speaking in Tongues: A Retrospective Appraisal," *The Luthera Quarterly,* 17 (November 1965): 316-29.

Horton, Stanley M. *Tongues and Prophecy: How to Know a Gift of Utterance Is in O der.* Gospel Publishing House, 1972.

Horton, Wade. *What Is the Good of Speaking with Tongues?* Assemblies of God Pu lishing House, 1960.

House, H. Wayne. "Tongues and the Mystery Religions of Corinth," *Bibliotheca Sacr* 140 (April-June 1983): 134-50.

Howard, Richard E. *Tongues Speaking in the New Testament.* Western Maine Graphi Publishing, 1980.

Hoyt, Herman. "Speaking in Tongues," *Brethren Missionary Herald,* 25 (1963): 1 57, 204-207.

Huffman, Jasper A. *Speaking in Tongues.* Bethel Publishing Company, 1910.

Hughes, Ray H. "Glossolalia in Contemporary Times," in *The Glossolalia Pheno enom,* Wade H. Horton, editor. Pathway Press, 1966. Pp. 143-77.

Hull, J. H. E. *The Holy Spirit in the Acts of the Apostles.* The World Publishing Co pany, 1968.

Hulme, A. J. Howard and Frederick H. Wood. *Ancient Egypt Speaks: A Miracle Tongues.* Rider and Company, 1940.

Humphreys, Fisher and Malcolm Tolbert. *Speaking in Tongues.* Christian Litho, 19

Hunt, George L. *Speaking in Tongues*. Gospel Hall, n.d.

Hunter, Harold. "Tongue-Speech: A Patristic Analysis," *Journal of Evangelical Theological Society*, 23:2 (1980): 125-37.

Hutch, Richard A. "The Personal Ritual of Glossolalia," *Journal for Scientific Study of Religion*, 19:3 (1980): 255-66.

Inglis, James. "Gift of Tongues, Another View," *Theological Monthly*, 5 (1891): 425-27.

Isbell, Charles D. "Glossolalia and Propheteialalia: A Study of 1 Corinthians 14," *Wesleyan Theological Journal*, 10 (Spring 1975): 15-22.

Jaquith, James R. "Toward a Typology of Formal Communicative Behavior: Glossolalia," *Anthropological Linguistics*, 9 (1967): 1-8.

Jaschke, H. "Λαλεῖν bei Lukas," *Biblische Zeitschrift*, 15:8 (1971): 109-14.

Jennings, George. "An Ethnological Study of Glossolalia," *Journal of the American Scientific Affiliation*, 20 (March 1968): 5-16.

Jividen, Jimmy. *Glossolalia: From God or Man?* Star Publications, 1971.

Johanson, Bruce C. "Tongues, A Sign for Unbelievers? A Structural and Exegetical Study of 1 Corinthians 14:20-25," *New Testament Studies*, 25 (January 1979): 180-203.

Johnson, S. Lewis. "The Gift of Tongues and the Book of Acts," *Bibliotheca Sacra*, 120 (October-December 1963): 309-11.

Jolley, Jennie A. *Bible Tongues*. Vantage Press, 1964.

Jones, Eli S. *The Holy Spirit and the Gift of Tongues*. United Christian Ashrams, n.d.

Jones, Kenneth E. *What about the Gift of Tongues?* Warner Press, 1962.

Jones, Lawrence Neale. "The Black Pentecostals," in *The Charismatic Movement*, Michael P. Hamilton, editor. Eerdmans, 1975. Pp. 145-58.

Joyce, J. Daniel. " 'Do All Speak with Tongues?'—No! 'Do Any Speak with Tongues?'—Maybe," *The Christian*, (May 30, 1971): 678-79.

Kaasa, Harris. "An Historical Evaluation," in "Symposium on Speaking in Tongues," *Dialog*, 2 (1963): 61-69.

Keiper, R. L. "Tongues and the Holy Spirit," *Moody Monthly*, 64 (September 1963): 61-69.

Kelsey, Morton T. *Discernment: A Study in Ecstasy and Evil*. Paulist Press, 1978.

_____. *Dreams: The Dark Speech of the Spirit*. Doubleday and Company, 1968.

_____. "Speaking in Tongues in 1971: An Assessment of Its Meaning and Value," *Review for Religious*, 30 (March 1971): 245-55.

_____. *Tongue Speaking: An Experiment in Spiritual Experience.* Doubleday and Company, 1964.

Kendall, E. L. "Speaking with Tongues," *Church Quarterly Review*, 168 (January-March 1967): 11-19.

Kildahl, John P. "Psychological Observations," in *The Charismatic Movement*, Michael P. Hamilton, editor. Eerdmans, 1975. Pp. 124-42.

_____. *The Psychology of Speaking in Tongues.* Harper & Row, 1972.

Kildahl, John P. and Paul A. Qualben. "Final Progress Report: Glossolalia and Mental Health." Research project supported by the Behavioral Sciences Research Branch of the National Institute of Mental Health, 1971.

_____. "Final Progress Report: Glossolalia and Mental Health." Unpublished paper, Brooklyn, n.d.

_____. "Relationships Between Glossolalia and Mental Health." A report of study done on a grant from the Behavioral Sciences Research Branch of the National Institute of Mental Health, Bethesda, 1971.

Killian, Matthew. "Speaking in Tongues," *The Priest*, 25 (November 1969): 611-16.

Kirkpatrick, Sherman. " 'Glossolalia' or 'the Gift of Tongues.' " Unpublished master's thesis, Phillips University, 1936.

Knox, Lloyd H. *Key Biblical Perspectives on Tongues.* Light and Life Press, 1974.

Knox, Ronald A. *Enthusiasm.* Oxford University Press, 1950.

Knudsen, Ralph E. "Speaking in Tongues," *Foundations*, 9 (January-March 1966): 4-57.

Koch, Kurt E. *Charismatic Gifts.* Association for Christian Evangelism, 1975.

_____. *The Strife of Tongues.* Kregel Publications, 1969.

Koenig, John. *Charismata: God's Gifts for God's People.* Westminster Press, 1978.

Krodel, Gerhard. "An Exegetical Examination," in "Symposium on Speaking in Tongues," *Dialog*, 2 (1963): 154-56.

Kucharsky, D. E. "Testing Tongues: Lutheran Medical Center Research Project," *Christianity Today*, 15 (June 4, 1971): 1-18.

Laffal, Julius, et al. "Communication of Meaning in Glossolalia," *Journal of Social Psychology*, 92 (April 1974): 277-91.

_____. *Pathological and Normal Language.* Atherton Press, 1965.

Lapsley, James N. and John H. Simpson. "Speaking in Tongues: Infantile Babble or Song of the Self?" *Pastoral Psychology*, 15 (September 1964): 16-24.

_____. "Speaking in Tongues: Token of Group Acceptance and Divine Approval," *Pastoral Psychology*, 15 (May 1964): 48-55.

_____. "Speaking in Tongues," *Princeton Seminary Bulletin*, 58 (February 1965): 1-18.

Laurentin, René. "The Birth of Catholic Pentecostalism," *Catholic Pentecostalism*. Doubleday and Company, 1977. Pp. 11-17.

_____. "Charismatische Erneuerung: Prophetische Erneuerung oder Neokonservatismus?" *Concilium*, 17:1 (1981): 27-33.

LeBarre, Weston. "Speaking in Tongues: Token of Group Acceptance and Divine Approval," *Pastoral Psychology*, 15 (May 1964): 48-55.

LeBarron, Albert. "A Case of Psychic Automation, Including 'Speaking with Tongues,' " *Proceedings of the Society for Psychical Research*, 12 (1896-1897): 277.

Lester, Andrew D. "Glossolalia: A Psychological Evaluation." Unpublished seminary paper, Southern Baptist Theological Seminary, 1965.

Lewis, I. M. *Ecstatic Religion*. Penguin Books, 1971.

Lhermitte, Jacques Jean. *True and False Possession*. Trans. P. J. Hepburne-Scott. Hawthorne Books, 1963.

Lightner, Robert Paul. *Speaking in Tongues and Divine Healing*. Regular Baptist Press, 1965.

_____. *The Tongues Tide*. Empire State Baptist Fellowship, 1964.

Lillie, David George. *Tongues Under Fire*. Fountain Trust, 1966.

Lindsay, George. *Twenty-One Reasons Why Christians Should Speak in Other Tongues*. Voice of Healing Publishing Company, 1959.

Lindsay, Gordon. *The Gift of Prophecy and the Gift of Interpretation of Tongues*. Voice of Healing Publishing Company, 1964.

Lindsell, Harold. "Tests for the Tongues Movement," in *Is the Whole Body a Tongue?* Don W. Hillis, editor. Eerdmans, 1974.

Lombard, Émile. *De la Glossolalie chez les premiers chrètiens et des phénomènes similaires*. Bridel, 1910.

_____. "Essai d'une classification des phénomènes de glossolalie," *Archives de Psychologie*, 7 (1908): 1-62.

Lovekin, Arthur Adams. "Glossolalia: A Critical Study of Alleged Origins, the New Testament and the Early Church." Unpublished master's thesis, University of the South, 1962.

Lovekin, Adams and H. Newton Malony. "Religious Glossolalia: A Longitudinal Study of Personality Changes," *Journal for the Scientific Study of Religion*, 16 (December 1977): 383-93.

Lowe, Harry W. *Speaking in Tongues: A Brief History of the Phenomenon Known as Glossolalia, or Speaking in Tongues*. Pacific Press Publishing Association, 1965.

Lyonnet, S. "De glossolalia Pentecotes eiusque Significatione," *Verbum domi* (1944): 65-75.

Lyons, Bobbye. "Charismatic Gifts: An Exegesis of 1 Corinthians 12:1-11." U lished master's thesis, Columbia Theological Seminary, 1965.

McCone, R. Clyde. *Culture and Controversy: An Investigation of the Tongues o tecost.* Dorrance, 1978.

McCready, William. "Les nouveaux pentecôtistes," *Concilium*, 72 (1972): 107-

McCrossan, T. J. *Speaking with Other Tongues: Sign or Gift—Which?* Christian lications, 1919.

MacDonald, William G. "Glossolalia in the New Testament," *Bulletin of the gelical Theological Society* 7 (1964): 59-68.

―――――. "The Place of Glossolalia in Neo-Pentecostalism," in *Speaking in Ton Let's Talk about It*, Watson E. Mills, editor. Word Books, 1973. Pp. 81-93.

McGee, John V. *Talking in Tongues.* W. Smith Publishers, 1963.

MacGorman, J. W. "Glossolalia Error and Its Correction: 1 Corinthians 12-14, *view and Expositor*, 80:3 (Summer 1983): 389-400.

Mackie, Alexander. *The Gift of Tongues.* George H. Doran Company, 1921.

McKinney, Joseph. "The Gift of Tongues: A School for Prayer and Ministry," *Covenant*, 10:12 (June 1981): 12-15.

McNamee, John J. "The Role of the Spirit in Pentecostalism: A Comparative Stu Doctor's dissertation, University of Tübingen, 1974.

Maeder, Alphonse. "La Langue d'un Aliéné: Analyse d'un Cas de Glossolalie, *chives de Psychologie*, 9 (March 1910): 208-16.

Malony, H. Newton. "Debunking Some of the Myths about Glossolalia," *Jourr the American Scientific Affiliation*, 34:3 (September 1982): 144-48.

Malony, H. Newton, Nelson Zwaanstra, and James W. Ramsey. "Personal and ational Determinants of Glossolalia: A Literature Review and Report of On Research." Paper presented at the International Congress of Religious Studies Angeles, 1972.

Maly, Karl. "Apostolische Gemeindeführung," *Theologie der Gegenwart*, 10 (1 219-22.

Manro, Philip. *Speaking in Tongues.* Reiner Publications, n.d.

Martin, Ira J. "1 Corinthians 13 Interpreted by Its Context," *The Journal of Bible Religion*, 18 (April 1950): 101-105.

―――――. "Glossolalia in the Apostolic Church," *Journal of Biblical Literatur* (1944): 123-30.

_____. *Glossolalia in the Apostolic Church: A Survey Study of Tongue-Speech.* Berea College Press, 1960.

_____. "The Place of Significance of Glossolalia in the New Testament." Unpublished doctor's dissertation, Boston University, 1942.

May, L. Carlyle. "A Survey of Glossolalia and Related Phenomena in Non-Christian Religions," *American Anthropologist*, 58 (February 1956): 75-96.

Mayers, Marvin K. "The Behavior of Tongues," in *Speaking in Tongues: Let's Talk about It*, Watson E. Mills, editor. Word Books, 1973. Pp. 112-27.

_____. "The Behavior of Tongues," *Journal of the American Scientific Affiliation*, 23 (September 1971): 89-95.

Meeks, Fred E. "Pastors and the Tongues Movement," *Southwestern Journal of Theology*, 19 (Spring 1977): 73-85.

_____. "Pastoral Care and Glossolalia: Implications of the Contemporary Tongues Movement in American Churches." Unpublished doctor's dissertation, Southwestern Baptist Theological Seminary, 1976.

Mehl, Roger. "Approche sociologique des mouvements charismatiques," *Bulletin de la Société du Protestantisme Francais*, (octobre-novembre-décembre 1974): 555-73.

Mensbrugghe, Francoise van der. "Les Mouvements de Renouveau Charismatique. Retour de l'Esprit? Retour de Dionysos?" Dissertation, Université de Genève, 1978.

Metz, Donald. *Speaking in Tongues: An Analysis.* Nazarene Publishing House, 1964.

Meyer, Johann A. G. *De charismatic των γλωσσων praesertim Act. ii et I Cor. xiv.* Lamminer, 1797.

Michael, John H. "The Gift of Tongues at Corinth," *The Expositor*, 4 (September 1907): 252-66.

Mills, Watson E. "Ecstaticism as a Background for Glossolalia," *Journal of the American Scientific Affiliation*, 27:4 (1975): 167-71.

_____. "Genesis of Glossolalia," *Averett Journal*, 4:2 (Fall 1972): 43-51.

_____. "Glossolalia: Christianity's Counterculture Amidst a Silent Majority," *Christian Century*, 89 (September 27, 1972): 949-51.

_____. "Glossolalia: Creative Sound or Destructive Fury," *Home Missions*, 43 (August 1972): 8-13.

_____. "Glossolalia: The New Language of Zion?" *People* (July 1973): 34-37.

_____. "Glossolalia as a Socio-Psychological Experience," *Search*, 3 (Winter 1973): 46-53.

_____. "Glossolalia: A Study of Origins." Unpublished paper presented at the national meeting of the Society of Biblical Literature, Atlanta, October 29, 1971.

_____. "Listening to the Glossolaliac: Going Beyond Words," *Western Recorder*, 145 (January 2, 1971): 10.

_____. "Literature on Glossolalia," *Journal of the American Scientific Affiliation*, 26:4 (December 1974): 169-73.

_____. "Reconstruction and Reappraisal," in *Understanding Speaking in Tongues* Watson E. Mills, editor. Eerdmans, 1972. Pp. 61-76.

_____, ed. *Speaking in Tongues: Let's Talk about It*. Word Books, 1973.

_____. "Spiritual Gifts in the New Testament," *Biblical Illustrator*, 1:2 (Sprin 1975): 29-33.

_____. "The Strange New Language of Christendom," in *The Lure of the Occul Watson E. Mills and M. Thomas Starkes, editors. Home Mission Board of th Southern Baptist Convention, 1974. Pp. 73-82.

_____. "A Theological Interpretation of Tongues in Acts and 1 Corinthians. Unpublished doctor's dissertation, Southern Baptist Theological Seminary, 1968.

_____. "Tongue Speech: Revolution or Renewal," *The Student*, 50 (Novemb 1970): 29-31.

_____, ed. *Understanding Speaking in Tongues*. Eerdmans, 1972.

Molenaar, D. G. *De doop met de Heilige Geest*. Kok, 1963.

Montague, George T. "Baptism in the Spirit and Speaking in Tongues: A Biblical A praisal," *Theology Digest*, 21 (1973): 342-60.

Moody, Dale. "Speaking in Tongues," *Proclaim*, 9 (1979): 13.

Moorehead, William G. "Tongues of Fire," *The International Standard Bible Enc clopedia*. 5 vols. 5 (The Howard-Severance Company, 1915): 2843-44.

Morentz, Paul. "Lecture on Glossolalia." Multilithed paper, University of Californi 1966.

Morris, Fred B. "Now I Want You All To Speak in Tongues," *The Christian Advocat 7 (July 4, 1963): 9-10.

Morris, John Warren. "The Charismatic Movement: An Orthodox Evaluation," *T Greek Orthodox Theological Review*, 28:2 (Summer 1983): 103-34.

Mosiman, Eddison. "A Dissertation on the Gift of Tongues in the New Testament Unpublished master's thesis, University of Chicago, 1910.

_____. *Das Zungenreden geschichtlich und psychologisch untersucht*. J. C. Mohr, 1911.

Motley, Michael T. "Glossolalia: Analyses of Selected Aspects of Phonology and M phology." Unpublished master's thesis, University of Texas, 1967.

Mountain, J. *Authority, Demons and Tongues*. Privately published, n.d.

Mueller, Theodore. "A Linguistic Analysis of Glossolalia," *Concordia Theological Monthly*, 45:3 (July 1981): 186-91.

Mühlen, Heribert. *Erfahrung mit dem Heiligen Geist*. Grünewald Verlag, 1979.

_____. "Gemeinsame Geist-Erfahrung: Hoffnung für die getrennten Kirchen," *Una Sancta*, 36:1 (1981): 20-32.

Müller, Alexander. "Die internationale Pfingstbewegung," *Informationsblatt*, 8 (May 22, 1959): 157-61.

Munk, Gerald W. "The Charismatic Experience in the Orthodox Tradition," *Theosis*, 1:7 (November 1978): 1-3.

Munro, John K. "The New Testament Spiritual Gifts." Unpublished master's thesis, Dallas Theological Seminary, 1940.

"My Experience of Speaking in Tongues," *Our Hope*, 33 (May 1927): 684-87.

Mueller, Theodore. "A Linguistic Analysis of Glossolalia," *Concordia Theological Monthly*, 45:3 (July 1981): 186-91.

Neely, B. G. *Bible vs. the Tongues Theory*. Nazarene Publishing House, n.d.

Neff, H. Richard. "The Cultural Basis for Glossolalia in the Twentieth Century," in *Speaking in Tongues: Let's Talk about It*, Watson E. Mills, editor. Word Books, 1973. Pp. 26-35.

Neighbor, R. E. *Talking in Tongues*. Gems of Gold Publishing Company, n.d.

Ness, William H. "Glossolalia in the New Testament," *Concordia Theological Monthly*, 32 (April 1961): 221-23.

Newport, John P. "Speaking in Tongues," *Home Missions*, 36 (May 1965): 7-9, 21-26.

Nevius, J. L. *Demon Possession and Allied Themes*. Revell, 1894.

Nida, Eugene A. "Glossolalia: A Case of Pseudo-Linguistic Structure." Unpublished paper delivered at the 39th Annual Meeting of the Linguistic Society of America, New York City, December 28, 1964.

_____. "Preliminary Report on Glossolalia." A paper presented at the Linguistic Society of America, New York, 1964.

Niesz, Nancy L. and Earl J. Kronenberger. "Self-Actualization in Glossolalic and Non-Glossolalic Pentecostals," *Sociological Analysis: A Journal in the Sociology of Religion*, 39 (Fall 1978): 250-56.

Northrup, Bernard E. *What You Should Know About . . . Tongues and Spiritual Gifts*. San Francisco Baptist Theological Seminary, n.d.

Nouwen, Henri. "The Pentecostal Movement: Three Perspectives," *Scholastic*, 109 (April 21, 1967): 15-17, 32.

Nunn, David O. *Manifestations of the Spirit: The Three Glorious Gifts of Utterance—Divine Kinds of Tongues, Interpretation of Tongues, Prophecy.* Bible Revival Evangelistic Association, n.d.

Oates, Wayne E. "Ecstaticism." Unpublished seminar paper, Duke University, 1943.

_____. "A Socio-Psychological Study of Glossolalia," in *Glossolalia: Tongue Speaking in Biblical, Historical, and Psychological Perspective*, Frank Stagg, E. Glenn Hinson, and Wayne E. Oates, editors. Abingdon Press, 1967. Pp. 76-99.

Ockenga, Harold J. *The Holy Spirit and Tongues.* Boston Park Street Church, 1965.

O'Connell, Daniel C. and Ernest T. Bryant. "Some Psychological Reflections on Glossolalia," *Review for Religious*, 31 (1972): 174-77.

Oesterreich, T. K. *Possession: Demonical and Other.* Trans. D. Ibberson. University Books, 1966.

Oke, Norman R. *Facing the Tongues Issue.* Beacon Hill Press, 1973.

Oman, John D. "On 'Speaking in Tongues': A Psychological Analysis," *Pastoral Psychology*, 14 (December 1963): 48-51.

Orr, William W. *If You Speak with Tongues—Here Are the Rules.* Grace Gospel Fellowship, n.d.

Osser, H. A., et al. "Glossolalic Speech from a Psycholinguistic Perspective," *Journal of Psycholinguistic Research*, 2 (1973): 9-19.

Palma, Anthony D. "Glossolalia in the Light of the New Testament and Subsequent History." Unpublished bachelor's thesis, Biblical Seminary, New York, 1960.

_____. "The Holy Spirit in the Corporate Life of the Pauline Congregation." Unpublished doctor's dissertation, Concordia Seminary, 1974.

_____. "Tongues and Prophecy: A Comparative Study in Charismata." Unpublished master's thesis, Concordia Seminary, 1966.

Palmer, Everett W. "Speaking in Tongues," *Christian Advocate*, 8 (October 22, 1964): 9-10.

_____. *Statement on the Tongues Movement.* Privately published, 1961.

Palmer, Gary. "Studies of Tension Reduction in Glossolalia." Unpublished paper, University of Minnesota, 1966.

_____. "Trance." Paper presented at the annual meeting of the Central States Anthropological Society, Chicago, April 27-29, 1967.

_____. "Trance and Dissociation: A Cross-Cultural Study in Psychophysiology." Master's thesis, University of Minnesota, 1966.

Panton, D. M. *Irvingism, Tongues, and the Gifts of the Holy Ghost.* Charles J. Thynne and Jarvis, n.d.

Pattison, E. Mansell. "Behavioral Research on the Nature of Glossolalia," *Journal of the American Scientific Affiliation*, 20 (September 1968): 73-86.

_____. "Speaking in Tongues and About Tongues," *Christian Standard*, 98 (February 15, 1964): 1-2.

Pattison, E. Mansell and Robert L. Casey. "Glossolalia: A Contemporary Mystical Experience," in *Clinical Psychiatry and Religion*, E. Mansell Pattison, editor. Little, Brown and Company, 1968. Pp. 133-48.

_____. "Glossolalia: A Contemporary Mystical Experience," *International Psychiatry Clinics*, 5 (1969): 133-48.

_____. "Ideological Support for the Marginal Middle Class: Faith Healing and Glossolalia," in *Religious Movements in Contemporary America*, Irving I. Zaretsky and Mark P. Leone, editors. Princeton University Press, 1974.

Pavelsky, Robert L. "The Psychological Correlates of Act and Process Glossolalia as a Function of Socioeconomic Class, Expectation of Glossolalia, and Frequency of Glossolalic Utterance." Unpublished doctor's dissertation, Fuller Theological Seminary, 1975.

Perkins, David W. "Superspirituality in Corinth," *The Theological Educator*, 14:1 (Fall 1983): 41-52.

Perkins, Jonathan E. *The Baptism of the Holy Spirit: An Explanation of Speaking in Other Languages as the Spirit Giveth Utterance*. B. N. Robertson Company, 1945.

Pfister, Oskar. "Die psycologische Enträtselung der Religiösen Glossolalie und der automatischen Kryptographie," *Jahrbuch für psychoanalytische und psychopathologische Forschungen*, 3 (1912): 427ff.

Pierce, Flora M. Johnson. "Glossolalia," *Journal of Religion and Psychical Research*, 4 (July-October 1981): 168-78.

Pierson, A. T. *Speaking with Tongues*. Gospel Publishing House, n.d.

_____. "Speaking with Tongues," *Missionary Review*, 20 (1907): 487, 682.

Pike, James A. "Pastoral Letter Regarding 'Speaking in Tongues,' " *Pastoral Psychology*, 15 (May 1964): 56-61.

Pikell, D. "Speaking in Tongues," *Cross and Crown*, 24 (September 1972): 280-85.

Pilkington, G. *The Unknown Tongues Discovered to be English, Spanish, and Latin: The Rev. Edward Irving Proved to be Erroneous in Attributing Their Utterance to the Influence of the Holy Spirit*. Privately published, 1831.

Pinnock, Clark H. and Grant R. Osborne. "A Truce Proposal for the Tongues Controversy," *Christianity Today*, 16 (October 8, 1971): 6-9.

Plog, Stanley C. "Preliminary Analysis of Group Questionnaires on Glossolalia." Unpublished data, University of California, 1966.

_____. "UCLA Conducts Research on Glossolalia," *Trinity*, 3 (Whitsuntide 1964): 38-39.

Polovina, Samuel Emil. "Light on the Tongues Movement," *Herald of Holiness*, 5 (December 13, 1916): 8.

Pope, R. Martin. "Gift of Tongues," in *A Dictionary of the Apostolic Church*, James Hastings, editor. 2 vols. 1 (Scribner's Sons, 1908): 598-99.

Poythress, Vern S. "Linguistic and Sociological Analyses of Modern Tongues-Speaking: Their Contributions and Limitations," *Westminster Theological Journal*, 42:2 (1980): 367-88.

"Preliminary Report, Study Commission on Glossolalia." Division of Pastoral Services, Diocese of California, May 2, 1963.

Preus, Klemet. "Nature of Glossolalia: Possible Options," *Westminster Theological Journal*, 40 (Fall 1977): 130-35.

_____. "Tongues: An Evaluation From a Scientific Perspective," *Concordia Theological Quarterly*, 46:4 (October 1982): 277-93.

"Protestant Episcopal Church in the U.S.A. Diocese of California." Division of Pastoral Services. Study Commission on Glossolalia, May 2, 1963.

Putnam, W. G. "Tongues, Gift of," in *New Bible Dictionary*, J. D. Douglas, editor. (Eerdmans, 1962): 1286-87.

Pyle, Hugh F. *Truth about Tongues*. Accent Books, 1976.

Quebedeaux, Richard. *The New Charismatics: The Origins, Development and Significance of Neo-Pentecostalism*. Doubleday and Company, 1976.

Radford, William F. *Apostolic Teaching Concerning Tongues*. Nazarene Publishing House, n.d.

Ramm, Bernard. *A Study of Some Special Problems in Reference to the Speaking in Tongues*. Bible Institute of Los Angeles, 1947.

_____. "The Word on Speaking in Tongues," *National Catholic Reporter*, 3 (April 26, 1967): 4.

Rarick, William John. "The Socio-Cultural Context of Glossolalia: A Comparison of Pentecostal and Neo-Pentecostal Religious Attitudes and Behavior." Unpublished doctor's dissertation, Fuller Theological Seminary, 1982.

Reid, Samuel Joseph. *What Saith the Scriptures: Concerning Healing of the Body "Tongues," Baptism of the Holy Spirit*. Privately published, n.d.

"Report of the Field Study Committee on Speaking in Tongues." Commission on Evangelism of the American Lutheran Church, 1972.

"Report of the Special Commission on Glossolalia." To the Right Reverend Gerald Francis Burrill, Bishop of Chicago, December 12, 1960.

"Report on Glossolalia." A report of the Commission on Evangelism of the American Lutheran Church, Minneapolis, 1962.

Rice, John R. "Speaking with Tongues," in *The Power of Pentecost*. Sword of the Lord Publishers, 1949. Pp. 203-76.

_____. *Speaking with Tongues*. Sword of the Lord Publishers, 1970.

Rice, Robert F. "Christian Glossolalia Through the Centuries," *View*, 1 (1964): 1-7.

Richardson, James T. "Psychological Interpretations of Glossolalia: A Reexamination of Research," *Journal for the Scientific Study of Religion*, 12 (1973): 199-207.

Richardson, James T. and M. T. V. Reidy. "Form and Fluidity into Contemporary Glossolalic Movements," *The Annual Review of the Social Sciences of Religion*, 4 (1980): 183-220.

Richet, Charles. "Xenoglossie: l'écriture automatique en langues étrangères," *Proceedings of the Society for Psychical Research*, 19 (1905-1907): 162-94.

Ridout, George W. *The Deadly Fallacy of Spurious Tongues*. Pentecostal Publishing House, n.d.

_____. *Spiritual Gifts, Including the Gift of Tongues: A Consideration of the Gifts of the Spirit and Particularly the Gift of Tongues, the "Pneumatika" and the "Charismata of 1 Corinthians."* Nazarene Publishing House, n.d.

Righter, James D. "A Critical Study of the Charismatic Experience of Speaking in Tongues." Unpublished doctor's dissertation, Wesley Theological Seminary, 1974.

Robers, Cleon L. "The Gift of Tongues in the Post Apostolic Church," *Bibliotheca Sacra*, 122 (April-June 1965): 134-43.

Roberts, Oral. *The Baptism with the Holy Spirit and the Value of Speaking in Tongues Today*. Privately Published, 1964.

Roberts, Peter. "A Sign: Christian or Pagan [1 Corinthians 14:21-25]?" *Expository Times*, 90 (April 1979): 199-203.

Robertson, Carl F. "The Nature of New Testament Glossolalia." Unpublished doctor's dissertation, Dallas Theological Seminary, 1975.

Robertson, O. Palmer. "Tongues: Sign of Covenantal Curse and Blessing," *Westminster Theological Journal*, 38:1 (1975): 43-53.

Robinson, D. W. B. "Charismata vs. Pneumatika: Paul's Method of Discussion," *Reformed Theological Review*, 31 (May-August 1972): 49-55.

Robison, Wayne A. *I Once Spoke in Tongues*. Forum House Publishers, 1973.

Roddy, Andrew Jackson. *Though I Spoke with Tongues: A Personal Testimony*. The Harvester, 1952.

Roehrs, Stephen Paul. "Glossolalia Phenomena." Unpublished master's thesis, Concordia Theological Seminary, 1971.

Ruble, Richard Lee. "A Spiritual Evaluation of Tongues in Contemporary Theology." Unpublished doctor's dissertation, Dallas Theological Seminary, 1964.

Runia, K. "The Forms and Functions of Nonsense Language," *Linguistics*, 50 (1969): 70-74.

_____. "Glossolalia as Learned Behavior," *Canadian Journal of Theology*, 15 (1969): 60-64.

_____. "Speaking in Tongues in the New Testament," *Vox Reformata* (May 1965): 20-29, 38-46.

Ruth, Christian W. "The Gift of Tongues," *Herald of Holiness*, 13 (December 24, 1924): 4-5.

Saake, H. "Paulus als Ekstatiker: Pneumatologische Beobachtungen zu 2 corinthians 12:1-10," *Biblica*, 53:3 (1972): 404-10.

_____. "Pneumatologia Paulina: zur Katholizität der Problematik des Charisma,' *Catholica*, 26:3 (1972): 212-23.

Sadler, A. W. "Glossolalia and Possession: An Appeal to the Episcopal Study Commission," *Journal for the Scientific Study of Religion*, 4 (1964): 84-90.

Samarin, William J. "Evolution in Glossolalic Private Language," *Anthropologica Linguistics*, 13 (1971): 55-67.

_____. "Evolution in Glossolalic Private Language." Unpublished manuscript n.d.

_____. "Forms and Functions of Nonsense Language," *Linguistics*, 50 (July 1969): 70-74.

_____. "Glossolalia as Learned Behavior," *Canadian Journal of Theology*, 1 (1969): 60-64.

_____. "Glossolalia as Learned Behavior." Unpublished paper presented to annual meeting of the Society for the Scientific Study of Religion, Montreal, 1968.

_____. "Glossolalia as Regressive Speech," *Language and Speech*, 16 (1973): 77-89.

_____. "Glossolalia as Regressive Speech." Unpublished paper presented at the Meeting of the Linguistic Society of America, Columbus, 1970.

_____. "Glossolalia as a Vocal Phenomenon," in *Speaking in Tongues: Let's Talk about It*, Watson E. Mills, editor. Word Books, 1973. Pp. 128-42.

_____. "The Glossolalist's 'Grammar of Use.' " Paper given at the Annual Meeting of the American Anthropological Association, San Diego, 1970.

_____. "The Language of Religion." A paper presented at the annual meeting of the Society for the Scientific Study of Religion, Chicago, 1971.

_____. "Language in Resocialization," *Practical Anthropology*, 17 (1970): 269-79.

_____. "The Linguisticality of Glossolalia," *The Hartford Quarterly*, 8 (1968): 49-75.

_____. "Religious Goals of a Neo-Pentecostal Group in a Non-Pentecostal Church," in *Perspectives on the New Pentecostalism*, Russell F. Spittler, editor. Baker Book House, 1976. Pp. 134-49.

_____. "Sociolinguistic vs. Neurophysiological Explanations for Glossolalia: Comment on Goodman's Paper," *Journal for the Scientific Study of Religion*, 11 (Spring 1972): 293-99.

_____. *Tongues of Men and Angels: The Religious Language of Pentecostalism.* Macmillan Publishing Company, 1972.

_____. "Variation and Variables in Religious Glossolalia," in *Language and Society*, Dell Haymes, editor. Cambridge University Press, 1972. Pp. 121-30.

_____. "Worship in Sign Language," *Acts*, 1:4 (1968): 27-28.

Sassaman, Marcus B. "An Investigation of the Interpretations of Glossolalia." Unpublished bachelor's thesis, Western Evangelical Seminary, 1966.

Satre, Lowell J. "Glossolalia in the New Testament," in *Reports and Actions of the Second General Convention of the American Lutheran Church*, 1964.

Schjelderup, Harald K. "Psychologische Analyse eines Falles von Zungenreden," *Zeitschrift für Psychologie*, 122 (1931): 1-12.

Schlauch, Margaret. *The Gift of Tongues*. Modern Age Books, 1942.

Schmidt, Karl L. *Die Pfingsterzählung und das Pfingstereignis*. Hindrich, 1919.

_____. "Das Pneuma Hagion als Person und als Charisma," *Eranos Jahrbuck*, 13 (1965): 187-231.

Scroggie, W. Graham. *The Baptism of the Holy Spirit and Speaking with Tongues*. Marshall, Morgan, and Scott, n.d.

_____. *Speaking with Tongues*. Book Stall, 1919.

Seamands, David A. *Tongues: Psychic and Authentic: A Biblical Study of the Holy Spirit and the Gift of Tongues*. Privately published, 1972.

Sebree, Herbert T. "Glossolalia," in *The Word and the Doctrine: Studies in Contemporary Wesleyan-Arminian Theology*, Kenneth E. Geiger, editor. Logos International, 1965. Pp. 335-51.

Seddon, A. E. "Edward Irving and Unknown Tongues," *Homiletic Review*, 57 (1957): 103.

Sherill, John L. *They Speak with Other Tongues*. McGraw-Hill Book Company, 1964.

Shuler, R. P. *McPhersonism: A Study of Healing Cults and Modern Day Tongues Movements*. Privately published, 1924.

Shumacher, W. R. "The Use of Ruah in the Old Testament and of Pneuma in the New Testament: A Lexicographical Study," *Journal of Biblical Literature*, 23 (1904): 13-67.

Shumway, Charles William. "A Critical History of Glossolalia." Unpublished doctor's dissertation, Boston University, 1919.

Siirala, Aarne. "A Methodological Proposal," in "Symposium on Speaking in Tongues," *Dialog*, 2 (1963): 158-59.

Simmons, J. P. *History of Tongues*. Privately published, n.d.

Slay, James L. "Glossolalia: Its Value to the Individual," in *The Glossolalia Phenomenon*, Wade H. Horton, editor. Pathway Press, 1966. Pp. 217-43.

Smalley, S. S. "Spiritual Gifts and 1 Corinthians 12-16," *Journal of Biblical Literature*, 88 (1968): 427-33.

Smith, B. L. "Tongues in the New Testament," *Churchman*, 87 (Winter 1973): 283-88.

Smith, Charles Russell. "Biblical Conclusions Concerning Tongues." Unpublished doctor's dissertation, Grace Theological Seminary, 1970.

Smith, D. Moody. "Glossolalia and Other Spiritual Gifts in a New Testament Perspective," *Interpretation*, 28 (July 1974): 307-20.

Smith, Daniel Stephen. "Glossolalia: The Personality Correlates of Conventional and Unconventional Subgroups." Unpublished doctor's dissertation, Rosemead Graduate School of Professional Psychology, 1977.

Smith, Frank W. "What Value Tongues?" *Message of the Open Bible*, 45 (June 1963): 4-5.

Smith, Swinburne. "Speaking with Tongues—The Gift and the Sign," *Pentecostal Evangel*, 44 (August 9, 1964): 7.

Smolchuck, Fred. *Tongues and Total Surrender*. Gospel Publishing House, 1974.

Smylie, James H. "Testing the Spirits in the American Context: Great Awakening, Pentecostalism, and the Charismatic Movements," *Interpretation*, 33:1 (1979): 32-46.

Soltan, George. "The Tongues Movement," *Our Hope*, 55 (June 1949): 751-55.

Speer, Blanche C. "A Linguistic Analysis of a Corpus of Glossolalia." Unpublished doctor's dissertation, University of Colorado at Boulder, 1971.

Stagg, Frank. "Glossolalia in the New Testament," in *Glossolalia: Tongue Speaking in Biblical, Historical, and Psychological Perspective*, Frank Stagg, E. Glenn Hinson, and Wayne E. Oates, editors. Abingdon Press, 1967. Pp. 20-44.

Stanger, Frank Bateman. *The Gifts of the Spirit*. Christian Publications, 1974.

Stanley, Arthur P. "The Gift of Tongues and the Gift of Prophesying," in *A Collection of Theological Essays from Various Authors*, George R. Noyes, compiler. William Crosby, 1856. Pp. 453-71.

Stanley, Gordon, et al. "Some Characteristics of Charismatic Experience: Glossolalia in Australia," *Journal for the Scientific Study of Religion*, 17 (Spring 1978): 269-77.

"A Statement with Regard to Speaking in Tongues," in *Reports and Actions of the Second General Convention of the American Lutheran Church*, 1964.

Steadman, J. M. "Anent the Gift of Tongues and Kindred Phenomena," *Methodist Quarterly Review*, 74 (October 1925): 688-715.

Stegall, Carroll, Jr. *The Modern Tongues and Healing Movement*. Privately published, n.d.

Stemme, Harry A. *Speaking with Other Tongues: Sign and Gift*. Northern Gospel Publishing House, 1946.

Stendahl, Krister. "The New Testament Evidence," in *The Charismatic Movement*, Michael Hamilton, editor. Eerdmans, 1975. Pp. 49-60.

Sterner, Russell Eugene. "Do All Speak in Tongues?" *Vital Christianity*, 94 (October 6, 1974): 15-17.

Sterrett, T. Norton. "The New Testament Charismata." Unpublished doctor's dissertation, Dallas Theological Seminary, 1947.

Stevenson, Ian. *Xenoglossy*. University of Virginia Press, 1974.

Stibbs, A. M. "Putting the Gift of Tongues in Its Place," *The Churchman*, 80 (Winter 1966): 295-303.

Stolee, Haakon, J. *Pentecostalism: The Problem of the Modern Tongues Movement*. Augsburg, 1936.

_____. *Speaking in Tongues*. Augsburg, 1963.

Stoll, R. F. "The First Christian Pentecost," *Ecclesiastical Review*, 108 (1943): 337-47.

Stone, D. D. "The Speaking in Tongues and the Episcopal Church," *Trinity*, 1 (Eastertide 1962): 10.

Stringer, Randy C. *What the Bible Teaches about the Purpose of Tongue Speaking*. Privately published, 1971.

Sullivan, Francis A. "Speaking in Tongues," *Lumen Vitae*, 31:2 (1976): 145-70.

Summers, Ray. "Unknown Tongues: 1 Corinthians 14." Unpublished paper, Souther Baptist Theological Seminary, 1960.

Sutcliff, J. P. " 'Credulous' and 'Skeptical' Views of Hypnotic Phenomena: Experiments on Esthesia, Hallucination, and Delusion," *Journal of Abnormal and Socic Psychology*, 62 (1961): 189-200.

Swank, J. Grant. "A Plea to Some Who Speak in Tongues," *Christianity Today*, 1 (February 28, 1975): 12-13.

Sweet, J. P. M. "A Sign for Unbelievers: Paul's Attitude to Glossolalia," *New Te. tament Studies*, 13 (April 1967): 240-57.

Taylor, James E. "A Perspective on Christian Glossolalia." Mimeographed paper, 1975.

Taylor, R. O. P. "The Tongues at Pentecost," *Expository Times*, 40 (1928-29): 30 303.

Taylor, Richard S. *Tongues: Their Purpose and Meaning*. Beacon Hill Press, 1973.

Teuber, Andrew S. *Tongues of Fire*. Privately published, 1966.

Thiselton, A. C. "The 'Interpretation' of Tongues: A New Suggestion in the Light Greek Usage in Phils and Josephus," *Journal of Theological Studies*, 30:1 (197ᵉ 15-36.

Thomas, K. "Speaking in Tongues." Unpublished paper, Berlin Suicide Preventi Center, 1965.

Thomas, Robert L. "The Holy Spirit and Tongues," *The King's Business*, 54 (M 1963): 9-11.

_____. "Tongues Will Cease," *Journal of the Evangelical Theological Socie.* 17:2 (1974): 81-89.

Thomson, W. S. "Tongues at Pentecost: Acts 2," *Expository Times*, 38 (1926): 28 86.

Tinney, James S. "Exclusivist Tendencies in Pentecostal Self-Definition: A Critiq from Black Theology," *Journal of Religious Thought*, 36:1 (1979): 32-49.

_____. *Is the Present "Tongues" Movement of God?* Bible Institute of Los A geles, n.d.

_____. "Right to Be Heard on Tongues," *Christianity Today*, 10 (September 1966): 46-47.

Toussaint, Stanley D. "1 Corinthians 13 and the Tongues Question," *Bibliotheca Sac* 120 (October-December 1963): 311-16.

Truluck, Rembert. "A Study of the Relationships Between Hellenistic Religious Ecstasy and Corinthian Glossolalia." Unpublished seminar paper, Southern Baptist Theological Seminary, 1965.

Tschiedel, Hans. "Ein Pfingstwunder im Apollonhymnos," *Zeitschrift für Religions— und Geistesgeschichte*, 27:1 (1975): 22-39.

Tugwell, Simon. "The Gift of Tongues in the New Testament," *Expository Times*, 84 (February 1973): 137-40.

Tuland, Carl G. "The Confusion about Tongues," *Christianity Today*, 13 (December 6, 1968): 207-209.

Turnbull, Grace H. *Tongues As of Fire: A Bible of Sacred Scriptures of the Pagan World.* Macmillan Publishing Company, 1929.

Turner, W. H. *Pentecost and Tongues.* Modern Publishing House, n.d.

Unger, Merrill F. *The Baptising Work of the Holy Spirit.* Van Campen Press, 1953.

_____. *New Testament Teaching on Tongues.* Kregel Publications, 1971.

Versteeg, John M. *Perpetuating Pentecost.* Willet, Clark and Colby, 1930.

Vivier, Lincoln Morse. "Glossolalia." Unpublished doctor's dissertation, University of Witwatersrand, 1960.

_____. "The Glossolalic and His Personality," in *Beiträge zur Ekstase*, T. H. Spoerri, editor. Basel, 1968.

Volz, Paul. *Der Geist gottes und die verwandten Erscheinungen im Alten Testament und im anschliessenden Judentum.* J. C. B. Mohr, 1910.

Wagner, C. P. "What about Tongue Speaking?" *Eternity*, 19 (March 1968): 24-26.

Walker, Dawson. *The Gift of Tongues and Other Essays.* T. & T. Clark, 1906.

Walters, Stanley D. "Speaking in Tongues," *Youth in Action* (May 1964): 8-11, 28.

Wansborough, Henry. "Speaking in Tongues," *The Way*, 14:3 (July 1974): 193-201.

Ward, Wayne E. "The Significance of Glossolalia for the Church," in *Speaking in Tongues: Let's Talk about It*, Watson E. Mills, editor. Word Books, 1973. Pp. 143-51.

Weber, Wilfried. "Charismatische Bewegung Theologie der Befreiung," *Zeitschrift für Missionswissenschaft und Relegionswissenschaft*, 62 (January 1978): 40-45.

Webster, Douglas. *Pentecostalism and Speaking with Tongues.* Highway Press, 1964.

Wedderburn, A. J. M. "Romans 8:26—Towards a Theology of Glossolalia?" *Scottish Journal of Theology*, 28:4 (1975): 369-77.

Weinel, Heinrich. *Die Wirkungen des Geistes und Geister im nachapostolischen Zeitalter bis auf Irenäus.* J. C. B. Mohr, 1899.

Weitbrecht, H. H. "Ekstatische Zustände bei Schizophrenen," *Beiträge zur Ekstase* T. H. Spoerri, editor. Karger, 1968.

Welliver, Kenneth Bruce. "Pentecost and the Early Church." Unpublished doctor' dissertation, Yale University, 1961.

Welmers, William E. "Glossolalia," *Christianity Today*, 7 (November 8, 1963): 19 20.

Westwood, Tom. "Speaking in Unknown Tongues," *Bible Treasury Notes*, 6 (Ma° 1949): 3-5.

White, Alma B. *Demons and Tongues.* Pillar of Fire Publishers, 1936.

Whitley, O. R. "When You Speak in Tongues: Some Reflections on the Contemporar Search for Ecstasy," *Encounter*, 35 (Spring 1974): 81-94.

Wietzke, Walter and Jack Hustad, eds. "A Report on Glossolalia." Reprinted in *Tc wards a Mutual Understanding of Neo-Pentecostalism.* Augsburg, 1973.

Willems, Emilio. "Validation of Authority in Pentecostal Sects of Chile and Brazil, *Journal for the Scientific Study of Religion*, 6 (1967): 253-58.

Willet, H. L. "Question Box: New Testament References to Glossolalia or Speaking i Other Tongues," *Christian Century*, 54 (March 24, 1937): 389.

Williams, Cyril G. "Ecstaticism in Hebrew Prophecy and Christian Glossolalia," *Stuc ies in Religion*, 3:4 (1973-1974): 320-38.

——————. "Glossolalia as a Religious Phenomenon: 'Tongues' at Corinth and Pe° tecost," *Religion*, 5 (Spring 1975): 16-32.

——————. *Tongues of the Spirit: A Study of Pentecostal Glossolalia and Related Ph nomena.* University of Wales Press, 1981.

Williams, George H. and Edith Waldvogel. "A History of Speaking in Tongues a° Related Gifts," in *The Charismatic Movement*, Michael Hamilton, editor. Eer mans, 1975. Pp. 61-113.

Willis, Lewis J. "Glossolalia in Perspective," in *The Glossolalia Phenomenon*, Wa H. Horton, editor. Pathway Press, 1966. Pp. 247-84.

Wolfram, Walter Andrew. "The Sociolinguistics of Glossolalia." Unpublished ma ter's thesis, Hartford Seminary, 1966.

Woolsey, Warren. "Speaking in Tongues: A Biblical, Theological and Practical Study Mimeographed paper, Houghton Wesleyan Church, 1971.

Wright, Arthur. "The Gift of Tongues: A New View," *Theological Monthly*, 5 (189 161-69, 272-80.

Zeller, George W. *God's Gift of Tongues: The Nature, Purpose and Duration of Tong° as Taught in the Bible.* Loizeaux Brothers, 1978.

INDEXES

2 Corinthians

Galatians

Ephesians

Philippians

Colossians

1 Thessalonians

2 Thessalonians

1 Timothy

2 Timothy

Titus

Philemon

Hebrews

James

1 Peter

1 John